R. Gupta's®

POPULAR MASTER GUIDE

Jawahar Navodaya Vidyalaya

Class **9**

Entrance Exam

Conducted by:

Navodaya Vidyalaya Samiti

- Specialised Study Material Prepared by Experts
- Numerous Solved Multiple Choice Questions (MCQs)
- According to Current Pattern of Examination

2027
EDITION

RAMESH PUBLISHING HOUSE, NEW DELHI

Published by

O.P. Gupta *for* Ramesh Publishing House

Admin. Office

12-H, New Daryaganj Road, Opp. Officers' Mess,
New Delhi-110002 ✆ 23275224, 23245124

E-mail: info@rameshpublishinghouse.com
For Online Shopping: www.rameshpublishinghouse.com

Showroom

- Balaji Market, Nai Sarak, Delhi-110006 ✆ 23282525 📱 9354373464
- 4457, Nai Sarak, Delhi-110006

Book Code: R-2020

ISBN: 978-93-88642-13-2

Price: ₹ 395

Printed at: Deepak Offset, Delhi

CONTENTS

□□□

COMPOSITION OF THE TEST

Selection Test will consist of questions from the subjects of Mathematics, General Science, English and Hindi. Difficulty level of the test paper shall be of Class VIII.

NATURE OF THE SELECTION TEST

Sl. No.	Subject	Marks
01	English	15
02	Hindi	15
03	Maths	35
04	Science	35
	TOTAL	100

- The test will be of objective type with 2½ hours duration without any break.
- Medium of Language for Examination will be English/Hindi.
- Students have to answer in OMR sheet.
- Merit List will be announced as per the NVS selection criteria.

❐❐❐

JAWAHAR NAVODAYA VIDYALAYA

Class-IX, Entrance Exam, 2026

(Exam held on 07-02-2026)

SECTION-I : हिन्दी भाषा

निर्देश (प्र.सं. 1 से 10 तक) : *प्रत्येक प्रश्न के लिए चार संभावित उत्तर विकल्प दिए गए हैं, जिनमें से केवल एक सही उत्तर चुनकर उसको ओ.एम.आर. उत्तर-पत्रिका पर उपयुक्त स्थान पर दर्शाना है।*

1. शुद्ध वाक्य का चयन कीजिए :

A. बिहार का राजधानी पटना है।
B. बिहार पटना की राजधानी है।
C. पटना बिहार की राजधानी है।
D. बिहार राजधानी की पटना है।

2. 'मन चंगा तो कठौती में गंगा' लोकोक्ति का अर्थ है :

A. इच्छा के अनुसार अपने आँगन में गंगा बहाना
B. शुद्ध या पवित्र मन ही तीर्थवत् होता है
C. मन में आए तो गाँठ में विपुल सम्पत्ति आ जाना
D. गंगा में स्नान से पाप धुल जाना

3. 'छोटा मुँह बड़ी बात' का अर्थ है :

A. बड़ी-बड़ी बातें करना
B. अपनी हैसियत से बढ़कर बात करना
C. ओछी बातें करना
D. आश्चर्य की बात कहना

4. मैंने आपको कहीं देखा है।

उपर्युक्त वाक्य में रेखांकित पद .... वाचक सर्वनाम है।

A. प्रथम पुरुष B. मध्यम पुरुष
C. उत्तम पुरुष D. अन्य पुरुष

5. नीचे दिए गए शब्दों में से कौन-सा शब्द अनेकार्थी है?

A. फल B. कान
C. आदमी D. जल

6. जिस वाक्य में एक उद्देश्य और एक विधेय रहता है। उस वाक्य को क्या कहते हैं?

A. साधारण वाक्य B. मिश्र वाक्य
C. संयुक्त वाक्य D. क्रियात्मक वाक्य

7. कोई मधुर गीत सुनाइए। रेखांकित शब्द है :

A. संज्ञा B. सर्वनाम
C. क्रिया D. विशेषण

8. शुद्ध रूप छाँटिए :

A. राष्ट्रीय B. राष्ट्रिय
C. राष्टीय D. राष्टींय

9. 'अनुराग' का विलोम शब्द है :

A. लगन B. राग
C. प्रेम D. विराग

10. 'नीच' का पर्यायवाची शब्द **नहीं** है :

A. खल B. दुष्ट
C. निकृष्ट D. नकली

निर्देश (प्र.सं. 11 से 15 तक) : *निम्नलिखित अनुच्छेद को पढ़कर प्रश्नों के लिए सर्वाधिक उपयुक्त उत्तर चुनिए।*

स्वाधीन भारत में चुपचाप बहुत कुछ बदल गया है। गाँव में एक माध्यमिक विद्यालय खुला है, डाकखाना है, गलियों में ईंटें बिछी हैं और बिजली की प्रकाश व्यवस्था हुई है। अब रहट, कहीं किसी क्षेत्र में दिखाई नहीं देता, सर्वत्र नलकूपों से सिंचाई हो रही है। फसलों, बीज और खाद में तथा औजारों में गुणात्मक सुधार हुआ है। सुबह-सुबह बैलों के कंधों पर हल कम दिखाई देने लगे हैं। खेत-खलिहानों में ट्रैक्टरों के अतिरिक्त भी नए यंत्र, औजार दिखाई देने लगे हैं। आधुनिकता और ग्रामीण अर्थतंत्र के इस बदलाव ने मेरे गाँव की मानसिकता और पारंपरिक आचार-व्यवहार को प्रभावित न किया हो, ऐसा भी नहीं है, तो भी दूर-दराज इस बड़े शहर में वर्षों से रहने वाला मैं अपने इस गाँव की मिट्टी में बसी ऐसी आत्मीय सुगंध के एहसास से अब भी पुलकित हो उठता हूँ जो मुझे बार-बार जब-तब यहाँ खींच लाती है। अपने इन

1. C **2.** B **3.** B **4.** B **5.** A **6.** A **7.** D **8.** A **9.** D **10.** D

अशिक्षित, गरीब आत्मीय जनों के सुख-दुःख में शामिल होकर मुझे जहाँ सुख मिलता है वहाँ कहीं भीतर से कुछ कुरेदता भी है, पीड़ा देता है। स्वाधीनता के इतने वर्ष बीत जाने पर भी इस परतापुर गाँव में इसके नर-नारियों और बच्चों में शिक्षा का अपेक्षित विकास नहीं हो पाया है। अभी भी रोजगार के विविध अवसरों और दिशाओं की खोज की प्यास इस गाँव में नहीं है और अभी भी विपन्नता और पिछड़ापन इसे घुन की तरह खाए जा रहा है। विकास हुआ है पर और अधिक विकास की आवश्यकता है।

11. अब रहट किसी क्षेत्र में दिखाई नहीं देता, क्योंकि :
- A. गलियों में ईंटें बिछ गई हैं।
- B. बिजली की प्रकाश व्यवस्था हो गई है।
- C. गाँव में माध्यमिक विद्यालय खुल गए हैं।
- D. सर्वत्र नलकूपों से सिंचाई हो रही है।

12. अनुच्छेद का लेखक गाँव को देखकर दुःखी है, क्योंकि :
- A. विपन्नता और पिछड़ापन इसे घुन की तरह खाए जा रहा है।
- B. चुपचाप बहुत कुछ बदल गया है।
- C. विविध अवसरों और दिशाओं की खोज हो रही है।
- D. आत्मीय जनों के सुख-दुःख में शामिल नहीं हो पा रहा है।

13. 'बैलों के कंधों पर हल कम दिखाई देने लगे हैं' कहा गया है, क्योंकि :
- A. बैल, कंधों पर हल नहीं रखने देते।
- B. बैलों के कंधे कमजोर हो गए हैं।
- C. बैलों की जगह ट्रैक्टर और नए यंत्र, औजार आ गए हैं।
- D. किसान बैलों को हल में नहीं जोतना चाहते।

14. गाँव की मानसिकता और पारंपरिक आचार-व्यवहार प्रभावित हुए हैं, क्योंकि :
- A. गाँव का आदमी पुरानी चीजें पसंद नहीं करता।
- B. गाँव में क्रांति हो गई है।
- C. गाँव के कुछ लोग शहर चले गए हैं।
- D. आधुनिकता और ग्रामीण अर्थतंत्र के बदलाव ने ग्रामीण समाज को प्रभावित किया है।

15. अनुच्छेद का लेखक पुलकित क्यों हो उठता है?
- A. गाँव के विकास को देखकर
- B. गाँव की मिट्टी को देखकर
- C. गाँव की मिट्टी में बसी आत्मीय सुगंध के एहसास से
- D. दूर-दराज बड़े शहर में रहने के कारण

SECTION-II : ENGLISH

Directions (Qs. No. 16-18): *Read the following passage carefully and answer questions by choosing the correct options from those that follow.*

Since the early 1900s, many glaciers around the world have been melting rapidly. Human activities are at the root of this phenomenon. Specifically, since the industrial revolution, carbon dioxide and other greenhouse gas emissions have raised temperatures, even higher in the poles, and as a result, glaciers are rapidly melting, calving off into the sea and retreating on land.

Scientists project that if emissions continue to rise unchecked, the Arctic could be ice free in the summer as soon as the year 2040 as ocean and air temperatures continue to rise rapidly.

16. The expression the 'Arctic could be ice free' means that ....
- A. there will be no Arctic Circle
- B. the Arctic will become a new land mass
- C. all Arctic ice will have melted
- D. the entire Arctic will be submerged

17. Human activities are at the root of this phenomenon. The term '*this phenomenon*' refers to ....
- A. industrial revolution
- B. melting of glaciers
- C. human activities
- D. greenhouse emissions

18. Temperatures are rising due to ....
- A. carbon dioxide and greenhouse gases
- B. unchecked emissions
- C. glaciers calving off
- D. glaciers retreating on land

Directions (Qs. No. 19-22): *Answer these questions by choosing the most appropriate options to complete the paragraph by filling in the blanks.*

The Lotus flower has been declared as ....(19).... National flower of India. It is a sacred flower and occupies a unique position in the art and mythology of ancient India and ....(20).... an auspicious symbol of Indian culture ....(21).... time immemorial. It is considered to be a survivor ....(22).... it pushes its way through muddy waters to reach out to the sunglight.

19. A. the B. an C. a D. any

20. A. have been B. has been C. had been D. will have been

21. A. from B. for C. before D. since

11. D	12. A	13. C	14. D	15. C	16. C	17. B	18. A	19. A	20. B	21. D

22. A. because B. although
C. and D. so

23. Choose the word <u>opposite</u> in meaning to the underlined word.

Lord Rama was <u>kind</u> to the squirrel.

A. happy B. sad
C. good D. cruel

24. Choose the word similar in meaning to the underlined word.

The traffic on the road kept him fully <u>occupied</u>.

A. stalled B. busy
C. worried D. delayed

25. Read the sentence given below and choose the option which correctly changes it into Passive Voice.

Beena forgot the cows.

A. The cows had been forgotten by Beena.
B. The cows were forgotten by Beena.
C. Beena had forgotten the cows.
D. The cows have been forgotten by Beena.

Directions (Qs. No. 26-28): *Answer these questions by choosing the most appropriate options to fill in the blanks.*

26. I .... I had not eaten a raw guava.

A. wish B. wishes
C. wished D. wishing

27. I am sorry there is .... sugar left.

A. the little B. very little
C. enough D. fewer

28. They .... gone out. I don't see any lights in the house.

A. shall have B. must have
C. can have D. will have

29. Choose one-word substitute for the following expression:

One who does not believe in the presence of God.

A. Theist B. Polytheist
C. Monotheist D. Atheist

30. Choose the option that has correctly changed the following sentence into indirect speech.

Venkat said, "Anitha, will you come with me to the market?"

A. Venkat asked Anitha if she will go with him to the market.
B. Venkat asked Anitha if she would go with him to the market.
C. Venkat asked Anitha would she come with him to the market.
D. Venkat asked Anitha if she would come with him to the market.

SECTION-III : MATHEMATICS

31. Which of the following will have 7 as unit's digit in their cube roots?

35937, 42875, 19683, 46656

A. 35937 B. 42875
C. 19683 D. 46656

32. Three numbers are in the ratio 2 : 3 : 5. The sum of their cubes is 54880. The numbers are:

A. 14, 21, 35 B. 12, 15, 17
C. 14, 18, 21 D. 21, 28, 32

33. The least number by which 648 is divided to get a perfect cube is:

A. 1 B. 2
C. 3 D. 4

34. A perfect square number can never have the following digit in its one's place:

A. 0 B. 4
C. 6 D. 8

35. Simplification of $\sqrt[3]{27} + \sqrt[3]{0.008} + \sqrt[3]{0.064}$ gives:

A. 3.24 B. 3.006
C. 3.06 D. 3.6

36. The compound interest on ₹ 2,000 for 3 years at 10% per annum, compounded annually is:

A. ₹ 331 B. ₹ 662
C. ₹ 242 D. ₹ 402

37. The price of a cricket bat is reduced by half and the resulting price is again reduced by 10%. What percentage of the original price is the final price?

A. 10% B. 30%
C. 45% D. 65%

22. A	23. D	24. B	25. B	26. A	27. B	28. B	29. D
30. B	31. C	32. A	33. C	34. D	35. D	36. B	37. C

38. $\left(\frac{7a}{3}+\frac{5b}{4}\right)\left(\frac{7a}{3}-\frac{5b}{4}\right)=$

A. $\frac{49}{9}b^2-\frac{25}{16}a^2$
B. $\frac{49}{9}a^2-\frac{25}{16}b^2$
C. $\frac{7}{9}a^2-\frac{5}{16}b^2$
D. $\frac{7}{3}a^2-\frac{25}{4}b^2$

39. 44 men can do a piece of work in 15 days. How many men will finish the same work in 11 days?

A. 50
B. 55
C. 60
D. 80

40. What sum will amount to ₹ 1,352 in 2 years at 4% compounded annualy?

A. ₹ 1,000
B. ₹ 1,200
C. ₹ 1,250
D. ₹ 1,300

41. The sum of four consecutive multiples of 7 is 294. The smallest multiple is:

A. 63
B. 77
C. 84
D. 98

42. A number whose seventh part exceeds its eighth part by 1, is:

A. 68
B. 64
C. 58
D. 56

43. Which of the following numbers is ***not*** a perfect cube?

A. 100
B. 216
C. 1000
D. 1000000

44. The value of $\sqrt{\sqrt{289}+\sqrt{64}}$ is:

A. 5
B. 7
C. 25
D. 8

45. If $\sqrt{1+\frac{25}{144}}=1+\frac{x}{12}$, then the value of '$x$' is:

A. 1
B. 5
C. 13
D. 17

46. 8 men can do a piece of work in 10 days. How long will 10 men take to do the same work?

A. 12 days
B. 8 days
C. 7 days
D. 6 days

47. A photograph of a bacteria enlarged 50,000 times attains a length of 5 cm. What is the actual length of the bacteria?

A. 10^3 cm
B. 10^4 cm
C. 10^{-4} cm
D. 2×10^{-4} cm

48. The value of $\left[12^{\frac{11}{5}} \div 12^{\frac{1}{5}}\right]$ is:

A. 12
B. 144
C. $(12)^{11}$
D. 120

49. If 30% of 140 = x% of 840, then the value of 'x' is:

A. 5
B. 15
C. 24
D. 60

50. Evaluate: $\frac{8^{-2}\times 5^3}{2^{-8}}$

A. $\frac{125}{8}$
B. 500
C. $\frac{250}{3}$
D. 125

51. The range of the following data is:
–7, –5, 1, 3, 5, 8, 9

A. 12
B. 16
C. 14
D. 8

52. The expenditure on rent was ₹ 4,000 out of total salary of ₹ 18,000. A pie chart depicting this information shows this by a sector with central angle equal to:

A. 60°
B. 70°
C. 80°
D. 90°

53. If ABCD is a rhombus in which the altitude from vertex D to side AB bisects AB, then ∠A and ∠B respectively, are:

A. 60°, 120°
B. 120°, 60°
C. 80°, 100°
D. 100°, 80°

54. The given pie chart gives the marks scored in an examination by a student in English, Hindi, Science, Social Science and Mathematics. If the total marks obtained by the student were 540, then the subject in which the student scored 105 marks is:

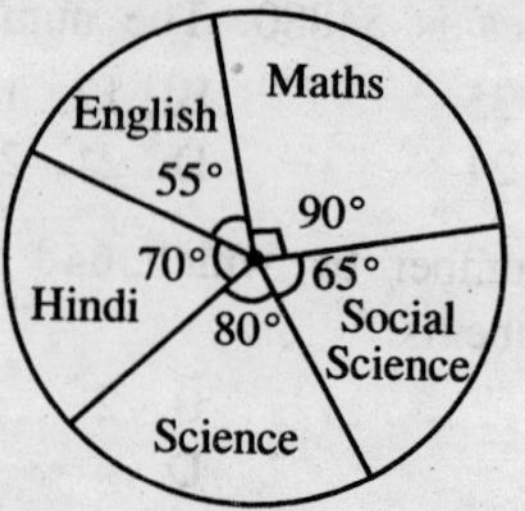

A. English
B. Hindi
C. Mathematics
D. Science

38. B	39. C	40. C	41. A	42. D	43. A	44. A	45. A	46. B
47. C	48. B	49. A	50. B	51. B	52. C	53. A	54. B	

55. In a ΔABC, $\angle ABC = 90°$ and $\angle CAB = 2\angle BCA$, then $\angle CAB$ equals:

A. 40° B. 30°
C. 90° D. 60°

56. The three angles of a triangle are in the ratio of 3 : 4 : 5. The largest angle of the triangle is:

A. 45° B. 60°
C. 75° D. 90°

57. A die is tossed once. The probability of getting a multiple of 3 is:

A. $\frac{1}{2}$ B. $\frac{1}{3}$
C. $\frac{1}{4}$ D. $\frac{1}{5}$

58. A square garden measuring 8 m on a side is surrounded by a 1 m wide footpath. The area of the footpath is:

A. 9 m^2 B. 8 m^2
C. 36 m^2 D. 28 m^2

59. The radius of a right circular cylinder is doubled and the height is made three times. The ratio between the volumes of the new cylinder and the original cylinder is:

A. 6 : 1 B. 12 : 1
C. 36 : 1 D. 18 : 1

60. The perimeter of a rectangular plot is 160 m. Its length is 5 m more than twice its breadth. The length of the plot is:

A. 25 m B. 40 m
C. 55 m D. 60 m

61. If $13x - 6(9 + 2x) + 2x = 6$, then x equals:

A. –20 B. 12
C. 20 D. 18

62. If $\frac{3y+4}{2-6y} + \frac{2}{5} = 0$, then $y = ?$

A. 8 B. –8
C. $\frac{16}{3}$ D. $-\frac{16}{3}$

63. Which of the following is same as $40x^3y^2z^3$?

A. $(5z^2)(2y^2)(4x^2)$ B. $(5z)(2y^3)(20x^2)$
C. $(5z^3)(4y^2)(2x^2)$ D. $(5z^3)(4y^2)(2x^3)$

64. If the area of a square is $(25y^2 + 16x^2 - 40xy)$, then the side of the square is:

A. $(5y + 4x)$ B. $(5x + 4y)$
C. $(5y - 4x)$ D. $(5x - 4y)$

65. Two numbers are in the ratio 3 : 5 and their difference is 46. The larger of the two numbers is:

A. 69 B. 230
C. 115 D. 184

SECTION-IV : GENERAL SCIENCE

66. Biodiversity refers to:

A. that part of the Earth in which living organisms exist.
B. that part of the Earth which supports life.
C. variety of foods/cuisines available to living organisms on Earth.
D. variety of organisms existing on Earth, their inter-relationships and their relationship with the environment.

67. Which one of the following options is ***not*** a reason for the migratory birds to fly to far away areas every year?

A. In search of food
B. To check their ability to fly
C. To avoid extreme cold climate condition
D. To lay eggs in areas with hospitable conditions

68. The image of an object formed by a plane mirror is:

A. inverted and diminished in size
B. erect and of same size as the object
C. erect and enlarged
D. inverted and enlarged

69. Select from the following the correct options which include changes at puberty seen in boys only:

1. Release of estrogen hormone
2. Adam's apple is small in size
3. Shoulders become broader and chest wider
4. Growth of facial hair

A. 1 and 2 B. 3 and 4
C. 1, 3 and 4 D. 2, 3, and 4

70. It was noticed in a water body that tadpoles did not metamorphose into adults for a long period of time. This may be due to lack of:

A. Adrenalin from the adrenal glands
B. Thyroxine from the thyroid gland
C. Insulin from the pancreas
D. Estrogen from the ovary

55. D	**56.** C	**57.** B	**58.** C	**59.** B	**60.** C	**61.** C	**62.** B
63. D	**64.** C	**65.** C	**66.** D	**67.** B	**68.** B	**69.** B	**70.** B

71. Which of the following statement(s) is/are ***incorrect*** in context of the process of reproduction in hens?

1. They exhibit internal fertilisation.
2. There are many protective layers formed around the developing embryo of a hen.
3. The embryo takes about 3 weeks to develop into a chick.
4. They are viviparous animals.

A. 4 only B. 1 and 3
C. 2 and 4 D. 1, 3 and 4

72. In which of the following animals do the young ones resemble their parents?

A. Frog B. Butterfly
C. Mosquito D. Cow

73. Given below are a few statements listing the chemical co-ordination in animals with the help of hormones:

1. They are secreted by the endocrine glands.
2. They are transported to the target site.
3. Endocrine glands release them into the blood-stream.
4. Target site responds to hormones and changes are observed in the body.

The correct sequence of events is:

A. 1, 2, 3, 4 B. 2, 3, 4, 1
C. 1, 3, 4, 2 D. 1, 3, 2, 4

74. When pressure on the bulb of a dropper (with its nozzle kept in water) is released, water rises in the dropper. This is due to:

A. Pressure of water B. Gravity of the Earth
C. Atmospheric pressure D. Shape of bulb

75. The correct increasing order of forces of static, rolling and sliding friction is:

A. Rolling, sliding, static
B. Sliding, static, rolling
C. Static, rolling, sliding
D. Rolling, static, sliding

76. To reduce friction between two surfaces, both the surfaces are:

A. made rough B. made smooth
C. grooved D. made hard

77. Audible frequency range for normal healthy human ear is:

A. 10 Hz to 10,000 Hz
B. 20 Hz to 20,000 Hz
C. 20 Hz to 10,000 Hz
D. 10 Hz to 20,000 Hz

78. Four close friends brought four containers/vessels of different shapes which contains coloured water. Volume of coloured water taken in each vessel is as shown below:

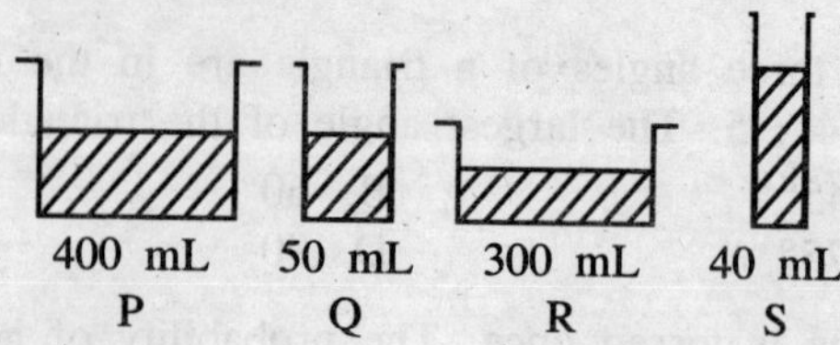

Arrange them in the order of increasing pressure at the base of each vessel:

A. $R < Q < P < S$ B. $S < R < P < Q$
C. $Q < S < P < R$ D. $P < R < S < Q$

79. There are four cylindrical rods A, B, C, D having the same mass and equal length but different areas of cross-section. Radius of a is 8 cm while B, C, D have radius 4 cm, 12 cm and 10 cm respectively. They are held vertically on the surface of sand in a large vessel. Which one of them will penetrate more?

A. B B. A C. D D. C

80. During the development of thunderstorm, positive charges collect near the:

A. Upper edge of the cloud
B. Lower edge of the cloud
C. Left edge of the cloud
D. Right edge of the cloud

81. Which one of the following Earth's layer is responsible for causing an earthquake?

A. Outer core B. Crust
C. Inner core D. Mantle

82. Which of the following is ***not*** used for electroplating metallic objects?

A. Nickel B. Silver
C. Chromium D. Sodium

83. Which one of the following can conduct electricity?

A. Vegetable oil B. Vinegar
C. Distilled Water D. Sugar Solution

84. An electric current can produce:

A. heating effect only
B. heating and chemical effect
C. chemical as well as magnetic effect
D. magnetic, heating and chemical effects

85. A body makes 15 oscillations in 30 s. Its frequency and time period respectively are:

A. 0.5 Hz, 0.2 s B. 2 Hz, 2 s
C. 0.5 Hz, 4 s D. 0.5 Hz, 2 s

71. A	**72.** D	**73.** D	**74.** C	**75.** A	**76.** B	**77.** B	**78.** A
79. A	**80.** A	**81.** B	**82.** D	**83.** B	**84.** D	**85.** D	

86. Tannistha is standing 12 m away in front of a large plane mirror. How far must she walk so that she is 6 m away from her image?

A. 7.5 m B. 9 m C. 6 m D. 15 m

87. A ray of light is incident on a plane mirror making an angle of 35° from its reflecting surface. The measure of the corresponding angle of reflection in this situation will be:

A. 35° B. 70° C. 55° D. 110°

88. A glass rod and a piece of silk are rubbed together. Which of the following happens according to convention?

A. Glass rod and piece of silk both acquire positive charge.
B. Glass rod and piece of silk both acquire negative charge.
C. Glass rod acquires positive charge and piece of silk acquires negative charge.
D. Glass rod acquires negative charge and piece of silk acquires positive charge.

89. Medicines called antibiotics which are used to kill or stop the growth of disease-causing micro-organisms are produced from:

A. Algae and Bacteria B. Fungi and Algae
C. Bacteria and Fungi D. Protozoa and Bacteria

90. Select the option that correctly matches the name of *human disease* given in Column I with its *mode of transmission* given in Column II.

Column I	Column II
I. Measles	1. Food/Water
II. Hepatitis A	2. Air
III. Cholera	3. Direct Contact/Air
IV. Chicken Pox	4. Water

A. I-4, II-3, III-1, IV-2
B. I-2, II-4, III-1, IV-3
C. I-3, II-4, III-2, IV-1
D. I-4, II-1, III-3, IV-2

91. The substance which is ***not*** obtained by processing of coal is:

A. Bitumen B. Coke
C. Coal tar D. Coal gas

92. The micro-organisms *Spirogyra* and *Chlamydomonas* belong to the group:

A. Bacteria B. Algae
C. Fungi D. Protozoa

93. 'Red Data Book' is the source book maintained to keep a record of:

A. all endangered plants and animals
B. all extinct plants and animals
C. all endemic plants and animals
D. all rare plants and animals

94. Consider the following statements in context of reproduction in humans:

1. Human sperm has a head, middle piece and a tail
2. The sperm is the beginning of a new individual.
3. Fertilisation takes place in the testes.
4. During fertilisation the egg moves towards the sperm.

The correct statement(s) is/are:

A. 1 only B. 1 and 3
C. 2 and 4 D. 1, 2 and 4

95. A combustion in which substances like phosphorus, when kept in air suddenly burns into flame without the application of any apparent cause, is known as:

A. Rapid combustion B. Explosion
C. Slow combustion D. Spontaneous combustion

96. The fires involving electrical equipment and inflammable material like petrol are best controlled by using:

A. Water B. Carbon dioxide
C. Fire extinguisher D. Sodium chloride

97. An example of inexhaustible natural resources is:

A. Minerals B. Natural gas
C. Sunlight D. Petroleum

98. The best time for removal of weeds from a field is:

A. before the weeds produce flowers and seeds.
B. after the weeds have produced flowers and seeds.
C. during the period of flowering and seed formation in weeds.
D. after the weeds have grown old and dried up in the fields.

99. Silos are used to:

A. Separate grain seeds from chaff.
B. grow crops in a field.
C. protect grains from rats and insects during storage.
D. supply water for irrigation of crops.

100. Consider the following statements:

1. Rhizobium bacteria is present in the nodules of roots of gram plant.
2. Fertilizers provide a lot of humus to the soil.
3. Mustard seeds are sown in the rainy season.
4. Using a seed drill to sow seeds ensures that the seeds get covered by the soil after sowing.

The correct statement(s) is/are:

A. 1 only B. 1 and 3
C. 2 and 3 D. 1 and 4

86. B	**87.** C	**88.** C	**89.** C	**90.** B	**91.** A	**92.** B	**93.** A
94. A	**95.** D	**96.** B	**97.** C	**98.** A	**99.** C	**100.** D	

EXPLANATORY ANSWERS

1. पटना बिहार की राजधानी है। यह वाक्य व्याकरण की दृष्टि से पूर्णतः शुद्ध है। इसमें कर्ता 'पटना' है और उसके बारे में सही संबंध 'बिहार की राजधानी' के रूप में व्यक्त किया गया है। अन्य विकल्पों में शब्द-क्रम और संबंध-वाचक रूप अशुद्ध हैं, इसलिए वे मानक हिंदी के अनुसार सही नहीं हैं।

2. शुद्ध या पवित्र मन ही तीर्थवत् होता है : इस लोकोक्ति का भाव यह है कि यदि मन पवित्र हो, तो साधारण स्थान भी तीर्थ के समान हो जाता है। यहाँ बाहरी आडंबर से अधिक आंतरिक शुद्धता को महत्व दिया गया है। इसलिए इसका सही आशय पवित्र मन को ही सबसे बड़ा तीर्थ मानना है।

3. 'छोटा मुँह बड़ी बात' का प्रयोग तब किया जाता है जब कोई व्यक्ति अपनी स्थिति, आयु या योग्यता से अधिक बड़ी बात कह दे। इसमें विनम्रता और आत्मसंकोच का भाव भी छिपा रहता है। इसलिए इसका सही अर्थ अपनी सीमा से बढ़कर बात करना है।

4. वाक्य में रेखांकित पद 'आपको' माना गया है। 'आप' उस व्यक्ति के लिए प्रयुक्त होता है जिससे सीधे संबोधन किया जा रहा हो। इसलिए यह मध्यम पुरुष वाचक सर्वनाम है।

5. अनेकार्थी शब्द वह होता है जिसके एक से अधिक अर्थ होते हैं। 'फल' के अनेक अर्थ हैं—*(i)* खाने वाला फल (जैसे आम, सेब), *(ii)* परिणाम या निष्कर्ष (कर्म का फल), *(iii)* किसी शस्त्र या उपकरण का अग्र भाग (नोक)। इस प्रकार 'फल' के विभिन्न अर्थ होने के कारण यह अनेकार्थी शब्द है।

6. जिस वाक्य में एक ही उद्देश्य और एक ही विधेय होता है, उसे साधारण वाक्य कहते हैं। इसमें केवल एक ही मुख्य कथन होता है, कोई आश्रित या संयुक्त उपवाक्य नहीं होता। इसलिए यह परिभाषा साधारण वाक्य की है।

7. वाक्य में रेखांकित शब्द 'मधुर' है, जो 'गीत' की विशेषता बता रहा है। जो शब्द संज्ञा या सर्वनाम की विशेषता प्रकट करे, वह विशेषण कहलाता है। इसलिए 'मधुर' विशेषण है।

8. 'राष्ट्रीय' ही इस शब्द का शुद्ध रूप है। यह 'राष्ट्र' शब्द से बना है और मानक हिंदी वर्तनी के अनुसार यही सही वर्तनात्मक रूप माना जाता है। बाकी सभी विकल्पों में वर्ण-विन्यास की अशुद्धि है।

9. 'अनुराग' का अर्थ प्रेम, स्नेह या लगाव होता है। इसका विलोम 'विराग' है, जिसका अर्थ है मोह या आसक्ति का अभाव। इसलिए 'विराग' इसका सही विपरीतार्थक शब्द है।

10. 'नीच' के पर्यायवाची शब्दों में खल, दुष्ट और निकृष्ट आते हैं, क्योंकि ये सभी हीन, बुरे या अधम अर्थ व्यक्त करते हैं। 'नकली' का अर्थ जाली या असली न होना है, जो 'नीच' का पर्याय नहीं है। इसलिए यही सही उत्तर है।

11. अनुच्छेद में स्पष्ट उल्लेख है कि अब रहट दिखाई नहीं देता क्योंकि उसकी जगह नलकूपों ने ले ली है। सिंचाई के आधुनिक साधनों के आने से पारंपरिक रहट अप्रचलित हो गया है, इसलिए उसका उपयोग समाप्त हो गया।

12. लेखक को गाँव की स्थिति देखकर दुःख इसलिए होता है क्योंकि विकास के बावजूद गरीबी और पिछड़ापन अभी भी बना हुआ है। शिक्षा और रोजगार के अवसरों की कमी भी इस पीड़ा को बढ़ाती है।

13. अनुच्छेद में बताया गया है कि अब खेतों में ट्रैक्टर और आधुनिक औजार दिखाई देने लगे हैं। इसी कारण बैलों द्वारा हल चलाने की परंपरा कम हो गई है, जिससे यह दृश्य दुर्लभ होता जा रहा है।

14. लेखक स्पष्ट रूप से कहता है कि आधुनिकता और आर्थिक परिवर्तन ने गाँव की मानसिकता और पारंपरिक व्यवहार को प्रभावित किया है। यह बदलाव तकनीकी और आर्थिक प्रगति के कारण आया है।

15. लेखक शहर में रहने के बावजूद गाँव की मिट्टी की आत्मीयता और अपनापन महसूस करता है। यही भावनात्मक जुड़ाव उसे बार-बार गाँव की ओर आकर्षित करता है और उसे पुलकित कर देता है।

16. The phrase "Arctic could be ice free" directly implies that during summer, the ice covering the Arctic region will disappear completely. It does not mean loss of the region itself, but specifically the melting of ice due to rising temperatures.

17. The term "this phenomenon" refers back to what was mentioned just before it, which is the rapid melting of glaciers. The sentence clearly connects human activities as the cause of glacier melting.

18. The passage explicitly states that emissions of carbon dioxide and other greenhouse gases have raised temperatures. These gases trap heat in the atmosphere, leading to global warming and rising temperatures.

19. The correct phrase is "declared as the National flower of India." The definite article "the" is used because it refers to a specific and unique designation.

20. The subject "It" (Lotus flower) is singular, so "has been" is grammatically correct. It indicates a continuous state from the past to the present.

21. The phrase "since time immemorial" is a standard expression meaning from an indefinite point in the past until now. Hence, "since" is the correct choice.

22. The sentence explains the reason why the lotus is considered a survivor. Therefore, "because" correctly connects the cause (pushing through muddy waters) with the result.

23. The word "kind" means gentle, compassionate, or benevolent. Its opposite is "cruel," which means harsh, unkind, or causing suffering. Hence, "cruel" is the correct antonym.

24. The word "occupied" in the sentence means being engaged or busy with something. Among the options, "busy" conveys the same meaning most accurately, indicating involvement in an activity.

25. The cows were forgotten by Beena.: The given sentence is in simple past tense. While changing to passive voice, the object "the cows" becomes the subject, and "were forgotten" is used as the correct past tense passive form.

26. The sentence expresses regret about a past action. In English, this pattern is written as "I wish + past perfect". Therefore, the correct sentence is "I wish I had not eaten a raw guava." Hence, wish is the correct option.

27. The sentence expresses scarcity of sugar. "Very little" correctly indicates an insufficient quantity, whereas "the little" would imply whatever small amount is enough.

28. The sentence expresses a strong logical assumption based on evidence (no lights). "Must have gone out" correctly indicates deduction about a past action.

29. An atheist is a person who does not believe in the existence of God. The other options refer to different types of belief in one or multiple gods.

30. While changing an interrogative sentence into indirect speech, "will" changes to "would". Also, "come" changes to "go" because the movement is reported from the speaker's point of view, not from Anitha's. Therefore, this is the correct indirect form.

31. $20^3 = 8000$

$30^3 = 27000,$

so the cube root lies between 20 and 30.

Now, $27^3 = 27 \times 27 \times 27$

$= 729 \times 27 = 19683.$

So, $\sqrt[3]{19683} = 27$, whose unit's digit is 7.

Hence, the required number is 19683.

32. Let the numbers be $2x$, $3x$, $5x$

Then,

$$(2x)^3 + (3x)^3 + (5x)^3 = 54880$$

$$8x^3 + 27x^3 + 125x^3 = 54880$$

$$160x^3 = 54880$$

$$x^3 = \frac{54880}{160} = 343$$

$$x = 7$$

Therefore, the numbers are 14, 21, 35.

33. $648 = 2^3 \times 3^4$

For a perfect cube, the power of each prime must be a multiple of 3.

Here, 2^3 is fine, but 3^4 is not.

Divide by 3: $\frac{648}{3} = 216 = 6^3$

So, the least number is 3.

34. The unit's digit of a perfect square can only be 0, 1, 4, 5, 6 or 9.

A perfect square never ends in 2, 3, 7 or 8.

Therefore, a perfect square number can never have 8 in its one's place.

35. $\sqrt[3]{27} = 3$

$$\sqrt[3]{0.008} = \sqrt[3]{(0.2)^3} = 0.2$$

$$\sqrt[3]{0.064} = \sqrt[3]{(0.4)^3} = 0.4$$

Adding,

$3 + 0.2 + 0.4 = 3.6.$

36. Principal, $P = 2000,$

Rate, $R = 10\%$, Time, $T = 3$ years

Amount, $A = P\left(1+\frac{R}{100}\right)^T = 2000\left(1+\frac{10}{100}\right)^3$

$= 2000(1.1)^3$

$= 2000 \times 1.331 = 2662$

Compound Interest,

$CI = A - P = 2662 - 2000 = 662.$

37. Let original price = 100

After reducing by half,

$= 100 \times \frac{1}{2} = 50$

Further reduction of 10%,

$= 50 \times \frac{90}{100} = 45$

Final price = 45% of original price.

38. $\left(\frac{7a}{3}+\frac{5b}{4}\right)\left(\frac{7a}{3}-\frac{5b}{4}\right)$

Using identity,

$(x + y)(x - y) = x^2 - y^2$

Here, $x = \frac{7a}{3}$, $y = \frac{5b}{4}$

So, $\left(\frac{7a}{3}\right)^2 - \left(\frac{5b}{4}\right)^2 = \frac{49a^2}{9} - \frac{25b^2}{16} = \frac{49}{9}a^2 - \frac{25}{16}b^2.$

39. Men $\times$ days = constant

$44 \times 15 = x \times 11$

$x = \frac{44 \times 15}{11}$

$x = 4 \times 15 = 60.$

40. Amount, $A = 1352,$

Rate, $R = 4\%,$

Time, $T = 2$ years

$$A = P\left(1+\frac{R}{100}\right)^T$$

$$1352 = P\left(1+\frac{4}{100}\right)^2$$

$$= P\left(\frac{104}{100}\right)^2 = P\left(\frac{26}{25}\right)^2 = P \times \frac{676}{625}$$

$$P = 1352 \times \frac{625}{676}$$

$$P = 2 \times 625 = 1250.$$

41. Let the four consecutive multiples of 7 be:

x, $x + 7$, $x + 14$, $x + 21$

Their sum is 294:

$$x + (x + 7) + (x + 14) + (x + 21) = 294$$

$$4x + 42 = 294$$

$$4x = 252$$

$$x = 63$$

So, the smallest multiple is 63.

42. Let the number be x

Its seventh part exceeds its eighth part by 1:

$$\frac{x}{7} - \frac{x}{8} = 1$$

$$\frac{8x - 7x}{56} = 1$$

$$\frac{x}{56} = 1$$

$$x = 56.$$

43.

$$216 = 6^3$$
$$1000 = 10^3$$
$$1000000 = 100^3$$

But 100 cannot be written in the form n^3 for any integer n.

So, 100 is not a perfect cube.

44. Given expression: $\sqrt{\sqrt{289} + \sqrt{64}}$

First evaluate inner square roots:

$$\sqrt{289} = 17$$

$$\sqrt{64} = 8$$

So, $\sqrt{17 + 8} = \sqrt{25}$

$$\sqrt{25} = 5.$$

45.

$$\sqrt{1 + \frac{25}{144}} = 1 + \frac{x}{12}$$

$$\sqrt{\frac{144 + 25}{144}} = 1 + \frac{x}{12}$$

$$\sqrt{\frac{169}{144}} = 1 + \frac{x}{12}$$

$$\frac{13}{12} = 1 + \frac{x}{12}$$

$$\frac{13}{12} - 1 = \frac{x}{12}$$

$$\frac{13}{12} - \frac{12}{12} = \frac{x}{12}$$

$$\frac{1}{12} = \frac{x}{12}$$

$$x = 1.$$

46. Total work $= 8 \times 10 = 80$ man-days

Required time for 10 men $= \frac{80}{10} = 8$ days.

47. Actual length $= \frac{5}{50,000}$ cm $= \frac{1}{10,000}$ cm

$$= 10^{-4} \text{ cm}.$$

48.

$$\frac{12^{11/5}}{12^{1/5}} = 12^{\frac{11}{5} - \frac{1}{5}} = 12^{\frac{10}{5}}$$

$$= 12^2 = 144.$$

49. 30% of 140 $= x$% of 840

$$\frac{30}{100} \times 140 = \frac{x}{100} \times 840$$

$$42 = \frac{840x}{100}$$

$$4200 = 840x$$

$$x = \frac{4200}{840} = 5.$$

50.

$$\frac{8^{-2} \times 5^3}{2^{-8}} = \frac{1}{8^2} \times 5^3 \times 2^8$$

$$= \frac{1}{64} \times 125 \times 256 = 125 \times \frac{256}{64}$$

$$= 125 \times 4 = 500.$$

51. Range = Maximum value − Minimum value

Maximum = 9, Minimum = −7

Range = 9 − (−7)

= 9 + 7 = 16.

52.

$$\text{Central angle} = \frac{\text{Part}}{\text{Whole}} \times 360°$$

$$= \frac{4000}{18000} \times 360° = \frac{2}{9} \times 360° = 80°.$$

53. DM ⊥ AB and AM = MB

ΔAMD ≅ ΔBDM

(∵ AM = MB, ∠AMD = ∠BMD = 90°m DM = DM)

∴ AB = AD = DB ⇒ ΔABD is equilateral

So, ∠A = 60° ⇒ ∠B = 120°.

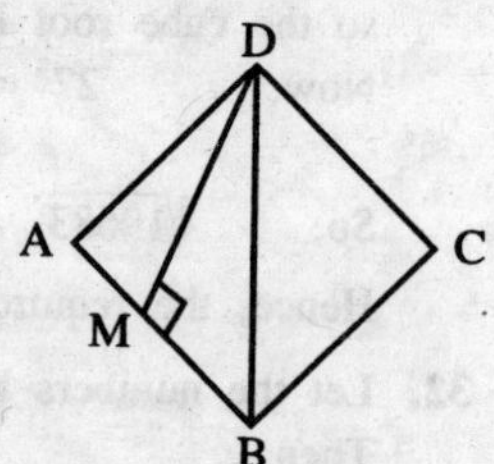

54. Total marks = 540

Central angle corresponding to 105 marks,

$$= \frac{105}{540} \times 360°$$

$$= \frac{105 \times 360}{540} = \frac{105 \times 2}{3} = 70°$$

From the pie chart, the sector of 70° represents Hindi, hence the required subject is Hindi.

55. Let ∠BCA = x

Then ∠CAB = $2x$ and ∠ABC = 90°

In ΔABC,

$$x + 2x + 90° = 180°$$

$$3x = 90° \Rightarrow x = 30°$$

$$\angle CAB = 2x = 60°.$$

56. Let the three angles be $3x$, $4x$, $5x$

Since the sum of angles of a triangle is 180°,

$$3x + 4x + 5x = 180°$$

$$12x = 180° \Rightarrow x = 15°$$

Largest angle $= 5x = 5 \times 15° = 75°$.

57. Numbers obtained when a die is rolled once

= 1, 2, 3, 4, 5, 6 (Total outcomes = 6)

Multiples of 3 = 3 and 6

Number of favorable outcomes = 2

$$\text{Probability} = \frac{2}{6} = \frac{1}{3}.$$

26. The sentence expresses regret about a past action. In English, this pattern is written as "I wish + past perfect". Therefore, the correct sentence is "I wish I had not eaten a raw guava." Hence, wish is the correct option.

27. The sentence expresses scarcity of sugar. "Very little" correctly indicates an insufficient quantity, whereas "the little" would imply whatever small amount is enough.

28. The sentence expresses a strong logical assumption based on evidence (no lights). "Must have gone out" correctly indicates deduction about a past action.

29. An atheist is a person who does not believe in the existence of God. The other options refer to different types of belief in one or multiple gods.

30. While changing an interrogative sentence into indirect speech, "will" changes to "would". Also, "come" changes to "go" because the movement is reported from the speaker's point of view, not from Anitha's. Therefore, this is the correct indirect form.

31. $20^3 = 8000$

$30^3 = 27000,$

so the cube root lies between 20 and 30.

Now, $27^3 = 27 \times 27 \times 27$

$= 729 \times 27 = 19683.$

So, $\sqrt[3]{19683} = 27$, whose unit's digit is 7.

Hence, the required number is 19683.

32. Let the numbers be $2x$, $3x$, $5x$

Then,

$$(2x)^3 + (3x)^3 + (5x)^3 = 54880$$
$$8x^3 + 27x^3 + 125x^3 = 54880$$
$$160x^3 = 54880$$
$$x^3 = \frac{54880}{160} = 343$$
$$x = 7$$

Therefore, the numbers are 14, 21, 35.

33. $648 = 2^3 \times 3^4$

For a perfect cube, the power of each prime must be a multiple of 3.

Here, 2^3 is fine, but 3^4 is not.

Divide by 3: $\frac{648}{3} = 216 = 6^3$

So, the least number is 3.

34. The unit's digit of a perfect square can only be 0, 1, 4, 5, 6 or 9.

A perfect square never ends in 2, 3, 7 or 8.

Therefore, a perfect square number can never have 8 in its one's place.

35. $\sqrt[3]{27} = 3$

$$\sqrt[3]{0.008} = \sqrt[3]{(0.2)^3} = 0.2$$
$$\sqrt[3]{0.064} = \sqrt[3]{(0.4)^3} = 0.4$$

Adding,

$3 + 0.2 + 0.4 = 3.6.$

36. Principal, $P = 2000,$

Rate, $R = 10\%$, Time, $T = 3$ years

Amount, $A = P\left(1+\frac{R}{100}\right)^T = 2000\left(1+\frac{10}{100}\right)^3$

$= 2000(1.1)^3$

$= 2000 \times 1.331 = 2662$

Compound Interest,

$CI = A - P = 2662 - 2000 = 662.$

37. Let original price = 100

After reducing by half,

$= 100 \times \frac{1}{2} = 50$

Further reduction of 10%,

$= 50 \times \frac{90}{100} = 45$

Final price = 45% of original price.

38. $\left(\frac{7a}{3}+\frac{5b}{4}\right)\left(\frac{7a}{3}-\frac{5b}{4}\right)$

Using identity,

$(x + y)(x - y) = x^2 - y^2$

Here, $x = \frac{7a}{3}$, $y = \frac{5b}{4}$

So, $\left(\frac{7a}{3}\right)^2 - \left(\frac{5b}{4}\right)^2 = \frac{49a^2}{9} - \frac{25b^2}{16} = \frac{49}{9}a^2 - \frac{25}{16}b^2.$

39. Men × days = constant

$44 \times 15 = x \times 11$

$$x = \frac{44 \times 15}{11}$$

$x = 4 \times 15 = 60.$

40. Amount, $A = 1352,$

Rate, $R = 4\%,$

Time, $T = 2$ years

$$A = P\left(1+\frac{R}{100}\right)^T$$
$$1352 = P\left(1+\frac{4}{100}\right)^2$$
$$= P\left(\frac{104}{100}\right)^2 = P\left(\frac{26}{25}\right)^2 = P \times \frac{676}{625}$$
$$P = 1352 \times \frac{625}{676}$$

$P = 2 \times 625 = 1250.$

41. Let the four consecutive multiples of 7 be:

$x, x + 7, x + 14, x + 21$

Their sum is 294:

$$x + (x + 7) + (x + 14) + (x + 21) = 294$$
$$4x + 42 = 294$$
$$4x = 252$$
$$x = 63$$

So, the smallest multiple is 63.

42. Let the number be x

Its seventh part exceeds its eighth part by 1:

$$\frac{x}{7} - \frac{x}{8} = 1$$

$$\frac{8x - 7x}{56} = 1$$

$$\frac{x}{56} = 1$$

$$x = 56.$$

43.

$$216 = 6^3$$

$$1000 = 10^3$$

$$1000000 = 100^3$$

But 100 cannot be written in the form n^3 for any integer n.

So, 100 is not a perfect cube.

44. Given expression: $\sqrt{\sqrt{289} + \sqrt{64}}$

First evaluate inner square roots:

$$\sqrt{289} = 17$$

$$\sqrt{64} = 8$$

So, $\sqrt{17 + 8} = \sqrt{25}$

$$\sqrt{25} = 5.$$

45.

$$\sqrt{1 + \frac{25}{144}} = 1 + \frac{x}{12}$$

$$\sqrt{\frac{144 + 25}{144}} = 1 + \frac{x}{12}$$

$$\sqrt{\frac{169}{144}} = 1 + \frac{x}{12}$$

$$\frac{13}{12} = 1 + \frac{x}{12}$$

$$\frac{13}{12} - 1 = \frac{x}{12}$$

$$\frac{13}{12} - \frac{12}{12} = \frac{x}{12}$$

$$\frac{1}{12} = \frac{x}{12}$$

$$x = 1.$$

46. Total work $= 8 \times 10 = 80$ man-days

Required time for 10 men $= \frac{80}{10} = 8$ days.

47. Actual length $= \frac{5}{50,000}$ cm $= \frac{1}{10,000}$ cm

$= 10^{-4}$ cm.

48.

$$\frac{12^{11/5}}{12^{1/5}} = 12^{\frac{11}{5} - \frac{1}{5}} = 12^{\frac{10}{5}}$$

$$= 12^2 = 144.$$

49. 30% of 140 $= x\%$ of 840

$$\frac{30}{100} \times 140 = \frac{x}{100} \times 840$$

$$42 = \frac{840x}{100}$$

$$4200 = 840x$$

$$x = \frac{4200}{840} = 5.$$

50.

$$\frac{8^{-2} \times 5^3}{2^{-8}} = \frac{1}{8^2} \times 5^3 \times 2^8$$

$$= \frac{1}{64} \times 125 \times 256 = 125 \times \frac{256}{64}$$

$$= 125 \times 4 = 500.$$

51. Range = Maximum value – Minimum value

Maximum = 9, Minimum = –7

Range = 9 – (–7)

= 9 + 7 = 16.

52. Central angle $= \frac{\text{Part}}{\text{Whole}} \times 360°$

$$= \frac{4000}{18000} \times 360° = \frac{2}{9} \times 360° = 80°.$$

53. DM ⊥ AB and AM = MB

$\Delta AMD \cong \Delta BDM$

(∵ AM = MB, ∠AMD = ∠BMD = 90°m DM = DM)

∴ AB = AD = DB ⇒ ΔABD is equilateral

So, ∠A = 60° ⇒ ∠B = 120°.

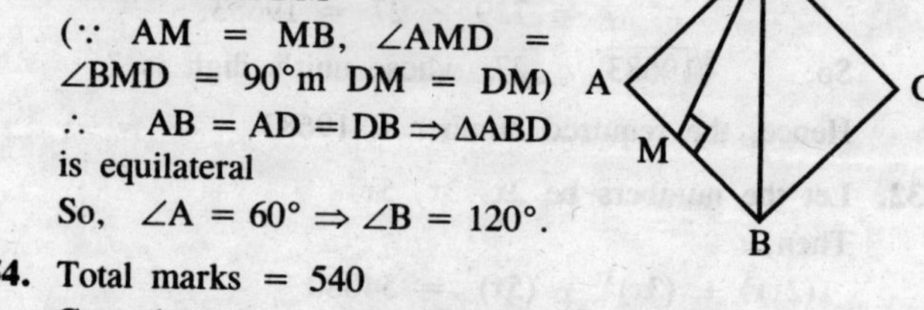

54. Total marks = 540

Central angle corresponding to 105 marks,

$$= \frac{105}{540} \times 360°$$

$$= \frac{105 \times 360}{540} = \frac{105 \times 2}{3} = 70°$$

From the pie chart, the sector of 70° represents Hindi, hence the required subject is Hindi.

55. Let ∠BCA = x

Then ∠CAB = $2x$ and ∠ABC = 90°

In ΔABC,

$$x + 2x + 90° = 180°$$

$$3x = 90° \Rightarrow x = 30°$$

$$\angle CAB = 2x = 60°.$$

56. Let the three angles be $3x$, $4x$, $5x$

Since the sum of angles of a triangle is 180°,

$$3x + 4x + 5x = 180°$$

$$12x = 180° \Rightarrow x = 15°$$

Largest angle $= 5x = 5 \times 15° = 75°$.

57. Numbers obtained when a die is rolled once = 1, 2, 3, 4, 5, 6 (Total outcomes = 6)

Multiples of 3 = 3 and 6

Number of favorable outcomes = 2

$$\text{Probability} = \frac{2}{6} = \frac{1}{3}.$$

58. Side of square garden = 8 m
Footpath is 1 m wide all around, so outer side
$= 8 + 1 + 1 = 10$ m
Area of outer square $= 10^2 = 100\ m^2$
Area of garden $= 8^2 = 64\ m^2$
Area of footpath $= 100 - 64 = 36\ m^2$.

59. Volume of a cylinder $= \pi r^2 h$
Original volume $= \pi r^2 h$
New radius $= 2r$, new height $= 3h$
New volume $= \pi(2r)^2\ (3h)$
$= \pi \times 4r^2 \times 3h = 12\pi r^2 h$
Required ratio $= 12\pi r^2 h : \pi r^2 h = 12 : 1$.

60. Perimeter of rectangle,
$2(l + b) = 160$
$l + b = 80$
Given, $l = 2b + 5$
So, $2b + 5 + b = 80$
$3b + 5 = 80$
$3b = 75 \Rightarrow b = 25$
Then, $l = 2(25) + 5$
$l = 50 + 5 = 55$ m.

61. $13x - 6(9 + 2x) + 2x = 6$
$13x - 54 - 12x + 2x = 6$
$3x - 54 = 6$
$3x = 60$
$x = 20$.

62. $\frac{3y+4}{2-6y} + \frac{2}{5} = 0$
$\frac{3y+4}{2-6y} = -\frac{2}{5}$
$5(3y + 4) = -2(2 - 6y)$
$15y + 20 = -4 + 12y$
$15y - 12y = -4 - 20$
$3y = -24$
$y = -8$.

63. $(5z^3)(4y^2)(2x^3) = (5 \times 4 \times 2)(x^3)(y^2)(z^3)$
$= 40x^3y^2z^3$
Hence, it is identical to $40x^3y^2z^3$.

64. Area of square $= 25y^2 + 16x^2 - 40xy$
Rearranging $= 25y^2 - 40xy + 16x^2$
$= (5y - 4x)^2$
Therefore, side of the square $= 5y - 4x$.

65. Let the numbers be $3x$ and $5x$
Their difference is 46,
So, $5x - 3x = 46$
$2x = 46$
$x = 23$
Larger number $= 5x = 5 \times 23 = 115$.

66. Biodiversity includes not only the variety of living organisms but also how they interact with each other and with their surroundings. It covers genetic, species, and ecosystem diversity, making option D the most comprehensive definition.

67. Migratory birds travel long distances mainly for survival reasons such as food availability, favorable climate, and reproduction. Testing their flying ability is not a biological reason for migration, hence this option is incorrect.

68. A plane mirror always forms an image that is upright (erect) and exactly equal in size to the object. The image is also virtual and laterally inverted, but size and position remain unchanged.

69. At puberty in boys, shoulders broaden and chest widens, and facial hair begins to grow. Estrogen is mainly a female hormone, and Adam's apple actually becomes prominent (not small), so only statements 3 and 4 are correct.

70. Metamorphosis of tadpoles into adult frogs is controlled by the hormone thyroxine. If this hormone is lacking, the transformation is delayed or does not occur, explaining the observed condition.

71. In hens, fertilisation takes place inside the body, so they show internal fertilisation. Protective layers are formed around the developing embryo, and the embryo takes about 3 weeks to develop into a chick. Hens lay eggs, so they are oviparous, not viviparous. Therefore, only statement 4 is incorrect.

72. In a cow, the young one resembles its parents because there is no larval stage or metamorphosis. In frog, butterfly, and mosquito, the young forms are very different from the adults during early stages. Hence, cow is the correct answer.

73. First, hormones are secreted by endocrine glands. Then these glands release them into the bloodstream, after which they are transported to the target site. Finally, the target site responds, and changes are observed in the body. So the correct sequence is 1,3,2,4.

74. When the bulb is pressed, air goes out of the dropper. When the pressure on the bulb is released, the pressure inside becomes lower, and atmospheric pressure acting on the water surface pushes water up into the dropper. Therefore, this happens due to atmospheric pressure.

75. Rolling friction is the least, sliding friction is greater than rolling friction, and static friction is the greatest among these three. Therefore, the correct increasing order is rolling friction, then sliding friction, then static friction.

76. Friction arises due to irregularities present on the surfaces in contact. When surfaces are made smooth, these irregularities are reduced, leading to less interlocking and hence reduced friction. Therefore, smoothing surfaces helps in minimizing friction.

77. The normal human ear can hear sounds within the frequency range of 20 Hz to 20,000 Hz. Sounds below 20 Hz are called infrasonic and above 20,000 Hz are ultrasonic, both of which are not audible to humans.

78. Pressure at the base of a liquid column depends only on height, $P = \rho gh$
From the figure, compare heights (not volumes):
R has the least height → least pressure
Q has more height than R

P has more height than Q
S has the maximum height → highest pressure
So, increasing order of pressure: R < Q < P < S.

79. Pressure $= \frac{\text{Force}}{\text{Area}}$

Since all four rods have the same mass, their weights are the same. Therefore, the rod with the smallest cross-sectional area will exert the greatest pressure on sand and will penetrate the most. Among radii 8 cm, 4 cm, 12 cm, and 10 cm, the smallest radius is 4 cm, so rod B will penetrate the most.

80. During a thunderstorm, charges separate inside the cloud. The lighter positive charges accumulate near the upper part of the cloud, while negative charges collect near the lower part. Hence, positive charges are found near the upper edge of the cloud.

81. Earthquakes are mainly caused by sudden movements in the Earth's crust. The crust is broken into tectonic plates, and when these plates move or slip, seismic waves are produced. Therefore, the crust is the layer responsible for causing earthquakes.

82. Electroplating is commonly done using metals such as nickel, silver, and chromium to improve appearance and prevent corrosion. Sodium is highly reactive and is not used for electroplating metallic objects. Hence, sodium is the correct answer.

83. Vinegar contains acetic acid and produces ions in solution, so it can conduct electricity. Vegetable oil is a poor conductor, distilled water has almost no ions, and sugar solution does not ionize in water. Therefore, vinegar can conduct electricity.

84. Electric current can produce heat in appliances such as heaters, magnetic effect in electromagnets, and chemical effect in processes like electrolysis. So electric current can produce all these three effects.

85. Frequency, $f = \frac{\text{Number of oscillations}}{\text{Time}}$

$$f = \frac{15}{30} = 0.5 \text{ Hz}$$

Time period, $T = \frac{1}{f} = \frac{1}{0.5} = 2\ s.$

86. Initial distance from mirror = 12 m
Distance between object and image = 2 × 12 = 24 m
Let she walks x m towards mirror,
New distance = $12 - x$
Distance between object and image = $2(12 - x) = 6$
$24 - 2x = 6$
$2x = 18$
$x = 9$ m.

87. Angle with reflecting surface = 35°
Angle with normal = 90° − 35° = 55°
Angle of reflection = angle of incidence = 55°.

88. When glass rod is rubbed with silk, electrons move from glass to silk.
Glass loses electrons → becomes positively charged.
Silk gains electrons → becomes negatively charged.

89. Antibiotics are substances produced by certain bacteria and fungi which inhibit or kill other microorganisms. For example, penicillin is produced by fungi.

90. Measles spreads through air via droplets released during coughing or sneezing, so I → 2.
Hepatitis A spreads mainly through contaminated water, so II → 4.
Cholera is caused by contaminated food or water (especially water-borne bacteria), so III → 1.
Chicken pox spreads through air and also by direct contact with infected person, so IV → 3.

91. Coal processing produces coke, coal tar, and coal gas as major products. Bitumen, however, is obtained from petroleum, not coal. Therefore, bitumen is not a product of coal processing.

92. Spirogyra and Chlamydomonas are simple, photosynthetic organisms that belong to the group algae. They are aquatic and perform photosynthesis like plants.

93. The Red Data Book is maintained to record species that are at risk of extinction. It mainly lists endangered plants and animals to help in their conservation and protection.

94. Human sperm consists of head, middle piece, and tail, so statement 1 is correct. A sperm alone is not a new individual, fertilisation occurs in the oviduct (not testes), and sperm moves towards egg, not vice versa. Hence only statement 1 is correct.

95. In spontaneous combustion, substances like phosphorus catch fire on their own when exposed to air without any external ignition source. This occurs due to low ignition temperature and reaction with oxygen.

96. Electrical fires and fires involving inflammable liquids like petrol cannot be controlled by water because water conducts electricity and spreads burning liquids. Carbon dioxide cuts off oxygen supply and does not conduct electricity, making it the safest option.

97. Inexhaustible resources are those that cannot be depleted by human use. Sunlight is continuously available and renewable, whereas minerals, petroleum, and natural gas are limited resources.

98. Weeds should be removed early before they flower and produce seeds, because once seeds are formed, they spread and increase weed growth in future crops.

99. Silos are storage structures designed to keep grains safe from pests, moisture, and insects. They help in maintaining quality during long-term storage.

100. Rhizobium bacteria live in root nodules of leguminous plants like gram and help in nitrogen fixation. Fertilizers do not add humus, mustard is a rabi crop (not sown in rainy season), and seed drills ensure proper covering of seeds with soil.

Previous Years' Paper

JAWAHAR NAVODAYA VIDYALAYA

Class-IX, Entrance Exam, 2025

(Exam held on 08-02-2025)

SECTION-I: हिन्दी

निर्देश (प्रश्न संख्या 1-15 तक): *प्रत्येक प्रश्न के लिए चार सम्भावित उत्तर विकल्प दिए गए हैं, जिनमें से केवल एक सही है। सही उत्तर चुनकर उसको ओ.एम.आर. उत्तर-पत्रिका पर उपयुक्त स्थान पर दर्शाना है।*

1. 'सावन हरे न भादों सूखे'—इस लोकोक्ति का अर्थ है :
A. सूखा पड़ने पर भी प्रसन्न रहना
B. हानि होने पर भी प्रसन्न रहना
C. सदा एकरस रहना
D. वर्षा ऋतु में चारों ओर हरा-भरा रहना

2. 'हाथ बँटाना' का अर्थ है :
A. सहायता लेना B. सहायता करना
C. काम करना D. काम देना

3. वह आँधी के समान आई और तूफान सी चली गई। उपर्युक्त वाक्य का भेद है :
A. सरल वाक्य B. संयुक्त वाक्य
C. मिश्र वाक्य D. क्रिया वाक्य

4. 'आमरण' शब्द में समास है :
A. तत्पुरुष समास
B. बहुव्रीहि समास
C. अव्ययीभाव समास
D. कर्मधारय समास

5. 'जो व्यक्ति किसी के उपकार को मानता हो'—उसके लिए कौन-सा शब्द उपयुक्त है?
A. कृतज्ञ B. कृतघ्न
C. ऋणी D. उपकृत

6. नीचे दिए गए शब्दों में से कौन-सा शब्द 'कमल' का पर्यायवाची नहीं है?
A. जलद B. जलज
C. पंकज D. राजीव

7. 'स्वाधीन' का विलोम है :
A. दास B. आजाद
C. पराधीन D. परवश

8. 'रस' शब्द में इया जोड़ने पर शब्द बनेगा :
A. रसीया B. रासीया
C. रसिया D. रासिया

9. निम्नलिखित में से कौन-सी वर्तनी शुद्ध है?
A. इतिहासिक B. ऐतिहासिक
C. एतिहासिक D. ऐतिहासिक

10. 'शैशव' शब्द से किस प्रकार की संज्ञा का बोध होता है?
A. समूहवाचक B. भाववाचक
C. जातिवाचक D. व्यक्तिवाचक

निर्देश (प्रश्न संख्या 11-15): *निम्नलिखित अनुच्छेद को पढ़कर सर्वाधिक उपयुक्त उत्तर चुनिए :*

सत्संग और निजी अनुभवों से कबीर ने ज्ञान तो प्राप्त कर लिया था, पर वे एक सद्गुरु का सहारा भी चाहते थे। उस समय स्वामी रामानंद काशी में ही रहते थे। उनका समाज में बड़ा आदर था। वे बड़े विद्वान और सिद्ध महात्मा माने जाते थे। कबीर उन्हीं को अपना गुरु बनाना चाहते थे। कबीर मुसलमान थे, इसलिए उनको भय था कि रामानंद जी उन्हें अपना शिष्य नहीं बनाएँगे। रामानंद रोज सवेरे गंगा स्नान करने जाते थे। एक दिन कबीर प्रातःकाल से पहले ही जाकर घाट की सीढ़ियों पर लेट गए। अँधेरे में रामानंद जी का पैर सीढ़ियों पर लेटे कबीर पर पड़ गया और उनके मुँह से ''राम-राम'' निकल पड़ा। बस कबीर ने इसी को गुरु-मंत्र मान लिया। उन्होंने बड़ी श्रद्धा से रामानंद जी के पैर पकड़ लिए। रामानंद जी ने भी कबीर को अपना शिष्य मान लिया। रामानंद जी की भाँति कबीर ने भी कहा था कि राम की भक्ति का सभी को अधिकार है। बिना किसी भेदभाव के सभी जातियों और संप्रदायों के लोग राम की उपासना कर सकते हैं। कबीर जाति-पाँति के भेदभाव के सख्त विरोधी थे। उनका कहना था

1. C **2.** B **3.** B **4.** C **5.** A **6.** A **7.** C **8.** C **9.** D **10.** B

कि ईश्वर ने ही सबको बनाया है। उसकी दृष्टि में सब समान हैं। न कोई ऊँचा है, न कोई नीचा है। जो लोग भेदभाव की भावना रखते हैं, वे ईश्वर के विरुद्ध काम करते हैं। कबीर मानते थे कि सब धर्मों और सम्प्रदायों का लक्ष्य एक ही है। लक्ष्य को प्राप्त करने के लिए मार्ग अलग-अलग हैं।

11. रामानंद जी का पैर सीढ़ियों पर लेटे कबीर पर पड़ा तो क्या हुआ?
A. कबीर को चोट लग गई।
B. रामानंद फिसल गए।
C. रामानंद के मुँह से "राम-राम" निकल पड़ा।
D. रामानंद गंगा-स्नान नहीं कर पाए।

12. कबीर जाति-पाँति के भेदभाव के सख्त विरोधी थे, क्योंकि :
A. कबीर को अपनी जाति का पता नहीं था।
B. कबीर मानते थे कि ईश्वर ने सबको नहीं बनाया।
C. जो लोग भेदभाव की बात करते हैं, वे ईश्वर में विश्वास नहीं करते हैं।
D. वे मानते थे कि ईश्वर ने ही सबको बनाया है, उसकी दृष्टि में सब समान हैं।

13. अनुच्छेद के अनुसार ऊँच-नीच और भेदभाव की भावना रखने वाले :
A. नास्तिक हैं।
B. आस्तिक हैं।
C. ईश्वर के विरुद्ध काम करते हैं।
D. सगुण के उपासक हैं।

14. रामानंद का समाज में बड़ा आदर था, क्योंकि :
A. वे कबीर के गुरु बनना चाहते थे।
B. वे निर्गुण सम्प्रदाय के थे।
C. वे बड़े सिद्ध महात्मा माने जाते थे।
D. वे काशी में रहते थे।

15. कबीर को भय था कि रामानंद जी उन्हें अपना शिष्य नहीं बनाएँगे, क्योंकि :
A. कबीर मुसलमान थे।
B. कबीर पढ़े लिखे नहीं थे।
C. रामानंद उनको नहीं जानते थे।
D. रामानंद निर्गुण के उपासक थे।

SECTION-II: ENGLISH

Directions (Qs. No. 16-30): *For each question, **four** possible answer choices have been given, out of which only **one** is correct. Select the correct answer and indicate it at the appropriate place in the OMR Answer Sheet.*

Directions (Qs. No. 16-19): *Answer these questions by choosing the most appropriate options to complete the paragraph by filling in the blanks.*

After Ram had saved (16) money for the rail ticket, his next problem was (17) to leave home (18) his parent's knowledge. He did not have the courage (19) ask them.

16. A. much B. few C. little D. enough

17. A. how B. where C. which D. who

18. A. for B. without C. on D. into

19. A. but B. and C. to D. too

20. Choose the word most similar in meaning to the word "stubborn".
A. obstinate B. proud
C. arrogant D. docile

21. Choose the word opposite in meaning to the underlined word.

He <u>dropped</u> the letter into the mailbox.
A. sank B. struck
C. lifted D. uncovered

22. Which of the following options correctly changes the sentence into passive voice?

If you want to enhance the taste of your cold coffee, add a scoop of vanilla ice cream to it.
A. If a scoop of vanilla ice cream is added to cold coffee, its taste is enhanced.
B. By adding a scoop of vanilla ice cream, you can enhance the taste of cold coffee.
C. To enhance the taste of cold coffee, add a scoop of vanilla ice cream to it.
D. Cold coffee taste is enhanced by adding a scoop of vanilla ice cream.

11. C **12.** D **13.** C **14.** C **15.** A **16.** D **17.** A **18.** B **19.** C **20.** A **21.** C **22.** A

Directions (Qs. No. 23-25): *Which option fit best to fill in the blanks.*

23. He as well as his friend ………… going to win the medal today.

A. is B. are
C. was D. were

24. Rashmi is ……… than any other girl in the class.

A. tall B. taller
C. tallest D. most tall

25. I think Chinese and Japanese are two of the …….. languages to learn.

A. very difficult B. most difficult
C. more difficult D. difficult

26. Choose the one-word substitute for the following expression.

'One who is all powerful'

A. Omnipresent B. Omniscient
C. Omnipotent D. Omnivorous

27. Select the alternative which best expresses the following sentence in indirect speech.

In his address to the nation, Prime Minister Modi said, "Do not forget to wear your mask and observe social distancing when you go out for any work."

A. In his address to the nation, Prime Minister Modi told his people not to forget wearing your masks and observe social distancing when you went out for any work.
B. In his address to the nation, Prime Minister Modi said to people they should not forget to wear their masks and observe social distancing when they go for any work.
C. In his address to the nation, Prime Minister Modi reminded people not to forget to wear masks and observe social distance when they goes out for any work.
D. In his address to the nation, Prime Minister Modi advised people not to forget to wear their masks and observe social distancing when they went out for any work.

Directions (Qs. No. 28-30): *Read the following passage carefully and answer the questions.*

The boat approached the tree. There was a boy in the boat who held on to one of the branches to steady himself, giving his free hand to Sita. She grasped it and slipped into the boat beside him. The boy placed his bare foot against the tree trunk and pushed it away. The little boat moved swiftly down the river. The big tree was left far behind.

28. How was Sita helped?

(*i*) The boy caught hold of a branch.
(*ii*) He gave his hand to Sita.

Options:

A. (*i*) is right and (*ii*) is wrong
B. (*i*) is wrong and (*ii*) is right
C. Both (*i*) and (*ii*) are right
D. Both (*i*) and (*ii*) are wrong

29. What did the boy do with the tree?

A. He pushed it away with his foot.
B. Both Sita and the boy pushed the tree away.
C. The boy cut down the tree.
D. He hit the tree with his boat.

30. Who helped Sita?

A. The boat B. The branches
C. A boy D. The tree

SECTION-III: MATHEMATICS

Directions (Qs. No. 31-65): *For each question, four possible answer choices have been given, out of which only* ***one*** *is correct. Select the correct answer and indicate it at the appropriate place in the OMR Answer Sheet.*

31. $(x + y)^2 - 4xy$ is equal to:

A. $(x + 2y)^2$ B. $(2x + y)^2$
C. $(x + y - 4xy)^2$ D. $(x - y)^2$

32. Which is the like term to $32ab^2c$?

A. $8 \times 4 \times 2 \times a \times b \times c \times b$
B. $16 \times 2 \times a \times b \times c$
C. $4 \times 4 \times 2 \times a \times b \times c \times c$
D. $4 \times 8 \times a \times b \times c \times a$

33. $(507)^2 - (497)^2 = ?$

A. 10040 B. 1004
C. 10140 D. 1014

34. When the price of a cycle was reduced by 20%, the number of cycles sold increased by 20%. The effect on the total sale of the shop is:

A. 4% decrease B. 4% increase
C. 10% increase D. 10% decrease

23. A **24.** B **25.** B **26.** C **27.** D **28.** C **29.** A **30.** C **31.** D **32.** A **33.** A **34.** A

35. The compound interest on ₹ 800 at 5% p.a. for 2 years is:

A. ₹ 82 B. ₹ 882
C. ₹ 820 D. ₹ 28

36. A bag has 4 red balls and 2 yellow balls. (The balls are identical in all respects other than colour). A ball is drawn from the bag without looking into the bag. The probability of getting a red ball is:

A. $\frac{1}{2}$ B. $\frac{2}{3}$
C. $\frac{1}{4}$ D. $\frac{1}{5}$

37. The given bar graph shows the number of students in a hostel speaking different languages. The total number of students in the hostel is:

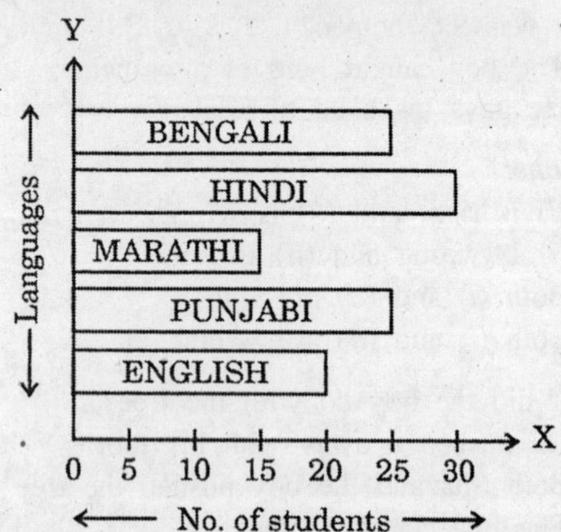

A. 120 B. 110
C. 105 D. 115

38. The probability of selecting a black queen from a well-shuffled pack of 52 cards is:

A. $\frac{1}{26}$ B. $\frac{1}{13}$
C. $\frac{1}{4}$ D. $\frac{1}{8}$

39. How many cubic meters of earth must be dug out to construct a well of depth 28 m and diameter 3 m?

A. 198 m^3 B. 128 m^3
C. 60 m^3 D. 72 m^3

40. Five years hence, a father's age will be three times the age of his son. Five years ago, the father was 7 times as old as his son then. The present age of the father (in years) is:

A. 10 B. 40
C. 35 D. 45

41. The sum of the digits of a 2-digit number is 11. The digits are reversed and the new number is subtracted from the original number, to get 27. The original number is:

A. 65 B. 92
C. 47 D. 74

42. Factors of $4a^2 + 9b^2 - 16c^2 - 12ab$ are:

A. $(2a - 3b - 4c)(2a + 3b + 4c)$
B. $(2a + 3b - 4c)(2a + 3b + 4c)$
C. $(2a - 3b - 4c)(2a - 3b + 4c)$
D. $(a + b + c)(4a - 9b + 4c)$

43. $\left(\frac{3}{11}\times\frac{5}{6}\right)-\left(\frac{9}{12}\times\frac{4}{3}\right)+\left(\frac{5}{13}\times\frac{6}{15}\right)$, on simplification, becomes:

A. $-\frac{177}{286}$ B. $-\frac{303}{40}$
C. $\frac{289}{492}$ D. $\frac{17}{24}$

44. The cube root of $-3\frac{3}{8}$ is:

A. $\frac{3}{2}$ B. $\frac{2}{3}$
C. $-\frac{2}{3}$ D. $-\frac{3}{2}$

45. Which of the following is the cube root of 0.027?

A. 0.003 B. 0.03
C. 0.3 D. 3

46. The length of a side of a cubical box whose volume is 1.331 cm^3 is:

A. 0.13 cm B. 0.11 cm
C. 1.1 cm D. 11 cm

47. If $3x + 4y = 18$ and $xy = 6$, then the value of $9x^2 + 16y^2$ is:

A. 324 B. 180
C. 170 D. 144

48. The square root of 218 lies between:

A. 12 and 13
B. 13 and 14
C. 14 and 15
D. 15 and 16

49. Which one of the following numbers ends with the digit 1?

A. 123^2 B. 149^2
C. 82^2 D. 117^2

35. A	**36.** B	**37.** D	**38.** A	**39.** A	**40.** B	**41.** D	**42.** C	**43.** A	**44.** D
45. C	**46.** C	**47.** B	**48.** C	**49.** B					

50. The value of $\sqrt{10+\sqrt{25+\sqrt{108+\sqrt{154+\sqrt{225}}}}}$ + $\left(\sqrt{\frac{225}{729}}-\sqrt{\frac{25}{144}}\right)\div\sqrt{\frac{16}{81}}$ is:

A. $\frac{69}{16}$ B. $\frac{31}{3}$
C. $\frac{54}{7}$ D. $\frac{108}{13}$

51. A regular polygon has 18 sides. The measure of an exterior angle of this polygon is:

A. 160° B. 18°
C. 36° D. 20°

52. The area of a square is $4x^2 + 4x + 1$. The perimeter of the square is:

A. $4(x + 1)$ B. $4(x - 1)$
C. $4(2x + 1)$ D. $4(2x - 1)$

53. The volume of a cube whose surface area is 600 m^2, is:

A. 100 m^3 B. 200 m^3
C. 500 m^3 D. 1000 m^3

54. The area of an equilateral triangle is $24\sqrt{3}$ sq. cm. The perimeter of this triangle (in cm) is:

A. $6\sqrt{6}$ B. $12\sqrt{6}$
C. $15\sqrt{6}$ D. $15\sqrt{3}$

55. ABCD is a rhombus in which ∠ABC = 80°. The measure of ∠CAD is:

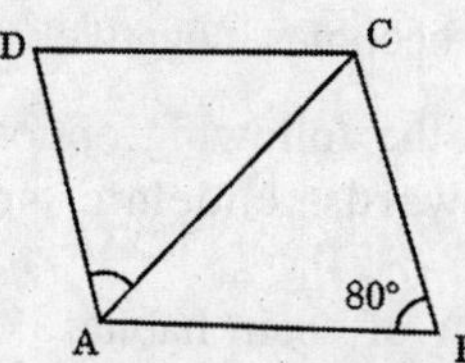

A. 45° B. 50°
C. 80° D. 100°

56. The number of sides of a regular polygon whose each exterior angle has a measure of 30° is:

A. 12 B. 6
C. 8 D. 10

57. The speed 30 m/s when converted into km/h is:

A. 30 km/h B. 60 km/h
C. 108 km/h D. 144 km/h

58. Hari wants to buy a rectangular field whose area is $(3a^2 + 5ab + 2b^2)$ sq. units. If one of its sides is $(a + b)$ units, then the length of the fence around the field is:

A. $(10a + 20b)$ units B. $(4a + 3b)$ units
C. $(2a + 2b)$ units D. $(8a + 6b)$ units

59. A man insures 90% of his property and pays $1\frac{2}{3}\%$ premium amounting to ₹ 360. The total value of the property is:

A. ₹ 18,000 B. ₹ 24,000
C. ₹ 30,000 D. ₹ 28,000

60. Which of the following values are equal?

P : 1^4; Q : 4^0; R : 0^4; S : 4^1

A. P and Q B. Q and R
C. P and R D. P and S

61. $[(2)^8 \div (2)^5]^3 \div 2^5$ on simplification, becomes:

A. 2^{14} B. 2^4
C. 2^{22} D. 2^{32}

62. The radii of the bases of two cylinders are in the ratio of 1 : 2 respectively and their heights are in the ratio 2 : 1 respectively. The ratio of their volumes is:

A. 1 : 2 B. 1 : 4
C. 2 : 1 D. 4 : 1

63. A 2-digit number is less than 20. The sum of the digits is double that of their product. The number is:

A. 12 B. 15
C. 11 D. 13

64. Which of the following is true?

A. $\frac{13}{16}+\frac{17}{18}=\frac{17}{18}+\frac{13}{16}$ B. $\frac{13}{16}\times\frac{17}{18}=\frac{16}{13}\times\frac{18}{17}$

C. $\frac{13}{16}-\frac{17}{18}=\frac{17}{18}-\frac{13}{16}$ D. $\frac{13}{16}\div\frac{17}{18}=\frac{17}{18}\div\frac{13}{16}$

65. Which of the following is **not** true?

A. $\left(\frac{2}{3}+\frac{3}{4}\right)+\frac{5}{7}=\frac{2}{3}+\left(\frac{3}{4}+\frac{5}{7}\right)$

B. $\left(\frac{2}{3}\times\frac{3}{4}\right)\times\frac{5}{7}=\frac{2}{3}\times\left(\frac{3}{4}\times\frac{5}{7}\right)$

C. $\left(\frac{2}{3}-\frac{3}{4}\right)-\frac{5}{7}=\frac{2}{3}-\left(\frac{3}{4}-\frac{5}{7}\right)$

D. $\left(\frac{2}{3}-\frac{3}{4}\right)-\frac{5}{7}=\frac{2}{3}-\left(\frac{3}{4}+\frac{5}{7}\right)$

50. A	**51.** D	**52.** C	**53.** D	**54.** B	**55.** B	**56.** A	**57.** C	**58.** D	**59.** B
60. A	**61.** B	**62.** A	**63.** C	**64.** A	**65.** C				

SECTION-IV: GENERAL SCIENCE

Directions (Qs. No. 66-100): *For each question, four possible answer choices have been given, out of which only* **one** *is correct. Select the correct answer and indicate it at the appropriate place in the OMR Answer Sheet.*

66. *Aspergillus* and *Penicillium* belong to the group:

A. Bacteria B. Fungi
C. Algae D. Protozoa

67. Put some seeds of wheat in a beaker containing water and stir well. Wait for some time. Which one of the following inferences is correct for this activity?

A. Healthy seeds being lighter, float on the surface of water
B. Damaged seeds being lighter, float on the surface of water.
C. Damaged seeds being heavier, settle down at the bottom of the beaker.
D. All seeds, healthy as well as damaged, float on the surface of water.

68. Mirror MM_1 and MM_2 are arranged as shown in the figure. A ray of light is incident on mirror MM_1, as shown. What angle does the reflected ray make from MM_2 as it reflects out from mirror MM_2?

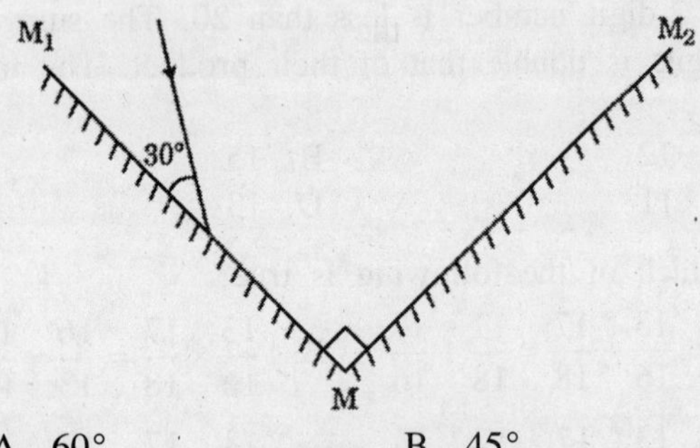

A. 60° B. 45°
C. 0° D. 30°

69. In making a kaleidoscope:

A. two identical rectangular strips of plane mirrors are kept inclined at an angle of 90° with each other.
B. three identical rectangular strips of plane mirrors are kept inclined at angles of 60° with each other.
C. two identical rectangular strips of plane mirrors are kept parallel to each other.
D. three identical rectangular strips of plane mirrors of different widths are used.

70. If in a classroom, large, same-sized plane mirrors are fixed on two adjacent walls, then a student will be able to see how many images of himself/herself?

A. 2 B. 12
C. 6 D. 3

71. Which of the following statements is true?

A. An earthquake of intensity 4 on the Richter scale is twice more devastating than an earthquake of intensity 2.
B. An earthquake of intensity 6 on the Richter scale is half as devastating as an earthquake of intensity 3.
C. An earthquake of intensity 4 on the Richter scale is 1000 times more devastating than an earthquake of intensity 3.
D. An earthquake of intensity 7 on the Richter scale is 1000 times more devastating than an earthquake of intensity 5.

72. Lightning strikes could destroy life and property. We can protect ourselves from lightning by:

A. avoiding bathing during a thunderstorm.
B. taking shelter under a tall tree.
C. watching TV programmes.
D. carrying an umbrella during a thunderstorm.

73. When a plastic straw is rubbed with polythene the:

A. straw and polythene both acquire negative charge.
B. straw becomes negatively charged and the polythene becomes positively charged.
C. straw and polythene both acquire positive charge.
D. straw becomes positively charged and the polythene becomes negatively charged.

74. Which one of the following options is an **incorrect** statement towards endemic species becoming endangered?

A. Destruction of their habitat
B. Increase in population of that species in the area
C. Introduction of new species in that area
D. Increased habitat protection for that species in the area

75. Which of the following is ***not*** true for a wildlife sanctuary?

A. Wildlife sanctuaries provide protection and suitable living conditions to wild animals.
B. People living in wildlife sanctuaries are allowed to collect medicinal plants, firewood, etc.
C. Poaching or capturing animals is allowed only to the people living in the wildlife sanctuary.
D. An area where animals are protected from any disturbance to them and their habitat.

66. B **67.** B **68.** D **69.** B **70.** D **71.** D **72.** A **73.** D **74.** D **75.** C

76. Metamorphosis in frogs is controlled by a hormone called:

A. Thyroxine B. Adrenalin
C. Growth hormone D. Insulin

77. By which one of the following ways can HIV virus **not** be transmitted from an infected person to a healthy person?

A. Sharing needles and syringes for injecting drugs.
B. From a mother to an infant through her milk.
C. Through sexual contact.
D. By shaking hands or sharing food.

78. Consider the following statements:

1. Human beings have 22 pairs of chromosomes in the nuclei of their body cells.
2. The unfertilized egg has one 'X' chromosome only.
3. The zygote would develop into a male child if the sperm contributes a 'Y' chromosome to the ovum at the time of fertilization.
4. Sex in all the living organisms is genetically determined.

The *incorrect* statements are:

A. 1 and 2 B. 2 and 3
C. 1 and 4 D. 1, 2 and 4

79. Identify the solution which does ***not*** conduct electricity.

A. Sugar solution
B. Vinegar solution
C. Lemon juice solution
D. Caustic soda solution

80. Which one of the following metals is used in electroplating an iron object to make it shiny and rust free?

A. Aluminium B. Copper
C. Zinc D. Chromium

81. Two experiments are performed taking similar electric bulbs and cells but two different solutions A and B as shown in the figure. It was found that the bulb in the set-up A glows more brightly as compared to that of set-up B. We can conclude that:

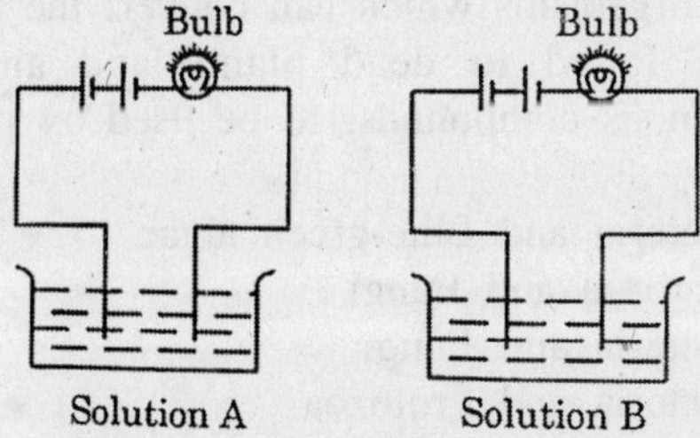

A. equal current is flowing through both the circuits.
B. set-up B may have some loose contacts.
C. solution A is a better conductor of electricity than solution B.
D. higher current is flowing through the circuit in set-up B.

82. Which one of the following can be treated as a contact force?

A. Muscular force B. Gravitational force
C. Electrostatic force D. Magnetic force

83. Srijana rolls a ball on dry marble floor, wet marble floor, newspaper and mat spread on the floor. The force of friction, acting on the rolling ball on different surfaces, in decreasing order will be:

A. Mat, newspaper, dry marble floor, wet marble floor.
B. Wet marble floor, dry marble floor, newspaper, mat.
C. Dry marble floor, wet marble floor, newspaper, mat.
D. Mat, wet marble floor, newspaper, dry marble floor.

84. Vineeta was driving a car and passing by a ploughed field in a rural area. Suddenly she felt that the brakes failed to work. The level of road was just above the level of the ploughed field. Which of the following actions would be scientifically correct for her to stop or slow down the car instantly?

A. Keep on honking while driving.
B. Search for a tree by the side of road so that the car can go and hit it.
C. Turning her car towards the ploughed field.
D. Screaming and shouting from the car to raise an alarm.

85. The necessary condition for a force to come into play is that we must have:

A. one object which must pull.
B. two objects to maintain a distance.
C. two objects to interact with each other.
D. one object which must push.

86. During winters some people sleep in a closed room with burning or smouldering coal fire which results in their death. The cause of their death is due to the formation of a very poisonous gas, which is:

A. Carbon dioxide B. Nitrogen dioxide
C. Carbon monoxide D. Sulphur dioxide

76. A **77.** D **78.** C **79.** A **80.** D **81.** C **82.** A **83.** A **84.** C **85.** C
86. C

87. Which of the following fuels has maximum calorific value?

A. Wood B. Coal
C. Hydrogen D. Petrol

88. Select from the following a group of products obtained by refining of petroleum:

A. Petrol, diesel, coal tar
B. Bitumen, detergents, polyester
C. Lubricating oil, paraffin wax, diesel
D. Acrylic, nylon, coke

89. The correct sequence of events during reproduction in human females is:

A. Ovulation → Fertilization → Zygote → Embryo → Foetus
B. Ovulation → Zygote → Fertilization → Embryo → Foetus
C. Fertilization → Zygote → Ovulation → Embryo → Foetus
D. Zygote → Embryo → Foetus → Ovulation → Fertilization

90. An ecosystem is made of:

A. only the plants, animals and microorganisms found in an area.
B. only the plants of an area and their interaction with the non-living components of that area.
C. only the animals of an area along with the decomposers present around them in the soil.
D. all the plants, animals and microorganisms in an area along with the non-living components like air, soil, etc.

91. The organism which reproduces asexually in the same way as yeast is:

A. Amoeba B. Hydra
C. Starfish D. Silkworm

92. Which of the following statement(s) is/are true reason(s) to explain the production of a large number of eggs and sperms in fishes?

1. Eggs and sperms are exposed to movement of water, rainfall and wind.
2. Production of more eggs and sperms ensures better chances of fertilization.
3. Large number of eggs are produced by aquatic animals due to plenty of food available in water.
4. Eggs may also be eaten by other animals in the pond.

A. 1 only B. 1, 2 and 4
C. 2 and 3 D. 3 and 4

93. Sound ***cannot*** travel through:

A. solids B. liquids
C. gases D. vacuum

94. The sound produced in a jal-tarang is due to the vibrations of the:

A. striking stick.
B. bowl or tumbler.
C. water in the bowl or tumbler.
D. air column above water in the bowl or tumbler.

95. When a force F is applied on a block A placed on a surface, it just tends to slide in the direction of the force. When another identical block B is placed on the top of A, the force required to achieve the same condition sliding will be:

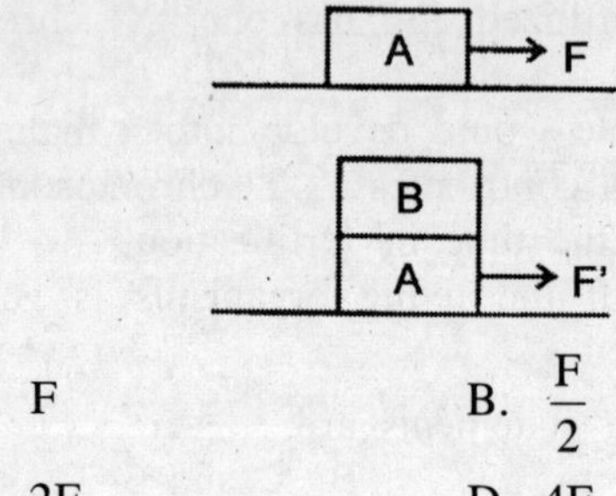

A. F B. $\frac{F}{2}$
C. 2F D. 4F

96. Select the option having correct matching of the food items given in Column I with their method of preservation given in Column II.

Column I	Column II
P. Amla	(*i*) Sodium metabisulphite
Q. Fish	(*ii*) Pasteurisation
R. Squashes	(*iii*) Salt
S. Milk	(*iv*) Oil and Vinegar

A. P-(*iv*), Q-(*ii*), R-(*i*), S-(*iii*)
B. P-(*ii*), Q-(*iv*), R-(*i*), S-(*iii*)
C. P-(*iii*), Q-(*iv*), R-(*i*), S-(*ii*)
D. P-(*iv*), Q-(*i*), R-(*iii*), S-(*ii*)

97. The substance that does ***not*** produce flame on burning is:

A. LPG B. Molten wax
C. Dry grass D. Charcoal

98. Micro-organisms which can convert the nitrogenous wastes found in dead plants and animals into nitrogenous compounds, to be used by plants again are:

A. Bacteria and Blue-green algae
B. Protozoa and Fungi
C. Bacteria and Fungi
D. Bacteria and Protozoa

87. C	**88.** C	**89.** A	**90** D	**91.** B	**92.** B	**93.** D	**94.** C	**95.** C	**96.** C
97. D	**98.** C								

99. The method of irrigation in which water falls on the crop from rotating nozzles like a rainfall is called:
A. Pulley system B. Drip system
C. Dhekli system D. Sprinkler system

100. It is important to remove weeds from the cultivated fields because they:
A. help the plants to grow.
B. attract animals pests to the fields.
C. compete with plants for essential requirements of water, nutrients, space and light.
D. secretes toxic substances that cause diseases in plants.

EXPLANATORY ANSWERS

1. (C): यह लोकोक्ति इस बात पर जोर देती है कि व्यक्ति या वस्तु पर बाहरी परिवर्तनों का प्रभाव नहीं पड़ता। 'सावन हरे' का अर्थ है हरी-भरी ऋतु और 'भादों सूखे' का संकेत सूखे या प्रतिकूल समय से है। इन दोनों विरोधाभासी स्थितियों के बावजूद कोई भी परिवर्तन न होना अर्थात् सदा एक-सा बने रहना। इस कथन से तात्पर्य है कि व्यक्ति को हर परिस्थिति में स्थिर और संतुलित व्यवहार रखना चाहिए।

2. (B): 'हाथ बँटाना' एक मुहावरा है जिसका अर्थ है—किसी के काम में सहयोग देना या उसकी मदद करना। जैसे—'मैंने रसोई में माँ का हाथ बँटाया।' इसका तात्पर्य हुआ कि मैंने माँ की सहायता की।

3. (B): यह वाक्य दो स्वतंत्र उपवाक्यों—'वह आँधी के समान आई' और 'तूफान सी चली गई'—से बना है, जिन्हें 'और' द्वारा जोड़ा गया है। इस प्रकार यह दो समान और स्वतंत्र खंडों को जोड़ने वाला वाक्य है, अतः इसे संयुक्त वाक्य कहते हैं।

4. (C): 'आमरण' शब्द 'आ + मरण' से बना है, जहाँ 'आ' उपसर्ग की तरह 'मरण' क्रिया पर जुड़ा है और समस्तपद भी अव्यय (क्रिया विशेषण) होता है। अव्ययीभाव समास की विशेषता है कि पहला पद अव्यय होता है और पूरा शब्द भी अव्ययी होता है। जैसे—'सदैव', 'सर्वत्र'। 'आमरण' का अर्थ होता है—मृत्यु तक।

5. (A): जो व्यक्ति किसी के उपकार को याद रखता है और उसे मान्यता देता है, उसे 'कृतज्ञ' कहते हैं। इसके विपरीत 'कृतघ्न' वह होता है जो उपकार भूल जाए। 'ऋणी' वह होता है जो किसी से उधार या सहायता लेकर उसका कर्जदार हो। लेकिन यहाँ संदर्भ 'उपकार मानने वाले' व्यक्ति का है, इसलिए 'कृतज्ञ' उपयुक्त उत्तर है।

6. (A): 'कमल' के पर्यायवाची शब्दों में 'जलज' (जो जल में उत्पन्न हुआ), 'पंकज' (कीचड़ में उत्पन्न), 'राजीव' (राजाओं के समान शोभायमान कमल) आते हैं। जबकि 'जलद' का अर्थ होता है—मेघ या बादल। अतः यह 'कमल' का पर्याय नहीं है।

7. (C): 'स्वाधीन' का अर्थ होता है—स्वतंत्र या अपने अधीन। इसका विलोम है 'पराधीन'—जो दूसरों के अधीन हो, स्वतंत्र न हो। 'परवश' भी इसका समानार्थी है, लेकिन सबसे शुद्ध व्याकरणिक विलोम 'पराधीन' है।

8. (C): 'रस' में 'इया' प्रत्यय जोड़ने पर जो शब्द बनता है, वह है—'रसिया'। यह शब्द भाव या गुणवाचक संज्ञा का विस्तार करता है। 'रसिया' का अर्थ होता है—जो रसिक हो, आनंद प्रेमी हो। शुद्ध वर्तनी भी यही है—'रसिया'। अन्य वर्तनी जैसे 'रसीया' या 'रासिया' अशुद्ध या प्रादेशिक उच्चारण के आधार पर हैं।

9. (D): शुद्ध वर्तनी 'ऐतिहासिक' है, जो संस्कृत शब्द 'इतिहास' से बना है और 'ऐ' उपसर्ग के साथ इसका उच्चारण होता है। हिंदी में यह 'ए' नहीं बल्कि 'ऐ' होता है, जैसे—'ऐतिहासिक घटना'। शेष सभी विकल्प अशुद्ध वर्तनी हैं।

10. (B): 'शैशव' शब्द किसी व्यक्ति या वस्तु को नहीं बल्कि जीवन की एक अवस्था (बाल्यावस्था) को दर्शाता है। यह कोई भौतिक वस्तु नहीं बल्कि एक अवस्था या भाव है। इसलिए यह भाववाचक संज्ञा है। 'शैशव' का प्रयोग जैसे—''शैशव काल व्यक्ति के चरित्र निर्माण का मूल होता है।''

11. (C): कबीर एक सच्चे गुरु की तलाश में थे और वे रामानंद जी को ही गुरु बनाना चाहते थे, परंतु मुसलमान होने के कारण उन्हें भय था कि रामानंद जी उन्हें स्वीकार नहीं करेंगे। इसलिए वे एक युक्ति से रामानंद जी के चरणों में गुरु-मंत्र प्राप्त करने का प्रयास करते हैं। एक दिन कबीर घाट की सीढ़ियों पर अँधेरे में लेट गए। प्रातःकाल गंगा स्नान के लिए आते रामानंद जी का पैर कबीर पर पड़ गया और अनायास उनके मुख से "राम-राम" निकल गया। कबीर ने इसी उच्चारण को गुरु-मंत्र मानकर उन्हें अपना गुरु स्वीकार कर लिया। यह विवरण स्पष्टतः अनुच्छेद में उल्लिखित है।

12. (D): कबीर सामाजिक भेदभाव और जातिप्रथा के घोर विरोधी थे। उनका मत था कि ईश्वर ने सभी मनुष्यों को समान रूप से बनाया है, इसलिए किसी को ऊँच या नीच नहीं कहा जा सकता। अनुच्छेद में स्पष्ट कहा गया है कि ''ईश्वर ने ही सबको बनाया है। उसकी दृष्टि में सब समान हैं।''इसीलिए वे जाति-पाँति के भेदभाव के विरोधी थे।

13. (C): कबीर के अनुसार वे लोग जो जाति, ऊँच-नीच और भेदभाव की भावना रखते हैं, वे न केवल सामाजिक दृष्टि से अनुचित आचरण करते हैं, बल्कि यह ईश्वर के विरुद्ध कार्य करने के

99. D **100.** C

समान है। अनुच्छेद में स्पष्टतः कहा गया है–"जो लोग भेदभाव की भावना रखते हैं, वे ईश्वर के विरुद्ध काम करते हैं।" अतः यही सर्वाधिक उपयुक्त उत्तर है।

14. (C): रामानंद जी काशी में रहते थे और समाज में उनका अत्यधिक आदर था। अनुच्छेद में उल्लेख है–"वे बड़े विद्वान और सिद्ध महात्मा माने जाते थे।" सिद्ध महात्मा होने के कारण उनका समाज में स्थान उच्च था और लोग उन्हें श्रद्धा से देखते थे। अतः सम्मान का कारण उनका साधुता और सिद्ध पुरुष होना था।

15. (A): कबीर रामानंद जी को अपना गुरु बनाना चाहते थे, लेकिन उन्हें यह चिंता थी कि रामानंद जी उन्हें अपना शिष्य नहीं बनाएँगे क्योंकि वे मुसलमान थे। उस काल में धार्मिक और जातीय भेदभाव बहुत अधिक था। अनुच्छेद में कहा गया है–"कबीर मुसलमान थे, इसलिए उनको भय था कि रामानंद जी उन्हें अपना शिष्य नहीं बनाएँगे।" यही इस प्रश्न का कारण और उत्तर दोनों है।

16. (D): Ram had saved enough money for the rail ticket. The word "enough" correctly expresses that he had saved a sufficient amount. "Much" and "little" are non-specific, and "few" refers to countable nouns, so they are inappropriate here.

17. (A): His next problem was how to leave home. The question is about the manner or method, hence "how" fits best. "Where" (place), "which" (choice), and "who" (person) are contextually incorrect.

18. (B): He wanted to leave home without his parents' knowledge. The preposition "without" indicates absence of knowledge or awareness, fitting the context perfectly.

19. (C): He did not have the courage to ask them. After "courage," the infinitive form is needed ("to ask"), not conjunctions like "but" or "and," and not the adverb "too."

20. (A): "Stubborn" means rigid or unwilling to change. Obstinate is its closest synonym. "Proud," "arrogant," and "docile" (which means submissive) are incorrect in this context.

21. (C): The opposite of dropped is lifted, as "drop" means to let something fall, and "lift" means to raise something up. "Sank" refers to going down in water, and "struck" or "uncovered" don't convey the opposite of dropping.

22. (A): This sentence most appropriately represents the passive voice transformation of the original sentence. It keeps the conditional structure and converts the main verb into passive form.

23. (A): He as well as his friend is going to win the medal. When two nouns are joined by "as well as," the verb agrees with the first subject. Since "he" is singular, "is" is correct.

24. (B): "Rashmi is taller than any other girl..." — this is a comparison between one and the rest, so the comparative form "taller" is used. "Tall" is base form, "tallest" is superlative used when comparing more than two or all.

25. (B): Chinese and Japanese are two of the most difficult languages... — when comparing within a group, especially with a superlative sense, "most difficult" is correct. "Very difficult" and "more difficult" are incorrect in this plural and comparative context.

26. (C): "One who is all powerful" is described by the word Omnipotent (Latin root omni = all, potent = powerful).

- Omnipresent = present everywhere
- Omniscient = all knowing
- Omnivorous = eats both plant and animal

27. (D): This option is grammatically correct, uses appropriate reported speech transformation, and conveys the advice tone fitting the original sentence. The verbs are properly backshifted (go → went), and pronouns adjusted (your → their).

28. (C): From the passage: "There was a boy in the boat who held on to one of the branches to steady himself, giving his free hand to Sita." This confirms (i) – he held the branch, and (ii) – he gave his hand to Sita. Both actions helped her board the boat safely.

29. (A): The passage states: "The boy placed his bare foot against the tree trunk and pushed it away." This clearly shows that the boy alone used his foot to push the tree, enabling the boat to drift down the river.

30. (C): It is explicitly mentioned that a boy helped Sita by steadying himself with a branch and giving her his hand. Neither the boat, tree, nor the branches acted independently to help her — the helper was the boy.

31. (D): $(x + y)^2 - 4xy$

$$= x^2 + y^2 + 2xy - 4xy$$
$$= x^2 + y^2 - 2xy = (x - y)^2$$

32. (A): $32ab^2c = \underline{2 \times 2 \times 2} \times \underline{2 \times 2} \times a \times b \times b \times c$

$$= 8 \times 4 \times 2 \times a \times b \times c \times b$$

$\therefore$ $8 \times 4 \times 2 \times a \times b \times c \times b$ is the like term of $32ab^2c$.

33. (A): $(507)^2 - (497)^2 = (507 + 497)(507 - 497)$

$$= 1004 \times 10 = 10040$$

34. (A): Price of a cycle was reduced by 20%, the number of cycles sold increased by 20%. The effect on the total sale of the shop

$$= \frac{20 \times 20}{100} = \frac{400}{100} = 4\% \text{ decrease.}$$

35. (A): $A = p\left(1+\frac{r}{100}\right)^t = 800\left(1+\frac{5}{100}\right)^2$

$= 800 \times \frac{21}{20} \times \frac{21}{20} = 2 \times 441 = 882$

$\therefore$ Compound interest = A – P

= 882 – 800 = ₹ 82

36. (B): No. of red balls = 4

No. of yellow balls = 2

No. of total balls = 4 + 2 = 6

Required probability $= \frac{4}{6} = \frac{2}{3}$

37. (D): The total number of students in the hostel = 20 + 25 + 15 + 30 + 25 = 115

38. (A): There are 2 black queen from a well-shuffled pack of 52 cards

$\therefore$ $n(A) = 2$

$p(A) = \frac{n(A)}{n(S)} = \frac{2}{52} = \frac{1}{26}$

39. (A): A well of diameter 3 m is dug 28 m deep. Volume of the earth taken out of it

$= \pi r^2 h = \pi\left(\frac{3}{2}\right)^2 \times 28$

$= \frac{22}{7} \times \frac{9}{4} \times 28 = 198 \text{ m}^3$

40. (B): Let present age of the father = x years and present age of his son = y years.

5 years ago, Father's age = x – 5 years

5 years ago, Son's age = y – 5 years

According to the question,

$x - 5 = 7(y - 5)$

$\Rightarrow$ $x - 5 = 7y - 35$

$\Rightarrow$ $x - 7y = -30$ ...(*i*)

After 5 years, father's age = x + 5 years

After 5 years, Son's age = y + 5 years

$x + 5 = 3(y + 5)$

$\Rightarrow$ $x + 5 = 3y + 15$

$\Rightarrow$ $x - 3y = 10$ ...(*ii*)

From (*i*) and (*ii*)

$x - 7y = -30$

$x - 3y = 10$

– + = 40

$\Rightarrow$ $y = \frac{40}{4} = 10$

Putting the value of y in (*i*)

$x - 7y = -30$

$x = 7y - 30$

$= 7 \times 10 - 30$

$= 70 - 30 = 40$

Hence, present age of the father = 40 years.

41. (D): Let ten's place digit no. = x

and unit's place digit no. = y

$\therefore$ Number = $10x + y$

New number = $10y + x$

$x + y = 11$ ...(*i*)

$x - y = 3$

$2x = 14$

$\Rightarrow$ $x = 7$

Putting the value of x in (*i*)

$x + y = 11$

$7 + y = 11$

$\Rightarrow$ $y = 11 - 7 = 4$

$\therefore$ Number = $10x + y$ = 74

42. (C): $4a^2 + 9b^2 - 12ab - 16c^2$

$= (2a)^2 + (3b)^2 - 2(2a)(3b) - (4c)^2$

$= (2a - 3b)^2 - (4c)^2$

$= (2a - 3b + 4c)(2a - 3b - 4c)$

43. (A): $\left(\frac{3}{11} \times \frac{5}{6}\right) - \left(\frac{9}{12} \times \frac{4}{3}\right) + \left(\frac{5}{13} \times \frac{6}{15}\right)$

$= \frac{5}{22} 1 + \frac{2}{13}$

$= \frac{65 - 286 + 44}{286} \frac{109 - 286}{286} = -\frac{177}{286}$

44. (D): The cube root of $-3\frac{3}{8}$

$= \sqrt[3]{-\frac{27}{8}} = \sqrt[3]{-\frac{3 \times 3 \times 3}{2 \times 2 \times 2}} = -\frac{3}{2}$

45. (C): The cube root of 0.027

$= \sqrt[3]{\frac{27}{1000}} = \sqrt[3]{\frac{3 \times 3 \times 3}{10 \times 10 \times 10}} = \frac{3}{10} = 0.3$

46. (C): Volume of cube = (side)^3

$\therefore$ side $= \sqrt[3]{\text{Volume}} = \sqrt[3]{1.331}$

$= \sqrt[3]{\frac{1331}{1000}} = \sqrt[3]{\frac{11 \times 11 \times 11}{10 \times 10 \times 10}}$

$= \frac{11}{10} = 1.1$ cm

47. (B): $\because$ $3x + 4y = 18$ and $xy = 6$

$\therefore$ value of $9x^2 + 16y^2 = (3x)^2 + (4y)^2$

$= (3x + 4y)^2 - 2(3x)(4y)$

$= (18)^2 - 24 \times 6 = 324 - 24 \times 6$

$= 324 - 144 = 180$

48. (C): Square root of 218

$= \sqrt{218} = 14.76$

1	$\overline{02}\,\overline{18}.\overline{00}\,\overline{00}$	14.76
1	1	
24	118	
4	96	
287	2200	
7	2009	
2946	×19100	
6	17676	
2952	1424	

Hence, square root of 218 lies between 14 and 15.

49. (B): A. $123^2 = 15129$

B. $149^2 = 22201$

C. $82^2 = 6724$

D. $117^2 = 13689$

Hence, the number 149^2 ends with the digit 1.

50. (A): The value of $\sqrt{10 + \sqrt{25 + \sqrt{108 + \sqrt{154 + \sqrt{225}}}}}$

$+ \left(\sqrt{\dfrac{225}{729}} - \sqrt{\dfrac{25}{144}}\right) \div \sqrt{\dfrac{16}{81}}$

$= \sqrt{10 + \sqrt{25 + \sqrt{108 + \sqrt{154 + 15}}}} + \left(\dfrac{15}{27} - \dfrac{5}{12}\right) \div \dfrac{4}{9}$

$= \sqrt{10 + \sqrt{25 + \sqrt{108 + \sqrt{169}}}} + \left(\dfrac{5}{9} - \dfrac{5}{12}\right) \div \dfrac{4}{9}$

$= \sqrt{10 + \sqrt{25 + \sqrt{108 + 13}}} + \left(\dfrac{60 - 45}{108}\right) \div \dfrac{4}{9}$

$= \sqrt{10 + \sqrt{25 + 11}} + \dfrac{15}{108} \times \dfrac{9}{4}$

$= \sqrt{10 + 6} + \dfrac{15}{12} \times \dfrac{1}{4} = 4 + \dfrac{5}{4} \times \dfrac{1}{4}$

$= 4 + \dfrac{5}{16} = \dfrac{64 + 5}{16} = \dfrac{69}{16}$

51. (D): Each interior angle of a polygon

$= \left(\dfrac{2n - 4}{n}\right) \times 90°$

where n = number of sides

$= \left[\dfrac{2(18) - 4}{18}\right] \times 90° = \left(\dfrac{36 - 4}{18}\right) \times 90° = \dfrac{32 \times 90°}{18}$

$= 32 \times 5 = 160°$

$\because$ Exterior angle + interior angle = 180°

$\therefore$ Exterior angle = 180° − 160° = 20°

52. (C): Area of a square = $(\text{side})^2$

Side of a square $= \sqrt{\text{Area}} = \sqrt{(2x)^2 + 2(2x) + 1^2}$

$= \sqrt{(2x + 1)^2} = 2x + 1$

Hence, perimeter of square = 4 × side

$= 4(2x + 1)$

53. (D): Surface area of cube $= 6(\text{side})^2$

$\Rightarrow$ $600 = 6a^2$

$\Rightarrow$ $a^2 = \dfrac{600}{6} = 100 \Rightarrow a = 10$ m

Volume of cube $= (a)^3 = (10)^3 = 10 \times 10 \times 10$

$= 1000$ m^3.

54. (B): Area of an equilateral triangle $= \dfrac{\sqrt{3}}{4}(\text{side})^2$

According to the question,

$\dfrac{\sqrt{3}}{4}(\text{side})^2 = 24\sqrt{3}$

$\text{Side}^2 = \dfrac{4 \times 24\sqrt{3}}{\sqrt{3}} = 96$

$\Rightarrow$ $\text{Side} = \sqrt{96} = 4\sqrt{6}$ cm

$\because$ perimeter of equilateral triangle = 3 × side

$= 3 \times 4\sqrt{6} = 12\sqrt{6}$ cm.

55. (B):

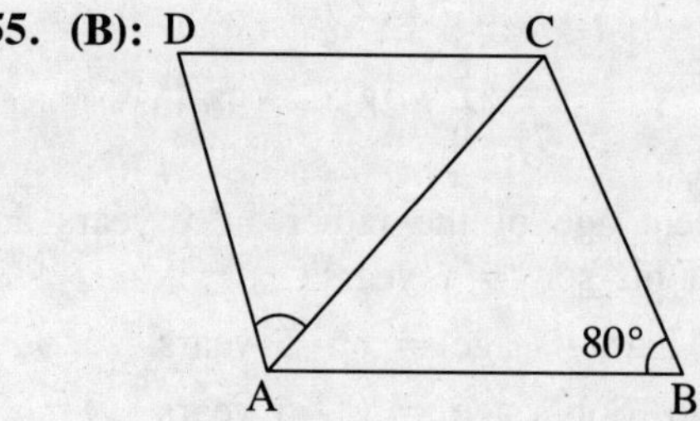

$\because$ ABCD is a rhombus in which AB = BC = CD = DA.

AC is diagonal

$\angle ABC = 80°$

In ΔABC, $\therefore$ $\angle B = 80°$, $\angle A = \angle C = 50°$

(AB = BC $\therefore$ $\angle A = \angle C$)

$\therefore$ CAD = 50° alternate angle are equal.

56. (A): $\because$ Exterior angle + Interior angle = 180°

30° + Interior angle = 180°

$\therefore$ Interior angle = 180° − 30° = 150

Each interior angle $= \dfrac{2n - 4}{n} \times 90° = \dfrac{180n - 360°}{n}$

$\Rightarrow$ $150 = \dfrac{180°n - 360°}{n} \Rightarrow 150n = 180n - 360°$

$\Rightarrow$ $30n = 360° \Rightarrow n = 12$

Hence, the number of sides = 12.

57. (C): Speed = 30 m/s

$$= 30 \times \frac{18}{5} \text{ km/h}$$

$$= 6 \times 18 \text{ km/h} = 108 \text{ km/h}$$

58. (D): Area of rectangular field = $l \times b$

$\Rightarrow (3a^2 + 5ab + 2b^2) = l \times b$ [where $l = a + b$]

$\Rightarrow (3a^2 + 3ab + 2ab + 2b^2) = (a + b) \times b$

$\Rightarrow 3a(a + b) + 2b(a + b) = (a + b) \times b$

$\Rightarrow (3a + 2b)(a + b) = (a + b) \times b$

$\Rightarrow b = 3a + 2b$

$\therefore$ breadth $= 3a + 2b$

Perimeter of rectangular field $= 2(l + b)$

$= 2(a + b + 3a + 2b)$

$= 2(4a + 3b) = 8a + 6b$ units

59. (B): Let the total value of the property = ₹ x

According to the question,

$$360 = \frac{5}{3}\% \text{ of } 90\% \text{ of } x$$

$$\Rightarrow 360 = \frac{5}{3 \times 100} \times \frac{90 \times x}{100}$$

$$\Rightarrow 360 = \frac{3x}{200} \Rightarrow x = \frac{360 \times 200}{3}$$

$$= 120 \times 200 = 24000$$

Hence, total value of the property = ₹ 24000.

60. (A): P : 1^4 = 1 Q : 4^0 = 1

R : 0^4 = 0 S : 4^1 = 4

Hence,the values of P and Q are equal.

61. (B): $[(2)^8 \div (2)^5]^3 \div 2^5$

$$= \left[\frac{2^8}{2^5}\right]^3 \div 2^5 = \left[2^{8-5}\right]^3 \div 2^5$$

$$= \left[2^3\right]^3 \div 2^5 = \frac{2^9}{2^5} = 2^{9-5} = 2^4$$

62. (A): Let radii of two cylinders are $1r$ and $2r$ and heights are $2h$ and $1h$.

Ratio of their volumes $= \dfrac{\pi(1r)^2 \times 2h}{\pi(2r)^2 \times 1h} = \dfrac{1}{2} = 1 : 2$

63. (C): Let ten's place digit number = x and unit's place digit number = y

$\therefore$ Number $= 10x + y$

$x + y = 1 + 1 = 2$ put $x = 1$, $y = 1$

$x \times y = 1 \times 1 = 1$

[sum of digits = 2 times their product]

$\therefore$ Number $= 10 \times 1 + 1 = 11$

64. (A): (A) $\dfrac{13}{16} + \dfrac{17}{18} = \dfrac{17}{18} + \dfrac{13}{16}$ is true

because $a + b = b + a$

(B) $\dfrac{13}{16} \times \dfrac{17}{18} = \dfrac{16}{13} \times \dfrac{17}{18}$ is not true.

because $a \times b \neq \dfrac{1}{a} \times \dfrac{1}{b}$

(C) $\dfrac{13}{16} - \dfrac{17}{18} = \dfrac{17}{18} - \dfrac{13}{16}$ is not true

because $a - b \neq b - a$

(D) $\dfrac{13}{16} \div \dfrac{17}{18} = \dfrac{17}{18} \div \dfrac{13}{16}$ is not true

because $a \div b \neq b \div a$.

65. (C): (A) $\left(\dfrac{2}{3} + \dfrac{3}{4}\right) + \dfrac{5}{7} = \dfrac{2}{3} + \left(\dfrac{3}{4} + \dfrac{5}{7}\right)$

is true because $(a + b) + c = a + (b + c)$

(B) $\left(\dfrac{2}{3} \times \dfrac{3}{4}\right) \times \dfrac{5}{7} = \dfrac{2}{3} \times \left(\dfrac{3}{4} \times \dfrac{5}{7}\right)$ is true

because $(a \times b) \times c = a \times (b \times c)$

(C) $\left(\dfrac{2}{3} - \dfrac{3}{4}\right) - \dfrac{5}{7} = \dfrac{2}{3} - \left(\dfrac{3}{4} - \dfrac{5}{7}\right)$ is not true

$(a - b) - c \neq a - (b - c)$

(D) $\left(\dfrac{2}{3} - \dfrac{3}{4}\right) - \dfrac{5}{7} = \dfrac{2}{3} - \left(\dfrac{3}{4} + \dfrac{5}{7}\right)$ is true

because $(a - b) - c = a - (b + c)$

66. (B): Aspergillus and Penicillium are well-known genera of fungi.

- Aspergillus includes several species that are used in fermentation and also some that can cause disease in humans (aspergillosis).
- Penicillium is famous for producing the antibiotic penicillin, discovered by Alexander Fleming in 1928.

Both are filamentous fungi and reproduce by forming spores. Hence, they belong to the Fungi kingdom.

67. (B): When wheat seeds are placed in water:

- Healthy seeds are usually denser and absorb water, causing them to sink.
- Damaged seeds often have hollow parts due to internal injury or insect infestation, making them less dense and hence, they float.

This simple floatation test is a common method used by farmers and scientists to separate viable (healthy) from non-viable (damaged) seeds.

68. (D): Let's analyze the path of the ray of light using the laws of reflection and geometry:

- The ray is incident on mirror MM_1 at an angle of 30° to the surface. Therefore, it makes an angle of 60° with the normal (since angle with normal = 90° − angle with surface).

- By the law of reflection, the angle of incidence = angle of reflection. So, the reflected ray from MM_1 makes an angle of 60° with the normal to MM_1.
- Now consider the V-shaped mirror system, where the mirrors MM_1 and MM_2 are inclined at 90° (as shown by the diagram—both inclined at 45° to the vertical).
- The reflected ray from MM_1 now strikes MM_2. We use geometry and reflection again:
  - Since MM_1 and MM_2 are at 90°, and the first reflected ray made a 60° angle with the normal on MM_1, the incident angle on MM_2 becomes:
    90° − 60° = 30° (with the normal to MM_2).
  - Therefore, by reflection, the ray reflects out making 30° with the normal to MM_2, which is the same angle it makes with the surface of MM_2.

So, the angle the reflected ray makes from MM_2 as it reflects out is 30°, measured with respect to the surface of MM_2.

Hence, the correct answer is D : 30°.

69. **(B):** In a kaleidoscope, three identical plane mirrors are typically arranged in a triangular tube, where each mirror is inclined at 60° to the adjacent ones. This arrangement produces symmetrical and multiple reflections, creating beautiful patterns. Thus, option B is correct.

70. **(D):** When two plane mirrors are placed on adjacent walls, the number of images formed depends on the angle between the mirrors. For two mirrors at 90°, the formula is:

$n = (360/\theta) - 1 \rightarrow (360/90) - 1 = 4 - 1 = 3$ images.

Therefore, the student will see 3 images of themselves.

71. **(D):** The Richter scale is logarithmic, meaning each whole number increase represents a 10-fold increase in amplitude and approximately 32 times more energy release.

From intensity 5 to 7, difference = 2 steps $\rightarrow 10^2$ = 100 times in amplitude,

But in terms of energy, $32 \times 32 = 1024$ times more.

So, 1000 times more is approximately correct.

72. **(A):** Water conducts electricity, and during a thunderstorm, lightning can strike plumbing or water pipes. Hence, it is advised to avoid bathing.

- Taking shelter under a tree (B) is dangerous.
- Watching TV (C) or using electronic devices during a storm can also be risky.
- Carrying an umbrella (D) increases chances of lightning strike due to the metal rod.

73. **(D):** When a plastic straw is rubbed with polythene, electrons are transferred from the straw to the polythene.

- Thus, polythene gains electrons → becomes negatively charged,
- Straw loses electrons → becomes positively charged.

This is a common example of triboelectric charging.

74. **(D):**

A. Destruction of their habitat: This is a correct statement leading to endangerment.

B. Increase in population of that species in the area: This can become a problem if the population surpasses the carrying capacity of the habitat, so this is also a correct statement leading to endangerment.

C. Introduction of new species in that area: This is a correct statement leading to endangerment.

D. Increased habitat protection for that species in the area: This is not a correct statement leading to endangerment. It would help the species, not harm it.

Therefore, the incorrect statement is: D. Increased habitat protection for that species in the area.

75. **(C):** This statement is false. Poaching and capturing wild animals is strictly prohibited in wildlife sanctuaries, regardless of who the person is.

Options A, B, and D correctly describe the function and allowances in sanctuaries.

76. **(A):** In frogs, metamorphosis (transformation from tadpole to adult frog) is controlled by the hormone thyroxine, which is secreted by the thyroid gland.

Other hormones:

Adrenalin: fight or flight response,

Growth hormone: controls growth but not metamorphosis,

Insulin: regulates blood sugar.

77. **(D):** HIV is not transmitted through casual contact like shaking hands or sharing food.

It spreads through:

- unprotected sex,
- blood transfusion,
- sharing needles,
- and mother-to-child via breast milk or during childbirth.

So, D is the correct safe method — no transmission through touch or food.

78. **(C):** Let's examine each statement:

Incorrect – Humans have 23 pairs of chromosomes (46 total). Out of these, 22 pairs are autosomes and 1 pair is sex chromosomes. Hence, this statement is misleading if interpreted as the total chromosome count.

Correct: The unfertilized egg always contains one X chromosome only.

Correct: The zygote develops into a male child only if the sperm contributes a Y chromosome. If the sperm contributes an X chromosome, the child will be female.

Incorrect: Sex is not genetically determined in all organisms. For example:

- In some reptiles, temperature during incubation determines sex.
- In bees, haplo-diploid system determines sex (haploid = male, diploid = female). Thus, it is incorrect to generalize that all organisms have genetically determined sex.

So, statements 1 and 4 are incorrect.

79. (A): Sugar solution does not conduct electricity because sugar is a covalent compound and does not dissociate into ions in water.

Whereas:

- Vinegar (acetic acid),
- Lemon juice (citric acid),
- Caustic soda (sodium hydroxide)

are all electrolytes that dissociate into ions and conduct electricity.

80. (D): Chromium is widely used to electroplate iron objects to give them a shiny, corrosion-resistant surface.

- This process is known as chrome plating.
- It provides aesthetic appeal and prevents rusting.

Other options:

- Aluminium is not used for plating; it's reactive.
- Copper is used for conductivity purposes, not rust protection.
- Zinc is used for galvanization, not specifically for shine.

81. (C): From the figure and description:

- Both setups use similar bulbs and cells (same power source and load).
- Bulb in Set-up A glows more brightly than in Set-up B.

Brightness of the bulb depends on the amount of current passing through the circuit. Greater the current → brighter the bulb.

Now, if Solution A allows more current to pass (resulting in brighter glow), it means:

- Solution A has lower resistance, or
- Solution A is a better conductor (i.e., it allows easier flow of electric charge than B).

Let's analyze other options:

A. equal current — Incorrect; if current were equal, bulb brightness would be same.

B. loose contacts — Not mentioned, and setups are stated to be identical except the solutions.

D. higher current in B — Incorrect, as the bulb in B glows dimmer, indicating lower current.

Hence, correct conclusion: C: solution A is a better conductor of electricity than solution B.

82. (A): Contact forces are those that require physical contact between two objects.

Muscular force involves physical contact — e.g., lifting, pushing.

Gravitational, electrostatic, and magnetic forces are non-contact forces.

Hence, muscular force is a contact force.

83. (A): Friction depends on surface roughness:

Mat: roughest → highest friction

Newspaper: less rough than mat

Dry marble floor: smooth

Wet marble floor: slippery → least friction

So, decreasing order: Mat > Newspaper > Dry Marble > Wet Marble

84. (C): Scientifically, ploughed field offers high resistance (friction) and soft ground, which helps slow down and stop the car more safely than hitting a tree or honking.

85. (C): For a force to come into play, interaction between two objects is essential. Whether it's push or pull, both involve interaction. So, C is correct.

86. (C): In closed rooms with incomplete combustion (like burning coal), carbon monoxide (CO) is produced, a highly poisonous gas that binds to hemoglobin and causes death due to oxygen deprivation.

87. (C): Calorific value is the amount of energy produced per unit mass of fuel.

Hydrogen has the highest calorific value (~150 kJ/g), much higher than:

Wood (~17 kJ/g)

Coal (~30 kJ/g)

Petrol (~47 kJ/g)

88. (C): These are all products of petroleum refining:

Diesel: obtained from fractional distillation

Paraffin wax and lubricating oil: heavier fractions

Others like coal tar and coke are from coal, and acrylic/nylon are synthetic polymers.

89. (A): Correct biological sequence in human reproduction:

Ovulation: release of ovum

Fertilization: sperm meets egg

Zygote forms

Embryo: early development

Foetus: later stage until birth

90. (D): An ecosystem includes biotic (living) and abiotic (non-living) components. It is defined by the interaction between organisms and their environment (soil, water, air).

So, D is the most comprehensive and correct definition.

91. (B): Hydra reproduces asexually by budding, the same method used by yeast. In this process, a new individual grows as an outgrowth (bud) from the parent.

Amoeba reproduces by binary fission.

Starfish can regenerate but not by budding like yeast.

Silkworm reproduces sexually.

92. (B): Fishes produce a large number of eggs and sperms due to the following reasons:

Correct – External fertilization exposes gametes to environmental factors like water flow, wind, and rainfall, which can reduce chances of successful fertilization.

Correct – More eggs and sperms increase probability of fertilization.

Incorrect – Food availability is not the primary reason for increased gamete production.

Correct – Eggs are often eaten by other organisms, so producing many increases chances that some will survive.

Hence, correct statements: 1, 2 and 4

93. (D): Sound requires a medium (solid, liquid, or gas) to travel by transmitting vibrations. In vacuum, where no particles exist, sound cannot propagate.

Therefore, sound cannot travel through vacuum.

94. (C): The sound produced in a jal-tarang is due to the vibrations of the water in the bowl or tumbler.

Here's why: A jal-tarang is a musical instrument consisting of bowls or tumblers filled with varying amounts of water.

When the bowls are struck with sticks, the water inside them vibrates.

The varying amounts of water in each bowl create different frequencies of vibration, resulting in different musical notes.

While the bowl and the air column also vibrate somewhat, the primary source of the sound is the vibrating water.

95. (C): In the first case, a force F is just enough to overcome friction and cause block A to slide. This means that F = limiting friction = μN, where μ is the coefficient of friction and N is the normal force on A. Let's now analyze the second case:

- An identical block B is placed on top of block A.
- Since both blocks are identical, the total weight on the contact surface with the ground doubles.
- Hence, the normal reaction force on the ground becomes 2N.
- Frictional force is $\mu \times$ normal force $= \mu \times$ 2N = 2F.

Therefore, to just make the blocks slide together (still assuming no relative motion between A and B), the required force must overcome the new, increased frictional force, which is 2F.

Hence, the correct answer is: C: 2F.

96. (C): Let's match the food items with their preservation methods:

P. Amla: Amla is often preserved by pickling, which involves using (*iii*) Salt.

Q. Fish: Fish can be preserved by pickling in (*iv*) Oil and Vinegar.

R. Squashes: Squashes are often preserved using chemical preservatives like (*i*) Sodium metabisulphite.

S. Milk: Milk is preserved through (*ii*) Pasteurisation.

Therefore, the correct matching is:

P - (*iii*), Q - (*iv*), R - (*i*), S - (*ii*)

97. (D): Charcoal burns without a flame because it is already a carbon-rich solid and undergoes glowing combustion, not flaming combustion.

LPG, molten wax, and dry grass all produce visible flames while burning.

98. (C): Decomposers like bacteria and fungi convert nitrogenous waste from dead organisms into ammonia and other compounds, which are eventually converted into nitrates usable by plants.

This is part of the nitrogen cycle.

99. (D): In the sprinkler irrigation system, water is sprayed on crops from rotating nozzles, simulating rainfall.

It is especially useful in sandy soils and uneven lands.

100. (C): Weeds are unwanted plants that compete with crops for vital resources like water, nutrients, space, and sunlight, thereby reducing crop yield.

They do not help plants (A)

Don't attract pests directly (B)

Don't secrete toxins that cause disease in general (D)

Previous Years' Paper

JAWAHAR NAVODAYA VIDYALAYA

Class-IX, Entrance Exam, 2024

(Exam held on 10-02-2024)

SECTION-I: हिन्दी

1. सही वर्तनी वाला शब्द चुनिए:

A. स्वछता B. स्वच्छता
C. स्वछ्छता D. स्वचछता

2. 'अँगूठा' का तत्सम रूप है:

A. अंगूठा B. अंगुस्ठ
C. अंगुष्ठ D. अंगुष्ठा

3. 'सुलभ' का विलोम शब्द है:

A. अलभ्य B. अलभ
C. दुर्लभ D. कुलभ

4. थॉमस अल्वा एडीसन ने बिजली के बल्ब ....।

वाक्य पूरा करने के लिए उपयुक्त विकल्प चुनिए:

A. की खोज की
B. का आविष्कार किया
C. का अनुसंधान किया
D. का संज्ञान किया

5. रेखांकित शब्द का पदभेद बताइए:

मेरे चाचा <u>भागलपुर</u> में रहते हैं।

A. संज्ञा B. सर्वनाम
C. क्रिया D. विशेषण

निर्देश (प्रश्न संख्या 6-10): *निम्नलिखित अनुच्छेद को पढ़कर दिए गए प्रश्नों के लिए सर्वाधिक उपयुक्त उत्तर चुनिए।*

योगाभ्यास मन को एकाग्र करने में सहायक होता है। यह भारत की बहुत प्राचीन वैज्ञानिक विधि है जिस पर आज सारी दुनिया मुग्ध है। मन और शरीर दोनों को स्वस्थ रखने में योगाभ्यास का महत्व सर्वविदित है। इसीलिए आज पूरे विश्व में लगभग दो अरब लोग योग का अभ्यास करते हैं और उससे लाभान्वित हो रहे हैं। योग केवल शारीरिक व्यायाम ही नहीं, मानसिक व्यायाम भी है। इसलिए इससे दोहरा लाभ है। इसके लिए विशेष तामझाम या मूल्यवान उपकरणों की भी आवश्यकता नहीं पड़ती। कोई चटाई, दरी या तौलिया बिछाकर या हरी दूब पर बैठकर घर या बाहर कहीं भी योगाभ्यास कर सकते हैं। आधे घंटे के योगाभ्यास से हमें दिनभर के लिए पर्याप्त ऊर्जा प्राप्त हो जाती है। स्वास्थ्य लाभ का इतना सस्ता और सरल उपाय और कोई नहीं हो सकता।

6. योग से दोहरा लाभ है, क्योंकि:

A. भारत के अलावा अन्य देशों में भी किया जाता है
B. शरीर और मन दोनों का व्यायाम है
C. तन और मन को एकाग्र रखता है
D. सस्ता और सुलभ है

7. अनुच्छेद में 'मन को एकाग्र करना' का आशय है:

A. केवल आगे की ओर देखना
B. मन को एक बात पर लगाना
C. एक बिंदु पर मन को स्थिर करना
D. एक व्यक्ति को मन से चाहना

8. 'योगाभ्यास' किन दो शब्दों से मिलकर बना है?

A. योगा + भ्यास B. योगा + अभ्यास
C. योग + अभ्यास D. योग + आभ्यास

9. दिनभर के लिए आवश्यक ऊर्जा पाने के लिए आवश्यक है:

A. पार्क में हरी दूब पर योगाभ्यास करना
B. चटाई या तौलिया बिछाकर योगाभ्यास करना
C. प्रतिदिन सुबह-शाम योगाभ्यास करना
D. प्रतिदिन आधे घंटे योगाभ्यास करना

10. योगाभ्यास के लिए आवश्यक **नहीं** है:

A. रंगीन चटाई B. नरम तौलिया
C. नई दरी D. महंगे उपकरण

1. B **2.** C **3.** C **4.** B **5.** A **6.** B **7.** C **8.** C **9.** D **10.** D

11. विद्यालय तुम्हें पुरस्कार देगा।

रेखांकित शब्द का सही पद-परिचय किस विकल्प में दिया गया है?

A. व्यक्तिवाचक संज्ञा B. जातिवाचक संज्ञा
C. भाववाचक संज्ञा D. समूहवाचक संज्ञा

12. शुद्ध वाक्य चुनिए:

A. यह काम कौन किया? B. यह काम किसने करा?
C. यह काम कौन ने किया? D. यह काम किसने किया?

13. मैं जानती हूँ कि माँ क्यों रूठी है।

A. सरल वाक्य B. संयुक्त वाक्य
C. मिश्र वाक्य D. प्रश्नार्थक वाक्य

14. मेल-जोल में बड़ी शक्ति है। इसलिए हमें .... काम पूरा करना चाहिए।

रिक्त स्थान के लिए उपयुक्त मुहावरा होगा।

A. एड़ी चोटी एक करके B. आँखें खोलकर
C. छाती ठोककर D. कंधे से कंधा मिलाकर

15. निम्नलिखित में से 'नाच न जाने आँगन टेढ़ा' लोकोक्ति का सही अभिप्राय है:

A. अपनी कमजारी छिपाने के लिए किसी अन्य की कमी निकालना
B. समय पर काम करने से कतराना
C. काम की बात न करना
D. अवसर पर चूक जाना

SECTION-II: ENGLISH

Directions (Qs. No. 16-18): *Read the following passage carefully and answer the questions.*

In a village, a shopkeeper used to sell his fruits at high prices, which brought him a lot of profit. But, he wasn't happy with it because he wanted to earn more. So, whenever a customer came to buy fruits from him, he cleverly reduced the weight a little. Now, he was earning more money. One day his friend came to buy some fruits from him and he did the same to his friend. When his friend got suspicious, the shopkeeper told him that it was his illusion.

16. How did the shopkeeper earn money?

A. By selling wood B. By selling vegetables
C. By selling fruits D. By selling grocery

17. The shopkeeper manipulated his customers because he was ______.

A. greedy B. ambitious
C. angry D. poor

18. The shopkeeper's friend grew ______.

A. merciful B. sympathetic
C. treacherous D. suspicious

Directions (Qs. No. 19-22): *Answer these questions by choosing the most appropriate options to complete the paragraph by filling in the blanks.*

Gulliver found that the strongest cables were no better than thin threads and the metal bars were like knitting needles. He made some strong cables by (19) multiple cables together. He also made some hooks by bending two-three metal bars together. He (20) tied the hooks at the ends of the cables and went to the shore with them. Before getting into the sea, Gulliver did not forget to put (21) his goggles to protect his eyes. Gulliver then waded through the sea water (22) was reaching only up to his chest.

19. A. twist B. twisted
C. twisting D. twists

20. A. then B. when
C. so D. but

21. A. out B. in
C. of D. on

22. A. who B. which
C. how D. while

23. Choose the word similar in meaning to the underlined word.

It will be hard for us to recoup the loss.

A. cut B. retain
C. spread D. recover

24. Read the sentence given below and choose the option which correctly changes it into Passive Voice.

Whom did you invite?

A. Whom was invited by you?
B. Who could be invited by you?
C. Who was invited by you?
D. Whom could be invited by you?

11. B	**12.** D	**13.** B	**14.** D	**15.** A	**16.** C	**17.** A	**18.** D	**19.** C	**20.** A
21. D	**22.** B	**23.** D	**24.** C						

25. The word which is **opposite** in meaning to 'mercilessly' is ________.
A. torturous B. cruelly
C. kindly D. heartlessly

Directions (Qs. No. 26-28): *Answer these questions by choosing the most appropriate options to fill in the blanks.*

26. The Amazon river in South America is the ________ river in the world.
A. longer B. longest
C. a long D. most longest

27. ________ seven Paralympians ran the hundred-metre race, but they were all declared winners.
A. None of the B. Neither of the
C. Either of the D. Some of the

28. He realised that he could not buy the jacket this month because he had very ________ money left after meeting all expenses.
A. few B. little
C. lesser D. some

29. Give one word substitute for the following expression:
'One who can be easily led to believe in something'.
A. Indelible B. Incredible
C. Gullible D. Invincible

30. Select the alternative that best expresses the following sentence in indirect speech:
Alan said, "After hearing the sad story of the laundry man, I quietly got up and walked back home."
A. Alan said to me that after hearing the laundry man's sad story I quietly got up and walked back home.
B. Alan said that after hearing the laundry man's sad story, he quietly got up and walked back home.
C. Alan was saying to me that after hearing the laundry man's sad story, he quietly got up and walked back home.
D. Alan said that after hearing the laundry man's sad story, I quietly to up and walked back home.

SECTION-III: MATHEMATICS

31. If the sum of five consecutive integers be S, then how is the greatest of these integers related to S?
A. $\frac{S-10}{5}$ B. $\frac{S+4}{4}$
C. $\frac{S+5}{4}$ D. $\frac{S+10}{5}$

32. Prem is 3 times older than his son Ashok. After 15 years, Prem will be twice the age of Ashok. What is the sum of their present ages?
A. 48 years B. 60 years
C. 64 years D. 72 years

33. In 24 coins, there are ₹ 1 coins, ₹ 2 coins and ₹ 5 coins. The value of these 24 coins is ₹ 62. If the number of ₹ 1 coins and the number of ₹ 5 coins is equal, then how many ₹ 5 coins are there?
A. 5 B. 7
C. 12 D. 16

34. If $x = 7-4\sqrt{3}$, then the value of $\left(x+\frac{1}{x}\right)$ is:
A. $3\sqrt{3}$ B. $8\sqrt{3}$
C. $14+8\sqrt{3}$ D. 14

35. If $a = \frac{\sqrt{5}+1}{\sqrt{5}-1}$ and $b = \frac{\sqrt{5}-1}{\sqrt{5}+1}$, then $\frac{a^2+ab+b^2}{a^2-ab+b^2}$ is:
A. 0.75 B. 1.25
C. $\frac{3}{5}$ D. $\frac{4}{3}$

36. The positive square root of
$\frac{(0.75)^3}{1-0.75}+[0.75+(0.75)^2+1]$ is:
A. 4 B. 3
C. 2 D. 1

37. The product of two positive numbers is $29\frac{31}{49}$ and one of them is three times the other. What is the greater number?
A. $\frac{22}{7}$ B. $\frac{66}{7}$
C. $\frac{37}{7}$ D. $\frac{68}{7}$

25. C **26.** B **27.** A **28.** B **29.** C **30.** B **31.** C **32.** B **33.** B **34.** D **35.** D **36.** C **37.** B

38. If $1^3 + 2^3 + 3^3 + 4^3 + ... + n^3 = \left[n\left(\frac{n+1}{2}\right)\right]^2$

where 'n' is a natural number, then $1^3 - 2^3 + 3^3 - 4^3 + 5^3 - 6^3 + 7^3 - 8^3 + 9^3 - 10^3$ is equal to:

A. 3025 B. –575
C. –1800 D. 2425

39. $\left(\frac{\sqrt[3]{8}}{\sqrt{16}} \div \frac{\sqrt{100}}{\sqrt{49}} \times \sqrt[3]{125}\right)$ is equal to:

A. 7 B. $\frac{7}{4}$
C. $\frac{7}{100}$ D. $\frac{4}{7}$

40. Three numbers are in the ratio 2 : 3 : 4 and sum of their cubes is 2673. The sum of these three numbers is:

A. 26 B. 27
C. 28 D. 29

41. If $(32)^{2x+1} = 8^{-x}4^{-4}$, then the value of x is:

A. 1 B. –1
C. 2 D. –2

42. $\left[\sqrt[3]{\sqrt[6]{5^9}}\right]^4 \left[\sqrt[6]{\sqrt[3]{5^9}}\right]^4$ is equal to:

A. 5^2 B. 5^4
C. 5^8 D. 5^{12}

43. $\sqrt[r]{\frac{9^{\left(r+\frac{1}{4}\right)}\sqrt{3.3^{-r}}}{\sqrt{3^{2-r}}}}$ is equal to:

A. 1 B. $\frac{1}{3}$
C. 3 D. 9

44. $\frac{2^x + 2^{x-1}}{2^{x+1} - 2^x}$ is equal to:

A. $\frac{1}{2}$ B. $\frac{3}{2}$
C. 1 D. $\frac{2}{3}$

45. A loaded truck covers 18 km in 35 minutes. At the same speed, how far can it travel in 7 hours?

A. 196 km B. 192 km
C. 216 km D. 212 km

46. If 28 people can do a work in 65 days, how many people can do the same work in 35 days?

A. 48 B. 46
C. 52 D. 56

47. Suppose L and M vary inversely. When L is 10, M is 6.

Which of the following is **not** a possible pair of corresponding values of L and M?

A. 12 and 5 B. 15 and 4
C. 45 and 1.3 D. 25 and 2.4

48. What percentage of profit should be added in the cost price of a commodity so as to gain a profit of 33% after allowing 5% discount to the customer?

A. 40 B. 45
C. 48 D. 52

49. On a certain sum, the simple interest at the end of $6\frac{1}{4}$ years becomes $\left(\frac{3}{8}\right)^{th}$ of the sum. The rate per cent is:

A. 7% B. 6%
C. 5% D. $5\frac{1}{2}\%$

50. A sum of money is kept at 5% p.a. compound interest for a period of 3 years. If the compound interest earned is ₹ 1,261, what is the sum of money invested?

A. ₹ 9,000 B. ₹ 8,400
C. ₹ 8,000 D. ₹ 7,500

51. The remainder obtained, on dividing $x^4 + 4x^2 + 10$ by $x^2 - 2x + 4$, is:

A. –6 B. 6
C. 4 D. –4

52. If $x + \frac{1}{x} = 5$, then the value of $\frac{2x}{3x^2 - 5x + 3}$ is:

A. 5 B. $\frac{1}{5}$
C. 4 D. $\frac{1}{4}$

53. If $\left(x + \frac{1}{x}\right)^2 = 3$, then the value of $x^{206} + x^{200} + x^{90} + x^{84} + x^{18} + x^{12} + x^6 + 1$, is:

A. 0 B. 1
C. 84 D. 206

38. B	**39.** B	**40.** B	**41.** B	**42.** B	**43.** D	**44.** B	**45.** C	**46.** C	**47.** C
48. A	**49.** B	**50.** C	**51.** A	**52.** B	**53.** A				

54. What is the value of x in the equation?

$$\frac{5(x+6)-15(2-x)}{3x-1}=10$$

A. $x = 1$
B. $x = -1$
C. $x = 2$
D. $x = -2$

55. If $\frac{1}{2}$ is subtracted from a number and the difference is multiplied by 8, the result is, 12. What is this number ?

A. 2 B. 3
C. 4 D. 8

56. If $\frac{5x}{3}-4=\frac{2x}{5}$, then the value of $(2x - 7)$ is:

A. $\frac{19}{13}$ B. $-\frac{13}{19}$
C. 0 D. $\frac{13}{19}$

57. The adjacent sides of a rectangle are in the ratio 5 : 3 and its area is 135 sq cm. The perimeter of the rectangle is:

A. 135 cm B. 54 cm
C. 81 cm D. 48 cm

58. ABCD is an isosceles trapezium, i.e. AD = BC. Then:

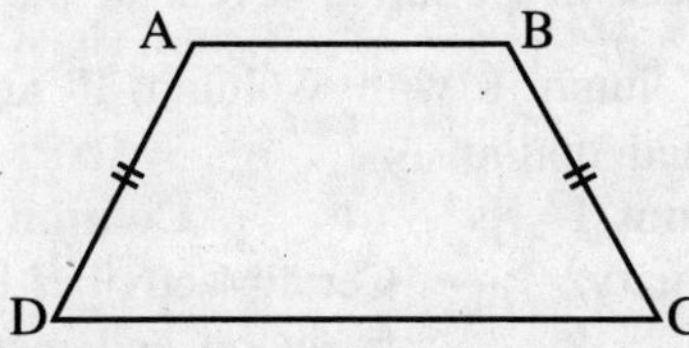

A. AD = CD B. ∠A = ∠B
C. ∠A = ∠D D. ∠A = ∠C

59. In the figure, ABCD is a rhombus. If ∠DMC = 90° and ∠DAB = 110°, then the measure of ∠BDC is:

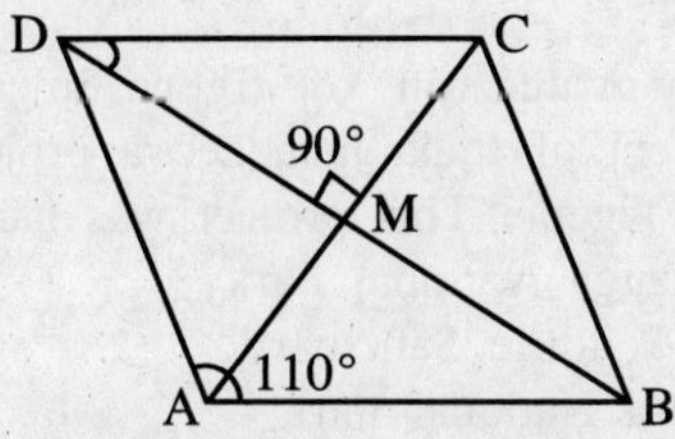

A. 30° B. 35°
C. 40° D. 45°

60. A rectangular sheet of paper 44 cm × 18 cm is rolled along its length and a cylinder is formed. What is the volume of that cylinder?

A. 2772 cu cm
B. 2722 cu cm
C. 2727 cu cm
D. 2277 cu cm

61. A beam of wood is 5 m long and 36 cm thick. It is made of 1.35 cu m of wood. What is the width of the beam?

A. 15 cm
B. 25 cm
C. 75 cm
D. 80 cm

62. The area of a school's rectangular playground is 38,400 sq m. If the ratio of its length to breadth is 3 : 2, then the perimeter of the playground is:

A. 500 m
B. 800 m
C. 1000 m
D. 1200 m

63. What is the ratio of the area of a square to the area of another square made on the diagonal of the first square?

A. $1:\sqrt{2}$ B. 1 : 2
C. 2 : 1 D. $\sqrt{2}:1$

64. Mohan spends 40% of his monthly income on food items, 20% on house rent and 30% on miscellaneous items. He saves 10% of his income every month. What is the central angle for house rent on a pie-chart?

A. 144° B. 36°
C. 72° D. 108°

65. One of the letters from the word "MOVEMENT" is chosen at random. What is the probability that this letter is M?

A. $\frac{1}{2}$ B. $\frac{1}{4}$
C. $\frac{2}{7}$ D. $\frac{1}{8}$

54. A	**55.** A	**56.** B	**57.** D	**58.** B	**59.** B	**60.** A	**61.** C	**62.** B	**63.** B
64. C	**65.** B								

SECTION-IV: GENERAL SCIENCE

66. One of the agricultural practices is preparation of soil resulting in loosening of soil initially. Which one of the following statements is **not** an advantage of this practice?
A. Allows the roots to breathe easily
B. Brings the nutrient-rich soil to the top
C. Helps in levelling the soil
D. Helps in the growth of earthworms and microbes

67. Select a group of two crops which are grown alternately in a field to replenish the soil with nutrients.
A. Paddy and Wheat B. Legumes and Wheat
C. Paddy and Maize D. Maize and Cotton

68. Weeding is done before sowing a crop by an agricultural practice known as:
A. Threshing B. Winnowing
C. Tilling D. Levelling

69. Match Column I and Column II and select the correct matching:

	Column I		Column II
A.	Lactobacillus	—	Fermentation
B.	Penicillium	—	Production of antibodies
C.	Blue green algae	—	Fixation of nitrogen
D.	Yeast	—	Food preservation

70. The two discoveries made by Louis Pasteur for the commercial use of microorganism respectively are:
A. pasteurisation and vaccines
B. fermentation and pasteurisation
C. pasteurisation and antibiotics
D. fermentation and vaccines

71. Given below are two columns - Column I and Column II:

Column I (Disease)	Column II (Causative Microorganism)
(*i*) Rust of wheat	(*a*) Protozoa
(*ii*) Typhoid	(*b*) Virus
(*iii*) Polio	(*c*) Fungi
(*iv*) Malaria	(*d*) Bacteria

Identify the option which correctly matches the disease with its causative microorganism:

	(*i*)	(*ii*)	(*iii*)	(*iv*)
A.	(*d*)	(*c*)	(*a*)	(*b*)
B.	(*b*)	(*a*)	(*c*)	(*d*)
C.	(*c*)	(*d*)	(*b*)	(*a*)
D.	(*a*)	(*b*)	(*d*)	(*c*)

72. Naphthalene balls used to repel moths and other insects are obtained from:
A. Coal-tar B. Coke
C. Coal gas D. Bitumen

73. Column I has some of the constituents of Petroleum and Column II has their uses. Correctly match the constituents with their uses:

Column I	Column II
(*i*) Paraffin wax	(*a*) Fuel for heavy motor vehicles
(*ii*) Bitumen	(*b*) Solvent for dry-cleaning
(*iii*) Diesel	(*c*) Paints
(*iv*) Petrol	(*d*) Vaseline

	(*i*)	(*ii*)	(*iii*)	(*iv*)
A.	(*d*)	(*c*)	(*b*)	(*a*)
B.	(*c*)	(*d*)	(*a*)	(*b*)
C.	(*d*)	(*c*)	(*a*)	(*b*)
D.	(*c*)	(*d*)	(*b*)	(*a*)

74. Which one amongst the following is a fuel with highest calorific value?
A. Petrol B. CNG
C. Diesel D. Wood

75. The consequence of deforestation is:
A. increase in the rainfall and fertility of the soil
B. increase in the ground water levels
C. increase of carbon dioxide levels in the atmosphere
D. decrease of pollution levels in the atmosphere

76. Match Column I with Column II and select the mismatched option:

	Column I		Column II
A.	Sanctuary	—	Certain activities like collecting firewood and medicinal plants allowed
B.	Fauna	—	Plants found in a particular area
C.	Endangered animals	—	Numbers decreasing due to loss of natural habitat
D.	Endemic species	—	Found exclusively in an area

77. For the protection of tigers in the country, Government of India launched a project known as "Project Tiger". This project was launched in:
A. Kaziranga National Park
B. Bori Wildlife Sanctuary
C. Satpura National Park
D. Pachmarhi Biosphere Reserve

66. C **67.** B **68.** C **69.** * **70.** B **71.** C **72.** A **73.** C **74.** B **75.** C
76. B **77.** *

78. Match the organs of human female reproductive system given in Column I with Column II giving the functions they perform:

Column I	Column II
(i) Ovaries	*(a)* Development of the baby takes place
(ii) Fallopian tubes	*(b)* Production of female gamete
(iii) Uterus	*(c)* Mature egg is released

	(i)	*(ii)*	*(iii)*
A.	*(a)*	*(b)*	*(c)*
B.	*(c)*	*(a)*	*(b)*
C.	*(a)*	*(c)*	*(b)*
D.	*(b)*	*(c)*	*(a)*

79. Reproduction in Hydra is similar to yeast as they both reproduce:
A. sexually
B. by binary fission
C. by budding
D. by external fertilisation

80. External fertilisation occurs in:
A. Frog B. Sparrow
C. Cat D. Crocodile

81. Which of the following produces a hormone which controls sugar in a person?
A. Adrenal gland B. Pancreas
C. Pituitary gland D. Thyroid gland

82. Which one of the following changes does **not** occur during adolescence?
A. Sudden increase in height
B. Growth of the larynx
C. Development of secondary sexual characters
D. Complexion/colour of the skin

83. Tadpoles **cannot** become adult frogs in the absence of which one of the following elements in water?
A. Carbon B. Chlorine
C. Iodine D. Nitrogen

84. The option containing contact forces only is:
A. Force of friction and muscular force
B. Electrostatic force and frictional force
C. Gravitational force and muscular force
D. Magnetic force and electrostatic force

85. A rectangular box of length 30 cm, breadth 15 cm and height 10 cm is kept on a table with its three faces of different areas touching the table. If the mass of the box is 100 kg, in all cases, the box exerts on the table:
A. same thrust and same pressure
B. same thrust but different pressure
C. different thrust but same pressure
D. different thrust and different pressure

86. Porters who carry heavy loads always have a long piece of cotton cloth with them. Before carrying the load on their heads they fold the cloth in the form of a round disc and place it on their heads. By doing this they:
A. decrease the thrust of the load.
B. save their heads from possible injury.
C. decrease the force exerted by the load on their heads.
D. increase the area of contact of the load with their heads.

87. Select the correct statement from the following:
A. Frictional force depends on the shape of the object and the nature of the fluid.
B. Frictional force on an object does not depend on its speed with respect to the fluid in which it moves.
C. Frictional force always acts in the direction of motion.
D. Because air is very light and thin, it does not exert any frictional force on the freely falling objects.

88. The audible range of frequencies for human ear is:
A. 10 Hz to 200 Hz
B. 20 Hz to 20,000 Hz
C. 1,000 Hz to 15,000 Hz
D. 20,000 Hz to 30,000 Hz

89. Amplitude and frequency are two important properties of any sound. When the amplitude of vibrations increases, the sound produced becomes:
A. low pitched B. more shrill
C. high pitched D. louder

90. In musical instruments 'Ektara' and 'Manjira' the vibrating parts are respectively:
A. The instrument itself and air-column
B. Air-column and stretched membrane
C. Stretched string and the instrument itself
D. Stretched membrane and the instrument itself

91. To change a feeble sound to a loud sound we will have to increase its:
A. Time period B. Velocity
C. Frequency D. Amplitude

78. D	**79.** C	**80.** A	**81.** B	**82.** D	**83.** C	**84.** A	**85.** B	**86.** D	**87.** A
88. B	**89.** D	**90.** C	**91.** D						

92. The factors on which the loudness and pitch of a sound respectively depend are:
A. Amplitude and speed of sound
B. Amplitude and frequency of sound
C. Frequency and amplitude of sound
D. Speed of sound and frequency

93. Which one is the example of chemical effect of electric current?
A. Deflection of magnetic needle when placed near a wire carrying electric current
B. Emission of heat and light from electric bulb when electric current is passed through it
C. Rotation of blades of fan, when current is passed through the fan
D. Appearance of gas bubbles near graphite electrodes immersed in water containing a little quantity of an acid when current is passed through the set-up

94. Earthquakes are mostly caused by:
A. volcanic eruption
B. collision of meteors with earth
C. underground nuclear explosion
D. movement of earth's plates in earth's crust

95. Study the following statements:
1. Lightning conductors can protect buildings from the effect of lightning.
2. Most earthquakes are caused due to nuclear explosions deep inside the earth.
3. During lightning, it is safer to use computers and TV, keeping doors and windows closed.
4. An electroscope is used to test whether an object is carrying charge or not.

The correct statements are:
A. 1 and 2 only B. 2 and 3 only
C. 3 and 4 only D. 1 and 4 only

96. Study the following statements:
1. Earthing is a process by which electric charge on charged objects is transferred to the earth.
2. During lightning electric discharge occurs between two charged clouds and also between the charged clouds and the earth.
3. During development of thunderstorms due to air currents, negative charges collect near the upper edge of the clouds and positive charges near the lower edges.
4. When positive and negative charges meet, streaks of bright light and sound are produced.

The correct statements are:
A. 1 and 2 only B. 3 and 4 only
C. 1, 2 and 4 D. 1, 3 and 4

97. The image formed by a convex mirror is always:
A. Real, erect and smaller than the size of the object
B. Virtual, inverted and of the same size as the object
C. Virtual, erect and magnified
D. Virtual, erect and smaller than the size of the object

98. If the angle between the incident ray and the reflected ray is 130°, the angle between the incident ray and the reflecting surface of the mirror is:
A. 25° B. 35°
C. 55° D. 65°

99. A ray of light is incident at a point on the reflecting surface of a plane mirror so that the angle between the incident ray and the reflected ray is 120°. If this ray is turned through an angle of 10° towards the reflecting surface keeping the point of incidence same, the angle between the incident ray and the new reflected ray will be:
A. 100° B. 110°
C. 130° D. 140°

100. The part of human eye which gives it a distinct colour is:
A. cornea B. iris
C. lens D. pupil

EXPLANATORY ANSWERS

1. (B): सही वर्तनी वाला शब्द "स्वच्छता" है। "स्वच्छता" हिंदी शब्द है जिसका अर्थ होता है शुद्धता या साफ-सुथराई। यह एक महत्वपूर्ण गुण है जो हमें स्वास्थ्य और हानिकारक रोगों से बचाता है।

2. (C): अंगूठा का तत्सम रूप "अंगुष्ठ है। तत्सम शब्द ऐसे शब्द होते हैं जिन्हें संस्कृत से बिना किसी परिवर्तन के हिंदी में प्रयुक्त किया जाता है।

3. (C): "सुलभ" का अर्थ होता है आसान या सरल, जबकि "दुर्लभ" का अर्थ होता है दुष्कर या मुश्किल। इसलिए, "सुलभ" और "दुर्लभ" एक-दूसरे के विलोम हैं। जब कोई कार्य आसानी से किया जा सकता है तो हम उसे "सुलभ" कहते हैं, जबकि जो कार्य मुश्किल होता है, उसे हम "दुर्लभ" कहते हैं।

4. (B): दिए गए सभी विकल्पों में थॉमस अल्वा एडीसन के लिए बिजली के बल्ब का आविष्कार करना सर्वाधिक उपयुक्त है।

92. C	**93.** D	**94.** D	**95.** D	**96.** D	**97.** D	**98.** A	**99.** D	**100.** B

अतः सही वाक्य है "थामस अल्वा एडीसन ने बिजली के बल्ब का आविष्कार किया।

5. (A): प्रश्न में दिया गया रेखांकित शब्द संज्ञा है। चुंकि किसी वस्तु, व्यक्ति, स्थान, भाव आदि को संज्ञा कहा जाता है। 'भागलपुर' एक भौगोलिक स्थान है अतः यह व्यक्तिवाचक संज्ञा होगा।

6. (B): अवतरण में स्पष्ट लिखा गया है कि "योग केवल शारीरिक व्यायाम ही नहीं, मानसिक व्यायाम भी है। इसलिए इससे दोहरा लाभ है।" अतः इसे शरीर और मन दोनों का व्यायाम माना गया है।

7. (C): 'मन को एकाग्र करना' का आशय एक बिन्दु पर मन को स्थिर करना है।

8. (C): दो समीपवर्ती वर्णों के मेल से जो विकार होता है वह सन्धि कहलाता है। इसके अलग-अलग भागों में विभक्त होकर विभिन्न अर्थ देना सन्धि-विच्छेद कहा जाता है। 'योगाभ्यास' का सन्धि-विच्छेद 'योग + अभ्यास' होगा। यह दीर्घ सन्धि का उदाहरण है।

9. (D): योग के महत्व पर प्रकाश डालते हुए कहा गया है कि आधे घण्टे के योगाभ्यास हमें दिनभर के लिए पर्याप्त ऊर्जा मिलती है। स्वास्थ्य लाभ का इतना सस्ता और सरल उपाय और कोई नहीं हो सकता।

10. (D): अवतरण में स्पष्ट लिखा गया है कि "योग के लिए विशेष तामझाम और मूल्यवान उपकरणों की भी आवश्यकता नहीं पड़ती। कोई चटाई, दरी या तौलिया बिछाकर या हरी दूब बैठकर घर या बाहर कहीं भी योगाभ्यास कर सकते हैं। स्वास्थ्य लाभ का इतना सरल और सस्ता उपाय और कोई नहीं हो सकता। अतः योगाभ्यास के लिए महंगे उपकरण की आवश्यकता नहीं है।

11. (B): दिए गए प्रश्न में रेखांकित शब्द 'पुरस्कार' शब्द जाति वाचक संज्ञा है। जिस शब्द से किसी जाति का बोध हो उसे जातिवाचक संज्ञा कहते हैं। जैसे—नदी, लड़का आदि।

12. (D): "यह काम किसने किया?" यहाँ पर "किसने" शब्द क्रिया के प्रकार को पूछता है, अर्थात कार्य का कर्त्ता कौन है। इस वाक्य में प्रश्न किया गया है कि काम किसने किया है। अतः सही उत्तर "यह काम किसने किया?" ही है।

13. (B): "मैं जानती हूँ कि माँ क्यों रूठी है।" एक संयुक्त वाक्य है। इसमें दो वाक्य हैं जो संयुक्त होकर एक विस्तृत अर्थ प्रकट करते हैं। पहला वाक्य है "मैं जानती हूँ" जो किसी कार्रवाई के सम्बन्ध में जानकारी प्रदान करता है, और दूसरा वाक्य है "माँ क्यों रूठी है" जो किसी स्थिति के कारण का प्रश्न करता है। इन दोनों वाक्यों का संयोग "कि" शब्द द्वारा होता है।

14. (D): दिए गए रिक्त स्थान के लिए कंधे से कंधा मिलाकर उपयुक्त मुहावरा है। कंधे से कंधा मिलाकर का सही अर्थ 'एक दूसरे के साथ सहयोग' करना है।

15. (A): 'नाच न जाने आँगन टेढ़ा' एक लोकोक्ति है। इसका अभिप्राय है—अपना दोष दूसरों के सिर मढ़ना या अपनी कमजोरी निकालने के लिए किसी और की कमी निकालना। वाक्य में प्रयोग – वह सबसे कहती-फिरती है कि वह नृत्य में माहिर है परन्तु जब नृत्य करने के लिए कहा गया तो बोली मंच खराब है। इसे कहते हैं नाच न जाने आंगन टेढ़ा।

16. (C): The passage clearly states that the shopkeeper used to sell his fruits at high prices. Therefore, the correct answer is (C).

17. (A): The passage mentions that the shopkeeper wanted to earn more money despite already making a profit. This indicates a desire for more wealth than he already had, which is characteristic of greed. Thus, the correct answer is (A).

18. (D): When the shopkeeper's friend came to buy fruits and the shopkeeper reduced the weight, the friend got suspicious. The passage explicitly states that his friend got suspicious of the shopkeeper's actions. Therefore, the correct answer is (D).

19. (C): The sentence needs a verb form that fits grammatically with "by" to indicate the method Gulliver used to make strong cables. The correct form is the gerund "twisting," which works as a noun in this context.

20. (A): The sentence describes a sequence of actions: making hooks, tying them, and then going to the shore. "Then" is the most appropriate word to indicate the sequence.

21. (D): The phrase "put on" is the correct verb phrase used when referring to wearing something like goggles.

22. (B): The sentence needs a relative pronoun to refer to "the sea water". "Which" is the appropriate choice as it introduces a non-restrictive relative clause that describes the sea water.

23. (D): The word "recoup" means to recover or make up for something that was lost. It is often used in financial contexts to describe the act of getting back money that was spent or lost. Since "recover" means to get back something that was lost, it is the word similar in meaning to "recoup".

24. (C): The original sentence asks "Whom did you invite?" This is in the active voice, with "you" as the subject performing the action (inviting). To convert it to passive voice, we need to focus on the recipient of the action (the one being invited). "Whom" is the object pronoun in the active voice, and it becomes the subject in the passive voice. The verb needs to be changed to the past participle ("invited") with the helping verb "was". The passive voice of the sentence is: Who was invited by you?

25. (C): Mercilessly means in a way that shows no mercy or pity. Kindly means in a friendly and pleasant way, which is the complete opposite of mercilessly.

26. (B): In this sentence, we're comparing the length of the Amazon River to all other rivers in the world. When making such a comparison, we use the superlative form of the adjective. "Longest" is the superlative form of "long," indicating the greatest length among all rivers.

27. (A): This option accurately reflects that out of a group of Paralympians, a portion of them participated in the hundred-metre race. "None of the" implies an unspecified subset of the larger group, which fits the context of the sentence where it suggests that a group of Paralympians, not necessarily all, participated in the race.

28. (B): The word "money" is an uncountable noun, which means we use different quantifiers and adjectives with it compared to countable nouns. "Little" is an adjective used to describe a small amount of an uncountable noun. In this context, it conveys the idea that there was not much money remaining after expenses were paid.

29. (C): "Gullible" describes someone who is easily persuaded to believe something. It implies a tendency to trust or believe things too readily and without proper evidence or critical thinking.

30. (B): This option accurately reflects the transformation of the sentence into indirect speech. In indirect speech, the pronouns and verb forms change to reflect the perspective of the speaker (Alan) rather than the listener. So, "I" changes to "he" to refer to Alan, who is the speaker.

31. (C): Let 5 consecutive integers be x, $x+1$, $x+2$, $x+3$ and $x+4$, where, $x = 1, 2, 3, \ldots$

Then, $S = x + x + 1 + x + 2 + x + 3 + x + 4$

$\Rightarrow \quad S = 5x + 10$

Let x be 2, then from given options

(A) $\frac{S-10}{5} = \frac{5x+10-10}{5} = \frac{5x}{5} = 2$

(B) $\frac{S+4}{4} = \frac{5x+10+4}{4} = \frac{5}{4}x + \frac{7}{2} = \frac{5}{2} + \frac{7}{2} = 6$

(C) $\frac{S+5}{4} = \frac{5x+10+5}{4} = \frac{5}{4}x + \frac{15}{4} = \frac{5}{2} + \frac{15}{4} = \frac{25}{4}$

(D) $\frac{S+10}{5} = \frac{5x+10+10}{5} = x + 4 = 2 + 4 = 6$

Here, option (C) is the greatest of these integers related to S.

32. (B): Let Ashok's present age be x years and prem's present age be $3x$.

Then, After 15 years,

$$2(x + 15) = 3x + 15$$
$$\Rightarrow 2x + 30 = 3x + 15$$
$$\Rightarrow 3x - 2x = 30 - 15$$
$$\Rightarrow x = 15$$

Hence, the sum of their present ages $= x + 3x = 4x = 4 \times 15 = 60$ years.

33. (B): Let the number of ₹ 1 coins $= x$

Then, the number of ₹ 5 coins $= x$

$\therefore$ The number of ₹ 2 coins $= 24 - 2x$

Now, ₹ 1 $\times x$ + ₹ 2 $(24 - 2x)$ + ₹ 5 $\times x$ = ₹ 62

$\Rightarrow x + 48 - 4x + 5x = 62$

$\Rightarrow 2x = 62 - 48$

$\Rightarrow 2x = 14 \Rightarrow x = 7$

Hence, the number of ₹ 5 coins $= x = 7$.

34. (D): Given, $x = 7 - 4\sqrt{3}$

$$\Rightarrow \frac{1}{x} = \frac{1}{7-4\sqrt{3}} \times \frac{7+4\sqrt{3}}{7+4\sqrt{3}}$$
$$= \frac{7+4\sqrt{3}}{7^2-(4\sqrt{3})^2} = \frac{7+4\sqrt{3}}{49-48}$$
$$= 7+4\sqrt{3}$$
$$\therefore \quad x+\frac{1}{x} = 7-4\sqrt{3}+7+4\sqrt{3}$$
$$= 7 + 7 = 14.$$

35. (D): Given, $a = \frac{\sqrt{5}+1}{\sqrt{5}-1}$

$$\Rightarrow a^2 = \left(\frac{\sqrt{5}+1}{\sqrt{5}-1}\right)^2 = \frac{5+1+2\sqrt{5}}{5+1-2\sqrt{5}}$$
$$\Rightarrow a^2 = \frac{3+\sqrt{5}}{3-\sqrt{5}}$$

and $\quad b = \frac{\sqrt{5}-1}{\sqrt{5}+1}$

$$\Rightarrow b^2 = \left(\frac{\sqrt{5}-1}{\sqrt{5}+1}\right)^2 = \frac{5+1-2\sqrt{5}}{5+1+2\sqrt{5}}$$

$\Rightarrow \quad b^2 = \frac{3-\sqrt{5}}{3+\sqrt{5}}$

and $\quad ab = \frac{\sqrt{5}+1}{\sqrt{5}-1} \times \frac{\sqrt{5}-1}{\sqrt{5}+1} = 1 \Rightarrow ab = 1$

$$\therefore \frac{a^2+ab+b^2}{a^2-ab+b^2} = \frac{\frac{3+\sqrt{5}}{3-\sqrt{5}}+1+\frac{3-\sqrt{5}}{3+\sqrt{5}}}{\frac{3+\sqrt{5}}{3-\sqrt{5}}-1+\frac{3-\sqrt{5}}{3+\sqrt{5}}}$$

$$= \frac{(3+\sqrt{5})^2+(3-\sqrt{5})^2+(3-\sqrt{5})(3+\sqrt{5})}{(3+\sqrt{5})^2+(3-\sqrt{5})^2-(3-\sqrt{5})(3+\sqrt{5})}$$

$$= \frac{9+5+6\sqrt{5}+9+5-6\sqrt{5}+9-5}{9+5+6\sqrt{5}+9+5-6\sqrt{5}-(9-5)}$$

$$= \frac{32}{24} = \frac{4}{3}.$$

36. (C): Let $A = \frac{(0.75)^3}{1-0.75} + [0.75+(0.75)^2+1]$

$$= \frac{(0.75)^3+(1-0.75)[0.75+(0.75)^2+1]}{(1-0.75)}$$

$$= \frac{(0.75)^3+1^3-(0.75)^3}{(1-0.75)}$$

$$= \frac{1^3}{(1-0.75)} = \frac{1}{0.25} = \frac{100}{25} = 4$$

$\Rightarrow \quad A = 4 \quad [\because a^3-b^3 = (a-b)(a^2+b^2+ab)]$

Hence, The positive square root of $A = \sqrt{4} = 2$.

37. (B): Let one number be x and other number be $3x$.

Then, $x \times 3x = 29\frac{31}{49} \Rightarrow 3x^2 = \frac{1452}{49}$

$\Rightarrow \quad x^2 = \frac{484}{49} \Rightarrow x = \frac{22}{7}$

Hence, the greater number $= 3x = 3\times\frac{22}{7} = \frac{66}{7}$.

38. (B): $1^3 - 2^3 + 3^3 - 4^3 + 5^3 - 6^3 + 7^3 - 8^3 + 9^3 - 10^3$

$= (1^3 - 2^3) + (3^3 - 4^3) + (5^3 - 6^3) + (7^3 - 8^3) + (9^3 - 10^3)$

$[a^3 - b^3 = (a - b)(a^2 + b^2 + ab)]$

$= (1 - 2)(1 + 4 + 2) + (3 - 4)(9 + 16 + 12) + (5 - 6)(25 + 36 + 30) + (7 - 8)(49 + 64 + 56) + (9 - 10)(81 + 100 + 90)$

$= -7 - 37 - 91 - 169 - 271$

$= -575.$

39. (B): $\left(\frac{\sqrt[3]{8}}{\sqrt{16}} \div \frac{\sqrt{100}}{\sqrt{49}} \times \sqrt[3]{125}\right)$

$$= \frac{2}{4} \div \frac{10}{7} \times 5 = \frac{1}{2} \times \frac{7}{10} \times 5 = \frac{1}{2} \times \frac{7}{2} = \frac{7}{4}.$$

40. (B): Let 3 numbers be $2x$, $3x$ and $4x$

Then, $(2x)^3 + (3x)^3 + (4x)^3 = 2673$

$\Rightarrow 8x^3 + 27x^3 + 64x^3 = 2673$

$\Rightarrow \quad 99x^3 = 2673 \Rightarrow x^3 = 27$

$\Rightarrow \quad x^3 = 3^3 \Rightarrow x = 3$

Hence, The sum of these 3 numbers

$= 2x + 3x + 4x = 9x = 9 \times 3 = 27.$

41. (B): Given, $\quad (32)^{2x+1} = 8^{-x}.4^{-4}$

$\Rightarrow \quad (2^5)^{2x+1} = (2^3)^{-x}.(2^2)^{-4}$

$\Rightarrow \quad 2^{10x+5} = 2^{-3x-8}$

$\therefore \quad 10x + 5 = -3x - 8$

$\Rightarrow \quad 10x + 3x = -8 - 5$

$\Rightarrow \quad 13x = -13$

$\Rightarrow \quad x = -1$

42. (B): $\left[\sqrt[3]{\sqrt[6]{5^9}}\right]^4 \left[\sqrt[6]{\sqrt[3]{5^9}}\right]^4$

$$= \left[(5^9)^{\frac{1}{3\times6}}\right]^4 \left[(5^9)^{\frac{1}{6\times3}}\right]^4 = \left[(5^9)^{\frac{1}{18}}\right]^4 \left[(5^9)^{\frac{1}{18}}\right]^4$$

$$= [5^{1/2}]^4 [5^{1/2}]^4 = [5^2][5^2] = 5^4.$$

43. (D): $\sqrt[r]{\frac{9^{\left(r+\frac{1}{4}\right)}\sqrt{3.3^{-r}}}{\sqrt{3^{2-r}}}} = \left[\frac{3^{2r+\frac{1}{2}}.3^{\frac{1-r}{2}}}{3^{\frac{2-r}{2}}}\right]^{\frac{1}{r}}$

$$= \left[\frac{3^{2r+\frac{1}{2}+\frac{1-r}{2}}}{3^{\left(1-\frac{r}{2}\right)}}\right]^{\frac{1}{r}} = \left[3^{2r+\frac{1}{2}+\frac{1}{2}-\frac{r}{2}-1+\frac{r}{2}}\right]^{\frac{1}{r}}$$

$$= [3^{2r+1-1}]^{\frac{1}{r}} = [3^{2r}]^{\frac{1}{r}} = 3^2 = 9.$$

44. (B): $\frac{2^x+2^{x-1}}{2^{x+1}-2^x} = \frac{2^x+2^x\cdot2^{-1}}{2^x\ 2^1\ 2^x}$

$$= \frac{2^x(1+2^{-1})}{2^x(2-1)} = \frac{1+\frac{1}{2}}{1} = \frac{3}{2}.$$

45. (C): Speed of a loaded truck $= \frac{\text{Distance}}{\text{Time}}$

$$= \frac{18 \text{ km}}{35 \text{ minutes}} = \frac{18 \text{ km}}{\frac{35}{60} \text{ hour}} = 18\times\frac{60}{35} \text{ km/h}$$

It can travel in 7 hours $= 18\times\frac{60}{35}$ km/h × 7 hrs

$= 18\times\frac{12}{7}\times 7$ km

$= 18 \times 12$ km $= 216$ km.

46. (C): More people, less day → Indirect proportion.
Let number of required people be x

People day

Then, $28 : x :: 35 : 65$

$\Rightarrow \quad 28\times 65 = x \times 35$

$\Rightarrow \quad x = \frac{28\times 65}{35} = \frac{4\times 65}{5}$

$= 4 \times 13 = 52$

$\Rightarrow \quad x = 52$ people.

47. (C): $\because$ $L \propto \frac{1}{M} \Rightarrow L = \frac{k}{M} \Rightarrow k = L\times M$

$\Rightarrow k = 10 \times 6$

$\Rightarrow k = 60$

(A) $k = 12 \times 5 = 60$

(B) $k = 15 \times 4 = 60$

(C) $k = 45 \times 1.3 = 58.5$

(D) $k = 25 \times 2.4 = 60$

Hence, option (C) is not a possible pair of corresponding values of L and M.

48. (A): Let the cost price be ₹ 100 and $x\%$ should be added in the cost price

Then, $(100+x)\times\frac{100-5}{100} = 133$

$\Rightarrow \quad (100+x)\times\frac{95}{100} = 133$

$\Rightarrow \quad (100+x)\times\frac{19}{20} = 133$

$\Rightarrow \quad 19(100 + x) = 133 \times 20$

$\Rightarrow \quad 1900 + 19x = 2660$

$\Rightarrow \quad 19x = 2660 - 1900 = 760$

$\Rightarrow \quad x = 40.$

49. (B): Let the sum be ₹ x

Then, Simple interest $=$ ₹ $\frac{3}{8}x$,

Given, $t = 6\frac{1}{4} = \frac{25}{4}$ years

$\therefore \quad \text{Rate} = \frac{\text{S.I.}\times 100}{\text{Sum}\times t} = \frac{\frac{3}{8}x\times 100}{x\times\frac{25}{4}}$

$= \frac{3}{8}\times 100\times\frac{4}{25}$

$= 3 \times 4 \times \frac{1}{2} = 6\%$

$\Rightarrow$ Rate $= 6\%$.

50. (C): Compound Interest $= P\left[\left(1+\frac{r}{100}\right)^n - 1\right]$

$\Rightarrow \quad 1261 = P\left[\left(1+\frac{5}{100}\right)^3 - 1\right]$

$\Rightarrow \quad 1261 = P\left[\left(1+\frac{1}{20}\right)^3 - 1\right]$

$\Rightarrow \quad 1261 = P\left[\left(\frac{21}{20}\right)^3 - 1\right]$

$\Rightarrow \quad 1261 = P\left[\frac{9261}{8000} - 1\right]$

$\Rightarrow \quad 1261 = P\left[\frac{1261}{8000}\right]$

$\Rightarrow \quad P = \frac{1261\times 8000}{1261} = 8000$

Hence, the sum of money invested $= P =$ ₹ 8000.

51. (A): Dividing $x^4 + 4x^2 + 10$ by $x^2 - 2x + 4$

$\therefore$
$$
\begin{array}{r|l|l}
(x^2 - 2x + 4) & x^4 + 4x^2 + 10 & x^2 + 2x + 4 \\
 & x^4 - 2x^3 + 4x^2 & \\
 & \underline{-\quad +\quad -} & \\
 & 2x^3 + 10 & \\
 & 2x^3 - 4x^2 + 8x & \\
 & \underline{-\quad +\quad -} & \\
 & 4x^2 - 8x + 10 & \\
 & 4x^2 - 8x + 16 & \\
 & \underline{-\quad +\quad -} & \\
 & -6 &
\end{array}
$$

$\therefore x^4 + 4x^2 + 10 = (x^2 - 2x + 4)(x^2 + 2x + 4) - 6$

Hence, the required remainder $= -6$.

52. (B): Given $x + \frac{1}{x} = 5$

$\therefore \quad \frac{2x}{3x^2 - 5x + 3} = \frac{\frac{2x}{x}}{\frac{3x^2 - 5x + 3}{x}} = \frac{2}{3x - 5 + \frac{3}{x}}$

$= \frac{2}{3\left(x + \frac{1}{x}\right) - 5} = \frac{2}{3(5) - 5} = \frac{2}{15 - 5}$

$= \frac{2}{10} = \frac{1}{5}.$

53. (A): Given, $\left(x+\frac{1}{x}\right)^2 = 3$

$\Rightarrow \quad x^2+2+\frac{1}{x^2} = 3 \Rightarrow x^2-1+\frac{1}{x^2} = 0$

$\Rightarrow \quad x^4 - x^2 + 1 = 0$

$\therefore x^{206} + x^{200} + x^{90} + x^{84} + x^{18} + x^{12} + x^6 + 1$

$= x^{200}(x^6 + 1) + x^{84}(x^6 + 1) + x^{12}(x^6 + 1) + (x^6 + 1)$

$= (x^{200} + x^{84} + x^{12} + 1)\ (x^6 + 1)$

$= (x^{200} + x^{84} + x^{12} + 1)\ [(x^2)^3 + 1^3]$

$= (x^{200} + x^{84} + x^{12} + 1)\ (x^2 + 1)(x^4 - x^2 + 1)$

$= (x^{200} + x^{84} + x^{12} + 1)\ (x^2 + 1) \times 0$

$= 0$

54. (A): $\frac{5(x+6)-15(2-x)}{3x-1} = 10$

$\Rightarrow 5(x + 6) - 15(2 - x) = 10(3x - 1)$

$\Rightarrow 5x + 30 - 30 + 15x = 30x - 10$

$\Rightarrow \quad 20x = 30x - 10$

$\Rightarrow \quad 30x - 20x = 10$

$\Rightarrow \quad 10x = 10$

$\Rightarrow \quad x = 1.$

55. (A): Let the number be x

Then, $\left(x-\frac{1}{2}\right)\times 8 = 12$

$\Rightarrow \quad \left(x-\frac{1}{2}\right) = \frac{12}{8}$

$\Rightarrow \quad \left(x-\frac{1}{2}\right) = \frac{3}{2}$

$\Rightarrow \quad x = \frac{1}{2}+\frac{3}{2} = \frac{4}{2}$

$\Rightarrow \quad x = 2.$

56. (B): Given, $\frac{5x}{3}-4 = \frac{2x}{5}$

$\Rightarrow \quad \frac{5x}{3}-\frac{2x}{5} = 4$

$\Rightarrow \quad \frac{25x-6x}{15} = 4$

$\Rightarrow \quad 19x = 60 \Rightarrow x = \frac{60}{19}$

$\therefore \quad (2x - 7) = 2\times\frac{60}{19}-7$

$= \frac{120}{19}-7 = \frac{120-133}{19} = \frac{-13}{19}$

Hence, $(2x - 7) = \frac{-13}{19}$.

57. (D): Let the sides of a rectangle be $5x$ cm and $3x$ cm.

Then, $l = 5x$ cm and $b = 3x$ cm.

$\therefore \quad \text{Area} = l \times b = 5x \times 3x$

$\Rightarrow \quad 135 = 15x^2$

$\Rightarrow \quad x^2 = 9 \Rightarrow x = 3$

Hence, perimeter of the rectangle

$= 2(l + b) = 2(5x + 3x)$

$= 16x = 16 \times 3 = 48$ cm.

58. (B): Given, ABCD is an isosceles trapezium.

i.e., AD = BC

and AB || DC

$\therefore$ ∠D = ∠C and ∠A = ∠B.

59. (B): Given, in the figure

ABCD is a rhombus, ∠DMC = 90°

and ∠DAB = 110°

$\because$ ∠DAB = ∠DCB and ∠ADC = ∠ABC

In rhombus

∠ADC + ∠DCB + ∠ABC + ∠DAB = 360°

⇒ ∠ABC + ∠DAB + ∠ABC + ∠DAB = 360°

⇒ 2∠ABC + 2∠DAB = 360°

⇒ 2∠ABC + 2 × 110° = 360°

⇒ 2∠ABC = 360° – 220°

⇒ ∠ABC = $\frac{140}{2}$ = 70°

⇒ ∠ADC = 70°

$\therefore$ ∠ADM + ∠CDM = 70°

⇒ ∠CDM + ∠CDM = 70°

[$\because$ ∠ADM = ∠CDM]

⇒ 2∠CDM = 70°

⇒ ∠CDM = 35°

$\therefore$ ∠BDC = 35°.

60. (A): Given, A rectangular sheet of paper

$l = 44$ cm, $b = 18$ cm

$\because$ Paper is rolled along its length and a cylinder is formed

$\therefore$ Perimeter of base of cylinder

= 44 cm and h = 18 cm

$\Rightarrow \quad 2\pi r = 44$ cm

$\Rightarrow \quad 2\times\frac{22}{7}r = 44$

$\Rightarrow \quad r = 7$ cm

Hence, the volume of the cylinder $= \pi r^2 h$

$= \frac{22}{7}\times 7^2 \times 18$

$= 22 \times 7 \times 18$

$= 154 \times 18$

$= 2772\ \text{cm}^3$

61. (C): Given A beam of wood,

$l = 5$ m, $h = 36$ cm $= \frac{36}{100}$ m

$\because$ Volume of beam $= lbh$

$\Rightarrow \quad 1.35$ cu m $= 5 \times b \times \frac{36}{100}$

$\Rightarrow 1.35 \times 100 \times 100 \times 100$ cu cm

$= 5 \times b \times \frac{36}{100} \times 100 \times 100$ cu cm

$\Rightarrow 135 \times 100 \times 100 = 5b \times 36 \times 100$

$\Rightarrow \quad 135 \times 100 = 5b \times 36$

$\Rightarrow \quad 13500 = 180b$

$\Rightarrow \quad b = \frac{13500}{180} = \frac{1350}{18} = \frac{150}{2} = 75$ cm

$\therefore$ The width of the beam $= 75$ cm.

62. (B): Let $l = 3x$ and $b = 2x$ be the length and breadth of a rectangular playground

Then, Area $= l \times b = 3x \times 2x$

$\Rightarrow \quad 38,400 = 6x^2$

$\Rightarrow \quad x^2 = 6400$

$\Rightarrow \quad x = 80$ m

$\therefore$ The perimeter of playground $= 2(l + b)$

$= 2(3x + 2x) = 10x$

$= 10 \times 80 = 800$ m.

63. (B): Let a be length of a side of a square

Then, Area of a square $= (\text{Side})^2 = a^2$

and its diagonal $= \text{Side}\sqrt{2} = a\sqrt{2}$

$\therefore$ Area of another square made on the diagonal

$= \left(a\sqrt{2}\right)^2 = 2a^2$

Hence, The required ratio $= a^2 : 2a^2 = 1 : 2$.

64. (C): In a pie-chart

$100 = 360°$

$\Rightarrow \quad 1 = \frac{360}{100}$ (20% on house rent)

$\Rightarrow \quad 20 = \frac{360}{100} \times 20 = 72°$

Hence, the central angle for house rent on a pie-chart $= 72°$.

65. (B): Given, word MOVEMENT

Total number of letters $= 8$

$\therefore \quad n(\text{S}) = 8$

and the number of letter M $= 2$

$\therefore$ Favourable number of out comes

$= 2 \Rightarrow n(\text{E}) = 2$

$\therefore \quad$ Probability $= \frac{n(\text{E})}{n(\text{S})} = \frac{2}{8} = \frac{1}{4}$.

66. (C): While loosening the soil can certainly aid in many aspects of agriculture, such as allowing roots to breathe easily, bringing nutrient-rich soil to the surface, and facilitating the growth of earthworms and microbes, it may not necessarily help in leveling the soil. In fact, loosening the soil can sometimes result in uneven terrain rather than leveling it.

67. (B): Legumes, such as peas, beans, or lentils, have the ability to fix nitrogen in the soil through symbiotic relationships with nitrogen-fixing bacteria in their root nodules. When grown alternately with crops like wheat, which require nitrogen for their growth, they help replenish the soil with this essential nutrient, promoting healthier growth in subsequent crops like wheat.

68. (C): Tilling involves the preparation of soil by breaking up the soil surface and turning it over to remove weeds, aerate the soil, and create a suitable seedbed for planting. Threshing (A) is the process of separating grains or seeds from the husks and straw. Winnowing (B) is the process of separating the lighter chaff from the heavier grains by tossing them in the air and letting the wind blow away the chaff. Levelling (D) is the process of making the surface of the soil even and smooth.

70. (B): Louis Pasteur's work on fermentation laid the foundation for the commercial use of microorganisms in industries such as brewing and winemaking. Pasteurization, a process named after him, involves heating beverages like milk and wine to kill bacteria and extend their shelf life.

71. (C):

***(i)* Rust of wheat – *(c)* Fungi:** Rust of wheat is a plant disease caused by various species of fungi belonging to the genus Puccinia. These fungi infect wheat plants, causing characteristic rust-colored pustules on the leaves, stems, and grains.

***(ii)* Typhoid – *(d)* Bacteria:** Typhoid fever is a bacterial infection caused by the bacterium Salmonella enterica serotype Typhi. It is typically transmitted through contaminated food or water and can lead to fever, abdominal pain, and in severe cases, intestinal perforation and death if left untreated.

***(iii)* Polio – *(b)* Virus:** Polio, short for poliomyelitis, is a viral infection caused by the poliovirus, which belongs to the family Picornaviridae. Poliovirus primarily affects the nervous system, leading to paralysis, muscle weakness, and in severe cases, respiratory failure.

(*iv*) **Malaria – (*a*) Protozoa:** Malaria is a parasitic disease caused by protozoa of the genus Plasmodium. The most common species that infect humans are Plasmodium falciparum, Plasmodium vivax, Plasmodium malariae, and Plasmodium ovale. Malaria is transmitted through the bite of infected Anopheles mosquitoes and can lead to symptoms such as fever, chills, and anemia.

72. (A): Naphthalene balls, also known as mothballs, are obtained from coal tar. Coal tar is a thick, black liquid that is a by product of coal. Naphthalene balls are white crystalline compounds that are flammable and potentially explosive. When placed in a closed container with material, the vapour from the naphthalene balls kills moths and other fiber insects to protect clothing. The naphthalene sublimes into a toxic, pungent smell that drives away insects.

73. (C):

(*i*) **Paraffin wax – (*d*) Vaseline:** Paraffin wax is used in the production of Vaseline (petroleum jelly), making option (*d*) correct.

(*ii*) **Bitumen – (*c*) Paints:** Bitumen is commonly used in the manufacturing of paints, so option (c) is correct.

(*iii*) **Diesel – (*a*) Fuel for heavy motor vehicles:** Diesel is indeed used as a fuel for heavy motor vehicles, aligning with option (*a*).

(*iv*) **Petrol – (*b*) Solvent for dry-cleaning:** Petrol (gasoline) is commonly used as a solvent in dry-cleaning processes, making option (*b*) correct.

74. (B): Compressed Natural Gas (CNG) typically has the highest calorific value among the options listed. It consists mainly of methane, which has a high calorific value compared to other fuels like petrol, diesel, or wood.

75. (C): Deforestation leads to the removal of trees, which are essential for absorbing carbon dioxide from the atmosphere during photosynthesis. When trees are cut down or burned, the stored carbon is released back into the atmosphere, contributing to increased levels of carbon dioxide, a greenhouse gas, which in turn exacerbates global warming and climate change.

76. (B): Fauna — Plants found in a particular area: This is the mismatched option. Fauna refers to the animal life of a particular region, including mammals, birds, reptiles, amphibians, and insects. Plants found in a particular area are typically referred to as flora, not fauna.

78. (D):

(*i*) **Ovaries — (*b*) Production of female gamete:** The ovaries are the female reproductive organs responsible for producing eggs (ova), which are the female gametes. In addition to producing eggs, the ovaries also produce female hormones such as estrogen and progesterone.

(*ii*) **Fallopian tubes — (*c*) Mature egg is released:** The fallopian tubes are the structures that transport the eggs from the ovaries to the uterus. When ovulation occurs, a mature egg is released from an ovary and enters the fallopian tube, where it may meet sperm for fertilization.

(*iii*) **Uterus — (*a*) Development of the baby takes place:** The uterus, also known as the womb, is the organ where the fertilized egg implants and develops into a baby. The lining of the uterus thickens each month to prepare for a potential pregnancy.

79. (C): Reproduction in Hydra is similar to yeast as they both reproduce by budding. In both Hydra and yeast, reproduction occurs through a process called budding, where a new individual grows from a certain part of the parent organism and eventually detaches to become a new independent organism.

80. (A): In frogs, fertilization takes place outside the female's body. The female releases eggs into the water, and the male releases sperm over the eggs to fertilize them externally. This is in contrast to sparrows, cats, and crocodiles, which all undergo internal fertilization.

81. (B): The organ that produces a hormone which controls sugar in a person is Pancreas. The pancreas produces insulin, a hormone that helps regulate blood sugar levels by facilitating the uptake of glucose into cells and lowering the blood glucose concentration.

82. (D): While adolescence involves many physical changes, such as a sudden increase in height (A), growth of the larynx (B), and development of secondary sexual characteristics (C), changes in the complexion or colour of the skin are not a characteristic feature of this developmental stage. Skin complexion is largely determined by genetics and may vary due to other factors such as sun exposure or medical conditions, but it is not specifically a change associated with adolescence.

83. (C): Iodine is essential for the production of thyroid hormones, which are critical for the metamorphosis of tadpoles into adult frogs. Without sufficient iodine, tadpoles may experience impaired development and fail to undergo the necessary changes to become adult frogs.

84. (A): The option containing contact forces only is Force of friction and muscular force. Both frictional force and muscular force require physical contact between objects to be exerted. Frictional force arises from the contact between two surfaces, and muscular force is generated by the muscles in the body when they exert force on an object.

86. (D): The action of porters using a long piece of cotton cloth folded into a round disc and placing it on their heads before carrying heavy loads serves to increase the area of contact of the load with their heads. Through this the pressure exerted by the load on their heads is distributed more evenly, reducing the risk of injury and discomfort. This method allows the weight of the load to be spread out over a larger surface area, making it more manageable and less likely to cause strain or injury to the porters.

87. (A): Friction is the force that resists the relative motion of material elements, fluid layers, and solid surfaces sliding against each other. It can have many consequences, such as wear, which can damage components or degrade performance, and the conversion of kinetic energy to thermal energy, which occurs when a viscous fluid is stirred.

88. (B): This range covers the frequencies that humans can typically hear, with 20 Hz being the lowest frequency that most people can perceive as a deep bass sound, and 20,000 Hz being the highest frequency that is typically audible, especially for younger individuals.

89. (D): Amplitude refers to the magnitude or intensity of the vibrations in a sound wave. When the amplitude increases, the energy carried by the sound wave increases, resulting in a louder sound. The pitch of the sound, which is determined by its frequency, does not change with changes in amplitude.

90. (C): In an Ektara, the vibrating part is a stretched string, typically made of a single piece of string attached to the instrument's body, which is plucked to produce sound.

In a Manjira, the vibrating part is the instrument itself. Manjiras are small cymbals or hand bells that are struck together to produce sound. The vibration occurs within the instrument's body when the bells are struck against each other.

91. (D): Amplitude refers to the magnitude or intensity of the vibrations in a sound wave. Increasing the amplitude of the sound wave increases its energy, resulting in a louder sound. This is why increasing the volume on a speaker or musical instrument amplifies the sound.

92. (C): Frequency determines the pitch of a sound. Higher frequencies result in higher pitch, while lower frequencies result in lower pitch.

Amplitude determines the loudness of a sound. Greater amplitudes result in louder sounds, while smaller amplitudes result in softer sounds.

93. (D): This phenomenon is known as electrolysis, where the passage of an electric current through a conducting solution (electrolyte) causes chemical reactions at the electrodes, resulting in the production of gas bubbles. In this case, the gas bubbles are likely hydrogen and oxygen, produced from the electrolysis of water.

94. (D): The movement of tectonic plates in the Earth's crust leads to the buildup of stress along faults, resulting in sudden releases of energy, which manifest as earthquakes. This movement can occur at plate boundaries, such as convergent, divergent, and transform boundaries, where the plates interact in various ways, leading to seismic activity.

95. (D): Statement 1: This statement is true. Lightning conductors, also known as lightning rods, are installed on buildings to provide a preferred path for lightning to strike, diverting the electrical charge safely into the ground and protecting the structure from damage.

Statement 4: This statement is true. An electroscope is a device used to detect the presence of electric charge on an object. When a charged object is brought near the electroscope, it causes the leaves of the electroscope to repel each other, indicating the presence of charge.

96. (D): Statement 1: This statement is true. Earthing is a safety measure used to prevent the buildup of excess electric charge on objects by providing a conducting path for the charge to flow into the Earth, thus neutralizing the object.

Statement 3: This statement is true. Thunderstorms involve the vertical movement of air currents, which leads to the separation of positive and negative charges within clouds, with negative charges typically collecting near the upper edge of the clouds and positive charges near the lower edges.

Statement 4: This statement is true. When positive and negative charges meet during a lightning strike, the rapid movement and collision of charged particles produce intense heat, light, and sound, resulting in a lightning flash and thunder.

97. (D): In a convex mirror, the reflected rays diverge away from each other, causing them to appear to originate from a point behind the mirror. This results in the formation of a virtual image that is erect (upright), diminished (smaller than the object), and located behind the mirror.

100. (B): The iris is the colored part of the eye that surrounds the pupil. It contains pigments that determine the colour of the eye. The colour of the iris varies from person to person, ranging from shades of blue, green, brown, and gray, depending on the amount and distribution of pigment melanin in the iris.

Previous Paper (Solved)

JAWAHAR NAVODAYA VIDYALAYA

Class-IX, Entrance Exam, 2023*

SECTION-I : हिन्दी

1. किस विकल्प में दोनों शब्द तत्सम हैं?

A. सूरज, अग्नि B. भानु, आसमान
C. आकाश, सितारा D. दिनकर, सूर्य

2. उस विकल्प का चयन कीजिए जिसमें दोनों शब्द 'बादल' के पर्यायवाची हैं :

A. मेघ, गगन B. शैल, व्योम
C. नभ, नग D. घन, जलद

3. निम्नलिखित वाक्य में रिक्त स्थान के लिए उपयुक्त शब्द चुनिए :

बैंक से ________ लिया है तो चुकाना भी पड़ेगा।

A. उदार B. उधार
C. उद्धार D. उधर

4. संज्ञा की विशेषता बताने वाले शब्द को कहा जाता है :

A. सर्वनाम B. विशेष्य
C. विशेषण D. क्रिया-विशेषण

5. शुद्ध वर्तनी वाला शब्द छाँटिए :

A. आविस्कार B. आविश्कार
C. अविष्कार D. आविष्कार

निर्देश (प्रश्न संख्या 6-10 तक): *निम्नलिखित अनुच्छेद को पढ़कर दिए गए प्रश्नों के सर्वाधिक उपयुक्त उत्तर चुनिए।*

आज हमारे अस्तित्व के लिए सबसे बड़ी चुनौती है—प्रदूषण। साँस लेते हुए, भोजन के साथ या पीने वाले पानी के साथ अत्यंत विषैले पदार्थ हमारे शरीर में पहुँच रहे हैं; वन काट देने से वर्षा अनियमित हो रही है—कहीं बाढ़, कहीं सूखा। तापमान बढ़ने से ग्लेशियर पिघल रहे हैं और समुद्रों में जल स्तर बढ़ रहा है। इसलिए संभव है सदी के अंत तक ग्लेशियर से निकलने वाली गंगा-यमुना जैसी नदियाँ ही सूख जाएँ। इसीलिए कहा जाता है कि अगला विश्वयुद्ध पानी के लिए होगा। प्रदूषण से अनेक प्रकार के असाध्य रोग बढ़ रहे हैं। वन कट रहे हैं और वनस्पतियाँ उजड़ रही हैं। वन्य जीव-जन्तुओं पर खतरा मँडरा रहा है और अंततः यह खतरा पूरे मानव समाज के लिए विनाशक होगा। मानव जाति को इस पृथ्वी से विलुप्त होने से रोकना है तो हमें जैसे भी हो प्रदूषण को शीघ्र ही रोकना होगा। अन्यथा कभी दूसरे ग्रह से आने वाले प्राणी पृथ्वी पर पहुँचकर कहेंगे—यहाँ कभी मनुष्य रहता था जो इतना मूर्ख था कि अपने पैरों पर स्वयं कुल्हाड़ी मारकर उजड़ गया।

6. हमारे शरीर में अत्यंत विषैले पदार्थ किसके द्वारा पहुँच रहे हैं?

A. हमारे अस्तित्व के द्वारा
B. हवा, जल और भोजन के द्वारा
C. गंगा-यमुना के जल के द्वारा
D. वन्य जीव-जन्तुओं के द्वारा

7. अनुच्छेद में आए किस शब्द का अर्थ 'संकट' है?

A. विनाशक B. अन्यथा
C. खतरा D. प्रदूषण

8. वन्य जीव-जन्तुओं के अस्तित्व पर खतरा होने का कारण है :

A. वनों का कटना
B. ग्लेशियर का पिघलना
C. नदियों का सूखना
D. समुद्रों में जल स्तर बढ़ना

9. कैसे कह सकते हैं कि गंगा-यमुना जैसी नदियाँ कभी सूख सकती हैं?

A. वन कट रहे हैं
B. बाढ़ें आ रही हैं
C. ग्लेशियर पिघल रहे हैं
D. समुद्रों का जल स्तर बढ़ रहा है

10. जिन रोगों की चिकित्सा असंभव हो, उन्हें कहा जाता है :

A. विनाशक B. असाध्य
C. असंभव D. विलुप्त

11. "रिया दूध पीकर सोने चली गई।"

उपर्युक्त वाक्य का संयुक्त वाक्य होगा :

A. रिया ने सोने से पहले दूध पिया।
B. रिया ने दूध पिया और सोने चली गई।
C. जब रिया ने दूध पी लिया तो सोने चली गई।
D. रिया, दूध पियो और सो जाओ।

12. निम्नलिखित वाक्य के लिए उपयुक्त मुहावरा चुनिए :

कितना समझाया था, पर इसके ________ ।

A. दाल नहीं गली
B. कान पर जूँ तक नहीं रेंगी

* Exam held on 11-02-2023.

C. कान नहीं भरे
D. कान फूट गए

13. किसी का नाम बड़ा हो पर उसमें उतने गुण न हों तो किस लोकोक्ति का प्रयोग ठीक रहेगा?
A. अंधों में काना राजा
B. मुँह में राम बगल में छुरी
C. ऊँची दुकान फीके पकवान
D. अधजल गगरी छलकत जाए

14. शुद्ध वाक्य छाँटिए :
A. हम तो पहले ही बता दिए थे।
B. हम तो पहले ही बताए थे।
C. हमने तो पहले ही बता ही दिए थे।
D. हमने तो पहले ही बता दिया था।

15. वह शब्द पहचानिए जिसमें कोई उपसर्ग **नहीं** है :
A. नियम B. निबंध
C. नित्य D. निर्वाचन

SECTION-II : ENGLISH

Directions (Qs. No. 16-18): *Read the following passage carefully and answer these questions.*

We turned to look in the direction pointed out, and there saw a penguin walking slowly along the shore with an egg under its tail. There were several others, we observed doing the same thing : and we found afterwards that these were a kind of penguins that always carried their eggs so. Indeed they had a most useful pocket for the purpose, just between the tail and the legs. We were very much struck with the regularity and order of this colony. The island seemed to be divided up into squares of which each penguin possessed one, and sat in stiff graveness in the middle of it, or took a slow march up and down the spaces in between. Some were sitting on their eggs, but others were feeding their young ones in a manner that caused us to laugh not a little. The mother stood on a raised rock, while the young one below her head uttered a number of loud unpleasant noises.

16. The penguins live:
A. on rocks B. in squares
C. on an island D. in a colony

17. The penguins carried their eggs in a pocket:
A. under their wings.
B. between the tail and legs.
C. on their backs.
D. on their tails.

18. The narrator and his friend could not help laughing when they saw:
A. the penguins carry their eggs.
B. the penguins do a slow march.
C. the mother penguins feeding their young ones.
D. a mother penguin standing on a raised rock and the young one making a loud noise below her.

Directions (Qs. No. 19-22): *Answer these questions by choosing the most appropriate options to complete the paragraph by filling in the blanks.*

Udhata, a thin donkey who was starved by his owner, a local fisherman, went in search ___(19)___ food with his friend, a jackal. The pair went ___(20)___ the village in the middle of the night until they stumbled upon a cucumber field. That night, they truly relished their meal and decided to pay a visit to the cucumber field every night. Udhata eventually ___(21)___ to look much healthier and was able to pick up more load. Once, after an appetizing and wholesome meal ___(22)___ cucumbers, the donkey started braying.

19. A. out B. of
C. into D. on

20. A. around B. out
C. for D. onto

21. A. begin B. beginning
C. began D. begun

22. A. on B. for
C. into D. of

23. The candidate said that his views have been deliberately <u>garbled.</u>

The word opposite in meaning to the underlined one is:
A. clarified B. slanted
C. distorted D. illustrated

24. Choose the word similar in meaning to the underlined word.

After a long and <u>arduous</u> drive on the hills, he felt fatigued.
A. easily B. effortless
C. difficult D. enjoyable

25. Read the sentence given below and choose the option which correctly changes it into Passive Voice.

She created twenty new dresses for the fashion show in just two days.
A. She had created twenty new dresses for the fashion show in just two days.
B. Twenty new dresses were created by her for the fashion show in just two days.

C. She had been creating twenty new dresses for the fashion show in just two days.

D. She will be creating twenty new dresses for the fashion show in just two days.

Directions (Qs. No. 26-28): *Answer these questions by choosing the most appropriate options to fill in the blanks.*

26. You can't depend on him; he knows _______ about finance.

A. a little B. few
C. little D. much

27. No other boy in the class is as _______ as Ram.

A. better B. good
C. best D. worse

28. He was sleeping well when the bell _______ .

A. has rung
B. rang
C. is ringing
D. would ring

29. Choose one-word substitute for the following expression:

Something that cures all illnesses or prolongs life.

A. Elixir B. Idyllic
C. Massif D. Masterpiece

30. Select the alternative which best expresses the following sentence in indirect speech:

The manager said to the clerk, "You may leave now. Don't forget to keep these files in the file cabinet."

A. The manager says to the clerk that you may leave then and asked not to forget to keep these files in the cabinet.

B. The manager told the clerk that he might leave then and ordered him not to forget to keep those files in the file cabinet.

C. The manager said to the clerk that he may leave now and ordered not to forget to keep those files in the cabinet.

D. The manager told to the clerk that he might leave then and ordered not to forget to keep these files in the cabinet.

SECTION-III : MATHEMATICS

31. If the price of an item is increased by 15% and the total sales of that item is reduced by 10%, then what will be the effect on the total earning of a shopkeeper?

A. 5% decrease
B. 1.5% increase
C. 2.5% decrease
D. 3.5% increase

32. A sum of money invested at simple interest triples itself in 8 years. How many times will it become in 20 years time?

A. 8 B. 7
C. 6 D. 9

33. At the rate of 5% annual interest on a sum of money, ₹ 1,261 compound interest is received in 3 years. The sum of money invested is:

A. ₹ 9,000 B. ₹ 8,400
C. ₹ 8,000 D. ₹ 7,500

34. A can do a work in 25 days and B can finish it in 20 days. They work together for 5 days. In how many days will B finish the remaining work?

A. 8 days B. 10 days
C. 11 days D. 13 days

35. If 5 men or 7 women can earn ₹ 1,372 per day, how much would 10 men and 5 women earn per day?

A. ₹ 3,724 B. ₹ 3,624
C. ₹ 3,524 D. ₹ 3,124

36. ABCD is a square. P, Q, R, S are the mid-points of AB, BC, CD and DA respectively. If the perimeter of square ABCD is $16\sqrt{2}$ cm, then the perimeter of the square PQRS is:

A. $16\sqrt{2}$ cm B. $8\sqrt{2}$ cm
C. 8 cm D. 16 cm

37. The perimeters of two squares are 40 cm and 32 cm. What is the perimeter of the third square whose area is equal to the difference of the areas of the first two squares?

A. 24 cm B. 26 cm
C. 25 cm D. 28 cm

38. A total of ₹ 50,000 is to be distributed as prizes to 200 persons. A prize is either of ₹ 100 or ₹ 500. What is the number of prizes of ₹ 100?

A. 50 B. 75
C. 125 D. 150

39. ABCD is a parallelogram having its sides, AB = $3x + 1$, BC = $2y + 3$, CD = 25 and DA = $y + 28$. Then, $(x + y)$ is equal to:

A. 29 B. 21
C. 25 D. 33

40. The four angles of a quadrilateral are in the ratio 2 : 3 : 5 : 8. What is the difference between the smallest and the greatest angles of the quadrilateral?

A. 80° B. 100°
C. 110° D. 120°

41. If $a^2 + b^2 + c^2 = 2(a - b - c) - 3$, then the value of $(2a - 3b + 4c)$ is:

A. 4 B. 3
C. 2 D. 1

42. The ages of Raju and Raman are in the ratio 5 : 8. If Raju was 5 years older and Raman 4 years younger, the age of Raju would have been the same as that of Raman. What is the age of Raju?

A. 15 years B. 16 years
C. 24 years D. 13 years

43. The difference between the digits of a 2-digit number is 3. If the digits are interchanged and the resulting number is added to the original number, we get 143. What is the original number?

A. 58 B. 47
C. 69 D. 96

44. If $\left(x - \frac{1}{x}\right)^2 = 36$, then what is the value of $x^4 + \frac{1}{x^4}$?

A. 1442 B. 1440
C. 1444 D. 1438

45. If one of the factors of $x^2 - y^2 + 2yz - z^2$ is $(x + y - z)$, then the other factor is:

A. $x + y - z$ B. $x - y + z$
C. $x + y + z$ D. $x - y - z$

46. The smallest square number which is divisible by each of the numbers 8, 15 and 20 is:

A. 900 B. 1600
C. 2500 D. 3600

47. If $1^3 + 2^3 + 3^3 + 4^3 + 5^3 = 225$, then $2^3 + 4^3 + 6^3 + 8^3 + 10^3$ is equal to:

A. 450 B. 900
C. 1800 D. $(225)^2$

48. $\sqrt[3]{0.008} + \sqrt[3]{0.343} - \sqrt{0.25}$ is equal to:

A. 0.4 B. 0.5
C. 0.7 D. 0.8

49. $\sqrt{\frac{9}{16}} + (0.008)^{-\frac{2}{3}} - \left(\frac{7}{10}\right)^0$ is equal to:

A. $11\frac{2}{3}$ B. $24\frac{3}{4}$
C. $18\frac{1}{3}$ D. $15\frac{2}{3}$

50. The greatest 4-digit number which is a perfect square, is:

A. 9801 B. 9816
C. 9824 D. 9864

51. Which of the following is a Pythagorean triplet?

A. (2, 3, 5) B. (5, 7, 9)
C. (6, 9, 11) D. (8, 15, 17)

52. The area of a square field is 60025 sq. m. A boy cycles along its boundary at 18 km/h. In how much time will he return to the starting point?

A. 166 seconds B. 176 seconds
C. 196 seconds D. 208 seconds

53. The unit place digit in 9^{201} is:

A. 9 B. 7
C. 3 D. 1

54. Four prime numbers are in ascending order. The product of the first three numbers is 455 and the product of the last three numbers is 1729. The greatest prime number amongst these four numbers is:

A. 7 B. 13
C. 19 D. 23

55. The smallest number which when added to the greatest 4-digit number makes the sum divisible by 345 is:

A. 5 B. 6
C. 50 D. 60

56. How many bricks of size 22 cm × 10 cm × 7 cm are required to construct a wall 33 m long, 3.5 m high and 40 cm thick if sand used in the construction occupies $\frac{1}{10}$th part of the wall?

A. 24,000 B. 25,000
C. 26,000 D. 27,000

57. An 8-faced fair die with numbers 1 to 8 is rolled. What is the probability of getting an even number?

A. $\frac{1}{2}$ B. $\frac{1}{3}$
C. $\frac{1}{4}$ D. $\frac{1}{6}$

58. The ages (in years) of 50 members of the junior cricket club in a town are given below:

15, 17, 14, 13, 14, 13, 14, 17, 17, 16, 17, 16, 15, 16, 15, 14, 13, 14, 15, 13, 18, 13, 15, 14, 15, 13, 14, 13, 13, 17, 15, 14, 14, 17, 16, 17, 15, 14, 17, 16, 16, 16, 14, 16, 13, 18, 16, 15, 14, 14

What percentage of members are in the 15-16 age group?

A. 28% B. 30%
C. 32% D. 36%

59. The area of a rectangular plot is 150 sq. m and perimeter is 50 m. The ratio of its length to breadth is:

A. 3 : 2 B. 50 : 3
C. 6 : 1 D. 7 : 2

60. A swimming pool is 260 m long and 140 m wide. If 54,600 cu m of water is pumped into it, What is the height of the water level in it?

A. 1 m B. 1.5 m
C. 2 m D. 2.5 m

61. What number should $(23)^{-3}$ be multiplied with so that the product becomes $(69)^{-1}$?

A. $\frac{529}{4}$ B. $\frac{529}{7}$

C. $\frac{529}{3}$ D. $\frac{529}{6}$

62. $(6 + 3) \times 9^{-1} \div 3^{-1} + 2^{-2}$ is equal to:

A. $\frac{5}{4}$ B. $\frac{7}{4}$

C. $\frac{13}{4}$ D. $\frac{7}{8}$

63. A pipe can fill a cistern in 9 hours. Due to a leak in its bottom, the cistern fills up in 10 hours. If the cistern is full, in how much time will it be emptied by the leak?

A. 60 hours B. 70 hours
C. 80 hours D. 90 hours

64. If $2^{2x-1} = \frac{1}{8^{x-3}}$, then the value of x is:

A. –2 B. –1
C. 2 D. 3

65. If $5^{2p} + 5^{p} + 5^{0} = 651$, then the value of p is:

A. 2 B. 3
C. 4 D. 5

SECTION-IV : GENERAL SCIENCE

66. Consider the following statements about chemical reactions:

1. During reaction sound may be produced.
2. During reaction heat may be produced but never absorbed.
3. During reaction a gas is always evolved.
4. The products formed may have different colour or physical state than the reactants.

The correct statement(s) is/are:

A. Only 4 B. Only 1 and 4
C. 1, 2 and 4 D. 2, 3 and 4

67. Consider the following adaptive features of animals:

1. Thick white fur
2. Layer of fat under the skin
3. Slippery body
4. Long curved and sharp claws

Out of these the adaptive features of a polar bear are:

A. Only 1 and 2
B. Only 3 and 4
C. 1, 2 and 4
D. 1, 2 and 3

68. Select the correct statement with reference to soil.

A. Loamy soil contains sand and clay only.
B. In loamy soil the percolation of water is very fast.
C. Weathering is a very fast process of soil formation.
D. Top soil contains maximum amount of humus.

69. A student has put a drop of dilute solution of sodium hydroxide first on a strip of blue litmus paper and then on a strip of red litmus paper. His observations must be:

A. Blue litmus paper turns red and red litmus paper turns blue.
B. No change in blue litmus paper but the red litmus paper turns blue.
C. Blue litmus paper turns red and no change in the red litmus paper.
D. Blue litmus paper and red litmus paper both become colourless.

70. Consider the following components of a food chain:

Frog, Eagle, Insects, Grass, Snake

In the food chain, the correct order of these components is:

A. Grass → Insects → Snake → Frog → Eagle
B. Grass → Frog → Insects → Snake → Eagle
C. Grass → Insects → Frog → Eagle → Snake
D. Grass → Insects → Frog → Snake → Eagle

71. Select the correct statement from the following:

A. Cotton and Mustard both are Kharif crops.
B. Cotton and Mustard both are Rabi crops.
C. Cotton is a Kharif crop and Mustard is a Rabi crop.
D. Cotton is a Rabi crop and Mustard is a Kharif crop.

72. Consider the following agricultural practices/ processes:

1. Ploughing
2. Crop Rotation
3. Field Fallow
4. Adding Manure and Fertilizer

The practices/processes which add nutrition to the soil are:

A. Only 2 and 4 B. 1, 3 and 4
C. 1, 2 and 4 D. 2, 3 and 4

73. Select from the following a group that comprises one element, one compound and one mixture:

A. Gold, sulphuric acid, air
B. Silver, carbon dioxide, sodium chloride
C. Oxygen, soil, milk
D. Silver, methane, manganese dioxide

74. An optical device (mirror or lens) can form real diminished as well as real enlarged images of an object on a screen placed on the same side as the object. This optical device is:

A. convex lens only
B. concave mirror only
C. either convex lens or concave mirror
D. either convex mirror or convex lens

75. According to the recommendations of the United Nations the amount of water for drinking, washing, cooking and maintaining proper hygiene per person per day is a minimum of:

A. 100 litres B. 50 litres
C. 25 litres D. 20 litres

76. Two plane mirrors 'A' and 'B' are placed at right angles to each other as shown. A ray of light PO incident at point O on the mirror 'A' at an angle of 30° falls on the mirror 'B' after reflection from the mirror 'A'. The angle of reflection for the ray reflected from the mirror B would be:

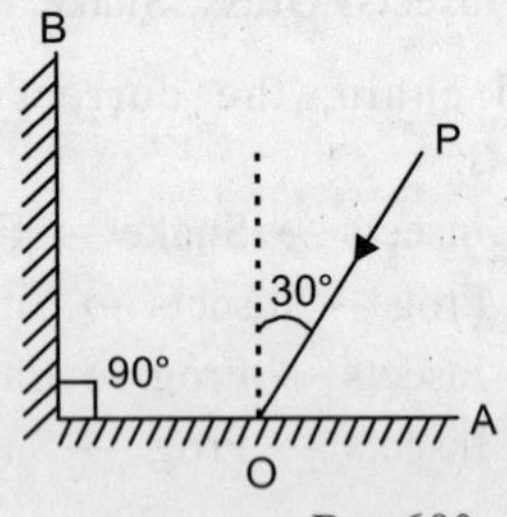

A. 30° B. 60°
C. 120° D. 150°

77. The correct sequence of three planets of the solar system in increasing order of their distance from the Sun is:

A. Venus, Mars, Saturn
B. Mercury, Venus, Mars
C. Mars, Mercury, Jupiter
D. Venus, Earth, Mars

78. A planet of our solar system which has no satellite of its own is:

A. Mars B. Neptune
C. Uranus D. Venus

79. Richter scale is used to measure the intensity of:

A. Lightning B. Earthquake
C. Tsunami D. Landslide

80. Four parallel rays of light are falling on surfaces S_1, S_2, S_3 and S_4 as shown in the figure. Surface(s) on which the angle of incidence is equal to angle of reflection is/are:

S_1 S_2
S_3 S_4

A. Only S_1 B. S_1, S_3 and S_4
C. S_3 and S_4 D. S_1, S_2, S_3 and S_4

81. The method used to obtain solid copper sulphate from copper sulphate solution is:

A. Condensation
B. Decantation
C. Evaporation
D. Sedimentation

82. The combination of features observed in grass is:

A. tap root and reticulate venation
B. fibrous root and parallel venation
C. tap root and parallel venation
D. fibrous root and reticulate venation

83. The mode of nutrition used by bread mould, mushroom and yeast is:

A. saprophytic B. parasitic
C. heterotrophic D. autotrophic

84. Human digestive system has more than ten organs. Select from the following combinations of three organs the one that does ***not*** carry out any of the digestive functions.

A. Buccal cavity, Oesophagus, Large intestine
B. Buccal cavity, Oesophagus, Rectum
C. Oesophagus, Large intestine, Rectum
D. Oesophagus, Pancreas, Small intestine

85. Consider the following edible plants:

1. Brinjal
2. Banana
3. Ladyfinger
4. Pumpkin

Out of these, a pair of plants having two or more edible parts is:

A. 1 and 2 B. 3 and 4
C. 2 and 4 D. 1 and 3

86. The fastest speed of falcon is 320 kilometers per hour. The correct method of expressing this speed using the correct unit symbols of distance and time is:
A. 320 kms/hr B. 320 KM/H
C. 320 KMS/HR D. 320 km/h

87. A bus moves with a speed of 36 kilometres per hour for 20 minutes and then with a speed of 54 kilometres per hour for the next 20 minutes. The total distance covered by the bus is:
A. 12 kilometres B. 18 kilometres
C. 30 kilometres D. 45 kilometres

88. Consider the electric circuit as shown. In this, AB is a thick copper wire. When the switch is ON current flows through the wire AB and the bulb starts glowing. We observe that the wire AB:

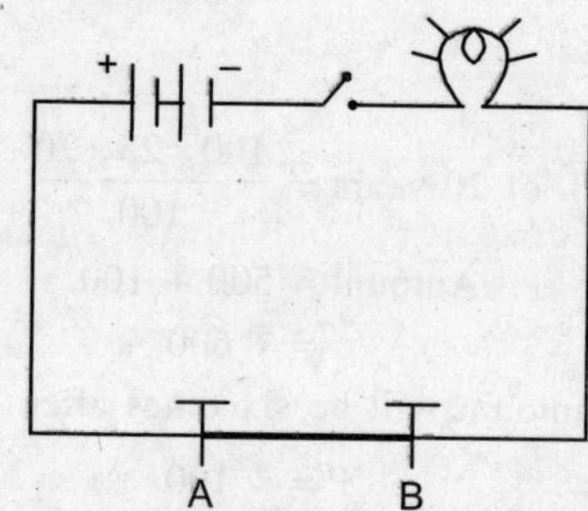

A. becomes red hot.
B. behaves like an electric fuse and melts immediately.
C. gives a severe shock on touching.
D. deflects a compass needle placed near it.

89. Sometimes the athletes suffer from muscle cramps. It is due to anaerobic respiration in which glucose is converted to:
A. lactic acid only
B. lactic acid and carbon dioxide
C. alcohol and carbon dioxide
D. alcohol and lactic acid

90. In human bodies the exchange of gases between blood and tissue and the absorption of nutrients takes place in the:
A. heart B. capillaries
C. arteries D. veins

91. Bryophyllum can reproduce by its:
A. Leaves B. Flowers
C. Roots D. Stem

92. Besides sunlight plants also need the following for photosynthesis:
A. Carbon monoxide, Water, Chlorophyll
B. Oxygen, Water, Chlorophyll
C. Nitrogen, Chlorophyll, Carbon dioxide
D. Chlorophyll, Water, Carbon dioxide

93. Silkworms secrete fibre made of:
A. protein
B. carbohydrates
C. cellulose only
D. starch + cellulose

94. A copper plate would feel cold as compared to a wooden table on a winter morning. It is due to the reason that the copper plate:
A. reflects more heat than the wooden table.
B. is made from metal whose density is more than that of wood.
C. is a better conductor of heat as compared to the wooden table.
D. is a poor conductor of heat as compared to the wooden table.

95. Consider the following statements:
1. Excretion takes place in plants.
2. Excretion takes place in both plants and animals.
3. Excretion is a process of getting rid of excess water only.
4. Secretion is one of the methods of excretion.

The correct statements are:
A. Only 1 and 2 B. Only 3 and 4
C. 1, 2 and 4 D. 1, 2 and 3

96. Transpiration is a process in which plants:
A. absorb water vapours from the atmospheric air.
B. release water vapours in the atmosphere.
C. receive water from the soil through roots.
D. receive water from the atmosphere for photosynthesis.

97. Select a pair of contact forces from the following:
A. Muscular force and Magnetic force
B. Muscular force and Frictional force
C. Frictional force and Electrostatic force
D. Gravitational force and Magnetic force

98. A water tank has four taps A, B, C and D as shown. If the tank is fully filled with water and the taps are opened simultaneously, the water will flow with the same pressure from the taps:

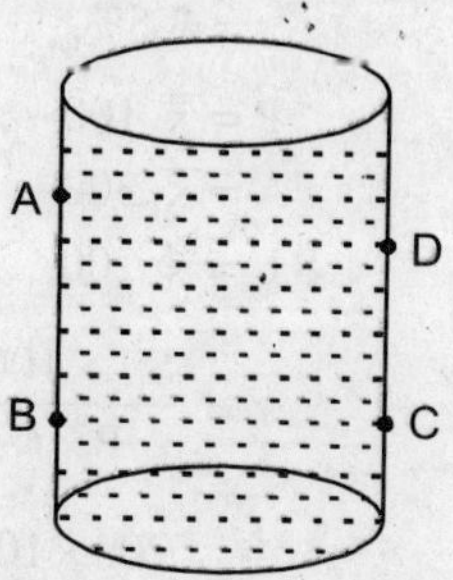

A. A and B B. C and D
C. B and C D. A and D

99. Consider the experimental set-up shown:

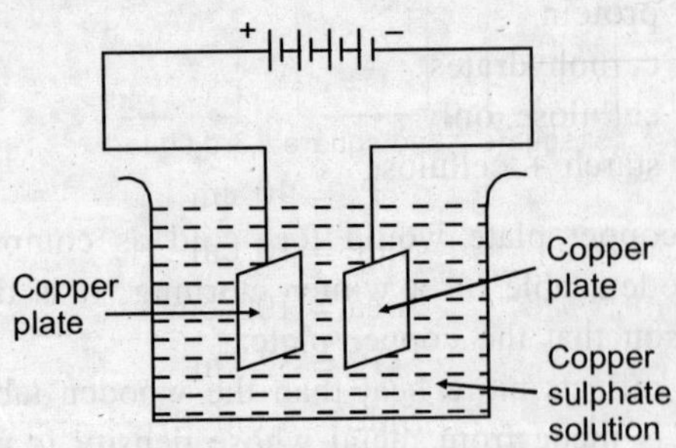

After passing current for about 15 minutes it is observed that:

A. the blue colour of the solution fades away.

B. both the electrodes gain copper from the solution.

C. copper gets transferred from the negatively charged electrode to the positively charged electrode.

D. copper gets transferred from the positively charged electrode to the negatively charged electrode.

100. Select from the following a gas where increased concentration in the environment may cause global warming:

A. Sulphur dioxide

B. Nitrogen dioxide

C. Carbon dioxide

D. Carbon monoxide

ANSWERS

1. (D)	**2. (D)**	**3. (B)**
4. (C)	**5. (D)**	**6. (B)**
7. (C)	**8. (A)**	**9. (C)**
10. (B)	**11. (B)**	**12. (B)**
13. (C)	**14. (D)**	**15. (C)**
16. (B)	**17. (C)**	**18. (C)**
19. (B)	**20. (A)**	**21. (A)**
22. (D)	**23. (C)**	**24. (B)**
25. (C)	**26. (B)**	**27. (B)**
28. (C)	**29. (B)**	**30. (A)**

31. (D): The effect on the total earning of a shopkeeper

$= 90 \times 115 - 100 \times 100$

$= 10350 - 10000$

$= ₹\ 350$

Hence, increased % $= \dfrac{350 \times 100}{100 \times 100}$

$= \dfrac{35}{10}\%$

$= 3.5\%.$

32. (C): Let, P = ₹ 100

A = ₹ 300

S.I. = ₹ 200

$$r = \frac{\text{S.I.} \times 100}{\text{P} \times t}$$

$$= \frac{200 \times 100}{100 \times 8}$$

$= 25\%$

S.I. of 20 years $= \dfrac{100 \times 25 \times 20}{100} = 500$

Amount $= 500 + 100$

$= ₹\ 600$

Hence, amount will be six times after 20 years.

33. (C): Let P = ₹ 100

$$A = 100\left(1 + \frac{5}{100}\right)^3$$

$$= 100 \times \frac{21}{20} \times \frac{21}{20} \times \frac{21}{20}$$

$= 115.7625$

$\therefore$ C.I. $= 115.7625 - 100$

$= ₹\ 15.7625$

When C.I. ₹ 15.7625 then P = ₹ 100

When C.I. ₹ 1261 then P

$$= ₹\ \frac{100}{15.7625} \times 1261$$

$= ₹\ 8000$

Hence, sum of money invested = ₹ 8000.

34. (C): A's 1 day work $= \dfrac{1}{25}$

B's 1 day work $= \dfrac{1}{20}$

(A + B)'s 1 day work $= \dfrac{1}{25} + \dfrac{1}{20}$

$$= \frac{4+5}{100} = \frac{9}{100}$$

$$(A + B)\text{'s 5 days work} = 5 \times \frac{9}{100} = \frac{9}{20}$$

$$\text{Remaining work} = 1 - \frac{9}{20} = \frac{11}{20}$$

$\frac{1}{20}$ part B can do in 1 day

$\frac{11}{20}$ part B can do in

$$\frac{1}{\frac{1}{20}} \times \frac{11}{20} = 20 \times \frac{11}{20}$$

$$= 11 \text{ days.}$$

35. (A): $\because$ 7 women = 5 men

$$5 \text{ women} = \frac{5}{7} \times 5 = \frac{25}{7} \text{ men}$$

$$10 \text{ men} + 5 \text{ women} = 10 + \frac{25}{7} = \frac{95}{7} \text{ men}$$

$\because$ 5 men can earn ₹ 1372 per day

$\therefore$ $\frac{95}{7}$ men can earn ₹ $\frac{1372}{5} \times \frac{95}{7}$ per day

= ₹ 196 × 19

= ₹ 3724 per day.

36. (D): Perimeter of square ABCD = $16\sqrt{2}$ cm

Side of ABCD = $4\sqrt{2}$ cm

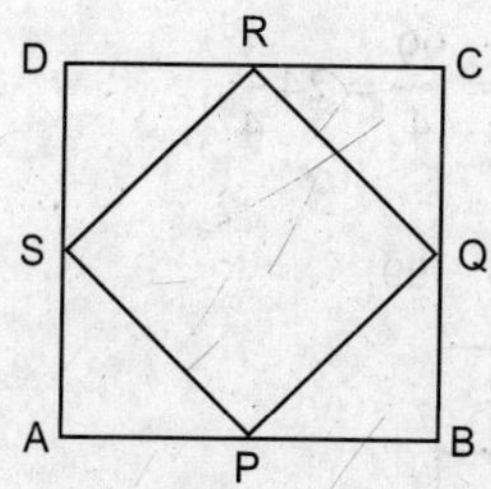

P, Q, R, S are the mid-point of AB, BC, CD and DA

$\therefore$ AP = BP

$\therefore$ Side of BP = $2\sqrt{2}$ cm

$$PQ^2 = \left(2\sqrt{2}\right)^2 + \left(2\sqrt{2}\right)^2$$

$$= 8 + 8$$

$$= 16$$

$\therefore$ PQ = 4 cm

$\therefore$ Side of PQRS = 4 cm

Perimeter of PQRS = 4 × 4

= 16 cm.

37. (A):

1st square 2nd square 3rd square

P_1 = 40 cm

Side = 10 cm

Area = 100 cm^2

P_2 = 32 cm

Side = 8 cm

Area = 64 cm^2

Area of 3rd square = 100 − 64

= 36 cm^2

Side of 3rd square = 6 cm

Hence, perimeter of 3rd square = 6 × 4 = 24 cm.

38. (C): Let number of prizes of ₹ 100 = x

$\therefore$ Number of prizes of ₹ 500 = 200 − x

According to the question,

$$100 \times x + 500(200 - x) = 50000$$

$$\Rightarrow 100x + 100000 - 500x = 50000$$

$$\Rightarrow 400x = 50000$$

$$\Rightarrow x = 125$$

Hence, number of prizes of ₹ 100 = 125.

39. (D):

D 25 C; $y + 28$; $2y + 3$; A $3x + 1$ B

$\because$ ABCD is a parallelogram

$\therefore$ $3x + 1 = 25$

$\Rightarrow$ $3x = 24$

$\Rightarrow$ $x = 8$

And $2y + 3 = y + 28$

$\Rightarrow$ $y = 25$

Hence, $x + y = 8 + 25 = 33$.

40. (D): Let angles are in the x ratios

$\because$ $2x + 3x + 5x + 8x = 360°$

$\Rightarrow$ $18x = 360°$

$\Rightarrow$ $x = 20°$

$2x = 2 \times 20 = 40°$

$3x = 3 \times 20 = 60°$

$5x = 5 \times 20 = 100°$

$8x = 8 \times 20 = 160°$

Greatest angle − Smallest angle = 160 − 40 = 120°.

41. (D): $\because$ $a^2 + b^2 + c^2 = 2(a - b - c) - 3$

$\Rightarrow (a^2 - 2a + 1) + (b^2 + 2b + 1) + (c^2 + 2c + 1) = 0$

$\Rightarrow (a - 1)^2 + (b + 1)^2 + (c + 1)^2 = 0$

$\therefore \quad a - 1 = 0$

$b + 1 = 0$

$c + 1 = 0$

$\Rightarrow \quad a = 1,$

$b = -1,$

$c = -1$

$\therefore \quad 2a - 3b + 4c = 2(1) - 3(-1) + 4(-1) = 1.$

42. (A): Let Raju's age = $5x$ years
and Raman's age = $8x$ years
According to the question,

$5x + 5 = 8x - 4$

$\Rightarrow \quad 3x = 9$

$\Rightarrow \quad x = 3$

Hence, Raju's age = 5×3
= 15 years.

43. (A): Let ten's place digit number = x
and one's place digit number = y

$\therefore \quad \text{Number} = 10x + y$

$y - x = 3 \quad \text{....}(i)$

$10y + x + 10x + y = 143$

$\Rightarrow \quad 11x + 11y = 143$

$\Rightarrow \quad x + y = 13 \quad \text{...}(ii)$

From (*i*) and (*ii*)

$x + y = 13$

$y - x = 3$

$2y = 16$

$\Rightarrow \quad y = 8$

$\therefore \quad x = 5$

$\therefore \quad \text{Number} = 58.$

44. (A): $\because \quad \left(x - \frac{1}{x}\right)^2 = 36$

$\Rightarrow \quad x^2 + \frac{1}{x^2} = 36 + 2 = 38$

Value of $x^4 + \frac{1}{x^4} = \left(x^2\right)^2 + \left(\frac{1}{x^2}\right)^2$

$= \left(x^2 + \frac{1}{x^2}\right)^2 - 2.x^2 \times \frac{1}{x^2}$

$= (38)^2 - 2$

$= 1444 - 2 = 1442.$

45. (B): $x^2 - y^2 + 2yz - z^2$

$= (x)^2 - (y^2 - 2yz + z^2)$

$= (x)^2 - (y - z)^2$

$= (x + y - z)\ (x - y + z)$

Hence, the other factor = $(x - y + z)$.

46. (D): L.C.M. of 8, 15 and 20

2	8,	15,	20
2	4,	15,	10
5	2,	15,	5
	2,	3,	1

L.C.M. = $2 \times 2 \times 5 \times 2 \times 3 = 120$

$\therefore$ Smallest square number = 3600
which is divisible by each of number 8, 15 and 20.

47. (C): $1^3 + 2^3 + 3^3 + 4^3 + 5^3 = 225$

$\therefore \quad 2^3 + 4^3 + 6^3 + 8^3 + 10^3$

$= 2^3\ (1^3 + 2^3 + 3^3 + 4^3 + 5^3)$

$= 8 \times 225$

$= 1800$

Hence, the value of $2^3 + 4^3 + 6^3 + 8^3 + 10^3$
= 1800.

48. (A): $\sqrt[3]{0.008} + \sqrt[3]{0.343} - \sqrt{0.25}$

$= \frac{2}{10} + \frac{7}{10} - \frac{5}{10}$

$= \frac{4}{10} = 0.4.$

49. (B): $\sqrt{\frac{9}{16}} + \left(\frac{2}{10}\right)^{3 \times \frac{-2}{3}} - 1 \qquad [\because x^0 = 1]$

$= \frac{3}{4} + \frac{100}{4} - 1$

$= \frac{3 + 100 - 4}{4} = \frac{99}{4} = 24\frac{3}{4}.$

50. (A):

9	9801	99
9	81	
189	1701	
9	1701	
198	×	

Hence, 9801 is a perfect square of the greatest 4-digit number.

51. (D): (2, 3, 5)

$2^2 + 3^2 \neq 5^2$

$4 + 9 \neq 25$

(5, 7, 9)

$5^2 + 7^2 \neq 9^2$

$25 + 49 \neq 81$

(6, 9, 11)

$6^2 + 9^2 \neq 11^2$

$36 + 81 \neq 121$

(8, 15, 17)

$$8^2 + 15^2 = 17^2$$
$$64 + 225 = 289$$
$$289 = 289$$

Hence, (8, 15, 17) is a Pythagorean triplet.

52. (C): Area of a square field = 60025 m^2

$\therefore$ Side of square = $\sqrt{60025}$

$= 245$ m

Perimeter of square = 4 × 245 = 980 m

Speed = 18 km/hr

$$= 18 \times \frac{5}{18} \text{ m/s} = 5 \text{ m/s}$$

$$\text{Required time} = \frac{980}{5} = 196 \text{ seconds.}$$

53. (A): Unit place of $(9)^1 = 9$

$(9)^2 = 1$

$(9)^3 = 9$

$(9)^4 = 1$

$(9)^5 = 9$

$(9)^6 = 1$

$\therefore$ Unit place of $(9)^{201} = 9$.

54. (C): Let four prime numbers are x_1, x_2, x_3, x_4

$$x_1 \times x_2 \times x_3 = 455$$

and $x_2 \times x_3 \times x_4 = 1729$

$$\frac{x_2 \times x_3 \times x_4}{x_1 \times x_2 \times x_3} = \frac{1729}{455}$$

$$\Rightarrow \quad \frac{x_4}{x_1} = \frac{247}{65} = \frac{19}{5}$$

$\therefore$ $x_4 = 19$

and $x_1 = 5$

$$x_2 \times x_3 = \frac{455}{5} = 91$$

$\therefore$ Numbers are 5, 7, 13 and 19

Hence, the greatest prime number = 19.

55. (B): The greatest 4-digit number = 9999

$$9999 + 6 = 10005$$
$$10005 \div 345 = 29$$

Hence, the required number = 6.

56. (D): Volume of the wall

$$= 33 \times \frac{35}{10} \times \frac{40}{100}$$
$$= 46.2 \text{ m}^3$$

Volume occupied by the sand

$$= \frac{1}{10} \times 46.2$$
$$= 4.62 \text{ m}^3$$

Volume occupied by the brick

$$= 46.2 - 4.62$$
$$= 41.58 \text{ m}^3$$

$$\text{Volume of each brick} = \frac{22}{100} \times \frac{10}{100} \times \frac{7}{100} \text{ m}^3$$

$$= \frac{154}{100000} \text{ m}^3$$

Required number of bricks

$$= 41.58 \times \frac{100000}{154}$$

$$= \frac{4158000}{154} = 27000.$$

57. (A): Required probability = $\frac{4}{8} = \frac{1}{2}$.

58. (D): Total members of 15-16 age group

$= 9 + 9 = 18$

$$\text{Required \%} = \frac{18}{50} \times 100 = 36\%.$$

59. (A):

$$l \times b = 150 \text{ m}^2$$
$$l + b = 25 \text{ m} \qquad ...(i)$$
$$(l - b)^2 = (l + b)^2 - 4lb$$
$$= (25)^2 - 4 \times 15$$
$$= 625 - 600 = 25$$
$$\Rightarrow \quad l - b = 5 \text{ m} \qquad ...(ii)$$

Solving (*i*) and (*ii*), then we get

$$l + b = 25$$
$$l - b = 5$$
$$2l = 30$$
$$l = 15 \text{ m},$$
$$b = 10 \text{ m}$$

$$\text{Required ratio} = \frac{15}{10} = 3 : 2.$$

60. (B):

$$h = \frac{54600}{260 \times 140}$$

$$= \frac{3}{2} \text{ m} = 1.5 \text{ m}$$

Hence, height of the water level = 1.5 m.

61. (C): $\frac{1}{69} \div \frac{1}{23^3} = \frac{1}{69} \times 23 \times 23 \times 23$

$= \frac{529}{3}.$

62. (C): $9 \times \frac{1}{9} \div \frac{1}{3} + \frac{1}{4} = 9 \times \frac{1}{9} \times \frac{3}{1} + \frac{1}{4}$

$= 3 + \frac{1}{4} = \frac{13}{4}.$

63. (D): The net part emptied in 1 hour

$= \frac{1}{9} - \frac{1}{10}$

$= \frac{10-9}{90}$

$= \frac{1}{90}$

Hence, time taken to emptied the cistern in 90 hours.

64. (C): $2^{2x-1} = \frac{1}{\left(2^3\right)^{(x-3)}}$

$= \frac{1}{2^{3x-9}}$

$\Rightarrow \quad 2^{2x-1} = 2^{-(3x-9)}$

$\Rightarrow \quad 2x - 1 = -3x + 9$

$\Rightarrow \quad x = 2.$

65. (A): $5^{2P} + 5^P = 650$

Let $5^P = x$

$x^2 + x - 650 = 0$

$\Rightarrow \quad x = 25$

$5^P = 5^2$

$\Rightarrow \quad P = 2$

Hence, the value of P = 2.

66. (D)	**67. (C)**	**68. (A)**
69. (B)	**70. (D)**	**71. (C)**
72. (C)	**73. (A)**	**74. (B)**
75. (B)	**76. (B)**	**77. (B)**
78. (D)	**79. (B)**	**80. (D)**
81. (B)	**82. (B)**	**83. (A)**
84. (C)	**85. (C)**	**86. (D)**
87. (C)	**88. (D)**	**89. (A)**
90. (B)	**91. (A)**	**92. (D)**
93. (A)	**94. (C)**	**95. (C)**
96. (B)	**97. (B)**	**98. (C)**
99. (D)	**100. (C)**	

MATHS

Rational Numbers

Rational Numbers

A rational number is defined as a rational number of the form $\frac{p}{q}$, where p and q are integers and $q \neq 0$.

The set of rational numbers encloses the set of integers and fractions. The rules given above for addition, subtraction, multiplication and division also apply on rational numbers.

Rational numbers that are not integral will have decimal values. These values can be of two types:

(a) Terminating (or Finite) Decimal Fractions:

For example : $\frac{17}{4} = 4.25$, $\frac{21}{5} = 4.2$ and so forth

(b) Non-terminating Decimal Fractions: Amongst non-terminating decimal fractions there are two types of decimal values:

(i) **Non-terminating Periodic Fractions:** These are non-terminating decimal fractions of the type $x.a_1a_2a_3...a_n\ a_1a_2a_3...a_n\ a_1a_2a_3...a_n$ written as $x.\overline{a_1\,a_2\,a_3...a_n}$

For example : $\frac{1}{3} = 0.3333\ ...\ = 0.\overline{3}$

$\frac{16}{3} = 5.333\ ....\ = 5.\overline{3}$ and so on.

(c) Non-terminating Non-periodic Fractions: These are the form $x.\ b_1b_2b_3...b_n\ \ c_1c_2c_3...\ c_n$

For example : 5.2731687143...

Pure Recurring Decimal : A decimal in which all the digits after the decimal point are repeated. For Example : $0.\overline{6}$, $0.\overline{16}$, ...$0.\overline{123}$.

Mixed Recurring Decimal : A decimal in which at least one of the digits after the decimal points is not repeated and then same digit and digits are repeated.

For example : $2.1\overline{6}$, $0.3\overline{5}$, $0.7\overline{85}$

Conversion of Pure Recurring of the form $\frac{p}{q}$:

Example 1: (i) $0.\overline{3}$, (ii) $0.\overline{35}$, (iii) $0.\overline{585}$

(i) Let $x = 0.\overline{3}$ Then,

$x = 0.3333...$ ...(i)

$10x = 3.3333...$ ...(ii)

On subtracting (i) from (ii), we get

$9x = 3$

$x = \frac{3}{9} = \frac{1}{3}$

$\Rightarrow 0.\overline{3} = \frac{1}{3}$ i.e., $0.333... = \frac{1}{3}$

(ii) Let $x = 0.\overline{35}$ Then,

$x = 0.353535...$ ...(i)

$100x = 35.3535...$ ...(ii)

On subtracting (i) from (ii), we get

$99x = 35$

$x = \frac{35}{99}$

$\therefore 0.\overline{35} = \frac{35}{99}$

(iii) Let $x = 0.\overline{585}$, Then

$x = 0.585\ 585\ 585$ ...(i)

$1000x = 585.585\ 585...$ ...(ii)

On subtracting (i) from (ii)

$999x = 585$

$x = \frac{585}{999}$

$\therefore 0.\overline{585} = \frac{585}{999}$

Shortcut : Write down the bar digit in numerator of a fraction and write down the same number of digit 9 in denominator of the fraction. For example:

$0.\overline{3} = \frac{3}{9}$, $0.\overline{35} = \frac{35}{99}$, $0.\overline{585} = \frac{585}{999}$,

$2.\overline{3} = 2 + 0.\overline{3} = 2 + \frac{3}{9} = 2 + \frac{1}{3} = 2\frac{1}{3} = \frac{7}{3}$

$15.\overline{32} = 15 + 0.\overline{32} = 15 + \frac{32}{99} = 15\frac{32}{99}$

Conversion of Mixed Recurring Fraction into $\frac{p}{q}$ form :

$0.235\ 35\ 35\ ...\ = 0.2\overline{35}$

Let $x = 0.2\overline{35}$

Then, $10x = 2.\overline{35}$

$10x = 2 + 0.\overline{35}$

$10x = 2 + \frac{35}{99}$

$10x = \frac{2 \times 99 + 35}{99} = \frac{198 + 35}{99}$

$10x = \frac{233}{99} \Rightarrow x = \frac{233}{990}$

(*ii*) $15.7\overline{12}$

Let $x = 15.7\overline{12}$

Then, $10x = 157.\overline{12}$

$10x = 157 + 0.\overline{12}$

$10x = 157 + \frac{12}{99}$

$10x = 157 + \frac{4}{33}$

$10x = \frac{157 \times 33 + 4}{33}$

$10x = \frac{5185}{33}$

$x = \frac{5185}{330}$

Irrational Numbers: A number is an irrational number, if it has a non-terminating and non-repeating decimal representation *i.e.*, irrational number can not be written in the form of $\frac{p}{q}$, where p and q are both integers and $q \neq 0$.

For example : $\sqrt{2}, \sqrt{3}$.

If a and b are two positive rational numbers such that ab is not a perfect square of a rational number then, $\sqrt{ab}$ is an irrational number lying between a and b. Also if a, b are rational numbers, then $\frac{a+b}{2}$ is a rational number between them.

Example 1 : Insert a rational and an irrational number between 2 and 3.

Sol. A rational Number between 2 and 3

$= \frac{2+3}{2} = 2.5$

An irrational Number between 2 and 3

$= \sqrt{2 \times 3} = \sqrt{6}$

Some useful results on Rational/Irrational Number

(*i*) $\sqrt{n}$ is rational number if n is a perfect square. For example, $\sqrt{4}, \sqrt{9}, \sqrt{16}$

(*ii*) Negative of an irrational number is an irrational number.

(*iii*) The sum of a rational number and an irrational number is an irrational number.

(*iv*) The product of a non-zero rational number and an irrational number is an irrational number.

(*v*) The sum, difference, product and quotient of two irrational number need not be an irrational number.

(*vi*) π is an irrational number.

(*vii*) Decimal expansion of a rational number is either terminating or non-terminating (recurring).

(*viii*) Decimal expansion of an irrational number is non-terminating non-recurring.

(*ix*) A real number is either rational or irrational number.

Comparison of Fraction

1. If the denominator of the fractions are same, the largest is one whose numerator is the largest.

Example : Which is the largest fraction among $\frac{3}{8}, \frac{7}{8}$ and $\frac{5}{8}$?

Solution: $\frac{7}{8}$

2. If the numerators of the fractions are same, the largest is one whose denominator is the smallest.

Example : Which is the largest fraction among $\frac{5}{2}, \frac{5}{7}$ and $\frac{5}{9}$?

Solution : $\frac{5}{2}$

3. If neither the numerators nor denominators of the fraction are same then they are converted into equivalent fractions of the same, denominator by taking the L.C.M. of the denominators of the given fractions. Then the fractions are compared according to (1).

Example : Which is the largest fraction among $\frac{1}{2}, \frac{2}{3}, \frac{4}{5}$ and $\frac{5}{8}$.

Solution : LCM of 2, 3, 5 and 8 = 120

Then, $\frac{1}{2} = \frac{1 \times 60}{2 \times 60} = \frac{60}{120}$

$\frac{2}{3} = \frac{2 \times 40}{3 \times 40} = \frac{80}{120}$

$$\frac{4}{5} = \frac{4 \times 24}{5 \times 24} = \frac{96}{120}$$

$$\frac{5}{8} = \frac{5 \times 15}{8 \times 15} = \frac{75}{120}$$

Largest fraction = $\frac{96}{120}$, that is $\frac{4}{5}$

4. Two fractions can also be compared by cross multiplication method.

Example : Which is greater $\frac{6}{13}$ or $\frac{5}{7}$?

Solution: Step 1 : Cross multiplying the two given fractions

$$\frac{6}{13} \times \frac{5}{7}$$

We get 6 × 7 = 42 and 13 × 5 = 65

Step 2 : Since 65 is greater than 42 and in 65, the numerator of $\frac{5}{7}$ is included.

$\therefore$ $\frac{5}{7}$ is greater than $\frac{6}{13}$.

5. If the difference of the numerator and denominator of each of the given fractions be same, then the fraction of the largest numerator is the largest.

Example : Which one of the following fractions is the largest $\frac{2}{3}, \frac{3}{4}, \frac{5}{6}$ and $\frac{9}{10}$?

Solution : Since in each of the given fractions the difference between the numerator and denominator is same and the largest numerator is 9. Therefore, the largest fraction is $\frac{9}{10}$.

Multiple Choice Questions

1. The decimal form of an irrational number is neither .... nor ....

A. terminating, repeating
B. terminating, non-repeating
C. non-terminating, non-repeating
D. non-terminating, repeating

2. π is a/an :

A. rational number
B. irrational number
C. neither rational nor irrational number
D. None of these

3. The decimal representation of a rational number is either .... or ....

A. terminating, recurring
B. non-terminating, non-recurring
C. terminating, non-terminating, recurring
D. None of these

4. Which one of the following statements is true?

A. The sum of two irrational numbers is always an irrational number.
B. The sum of two irrational numbers is always a rational number.
C. The sum of two irrational numbers may be a rational number or an irrational number.
D. The sum of two irrational numbers is always an integer.

5. Which of the following is a correct statement?

A. Sum of two irrational numbers is always irrational.
B. Sum of a rational and irrational number is always an irrational number.
C. Square of an irrational number is always a rational number.
D. Sum of two rational numbers can never be an integer.

6. Which of the following statements is true?

A. Product of two irrational numbers is always irrational.
B. Product of a rational and an irrational number is always irrational.
C. Sum of two irrational numbers can never be irrational.
D. Sum of an integer and a rational number can never be an integer.

7. Which of the following is irrational?

A. $\sqrt{\frac{4}{9}}$ B. $\frac{4}{5}$
C. $\sqrt{7}$ D. $\sqrt{81}$

8. Which of the following is irrational?

A. 0.14
B. $0.14\overline{16}$
C. $0.\overline{1416}$
D. 0.1014001400014

9. Which of the following is rational?

A. $\sqrt{3}$ B. π
C. $\frac{4}{0}$ D. $\frac{0}{4}$

10. The number 0.318564318564318564.... is:
A. a natural number
B. an integer
C. a rational number
D. an irrational number

11. If n is a natural number, then $\sqrt{n}$ is:
A. always a natural number
B. always an irrational number
C. always an irrational number
D. sometimes a natural number and sometimes an irrational number

12. Which of the following numbers can be represented as non-terminating, repeating decimals?
A. $\frac{39}{24}$ B. $\frac{3}{16}$
C. $\frac{3}{11}$ D. $\frac{137}{25}$

13. Every point on a number line represents:
A. a unique real number
B. a natural number
C. a rational number
D. an irrational number

14. An irrational number between 2 and 2.5 is:
A. $\sqrt{11}$ B. $\sqrt{5}$
C. $\sqrt{22.5}$ D. $\sqrt{12.5}$

15. Which of the following is irrational?
A. 0.15 B. 0.01516
C. $0.\overline{1516}$ D. 0.5015001500015

16. The number of consecutive zeros in $2^3 \times 3^4 \times 7$, is:
A. 3 B. 2
C. 4 D. 5

17. The number $1.\overline{27}$ in the form $\frac{p}{q}$, where p and q are integers and $q \neq 0$, is:
A. $\frac{14}{9}$ B. $\frac{14}{11}$
C. $\frac{14}{13}$ D. $\frac{14}{15}$

18. The number $0.\overline{3}$ in the form $\frac{p}{q}$, where p and q are integers and $q \neq 0$, is:
A. $\frac{33}{100}$ B. $\frac{3}{10}$
C. $\frac{1}{3}$ D. $\frac{3}{100}$

19. The smallest rational number by which $\frac{1}{3}$ should be multiplied so that its decimal expansion terminates after one place of decimal, is:
A. $\frac{1}{10}$ B. $\frac{3}{10}$
C. 3 D. 30

20. $0.3\overline{2}$ when expressed in the form $\frac{p}{q}$ (p, q are integers, $q \neq 0$), is:
A. $\frac{8}{25}$ B. $\frac{29}{90}$
C. $\frac{32}{99}$ D. $\frac{32}{199}$

21. $23.\overline{43}$ when expressed in the form $\frac{p}{q}$ (p, q are integers, $q \neq 0$), is:
A. $\frac{2320}{99}$ B. $\frac{2343}{100}$
C. $\frac{2343}{999}$ D. $\frac{2320}{199}$

22. $0.\overline{001}$ when expressed in the form $\frac{p}{q}$ (p, q are integers, $q \neq 0$), is:
A. $\frac{1}{1000}$ B. $\frac{1}{100}$
C. $\frac{1}{1999}$ D. $\frac{1}{999}$

23. The value of $0.\overline{23}+0.\overline{22}$ is:
A. $0.\overline{45}$ B. $0.\overline{43}$
C. $0.\overline{42}$ D. 45

24. $5.\overline{23}+6.\overline{33}-3.\overline{11} = ?$
A. $8.\overline{55}$ B. $7.\overline{45}$
C. $8.\overline{45}$ D. $9.\overline{25}$

25. If $\sqrt{12} = 3.464$, value of $\sqrt{\frac{3}{4}}+2\sqrt{\frac{4}{3}}$ is:
A. 3.17
B. 3.464
C. 3.1753
D. None of these

ANSWERS

1	2	3	4	5	6	7	8	9	10
A	B	C	C	B	B	C	D	D	C
11	**12**	**13**	**14**	**15**	**16**	**17**	**18**	**19**	**20**
D	C	A	B	D	A	B	C	B	B
21	**22**	**23**	**24**	**25**					
A	D	A	C	C					

EXPLANATORY ANSWERS

7. $\sqrt{\frac{4}{9}} = \frac{2}{3},\ \frac{p}{q}$ form $q \neq 0$ rational number

$\frac{4}{5}, \frac{p}{q}$ form, $q \neq 0$ rational number

$\sqrt{7}, \sqrt{7}$ is not an integer $\therefore$ Irrational number

$\sqrt{81} = \frac{9}{1},\ \frac{p}{q}$ form, $q \neq 0$, rational number

10. 0.318564318564318 ....

$0.\overline{31854}$ (Recurring form)

$\therefore$ This is a rational number

14. An irrational number between 2 and 2.5 is $= \sqrt{2 \times 2.5} = \sqrt{5}$

16. We get zero if $2 \times 5 = 10$

$\therefore \quad 2^3 \times 5^3 = 1000$

we get three zero.

17. $1.\overline{27} = 1 + 0.\overline{27} = 1 + \frac{27}{99} = 1 + \frac{3}{11} = \frac{14}{11}$

18. $0.\overline{3} = \frac{3}{9} = \frac{1}{3}$

20. $\dot{0}.3\overline{2} = \frac{32-3}{90} = \frac{29}{90}$

21. $23.\overline{43} = 23 + 0.\overline{43} = 23 + \frac{43}{99}$

$= \frac{23 \times 99 + 43}{99} = \frac{2277 + 43}{99} = \frac{2320}{99}$

23. $0.\overline{23} + 0.22 = \frac{23}{99} + \frac{22}{99}$

$= \frac{23 + 22}{99} = \frac{45}{99} = 0.\overline{45}$

24. $5 + 0.\overline{23} + 6 + 0.\overline{33} - 3 - 0.\overline{11}$

$= 8 + 0.\overline{56} - 0.\overline{11} = 8 + 0.\overline{45} = 8.\overline{45}$

25. $\sqrt{\frac{3}{4}} + 2\sqrt{\frac{4}{3}} = \sqrt{\frac{9}{12}} + 2 \times \sqrt{\frac{12}{9}}$

$= \frac{3}{\sqrt{12}} + 2 \times \frac{\sqrt{12}}{3} = \frac{3}{3.464} + 2 \times \frac{3.464}{3}$

$= 0.8660 + 2.3093$

$= 3.1753$

□□□□□

2

Square and Square Root

☛ Points To Remember

- A number n is a perfect square number, if $n = m^2$
- A perfect square number is never negative.
- A square number never ends in 2, 3, 7 or 8.
- The number of zeros at the end of a perfect square is even.
- The square of an even number is even.
- The square of an odd number is odd.
- There are no natural number p and q such that $p^2 = 2q^2$.
- A number m is a square root of n, if $n = m \times m = m^2$. Positive square root of n is written as $\sqrt{n}$.
- If p and q are perfect squares ($q \neq 0$), then

  (*i*) $\sqrt{p \times q} = \sqrt{p} \times \sqrt{q}$

  (*ii*) $\sqrt{\dfrac{p}{q}} = \dfrac{\sqrt{p}}{\sqrt{q}}$
- A perfect squares leaves remainder 0 or 1 on division by 3.

  The following table gives the possible remainders for some other prime divisors.

Divisor	Possible Remainders
3	0, 1
5	0, 1, 4
7	0, 1, 2, 4
11	0, 1, 3, 4, 5, 9
13	0, 1, 3, 4, 9, 10, 12

- The unit's digit of the square of a natural number is the unit's digit of the square of the digit at unit's place of the given natural number.

Unit's digit of the number	Unit's digit of the square of the number
0	0
1 or 9	1
2 or 8	4
3 or 7	9
4 or 6	6
5	5

- For every natural number n,

  $(n + 1)^2 - n^2 = (n + 1) + n$

  e.g.; $9^2 - 8^2 = 9 + 8 = 17$

  $19^2 - 18^2 = 19 + 18 = 37$
- The square of a natural number n is equal to the sum of first n odd natural numbers.

  e.g.; $2^2 = 1 + 3$

  $4^2 = 1 + 3 + 5 + 7 = 16$

  n^2 = Sum of first n odd natural numbers.
- A triplet (m, n, p) of three natural numbers m, n and p is called a pythagorean triplet if $m^2 + n^2 = p^2$
- The square root of a perfect square number can be obtained by :

  (*i*) the prime factorization.

  (*ii*) the division method.
- If n is not a perfect square, then $\sqrt{n}$ is not a rational number.
- Squares of natural numbers having all digits 1 have a following pattern:

$$
\begin{aligned}
1^2 &= 1\\
11^2 &= 1\,\mathbf{2}\,1\\
111^2 &= 1\,2\,\mathbf{3}\,2\,1\\
1111^2 &= 1\,2\,3\,\mathbf{4}\,3\,2\,1\\
11111^2 &= 1\,2\,3\,4\,\mathbf{5}\,4\,3\,2\,1\\
111111^2 &= 1\,2\,3\,4\,5\,\mathbf{6}\,5\,4\,3\,2\,1\\
\vdots \quad & \quad \vdots \qquad \vdots\\
111111111^2 &= 1\,2\,3\,4\,5\,6\,7\,8\,\mathbf{9}\,8\,7\,6\,5\,4\,3\,2\,1
\end{aligned}
$$

In this pattern the sum of the digits of every number on the right hand side is a perfect square at given below:

$$
\begin{aligned}
1 + 2 + 1 &= 4 = 2^2\\
1 + 2 + 3 + 2 + 1 &= 9 = 3^2\\
1 + 2 + 3 + 4 + 3 + 2 + 1 &= 16 = 4^2
\end{aligned}
$$

. . . .

$1 + 2 + 3 + 4 + 5 + 6 + 7 + 8 + 9 + 8 + 7 + 6 + 5 + 4 + 3 + 2 + 1 = 81 = 9^2$.

- Observe the following pattern

$$
\begin{aligned}
11^2 &= 121\\
101^2 &= 10201\\
1001^2 &= 1002001\\
10001^2 &= 100020001
\end{aligned}
$$

- Observe the following pattern

$$11^2 = 121$$
$$101^2 = 10201$$
$$10101^2 = 102030201$$
$$1010101^2 = 1020304030201$$
$$101010101^2 = 10203040504030201$$

- **Short Cut Method to find Squares Column Method**

Using $(a + b)^2 = a^2 + 2ab + b^2$.

Make three columns: What is square of 86

$a = 8, b = 6$

Step	Column I (a^2)	Column II $2ab$	Column III b^2
I	$(8)^2 = 64$	$2 \times 8 \times 6 = 96$	$(6)^2 = 36$
II	64	96 + 3 99	**36**
III	64 + 9 **73**	**96** + 3 99	**36**

The bold digits give the required square $86^2 = 7396$.

Square Root

Square root of a given number is that number which is multiplied by itself is equal to the given number.

For example, square root of 81 is 9 because 92 = 9 × 9 = 81.

Methods of Finding the square root

(a) Prime Factorization Method

(*i*) Prime Factorization Method

(*ii*) Group the Factors in Paris

(*iii*) Take one number from each pair of factors and then multiply them together.

Example: Find the square root of 4761?

Solution: $4761 = \underbrace{23 \times 23} \times \underbrace{3 \times 3}$

$\therefore \quad \sqrt{4761} = 23 \times 3 = 69.$

(b) Method of Division: This method is used when the number is large and the factors cannot be easily determined.

Example: Find the square root of 226576?

Solution:

	476
4	226516
4	16
87	665
7	609
946	5676
6	5676
	×

$\sqrt[2]{226576} = 476.$

Multiple Choice Questions

1. $\sqrt{53824} = ?$

A. 202 B. 232
C. 242 D. 332

2. The value of $\sqrt{10+\sqrt{25+\sqrt{108+\sqrt{154+\sqrt{255}}}}}$ is:

A. 4 B. 6
C. 8 D. 10

3. Evaluate : $\sqrt{41-\sqrt{21+\sqrt{19-\sqrt{9}}}}$.

A. 3 B. 5
C. 6 D. 6.4

4. $\left(\frac{\sqrt{625}}{11} \times \frac{14}{\sqrt{25}} \times \frac{11}{\sqrt{196}}\right)$ is equal to:

A. 5 B. 6
C. 8 D. 11

5. If $x * y = x + y + \sqrt{xy}$, the value of 6*24 is:

A. 41 B. 42
C. 43 D. 44

6. $\sqrt{\frac{25}{81} - \frac{1}{9}} = ?$

A. $\frac{2}{3}$ B. $\frac{4}{9}$
C. $\frac{16}{81}$ D. $\frac{25}{81}$

7. The value of $\sqrt{0.01} + \sqrt{0.81} + \sqrt{1.21} + \sqrt{0.0009}$ is:

A. 2.03 B. 2.1
C. 2.11 D. 2.13

8. If $\sqrt{18225} = 135$, then the value of $\left(\sqrt{182.25} + \sqrt{1.8225} + \sqrt{0.018225} + \sqrt{0.00018225}\right)$ is:

A. 1.49985 B. 14.9985
C. 149.985 D. 1499.85

9. If $\sqrt{3^n} = 729$, then the value of n is:

A. 6 B. 8
C. 10 D. 12

10. If $\sqrt{1+\frac{x}{169}} = \frac{14}{13}$, then x is equal to:

A. 1 B. 13
C. 27 D. None of these

11. If $\sqrt{1+\frac{55}{729}} = 1+\frac{x}{27}$, then the value of x is:

A. 1 B. 3
C. 5 D. 7

12. The value of $\frac{\sqrt{80}-\sqrt{112}}{\sqrt{45}-\sqrt{63}}$ is:

A. $\frac{3}{4}$ B. $1\frac{1}{3}$
C. $1\frac{7}{9}$ D. $1\frac{3}{4}$

13. Given $\sqrt{2} = 1.414$. The value of $\sqrt{8}+2\sqrt{32}-3\sqrt{128}+4\sqrt{50}$ is:

A. 8.426 B. 8.484
C. 8.526 D. 8.876

14. $\sqrt{\frac{0.081\times 0.324\times 4.624}{1.5625\times 0.0289\times 72.9\times 64}}$ is equal to:

A. 0.024 B. 0.24
C. 2.4 D. 24

15. The value of $\sqrt{\frac{(0.03)^2+(0.21)^2+(0.065)^2}{(0.003)^2+(0.021)^2+(0.0065)^2}}$ is:

A. 0.1 B. 10
C. 10^2 D. 10^3

16. The square root of $\left(7+3\sqrt{5}\right)\left(7-3\sqrt{5}\right)$ is:

A. $\sqrt{5}$ B. 2
C. 4 D. $3\sqrt{5}$

17. $\left(\sqrt{3}-\frac{1}{\sqrt{3}}\right)^2$ simplifies to:

A. $\frac{3}{4}$ B. $\frac{4}{\sqrt{3}}$
C. $\frac{4}{3}$ D. None of these

18. $\left(\sqrt{2}+\frac{1}{\sqrt{2}}\right)^2$ is equal to :

A. $2\frac{1}{2}$ B. $3\frac{1}{2}$
C. $4\frac{1}{2}$ D. $5\frac{1}{2}$

19. If $3a = 4b = 6c$ and $a + b + c = 27\sqrt{29}$, then $\sqrt{a^2+b^2+c^2}$ is:

A. $3\sqrt{29}$ B. 81
C. 87 D. None of these

20. The square root of $0.\overline{4}$ is:

A. $0.\overline{6}$ B. $0.\overline{7}$
C. $0.\overline{8}$ D. $0.\overline{9}$

21. Which one of the following numbers has rational square root?

A. 0.4 B. 0.09
C. 0.9 D. 0.025

22. The value of $\sqrt{0.4}$ is:

A. 0.02 B. 0.2
C. 0.51 D. 0.63

23. The greatest four-digit perfect square number is:

A. 9000 B. 9801
C. 9900 D. 9981

24. The least number of 4 digits which is a perfect square, is:

A. 1000 B. 1016
C. 1024 D. 1036

25. If $x = \left(7-4\sqrt{3}\right)$, then the value of $\left(x+\frac{1}{x}\right)$ is:

A. $3\sqrt{3}$ B. $8\sqrt{3}$
C. 14 D. $14+8\sqrt{3}$

26. If $x = \frac{\sqrt{3}+1}{\sqrt{3}-1}$ and $y = \frac{\sqrt{3}-1}{\sqrt{3}+1}$, then the value of $(x^2 + y^2)$ is:

A. 10 B. 13
C. 14 D. 15

27. If $a = \frac{\sqrt{5}+1}{\sqrt{5}-1}$ and $b = \frac{\sqrt{5}-1}{\sqrt{5}+1}$, the value of $\left(\frac{a^2+ab+b^2}{a^2-ab+b^2}\right)$ is:

A. $\frac{3}{4}$ B. $\frac{4}{3}$
C. $\frac{3}{5}$ D. $\frac{5}{3}$

28. The least number by which 294 must be multiplied to make it a perfect square, is:

A. 2 B. 3
C. 6 D. 24

29. What is the smallest number by which 5808 should be multiplied so that the product becomes a perfect square?

A. 2 B. 3
C. 7 D. 11

30. The least number by which 1470 must be divided to get a number which is a perfect square, is:

A. 5 B. 6
C. 15 D. 30

31. What is the least number which should be subtracted from 549162 in order to make it a perfect square?

A. 28 B. 36
C. 62 D. 81

32. If $\sqrt{\left(1+\frac{27}{169}\right)} = 1+\frac{x}{13}$, then x equals:

A. 1 B. 3
C. 5 D. 7

33. $\sqrt{3\sqrt{3\sqrt{3\sqrt{3\sqrt{3\sqrt{3}}}}}} = ?$

A. $3^{\frac{31}{64}}$ B. $3^{\frac{31}{32}}$
C. $3^{\frac{1}{64}}$ D. None of these

34. $\sqrt{248+\sqrt{52+\sqrt{144}}} = ?$

A. 14 B. 16
C. 16.6 D. 18.8

35. Given that $\sqrt{4096} = 64$, the value of $\sqrt{4096} + \sqrt{40.96} + \sqrt{.004096}$ is:

A. 70.4 B. 70.464
C. 71.104 D. 71.4

36. If $\sqrt{0.03\times 0.3\times a} = 0.03\times 0.3\times\sqrt{b}$, then the value of $\frac{a}{b}$ is:

A. 0.009 B. 0.03
C. 0.09 D. None of these

37. If $\sqrt{1+\sqrt{1-\frac{2176}{2401}}} = 1+\frac{x}{7}$, then the value of x is:

A. 3 B. 1
C. 5 D. 7

38. If $a = \frac{\sqrt{5}+1}{\sqrt{5}-1}$ and $b = \frac{\sqrt{5}-1}{\sqrt{5}+1}$; then the value of $\frac{a^2+ab+b^2}{a^2-ab+b^2}$ is:

A. $\frac{3}{4}$ B. $\frac{4}{3}$
C. $\frac{3}{5}$ D. $\frac{5}{3}$

39. The smallest number by which 3600 must be multiplied to make if perfect cube, is:

A. 40 B. 60
C. 20 D. 15

40. If $\sqrt{12} = 3.464$, then the value of $\sqrt{\frac{3}{4}}+2\sqrt{\frac{4}{3}}$ is:

A. 3.17 B. 3.464
C. 3.1753 D. None of these

ANSWERS

1	2	3	4	5	6	7	8	9	10
B	A	C	A	B	B	D	B	D	C
11	**12**	**13**	**14**	**15**	**16**	**17**	**18**	**19**	**20**
A	B	B	A	B	B	C	C	C	A
21	**22**	**23**	**24**	**25**	**26**	**27**	**28**	**29**	**30**
B	D	B	C	C	C	B	C	B	D
31	**32**	**33**	**34**	**35**	**36**	**37**	**38**	**39**	**40**
D	A	B	B	B	A	B	B	B	C

EXPLANATORY ANSWERS

1.

```
    2 | 53824 (232
      | 4
   43 | 138
      | 129
  462 |  924
      |  924
      |   ×
```

$\therefore \sqrt{53824} = 232.$

2. Given exp. $= \sqrt{10+\sqrt{25+\sqrt{108+\sqrt{154+15}}}}$

$= \sqrt{10+\sqrt{25+\sqrt{108+\sqrt{169}}}}$

$= \sqrt{10+\sqrt{25+\sqrt{108+13}}} = \sqrt{10+\sqrt{25+\sqrt{121}}}$

$= \sqrt{10+\sqrt{25+11}} = \sqrt{10+\sqrt{36}}$

$= \sqrt{10+6} = \sqrt{16} = 4$

3. Given exp. $= \sqrt{41-\sqrt{21+\sqrt{19-3}}}$

$= \sqrt{41-\sqrt{21+\sqrt{16}}} = \sqrt{41-\sqrt{21+4}}$

$= \sqrt{41-\sqrt{25}} = \sqrt{41-5} = \sqrt{36} = 6$

4. Given exp. $= \frac{25}{11}\times\frac{14}{5}\times\frac{11}{14} = 5$

5. $6*24 = 6 + 24 + \sqrt{6\times24} = 30+\sqrt{144} = 30+12 = 42$

6. $\sqrt{\frac{25}{81}-\frac{1}{9}} = \sqrt{\frac{25-9}{81}} = \sqrt{\frac{16}{81}} = \frac{\sqrt{16}}{\sqrt{81}} = \frac{4}{9}$

7. Given exp. $= \sqrt{\frac{1}{100}}+\sqrt{\frac{81}{100}}+\sqrt{\frac{121}{100}}+\sqrt{\frac{9}{10000}}$

$= \frac{1}{10}+\frac{9}{10}+\frac{11}{10}+\frac{3}{100}$

$= 0.1 + 0.9 + 1.1 + 0.03 = 2.13$

8. Given exp. $= \sqrt{\frac{18225}{10^2}}+\sqrt{\frac{18225}{10^4}}+\sqrt{\frac{18225}{10^6}}+\sqrt{\frac{18225}{10^8}}$

$= \sqrt{\frac{18225}{10}}+\sqrt{\frac{18225}{10^2}}+\sqrt{\frac{18225}{10^3}}+\sqrt{\frac{18225}{10^4}}$

$= \frac{135}{10}+\frac{135}{100}+\frac{135}{1000}+\frac{135}{10000}$

$= 13.5 + 1.35 + 0.135 + 0.0135 = 14.9985$

9. $\sqrt{3^n} = 729 = 3^6 \Leftrightarrow \left(\sqrt{3^n}\right)^2 = (3^6)^2$

$\Leftrightarrow 3^n = 3^{12} \Leftrightarrow n = 12$

10. $\sqrt{1+\frac{x}{169}} = \frac{14}{13} \Rightarrow 1+\frac{x}{169} = \frac{196}{169}$

$\Rightarrow \frac{x}{169} = \left(\frac{196}{169}-1\right) = \frac{27}{169} \Rightarrow x = 27.$

11. $\sqrt{1+\frac{55}{729}} = 1+\frac{x}{27} \Rightarrow \sqrt{\frac{784}{729}} = \frac{27+x}{27}$

$\Rightarrow \frac{28}{27} = \frac{27+x}{27} \Rightarrow 27 + x = 28 \Rightarrow x = 1$

12. $\frac{\sqrt{80}-\sqrt{112}}{\sqrt{45}-\sqrt{63}} = \frac{\sqrt{16\times5}-\sqrt{16\times7}}{\sqrt{9\times5}-\sqrt{9\times7}}$

$= \frac{4\sqrt{5}-4\sqrt{7}}{3\sqrt{5}-3\sqrt{7}} = \frac{4\left(\sqrt{5}-\sqrt{7}\right)}{3\left(\sqrt{5}-\sqrt{7}\right)} = \frac{4}{3} = 1\frac{1}{3}$

13. Given exp. $= \sqrt{4\times2}+2\sqrt{16\times2}-3\sqrt{64\times2}+4\sqrt{25\times2}$

$= 2\sqrt{2}+8\sqrt{2}-24\sqrt{2}+20\sqrt{2}$

$= 6\sqrt{2} = 6 \times 1.414 = 8.484$

14. Given exp. $= \sqrt{\frac{81\times324\times4624}{15625\times289\times729\times64}}$

$= \frac{9\times18\times68}{125\times17\times27\times8} = \frac{3}{125} = 0.024$

15. Given exp. $= \sqrt{\frac{(0.03)^2+(0.21)^2+(0.065)^2}{\left(\frac{0.03}{10}\right)^2+\left(\frac{0.21}{10}\right)^2+\left(\frac{0.065}{10}\right)^2}}$

$= \sqrt{\frac{100\ [(0.03)^2+(0.21)^2+(0.065)^2}{(0.03)^2+(0.21)^2+(0.065)^2}}$

$= \sqrt{100} = 10$

16. $\sqrt{(7+3\sqrt{5})(7-3\sqrt{5})} = \sqrt{(7)^2-(3\sqrt{5})^2}$

$= \sqrt{49-45} = \sqrt{4} = 2$

17. $\left(\sqrt{3}-\frac{1}{\sqrt{3}}\right)^2 = \left(\sqrt{3}\right)^2+\left(\frac{1}{\sqrt{3}}\right)^2 - 2\times\sqrt{3}\times\frac{1}{\sqrt{3}}$

$= 3+\frac{1}{3}-2 = 1+\frac{1}{3} = \frac{4}{3}$

18. $\left(\sqrt{2}+\frac{1}{\sqrt{2}}\right)^2 = \left(\sqrt{2}\right)^2+\left(\frac{1}{\sqrt{2}}\right)^2 + 2\times\sqrt{2}\times\frac{1}{\sqrt{2}}$

$= 2+\frac{1}{2}+2 = 4+\frac{1}{2} = 4\frac{1}{2}$

19. $4b = 6c \Rightarrow b = \frac{3}{2}c$ and $3a = 4b$

$\Rightarrow \quad a = \frac{4}{3}b = \frac{4}{3}\left(\frac{3}{2}c\right) = 2c$

$a + b + c = 27\sqrt{29}$

$2c+\frac{3}{2}c+c = 27\sqrt{29}$

$\Rightarrow \quad \frac{9}{2}c = 27\sqrt{29} \Rightarrow c = 6\sqrt{29}$

$\therefore \sqrt{a^2+b^2+c^2} = \sqrt{(a+b+c)-2(ab+bc+ca)}$

$= \sqrt{\left(27\sqrt{29}\right)^2-2\left(2c\times\frac{3}{2}c+\frac{3}{2}c\times c+c\times2c\right)}$

$= \sqrt{(729\times29)-2\left(3c^2+\frac{3}{2}c^2+2c^2\right)}$

$= \sqrt{(729\times29)-2\times\frac{13}{2}c^2}$

$= \sqrt{(729\times29)-13\times\left(6\sqrt{29}\right)^2}$

$= \sqrt{29(729-468)}$

$= \sqrt{29 \times 261} = \sqrt{29 \times 29 \times 9} = 29 \times 3 = 87$

20. $\sqrt{0.\overline{4}} = \sqrt{\frac{4}{9}} = \frac{2}{3} = 0.666.... = 0.\overline{6}$.

21. $\sqrt{0.09} = \sqrt{\frac{9}{100}} = \frac{3}{10} = 0.3$, which is rational.

$\therefore$ 0.09 has rational square root.

22.

$$\begin{array}{r|l} 6 & 0.\overline{40}\,\overline{00}\,\overline{00}\ (0.63 \\ & 36 \\ \hline 123 & \ \ 400 \\ & \ \ 369 \\ \hline \end{array}$$

23. Greatest number of four digits is 9999.

$$\begin{array}{r|l} 9 & \overline{99}\,\overline{99}\ (99 \\ & 81 \\ \hline 189 & 1899 \\ & 1701 \\ \hline & \ \ 198 \end{array}$$

$\therefore$ Required number = (9999 – 198) = 9801.

24. Least number of 4 digits is 1000.

$$\begin{array}{r|l} 3 & \overline{10}\,\overline{00}\ (31 \\ & 9 \\ \hline 61 & 100 \\ & \ \ 61 \\ \hline & \ \ 39 \end{array}$$

$\therefore (31)^2 < 1000 < (32)^2$.

Hence, required number = $(32)^2 = 1024$.

25. $x + \frac{1}{x} = (7-4\sqrt{3}) + \frac{1}{(7-4\sqrt{3})} \times \frac{(7+4\sqrt{3})}{(7+4\sqrt{3})}$

$= (7-4\sqrt{3}) + \frac{(7+4\sqrt{3})}{(49-48)}$

$= (7-4\sqrt{3}) + (7+4\sqrt{3}) = 14$

26. $x = \frac{(\sqrt{3}+1)}{(\sqrt{3}-1)} \times \frac{(\sqrt{3}+1)}{(\sqrt{3}+1)} = \frac{(\sqrt{3}+1)^2}{(3-1)}$

$= \frac{3+1+2\sqrt{3}}{2} = 2+\sqrt{3}$

$y = \frac{(\sqrt{3}-1)}{(\sqrt{3}+1)} \times \frac{(\sqrt{3}-1)}{(\sqrt{3}-1)} = \frac{(\sqrt{3}-1)^2}{(3-1)}$

$= \frac{3+1-2\sqrt{3}}{2} = 2-\sqrt{3}$

$\therefore x^2 + y^2 = (2+\sqrt{3})^2 + (2-\sqrt{3})^2$

$= 2(4 + 3) = 2 \times 7 = 14$

27. $a = \frac{(\sqrt{5}+1)}{(\sqrt{5}-1)} \times \frac{(\sqrt{5}+1)}{(\sqrt{5}+1)} = \frac{(\sqrt{5}+1)^2}{(5-1)}$

$= \frac{5+1+2\sqrt{5}}{4} = \left(\frac{3+\sqrt{5}}{2}\right)$

$b = \frac{(\sqrt{5}-1)}{(\sqrt{5}+1)} \times \frac{(\sqrt{5}-1)}{(\sqrt{5}-1)} = \frac{(\sqrt{5}-1)^2}{(5-1)}$

$= \frac{5+1-2\sqrt{5}}{4} = \left(\frac{3-\sqrt{5}}{2}\right)$

$\therefore a^2 + b^2 = \frac{(3+\sqrt{5})^2}{4} + \frac{(3-\sqrt{5})^2}{4}$

$= \frac{(3+\sqrt{5})^2 + (3-\sqrt{5})^2}{4}$

$= \frac{2(9+5)}{4} = 7$

Also, $ab = \frac{(3+\sqrt{5})}{2} \cdot \frac{(3-\sqrt{5})}{2} = \frac{(9-5)}{4} = 1$.

$\therefore \frac{a^2+ab+b^2}{a^2-ab+b^2} = \frac{(a^2+b^2)+ab}{(a^2+b^2)-ab}$

$= \frac{7+1}{7-1} = \frac{8}{6} = \frac{4}{3}$

28. 294 = 7 × 7 × 2 × 3.

To make it a perfect square, it must be multiplied by 2 × 3 *i.e.,* 6.

$\therefore$ Required number = 6.

29. 5808 = 2 × 2 × 2 × 2 × 3 × 11 × 11

$= 2^2 \times 2^2 \times 3 \times 11^2$

To make it a perfect square, it must be multiplied by 3.

30. 1470 = 7 × 7 × 5 × 6. To make it a perfect square, it must be divided by 5 × 6, *i.e.,* 30.

31.

$$\begin{array}{r|l} 7 & \overline{54}\,\overline{91}\,\overline{62}\ (741 \\ & 49 \\ \hline 144 & \ \ 591 \\ & \ \ 576 \\ \hline 1481 & \ \ \ 1562 \\ & \ \ \ 1481 \\ \hline & \ \ \ \ \ 81 \end{array}$$

$\therefore$ Required number to be subtracted = 81.

32. $\sqrt{1+\frac{27}{169}} = 1 + \frac{x}{13}$

$\sqrt{\frac{196}{169}} = \frac{13+x}{13}$

$$\frac{14}{13} = \frac{13+x}{13}$$

$$14 = 13 + x$$

$$\therefore \quad x = 1$$

33. $\sqrt{3\sqrt{3\sqrt{3\sqrt{3.3^{\frac{1}{2}}}}}} = \sqrt{3\sqrt{3\sqrt{3.3^{\frac{3}{4}}}}} = \sqrt{3\sqrt{3.3^{\frac{7}{8}}}}$

$$= \sqrt{3.3^{\frac{15}{16}}} = 3^{\frac{31}{32}}$$

34. $\sqrt{248+\sqrt{52+12}} = \sqrt{248+\sqrt{64}}$

$$= \sqrt{248+8} = \sqrt{256} = 16$$

35. $\sqrt{4096} + \sqrt{\frac{4096}{100}} + \sqrt{\frac{4096}{1000000}}$

$$= 64 = \frac{64}{10} + \frac{64}{1000}$$

$$= 64 + 6.4 + 0.064$$

$$= 70.464$$

36. $\sqrt{0.03 \times 0.3 \times a} = 0.03 \times 0.3 \times \sqrt{b}$

Taking square of both sides, we get

$0.03 \times 0.3 \times a = 0.03 \times 0.3 \times 0.03 \times 0.3 \times b$

$$\frac{a}{b} = \frac{0.03 \times 0.3}{1} = 0.009$$

37. We have,

$$\sqrt{1+\sqrt{\frac{225}{2401}}} = 1+\frac{x}{7}$$

$$\sqrt{1+\frac{15}{49}} = 1+\frac{x}{7}$$

$$\sqrt{\frac{64}{49}} = 1+\frac{x}{7}$$

$$\frac{8}{7} = 1+\frac{x}{7}$$

$$1+\frac{1}{7} = 1+\frac{x}{7}$$

$$\therefore \quad x = 1$$

38. $a + b = \frac{\sqrt{5}+1}{\sqrt{5}-1} + \frac{\sqrt{5}-1}{\sqrt{5}+1}$

$$= \frac{(\sqrt{5}+1)^2 + (\sqrt{5}-1)^2}{(\sqrt{5})^2 - (1)^2}$$

$$\therefore \quad = \frac{2(\sqrt{5})^2 + (1)^2}{5-1} = \frac{6}{2} = 3$$

$$ab = \frac{\sqrt{5}+1}{\sqrt{5}-1} \times \frac{\sqrt{5}-1}{\sqrt{5}+1} = 1$$

$$\frac{a^2+ab+b^2}{a^2-ab+b^2} = \frac{(a+b)^2 - 2ab + ab}{(a+b)^2 - 2ab - ab}$$

$$= \frac{(a+b)^2 - ab}{(a+b)^2 - 3ab}$$

$$= \frac{(3)^2 - 1}{(3)^2 - 3 \times 1} = \frac{9-1}{9-3} = \frac{8}{6} = \frac{4}{3}$$

39.

3	3600
3	1200
2	400
2	200
2	100
2	50
5	25
5	5
5	1

$$3600 = 3 \times 3 \times 2 \times 2 \times 2 \times 2 \times 5 \times 5$$

$$= 3 \times 2 \times 2 \times 5$$

$$= 60$$

40. $\sqrt{\frac{3}{4}} + 2\sqrt{\frac{4}{3}} = \sqrt{\frac{12}{16}} + 2\sqrt{\frac{12}{9}}$

$$= \frac{\sqrt{12}}{4} + 2 \times \frac{\sqrt{12}}{3}$$

$$= \frac{3.464}{4} + 2 \times \frac{3.464}{3}$$

$$= 0.866 + 2.3093$$

$$= 3.1753$$

□□□□□

3

Cubes and Cube Roots

☛ Points To Remember

- If n is a perfect cube and $n = m^3$, then m is a cube root of n. A cube root of n is written as $\sqrt[3]{n}$ or $(n)^{1/3}$.
- The cube root of a perfect cube can be obtained by prime factorization of the number.
- The cube root of a product of two perfect cubes is the product of the cube roots of the perfect cubes *i.e.,* $\sqrt[3]{ab} = \sqrt[3]{a} \cdot \sqrt[3]{b}$
- The cube root of a Quotient of two perfect cubes is the quotient of their cube roots *i.e.,* $\sqrt[3]{\frac{a}{b}} = \frac{\sqrt[3]{a}}{\sqrt[3]{b}}$, $b \neq 0$, where a and b are perfect cubes.
- The cube root of a negative perfect cube is negative.

Number m	Perfect cubes m^3	Cube roots $\sqrt[3]{m^3}$
1	1	1
2	8	2
3	27	3
4	64	4
5	125	5
6	216	6
7	343	7
8	512	8
9	729	9
10	1000	10

Cube Root

The cube root of a given number is that number which when raised to the third power produces the given number, that is the cube root of a number x is the number whose cube is x.

The cube root of x is written as $\sqrt[3]{x}$

For example, cube root of 64 is 4 as $4 \times 4 \times 4 = 64$.

Method to find Cube Root

Method of Factorisation

(1) Write a given number as product of prime factors.

(2) Take the product of prime numbers; choosing one out of three of each type.

This product gives the cube root of the given number.

Example: Find the cube root of 42875.

Solution: Resolving 42875 into prime factors, we get

$$42875 = \underbrace{5 \times 5 \times 5}\times\underbrace{7 \times 7 \times 7}$$

$$\therefore \quad \sqrt[3]{4287} = 5 \times 7 = 35.$$

Multiple Choice Questions

1. What is the cube root of 2197?

A. 13 B. 15
C. 17 D. 19

2. What is the cube root of 117649?

A. 39 B. 49
C. 59 D. 65

3. What is the cube root of $\frac{343}{125}$?

A. $\frac{5}{7}$ B. $\frac{9}{11}$
C. $\frac{7}{5}$ D. $\frac{9}{5}$

4. What is the cube root of $-\frac{2197}{1331}$?

A. $-\frac{13}{11}$ B. $-\frac{13}{9}$
C. $-\frac{11}{13}$ D. $-\frac{13}{17}$

5. What is the unit digits of the cube root of 226981?

A. 1 B. 9
C. 6 D. 8

6. What is the unit digits of the cube root of 175616?

A. 2 B. 4
C. 6 D. 8

7. What is the smallest number by which 392 must be multiplied so that the product is a perfect cube?

A. 2 B. 5
C. 7 D. 9

8. What is the smallest number by which 3087 must be divided so that the quotient is a perfect cube?

A. 7 B. 9
C. 11 D. 13

9. What is the value of following expression $= [(5^2 + 12^2)^{1/2}]^3$

A. 2197 B. 14615
C. 15620 D. 16625

10. $[(6^2 + 8^2)^{1/2}]^3$

A. 4812 B. 1000
C. 5913 D. 4313

11. $\sqrt[3]{0.1\times0.1\times0.1\times13\times13\times13}$

A. 1.4 B. 1.2
C. 1.3 D. 1.7

12. $\sqrt[3]{\dfrac{0.027}{0.008}} - \sqrt[3]{\dfrac{0.09}{0.04}} - 1$

A. –1 B. –2
C. –3 D. 1

13. Three numbers are in the ratio 1 : 2 : 3. The sum of their cubes is 98784. What is the smallest number?

A. 12 B. 14
C. 16 D. 18

14. What is the volume of a cube whose surface area is 150 m^2?

A. 120 m^3 B. 122 m^3
C. 125 m^3 D. 135 m^3

15. The volume of a cube is 9261000 m^3. What is the side of the cube?

A. 210 m B. 220 m
C. 230 m D. 245 m

16. if $\sqrt[3]{3^n}$ = 729, then value of n is:

A. 16 B. 18
C. 20 D. 22

17. The cube root of .000216 is:

A. .6 B. .06
C. .006 D. None of these

18. $\sqrt[3]{4\dfrac{12}{125}} = ?$

A. $1\frac{2}{5}$ B. $1\frac{3}{5}$
C. $1\frac{4}{5}$ D. $2\frac{2}{5}$

19. $\sqrt[3]{\sqrt{.000064}} = ?$

A. .02 B. .2
C. 2 D. None of these

20. The largest four-digit number which is a perfect cube, is:

A. 8000 B. 9261
C. 9999 D. None of these

21. By what least number 675 be multiplied to obtain a number which is a perfect cube?

A. 5 B. 6
C. 7 D. 8

22. What is the smallest number by which 3600 be divided to make it a perfect cube?

A. 9 B. 50
C. 300 D. 450

23. $\sqrt[3]{0.000216}$ is equal to:

A. 0.0006 B. 0.006
C. 0.06 D. 0.6

24. If $1^3 + 2^3 + 3^3 + ... + 10^3 = 3025$, then the value of $2^3 + 4^3 + 6^3 + ... + 20^3$ is equal to:

A. 6050 B. 9075
C. 12100 D. 24200

25. $\sqrt[3]{333+\sqrt[3]{987+\sqrt[3]{2197}}}$

A. 21 B. 18
C. 7 D. 3

ANSWERS

1	2	3	4	5	6	7	8	9	10
A	B	C	A	A	C	C	B	A	B
11	**12**	**13**	**14**	**15**	**16**	**17**	**18**	**19**	**20**
C	A	B	C	A	B	B	B	B	B
21	**22**	**23**	**24**	**25**					
A	D	C	A	C					

EXPLANATORY ANSWERS

1. $(2197)^{1/3} = (13 \times 13 \times 13)^{1/3}$

$= [(13)^3]^{1/3} = (13)^{3 \times 1/3}$

13	2197
13	169
13	13
	1

$= 13.$

Other Method: 2197, here unit digit is 7. Unit digit is cube root of 3, after striking out the last three digit from the right, the number is 2. 1 is the largest number whose cube is less than 2. The required cube root is 13.

2. $(117649)^{1/3} = 49$

3. $\sqrt[3]{\frac{343}{125}} = \sqrt[3]{\frac{7 \times 7 \times 7}{5 \times 5 \times 5}} = \frac{7}{5}$

4. $-\sqrt[3]{\frac{2197}{1331}} = -\sqrt[3]{\frac{13 \times 13 \times 13}{11 \times 11 \times 11}}$

13	2197
13	169
13	13
	1

$= -\frac{13}{11}$

5. Unit digit of 226981 is

$(1)^3 = 1$

6. Unit digit of 175616 is

$(6)^3 = 6$

7. Resolving 392 into prime factor.

$392 = 2 \times 2 \times 2 \times 7 \times 7$

2	392
2	196
2	98
7	49
7	7
	1

For perfect cube, given number must be multiplied by 7.

8. Resolving 3087 into prime factor

$3087 = 7 \times 7 \times 7 \times 3 \times 3$

3	3087
3	1029
7	343
7	49
7	7
	1

For perfect cube given number must divided by $3 \times 3 = 9$.

9. $\left[(5^2 + 12^2)^{1/2}\right]^3 = \left[(25 + 144)^{1/2}\right]^3$

$= \left[(169)^{1/2}\right]^3$

$= \left[(13)^{1/2}\right]^3$

$= (13)^3 = 2197$

10. $\left[(6^2 + 8^2)^{1/2}\right]^3 = \left[(36 + 64)^{1/2}\right]^3$

$= \left[(100)^{1/2}\right]^3 = (10)^3$

$= 1000.$

11. $\sqrt[3]{0.1 \times 0.1 \times 0.1 \times 13 \times 13 \times 13}$

$= 0.1 \times 13 = 1.3.$

12. $\sqrt[3]{\frac{0.027}{0.008}} = \sqrt[3]{\frac{27}{8}} = \sqrt[3]{\frac{3 \times 3 \times 3}{2 \times 2 \times 2}} = \frac{3}{2}$

$\sqrt{\frac{.09}{.04}} = \sqrt{\frac{9}{4}} = \frac{3}{2}.$

Required expression

$\frac{3}{2} - \frac{3}{2} - 1 = -1$

13. Let the number be

x^3, $2x^3$ and $3x^3$.

According to question

$x^3 + (2x)^3 + (3x)^3 = 98784$

$x^3 + 8x^3 + 27x^3 = 98784$

$36x^3 = 98784$

$x^3 = \frac{98784}{36} = 2744$

$x = (2744)^{1/3}$

$= (14^3)^{1/3} = 14.$

Smallest number = 14.

14. Surface area of cube $= 150\ m^2$.

$6l^2 = 150$

$$l^2 = \frac{150}{6} = 25$$

$$l = \sqrt{25} = 5.$$

Volume of cube $= l^3 = 5^3$

$= 125\ m^3$

15. Volume of a cube $= 9261000\ m^3$

$l^3 = 9261000$

$= 210^3$

$l = (210^3)^{1/3}$

$= 210\ m$

16. $(3)^{n/3} = (3)^6$

$\frac{n}{3} = 6$

$n = 18$

17. $(.000216)^{1/3} = \left(\frac{216}{10^6}\right)^{1/3} = \left(\frac{6 \times 6 \times 6}{10^2 \times 10^2 \times 10^2}\right)^{1/3}$

$= \frac{6}{10^2} = \frac{6}{100} = .06$

18. $\sqrt[3]{4\frac{12}{125}} = \sqrt[3]{\frac{512}{125}} = \left(\frac{8 \times 8 \times 8}{5 \times 5 \times 5}\right)^{1/3} = \frac{8}{5} = 1\frac{3}{5}$

19. $\sqrt{.000064} = \sqrt{\frac{64}{10^6}} = \frac{8}{10^3} = \frac{8}{1000} = .008$

$\therefore \sqrt[3]{\sqrt{.000064}} = \sqrt[3]{.008} = \sqrt[3]{\frac{8}{1000}} = \frac{2}{10} = 0.2$

20. Clearly, 9261 is a perfect cube satisfying the given property.

21. $675 = 5 \times 5 \times 3 \times 3 \times 3.$

To make it a perfect cube, it must be multiplied by 5.

22. $3600 = 2^3 \times 5^2 \times 3^2 \times 2.$

To make it a perfect cube, it must be divided by $5^2 \times 3^2 \times 2$ *i.e.*, 450.

23. $\sqrt[3]{\frac{216}{1000000}} = \frac{6}{100} = 0.06$

24. $2^3 + 4^3 + 6^3 + ... + 20^3$

$= 2(1^3 + 2^3 + 3^3 + ... + 10^3$

$= 2 \times 3025 = 6050$

25. $\sqrt[3]{333 + \sqrt[3]{987 + \sqrt[3]{(13)^3}}}$

$= \sqrt[3]{333 + \sqrt[3]{987 + 13}} = \sqrt[3]{333 + \sqrt[3]{1000}}$

$= \sqrt[3]{333 + 10} = \sqrt[3]{343} = 7$

□□□□□

4

Exponents and Powers

Points To Remember

- If n is a positive integer and a is a rational number, then $a^n = a \times a \times a \times ... \times a$ (n times)

  a^n is called the nth power of a. The rational number a is called **base** and n is called **Index** or **exponent** of the nth power of a.
- If $a^n = x$ then

  $a = (x)^{1/n}$.

  $(x)^{1/n}$ is also written in the form as $\sqrt[n]{x}$ and it is read as nth root of x. $\sqrt[n]{x}$ is called **Surd** and n is known as the **index of the Surd.**
- **Laws of indices :** If a and b be any two rational numbers and m, n are integer, then:

  (i) $a^m \times a^n = a^{m+n}$

  (ii) $a^m \div a^n = a^{m-n}$

  (iii) $a^m \div a^m = a^{m-m} = a^0 = 1$

  (iv) $(a \times b)^m = a^m \times b^m$

  (v) $(a^m)^n = a^{mn}$

  (vi) $(-a)^m = (-1)^m a^m$

  (vii) $\left(\frac{p}{q}\right)^m = \frac{p^m}{q^m}$, where p, q are integers and $q \neq 0$.

  (viii) $\left(\frac{p}{q}\right)^{-m} = \left(\frac{q}{p}\right)^m$

  (ix) $\left(\frac{p}{q}\right)^m \times \left(\frac{p}{q}\right)^n = \left(\frac{p}{q}\right)^{m+n}$

  (x) $\left(\frac{p}{q}\right)^m \div \left(\frac{p}{q}\right)^n = \left(\frac{p}{q}\right)^{m-n}$

  (xi) $\left[\left(\frac{p}{q}\right)^m\right]^n = \left(\frac{p}{q}\right)^{mn}$
- If a is a negative rational number and n is an odd positive integer, then the nth root of a is minus of the nth root of $|a|$.
- If a is a negative rational number and n is an even positive integer, then the nth root of a is not defined.
- Let a be any positive rational number and $\frac{m}{n}$ be a positive rational number in the lowest form. Then $a^{\frac{m}{n}}$ is defined as the nth root of a^m. *i.e.*, $a^{m/n} = (a^m)^{1/n}$.

  $$a^{-m/n} = \frac{1}{a^{m/n}}.$$
- If a is a rational number and n is a positive integer such that nth root of a *i.e.*, $(a)^{1/n}$ or $\sqrt[n]{a}$ is an irrational number, then $a^{1/n}$ is called a radical or a Surd of index n and a is called the radical.
- A radical that contains no rational factor other than 1, is called a pure radical.
- A radical which has a rational factor other than unity, the other factor being irrational, is called a mixed radical.
- A square root radical is said to be in simplest form, if

  (*i*) there is no fraction in the radicand

  (*ii*) no perfect square is a factor of radicand.

  (*iii*) there is no radical in the denominator.

Rationalisation

Some Identities : Let a and b be positive real numbers, then

(i) $\left(\sqrt{a}\right)^2 = a$

(ii) $\sqrt{a}\,\sqrt{b} = \sqrt{ab}$

(iii) $\frac{\sqrt{a}}{\sqrt{b}} = \sqrt{\frac{a}{b}}$

(iv) $\left(\sqrt{a}+\sqrt{b}\right)\left(\sqrt{a}-\sqrt{b}\right) = a - b$

(v) $\left(a+\sqrt{b}\right)\left(a-\sqrt{b}\right) = a^2 - b$

(vi) $\left(\sqrt{a} \pm \sqrt{b}\right)^2 = a \pm 2\sqrt{ab} + b$

(vii) $\left(\sqrt{a}+\sqrt{b}\right)\left(\sqrt{c}+\sqrt{d}\right) = \sqrt{ac}+\sqrt{ad}+\sqrt{bc}+\sqrt{bd}$

Rationalisation factor for $\frac{1}{\sqrt{a}}$ is $\sqrt{a}$ and for $\frac{1}{a \pm \sqrt{b}}$, the rationalisation factor is $a \mp \sqrt{b}$ [if $a^2 - b^2 = 1$]

Rationalisation factor for $\frac{1}{\sqrt{a} \pm \sqrt{b}}$ is $\sqrt{a} \mp \sqrt{b}$

[if $a^2 - b^2 = 1$)

Comparison of Surd

(*i*) If two surds are of the same order, then the one whose radicand is larger, is the larger of the two.

Ex: $\sqrt[3]{19} > \sqrt[3]{15}, \sqrt{7} > \sqrt{5}$ etc.

(*ii*) If two surds are distinct order, we change them into the surds of the same order.
This order is the L.C.M. of the orders of the given surds.

Ex. Which is the greatest out of $\sqrt[3]{5}, \sqrt[4]{3}, \sqrt[5]{4}$?

$$\sqrt[3]{5} = (5)^{\frac{1}{3}}$$

$$\sqrt[4]{3} = (3)^{\frac{1}{4}}$$

$$\sqrt[5]{4} = (4)^{\frac{1}{5}}$$

$\therefore$ LCM of (3, 4, 5) = 60

$$\sqrt[3]{5} = (5)^{\frac{1}{3}} = (5)^{\frac{20}{60}} = \sqrt[60]{(5)^{20}}$$

$$\sqrt[4]{3} = (3)^{\frac{1}{4}} = (3)^{\frac{15}{60}} = \sqrt[60]{(3)^{15}}$$

$$\sqrt[5]{4} = (4)^{\frac{1}{5}} = (4)^{\frac{12}{60}} = \sqrt[60]{(4)^{12}}$$

$\therefore \sqrt[3]{5}$ is the greates.

Multiple Choice Questions

1. The value of $\{2 - 3\ (2 - 3)^3\}^3$ is:
A. 5 B. 125
C. 1/5 D. −125

2. $(256)^{0.16} \times (256)^{0.09}$:
A. 4 B. 16
C. 64 D. 256.25

3. If $10^{2y} = 25$, then 10^{-y} equals:
A. $-\frac{1}{5}$ B. $\frac{1}{50}$
C. $\frac{1}{625}$ D. $\frac{1}{5}$

4. The value of $x - y^{x-y}$ when $x = 2$ and $y = -2$ is:
A. 18 B. −18
C. 14 D. −14

5. If $9^{x+2} = 240 + 9^x$, then $x =$
A. 0.5 B. 0.2
C. 0.4 D. 0.1

6. If $8^{x+1} = 64$, what is the value of 3^{2x+1}?
A. 1 B. 3
C. 9 D. 27

7. If $4^x - 4^{x-1} = 24$, then $(2x)^x$ equals:
A. $5\sqrt{5}$ B. $\sqrt{5}$
C. $25\sqrt{5}$ D. 125

8. $\dfrac{5^{n+2} - 6 + 5^{n+1}}{13 \times 5^n - 2 \times 5^{n+1}}$ is equal to:
A. $\frac{5}{3}$ B. $-\frac{5}{3}$
C. $\frac{3}{5}$ D. $-\frac{3}{5}$

9. If $\left(\frac{2}{3}\right)^x \left(\frac{3}{2}\right)^{2x} = \frac{81}{16}$, then $x =$
A. 2 B. 3
C. 4 D. 1

10. If $(16)^{2x+3} = (64)^{x+3}$, then $4^{2x-2} =$
A. 64 B. 256
C. 32 D. 512

11. If $\dfrac{3^{5x} \times 81^2 \times 6561}{3^{2x}} = 3^7$, then $x =$
A. 3 B. −3
C. $\frac{1}{3}$ D. $-\frac{1}{3}$

12. If $x = \sqrt{5} + 2$, then $x - \frac{1}{x}$ equals:
A. $2\sqrt{5}$ B. 4
C. 2 D. $\sqrt{5}$

13. If $\dfrac{\sqrt{3} - 1}{\sqrt{3} + 1} = a - b\sqrt{3}$, then:
A. $a = 2, b = 1$ B. $a = 2, b = -1$
C. $a = -2, b = 1$ D. $a = b = 1$

14. If $x = \dfrac{2}{3 + \sqrt{7}}$, then $(x - 3)^2 =$
A. 1 B. 3
C. 6 D. 7

15. If $x = 7 + 4\sqrt{3}$ and $xy = 1$, then $\frac{1}{x^2} + \frac{1}{y^2} =$
A. 64 B. 134
C. 194 D. 1/49

16. If $x + \sqrt{15} = 4$, then $x + \frac{1}{x} =$
A. 2 B. 4
C. 8 D. 1

17. If $x=\sqrt[3]{2+\sqrt{3}}$, then $x^3+\frac{1}{x^3}=$

A. 2 B. 4
C. 8 D. 9

18. If $x=\frac{\sqrt{5}+\sqrt{3}}{\sqrt{5}-\sqrt{3}}$ and $y=\frac{\sqrt{5}-\sqrt{3}}{\sqrt{5}+\sqrt{3}}$, then $x + y + xy =$

A. 9 B. 5
C. 17 D. 7

19. If $x=\frac{\sqrt{3}-\sqrt{2}}{\sqrt{3}+\sqrt{2}}$ and $y=\frac{\sqrt{3}+\sqrt{2}}{\sqrt{3}-\sqrt{2}}$, then $x^2 + xy + y^2 =$

A. 101 B. 99
C. 98 D. 102

20. The value of $\sqrt{3-2\sqrt{2}}$ is:

A. $\sqrt{2}-1$ B. $\sqrt{2}+1$
C. $\sqrt{3}-\sqrt{2}$ D. $\sqrt{3}+\sqrt{2}$

21. The Value of $\sqrt{5+2\sqrt{6}}$ is:

A. $\sqrt{3}-\sqrt{2}$ B. $\sqrt{3}+\sqrt{2}$
C. $\sqrt{5}+\sqrt{6}$ D. None of these

22. If $x=\sqrt{6}+\sqrt{5}$, then $x^2+\frac{1}{x^2}-2=$

A. $2\sqrt{6}$ B. $2\sqrt{5}$
C. 24 D. 20

23. If $\sqrt{13-a\sqrt{10}}=\sqrt{8}+\sqrt{5}$, then $a =$

A. –5 B. –6
C. –4 D. –2

24. If $\frac{5-\sqrt{3}}{2+\sqrt{3}}=x+y\sqrt{3}$, then

A. $x = 13, y = -7$ B. $x = -13, y = 7$
C. $x = -13, y = -7$ D. $x = 13, y = 7$

25. Simplify : $18-\left[5-\left\{6+2\left(7-\overline{8-5}\right)\right\}\right]$

A. 13 B. 15
C. 27 D. 32

26. If $x * y = x^2 + y^2 - xy$, then the value of $9 * 11$ is:

A. 93 B. 103
C. 113 D. 121

27. $\dfrac{3\frac{1}{4}-\frac{4}{5}\text{ of }\frac{5}{6}}{4\frac{1}{3}\div\frac{1}{5}-\left(\frac{3}{10}+21\frac{1}{5}\right)}$ is equal to:

A. $\frac{1}{6}$ B. $2\frac{7}{12}$
C. $15\frac{1}{2}$ D. $21\frac{1}{2}$

28. If $\frac{x}{2y}=\frac{6}{7}$, then the value of $\frac{x-y}{x+y}+\frac{14}{19}$ is:

A. $\frac{13}{19}$ B. $\frac{15}{19}$
C. 1 D. $1\frac{1}{19}$

29. The value of $\dfrac{1}{2+\dfrac{1}{2+\dfrac{1}{2-\frac{1}{2}}}}$ is:

A. $\frac{3}{8}$ B. $\frac{19}{8}$
C. $\frac{8}{3}$ D. $\frac{8}{19}$

30. If $2=x+\dfrac{1}{1+\dfrac{1}{3+\frac{1}{4}}}$, then the value of x is:

A. $\frac{12}{17}$ B. $\frac{13}{17}$
C. $\frac{18}{17}$ D. $\frac{21}{17}$

31. If $\frac{37}{13}=2+\dfrac{1}{x+\dfrac{1}{y+\frac{1}{z}}}$, where x, y, z are natural numbers, then x, y, z are:

A. 1, 2, 5 B. 1, 5, 2
C. 5, 2, 11 D. 11, 2, 5

32. When simplified, the product $\left(1-\frac{1}{2}\right)\left(1-\frac{1}{3}\right)\left(1-\frac{1}{4}\right)....\left(1-\frac{1}{n}\right)$ gives:

A. $\frac{1}{n}$ B. $\frac{2}{n}$
C. $\frac{2(n-1)}{n}$ D. $\frac{2}{n(n+1)}$

33. The value of $\left(1+\frac{1}{2}\right)\left(1+\frac{1}{3}\right)\left(1+\frac{1}{4}\right)...\left(1+\frac{1}{120}\right)$ is:

A. 30 B. 40.5
C. 60.5 D. 121

34. What is the sum :

$\frac{1}{2}+\frac{1}{6}+\frac{1}{12}+\frac{1}{20}+\frac{1}{30}+\frac{1}{42}+\frac{1}{56}+\frac{1}{72}+\frac{1}{90}+\frac{1}{110}+\frac{1}{132}$

A. $\frac{7}{8}$ B. $-\frac{1}{4}$

C. $\frac{1}{4}$ D. None of these

35. The value of $999\frac{995}{999}\times 999$ is:

A. 990809 B. 998996
C. 998999 D. 999824

36. $\left(999\frac{1}{7}+999\frac{2}{7}+999\frac{3}{7}+999\frac{4}{7}+999+\frac{5}{7}+999\frac{6}{7}\right)$

is simplified to:

A. 2997 B. 5979
C. 5994 D. 5997

37. The value of $1+\frac{1}{4\times 3}+\frac{1}{4\times 3^2}+\frac{1}{4\times 3^3}$ is:

A. $\frac{121}{108}$ B. $\frac{3}{2}$

C. $\frac{31}{2}$ D. None of these

38. $\left(\frac{785\times 785\times 785+435\times 435\times 435}{785\times 785+435\times 435-785\times 435}\right)$ simplifies to:

A. 350 B. 785
C. 1220 D. 1320

39. $\frac{1}{5}+999\frac{494}{495}\times 99=?$

A. 90000 B. 90900
C. 99000 D. 99990

40. $\left(1+\frac{1}{x+1}\right)\left(1+\frac{1}{x+2}\right)\left(1+\frac{1}{x+3}\right)\left(1+\frac{1}{x+4}\right)=?$

A. $\frac{x+5}{x+1}$ B. $\left(x+\frac{1}{x+5}\right)$

C. $\frac{1}{(x+5)}$ D. $\left(1+\frac{1}{x+5}\right)$

ANSWERS

1	2	3	4	5	6	7	8	9	10
B	A	D	D	A	D	C	B	C	B
11	**12**	**13**	**14**	**15**	**16**	**17**	**18**	**19**	**20**
B	B	A	D	C	C	B	A	B	A
21	**22**	**23**	**24**	**25**	**26**	**27**	**28**	**29**	**30**
B	D	C	A	C	B	C	C	D	D
31	**32**	**33**	**34**	**35**	**36**	**37**	**38**	**39**	**40**
B	A	C	B	B	D	A	C	C	A

EXPLANATORY ANSWERS

2. $(256)^{0.16+0.09} = (256)^{0.25} = (256)^{\frac{1}{4}} = 4$

3. We have, $10^{2y} = 25$

$(10^y)^2 = 25$

$10^y = \sqrt{25} = 5$

$10^{-y} = \frac{1}{5}$

4. $2-(-2)^{2-(-2)} = 2-(-2)^4$

$= 2 - 16 = -14$

5. $9^x \times 9^2 = 240 + 9^x$

$81 \times 9^x = 240 + 9^x$

$80 \times 9^x = 240$

$9^x = 3$

$3^{2x} = 3^1$

$2x = 1$

$x = \frac{1}{2} = 0.5$

6. $8^{x+1} = 8^2$

$x + 1 = 2$

$x = 1$

$3^{2x+1} = 3^{2\times 1+1} = 3^3 = 27$

7. $4^x - 4^{x-1} = 24$

$4^x - \frac{4^x}{4} = 24$

$4 \times 4^x - 4^x = 96$

$3 \times 4^x = 96$

$4^x = 32$

$2^{2x} = 2^5$

$2x = 5$

$$x = \frac{5}{2}$$

$$(2x)^x = \left(2\frac{5}{2}\right)^{5/2} = (5^5)^{\frac{1}{2}} = 25\sqrt{5}$$

8. $$\frac{5^{n+1}(5-6)}{5^{n+1}(13\times 5^{-1})-2} = \frac{-1}{\frac{13}{5}-2} = -\frac{5}{3}$$

9. $$\left(\frac{3}{2}\right)^{-x}\left(\frac{3}{2}\right)^{2x} = \left(\frac{3}{2}\right)^{4}$$

$$-x + 2x = 4$$

$$x = 4$$

10. $$(4)^{2\,(2x+3)} = (4)^{3(x+3)}$$

$$4x + 6 = 3x + 9$$

$$x = 3$$

$$4^{2x-2} = 4^{2\times 3-2}$$

$$= 4^4 = 256$$

11. $$\frac{3^{5x}\times 81^2\times 6561}{3^{2x}} = 3^7$$

$$\frac{3^{5x}\times 3^{4\times 2}\times 3^8}{3^{2x}} = 3^7$$

$$3^{5x+8+8-2x} = 3^7$$

$$3x + 16 = -7$$

$$3x = -9$$

$$x = -3$$

12. $$x = \sqrt{5}+2$$

$$\frac{1}{x} = \sqrt{5}-2$$

$$x - \frac{1}{x} = 4$$

13. After Rationalisation, we get

$$\frac{\sqrt{3}-1}{\sqrt{3}+1}\times\frac{\sqrt{3}-1}{\sqrt{3}-1} = \frac{\left(\sqrt{3}-1\right)^2}{\left(\sqrt{3}\right)^2-(1)^2} = \frac{3+1-2\sqrt{3}}{3-1}$$

$$= \frac{4-2\sqrt{3}}{2} = 2-\sqrt{3}$$

After comparison, $a = 2$, $b = 1$ with $a - b\sqrt{3}$

14. $$x = \frac{2}{3+\sqrt{7}}\times\frac{3-\sqrt{7}}{3-\sqrt{7}} = \frac{2\left(3-\sqrt{7}\right)}{(3)^2-\left(\sqrt{7}\right)^2}$$

$$x = 3-\sqrt{7}$$

$$(x-3)^2 = \left(3-\sqrt{7}-3\right)^2 = \left(-\sqrt{7}\right)^2 = 7$$

15. $$x = 7+4\sqrt{3}$$

$$\frac{1}{x} = 7-4\sqrt{3}$$

$$x+\frac{1}{x} = 14 \qquad ...(1)$$

$$\because \quad xy = 1 \quad \therefore \quad \frac{1}{y} = x$$

$$\frac{1}{x^2}+\frac{1}{y^2} = x^2+\frac{1}{x^2}$$

Taking square of eq. (1), we get

$$x^2+\frac{1}{x^2}+2 = 196$$

$$x^2+\frac{1}{x^2} = 194$$

16. $$x+\sqrt{15} = 4$$

$$x = 4-\sqrt{15}$$

$$\frac{1}{x} = 4+\sqrt{15}$$

$$x+\frac{1}{x} = 8$$

17. We have,

$$x = \sqrt[3]{2+\sqrt{3}}$$

$$x^3 = 2+\sqrt{3}$$

$$\frac{1}{x^3} = 2-\sqrt{3}$$

$$x^3+\frac{1}{x^3} = 4$$

18. $$xy = 1$$

$$x + y = \frac{\sqrt{5}+\sqrt{3}}{\sqrt{5}-\sqrt{3}}+\frac{\sqrt{5}-\sqrt{3}}{\sqrt{5}+\sqrt{3}}$$

$$= \frac{\left(\sqrt{5}+\sqrt{3}\right)^2+\left(\sqrt{5}-\sqrt{3}\right)^2}{\left(\sqrt{5}\right)^2-\left(\sqrt{3}\right)^2}$$

$$= \frac{2(5+3)}{5-3} = 8$$

$$\therefore \quad x + y + xy = 8 + 1 = 9$$

19. $$x^2 + y^2 + xy = (x+y)^2 - xy$$

$$xy = 1$$

$$x + y = \frac{\sqrt{3}-\sqrt{2}}{\sqrt{3}+\sqrt{2}}+\frac{\sqrt{3}+\sqrt{2}}{\sqrt{3}-\sqrt{2}}$$

$$= \frac{\left(\sqrt{3}-\sqrt{2}\right)^2+\left(\sqrt{3}+\sqrt{2}\right)^2}{\left(\sqrt{3}\right)^2-\left(\sqrt{2}\right)^2}$$

$$= \frac{2(3+2)}{3-2} = 10$$

$$(x + y)^2 - xy = (10)^2 - 1$$
$$= 99$$

20. $\sqrt{3-2\sqrt{2}} = \sqrt{\left(\sqrt{2}\right)^2+(1)^2-2\times\sqrt{2}\times 1}$

$a^2+b^2 \quad 2\times a\times b = \sqrt{\left(\sqrt{2}-1\right)^2} = \sqrt{2}-1$

22. $x = \sqrt{6}+\sqrt{5}$

$$\frac{1}{x} = \sqrt{6}-\sqrt{5}$$

$$x+\frac{1}{x} = 2\sqrt{6}$$

Taking square of both sides, we get

$$x^2+\frac{1}{x^2}+2 = 24$$

$$x^2+\frac{1}{x^2} = 22$$

$$\therefore \quad x^2+\frac{1}{x^2}-2 = 22 - 2 = 20$$

23. $\sqrt{13-a\sqrt{10}} = \sqrt{8}+\sqrt{5}$

Taking square of both sides, we get

$$13-a\sqrt{10} = 8+5+2\sqrt{40}$$

$$13-a\sqrt{10} = 13+4\sqrt{40}$$

After comparing both sides, we get

$$a = -4$$

24. $\frac{5-\sqrt{3}}{2+\sqrt{3}} = x+y\sqrt{3}$

After Rationalisation, we get

$$\frac{5-\sqrt{3}}{2+\sqrt{3}}\times\frac{2-\sqrt{3}}{2-\sqrt{3}} = \frac{\left(5-\sqrt{3}\right)\left(2-\sqrt{3}\right)}{(2)^2-\left(\sqrt{3}\right)^2}$$

$$= \frac{10-5\sqrt{3}-2\sqrt{3}+3}{1}$$

$$= 13-7\sqrt{3}$$

After comparing with $x+y\sqrt{3}$, we get

$$x = 13,\ y = -7$$

25. Given exp. $= 18 - [5 - \{6 + 2\,(7 - 3)\}]$
$= 18 - [5 - \{6 + 2 \times 4\}]$
$= 18 - [5 - \{6 + 8\}]$
$= 18 - [5 - 14\}] = 18 - [-9]$
$= 18 + 9 = 27$

26. $9 * 11 = 9^2 + (11)^2 - 9 \times 11$
$= 81 + 121 - 99 = 103.$

27. Given exp. $= \dfrac{\frac{13}{4}-\frac{1}{4}\text{ of }\frac{5}{6}}{\frac{13}{3}\div\frac{1}{5}-\left(\frac{3}{10}+\frac{106}{5}\right)}$

$$= \frac{\frac{13}{4}-\frac{2}{3}}{\frac{13}{3}\times 5-\frac{215}{10}} = \frac{\frac{31}{12}}{\frac{65}{3}-\frac{43}{2}}$$

$$= \left(\frac{31}{12}\times 6\right) = \frac{31}{2} = 15\frac{1}{2}$$

28. $\frac{x}{2y} = \frac{6}{7}$

$$\Rightarrow \quad \frac{x}{y} = \left(2\times\frac{6}{7}\right) = \frac{12}{7}$$

$$\therefore \quad \frac{x-y}{x+y}+\frac{14}{19} = \frac{\frac{x}{y}-1}{\frac{x}{y}+1}+\frac{14}{19}$$

$$= \frac{\frac{12}{7}-1}{\frac{12}{7}+1}+\frac{14}{19} = \frac{(5/7)}{(19/7)}+\frac{14}{19}$$

$$\left(\frac{5}{7}\times\frac{7}{19}\right)+\frac{14}{19} = \frac{5}{19}+\frac{14}{19} = \frac{19}{19} = 1$$

29. Given exp. $= \dfrac{1}{2+\dfrac{1}{2+\dfrac{1}{(3/2)}}} = \dfrac{1}{2+\dfrac{1}{2+\dfrac{2}{3}}}$

$$= \frac{1}{2+\frac{1}{(8/3)}} = \frac{1}{2+\frac{3}{8}} = \frac{1}{(19/8)} = \frac{8}{19}$$

30. $x = 2-\dfrac{1}{1+\dfrac{1}{(13/4)}} = 2-\dfrac{1}{1+\dfrac{4}{13}}$

$$= 2-\frac{1}{(17/13)} = 2-\frac{13}{17} = \frac{21}{17}$$

31. $2+\cfrac{1}{x+\cfrac{1}{y+\cfrac{1}{z}}} = \frac{37}{13} = 2\frac{11}{13} + 2 + \frac{11}{13}$

$\Rightarrow \quad \cfrac{1}{x+\cfrac{1}{y+\cfrac{1}{z}}} = \frac{11}{13}$

$\Rightarrow \quad x+\cfrac{1}{y+\cfrac{1}{z}} = \frac{13}{11}$

$\Rightarrow \quad x+\cfrac{1}{y+\cfrac{1}{z}} = 1+\frac{2}{11}$

$\Rightarrow x = 1,\ y+\frac{1}{z} = \frac{11}{2} = 5\frac{1}{2} = 5+\frac{1}{2}$

$\Rightarrow \quad x = 1,\ y = 5,\ z = 2$

32. Given exp. $= \frac{1}{2}\times\frac{2}{3}\times\frac{3}{4}\times....\times\frac{(n-1)}{n} = \frac{1}{n}$

33. Given exp. $= \frac{3}{2}\times\frac{4}{3}\times\frac{5}{4}\times....\times\frac{121}{120} = \frac{121}{2} = 60.5$

34. Given exp. $= \left(1-\frac{1}{2}\right)+\left(\frac{1}{2}-\frac{1}{3}\right)+\left(\frac{1}{3}-\frac{1}{4}\right)+\left(\frac{1}{4}-\frac{1}{5}\right)+....$

$+\left(\frac{1}{11}-\frac{1}{12}\right) = \left(1-\frac{1}{12}\right) = \frac{11}{12}$

35. Given exp. $= \left(1000-\frac{4}{999}\right)\times 999$

$= 999000 - 4 = 998996$

36. Given exp. $= \left(1000-\frac{6}{7}\right)+\left(1000-\frac{5}{7}\right)+\left(1000-\frac{4}{7}\right)+$

$\left(1000-\frac{3}{7}\right)+\left(1000-\frac{2}{7}\right)+\left(1000-\frac{1}{7}\right)$

$= 6000-\left(\frac{6}{7}+\frac{5}{7}+\frac{4}{7}+\frac{3}{7}+\frac{2}{7}+\frac{1}{7}\right)$

$= 6000-\frac{21}{7} = 6000-3 = 5997$

37. Given exp. $= \frac{4\times 3^3+3^2+3+1}{4\times 3^3}$

$= \frac{108+9+3+1}{108} = \frac{121}{108}$

38. Given exp. $= \left(\frac{a^3+b^3}{a^2+b^2-ab}\right) = (a+b),$

where $a = 785,\ b = 435$

$= (785 + 435) = 1220$

39. $\frac{1}{5}+\left(999+\frac{494}{495}\right)\times 99$

$= \frac{1}{5}+(999\times 99)+\frac{494}{495}\times 99$

$= \frac{1}{5}+\frac{494}{5}+999\times 99$

$= \frac{495}{5}+(1000-1)\times 99$

$= 99 + 99000 - 99 = 99000$

40. $\left(\frac{x+2}{x+1}\right)\left(\frac{x+3}{x+2}\right)\left(\frac{x+4}{x+3}\right)\left(\frac{x+5}{x+4}\right) = \frac{x+5}{x+1}$

□□□□□

5

Direct and Inverse Proportions

Important Facts and Formulae

1. **Direct Proportion:** Two quantities are said to be directly proportional, if on the increase (or decrease) of the one, the other increases (or decreases) to the same extent.

   Ex. 1. Cost is directly proportional to the number of articles.
   (*More Articles, More Cost*)

   Ex. 2. Work done is directly proportional to the number of men working on it.
   (*More Men, More Work*)

2. **Indirect Proportion :** Two quantities are said to be indirectly proportional, if on the increase of the one, the other decreases to the same extent and vice-versa.

   Ex. 1. The time taken by a car in covering a certain distance is inversely proportional to the speed of the car.
   (*More speed, Less is the time taken to cover a distance*)

   Ex. 2. Time taken to finish a work is inversely proportional to the number of persons working at it.
   (*More persons, Less is the time taken to finish a job.*)

Remark : In solving questions by chain rule, we compare every item with the term to be found out.

Formulae:

(*i*) If $W_1 = W_2$

$$M_1 \times D_1 \times T_1 \times E_1 = M_2 \times D_2 \times T_2 \times E_2$$

(*ii*) If $W_1 \neq W_2$

$$\frac{M_1 \times D_1 \times T_1 \times E_1}{W_1} = \frac{M_2 \times D_2 \times T_2 \times E_2}{W_2}$$

where M → Number of Men
D → Number of Days
T → Time
E → Efficiency
W → Work

Multiple Choice Questions

1. If the cost of x metres of wire is d rupees, then what is the cost of y metres of wire at the same rate?

   A. ₹ $\left(\frac{xy}{d}\right)$ B. ₹ (xd)
   C. ₹ (yd) D. ₹ $\left(\frac{yd}{x}\right)$

2. If the price of 6 toys is ₹ 264.37, what will be the approximate price of 5 toys?

   A. ₹ 140 B. ₹ 100
   C. ₹ 200 D. ₹ 220

3. The price of 357 mangoes is ₹ 1517.25. What will be the approximate price of 9 dozens of such mangoes?

   A. ₹ 3000 B. ₹ 3500
   C. ₹ 4000 D. ₹ 2500

4. If a quarter kg of potato costs 60 paise, how many paise will 200 gm cost?

   A. 48 paise B. 54 paise
   C. 56 paise D. 72 paise

5. If 11.25 m of uniform iron rod weighs 42.75 kg, what will be the weight of 6 m of the same rod?

   A. 22.8 kg B. 25.6 kg
   C. 28 kg D. 26.5 kg

6. On a scale of map, 0.6 cm represents 6.6 km. If the distance between the points on the map is 80.5 cm, the actual distance between these points is:

   A. 9 km B. 72.5 km
   C. 190.75 km D. 885.5 km

7. An industrial loom weaves 0.128 metres of cloth every second. Approximately, how many seconds will it take for the loom to weave 25 metres of cloth?

   A. 178 B. 195
   C. 204 D. 488

8. A flagstaff 17.5 m high casts a shadow of length 40.25 m. The height of the building, which casts a shadow of length 28.75 m under similar conditions will be:

   A. 10 m B. 12.5 m
   C. 17.5 m D. 21.25 m

9. A man completes $\frac{5}{8}$ of a job in 10 days. At this rate, how many more days will it take him to finish the job?

A. 5 B. 6

C. 7 D. $7\frac{1}{2}$

10. 36 men can complete a piece of work in 18 days. In how many days will 27 men complete the same work?

A. 12 B. 18

C. 22 D. 24

11. A fort had provision of food for 150 men for 45 days. After 10 days, 25 men left the fort. The number of days for which the remaining food will last, is :

A. $29\frac{1}{5}$ B. $37\frac{1}{4}$

C. 42 D. 54

12. A wheel that has 6 cogs is meshed with a larger wheel of 14 cogs. When the smaller wheel has made 21 revolutions, then the number of revolutions made by the larger wheel is:

A. 4 B. 9

C. 12 D. 49

13. In a camp, there is a meal for 120 men or 200 children. If 150 children have taken the meal, how many men will be catered to with the remaining meal?

A. 20 B. 30

C. 40 D. 50

14. The cost of 16 packets of salt, each weighing 900 grams is ₹ 28. What will be the cost of 27 packets, if each packet weighs 1 kg?

A. ₹ 52.50 B. ₹ 56

C. ₹ 58.50 D. ₹ 64.75

15. 4 mat-weavers can weave 4 mats in 4 days. At the same rate, how many mats would be woven by 8 mat-weavers in 8 days?

A. 4 B. 8

C. 12 D. 16

16. Running at the same constant rate, 6 identical machines can produce a total of 270 bottles per minute. At this rate, how many bottles could 10 such machines produce in 4 minutes?

A. 648 B. 1800

C. 2700 D. 10800

17. In a dairy farm, 40 cows eat 40 bags of husk in 40 days. In how many days one cow will eat one bag of husk?

A. 1 B. $\frac{1}{40}$

C. 40 D. 80

18. 12 men working 8 hours per day complete a piece of work in 10 days. To complete the same work in 8 days, working 15 hours a day, the number of men required, is:

A. 4 B. 5

C. 6 D. 8

19. 10 men, working 6 hours a day can complete a work in 18 days. How many hours a day must 15 men work to complete the same work in 12 days?

A. 6 B. 10

C. 12 D. 15

20. 39 persons can repair a road in 12 days, working 5 hours a day. In how many days will 30 persons, working 6 hours a day, complete the work?

A. 10 B. 13

C. 14 D. 15

21. If 7 spiders make 7 webs in 7 days, then 1 spider will make 1 web in how many days?

A. 1 B. $\frac{7}{2}$

C. 7 D. 49

22. If 18 binders bind 900 books in 10 days, how many binders will be required to bind 660 books is 12 days?

A. 22 B. 14

C. 13 D. 11

23. If 18 pumps can raise 2170 tonnes of water in 10 days, working 7 hours a day, in how many days will 16 pumps raise 1736 tonnes, working 9 hours a day?

A. 9 days B. 8 days

C. 7 days D. 6 days

24. 120 men had provisions for 200 days. After 5 days, 30 men died due to an epidemic. The remaining food will last for:

A. 150 days B. $146\frac{1}{4}$ days

C. 245 days D. 260 days

25. A garrison of 500 men had provisions for 24 days. However, a reinforcement of 300 men arrived. The food will now last for:

A. 18 days B. $17\frac{1}{2}$ days

C. 16 days D. 15 days

26. A garrison had provisions for a certain number of days. After 10 days (1/5)th of the men desert and it is found that the provisions will now last just as long as before. How long was that?

A. 35 days B. 15 days

C. 25 days D. 50 days

27. 20 men complete one-third of a piece of work in 20 days. How many more men should be employed to finish the rest of the work in 25 more days?

A. 10 B. 12
C. 15 D. 20

28. If 17 labourers can dig a ditch 26 metres long in 18 days, working 8 hours a day, how many more labourers should be engaged to dig a similar ditch 39 metres long in 6 days, each labourer working 9 hours a day?

A. 51 B. 68
C. 85 D. 34

29. If x men working x hours per day can do x units of a work in x days, then y men working y yours per day would be able to complete in y days:

A. $\frac{x^2}{y^3}$ units of work B. $\frac{x^3}{y^2}$ units of work

C. $\frac{y^2}{x^3}$ units of work D. $\frac{y^3}{x^2}$ units of work

30. A contractor undertakes to do a piece of work in 40 days. He engages 100 men at the beginning and 100 more after 35 days and completes the work in stipulated time. If he had not engaged the additional men, how many days behind schedule would it be finished?

A. 5 B. 6
C. 3 D. 9

ANSWERS

1	2	3	4	5	6	7	8	9	10
D	D	D	A	A	D	B	B	B	D
11	**12**	**13**	**14**	**15**	**16**	**17**	**18**	**19**	**20**
C	B	B	A	D	B	C	D	A	B
21	**22**	**23**	**24**	**25**	**26**	**27**	**28**	**29**	**30**
C	D	C	D	D	D	B	A	D	A

EXPLANATORY ANSWERS

1. Cost of x metres = ₹ d. Cost of 1 metre

$$= ₹\left(\frac{d}{x}\right)$$

Cost of y meters = $₹\left(\frac{d}{x}\times y\right) = ₹\left(\frac{dy}{x}\right)$.

2. Let the required price be ₹ x. Then,

Less toys, Less cost (Direct proportion)

$\therefore$ 6 : 5 : : 264.37 : x ⇔ $6x = (5 \times 264.37)$

⇔ $x = \frac{(5\times 264.37)}{6}$

⇔ $x = 220.308$

$\therefore$ Approximate price of 5 toys = ₹ 220.

3. Let the required price be ₹ x. Then, *More mangoes, More price (Direct Proportion)*

$\therefore$ 357 : (49 × 12) : : 1517.25 : x

⇔ $357x = (49 \times 12 \times 1517.25)$

⇔ $x = \frac{(49\times 12\times 1517.25)}{357}$ ⇔ $x = 2499$.

Hence, the approximate price is ₹ 2500.

4. Let the required cost be x paise. *Less weight, Less cost (Direct Proportion)*

$\therefore$ 250 : 200 : : 60 : x

⇔ $250 \times x = (200 \times 60)$

$x = \frac{(200\times 60)}{250}$ ⇔ $x = 48$.

5. Let the required weight be x kg. Then, *Less length, Less weight (Direct Proportion)*

$\therefore$ 11.25 : 6 : : 42.75 : x

⇔ $11.25 \times x = 6 \times 42.75$

⇔ $x = \frac{(6\times 42.75)}{11.25}$

⇔ $x = 22.8$.

6. Let the actual distance be x km. Then,

More distance on the map. *More is the actual distance (Direct Proportion)*

$\therefore$ 0.6 : 80.5 : : 6.6 : x

⇔ $0.6x = 80.5 \times 6.6$

⇔ $x = \frac{80.5\times 6.6}{0.6}$

⇔ $x = 885.5$.

7. Let the required time be x seconds. *Then, More metres, more time (Direct Proportion)*

$\therefore$ 0.128 : 25 : : 1 : x

⇔ $0.128 \times x = 25 \times 1$

$\Leftrightarrow \quad x = \dfrac{25}{0.128} = \dfrac{25 \times 1000}{128}$

$\Leftrightarrow \quad x = 195.31$

$\therefore$ Required time = 195 sec (approximately).

8. Let the height of the building be x metres.

Less lengthy shadow, *Less is the height (Direct Proportion)*

$\therefore$ 40.25 : 28.75 : : 17.5 : x

$\Leftrightarrow \quad 40.25 \times x = 28.75 \times 17.5$

$\Leftrightarrow \quad x = \dfrac{(28.75 \times 17.5)}{40.25} \Leftrightarrow x = 12.5$

9. Work done $= \dfrac{5}{8}$. Balance work $= \left(1 - \dfrac{5}{8}\right) = \dfrac{3}{8}$.

Less work, Less days (Direct Proportion)

Let the required number of days be x

Then $\dfrac{5}{8} : \dfrac{3}{8} :: 10 : x \Leftrightarrow \dfrac{5}{8} \times x = \dfrac{3}{8} \times 10$

$\Leftrightarrow \quad x = \left(\dfrac{3}{8} \times 10 \times \dfrac{8}{5}\right) = 6.$

10. Let the required number of days be x.

Then, *Less men, More days (Indirect Proportion)*

$\therefore$ 27 : 36 : : 18 : x

$\Leftrightarrow \quad 27 \times x = 36 \times 18$

$\Leftrightarrow \quad x = \dfrac{36 \times 18}{27} \Leftrightarrow x = 24.$

11. After 10 days : 150 men had food for 35 days.

Suppose 125 men had food for x days. Now, *Less men, more days (Indirect Proportion)*

$\therefore$ 125 : 150 : : 35 : x

$\Leftrightarrow \quad 125 \times x = 150 \times 35$

$\Leftrightarrow \quad x = \dfrac{150 \times 35}{125} \Leftrightarrow x = 42.$

Hence, the remaining food will last for 42 days.

12. Let the required number of revolutions made by larger wheel be x.

Then, *More cogs, Less revolutions (Indirect Proportion)*

$\therefore$ 14 : 6 : : 21 : x

$\Leftrightarrow \quad 14 \times x = 6 \times 21$

$\Leftrightarrow \quad x = \left(\dfrac{6 \times 21}{14}\right) = 9.$

13. There is a meal for 200 children. 150 children have taken the meal. Remaining meal is to be catered to 50 children.

Now, 200 children ≡ 120 men

50 children $\equiv \left(\dfrac{120}{200} \times 50\right)$ men = 30 men.

14. Let the required cost be ₹ x. Then,

More packets, More cost *(Direct Proportion)*

More weight, More cost *(Direct Proportion)*

$\left.\begin{array}{ll}\text{Packets} & 16:27 \\ \text{Weight} & 900:1000\end{array}\right\} :: 28 : x$

$\therefore \quad (16 \times 900 \times x) = (27 \times 1000 \times 28)$

$\Leftrightarrow \quad x = \dfrac{(27 \times 1000 \times 28)}{16 \times 900}$

$= \dfrac{105}{2} = ₹\,52.50$

15. Let the required number of mats be x.

More weavers, More mats *(Direct Proportion)*

More days, More mats *(Direct Proportion)*

$\left.\begin{array}{ll}\text{Weavers} & 4:8 \\ \text{Days} & 4:8\end{array}\right\} :: 4 : x$

$\therefore \quad 4 \times 4 \times x = 8 \times 8 \times 4$

$\Leftrightarrow \quad x = \dfrac{(8 \times 8 \times 4)}{(4 \times 4)} = 16.$

16. Let the required number of bottles be x.

More machines, More bottles *(Direct Proportion)*

More minutes, More bottles *(Direct Proportion)*

$\left.\begin{array}{ll}\text{Machines} & 6 : 10 \\ \text{Time (in Minutes)} & 1 : 4\end{array}\right\} :: 270 : x$

$\therefore \quad 6 \times 1 \times x = 10 \times 4 \times 270$

$\Leftrightarrow \quad x = \dfrac{10 \times 4 \times 270}{6} \Leftrightarrow x = 1800.$

17. Let the required number of days be x.

Less cows, More days *(Indirect Proportion)*

Less bags, Less days *(Direct Proportion)*

$\left.\begin{array}{ll}\text{Cows} & 1:40 \\ \text{Bags} & 40:1\end{array}\right\} :: 40 : x$

$\therefore \quad 1 \times 40 \times x = 40 \times 1 \times 40 \Leftrightarrow x = 40.$

18. Let the requred number of men be x.

Less days, More men *(Indirect Proportion)*

More working hrs per day, Less men *(Indirect Proportion)*

$\left.\begin{array}{ll}\text{Days} & 8:10 \\ \text{Working Hrs} & 15:8\end{array}\right\} :: 12 : x$

$\therefore \quad 8 \times 15 \times x = 10 \times 8 \times 12$

$\Leftrightarrow \quad x = \dfrac{10 \times 8 \times 12}{8 \times 15} \Leftrightarrow x = 8.$

19. Let the required number of hours per day be x.

More men, Less hours per day *(Indirect Proportion)*

Less days, More hours per day *(Indirect Proportion)*

$\left.\begin{array}{ll}\text{Men} & 15:10 \\ \text{Days} & 12:18\end{array}\right\} :: 6 : x$

$\therefore \quad 15 \times 12 \times x = 10 \times 18 \times 6$

$\Leftrightarrow \quad x = \frac{10 \times 18 \times 6}{15 \times 12} \quad \Leftrightarrow x = 6.$

20. Let the required number of days be x.

Less persons, More days (Indirect Proportion)

More working hrs per day, Less days (Indirect Proportion)

$$\left.\begin{array}{ll}\text{Persons} & 30:39\\ \text{Working hrs/day} & 6:5\end{array}\right\}::12:x$$

$\therefore \quad 30 \times 6 \times x = 39 \times 5 \times 12$

$\Leftrightarrow \quad x = \frac{39 \times 5 \times 12}{30 \times 6} \quad \Leftrightarrow x = 13.$

21. Let the required number of days be x. Then,

Less spiders, More days (Indirect Proportion)

Less webs, Less days (Direct Proportion)

$$\therefore \left.\begin{array}{ll}\text{Spiders} & 1:7\\ \text{Webs} & 7:1\end{array}\right\}::7:x$$

$\therefore \quad 1 \times 7 \times x = 7 \times 1 \times 7 \Leftrightarrow x = 7.$

22. Let the required number of binders be x.

Less books, Less binders (Direct Proportion)

More days, Less binders (Indirect Proportion)

$$\left.\begin{array}{ll}\text{Books} & 900:600\\ \text{Days} & 12:10\end{array}\right\}::18:x$$

$\therefore \quad (900 \times 20 \times x) = (600 \times 10 \times 18)$

$\Leftrightarrow \quad x = \frac{600 \times 10 \times 18}{900 \times 12} = 11.$

23. *Less pumps, more days* (Indirect)

Less Water, less days (Direct)

More working hrs., less days (Indirect)

$$\left.\begin{array}{ll}\text{Pumps} & 16:18\\ \text{Water} & 2170:1736\\ \text{Working hours} & 9:7\end{array}\right\}::10:x$$

$\therefore \quad x = \left(\frac{18 \times 1736 \times 7 \times 10}{16 \times 2170 \times 9}\right) = 7 \text{ days}.$

24. The remaining food is sufficient for 120 men for 195 days.

But, now remaining men = 90.

Less men, more days (Indirect)

$\therefore \quad 90 : 120 :: 195 : x$

or $\quad x = \left(\frac{120 \times 195}{90}\right) = 260 \text{ days}.$

25. More men, less number of days (Indirect)

$800 : 500 :: 24 : x$

or $\quad x = \left(\frac{500 \times 24}{800}\right) = 15 \text{ days}.$

26. Let, initially there be x men having provisions for y days.

After 10 days, x men had provisions for $(y - 10)$ days.

These provisions were for $\left(x - \frac{x}{5}\right)$ *i.e.*, $\frac{4x}{5}$ men for y days.

$\therefore \quad x(y - 10) = \frac{4x}{5}y$ or $xy - 50x = 0$

or $\quad x(y - 50) = 0$ or $y - 50 = 0$ *i.e.* $y = 50$ days.

27. Work done $= \frac{1}{3}$, work to be done $= \frac{2}{3}$.

Now, more work, more men (*Direct*)

More days, less men (*Indirect*)

$$\left.\begin{array}{ll}\text{Work} & \frac{1}{3}:\frac{2}{3}\\ \text{Days} & 25:20\end{array}\right\}::20:x$$

$\therefore \quad x = \left(\frac{2}{3} \times 20 \times 20 \times \frac{3}{25}\right) = 32 \text{ men}.$

So, 12 more men should be employed.

28. More length, more labourers (*Direct*)

More daily hours, less labourers (*Indirect*)

Less days, more labourers (*Indirect*)

$$\left.\begin{array}{ll}\text{Length} & 26:39\\ \text{Daily hrs.} & 9:8\\ \text{Days} & 6:18\end{array}\right\}::17:x$$

or $\quad x = \left(\frac{39 \times 8 \times 18 \times 17}{26 \times 9 \times 6}\right) = 68.$

So, more labourers to be engaged = (68 – 17) = 51.

29. More men, more work (*Direct*)

More working hrs., more work (*Direct*)

More days, more work (*Direct*)

$$\left.\begin{array}{ll}\text{Men} & x:y\\ \text{Working hrs.} & x:y\\ \text{Days} & x:y\end{array}\right\}::x:z$$

$\therefore \quad z = \left(\frac{y \times y \times y \times x}{x \times x \times x \times x}\right) = \frac{y^3}{x^2}$ units of work.

30. [(100 × 35) + (200 × 5)] working for 1 day can finish the work.

Thus, 4500 men can finish it in 1 day.

So, 100 men can finish it in $\left(\frac{4500}{100}\right) = 45$ days,

i.e., 5 days behind schedule.

❑❑❑❑❑

6

Comparing Quantities

Percentage

I. Concept of Percentage : By a certain percent, we mean that many hundredths. Thus, x percent means x hundredths, written as $x\%$.

To express $x\%$ as a fraction : We have, $x\% = \frac{x}{100}$.

Thus, $20\% = \frac{20}{100} = \frac{1}{5}$; $48\% = \frac{48}{100} = \frac{12}{25}$, etc.

To express $\frac{a}{b}$ as a percent : We have, $\frac{a}{b} = \left(\frac{a}{b} \times 100\right)\%$.

Thus, $\frac{1}{4} = \left(\frac{1}{4} \times 100\right)\% = 25\%$;

$0.6 = \frac{6}{10} = \frac{3}{5} = \left(\frac{3}{5} \times 100\right)\% = 60\%$.

II. If the price of a commodity increases by R%, then the reduction in consumption so as not to increase the expenditure is

$$\left[\frac{R}{(100+R)} \times 100\right]\%$$

If the price of a commodity decreases by R%, then the increase in consumption so as not to decrease the expenditure is

$$\left[\frac{R}{(100-R)} \times 100\right]\%$$

III. Results on Population : Let the population of a town be P now and suppose it increases at the rate of R% per annum, then :

1. Population after n years $= P\left(1+\frac{R}{100}\right)^n$.

2. Population n years ago $= \frac{P}{\left(1+\frac{R}{100}\right)^n}$.

IV. Results on Depreciation : Let the present value of a machine be P. Suppose it depreciates at the rate of R% per annum. Then :

1. Value of the machine after n years $= P\left(1-\frac{R}{100}\right)^n$.

2. Value of the machine n years ago $= \frac{P}{\left(1-\frac{R}{100}\right)^n}$.

V. If A is R% more than B, then B is less than A by

$$\left[\frac{R}{(100+R)} \times 100\right]\%$$

If A is R% less than B, then B is more than A by

$$\left[\frac{R}{(100-R)} \times 100\right]\%.$$

Multiple Choice Questions

1. If the cost of a book worth ₹ 50 is increased by ₹ 25. What is the rate of increase?

A. 50% B. 60%
C. 70% D. 80%

2. A number decreases by $72\frac{1}{2}\%$ gives 87. What is the number?

A. 90 B. 100
C. 120 D. 140

3. 25% of a number is less than 18% of 650 by 19. What is the number?

A. 193 B. 392
C. 396 D. 492

4. Two candidates fought an election, one get 65% of the votes and won by 300 votes. What is the total number of votes polled?

A. 1000 B. 1200
C. 1400 D. 1500

5. 96% of the population of a town is 23040. What is the total number of population?

A. 21000 B. 24000
C. 26000 D. 24000

6. If 75% of students in a school are boys and the number of girls is 420. What is the number of boys?

A. 1160 B. 1170
C. 1260 D. 1420

7. The population of a village is 5000; and it increase at the rate of 2% every year. What will be the population after 2 years?

A. 5200 B. 5400
C. 5202 D. 6300

8. The population of a town increases by 5% annually. If it is 15435 now, what was the population 2 years ago?

A. 8400 B. 9300
C. 9700 D. 9850

9. The population of a town is 8000. It increases by 10% during first year and by 20% during second year. What will be the population after 2 years.

A. 10,120 B. 10,560
C. 11,420 D. 12,460

10. Kavita went to school for 216 days in a year. If her attendance was 90%, then find out the number of days the school was open in that year?

A. 100 days
B. 140 days
C. 240 days
D. 280 days

11. Dinesh spends 23% of his monthly income on his children's education and donates 2% of it to an organisation. If he spends ₹ 2500 in one month on these two, then find his monthly income?

A. ₹ 9000 B. ₹ 10,000
C. ₹ 11,000 D. ₹ 17,000

12. In a school the number of students increased by 6% of the number at the beginning. If this increases in the number of students is 150, then find the number of students in the school before the increase and after the increase?

A. 2500, 2650 B. 2450, 2730
C. 2400, 2750 D. 2600, 2710

13. There are 1500 trees in a garden, out of which 15% are mango trees, 18% are lemon trees and the remaining are orange trees. What is the number of orange trees?

A. 1005 B. 1102
C. 1010 D. 1002

14. In an examination 70% students were successful. What is the total number of students, if the number of successful students was 210.

A. 90 B. 150
C. 300 D. 350

15. A cricket team won 60% of the matches played in a year. What is the total number of matches played in the year if the team lost 10 matches and no match ended in a draw?

A. 22 B. 25
C. 27 D. 29

Profit & Loss

Cost Price : The price at which an article is purchased, is called its cost price, abbreviated as C.P.

Selling Price : The price at which an article is sold, is called its selling price, abbreviated as S.P.

Profit or Gain : If S.P. is greater than C.P., the seller is said to have a profit or gain.

Loss : If S.P. is less than C.P., the seller is said to have incurred a loss.

Formulae :

1. Gain = (S.P.) – (C.P.)
2. Loss = (C.P.) – (S.P.)
3. Loss or gain is always reckoned on C.P.
4. Gain % = $\left(\frac{\text{Gain} \times 100}{\text{C.P.}}\right)$
5. Loss % = $\left(\frac{\text{Loss} \times 100}{\text{C.P.}}\right)$
6. S.P. = $\frac{(100 + \text{Gain\%})}{100} \times \text{C.P.}$
7. S.P. = $\frac{(100 - \text{Loss\%})}{100} \times \text{C.P.}$
8. C.P. = $\frac{100}{(100 + \text{Gain\%})} \times \text{S.P.}$
9. C.P. = $\frac{100}{(100 - \text{Loss\%})} \times \text{S.P.}$
10. If an article is sold at a gain of say, 35%, then S.P. = 135% of C.P.

11. If an article is sold at a loss of say, 35%, then S.P. = 65% of C.P.

12. When a person sells two similar items, one at a gain of say, $x\%$, and the other at a loss of $x\%$, then the seller always incurs a loss given by:

$$\text{Loss } \% = \left(\frac{\text{Common Loss and Gain\%}}{10}\right)^2 = \left(\frac{x}{10}\right)^2.$$

13. If a trader professes to sell his goods at cost price, but uses false weights, then

$$\text{Gain\%} = \left[\frac{\text{Error}}{(\text{True Value}) - (\text{Error})} \times 100\right]\%.$$

Multiple Choice Questions

1. A former sold two bullocks for ₹ 18000 each. On one bullock he gained 20% and on the other he lost 20%. What is his total loss or gain?

A. ₹ 1500 B. ₹ 1600
C. ₹ 1750 D. ₹ 1520

2. By selling 144 hens, Mukesh lost the S.P. of 6 hens. What is the loss per cent?

A. 2% B. 4%
C. 6% D. 8%

3. A shopkeeper purchased 100 blankets at ₹ 2000 each. He found that 10 blankets were defective and he sold these at ₹ 1200 each. At what rate should he sell the remaining blankets so as to gain 14% on the whole?

A. ₹ 2400 B. ₹ 2600
C. ₹ 2800 D. ₹ 3200

Directions (4 and 5) : *A goldsmith bought 100g of gold for ₹ 54000 from a wholesaler. He then sold it at a gain of 10%.*

4. S.P. of 10g of gold for the goldsmith.

A. ₹ 5820 B. ₹ 5460
C. ₹ 5370 D. ₹ 5940

5. C.P. of 10g of gold for the wholesaler, if his profit is 8%.

A. ₹ 2000 B. ₹ 4000
C. ₹ 5000 D. ₹ 5500

Directions (6 to 8) : *William sells a quintal of wheat for ₹ 924 and earns a profit of 12%. By selling a quintal of rice for the same amount he loses 12%. Find,*

6. C.P. of wheat :

A. ₹ 825 B. ₹ 935
C. ₹ 945 D. ₹ 1025

7. C.P. of rice :

A. ₹ 920 B. ₹ 980
C. ₹ 1050 D. ₹ 1120

8. Gain or loss per cent on the whole transaction.

A. ₹ 23 B. ₹ 25
C. ₹ 27 D. ₹ 29

9. A tricycle is sold at a gain of 16%. Had it been sold for ₹ 100 more, the gain would have been 20%. What is the C.P. of the tricycle?

A. ₹ 2500 B. ₹ 2210
C. ₹ 2350 D. ₹ 2400

10. Manish bought 20 dining tables for ₹ 1,20,000 and sold these at a profit equal to the selling price of 4 dining tables. What is the S.P. of one dining table?

A. ₹ 5500 B. ₹ 7500
C. ₹ 8500 D. ₹ 9000

11. Yogita sold a plot of land at 20% gain to Dimpi. Dimpi sold it to Anjali at 10% profit. If Anjali had to pay ₹ 3,30,000 for the plot. What is the C.P. of the plot for Yogita?

A. ₹ 2,50,000 B. ₹ 2,45,000
C. ₹ 2,70,000 D. ₹ 2,90,500

12. A man buys a plot of agricultural land for ₹ 3,00,000. He sells one-third at a loss of 20% and two-fifths at a gain of 25%. At what price must he sell the remaining land so as to make an overall profit of 10%?

A. ₹ 75,000 B. ₹ 95,000
C. ₹ 1,00,000 D. ₹ 1,50,000

13. A dishonest dealer professes to sell his goods at cost price, but he uses a weight of 960 grams for 1 kg. What is the gain per cent?

A. $4\frac{1}{6}\%$ B. $5\frac{1}{7}\%$
C. $7\frac{1}{6}\%$ D. $9\frac{1}{3}\%$

14. A man purchase two fans for ₹ 2160. By selling one fan at a profit of 15% and the other at a loss of 9% he neither gains nor losses in the whole transaction. What is the cost price of fan which is sold at 9% less?

A. ₹ 1150 B. ₹ 1200
C. ₹ 1350 D. ₹ 1400

15. By reducing the selling price of an article by ₹ 50, a gain of 5% turns into a loss of 5%. What is the original selling price of the article?

A. ₹ 425 B. ₹ 525
C. ₹ 650 D. ₹ 720

16. If the selling price of 10 pens is equal to cost price of 14 pens. What is the gain per cent?
A. 40% B. 50%
C. 60% D. 70%

17. If selling price is doubled, the profit triples. What is the profit per cent?
A. $66\frac{2}{3}$ B. 100
C. $105\frac{1}{3}$ D. 120

18. If the cost price of 12 pens is equal to the selling price of 8 pens, the gain per cent is:
A. 25% B. $33\frac{1}{3}$%
C. 50% D. $66\frac{2}{3}$%

19. The cost price of 20 articles is the same as the selling price of x articles. If the profit is 25%, then the value of x is:
A. 15 B. 16
C. 18 D. 25

20. A man bought apples at the rate of 8 for ₹ 34 and sold them at the rate of 12 for ₹ 57. How many apples should be sold to earn a net profit of ₹ 45?
A. 90 B. 100
C. 135 D. 150

21. Some articles were bought at 6 for ₹ 5 and sold at 5 for ₹ 6. Gain per cent is:
A. 30% B. $33\frac{1}{3}$%
C. 35% D. 44%

22. A trader mixes 26 kg of rice at ₹ 20 per kg with 30 kg of rice of other variety at ₹ 36 per kg and sells the mixture at ₹ 30 per kg. His profit per cent is:
A. No profit, no loss B. 5%
C. 8% D. 10%

23. A dishonest dealer uses a scale of 90 cm instead of a metre scale and claims to sell at cost price. His profit is:
A. 9% B. 10%
C. 12% D. None of these

24. A sells a bicycle to B at a profit of 20%. B sells it to C at a profit of 25%. If C pays ₹ 225 for it, the cost price of the bicycle for A is:
A. ₹ 110 B. ₹ 120
C. ₹ 125 D. ₹ 150

25. A shopkeeper sells two watches for ₹ 308 each. On one he gets 12% profit and on the other 12% loss. His profit or loss in the entire transaction was:
A. Neither profit, nor loss B. $1\frac{11}{25}$% loss
C. $1\frac{11}{25}$% profit D. $3\frac{2}{25}$% loss

Discount

Market Price (M.P.)—The attached price is called the market price (M.P.) or list price (L.P.) of the article and the reduction allowed in the price is called the **discount**.

(*i*) Discount = M.P. – S.P.

(*ii*) $\text{Discount \%} = \dfrac{\text{Discount} \times 100}{\text{M.P.}}$

(*iii*) $\text{S.P.} = \text{M.P.} - \dfrac{\text{Discount\%} \times \text{M.P.}}{100}$

(*iv*) $\text{S.P.} = \text{M.P.} \times \left(1 - \dfrac{\text{Discount\%}}{100}\right)$

(*v*) $\text{M.P.} = \dfrac{100 \times \text{S.P.}}{100 - \text{Discount\%}}$

$\text{S.P.} = \text{M.P.}\left(\dfrac{100 - \text{Discount\%}}{100}\right)$

$\text{M.P.} - \text{S.P.} = \dfrac{\text{M.P.} \times \text{Discount\%}}{100}$

$\text{Discount\%} = \left(\dfrac{\text{M.P.} - \text{S.P.}}{\text{M.P.}}\right) \times 100$

Multiple Choice Questions

1. A cloth merchant offers 15% festival discount on every saree sold. If a certain saree is sold for ₹ 680, what is its marked price?
A. ₹ 800 B. ₹ 900
C. ₹ 1250 D. ₹ 1300

2. A shopkeeper offers 10% discount on an article and still makes a profit of 20%. What is the C.P. of the article if the marked price is ₹ 350?
A. ₹ 259.20 B. ₹ 262.50
C. ₹ 265.75 D. ₹ 272.5

3. A manufactures marks his goods in such a way that after allowing 20% discount, he makes a profit of 18%. What is the marked price of an item which costs him ₹ 200?

A. ₹ 295 B. ₹ 310
C. ₹ 315 D. ₹ 375

4. The marked price of a brand of coffee is ₹ 35 for 100g. But the shopkeeper gives a cup costing ₹ 7.50 free with it. Even then he gets a gain of 10%. What is the cost price of 100g of coffee?

A. ₹ 15 B. ₹ 25
C. ₹ 35 D. ₹ 65

5. A car is marked at ₹ 2,25,000. The manufacturer gives a discount of 10%. The dealer also gives a discount of 5%. What is the S.P. of the car?

A. ₹ 1,72,369 B. ₹ 1,64,370
C. ₹ 1,52,393 D. ₹ 1,92,375

6. A cycle merchant allows 25% commission on his advertised price and still makes a profit of 20%. If he gains ₹ 60 over the sale of one cycle. What is his advertised price?

A. ₹ 290 B. ₹ 310
C. ₹ 480 D. ₹ 520

7. The marked price of a shirt was ₹ 165 and it was at a discount of 12%. What the selling price of the shirt?

A. ₹ 145.20 B. ₹ 155.30
C. ₹ 165.20 D. ₹ 175.25

8. A trader marks his goods 40% above the cost price and gives a discount of 20% on the marked price. What is his gain per cent?

A. 8% B. 9%
C. 12% D. 15%

9. How much per cent more than the C.P. should a manufacturer mark his goods so that after allowing a discount of 20% on the marked price, he gains 10%.

A. 34.5% B. 27.5%
C. 37.5% D. 38.5%

10. A shopkeeper allows a discount of 10% to his customers and still gains 20%. What is the marked price of an article which costs ₹ 450 to the shopkeeper?

A. ₹ 600 B. ₹ 700
C. ₹ 800 D. ₹ 900

11. A dealer of scientific instruments allows 20% discount on the marked price of the instruments and still makes a profit of 25%. If his gain over the sale of an instrument is ₹ 150. What is the marked price of the instrument?

A. ₹ 917.25 B. ₹ 937.50
C. ₹ 945.75 D. ₹ 947.25

12. Jyoti and Meena run a ready-made garment shop. They mark the garments at such a price that even after allowing a discount of 12.5%, they make a profit of 10%. What is the marked price of a suit which costs them ₹ 1470?

A. ₹ 1820 B. ₹ 1848
C. ₹ 1868 D. ₹ 1948

Simple Interest

Important Facts and Formulae

1. **Principal :** The money borrowed or lent out for a certain period is called the **principal** or the sum.
2. **Interest :** Extra money paid for using other's money is called **interest**.
3. **Simple Interest (S.I.) :** If the interest on a sum borrowed for a certain period is reckoned uniformly, then it is called **simple interest**.

Let Principal = P, Rate = R% per annum (p.a.) and Time = T years. Then,

(i) $\text{S.I.} = \left(\frac{P \times R \times T}{100}\right)$

(ii) $P = \left(\frac{100 \times \text{S.I.}}{R \times T}\right)$; $R = \left(\frac{100 \times \text{S.I.}}{P \times T}\right)$

and $T = \left(\frac{100 \times \text{S.I.}}{P \times R}\right)$

Multiple Choice Questions

1. What is the interest on ₹ 2000 for 3 years at 8% per annum?

A. 480 B. 490
C. 510 D. 420

2. What is the simple interest on ₹ 4000 for 3 years at the rate of 10% p.a.?

A. ₹ 1200 B. ₹ 1300
C. ₹ 2200 D. ₹ 1424

3. What is the simple interest on ₹ 9280 at the rate of $4\frac{1}{2}$% per annum for 5 months?

A. ₹ 374 B. ₹ 174
C. ₹ 184 D. ₹ 192

4. Pawan borrowed ₹ 3000 from a friend at simple interest. After 5 years he paid ₹ 4500; and cleared his debt. What is the rate of interest?
A. 12% B. 15%
C. 10% D. 20%

5. In what time will a sum amount to 5 times of itself at the rate of $7\frac{1}{2}$% per annum?
A. 2 years B. $5\frac{1}{2}$ years
C. $13\frac{1}{3}$ years D. $53\frac{1}{3}$ years

6. A sum was put at simple interest at a certain rate for 2 years. Had it been put at 3% higher rate, it would have fetched ₹ 300 more. What is the sum?
A. ₹ 6000 B. ₹ 5000
C. ₹ 5500 D. ₹ 6500

7. What simple interest will discharge a debt of ₹ 2210 due in 4 years at 7% per annum?
A. ₹ 628.2 B. ₹ 638.4
C. ₹ 618.8 D. ₹ 698.2

8. ₹ 800 amount to ₹ 920 in 3 years at simple interest. If the interest rate is increased by 3%. What is the amount?
A. ₹ 892 B. ₹ 992
C. ₹ 1002 D. ₹ 782

9. Kamal lent ₹ 600 to Meena for 2 years and ₹ 150 to Anil for 4 years and received altogether from both ₹ 90 as simple interest. What is the rate of interest?
A. 6% p.a. B. 5% p.a.
C. $8\frac{1}{2}$% p.a. D. 10% p.a.

10. The difference between the interest received from two different banks on ₹ 500 for 2 years is ₹ 2.50. What is the difference between their rates?
A. 0.35% B. 0.55%
C. 0.25% D. 0.65%

11. A sum was put at simple interest at a certain rate for 2 years. Had it been put at 1% higher rate, it would have fetched ₹ 24 more. What is the sum?
A. ₹ 1200 B. ₹ 1400
C. ₹ 1500 D. ₹ 1600

12. In what time will the simple interest on ₹ 780 at 5% be equal to the simple interest on ₹ 600 at $6\frac{1}{2}$% ?
A. 2 years B. 5 years
C. 8 years D. All of these

13. In what time will a sum of money double itself at $6\frac{1}{4}$% p.a. simple interest?
A. 12 years B. 16 years
C. 18 years D. 22 years

14. A sum of money doubles itself in 10 years. In how many years would it treble itself?
A. 10 years B. 15 years
C. 20 years D. 25 years

15. The simple interest on a sum of money at 8% per annum for 6 years is half the sum. What is the sum?
A. ₹ 1000 B. ₹ 1200
C. ₹ 1500 D. Data in adequate

Compound Interest

Compound Interest : Sometimes it so happens that the borrower and the lender agree to fix up a certain unit of time, say yearly or half-yearly or quarterly to settle the previous account.

In such cases, the amount after first unit of time becomes the principal for the second unit, the amount after second unit becomes the principal for the third unit and so on.

After a specified period, the difference between the amount and the money borrowed is called the Compound Interest (*abbreviated* as C.I.) for that period.

Important Facts and Formulae

Let Principal = P, Rate = R% per annum, Time = n years.

I. When interest is compound Annually:

$$\text{Amount} = P\left(1+\frac{R}{100}\right)^n$$

II. When interest is compounded Half-yearly :

$$\text{Amount} = P\left[1+\frac{(R/2)}{100}\right]^{2n}$$

III. When interest is compounded Quarterly :

$$\text{Amount} = P\left[1+\frac{(R/4)}{100}\right]^{4n}$$

IV. When interest is compounded Annually but time is in fraction, say $3\frac{2}{5}$ years.

$$\text{Amount} = P\left(1+\frac{R}{100}\right)^3 \times \left(1+\frac{\frac{2}{5}R}{100}\right)$$

V. When Rates are different for different years, say $R_1\%$, $R_2\%$, $R_3\%$ for 1st, 2nd, 3rd year respectively.

Then, Amount = $P\left(1+\frac{R_1}{100}\right)\left(1+\frac{R_2}{100}\right)\left(1+\frac{R_3}{100}\right)$.

VI. Present worth of Rs. x due n years hence is given by :

Present Worth = $\frac{x}{\left(1+\frac{R}{100}\right)^n}$.

Multiple Choice Questions

1. What is the amount of ₹ 6000 lent at 5% per annum for 2 years if the interest is compounded annually?
A. ₹ 6615 B. ₹ 6720
C. ₹ 6625 D. ₹ 6612

2. What is the compound interest on ₹ 25600 for 2 years at 6.25% per annum?
A. ₹ 3300 B. ₹ 3500
C. ₹ 4000 D. ₹ 3350

3. What is the amount and compound interest on ₹ 16000 for 3 years, if the rate of interest is 2% per annum?
A. ₹ 989.2 B. ₹ 987.43
C. ₹ 979.33 D. ₹ 991.24

4. Simple interest on a sum of money for 3 years at $6\frac{1}{4}\%$ per annum is ₹ 2400. What will be the compound interest on that sum at the same rate for the same period?
A. ₹ 2430.43 B. ₹ 2553.13
C. ₹ 2522.17 D. ₹ 2532.19

5. The difference between the compound interest and the simple interest on a certain sum for 2 years at 10% per annum is ₹ 300. What is the sum?
A. ₹ 20,000 B. ₹ 25,000
C. ₹ 30,000 D. ₹ 35,000

6. A certain sum amounts to ₹ 5832 in 2 years at 8% compound interest. What is the sum?
A. ₹ 4000 B. ₹ 5000
C. ₹ 7000 D. ₹ 9000

7. At what rate per cent will a sum of ₹ 1000 amount to ₹ 1102.50 in 2 years at compound interest?
A. 7% p.a. B. 8% p.a.
C. 5% p.a. D. 10% p.a.

8. The difference between the compound interest and simple interest on a certain sum for 2 years at 7.5% per annum is ₹ 360. What is the sum?
A. ₹ 54,000 B. ₹ 64,000
C. ₹ 63,500 D. ₹ 62,500

9. The difference in simple interest and compound interest on a certain sum of money at $6\frac{2}{3}\%$ per annum for 3 years is ₹ 46. What is the sum?
A. ₹ 3375 B. ₹ 3250
C. ₹ 3340 D. ₹ 3450

10. A sum of money deposited at 2% per annum compounded annually becomes ₹ 10404 at the end of 2 years. What is the sum deposited?
A. ₹ 11,000 B. ₹ 10,000
C. ₹ 12,500 D. ₹ 13,600

11. A sum of money amounts to ₹ 4,53,690 in 2 years at 6.5% p.a. compounded annually. What is the sum?
A. ₹ 3,50,000 B. ₹ 4,00,000
C. ₹ 2,25,000 D. ₹ 5,50,000

12. What sum of money will amount to ₹ 45,582.25 at $6\frac{3}{4}\%$ p.a. in two years interest being compounded annually?
A. ₹ 30,000 B. ₹ 35,000
C. ₹ 40,000 D. ₹ 42,000

13. At what rate per cent per annum will a sum of ₹ 4000 yield compound interest of ₹ 410 in 2 years?
A. 6% p.a. B. 5% p.a.
C. 10% p.a. D. 12% p.a.

14. In how much time will a sum of ₹ 1600 amount to ₹ 1852.20 at 5% per annum compound interest?
A. 2 years B. 3 years
C. 4 years D. 5 years

15. Reena invested a sum of ₹ 12,000 at 5% per annum compound interest she received an amount of ₹ 13,230 after n years. What is the value of n?
A. 2 years B. 3 years
C. 5 years D. 9 years

16. What is the compound interest on ₹ 12000 for 3 years at 10% per annum compound annually?
A. ₹ 3732 B. ₹ 3827
C. ₹ 3972 D. ₹ 4000

17. Abhay lent ₹ 8000 to his friend for 3 years at the rate of 5% per annum compound interest. What amount does Abhay get after 3 years?
A. ₹ 9241 B. ₹ 9261
C. ₹ 9132 D. ₹ 9232

18. Vijay obtains a loan of ₹ 64,000 against his fixed deposits. If the rate of interest be 2.5 paise per rupee per annum, calculate the compound interest payable after 3 years.
A. ₹ 68,421 B. ₹ 67,431
C. ₹ 68,921 D. ₹ 66,921

19. What is the compound interest at the rate of 10% per annum for four years on the principal which in four years at the rate of 4% per annum gives ₹ 1600 as simple interest?
A. ₹ 1557.78
B. ₹ 1697.79
C. ₹ 1798.22
D. ₹ 1696.23

20. What is the compound interest of ₹ 12,000 for 2 years at 20% per annum when compounded half-yearly?
A. 5569.2
B. 5562.3
C. 5571.4
D. 5671.2

ANSWERS

Percentage

1	2	3	4	5	6	7	8	9	10
A	C	B	A	B	C	C	A	B	C
11	**12**	**13**	**14**	**15**					
B	A	A	C	B					

Profit & Loss

1	2	3	4	5	6	7	8	9	10
A	B	A	D	C	A	C	C	A	B
11	**12**	**13**	**14**	**15**	**16**	**17**	**18**	**19**	**20**
A	C	A	C	B	A	B	C	B	A
21	**22**	**23**	**24**	**25**					
D	B	D	D	B					

Discount

1	2	3	4	5	6	7	8	9	10
A	B	A	B	D	C	A	C	C	A
11	**12**								
B	B								

Simple Interest

1	2	3	4	5	6	7	8	9	10
A	A	B	C	D	B	C	B	B	C
11	**12**	**13**	**14**	**15**					
A	D	B	C	D					

Compound Interest

1	2	3	4	5	6	7	8	9	10
A	A	C	B	C	B	C	B	A	B
11	**12**	**13**	**14**	**15**	**16**	**17**	**18**	**19**	**20**
B	C	B	B	A	C	B	C	B	A

EXPLANATORY ANSWERS

Percentage

1. Cost price = ₹ 50
Increase = ₹ 25

Rate of increase = $\frac{25 \times 100}{50} = 50\%$

2. Let Number = x

$72\frac{1}{2}\%$ of $x = 87$

$\frac{145}{2 \times 100} \times x = 87$

$x = \frac{87 \times 2 \times 100}{145} = 120$

3. Let number = x
18% of 650 – $x \times 25\%$ = 19

$\frac{18}{100} \times 650 - 19 = \frac{25x}{100}$

$117 - 19 = \frac{x}{4}$

$98 \times 4 = x$

$x = 392$

4. Let total number of votes = x
65% of x – 35% of x = 300
30% x = 300

$\frac{30}{100} \times x = 300 \Rightarrow x = \frac{300 \times 100}{30}$

$x = 1000$

5. Let total population = x
96% of x = 23040

$\frac{96}{100} \times x = 23040$

$x = \frac{23040 \times 100}{96}$

$= 960 \times 25$
$= 24000$

6. Per cent of girls = 25%
Let total number of students = x
25% of x = 420

$\frac{25}{100} \times x = 420$

$x = 420 \times 4 = 1680$

Total number of students = 1680.
No. of boys = 75% of 1680

$= \frac{75}{100} \times 1680$

$= 1260$

7. Population = 5000

Increase in 1st year = $5000 \times \frac{2}{100} = 100$

Population after 1 year = 5000 + 100 = 5100
Increase in population in 2nd year

$= 5100 \times \frac{2}{100}$

$= 102$

Population of 2 years
= 5100 + 102
= 5202

8. Population = 15435
Time = 2 yrs.
Rate = 5% p.a.
Population after 2 years

$$= \frac{P}{\left(1+\frac{r}{100}\right)^n} = \frac{15435}{\left(1+\frac{5}{100}\right)^2}$$

$$= \frac{15435}{\left(\frac{21}{20}\right)^2} = \frac{15435 \times 20 \times 20}{21 \times 21}$$

= 21 × 400
= 8400

9. P = 8000
r_1 = 10%
r_2 = 20%
Time = 2 years
Population after two years

$$= P\left(1+\frac{r_1}{100}\right)\left(1+\frac{r_2}{100}\right)$$

$$= 8000\left(1+\frac{10}{100}\right)\left(1+\frac{20}{100}\right)$$

$$= 8000 \times \frac{11}{10} \times \frac{6}{5}$$

= 10560

10. Let total no. of days = x
90% of x = 216

$\frac{90}{100} x = 216$

$x = \frac{216 \times 10}{9} = 240$ days

11. Let total income = ₹ x
25% of x = 2500

$\frac{25}{100} \times x = 2500$

$x = \frac{2500 \times 100}{25} =$ ₹ 10000

12. Let number of student in beginning = x

6% of x = 150

$$\frac{6}{100}\times x = 150 \Rightarrow x = \frac{150\times100}{6}$$

x = 2500

Increased number of student

= 2500 + 150 = 2650

13. Total trees = 1500

Nos. of Mangoes = 1500 × 15%

$$= 1500\times\frac{15}{100} = 225.$$

Nos. of Lemon trees = 1500 × 18%

$$= 1500\times\frac{18}{100}$$

= 15 × 18 = 270.

Nos. of Orange trees = 1500 – (225 + 270)

= 1500 – 495 = 1005

14. Let total nos. of students = x

70% of x = 210

$$\frac{70}{100}\times x = 210 \Rightarrow x = \frac{210\times100}{70}$$

x = 300

15. Let total number of matches = x

40% of x = 10

$$\frac{40}{100}\times x = 10$$

$$x = \frac{10\times5}{2}$$

x = 25

Total number of matches = 25

Profit & Loss

1. S.P. = 18000

Profit = 20%

Let C.P. = x

$x + x \times 20\%$ = 18000

$$\frac{120}{100}x = 18000$$

$$x = \frac{18000\times5}{6} = 15000$$

C.P. of 1st bullock = 15000

Again,

S.P. = 18000

Loss = 20%

Let C.P. = x

$$x - x\times\frac{20}{100} = 18000$$

$$\frac{80}{100}x = 18000$$

$$x = \frac{18000\times5}{4}$$

x = 22500

Total C.P. = 22500 + 15000

= 37500

Total S.P. = 18000 + 18000 = 36000

Loss = 37500 – 36000

= ₹ 1500

2. Let S.P. of 1 hen = ₹ 1

S.P. of 144 hens = ₹ 144

Loss = S.P. of 6 hens = 6 × 1 = ₹ 6

C.P. of 144 hens = 144 + 6 = ₹ 150

$$\text{Loss\%} = \frac{\text{loss}\times100}{\text{C.P}} = \frac{6\times100}{150}$$

= 4%

3. C.P. of 100 blankets = 100 × 2000

= ₹ 200000

Profit = 14%

$$\text{S.P.} = 200000 + 200000\times\frac{14}{100}$$

= 228000

S.P. of 10 blankets = 1200 × 10

= 12000

Remaining S.P. = 228000 – 12000

S.P. of 90 blankets = 216000

$$\text{S.P. of 1 blanket} = \frac{216000}{90}$$

= ₹ 2400

Direction (4 and 5): C.P. of 100g. gold = ₹ 54000

Profit = 10%

$$\text{S.P. of 100g. gold} = 54000 + 54000\times\frac{10}{100}$$

= 54000 + 5400

= 59400

4. $$\text{S.P. of 100g. gold} = \frac{59400}{100}\times10$$

= ₹ 5940

5. $$\text{S.P. of wholesaler (10 gm.)} = \frac{54000}{100}\times10$$

= 5400.

C.P. of wholesaler for 10g. = x

$x + x \times 8\%$ = 5400

$$\frac{108}{100}\times x = 5400$$

$$x = \frac{5400\times100}{108}$$

= ₹ 5000

Directions (6 to 8) : Let C.P. of Wheat = ₹ x

6. $x + x \times 12\% = 924$

$\frac{112}{100}x = 924$

$x = \frac{924 \times 100}{112}$

$x = ₹\ 825$

7. Let C.P. of Rice = ₹ x

$x - x \times \frac{12}{100} = 924$

$\frac{88}{100}x = 924$

$x = \frac{924 \times 100}{88} = ₹\ 1050$

8. Total S.P. = 924 + 924 = 1848

Total C.P. = 825 + 1050

= 1875

Profit = 1875 – 1848

= ₹ 27

9. Let C.P. of tricycle = ₹ x

116% of $x + 100 = 120\%\ x$

$\frac{116}{100} \times x + 100 = \frac{120}{100}x$

$\frac{6}{5}x - \frac{29}{25}x = 100$

$\frac{30x - 29x}{25} = 100 \Rightarrow x = 100 \times 25$

$\Rightarrow \quad x = ₹\ 2500$

10. C.P. of 20 dining tables = ₹ 120000

C.P. of 1 dining table $= \frac{120000}{20}$

= ₹ 6000.

Let his profit = ₹ x per dining table

S.P. of 1 dining table = 6000 + x

Total profit = 4 (6000 + x)

= 24000 + 4x

S.P. price of 20 dining table

= 120000 + 24000 + 4x

= 144000 + 4x.

S.P. price of 1 dining table

$\frac{6000 + x}{1} = \frac{144000 + 4x}{20}$

$120000 + 20x = 144000 + 4x$

$16x = 144000 - 120000$

$16x = 24000$

$x = \frac{24000}{16}$

Profit = 1500

S.P. of 1 dining table

= 6000 + 1500 = ₹ 7500

11. Let C.P. of Dimpi = ₹ x

$x + x \times 10\% = 330000$

$\frac{110}{100}x = 330000$

$x = \frac{330000}{11} \times 10 = 300000$

Let C.P. of Yogita = ₹ y

$y + y \times 20\% = 300000$

$\frac{120}{100}y = 300000$

$y = \frac{300000}{12} \times 10$

$y = ₹\ 250000$

12. C.P. of entire land = ₹ 300000

Profit = 10%

S.P. $= 300000 + 300000 \times \frac{10}{100}$

= ₹ 330,000

C.P. of $\frac{1}{3}$rd land $= \frac{1}{3} \times 300000$

= 100000

Loss = 20%

S.P. $= 100000 - 100000 \times \frac{20}{100}$

= 80000

C.P. of 2/5rd land $= \frac{2}{5} \times 300000$

= ₹ 120000

Gain = 25%

S.P. $= 120000 + 120000 \times \frac{25}{100}$

= 150000

Remaining S.P. = 330000 – (150000 + 80000)

= 330000 – 230000

= ₹ 100000

13. Gain = 1000g – 960g = 40g.

Gain % $= \frac{40 \times 100}{960} = \frac{25}{6}$

$= 4\frac{1}{6}\%$

14. Let C.P. of 1st Fan = ₹ x

C.P. of other = $(2160 - x)$

$115\%\ x + 91\%\ (2160 - x) = 2160$

$\frac{115}{100} \times x + \frac{91}{100}(2160 - x) = 2160$

$\frac{23}{20}x - \frac{91}{100}x = 2160 - 2160 \times \frac{91}{100}$

$\frac{115x - 91x}{100} = 2160\left(\frac{100 - 91}{100}\right)$

$$\frac{24x}{100} = \frac{2160 \times 9}{100}$$

$$x = \frac{2160 \times 9}{24} = 810$$

C.P. of 1st fan = ₹ 810

C.P. of 2nd fan = 2160 – 810 = ₹ 1350

15. Let C.P. = ₹ x

$$105\% \text{ of } x - 50 = 95\%\ x$$

$$105\% \text{ of } x - 95\% x = 50$$

$$10\% \text{ of } x = 50$$

$$x = \frac{50 \times 100}{10} = ₹\ 500$$

$$\text{Original S.P.} = 105\%\ x = \frac{105}{100} \times 500 = ₹\ 525$$

16. Gain = 14 – 10 = 4

$$\text{Gain \%} = \frac{4 \times 100}{10} = 40\%$$

17. Let C.P. be ₹ x and S.P. be ₹ y.

Then, $3(y - x) = (2y - x) \Rightarrow y = 2x$

Profit = ₹ $(y - x)$ = ₹ $(2x - x)$ = ₹ x.

$$\therefore \quad \text{Profit\%} = \left(\frac{x}{y} \times 100\right)\% = 100\%$$

18. Let C.P. of each pen be ₹ 1. Then, C.P. of 8 pens = ₹ 8; S.P. of 8 pens = ₹ 12.

$$\therefore \quad \text{Gain\%} = \left(\frac{4}{8} \times 100\right)\% = 50\%.$$

19. Let C.P. of each article be ₹ 1. C.P. of x articles = ₹ x, S.P. of x articles = ₹ 20. Profits = ₹ = $(20 - x)$.

$$\therefore \quad \frac{20 - x}{x} \times 100 = 25 \Rightarrow 2000 - 100x = 25x$$

$$\Rightarrow \quad 125x = 2000 \Rightarrow x = 16.$$

20. C.P. of 1 apple = ₹ $\left(\frac{34}{8}\right)$ = ₹ 4.25. S.P. of 1 apple = ₹ $\left(\frac{57}{12}\right)$ = ₹ 4.75. Profit on each apple = ₹ 0.50

$$\therefore \text{ Number of apples required} = \left(\frac{45}{0.50}\right) = 90.$$

21. Suppose, number of articles bought = L.C.M. of 6 and 5 = 30.

C.P. of 30 articles = ₹ $\left(\frac{5}{6} \times 30\right)$ = ₹ 25. S.P. of 30 articles = ₹ $\left(\frac{6}{5} \times 30\right)$ = ₹ 36.

$$\therefore \text{ Gain \%} = \left(\frac{11}{25} \times 100\right)\% = 44\%.$$

22. C.P. of 56 kg rice = ₹ (26 × 20 + 30 × 36) = ₹ (520 + 1080) = ₹ 1600.

S.P. of 56 kg rice = ₹ (56 × 30) = ₹ 1680.

$$\therefore \text{ Gain} = \left(\frac{80}{1600} \times 100\right)\% = 5\%.$$

23. $\text{Gain \%} = \left(\frac{10}{90} \times 100\right)\% = 11\frac{1}{9}\%$

24. 125% of 120% of A = 225

$$\Rightarrow \quad \frac{125}{100} \times \frac{120}{100} \times A = 225$$

$$\Rightarrow \quad A = \left(225 \times \frac{2}{5}\right) = ₹\ 150.$$

25.

$$\text{Loss\%} = \left(\frac{\text{Common Loss and Gain\%}}{10}\right)^2 \%$$

$$= \left(\frac{12}{10}\right)^2 \% = \frac{36}{25}\% = 1\frac{11}{25}\%.$$

Discount

1. S.P. = ₹ 680

Discount = 15%

$$\text{M.P.} = \frac{100 \times \text{S.P.}}{100 - \text{Discount\%}}$$

$$= \frac{100 \times 680}{100 - 15} = \frac{100 \times 680}{85} = ₹\ 800$$

2. C.P. = ₹ x

$$120\% \text{ of } x = 350 - 350 \times 10\%$$

$$\frac{120}{100} \times x = 350 - 35 = 315.$$

$$x = \frac{315 \times 5}{6} = \frac{525}{2}$$

C.P. = ₹ 262.50

3. Let M.P. = ₹ x

$$80\%\ x = 118\% \text{ of } 200$$

$$\frac{80}{100} \times x = \frac{118}{100} \times 200$$

$$x = \frac{236 \times 5}{4} = ₹\ 295$$

4. Let C.P. of 100 gm coffee = ₹ x

110% of x = 35 – 7.50 = 27.50

$$\frac{110}{100}\times x = 27.50$$

$$x = \frac{27.50\times100}{110\times100}$$

C.P. = ₹ 25.

5. M.P. = ₹ 225000

$$\text{1st S.P.} = 225000 - 225000 \times \frac{10}{100}$$

= 225000 – 22500 = 202500

$$\text{2nd S.P.} = 202500 - 202500 \times \frac{5}{100}$$

= 202500 – 10125 = ₹ 192375

6. Let M.P. = 100

Commission = 25%

S.P. = 100 – 25 = 75

Profit = 20%

$$\text{C.P.} = \frac{100}{120}\times 75 = \frac{375}{6} = 62.50$$

Gain = 75 – 62.50 = ₹ 12.50

$$\text{M.P.} = \frac{100}{12.50}\times 60 = ₹\ 480$$

7.
$$\text{S.P.} = \frac{\text{M.P.}(100-\text{Discount})}{100}$$

$$= \frac{165\times(100-12)}{100} = \frac{165\times 88}{100}$$

= 33 × 4.4 = ₹ 145.20

8. Let C.P. = 100

M.P. = 140

Discount = 20%

$$\text{S.P.} = 140 - 140\times\frac{20}{100}$$

= 140 – 28 = 112

Profit = 112 – 100 = 12

$$\text{Profit \%} = \frac{12\times100}{100} = 12\%$$

9. Let C.P. = ₹ x

$$\text{S.P.} = 110\% \text{ of } x = \frac{110}{100}\times x = \frac{11}{10}x.$$

Discount = 20%

$$\text{M.P.} = \frac{100\times\frac{11}{10}x}{100-20} = \frac{100\times\frac{11}{10}x}{80} = \frac{11}{8}x.$$

$$\text{Required \%} = \frac{\frac{11x}{8}-x}{x}\times100 = \frac{3x\times100}{8x} = 37.5\%$$

10. C.P. = 450

Gain = 20%

$$\text{S.P.} = 450 + 450\times\frac{20}{100}$$

= 450 + 90 = 540

Discount = 10%

$$\text{M.P.} = \frac{100\times\text{S.P.}}{100-\text{Discount}} = \frac{100\times540}{100-10}$$

$$= \frac{100\times540}{90} = ₹\ 600$$

11. Gain % = 25

Gain = ₹ 150

C.P. = x

25% of x = 150

$$x = \frac{150\times100}{25} = 600$$

C.P. = 600

S.P. = 600 + 150 = 750

$$\text{M.P.} = \frac{100\times750}{100-20} = \frac{100\times750}{80}$$

M.P. = 5 × 187.50 = ₹ 937.50

12. C.P. = 1470

Gain = 10%

$$\text{S.P.} = 1470 + 1470\times\frac{10}{100}$$

= 1470 + 147 = 1617

$$\text{M.P.} = \frac{100\times1617}{100-12.5} = \frac{100\times1617}{87.5}$$

M.P. = ₹ 1848

Simple Interest

1. P = ₹ 2000

T = 3 yrs

R = 8% p.a.

$$\text{Interest} = \frac{\text{PRT}}{100} = \frac{2000\times8\times3}{100} = ₹\ 480$$

2. P = ₹ 4000

T = 3 yrs.

R = 10% p.a.

$$\text{S.I.} = \frac{\text{PRT}}{100} = \frac{4000\times10\times3}{100}$$

= ₹ 1200

3. P = 9280

$$R = \frac{9}{2}\%\ \text{p.a.}$$

$$T = \frac{5}{12} \text{ yr.}$$

$$S.I. = \frac{PRT}{100} = \frac{9280 \times 9 \times 5}{100 \times 2 \times 12}$$

$$= 58 \times 3 = ₹\ 174$$

4. $P = ₹\ 3000$

$A = ₹\ 4500$

$S.I. = A - P = 4500 - 3000 = 1500$

$T = 5$ yrs.

$$R = \frac{S.I. \times 100}{P \times T} = \frac{1500 \times 100}{3000 \times 5} = 10\%$$

5. $P = ₹\ 100$

$A = ₹\ 500$

$S.I. = 500 - 100 = ₹\ 400$

$$R = \frac{15}{2}\% \text{ p.a.}$$

$$T = \frac{S.I. \times 100}{P \times R}$$

$$= \frac{400 \times 100 \times 2}{100 \times 15} = \frac{160}{3} = 53\frac{1}{3} \text{ yrs.}$$

6. Let Rate = $x\%$

$$\frac{P \times (x+3) \times 2}{100} - \frac{P \times x \times 2}{100} = 300$$

$$\frac{2P(x+3)}{100} - \frac{2Px}{100} = 300$$

$$2Px + 6P - 2Px = 30000$$

$$P = \frac{30000}{6}$$

Principle = ₹ 5000

7. $P = 2210$

$R = 7$

$T = 4$

$$S.I. = \frac{PRT}{100} = \frac{2210 \times 7 \times 4}{100} = ₹\ 618.80$$

8. $P = 800$

$A = 920$

$T = 3$ yrs.

$S.I. = 920 - 800 = 120$

$$R = \frac{S.I. \times 100}{P \times T} = \frac{120 \times 100}{800 \times 3} = 5\% \text{ p.a.}$$

New rate = 5 + 3 = 8%

$$S.I. = \frac{PRT}{100} = \frac{800 \times 8 \times 3}{100} = ₹\ 192$$

$$A = P + S.I. = 800 + 192 = ₹\ 992$$

9. $$\frac{600 \times 2 \times R}{100} + \frac{2150 \times 4 \times R}{100} = 90$$

$$12\,R + 6\,R = 90$$

$$18\,R = 90$$

$$R = \frac{90}{18}$$

$$R = 5\% \text{ p.a.}$$

10. $$\frac{500 \times r_1 \times 2}{100} - \frac{500 \times r_2 \times 2}{100} = 2.50$$

$$10\,(r_1 - r_2) = 2.50$$

$$r_1 - r_2 = \frac{2.50}{10}$$

$$r_1 - r_2 = 0.25\%$$

11. $$\frac{P \times (x+1) \times 2}{100} - \frac{P \times x \times 2}{100} = 24$$

$$2Px + 2P - 2Px = 2400$$

$$P = ₹\ 1200$$

12. $T = ?$

$P_1 = ₹\ 780$

$R_1 = ₹\ 5\%$

$P_2 = ₹\ 600$

$$R_2 = \frac{13}{2}\%$$

According to question

$$\frac{P_1R_1T_1}{100} = \frac{P_2R_2T_2}{100}$$

$$\frac{780 \times 5 \times T_1}{100} = \frac{600 \times 13 \times T_2}{100 \times 2}$$

$$T_1 = T_2$$

It is true for all values of T.

13. Let sum = 100

Amount = 200

$S.I. = 200 - 100 = ₹\ 100$

$$R = \frac{25}{4}\% \text{ p.a.}$$

$$T = \frac{S.I. \times 100}{P \times R} = \frac{100 \times 100 \times 4}{100 \times 25}$$

$= 16$ yrs.

14. Let sum = ₹ 100

Amount = ₹ 200

S.I. = ₹ 100

T = 10 years

$$R = \frac{S.I. \times 100}{P \times T} = \frac{100 \times 100}{100 \times 10}$$

R = 10% p.a.

Again, P = ₹ 100

A = ₹ 300

S.I. = ₹ 200

R = 10% p.a.

T = ?

$$T = \frac{S.I. \times 100}{P \times R} = \frac{200 \times 100}{100 \times 10}$$

T = 20 years.

15. Let sum = ₹ x

S.I. = ₹ $x/2$

R = 8% p.a.

T = 6 years.

$$\text{S.I.} = \frac{\text{PRT}}{100}$$

$$x/2 = \frac{x\times8\times6}{100} = \frac{12x}{25}$$

$$\Rightarrow \quad \frac{1}{2} = \frac{12}{25}, \text{ which is false.}$$

So, data is inadequate.

Compound Interest

1. P = ₹ 6000

R = 5% p.a.

T = 2 years

$$A = P\left(1+\frac{r}{100}\right)^n = 6000\left(1+\frac{5}{100}\right)^2$$

$$= 6000 \times \frac{21}{20}\times\frac{21}{20}$$

$$= 15 \times 21 \times 21 = ₹\ 6615$$

2. P = ₹ 25600

R = 6.25 p.a.

T = 2 years

$$A = P\left(1+\frac{r}{100}\right)^n = 25600\left(1+\frac{6.25}{100}\right)^2$$

$$= 25600\left(\frac{17}{16}\right)^2$$

$$= 25600\ \frac{17}{16}\times\frac{17}{16}$$

$$= 28900$$

C.I. = A – P = 28900 – 25600

= ₹ 3300

3. P = ₹ 16000

n = 3 years

R = 2% p.a.

$$A = P\left(1+\frac{R}{100}\right)^n = 16000\left(1+\frac{2}{100}\right)^3$$

$$= 16000 \times \frac{51}{50}\times\frac{51}{50}\times\frac{51}{50}$$

$$= \frac{16\times51\times51\times51}{125} = \frac{2122416}{125}$$

= ₹ 16979. 33

C.I. = A – P

= 16979.33 – 16000

= ₹ 979.33

4. S.I. = ₹ 24000

$$R = \frac{25}{4}\%\ \text{p.a.}$$

T = 3 years

$$P = \frac{\text{S.I.} \times 100}{R \times T} = \frac{2400\times100\times4}{25\times3}$$

= ₹ 12800.

$$A = P\left(1+\frac{r}{100}\right)^n = 12800\left(1+\frac{25}{400}\right)^3$$

$$= ₹\ 12800 \times \frac{17}{16}\times\frac{17}{16}\times\frac{17}{16} = \frac{245650}{16}$$

= 15353.13

C.I. = A – P

= 15353.13 – 12800 = ₹ 2553.13

5. $$P\left[\left(1+\frac{r}{100}\right)^n - 1\right] - \frac{PRT}{100} = 300$$

$$P\left[\left(1+\frac{10}{100}\right)^2 - 1\right] - \frac{P\times10\times2}{100} = 300$$

$$P\left(\frac{121}{100} - 1\right) - \frac{P}{5} = 300$$

$$P\times\frac{21}{100} - \frac{P}{5} = 300$$

$$\frac{21P - 20P}{100} = 300$$

P = 300 × 100

= ₹ 30,000

6. $$A = P\left(1+\frac{r}{100}\right)^n$$

$$5832 = P\left(1+\frac{8}{100}\right)^2$$

$$= P\times\frac{108}{100}\times\frac{108}{100}$$

$$P = \frac{5832\times100\times100}{108\times108}$$

= ₹ 5000

7. $$1102.50 = 1000\left(1+\frac{r}{100}\right)^2$$

$$\frac{1102.50}{1000} = \left(1+\frac{r}{100}\right)^2$$

$$\left(\frac{21}{20}\right)^2 = \left(1+\frac{r}{100}\right)^2$$

$$\frac{21}{20} = 1+\frac{r}{100}$$

$$\frac{1}{20} = \frac{r}{100}$$

$$r = \frac{100}{20} = 5\% \text{ p.a.}$$

8. $$P\left[\left(1+\frac{r}{100}\right)^n-1\right] - \frac{PRT}{100} = 360$$

$$P\left[\left(1+\frac{7.5}{100}\right)^2-1\right] - \frac{P\times 7.5\times 2}{100} = 360$$

$$P\left[\frac{43}{40}\times\frac{43}{40}-1\right] - \frac{6P}{40} = 360$$

$$P\times\frac{43\times43-40\times40}{40\times40} - \frac{6P}{40} = 360$$

$$P\times\frac{1849-1600}{1600} - \frac{6P}{40} = 360$$

$$\frac{249}{1600}P - \frac{6P}{40} = 360$$

$$\frac{249\,P-240\,P}{1600} = 360$$

$$9P = 360\times1600$$

$$P = \frac{360\times1600}{9}$$

$$P = 40\times1600 = ₹\ 64000$$

9. $$P\left[\left(1+\frac{r}{100}\right)^n-1\right] - \frac{PRT}{100} = 46$$

$$P\left[\left(1+\frac{20}{300}\right)^3-1\right] - \frac{P\times20\times3}{100\times3} = 46$$

$$P\left(\frac{16}{15}\times\frac{16}{15}\times\frac{16}{15}-1\right) - \frac{P}{5} = 46$$

$$P\left(\frac{16\times16\times16-15\times15\times15}{15\times15\times15}\right) - \frac{P}{5} = 46$$

$$P\left(\frac{4096-3375}{3375}\right) - \frac{P}{5} = 46$$

$$P\times\frac{721}{3375} - \frac{P}{5} = 46$$

$$\frac{721\,P-675\,P}{3375} = 46$$

$$\frac{46P}{3375} = 46$$

$$P = \frac{46\times3375}{46} = ₹\ 3375$$

10. $$A = P\left(1+\frac{r}{100}\right)^n$$

$$10404 = P\left(1+\frac{2}{100}\right)^2 = P\times\frac{51}{50}\times\frac{51}{50}$$

$$P = \frac{10404\times50\times50}{51\times51}$$

$$= 4\times2500 = 10000$$

$$P = ₹\ 10000$$

11. $$A = P\left(1+\frac{r}{100}\right)^n$$

$$453690 = P\left(1+\frac{6.5}{100}\right)^2 = P\times\frac{1065\times1065}{1000\times1000}$$

$$P = \frac{453690\times1000000}{1065\times1065}$$

$$P = 400000$$

12. $$A = P\left(1+\frac{r}{100}\right)^n$$

$$45582.25 = P\left(1+\frac{27}{400}\right)^2 = P\times\frac{427}{400}\times\frac{427}{400}$$

$$P = \frac{45582.25\times400\times400}{427\times427}$$

$$= 25\times400\times4 = ₹\ 40000$$

13. $$\text{C.I.} = P\left[\left(1+\frac{r}{100}\right)^n-1\right]$$

$$410 = P\left[\left(1+\frac{r}{100}\right)^2-1\right]$$

$$410 = 4000\left[\left(1+\frac{r}{100}\right)^2-1\right]$$

$$\frac{410}{4000} = \left(1+\frac{r}{100}\right)^2-1$$

$$\frac{41}{400}+1 = \left(1+\frac{r}{100}\right)^2$$

$$\frac{441}{400} = \left(1+\frac{r}{100}\right)^2$$

$$\left(\frac{21}{20}\right)^2 = \left(1+\frac{r}{100}\right)^2$$

$$1+\frac{r}{100} = \frac{21}{20} \Rightarrow \frac{r}{100} = \frac{21}{20}-1 = \frac{1}{20}$$

$$r = \frac{100}{20} = 5\% \text{ p.a.}$$

14. $$A = P\left(1+\frac{r}{100}\right)^n$$

$$1852.20 = 1600\left(1+\frac{5}{100}\right)^n$$

$$\frac{1852.20}{1600} = \left(1+\frac{1}{20}\right)^n = \left(\frac{21}{20}\right)^n$$

$$\frac{9261}{8000} = \left(\frac{21}{20}\right)^n$$

$$\left(\frac{21}{20}\right)^3 = \left(\frac{21}{20}\right)^n \Rightarrow n = 3 \text{ years}$$

15. $$13230 = 12000\left(1+\frac{5}{100}\right)^n$$

$$\frac{13230}{12000} = \left(\frac{21}{20}\right)^n$$

$$\left(\frac{21}{20}\right)^2 = \left(\frac{21}{20}\right)^n$$

$\Rightarrow$ $n = 2$ years

16. $$C.I. = P\left[\left(1+\frac{r}{100}\right)^n - 1\right]$$

$$= 12000\left[\left(1+\frac{10}{100}\right)^3 - 1\right]$$

$$= 12000\left(\frac{11\times11\times11}{1000} - 1\right)$$

$$= 12000\left(\frac{1331-1000}{1000}\right) = 12000\times\frac{331}{1000}$$

$$= 12 \times 331 = ₹\ 3972$$

17. $$A = P\left(1+\frac{r}{100}\right)^n$$

$$= 8000\left(1+\frac{5}{100}\right)^3$$

$$= 8000\times\frac{21\times21\times21}{20\times20\times20}$$

$$= ₹\ 9261$$

18. R = 2.5 paise per rupee per annum
= 2.5% per annum

$$A = P\left(1+\frac{r}{100}\right)^n = 64000\left(1+\frac{2.5}{100}\right)^3$$

$$= 64000\times\frac{41}{40}\times\frac{41}{40}\times\frac{41}{40}$$

$$= 41\times41\times41 = ₹\ 68921$$

19. $$S.I. = \frac{PRT}{100}$$

$$P = \frac{S.I.\times100}{R\times T} = \frac{1600\times100}{4\times4}$$

$$P = 10000$$

$$C.I. = P\left[\left(1+\frac{r}{100}\right)^n - 1\right]$$

$$= 10000\left[\left(1+\frac{4}{100}\right)^4 - 1\right]$$

$$= 10000\left(\frac{26}{25}\times\frac{26}{25}\times\frac{26}{25}\times\frac{26}{25} - 1\right)$$

$$= 10000\left(\frac{26\times26\times26\times26 - 25\times25\times25\times25}{25\times25\times25\times25}\right)$$

$$= 10000\left(\frac{456976-390625}{390625}\right)$$

$$= \frac{10000\times66351}{390625} = ₹\ 1697.79$$

20. $n = 4$

$$r = \frac{20}{2}\% = 10\%$$

$$P = 12000$$

$$A = P\left(1+\frac{r}{100}\right)^n = 12000\left(1+\frac{10}{100}\right)^4$$

$$= 12000\times\frac{11}{10}\times\frac{11}{10}\times\frac{11}{10}\times\frac{11}{10}$$

$$= 1.2\times11\times11\times11\times11$$

$$= 17569.2$$

$$C.I. = A - P = 17569.2 - 12000$$

$$= ₹\ 5569.20$$

□□□□□

7

Algebraic Expressions and Identities Including Factorization

Algebric Identies

Some Important Formula

(*i*) $(a + b)^2 = a^2 + 2ab + b^2$

(*ii*) $(a - b)^2 = a^2 - 2ab + b^2$

(*iii*) $a^2 - b^2 = (a - b)(a + b)$

(*iv*) $(a + b + c)^2 = a^2 + b^2 + c^2 + 2ab + 2bc + 2ca$

(*v*) $(a + b - c)^2 = a^2 + b^2 + c^2 + 2ab - 2bc - 2ca$

(*vi*) $(a - b + c)^2 = a^2 + b^2 + c^2 - 2ab - 2bc + 2ca$

(*vii*) $(-a + b + c)^2 = a^2 + b^2 + c^2 - 2ab + 2bc - 2ca$

(*viii*) $(a + b)^3 = a^3 + b^3 + 3ab(a + b)$ or
$= a^3 + b^3 + 3a^2b + 3ab^2$

(*ix*) $(a - b)^3 = a^3 - b^3 - 3ab\ (a - b)$ or
$= a^3 - b^3 - 3a^2b + 3ab^2$

(*x*) $a^3 + b^3 = (a + b)\ (a^2 + b^2 - ab)$ or
$= (a + b)^3 - 3ab(a + b)$

(*xi*) $a^3 - b^3 = (a - b)\ (a^2 + b^2 + ab)$ or
$= (a - b)^3 + 3ab\ (a - b)$

(*xii*) $a^3 + b^3 + c^3 - 3abc = (a + b + c)(a^2 + b^2 + c^2 - ab - bc - ca)$

If $a + b + c = 0$
$a^3 + b^3 + c^3 = 3abc$

(*xiii*) $(x + a)\ (x + b) = x^2 + (a + b)x + ab$

(*xiv*) $(a + b)^2 + (a - b)^2 = 2(a^2 + b^2)$

(*xv*) $(a + b)^2 - (a - b)^2 = 4ab$

(*xvi*) $(a + b)^3 + (a - b)^3 = 2(a^3 + 3ab^2)$

(*xvii*) $(a + b)^3 - (a - b)^3 = (2(b^3 + 3a^2b)$

(*xviii*) If $x + \frac{1}{x} = t$

Then, $x^2 + \frac{1}{x^2} = t^2 - 2$

(*xix*) If $x - \frac{1}{x} = t$

Then, $x^2 + \frac{1}{x^2} = t^2 + 2$

(*xx*) $x^3 + \frac{1}{x^3} = \left(x + \frac{1}{x}\right)^3 - 3\left(x + \frac{1}{x}\right)$

(*xxi*) $x^2 - \frac{1}{x^3} = \left(x - \frac{1}{x}\right)^3 + 3\left(x - \frac{1}{x}\right)$

(*xxii*) $x + \frac{1}{x} = \sqrt{x^2 + \frac{1}{x^2} + 2}$

(*xxiii*) $x - \frac{1}{x} = \sqrt{x^2 + \frac{1}{x^2} - 2}$

Factorization of Algebraic Expressions

Factorization : The process of writing an algebraic expression as the product of two or more algebraic expressions is called factorization.

Factors : The algebraic expressions that may be multiplied to obtain the given algebraic expressions are called factors of the given expression.

Factor Theorem : If $f(x)$ is completely divisible by $(x - a)$ then $f(a) = 0$, $(x - a)$ is called factor of $f(x)$, if and only if $f(a) = 0$

Remainder Theorem : If an expression $f(x)$ is divided by $(x - a)$ then the remainder is $f(a)$.

e.g., $f(x) = ax^3 + bx + cx + d$

$f(a) = a \cdot a^3 + b \cdot a + c \cdot a + d$ is known as remainder of the given polynomials.

Multiple Choice Questions

1. $(28)^3 + (-15)^3 + (-13)^3 = ?$

A. 16380 B. 16250
C. 16420 D. 16280

2. If $x + \frac{1}{x} = 5$, What is the value of $x^3 + \frac{1}{x^3}$:

A. 120 B. 210
C. 110 D. 105

3. If $x^2 + \frac{1}{x^2} = 83$, what is the value of $x^3 - \frac{1}{x^3} = ?$

A. 756 B. 754
C. 856 D. 932

4. $23^3 - 17^3 = ?$
A. 7254
B. 7153
C. 7271
D. 7154

5. If $x + \frac{1}{x} = 15$, then the value of $x^2 + \frac{1}{x^2}$ will be:
A. 228
B. 230
C. 323
D. 223

6. If $x = 12$ and $y = 4$, the value of $(x+y)^{x/y}$ will be:
A. 4096
B. 3896
C. 4196
D. 5086

7. If $x + y = 2z$, then the value of $\left(\frac{x}{x-z}+\frac{z}{y-z}\right)$ will be:
A. 1
B. 4
C. 3/2
D. 2

8. If $x + y + z = 0$, then the value of $\frac{(x+y)(y+z)(z+x)}{xyz}$ will be:
A. –3
B. –2
C. 0
D. –1

9. If $x + \frac{1}{x} = 3$, the value of $x^4 + \frac{1}{x^4}$ will be:
A. 49
B. 47
C. 37
D. 42

10. If $\left(x+\frac{1}{x}\right)^2 = 0$, then the value of $\left(x^2+\frac{1}{x^2}\right)$ will be:
A. 1
B. –1
C. 2
D. –2

11. If $\left(a+\frac{2}{a}\right) = 3$, then the value of $\left(a-\frac{2}{a}\right)$ will be:
A. ± 4
B. ± 5
C. ± 2
D. ± 1

12. If $\sqrt{a}+\frac{1}{\sqrt{a}} = 4$, then the value of $a^2 + \frac{1}{a^2}$ will be:
A. 194
B. 199
C. 178
D. 192

13. Factors of $x^2 - 25$ are:
A. $(x-1)(x-25)$
B. $(x+25)(x-1)$
C. $(x+5)(x-5)$
D. $(x-5)(x-5)$

14. Square of $\left(x-\frac{1}{x}\right)$ will be
A. $x^2 - 2 - \frac{1}{x^2}$
B. $x^2 - 2 + \frac{1}{x^2}$
C. $x^2 - 4 - \frac{1}{x^2}$
D. $x^2 - 2 + \frac{1}{x}$

15. Factors of $36 - 9x^2$ will be:
A. $(6+3x)(6-3x)$
B. $(3x-6)(6-3x)$
C. $(3x+6)(3x-6)$
D. $(12x-3x)(3+3x)$

16. Factors of $8x^3 + y^3$ are:
A. $(2x+y)(4x^2-2xy+y^2)$
B. $(2x+y)(4x^2+2xy+y^2)$
C. $(2x-y)(4x^2-2xy+y^2)$
D. $(2x+y)(4x^2-2xy-y^2)$

17. If the expression $x^3 + 5x^2 - 2 + k$ is completely divisible by $(x-1)$, the value of k will be:
A. –3
B. –8
C. –3
D. –4

18. What is the factors of $x^2 + 3x - 10$
A. $(x-1)(x-10)$
B. $(x-2)(x+5)$
C. $(x+2)(x-5)$
D. $(x+2)(x+5)$

19. Factors of $(x+y)^3 - x - y$ are:
A. $(x-y)[(x-y)^2-1]$
B. $(x+y)[(x+y)^2-1]$
C. $(x+y)[(x+y)^2+1]$
D. $(x-y)[(x+y)^2+1]$

20. Factors of $x^3y^3z^3 - 27$ are:
A. $(xyz-3)(x^2y^2z^2+3xyz+9)$
B. $(xyz+3)(x^2y^2z^2+3xyz+9)$
C. $(3-xyz)(x^2y^2z^2-3xyz+9)$
D. $(xyz-3)(x^2y^2+y^2z^2+z^2x^2)$

21. If $x = \sqrt{3}$, the value of $x^4 + 2 + \frac{1}{x^4}$ will be:
A. $\frac{9}{100}$
B. $\frac{81}{100}$
C. $\frac{101}{9}$
D. $\frac{100}{9}$

22. Factors of $4x^2 + 8x - 5$ will be:
A. $(2x-1)(2x+5)$
B. $(2x+1)(2x+5)$
C. $(2x-5)(2x-1)$
D. $(2x+5)(1-2x)$

23. Factors of $a^2 + \frac{1}{4} + a$ will be:
A. $\left(a+\frac{1}{2}\right)\left(a-\frac{1}{2}\right)$
B. $\left(a+\frac{1}{2}\right)^2$
C. $\left(a+\frac{1}{2}\right)^3$
D. $\left(a+\frac{1}{2}\right).a$

24. If $(x-2)$ is a factor of $x^2 + 2x - a$, the value of a will be:
A. 8
B. 6
C. 11
D. 3

25. Factors of $x^8 - x^4 - 30$ will be:
A. $(x^4-5)(x^4+6)$
B. $(x^4+5)(x^4-6)$
C. $(x^4+5)(x^4+6)$
D. $(x^4-10)(x^4+3)$

ANSWERS

1	2	3	4	5	6	7	8	9	10
A	C	A	A	D	A	A	D	B	D
11	**12**	**13**	**14**	**15**	**16**	**17**	**18**	**19**	**20**
D	A	C	B	A	A	D	B	B	A
21	**22**	**23**	**24**	**25**					
D	A	B	A	B					

EXPLANATORY ANSWERS

1. Let $a = 28$, $b = -15$ and $c = -13$. Then

$$a + b + c = 28 - 15 - 13 = 0$$

$$a^3 + b^3 + c^3 = 3abc$$

$$(28)^3 + (-15)^3 + (-13)^3 = 3 \times 28 \times (-15) \times (-13) = 16380$$

2. $x^3 + \frac{1}{x^3} = \left(x+\frac{1}{x}\right)^3 - 3\left(x+\frac{1}{x}\right)$

$$= (5)^3 - 3 \times 5$$

$$= 125 - 15$$

$$= 110$$

3. If $x^2 + \frac{1}{x^2} = 83$, what is the value of $x^3 - \frac{1}{x^3} = ?$

$$\left(x-\frac{1}{x}\right)^2 = x^2 + \frac{1}{x^2} - 2$$

$$x - \frac{1}{x} = \sqrt{83-2} = \sqrt{81}$$

$$x - \frac{1}{x} = 9$$

$$\therefore \left(x^3 - \frac{1}{x^3}\right) = \left(x-\frac{1}{x}\right)^3 + 3\left(x-\frac{1}{x}\right)$$

$$= (9)^3 + 3 \times 9$$

$$= 729 + 27$$

$$= 756$$

4. $23^3 - 17^3 = (20 + 3)^3 - (20 - 3)^3$

$$= 2(3^3 + 3 \times 20^2 \times 3)$$

$$[\because (a + b)^3 - (a - b)^3 = 2(b^3 + 3a^2b)]$$

$$= 2\ (27 + 3600)$$

$$= 54 + 7200 = 7254$$

5. $\because x + \frac{1}{x} = 15$

$$\Rightarrow \left(x+\frac{1}{x}\right)^2 = (15)^2 \Rightarrow x^2 + \frac{1}{x^2} + 2.x\frac{1}{x} = 225$$

$$\therefore x^2 + \frac{1}{x^2} = 225 - 2 = 223.$$

6. $(x+y)^{x/y} = (12+4)^{12/4} = (16)^3 = 4096.$ $[\because x = 12, y = 4]$

7. $\because x + y = 2z \Rightarrow x - z = z - y = -(y - z)$

$$\therefore \frac{x}{x-z} + \frac{z}{y-z} = \frac{x}{-(y-z)} + \frac{z}{y-z} = \frac{z-x}{y-z} = 1.$$

$$[\because x - z = z - y]$$

8. $\because x + y + z = 0 \Rightarrow x + y = -z$

$$x + y + z = 0 \Rightarrow y + z = -x$$

and $x + y + z = 0 \Rightarrow z + x = -y$

$$\therefore \frac{(x+y)(y+z)(z+x)}{xyz} = \frac{(-z)(-x)(-y)}{xyz} = -1.$$

9. $\because x + \frac{1}{x} = 3 \Rightarrow \left(x+\frac{1}{x}\right)^2 = (3)^2$

$$\Rightarrow x^2 + \frac{1}{x^2} + 2.x.\frac{1}{x} = 9 \Rightarrow x^2 + \frac{1}{x^2} = 9 - 2 = 7$$

$$\because x^2 + \frac{1}{x^2} = 7 \Rightarrow \left(x^2+\frac{1}{x^2}\right)^2 = (7)^2$$

$$\Rightarrow x^4 + \frac{1}{x^4} + 2.x^2.\frac{1}{x^2} = 49$$

$$\therefore x^4 + \frac{1}{x^4} = 49 - 2 = 47.$$

10. $\left(x+\frac{1}{x}\right)^2 = 0 \Rightarrow x^2 + \frac{1}{x^2} + 2x.\frac{1}{x} = 0$

$$\Rightarrow x^2 + \frac{1}{x^2} = -2.$$

11. $\because \left(a-\frac{2}{a}\right)^2 = \left(a+\frac{2}{a}\right)^2 - 4.a.\frac{2}{a} = (3)^2 - 8 = 9 - 8 = 1$

$$\therefore \left(a-\frac{2}{a}\right) = \pm\sqrt{1} = \pm 1.$$

12. $\because \sqrt{a} + \frac{1}{\sqrt{a}} = 4$

$$\Rightarrow \left(\sqrt{a}+\frac{1}{\sqrt{a}}\right)^2 = (4)^2 \Rightarrow a + \frac{1}{a} + 2.\sqrt{a}.\frac{1}{\sqrt{a}} = 16$$

$$\because \left(a+\frac{1}{a}\right) = 14 \Rightarrow \left(a+\frac{1}{a}\right)^2 = (14)^2$$

$\Rightarrow \quad a^2 + \frac{1}{a^2} + 2.a.\frac{1}{a} = 196$

$\therefore \quad a^2 + \frac{1}{a^2} = 196 - 2 = 194.$

13. $x^2 - 25 = (x)^2 - (5)^2$, [which is of the form $a^2 - b^2$]
$= (x + 5)(x - 5).$

14. According to question:

Square of $\left(x - \frac{1}{x}\right) = \left(x - \frac{1}{x}\right)^2$

$= x^2 - 2.x.\frac{1}{x} + \left(\frac{1}{x}\right)^2 = x^2 - 2 + \frac{1}{x^2}.$

15. $36 - 9x^2 = (6)^2 - (3x)^2$ [which is of the form $a^2 - b^2$]
$= (6 + 3x)(6 - 3x).$

16. $8x^3 + y^3 = (2x)^3 + (y)^3$ [which is of the form $a^3 + b^3$]
$= (2x + y)[(2x)^2 - 2x.y + (y)^2]$
$= (2x + y)(4x^2 - 2xy + y^2).$

17. Since the expression $x^3 + 5x^2 - 2 + k$ is completely divisible by $(x - 1)$

$\therefore$ on substituting $x = 1$ in the given expression, its value will be zero

i.e., $(1)^3 + 5(1)^2 - 2 + k = 0 \Rightarrow 1 + 5 - 2 + k = 0$

$\Rightarrow \quad 4 + k = 0 \Rightarrow k = -4$

Hence value of k is -4.

18. $\because x^2 + 3x - 10 = x^2 + 5x - 2x - 10$
$= x(x + 5) - 2(x + 5) = (x - 2)(x + 5)$

19. $\because (x + y)^3 - x - y = (x + y)^3 - (x + y) = (x + y)[(x + y)^2 - 1].$

20. $\because x^3y^3z^3 - 27 = (xyz)^3 - (3)^3$[which is of the form $a^3 - b^3$]
$= (xyz - 3)[(xyz)^2 + xyz.3 + (3)^2]$
$= (xyz - 3)(x^2y^2z^2 + 3xyz + 9).$

21. $\because x^4 + 2 + \frac{1}{x^4} = (x^2)^2 + 2.x^2.\frac{1}{x^2} + \left(\frac{1}{x^2}\right)^2 = \left(x^2 + \frac{1}{x^2}\right)^2$

$\therefore$ On substituting $x = \sqrt{3}$

$= \left((\sqrt{3})^2 + \frac{1}{(\sqrt{3})^2}\right)^2 = \left(3 + \frac{1}{3}\right)^2$

$= \left(\frac{10}{3}\right)^2 = \frac{100}{9}.$

22. $\because \quad 4x^2 + 8x - 5 = 4x^2 + 10x - 2x - 5$
$= 2x(2x + 5) - 1(2x + 5)$
$= (2x - 1)(2x + 5).$

23. $\because \quad a^2 + \frac{1}{4} + a = (a)^2 + 2.\frac{1}{2}.a + \left(\frac{1}{2}\right)^2 = \left(a + \frac{1}{2}\right)^2.$

24. Since $(x - 2)$ is a factor of $x^2 + 2x - a$

$\therefore$ On substituting $x = 2$ in the expression, the result obtained will be zero

$\therefore \quad (2)^2 + 2.2 - a = 0$

or $\quad 4 + 4 - a = 0$

or $\quad a = 8$

25. $\because \quad x^8 - x^4 - 30 = x^8 - 6x^4 + 5x^4 - 30$
$= x^4(x^4 - 6) + 5(x^4 - 6)$
$= (x^4 + 5)(x^4 - 6).$

□□□□□

8

Linear Equations in One Variable

An equation is called linear equation in one variable or an equation of degree one in one variable, if only a single variable with degree one occurs in the equation. For example,

$x + 3 = 0$, $3x + 5 = 8$, $2t + 3 = t + 16$

Multiple Choice Questions

1. The difference between two numbers is 8. If 2 is added to the greater number, the result will be three times the smaller. What are the numbers?
   A. 13, 5 B. 5, 13
   C. 12, 6 D. 13, 6

2. Find three consecutive numbers such that if they are divided by 4, 7 and 11 respectively, the sum of the quotients will be 10.
   A. 20, 21, 22 B. 22, 23, 24
   C. 25, 26, 27 D. 28, 29, 30

3. In a bag one-fifth of the balls are black and one-third are red, there are 15 dozen green balls and 30 blue balls. What is the number of black balls and red balls in the bag?
   A. 90, 110 B. 90, 150
   C. 80, 150 D. 150, 110

4. The sum of the ages of A and B is 30 years. Five years hence, A will be three times as old as B. What is their present ages?
   A. 25 years, 8 years B. 30 years, 9 years
   C. 25 years, 5 years D. 30 years, 10 years

5. Two persons A and B start walking in opposite directions at 8 a.m. from two places which are 27 km. apart. Both of them meet at 11 a.m. If A's speed is 3 km/hr more than that of B, find their respective speeds?
   A. 3 km/hr, 6 km/hr B. 4 km/hr, 6 km/h
   C. 3 km/h, 5 km/hr D. 5 km/h, 7 km/h

6. The length of a room exceeds its breadth by 30 cm. If the length is increased by 30 cm and the breadth is decreased by 20 cm, the area remains the same. What is the length and breadth of the room?
   A. 120 cm, 150 cm B. 140 cm, 160 cm
   C. 130 cm, 150 cm D. 120 cm, 140 cm

7. One number exceeds another by 5. Their sum is 29. What are the numbers?
   A. 13, 14 B. 14, 16
   C. 12, 17 D. 15, 18

8. The sum of two number is 8, if 22 is added to the smaller number then it becomes five times the other. What are the numbers?
   A. 4, 5 B. 3, 5
   C. 3, 7 D. 5, 8

9. A motorboat goes downstream in a river and covers the distance between two coastal towns in five hours. It covers this distance upstream in six hours. If the speed of the stream is 2 km/hr., find the speed of the boat in still water.
   A. 11 km/hr B. 20 km/hr
   C. 22 km/hr D. 32 km/hr

10. A race-boat covers a distance of 66 km downstream in 110 minutes. It covers this distance upstream in 120 minutes. The speed of the boat in still water is 34.5 km/hr, find the speed of the stream.
    A. 1.5 km/hr B. 2.5 km/hr
    C. 3.0 km/hr D. 4.5 km/hr

11. A steamer, going down stream in a river, covers the distance between two towns in 20 hours. Coming back up stream, it covers this distance in 25 hours. The speed of water is 4 km/hr, find the distance between the two towns.
    A. 600 km B. 700 km
    C. 800 km D. 900 km

12. The sum of two numbers is 2490. If 6.5% of one number is equal to 8.5% of the other, find the numbers.
    A. 1412, 1072 B. 1411, 1079
    C. 1415, 1092 D. 1417, 1095

13. The distance between two stations A and B is 230 km. Two motor cyclists start simultaneously from A and B in the opposite directions and the distance between them after three hours is 20 km. If the speed of one motor cyclist is less than that of the other by 10 km/hr, find the speed of each motor cyclist.
    A. 30 km/hr, 40 km/hr B. 30 km/hr, 50 km/hr
    C. 40 km/hr, 60 km/hr D. 50 km/hr, 70 km/hr

14. Divide ₹ 1380 among Ahmed, John and Mamta so that the amount Ahmed receives is 5 times as much as Mamta's share and is 3 times as much as John's share. What is John's share?
    A. ₹ 180 B. ₹ 300
    C. ₹ 920 D. ₹ 900

15. The length of a rectangle is 15 cm. more than its width. The perimeter is 150 cm, find the dimensions of the rectangle.
A. 30 cm, 25 cm B. 20 cm, 25 cm
C. 30 cm, 45 cm D. 32 cm, 42 cm

16. An altitude of a triangle is five-thirds the length of its corresponding base. If the altitude were increased by 4 cm. and the base be decreased by 2 cm, the area of the triangle would remain the same. What is the base and the altitude of the triangle?
A. 12 cm, 16 cm B. 12 cm, 20 cm
C. 14 cm, 18 cm D. 12 cm, 24 cm

17. The perimeter of a triangle measuring 49 cm. The one side 7 cm. longer than the other and 5 cm. shorter than the third. What is the length of smaller side of the triangle?
A. 5 cm B. 17 cm
C. 22 cm D. 10 cm

18. If I add ten to four times a number, the result is five less than five times the number. What is my number?
A. 13 B. 14
C. 15 D. 21

19. The denominator of a rational number is greater than its numerator by 3. If 3 is subtracted from the numerator and 2 is added to its denominator, the new number becomes $\frac{1}{5}$. What is the original number?
A. $\frac{5}{8}$ B. $\frac{7}{8}$
C. $\frac{9}{11}$ D. $\frac{8}{13}$

20. The denominator of a rational number is greater than its numerator by 5. If the numerator is increased by 11 and the denominator decreased by 14, the new number becomes 5. What is the original number?
A. $\frac{14}{39}$ B. $\frac{12}{23}$
C. $\frac{14}{19}$ D. $\frac{14}{29}$

ANSWERS

1	2	3	4	5	6	7	8	9	10
A	A	B	C	A	A	C	B	C	A
11	**12**	**13**	**14**	**15**	**16**	**17**	**18**	**19**	**20**
C	B	A	B	C	B	D	C	A	C

EXPLANATORY ANSWERS

1. According to question.

$x - y = 8$ ...(i)

$x + 2 = 3y \Rightarrow x - 3y = -2$ ...(ii)

Eqn. (i) and (ii)

$x - y = 8$

$x - 3y = -2$

$- \quad + \quad +$

$2y = 10 \Rightarrow y = 5$

Eqn (i)

$\Rightarrow x - 5 = 8 \Rightarrow x = 13$ and $y = 5$

2. Let three consecutive numbers

$x, x + 1, x + 2$

$$\frac{x}{4}+\frac{x+1}{7}+\frac{x+2}{11} = 10$$

$$\frac{77x+44x+44+28x+56}{308} = 10$$

$$\frac{149x+100}{308} = \frac{10}{1}$$

$149x + 100 = 3080$

$\Rightarrow 149x = 2980$

$$\Rightarrow x = \frac{2980}{149} = 20$$

Required Numbers

$x = 20, x + 1 = 20 + 1 = 21$ and

$x + 2 = 20 + 2 = 22,$

i.e. 20, 21, 22

3. Let total number of balls be x

According to question,

$$\frac{x}{5}+\frac{x}{3}+15\times12+30 = x$$

$$\frac{x}{5}+\frac{x}{3}+210 = x$$

$$x-\frac{x}{5}-\frac{x}{3} = 210$$

$$\Rightarrow \frac{15x-3x-5x}{15} = 210$$

$$\Rightarrow \frac{7}{15}x = 210 \Rightarrow x = \frac{210\times15}{7}$$

$x = 450$

$$\text{Black balls} = \frac{x}{5} = \frac{450}{5} = 90$$

Red balls $= \frac{x}{3} = \frac{450}{3} = 150$

4. Let present age of A = x yrs.
then B = 30 – x yrs.
According to question,

$$x + 5 = 3\,(35 - x) = 105 - 3x$$
$$4x = 100 \Rightarrow x = 25$$

A's present age = 25 yrs.
B's present age = 30 – 25 = 5 yrs.

5. Let B's speed be x km/hr.
A's speed = $(x + 3)$ km/hr.
According to question,

$$3x + 9 + 3x = 27$$
$$6x = 18 \Rightarrow x = 3 \text{ km/hr}$$

B's speed = 3 km/hrs.
A's speed = 6 km/hr.

6. Let breadth = x cm.
length = $(x + 30)$ cm.
Area = $x\,(x + 30) = (x^2 + 30x)$ cm^2
New breadth = x – 20 and New length
= x + 60 cm.
New Area = $(x - 20)(x + 60)$
$= x^2 + 40x - 1200$

According to question

$$x^2 + 40x - 1200 = x^2 + 30x$$
$$10x = 1200$$
$$x = 120 \text{ cm.}$$

Breadth = 120 cm.
Length = 120 + 30 = 150 cm.

7. Let another number = x
One number = $x + 5$

$$x + x + 5 = 29$$
$$2x + 5 = 29$$
$$2x = 24 \Rightarrow x = 12$$

Required Number,
12, 17

8. Let smaller number = x
Other number = $8 - x$

$$x + 22 = 5\,(8 - x) = 40 - 5x$$
$$6x = 40 - 22 = 18$$
$$x = 3$$

Required Numbers
3, 5

9. Let speed of still water = x km/hr.
Speed of stream = 2 km/hr.
Downstream = $(x + 2)$ km/hr.
Upstream = $(x - 2)$ km/hr.
According to question

$$5\,(x + 2) = 6\,(x - 2)$$
$$5x + 10 = 6x - 12$$
$$x = 22 \text{ km/hr.}$$

Speed in still water = 22 km/hr.

10. Let speed of stream = x km/hr.
Downstream = $(34.5 + x)$ km/hr.
Upstream = $(34.5 - x)$ km/hr.

$$\text{Downstream} = \frac{\frac{66}{110}}{60} = \frac{66 \times 6}{11}$$
$$= 36 \text{ km/hr.}$$
$$34.5 + x = 36$$
$$x = 36 - 34.5 = 1.5 \text{ km/hr.}$$

Speed of stream = 1.5 km/hr.

11. Let distance = x km.

Downstream $= \frac{x}{20}$ km/hr.

Upstream $= \frac{x}{25}$ km/hr.

Speed of water = 4 km/hr.

Speed of water $= \frac{1}{2}$ (down stream – up stream)

$$4 = \frac{1}{2}\left(\frac{x}{20} - \frac{x}{25}\right)$$
$$8 = \frac{5x - 4x}{100} = \frac{x}{100}$$
$$x = 8 \times 100 = 800 \text{ km.}$$

12. Let 1st number = x
Other number = 2490 – x
According to question

$$6.5\%\, x = 8.5\%\,(2490 - x)$$
$$\frac{65}{1000}x = \frac{85}{1000}(2490 - x)$$
$$13x + 17x = 17 \times 2490$$
$$30x = 17 \times 2490$$
$$x = \frac{17 \times 2490}{30} = 17 \times 83$$
$$x = 1411$$

Other number = 2490 – 1411
= 1079

Required nos. 1411 and 1079

13.

x km/hr. (A) ———— (B) $(x + 10)$ km/hr.

← 230 km. →

Relative speed = $x + x + 10 = (2x + 10)$ km/hr.
Distance after three hours = 230 – 20
= 210 km.

According to question,

$$3\,(2x + 10) = 210$$
$$2x + 10 = 70$$
$$2x = 60$$
$$\Rightarrow x = 30$$

Speed of each motorcyclist is 30 km/hr. and 40 km/hr.

14. Let Mamta's share = ₹ x

Then,

Ahmed's share = $5x$

John's share = $1380 - 6x$

Hence,

$$5x = 3\,(1380 - 6x) = 4140 - 18x$$
$$23x = 4140$$
$$x = \frac{4140}{23} = 180$$

Mamta's share = ₹ 180

Ahmed's share = 5 × 180 = ₹ 900

John's share = 1380 − 1080 = ₹ 300

15. Let width = x cm.

Length = $x + 15$ cm.

$$2\,(x + x + 15) = 150$$
$$2x + 15 = 75$$
$$2x = 60$$
$$x = 30$$

width = 30 cm. and length = 45 cm.

16.

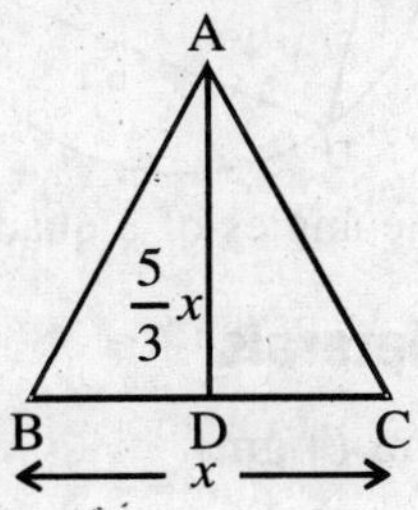

According to question

$$\frac{1}{2}x\times\frac{5}{3}x = \frac{1}{2}\left(\frac{5}{3}x+4\right)(x-2)$$

$$2\times\frac{5}{6}x^2 = \frac{5}{3}x^2-\frac{10}{3}x+4x-8$$

$$\frac{5}{3}x^2 = \frac{5}{3}x^2-\frac{10}{3}x+4x-8$$

$$4x-\frac{10}{3}x = 8 \Rightarrow \frac{2}{3}x=8$$

$$\Rightarrow \quad 2x = 8\times 3 \;\Rightarrow\; x=\frac{8\times3}{2}=4\times3$$

$$x = 12 \text{ cm.}$$

Base = 12 cm.

$$\text{Altitude} = \frac{5}{3}\times12 = 20 \text{ cm.}$$

17. Let other side = x cm.

One side = $(x + 7)$ cm.

Third side = $x + 12$ cm.

According to question

$$x + x + 7 + x + 12 = 49$$
$$3x = 49 - 19 = 30$$
$$x = 10$$

Hence smaller side is 10 cm.

18. Let number be x

Then,

$$4x + 10 = 5x - 5$$
$$x = 10 + 5 = 15$$

19. Let numerator = x

Denominator = $x + 3$

$$\frac{x-3}{x+3+2} = \frac{1}{5} \;\Rightarrow\; \frac{x-3}{x+5}=\frac{1}{5}$$

$$\Rightarrow \quad 5x - 15 = x + 5$$
$$4x = 20 \;\Rightarrow x = 5$$

Required fraction = 5/8

20. Let Numerator = x

denominator = $x + 5$

Hence,

$$\frac{x+11}{x+5-14} = \frac{5}{1}$$

$$\Rightarrow \quad \frac{x+11}{x-9}=\frac{5}{1}$$

$$\Rightarrow \quad 5x - 45 = x + 11$$
$$4x = 56 \Rightarrow x = 14.$$

$$\text{Required fraction} = \frac{x}{x+5} = \frac{14}{14+5} = \frac{14}{19}$$

❑❑❑❑❑

9

Understanding Quadrilaterals

(Parallelogram, Rhombus, Rectangle, Square, Kite)

Area

(*a*) Area = $\frac{1}{2}$ (Product of diagonals) × (sine of the angle between them)

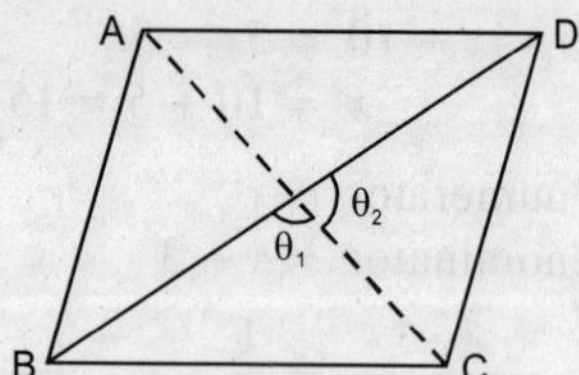

If θ_1 and θ_2 are the two angles made between themselves by the two diagonals, we have by the property of intersecting lines

$\Rightarrow$ $\theta_1 + \theta_2 = 180°$

Then, the area of quadrilateral

$$= \frac{1}{2}\, d_1 d_2 \sin\theta_1$$

$$= \frac{1}{2} d_1 d_2 \sin\theta_2$$

(*b*) Area = $\frac{1}{2}$ × diagonal × sum of the perpendiculars to it from opposite vertices = $\frac{d(h_1 + h_2)}{2}$

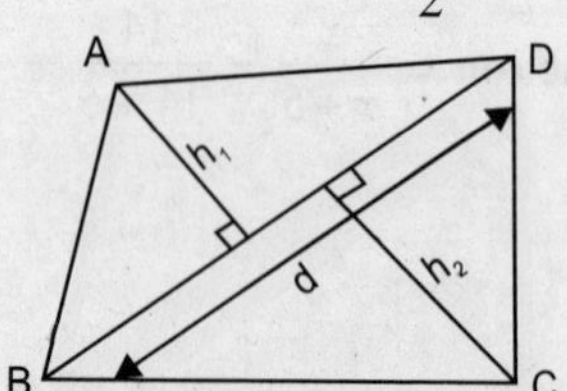

(*c*) Area of circumscribed quadrilateral

$$A = \sqrt{S(S-a)(S-b)(S-c)(S-d)}$$

Where $S = \frac{a+b+c+d}{2}$

where, *a*, *b*, *c* and *d* are the length of the sides.

Properties

1. In a convex quadrilateral inscribed in a circle, the product of the diagonals is equal to the sum of the products of the opposite sides. For example, in the figure below:

   $(a \times c) + (b \times d) = AC \times BD$

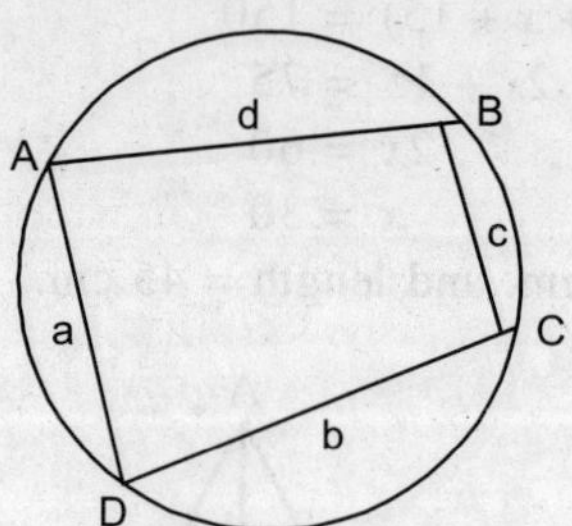

2. Sum of all the angles of a quadrilateral = 360°.

Types of Quadrilaterals

1. Parallelogram (|| gm)

A parallelogram is a quadrilateral with opposite sides parallel (as shown in figure below)

(*a*) Area = Base (*b*) × height (*h*) = *bh*

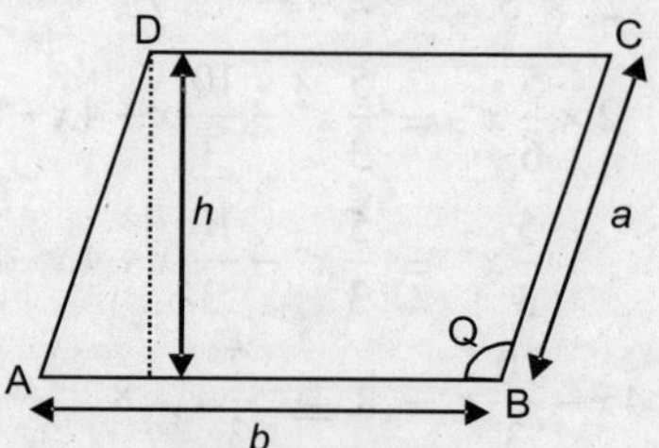

(*b*) Area = product of any two adjacent sides × sine of the included angle

$= ab \sin Q$

(*c*) Perimeter = $2(a + b)$

where *a* and *b* are any two adjacent sides.

Properties

1. Diagonals of a parallelogram bisect each other.
2. Bisectors of the angles of a parallelogram form a rectangle.
3. A parallelogram inscribed in a circle is a rectangle.
4. A parallelogram circumscribed about a circle is a rhombus.
5. The opposite angles in a parallelogram are equal.

6. The sum of the squares of the diagonals is equal to the sum of the squares of the four sides in the figure:

$AC^2 + BD^2 = AB^2 + BC^2 + CD^2 + AD^2$
$= 2(AB^2 + BC^2)$

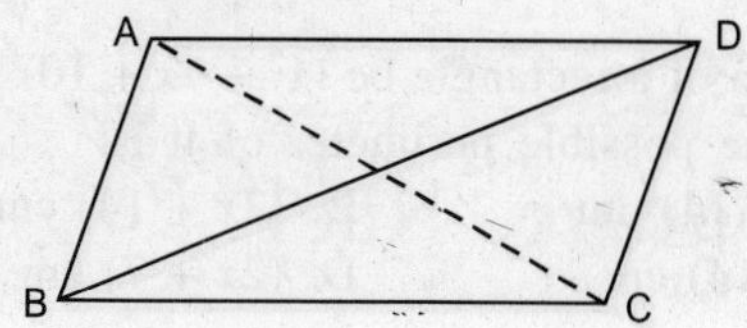

Rectangles

A rectangle is a parallelogram with all angles 90°

(a) Area = Base × Height = $b \times h$

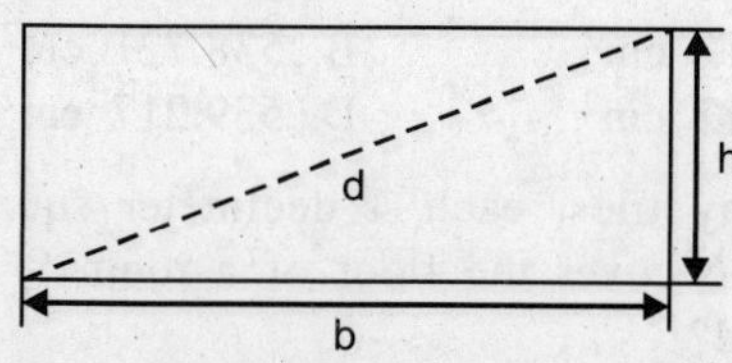

Note : Base and height are also referred to as the length and the breadth in a rectangle.

(b) Diagonal (d) = $\sqrt{b^2 + h^2}$ → by Pythagoras theorem

Properties

1. Diagonals are equal and bisect each other.
2. Bisectors of the angles of a rectangle (a parallelogram) form another rectangle.
3. All rectangles are parallelograms but the reverse is not true.

Rhombus

A parallelogram having all the sides equal is a rhombus.

(a) Area = $\frac{1}{2}$ × product of diagonals × sine of the angle between them.

$= \frac{1}{2} \times d_1 \times d_2 \sin 90°$

(Diagonals in a rhombus intersect at right angles) (since sin 90° = 1)

$= \frac{1}{2} \times d_1 d_2$

(b) Area = product of adjacent sides × sine of the angle between them.

Properties

1. Diagonals bisect each other at right angles.
2. All rhombuses are parallelograms but the reverse is not true.
3. A rhombus may or may not be a square but all squares are rhombuses.

Square

A square is a rectangle with adjacent sides equal or a rhombus with each angle 90°.

(a) Area = base × height = a^2

(b) Area = 1/2 (diagonal)^2 = 1/2 d^2 (square is a rhombus too).

(c) Perimeter = $4a$ (a = side of the square)

(d) Diagonal = $a\sqrt{2}$

(e) In radius = $\frac{a}{2}$

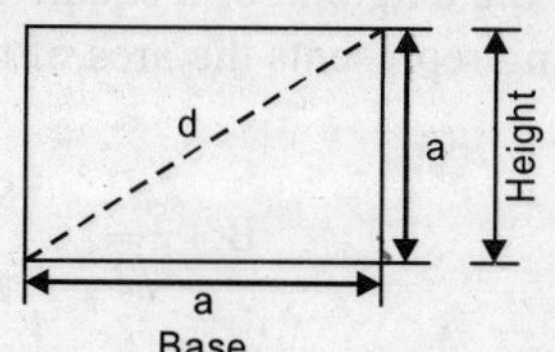

Properties

1. Diagonals are equal and bisect each other at right angles.
2. Side is the diameter of the inscribed circle.
3. Diagonal is the diameter of the circumscribing circle.

⇒ Diameter = $a\sqrt{2}$

Circumradius = $\frac{a}{\sqrt{2}}$

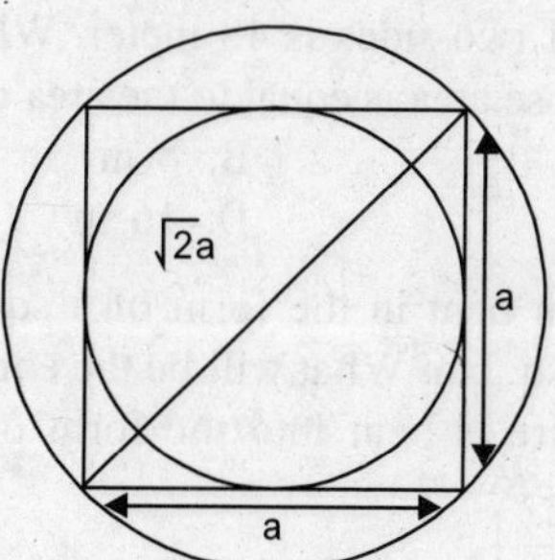

Trapezium

A trapezium is a quadrilateral with only two sides parallel to each other.

(a) Area = $\frac{1}{2}$ × sum of parallel sides × heights = $\frac{1}{2}$ (AB + DC) × h — For the figure below.

(b) Median = $\frac{1}{2}$ × sum of the parallel sides (median is the line equidistant from the parallel sides). For any line EF parallel to AB

$$EF = \frac{\{[P \times (AB)] + Q \times (DC)]\}}{AD}$$

D C P E h F Q A B

Properties

1. If the non-parallel sides are equal then diagonals will be equal too.

Multiple Choice Questions

1. If the length of the diagonal AC of a square ABCD is 5.2 cm, then the area of the square is:
A. 15.12 sq. cm B. 13.52 sq. cm
C. 12.62 sq. cm D. 10.00 sq. cm

2. The length of the diagonal of a square is 'a' cm. Which of the following represents the area of the square (in sq. cm)?
A. $2a$ B. $\frac{a}{\sqrt{2}}$
C. $\frac{a^2}{2}$ D. $\frac{a^2}{4}$

3. What is the length of the largest rod that can be placed in a room 16 m long, 12 m broad and $10\frac{2}{3}$ m high?
A. 123 m B. 68 m
C. $22\frac{2}{3}$ m D. $22\frac{1}{3}$ m

4. The perimeter of a rectangle is 160 meter and the difference of two sides is 48 meter. What is the side of a square whose area is equal to the area of this rectangle?
A. 32 m B. 8 m
C. 4 m D. 16 m

5. A wire when bent in the form of a square encloses an area of 484 sq. cm. What will be the enclosed area when the same wire is bent into the form of a circle? $\left(\text{Take } \pi = \frac{22}{7}\right)$
A. 125 cm^2 B. 230 cm^2
C. 550 cm^2 D. 616 cm^2

6. A took 15 sec. to cross a rectangular field diagonally walking at the ratio of 52 m/min and B took the same time to cross the same field along its sides walking at the rate of 68 m/min. The area of the field is:
A. 30 m^2 B. 40 m^2
C. 50 m^2 D. 60 m^2

7. The difference between the length and breadth of a rectangle is 23 m. If its perimeter is 206 m, then its area is:
A. 1520 m^2 B. 2420 m^2
C. 2480 m^2 D. 2520 m^2

8. A path of uniform width runs round the inside of a rectangular field 38 m long and 32 m wide. If the path occupies 600 m^2, then the width of the path is:
A. 30 m B. 5 m
C. 18.75 m D. 10 m

9. The perimeter of the floor of a room is 18 m. What is the area of the walls of the room, if the height of the room is 3 m?
A. 21 m^2 B. 42 m^2
C. 54 m^2 D. 108 m^2

10. If the area of a rectangle be $(x^2 + 7x + 10)$ sq. cm, then one of the possible perimeter of it is:
A. $(4x + 14)$ cm B. $(2x + 14)$ cm
C. $(x + 14)$ cm D. $(2x + 7)$ cm

11. A kite in the shape of a square with a diagonal 32 cm attached to an equilateral triangle of the base 8 cm. Approximately how much paper has been used to make it? (Use $\sqrt{3} = 1.732$)
A. 539.712 cm^2 B. 538.721 cm^2
C. 540.712 cm^2 D. 539.217 cm^2

12. How many tiles, each 4 decimeter square, will be required to cover the floor of a room 8 m long and 6 m broad?
A. 200 B. 260
C. 280 D. 300

13. If each edge of a square be doubled, then the increase percentage in its area is:
A. 200% B. 250%
C. 280% D. 300%

14. The length of a room is 3 m more than its breadth. If the area of a floor of the room is 70 m^2, then the perimeter of the floor will be:
A. 14 metres B. 28 metres
C. 34 metres D. 17 metres

15. The diagonals of a rhombus are 32 cm and 24 cm respectively. The perimeter of the rhombus is:
A. 80 cm B. 72 cm
C. 68 cm D. 64 cm

16. The perimeter of a rhombus is 40 cm. If one of the diagonals be 12 cm long, what is the length of the other diagonal?
A. 12 cm B. $\sqrt{136}$ cm
C. 16 cm D. $\sqrt{44}$ cm

17. A parallelogram ABCD has sides AB = 24 cm and AD = 16 cm. The distance between the sides AB and DC is 10 cm. What is the distance between the sides AD and BC?
A. 15 cm B. 18 cm
C. 16 cm D. 9 cm

18. The adjacent sides of a paralleogram are 36 cm and 27 cm in length. If the distance between the shorter sides is 12 cm, then the distance between the longer sides is:
A. 10 cm B. 12 cm
C. 16 cm D. 9 cm

19. ABCD is a trapezium in which AB || DC and AB = 2 CD. The diagonals AC and BD meet at O. The ratio of area of triangles AOB and COD is:

A. 1 : 1 B. 1 : $\sqrt{2}$
C. 4 : 1 D. 1 : 4

20. The length of each side of a rhombus is equal to the length of the side of a square whose diagonal is $40\sqrt{2}$ cm. If the length of the diagonals of the rhombus are in the ratio 3 : 4, then its area (in cm^2) is:

A. 1550 B. 1600
C. 1535 D. 1536

21. The area of a rhombus is 216 cm^2 and the length of its one diagonal is 24 cm. The perimeter (in cm) of the rhombus is:

A. 52 B. 60
C. 120 D. 100

22. The area of a rhombus is 256 sq. cm. and one of its diagonal is twice the other in length. Then length of its larger diagonal is:

A. 32 cm B. 48 cm
C. 36 cm D. 24 cm

23. The floor of a corridor is 100 cm long and 3 m wide. Cost of covering the floor with carpet 50 cm wide at the ratio of ₹ 15 per m is:

A. ₹ 4500 B. ₹ 9000
C. ₹ 7500 D. ₹ 1900

24. The length and breadth of a rectangle are increased by 12% and 15% respectively. Its area will be increased by:

A. $27\frac{1}{5}\%$ B. $28\frac{4}{5}\%$
C. 27% D. 28%

25. The length of rectangle is increased by 60%. By what per cent would the breadth to be decreased to maintain the same area?

A. $37\frac{1}{2}\%$ B. 60%
C. 75% D. 120%

ANSWERS

1	2	3	4	5	6	7	8	9	10
B	C	C	A	D	D	D	B	C	A
11	**12**	**13**	**14**	**15**	**16**	**17**	**18**	**19**	**20**
A	D	D	C	A	C	A	D	C	D
21	**22**	**23**	**24**	**25**					
B	A	B	B	A					

EXPLANATORY ANSWERS

1. Side of a square = $\frac{\text{Diagonal}}{\sqrt{2}}$

Area of square = $\left(\frac{\text{Diagonal}}{\sqrt{2}}\right)^2$

$$= \frac{(5.2)^2}{2} = \frac{5.2 \times 5.2}{2}$$

$= 2.6 \times 5.2 = 13.52$ cm^2.

2. Area of square = $\frac{\text{Diagonal}^2}{2} = \frac{a^2}{2}$

3. Since the room is in cuboid shape

Length of largest rod = Diagonal of cuboid

$$= \sqrt{l^2 + b^2 + h^2}$$

$$= \sqrt{16^2 + 12^2 + \frac{32^2}{3^2}}$$

$$= \sqrt{256 + 144 + \frac{1024}{9}}$$

$$= \sqrt{\frac{2304 + 1296 + 1024}{9}}$$

$$= \sqrt{\frac{4624}{9}} = \frac{68}{3} = 22\frac{2}{3} \text{ m.}$$

4. According to question,

$2(l + b) = 160$

$l + b = 80$ ...(*i*)

$l - b = 48$ ...(*ii*)

on solving (*i*) and (*ii*)

$l = 64, \quad b = 16$

area of square = area of rectangle

(side)^2 = 64 × 16

side = $\sqrt{64 \times 16}$

= 32 m.

5. $(\text{side})^2 = 484$ cm

side $= 22$ cm

perimeter of square $= 4 \times 22 = 88$ cm

According to question,

$2\pi r = 88$ cm

$r = \dfrac{88 \times 7}{2 \times 22} = 14$ cm

area of circle $= \pi r^2 = \dfrac{22}{7} \times 14 \times 14 = 616$ cm^2.

6. 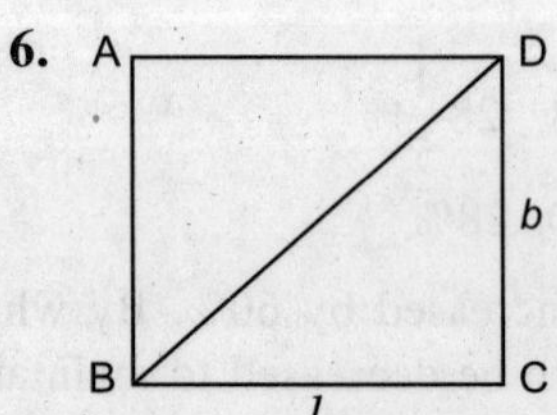

BD = length of diagonal = speed × time

$= \dfrac{52}{60} \times 15 = 13$ m

$BD = \sqrt{l^2 + b^2}$

$\Rightarrow \quad l^2 + b^2 = 13^2 = 169$

Again, $\quad l + b = \dfrac{68}{60} \times 15 = 17$

$(l + b)^2 = l^2 + b^2 + 2\,lb$

$17^2 = 169 + 2\,lb$

$lb = \dfrac{120}{2} = 60$ m^2.

7. Let the breadth be $= x$ m

$\therefore$ length $= (23 + x)$ m

$\Rightarrow \quad 2(x + 23 + x) = 206$

$4x = 206 - 46$

$x = \dfrac{160}{4} = 40$ m

$\therefore$ length $= 40 + 23 = 63$ m

$\therefore$ Required area $= 63 \times 40 = 2520$ m^2.

8. 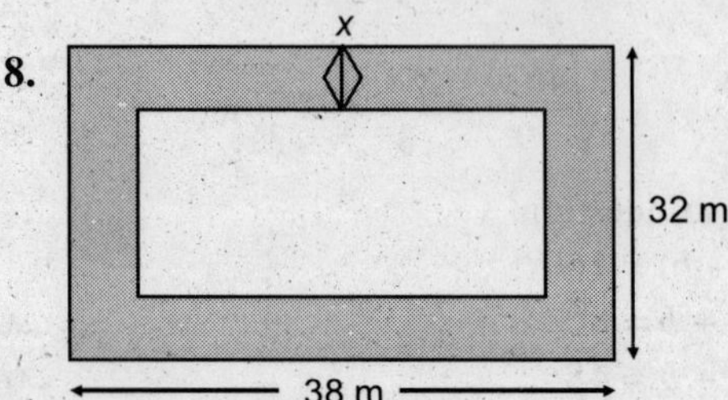

area of path $= 600$ m^2

$(l + b - 2x)2x = 600$

$(38 + 32 - 2x)2x = 600$

$(70 - 2x)2x = 600$

$(70 - 2x)x = \dfrac{600}{2} = 300$

$70x - 2x^2 = 300$

$2x^2 - 70x + 300 = 0$

$x^2 - 35x + 150 = 0$

$x^2 - 30x - 5x + 150 = 0$

$x(x - 30) - 5(x - 30) = 0$

$(x - 30)(x - 5) = 0$

$x = 30$ not possible

$x = 5$ (right).

9. Area of walls = Perimeter of base × heaght

$= 18 \times 3 = 54$ m^2.

10. $x^2 + 7x + 10 = x^2 + 5x + 2x + 10$

$= x(x + 5) + 2(x + 5)$

$= (x + 2)(x + 5)$

$\therefore$ Two sides of rectangle

$= (x + 2)(x + 5)$

$\therefore$ Perimeter $= 2(x + 2 + x + 5)$

$= 2(2x + 7) = (4x + 14)$ cm.

11. 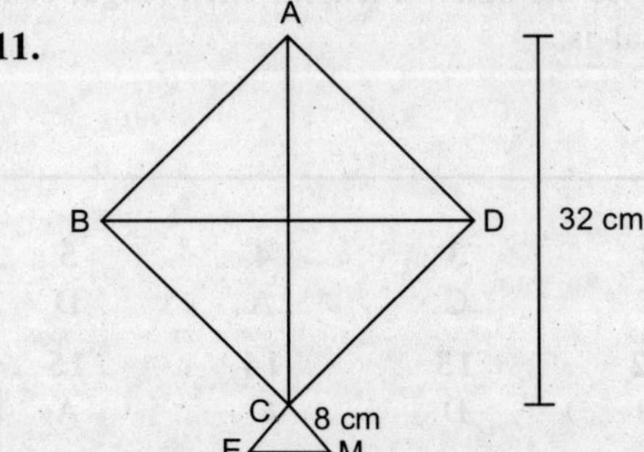

area of square $= \dfrac{1}{2}$ (Diagonal)^2

$= \dfrac{1}{2}(32)^2 = \dfrac{1}{2} \times 32 \times 32 = 16 \times 32$

$= 512$ cm^2

area of triangle $= \dfrac{\sqrt{3}}{4} 8^2 = \dfrac{1.732 \times 8 \times 8}{4}$

$= 1.732 \times 2 \times 8 = 27.712$ cm^2

Required are $= (512 + 27.712)$ cm^2

$= 539.712$ cm^2.

12. Area of the floor $= 8 \times 6 = 48$ m^2

$= 4800$ dm^2 (1 m = 10 dm)

Area of square tile $= 4 \times 4 = 16$ dm^2

No. of tiles $= \dfrac{4800}{16} = 300$.

13. Percentage increase in area

$= \left(x + y + \dfrac{xy}{100}\right)\%$

Here, $x = 100\%$, $y = 100\%$

$= \left(100 + 100 + \dfrac{100 \times 100}{100}\right)\% = 300\%$.

14. Let the breadth of floor = x m

Then the length of floor = $(x + 3)$ m

A.T.Q.

$$x \times (x + 3) = 70$$
$$x^2 + 3x - 70 = 0$$
$$x^2 + 10x - 7x - 70 = 0$$
$$(x + 10)(x - 7) = 0$$
$$x = 7, x = -10$$

Breadth = 7 m

Length = 10 m

Perimeter of floor = 2 (L + B)

= 2(10 + 7) = 34 m.

15. We know that rhombus is parallelogram whose all four sides are equal and its diagonals bisect each other at 90°.

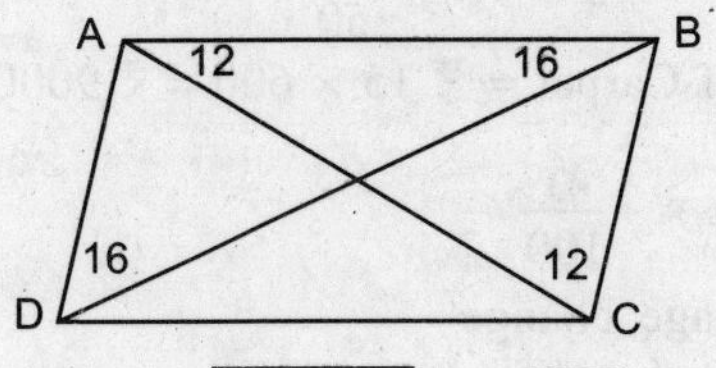

$\therefore$ $AB = \sqrt{16^2 + 12^2} = \sqrt{400} = 20$ cm

= side of rhombus

$\therefore$ perimeter of the rhombus

= 20 × 4 = 80 cm.

16. 4 × side = 40 cm (given)

$$\text{side} = \frac{40}{4} = 10 \text{ cm}$$

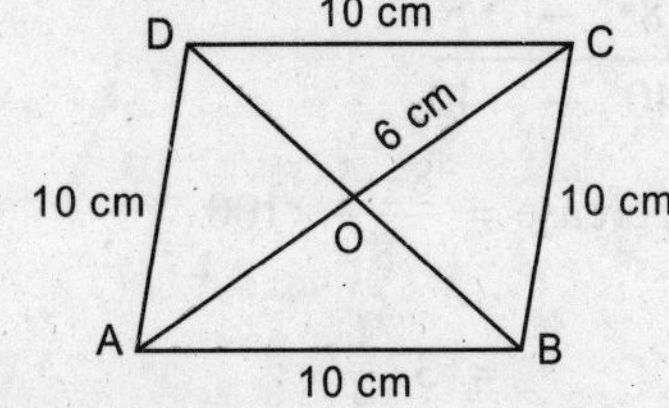

In Δ AOB,

$$OB = \sqrt{10^2 - 6^2} = \sqrt{100 - 36}$$
$$= \sqrt{64} = 8 \text{ cm}$$

Diagonal BD = 8 × 2 = 16 cm.

17.

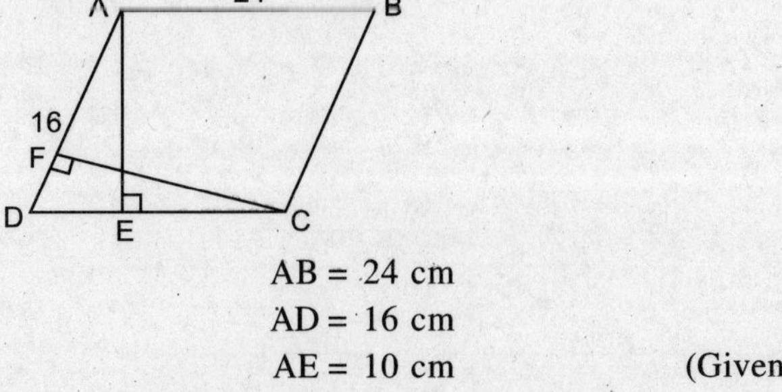

AB = 24 cm

AD = 16 cm

AE = 10 cm (Given)

Area of Parallelogram

= AE × DC = 10 × 24

= 240 cm^2

also, area of Parallelogram

= FC × AD = 240

FC × 16 = 240

FC = 15

$\therefore$ Distance between AD and BC = 15 cm.

18.

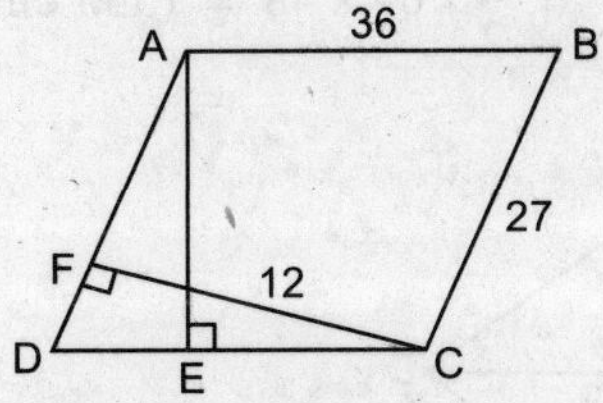

Area of parallelogram

= AE × DC = CF × AD

AE × 36 = 12 × 27

= AE = 9 cm

$\therefore$ Distance between bigger sides = 9 cm.

19.

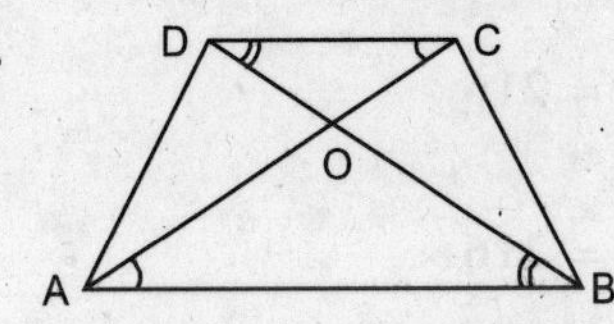

$\therefore$ AB = 2 CD

$$\frac{AB}{CD} = \frac{2}{1}$$

$$\frac{ar(\Delta AOB)}{ar(\Delta COD)} = \left(\frac{2}{1}\right)^2 = \frac{4}{1} = 4:1$$

(Δ AOB ~ Δ COD).

20.

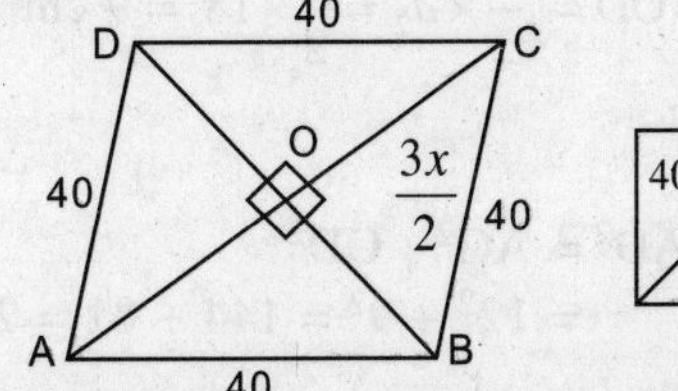

Let AC = $4x$ and BD = $3x$

$\therefore$ OA = $2x$ and OB = $\frac{3x}{2}$

In Right Δ OAB

$$\sqrt{(2x)^2 + \left(\frac{3x}{2}\right)^2} = 40$$

$$4x^2 + \frac{9x^2}{4} = 40^2 = 1600$$
$$16x^2 + 9x^2 = 1600 \times 4$$
$$25x^2 = 6400$$
$$x^2 = \frac{6400}{25}$$
$$x = \sqrt{\frac{6400}{25}} = \frac{80}{5} = 16$$

$\therefore$ $AC = 4x = 4 \times 16 = 64$

$BD = 3x = 3 \times 16 = 48$

$$\text{area} = \frac{1}{2} \times AC \times BD$$

$$= \frac{1}{2} \times 64 \times 48 = 1536 \text{ cm}^2.$$

21. 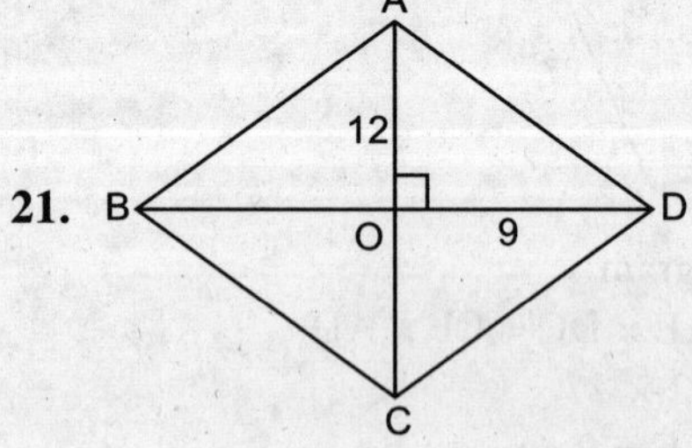

$d_1 = 24$ cm

area of Rhombus = 216

$$\frac{1}{2} \times d_1 \times d_2 = 216$$

$$\frac{1}{2} \times 24 \times d_2 = 216$$

$$d_2 = \frac{216 \times 2}{24} = 18 \text{ cm}$$

$$OA = \frac{1}{2} \times d_1 = \frac{1}{2} \times 24 = 12 \text{ cm}$$

$\therefore$ Diagonals of Rhombus bisect each other at right angle

$$OD = \frac{1}{2} \times d_2 = \frac{1}{2} \times 18 = 9 \text{ cm}$$

Now,

In Right Δ AOD

$$AD^2 = AO^2 + OD^2$$

$$= 12^2 + 9^2 = 144 + 81 = 225$$

$$AD = \sqrt{225} = 15 \text{ cm}$$

$\therefore$ Perimeter of Rhombus

$$= 4 \times AD = 4 \times 15 = 60 \text{ cm.}$$

22. Let the diagonal of rhombus

$$d_1 = x \ \& \ d_2 = 2x$$

$$\text{Area of rhombus} = \frac{1}{2} d_1 d_2$$

$$256 = \frac{1}{2}(x)(2x)$$

$$16 = x$$

Longer diagonal = $2x = 2(16) = 32$ cm.

23. Area of corridor = $100 \times 3 = 300$ m^2

$$\text{Carpet length} = \frac{300 \times 100}{50} = 600 \text{ cm}$$

Cost of Carpet = ₹ 15×600 = ₹ 9000.

24. Use $x + y + \frac{xy}{100}$

percentage change

$$= 12 + 15 + \frac{12 \times 15}{100}$$

$$= 27 + \frac{9}{5}$$

$$= 27 + 1 + \frac{4}{5} = 28\frac{4}{5}\%.$$

25.

Length	5	→	8
Breadth	8	→	5
Area	40	→	40

$$\Rightarrow \% \text{ Decrease} = \frac{8-5}{8} \times 100$$

$$= 37\frac{1}{2}\%.$$

□□□□□

10

Geometry

LINES AND ANGLES

A line is made up of an infinite number of points and it has only length. *i.e.*, A line has no end points on either side. A line segment has two end points. A ray has one end point.

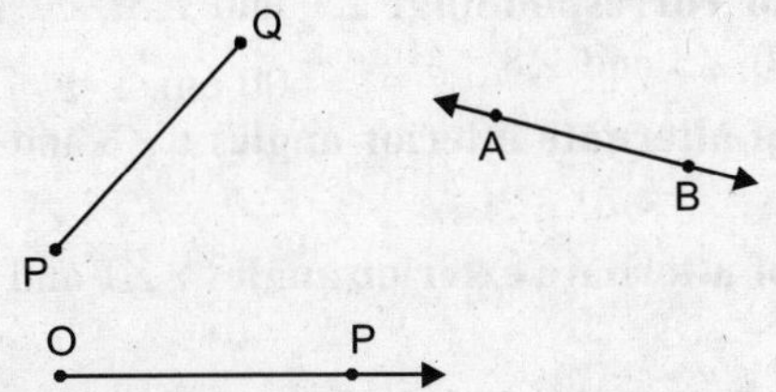

Line Segment Line Ray

- A line segment PQ is generally denoted by $\overline{PQ}$
- A line AB is denoted by $\overleftrightarrow{AB}$
- And the ray OP is denoted by $\overrightarrow{OP}$
- **Collinear points :** Three or more than three points are said to be collinear if there is a line which contains them all.

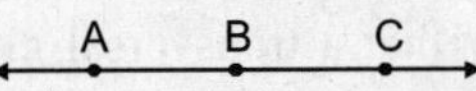

Here A, B and C are collinear points.

- **Concurrent lines :** Three or more than three lines are said to be concurrent if there is a point which lies on all of them.

AB, CD and EF are concurrent lines.

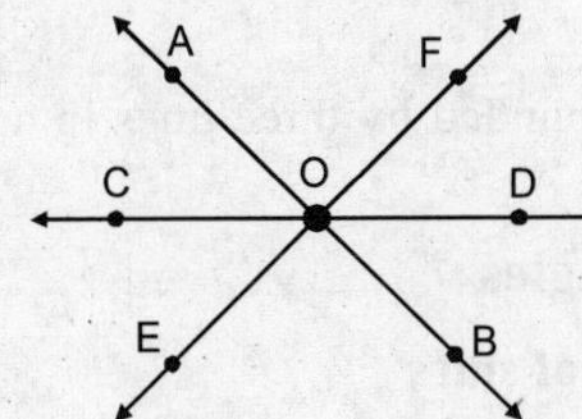

Recall that an "angle" is formed when lines or line segments meet.

E.g.

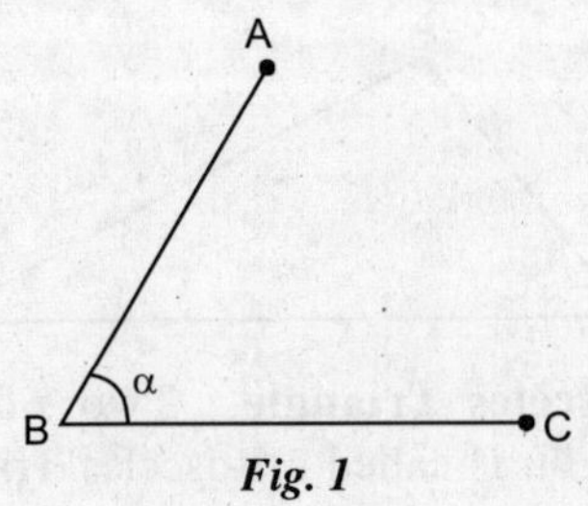

Fig. 1

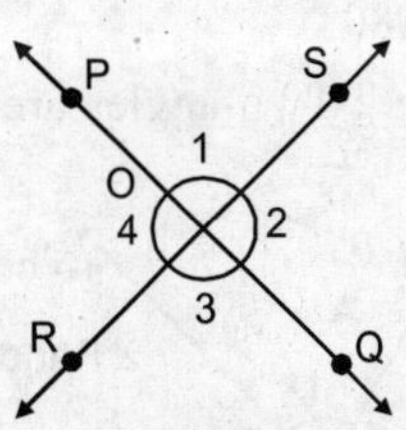

Fig. 2

in figure (1) ∠α fomed by AB and BC in figure (2) ∠1, ∠2, ∠3 and ∠4 are formed by PQ and RS.

Related Angles

- **Acute Angle :** x $0° < x < 90°$
- **Right Angle :** y $y = 90°$
- **Obtuse Angle :** z $180° < z < 360°$
- **Straight Angle :** t $t = 180°$
- **Reflex Angle :** r $180° < r < 360°$
- **Complementary Angles :** When the sum of the measures of the two angles is 90°, the angles are called "Complementary Angles".

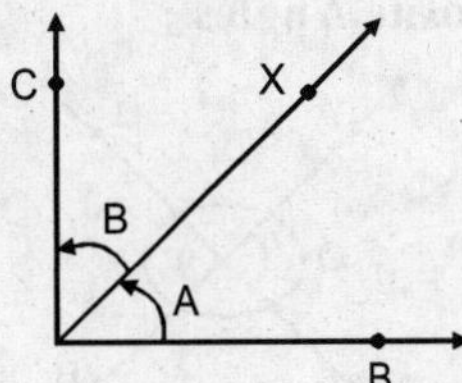

i.e. $\angle A + \angle B = 90°$ or $\angle A = \angle 90° - \angle B$

- **Supplementary Angles :** Sum of two angles which are supplementary is 180°.

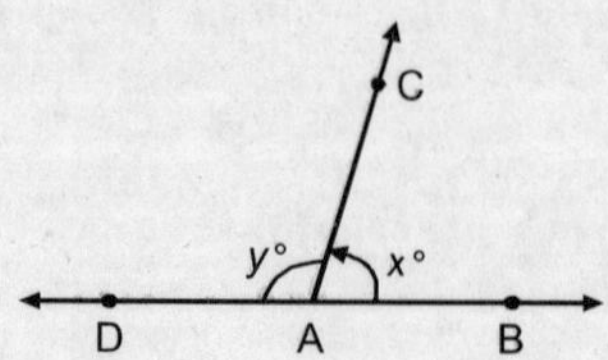

i.e. $\angle x + \angle y = 180°$

- **Adjacent Angles :** Two angles are said to be adjacent if

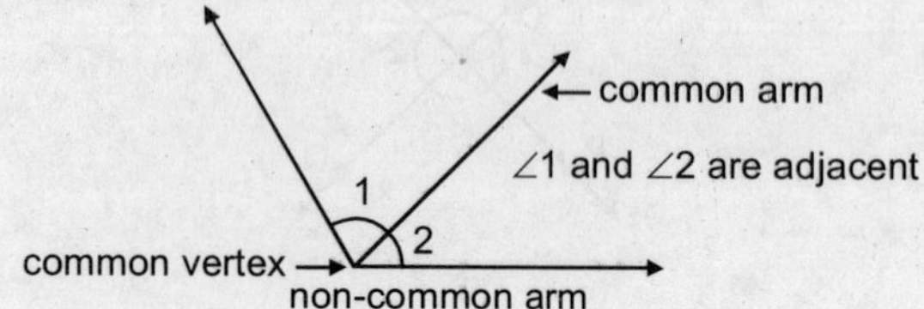

1. They have a common vertex;
2. They have a common arm; and
3. The non-common arms are on either side of the common arm.

- **Linear pair :** A linear pair is a pair of adjacent angles whose non-common sides are opposite rays.

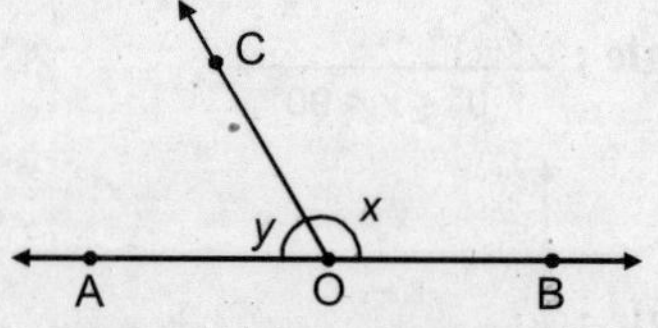

$\angle x$, $\angle y$ and A linear pair and $\angle x + \angle y = 180°$

i.e. linear pair Angles are supplementary.

- **Parallel Lines :** If two lines have no point in common they are said to be

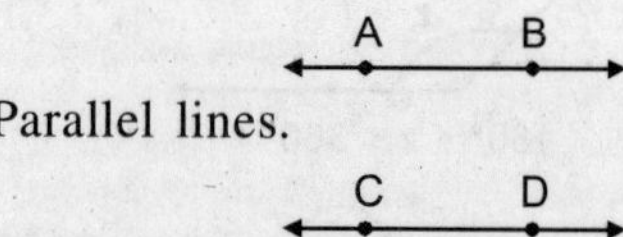

- **Intersecting Lines :** If two lines have a point in common, they are said to be intersecting lines. Two lines can intersect at the most at one point.

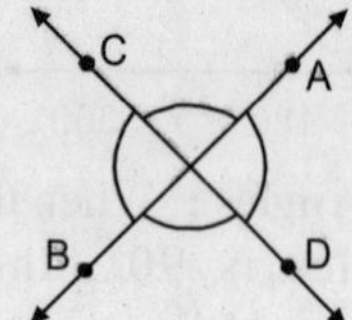

- **Vertically opposite Angles :**

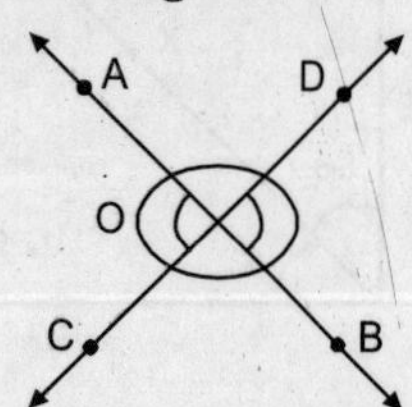

$\angle AOD$ $\angle BOC$, $\angle AOC$ $\angle BOD$ } are vertically opposite angles

- **Angles made by a transversal line :**

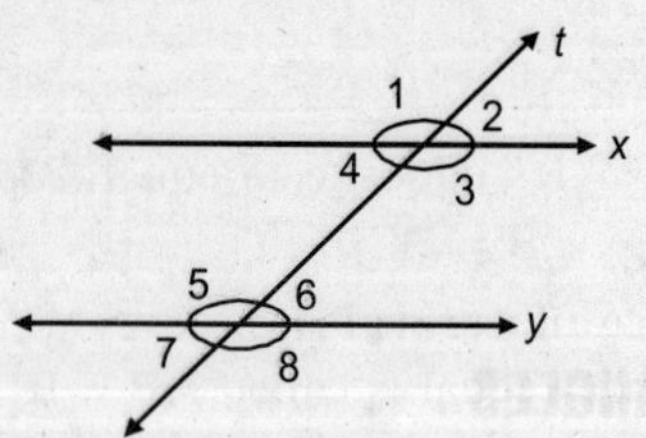

Interior Angles : $\angle 3, \angle 4, \angle 5, \angle 6$

Exterior Angles : $\angle 1, \angle 2, \angle 7, \angle 8$

Pairs of corresponding: $\angle 1$ and $\angle 5$, $\angle 2$ and $\angle 6$, $\angle 4$ and $\angle 7$, $\angle 3$ and $\angle 8$

Pairs of alternate interior angles : $\angle 3$ and $\angle 5$, $\angle 4$ and $\angle 6$

Pairs of alternate exterior angles : $\angle 1$ and $\angle 8$, $\angle 2$ and $\angle 7$

Pairs of interior angles on the same side of the transversal : $\angle 3$ and $\angle 6$, $\angle 4$ and $\angle 5$

→ If two parallel lines are interested by a transversal then:
1. Each pair of corresponding angles are eqal.
2. Each pair of alternate interior are equal.
3. Interior angles on the same side of the transversal are supplementary.

→ **Checking for parallel lines:** If two lines are parallel, then you know that a transversal gives rise to

- pairs of equal corresponding angles
- pairs of equal alternate interior angles and
- interior angles on the same side of the transversal being Supplementary.

TRIANGLES

A plane figure bounded by three lines in a plane is called a triangle.

Type of Triangles

1. On the basis of sides

(*i*) **Scalene Triangle :** All three sides are of different lengths is called a Scalene Triangle.

$AB \neq BC \neq CA$

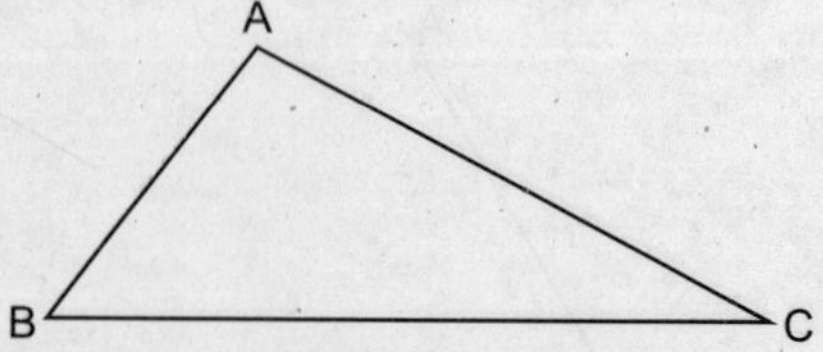

(*ii*) **Isosceles Triangle :** Two sides are of equal length, is called a Isosceles Triangle.

$AB = AC$

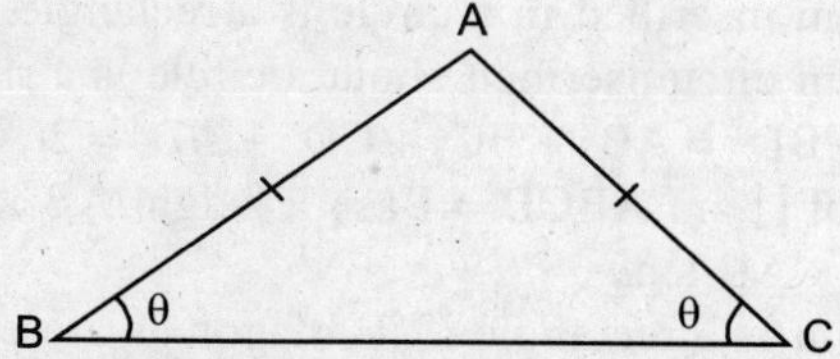

→ Angles opposite to equal sides are equal.
i.e. $\angle B = \angle C$

(iii) **Equilateral Triangle :** A triangle having all sides equal is called AB = BC = CA

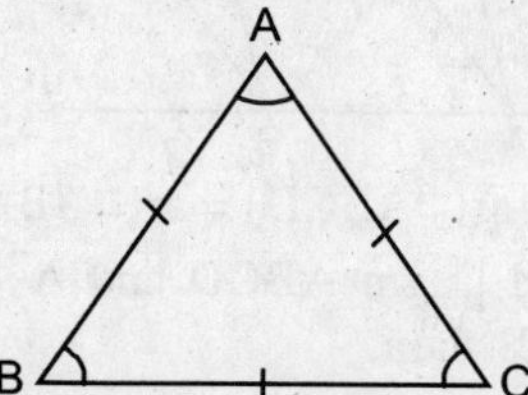

All angles are equal and is equal to 60°.

$\angle A = \angle B = \angle C = 60°$

2. On the basis of Angles

(i) **Right-angled Triangle :** In a triangle, in which one of the angles measures 90° is called a right-angled triangle.

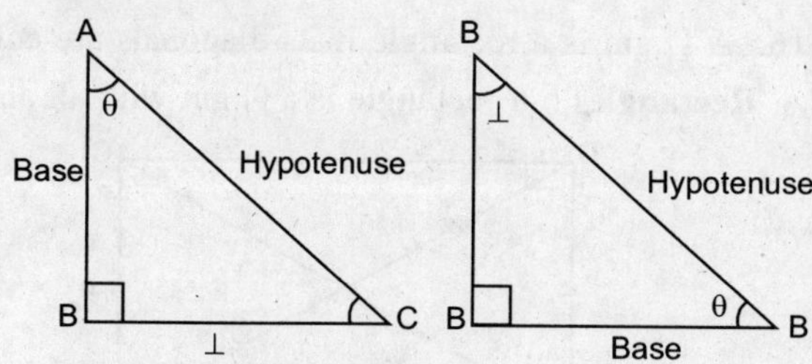

(ii) **Acute-angled Triangle :** A triangle in which every angle is more than 0° and less than 90° is called an acute-angle triangle.

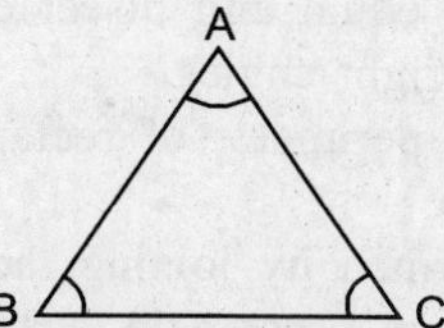

(iii) **Obtuse-angled Triangle :** A triangle in which one of the angles is more than 90° is called an obtuse-angle triangle.

Note : An equilateral triangle is an isosceles triangle but the converse is not true.

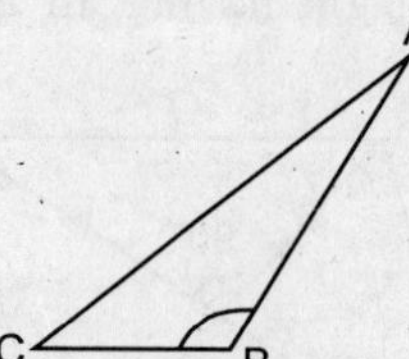

- **Perimeter of Triangle (2*s*) :** The sum of lengths of three sides of a triangle is called its perimeter.

$2s = a + b + c$

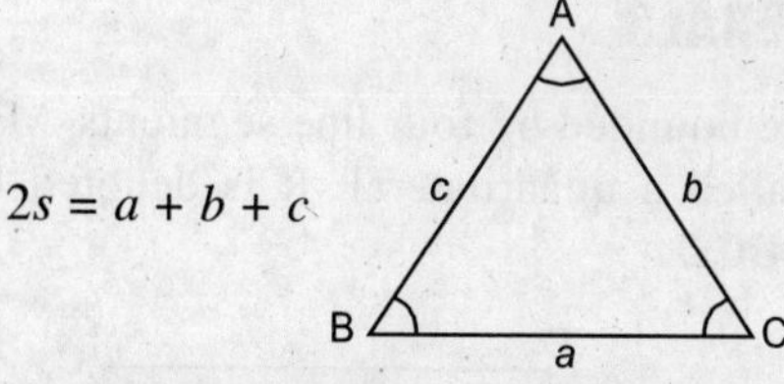

- **Types of Triangles:** Angle Sum property of a triangle:

Theorem 1: The sum of the angles of a Δ is 180°.

Theorem 2: (Exterior angle Theorem): If a side of a triangle is produced, the exterior angle so formed is equal to the sum of the two interior opposite angles.

$$\angle ACD = \angle ABC + \angle BAC$$

$$\Rightarrow \quad \angle 4 = \angle 1 + \angle 2$$

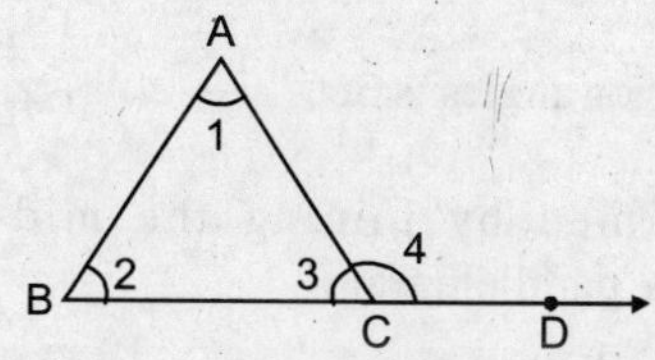

Note : An exterior angle of a triangle is greater than either of the interior opposite angles.

i.e. 4 > 1, and 4 > 2

If three sides of triangle be produced in order then sum of exterior angles so formed is 360°.

$\angle 1 + \angle 2 + \angle 3 = 360°$

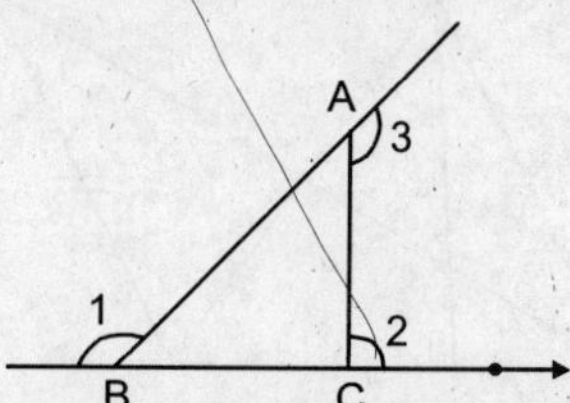

→ **Some properties of triangle:**

Theorem 3: Angles opposite to equal sides of an isosceles triangle are equal.

Here Δ ABC is an isosceles Δ *i.e.* AB = AC

$\angle ABC = \angle BCA$

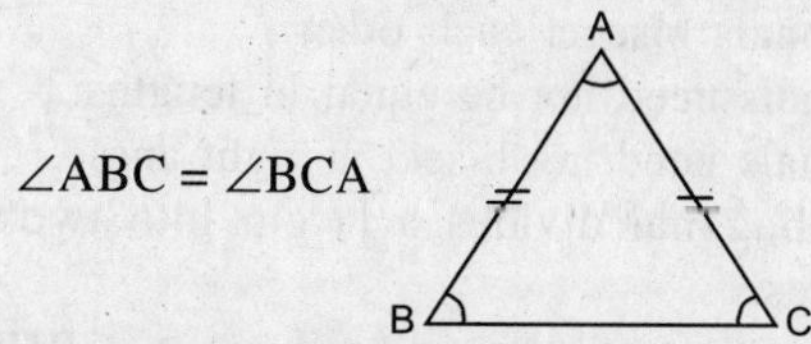

Theorem 4: The sides opposite to equal angles of a triangle are equal.

Here, $\angle B = \angle C \Rightarrow \angle 1 = \angle 2$

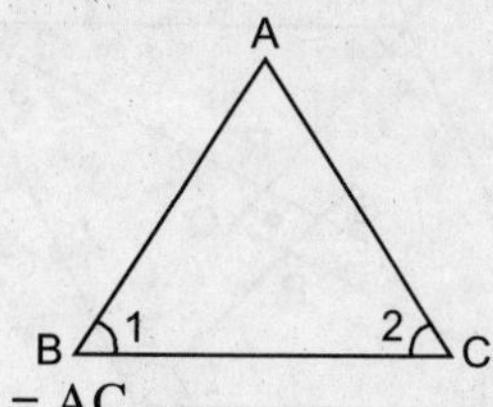

$\therefore$ AB = AC

QUADRILATERALS

A plane figure bounded by four line segments AB, BC, CD, and DA is called a quadrilateral. It is denoted by symbol '□' *i.e.* □ ABCD.

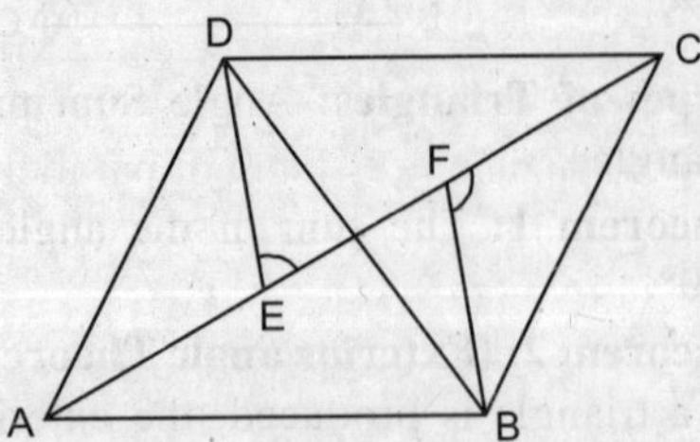

pairs of consecutive (adjacent) angles:
(∠A, ∠B), (∠B, ∠C), (∠C, ∠D), (∠D, ∠A)
(AB, BC), (BC, CD), (CD, DA) and (DA, AB)

Properties

Sum of four interior angles is 360°. *i.e.* ∠A + ∠B + ∠C + ∠D = 360°.

The figure formed by joining the mid-points of a quadrilateral is a parallelogram.

Area of ABCD = $\frac{1}{2}$AC × (DE + BF)

Types of Quadrilaterals

1. **Parallelogram (| | gm) :** A quadrilateral whose opposite sides are parallel.

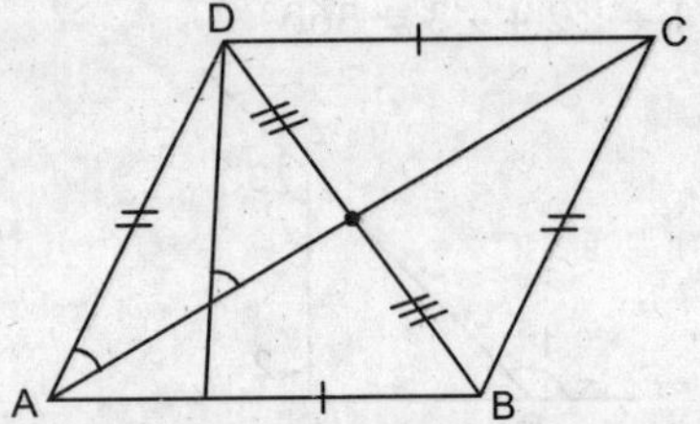

Properties

1. The opposite sides are equal and parallel.
2. Opposite angles are equal. (∠A = ∠C) and (∠B = ∠D)
3. Sum of any two adjacent angles is 180°.
4. Diagnonals bisecet each other.
5. Diagonals need not be equal in lengths.
6. Diagonals need not bisect at right angle.
7. Each diagonal divides a | | gm into two congruent triangles.
   i.e., Δ ABC ≅ Δ ADC and Δ ABD ≅ Δ BCD
8. Bisectors of the angles of a | | gm form a rectangle. *i.e.* PQRS is rectangle.

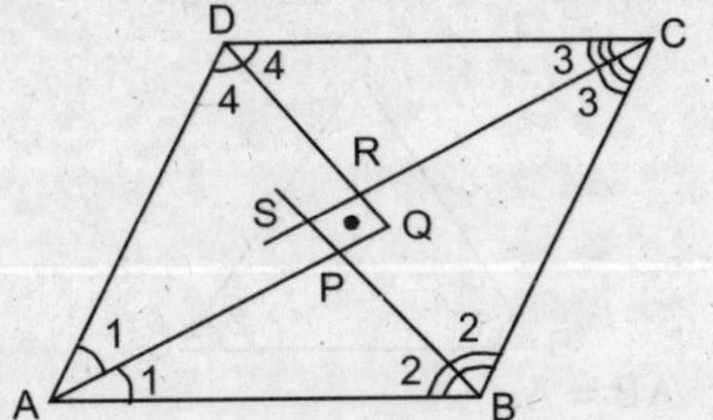

9. A | | gm inscribed in a circle is a rectangle.
10. A | | gm circumscribed about a circle is a rhombus.
11. $AC^2 + BD^2 = AB^2 + BC^2 + CD^2 + AD^2 = 2(AB^2 + BC^2)$
12. Area of | | gm ABCD = Base × height AB × h
    = AB × AD sin$q$
13. A | | gm is a rectangle if its diagonals are equal.
14. | | gm that lie on the same base and between the same parallel lines are equal in area, *i.e.*

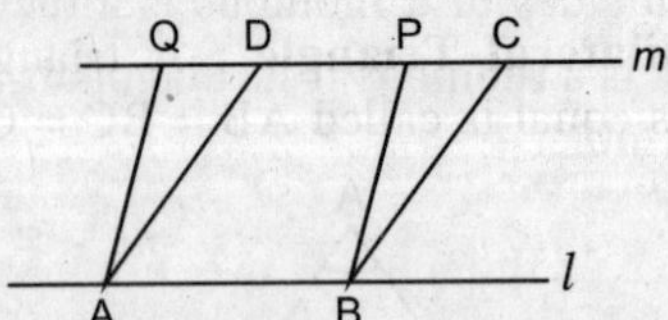

if l | | m, then ar(□ABCD) = ar(□ABPQ)

15. If l | | m, and | | gm ABCD and Δ APB made on the same base AB then,

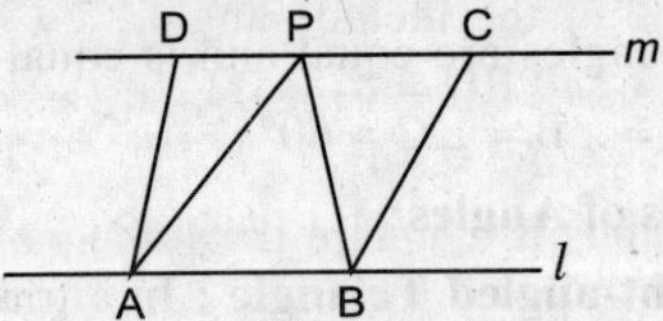

ar(Δ APB) = $\frac{1}{2}ar$ (□ABCD)

16. A | | gm is a rectangle if its diagonals are equal.

2. **Rectangles :** A rectangle is a | | gm with all angles 90°.

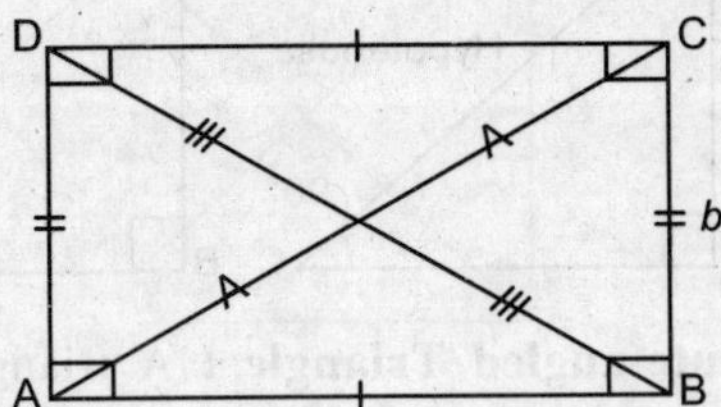

Properties

1. Diagonals are equal and bisect each other, but not necessarily at right angles.
2. For the given perimeter of rectangles, a square has maximum area.
3. The figure formed by joining the mid-points of the adjacent sides of a rectangle is rhombus.
4. Area of rectangles ABCD = length × breadth = $l \times b$
5. Diagonals of a rectangle = $\sqrt{l^2 + b^2}$
6. Bisectors of the angles of a rectangle (a | | gm) form another rectangle.

3. **Rhombus :** A | | gm having all the sides equal is a "rhombus".

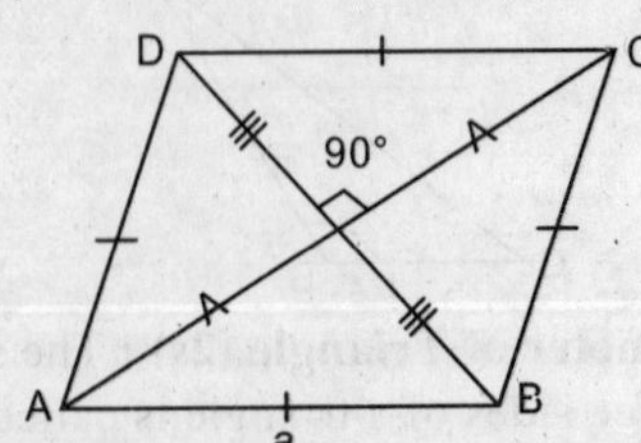

Properties

1. AB = BC = CD = DA = a (say)
2. Diagonals bisect each other at right angle, but they are not necessarily equal.
3. A rhombus may or may not be a square but all squares are rhombus.
4. The figure formed by joining the mid-points of the adjacent sides of a rhombus is a rectangle.
5. A || gm is a rhombus if its diagonals are perpendicular to each other.
6. (*a*) Area of rhombus = $\frac{1}{2}$ × product of diagonals

   $= \frac{1}{2} \times d_1 d_2$

   (*b*) Area of rhombus = product of adjacent sides × sine of the include angle.
7. AC = d_1 and BD = d_2 (say) then, $d_1^2 + d_2^2 = 4a^2$
8. A rhombus is a square if its diagonals are equal. *i.e.* if $d_1 = d_2 \Rightarrow$ ABCD is a square.

4. Square : A square is a rectangle with adjacent sides equal or a rhombus with each angle 90°.

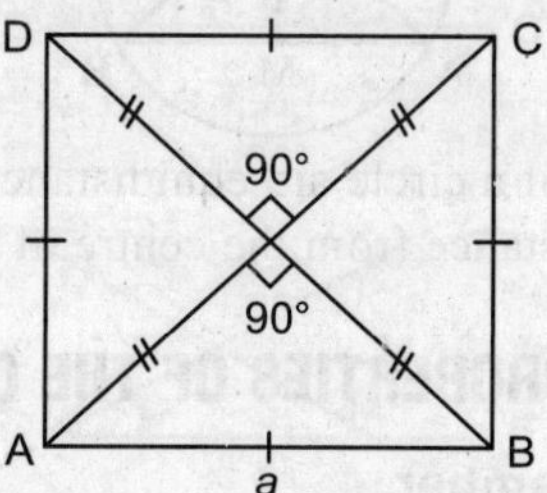

Properties

1. AB = BC = CD = AD = a (say) & ∠A = ∠B = ∠C = ∠D = 90°
2. Diagonals are equal and bisect each other at right angle.
3. The figure formed by joining the mid-points of the adjacent sides of a square is a square.
4. Area = (side)^2 = $a^2 = \frac{d^2}{2}$, and diagonal (*d*) = $a\sqrt{2}$.

5. Trapezium : A trapezium is a quadrilateral with only two sides parallel to each other.

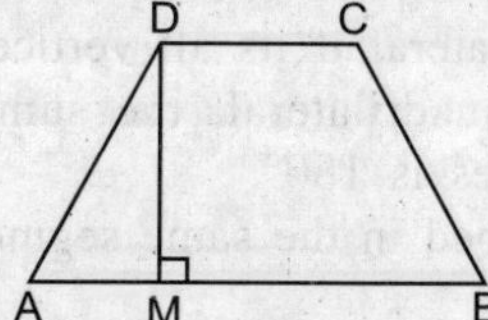

Properties

1. ∠A + ∠D = ∠B + ∠C = 180°
2. If E and F are the mid-points of two non-parallel sides AD and BC respectively, then,

   Median (EF) = $\frac{1}{2}$(AB + DC)

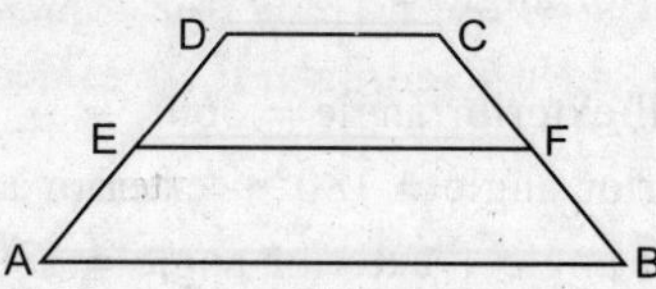

3. Area of trapezium = $\frac{1}{2}$ (sum of parallel sides) × height

   $= \frac{1}{2} \times (AB + CD) \times DM = \frac{1}{2}(AB + CD) \times h$
4. Sum of square of diagonals = (sum of squares of non-parallel side) + 2(product of || sides)

   i.e. $AC^2 + BD^2 = BC^2 + AD^2 + 2AB.CD$
5. By joining the mid-points of adjacent sides of a trapezium four similar triangles are obtained.
6. $\frac{AO}{OC} = \frac{BO}{OD}$

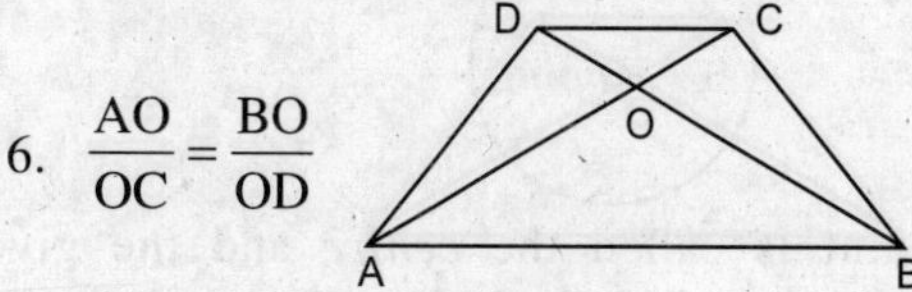

The mid-point Theorem:

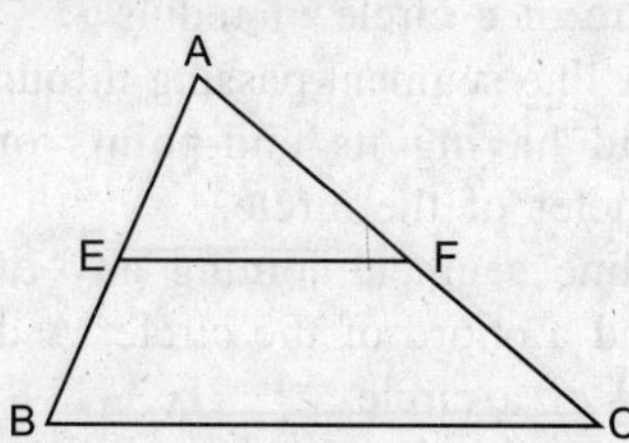

E and F are the mid-points of side AB and AC respectively then,

EF = $\frac{1}{2}$BC and EF || BC

Polygons : A closed-figure bounded by three or more than three straight lines.

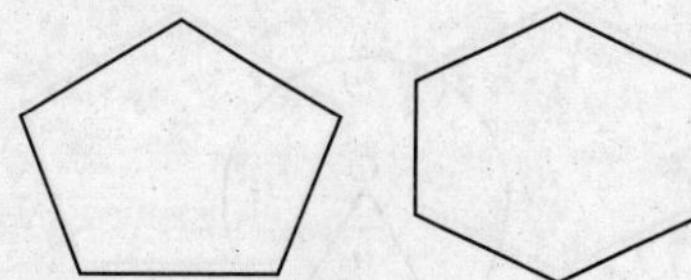

e.g. No. of sides	Name
3	Triangle
4	Quadrilateral
5	Pentagon
6	Hexagon
7	Heptagon
8	Octagon
9	Nonagon
10	Decagon

Regular Polygon : A polygon in which all the sides are equal and also the interor angles are equal, is called a 'Regular polygon'.

if *n* = total no. of sides of a regular polygon, then:

1. Sum of interor angles = $(n - 2) \times 180°$
2. Each exterior angle = $\left(\frac{360°}{n}\right)$
3. Sum of all exterior angle = 360°
4. Each interior angle = 180° – exterior angle
   ⇒ interior angle + exterior angle = 180°
5. Number of diagonals = $\frac{n(n-3)}{2}$

CHORDS OF A CIRCLE

Points To Remember

- **Circle :** A circle is a set of those points in a plane that are at a given constant distance from a given fixed point in the plane.

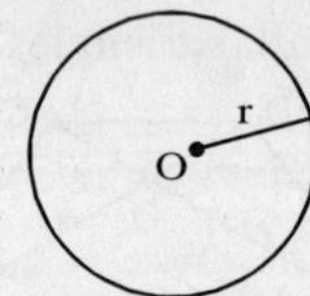

The fixed point is called the *centre* and the given constant distance is called the radius of the circle.
O is the centre of a circle of radius *r*.

- **Diameter :** A line segment passing through the centre of the circle and having its end-points on the circle is called a diameter of the circle.
- **Chord :** A line segment joining any two points on a circle is called a chord of the circle. A diameter is the longest chord of a circle.
- **Secant :** A secant is a line segment that intersects a circle at two points.
- **Circumference of a circle :** The perimeter of a circle is called its circumference.
  Perimeter of a circle (C) = $2\pi r$.
- **Degree Measure of An Arc :** The degree of an arc is the measure of its central angle in degrees.
  $m\ \widehat{(AB)} = \theta°$.

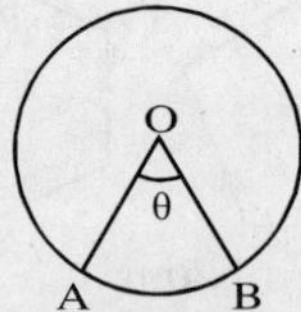

- **Sector of a Circle :** A sector of a circle is the region enclosed by an arc of the circle and the two radii of its end-point.

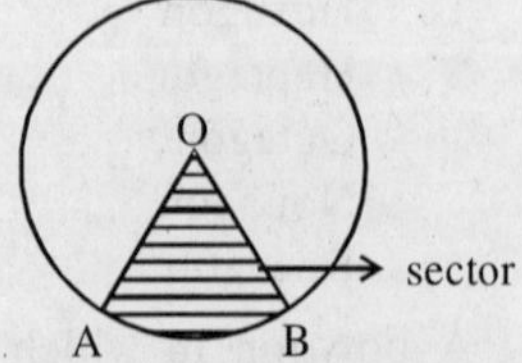

- **Segment of a Circle :** The segment of a circle is the region bounded by an arc of the circle and the chord joining the end-points of the arc.

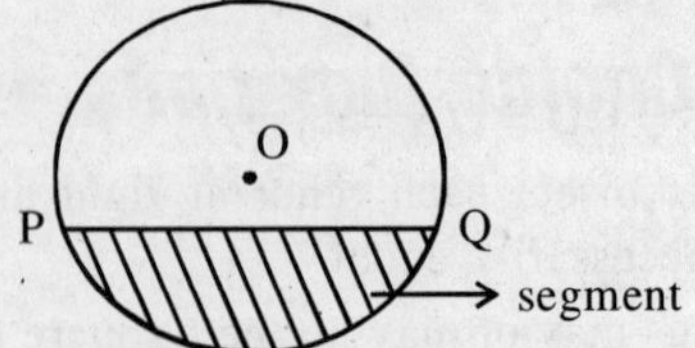

Properties of Chord of a Circle

- The perpendicular from the centre of a circle to a chord bisects the chord.
  i.e. AC = BC

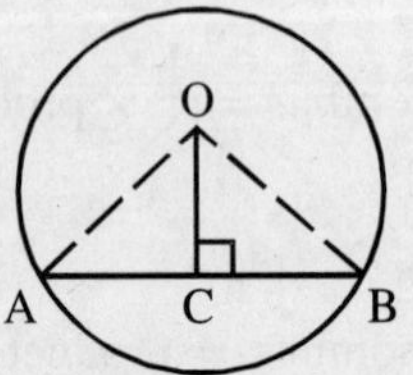

- The line joining the centre of a circle to the mid-point of a chord is perpendicular to the chord.
  i.e. AM = BM
  then OM ⊥ AB

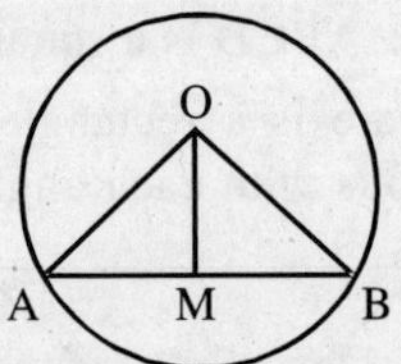

- Equal chords of a circle are equidistance from the centre.
- Chords equidistance from the centre of a circle are equal.

SOME ANGLE PROPERTIES OF THE CIRCLE

Points To Remember

- **Intercepted Arc :** An arc of a circle is said to be intercepted by a circle if,
  (*i*) the end-point of the arc lie on the arms of the circle.
  (*ii*) each arm of the angle contains at least one end-point of the arc.
  (*iii*) the arc lies in the interior of the angle, except for the end-point of the arc.
- The angle subtended by an arc of a circle at the centre of the circle is double the angle it subtends at any point on the remaining part of the circle.
- **Cyclic Quadrilateral :** A quadrilateral is called a cyclic quadrilateral if its all vertices lie on a circle.
- In a cyclic quadrilateral, the sum of each pair of opposite angles is 180°.
- Angles inscribed in the same segment of a circle are equal.
- Angle of a semi-circle is a right angle.
- Equal chords of a circle subtend equal angles at the centre.
- Chords of a circle which subtend equal angles at the centre are equal.

Multiple Choice Questions

1. What is the measures of an angle which is complement of itself?

A. 40° B. 30°
C. 45° D. 50°

2. Determine the value of y.

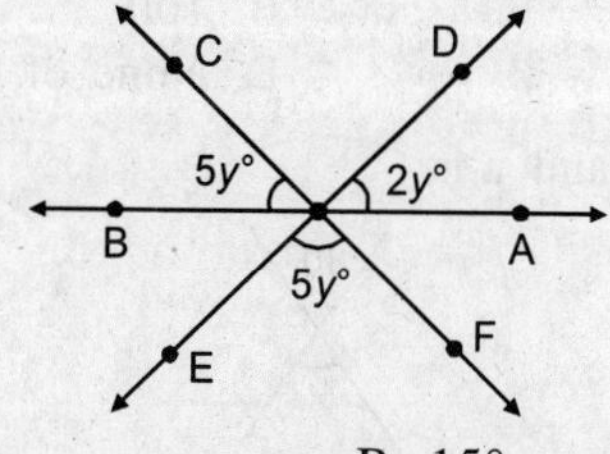

A. 17° B. 15°
C. 20° D. 25°

3. In the given figure, the arms of two angles are parallel. If ∠ABC = 70°, then find ∠DGC and ∠DEF :

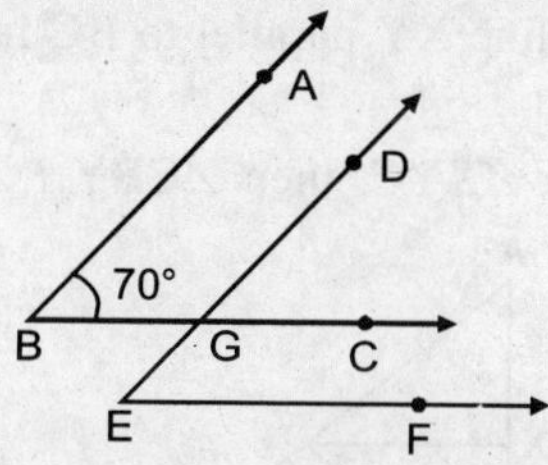

A. 70°, 60° B. 60°, 50°
C. 70°, 70° D. None of these

4. In the given figure, AB || CD, then X is equal to:

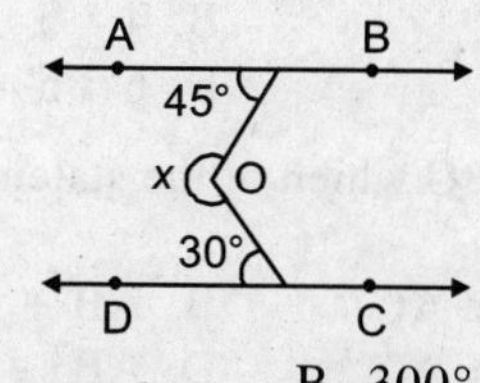

A. 290° B. 300°
C. 280° D. 285°

5. In the given two straight lines PQ and RS intersect each other at 'O'. If ∠SOT = 75°, find the value of a, b and c:

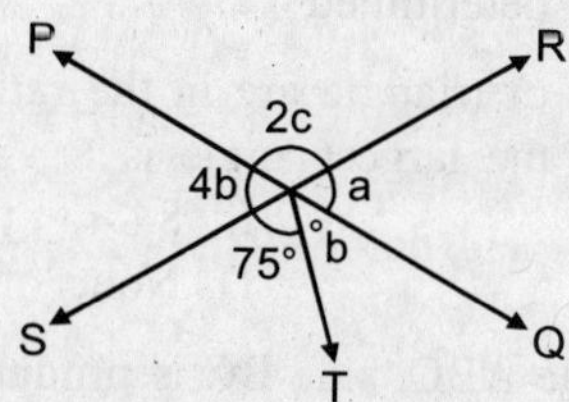

A. a = 84°, b = 21°, c = 48°
B. a = 48°, b = 20°, c = 50°
C. a = 72°, b = 24°, c = 54°
D. a = 64°, b = 28°, c = 45°

6. In the given figure XY and MN intersect at O. If POY = 90° and $a : b$ = 2 : 3, then find c:

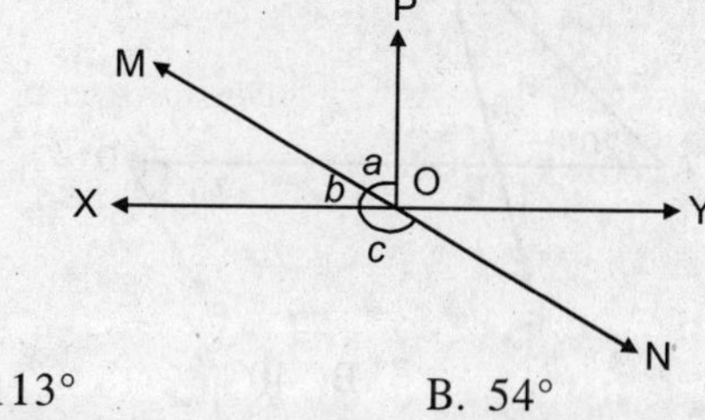

A. 113° B. 54°
C. 126° D. 48°

7. In the given diagram AB || GH || DE and GF || BD || HI, ∠FGC = 80°. What is the value of ∠CHI?

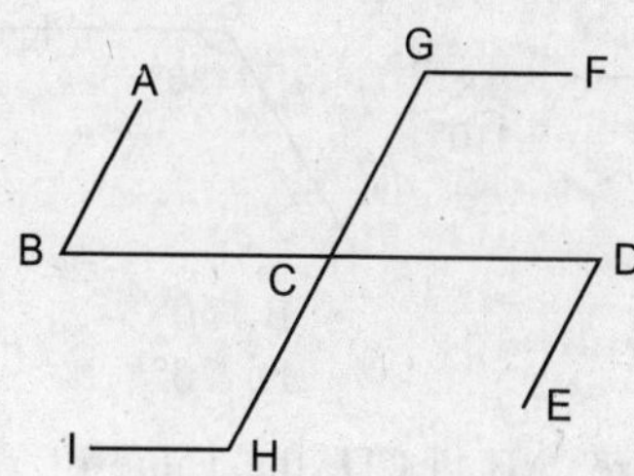

A. 80° B. 120°
C. 100° D. 160°

8. An Angle is equal to one-third of its supplement. What is its measure?

A. 45° B. 50°
C. 55° D. None of these

9. Lines 1 || m, p || q. What are a, b, c, d?

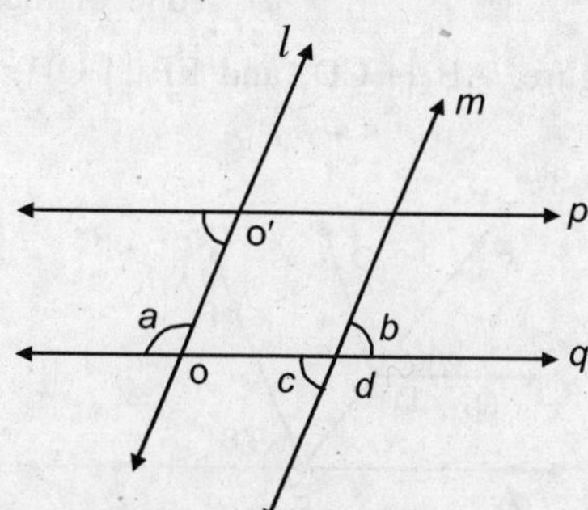

A. a = 120°, b = 60°, c = 60°, d = 120°
B. a = 120°, b = 120°, c = 60°, d = 120°
C. a = 120°, b = 60°, c = 120°, d = 60°
D. None of these

10. In figures, AB || CD. What is θ ?

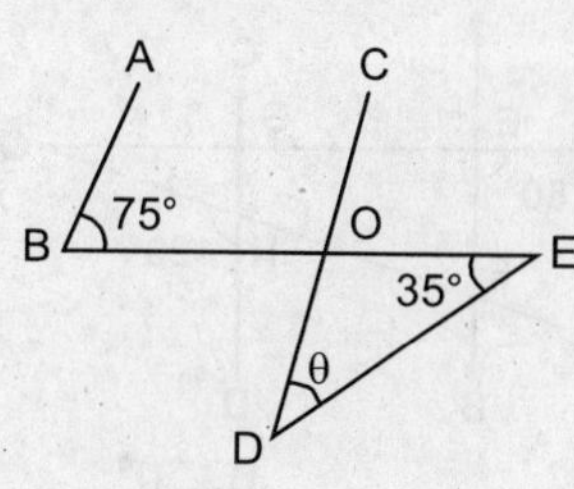

A. 30° B. 35°
C. 40° D. 45°

11. From the given figure, find $\angle ABC$, if BE || DE :

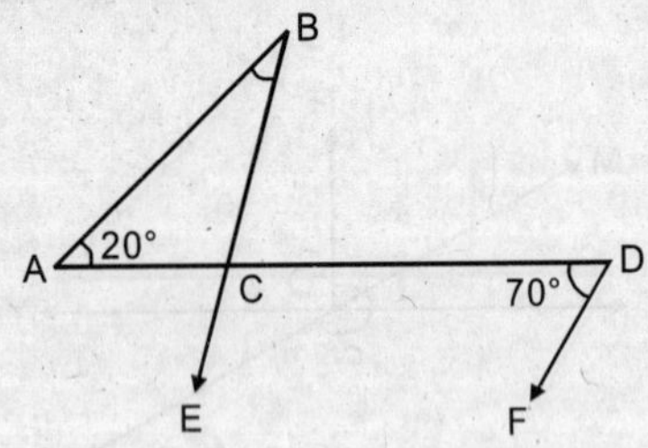

A. 50° B. 40°
C. 35° D. None of these

12. In the figure, if PQ || ST, $\angle PQR = 110°$ and $\angle RST = 130°$, find $\angle QRS$.

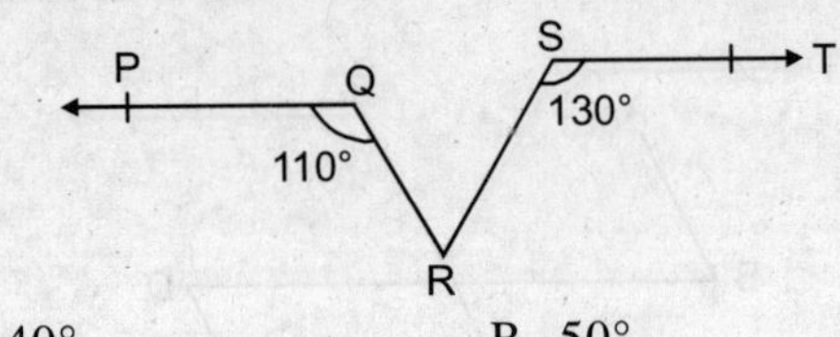

A. 40° B. 50°
C. 60° D. 70°

13. In the figure, AB || CD, the value of x is :

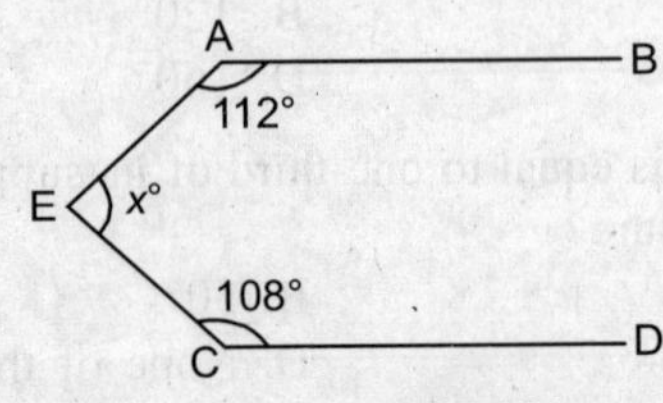

A. 220° B. 140°
C. 150° D. None of these

14. In the figure, AB || CD, and EF || QD, the value of $\angle PDQ$ is :

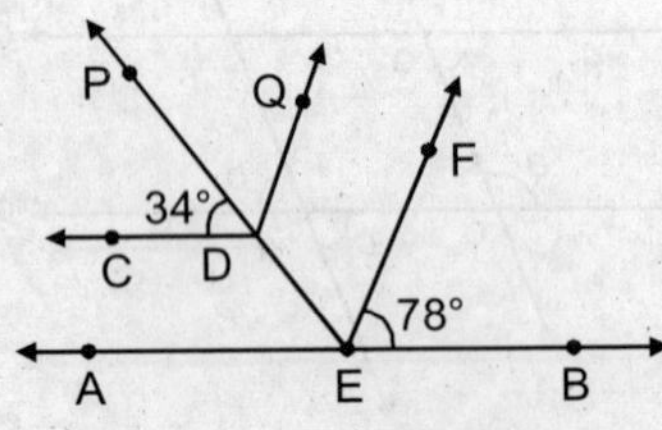

A. 68° B. 78°
C. 56° D. None of these

15. In the given figure AB || CD, given that $\angle PEB = 80°$, $\angle QHD = 120°$ and $\angle PQR = X°$, find the value of x:

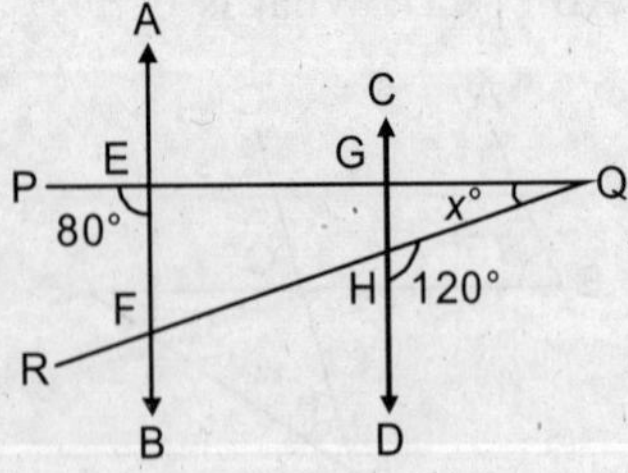

A. 40° B. 20°
C. 100° D. 30°

16. In the given figure, if $\angle ABC = 90°$, and $\angle A = 30°$, then $\angle ACD =$

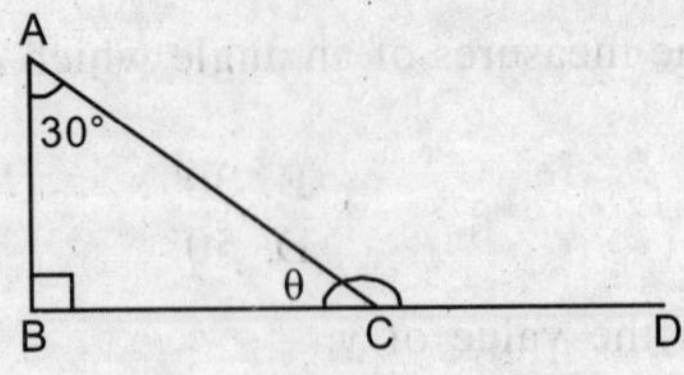

A. 120° B. 100°
C. 110° D. None of these

17. Value of x and y is :

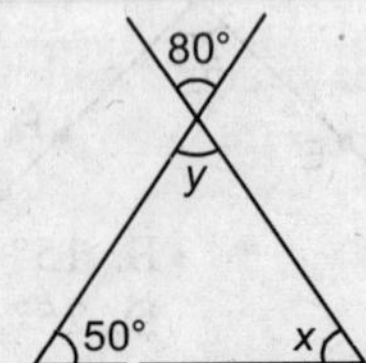

A. $x = 60°, y = 80°$ B. $x = 80°, y = 50°$
C. $x = 50°, y = 80°$ D. None of these

18. In Δ ABC, a line XY parallel to BC intersects AB at X and AC at Y:

If BY bisects $\angle XYC$, then $\angle CBY : \angle CYB$ is :

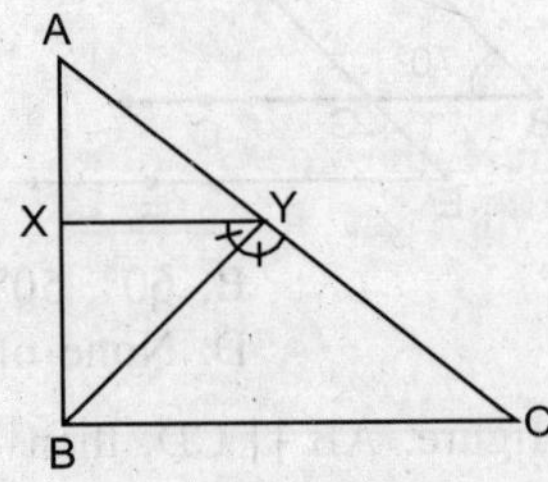

A. 5 : 4 B. 4 : 3
C. 1 : 1 D. 6 : 5

19. In a triangle ABC which of the statements is necessarily true?

A. AB + BC < AC B. AB + BC > AC
C. AB + BC = AC D. $AB^2 + BC^2 = AC^2$

20. In ΔABC, $\angle A > 90°$, then $\angle B$ and $\angle C$ must be :

A. acute
B. obtuse
C. one acute and one abtuse
D. Can't be determined

21. If the angles of triangle are in the ratio 1 : 4 : 7, then the value of the largest angle is :

A. 135° B. 84°
C. 105° D. None of these

22. In the triangle ABC, side BC is produced to D, $\angle ACD = 100°$ if BC = AC, then find $\angle ABC$ is :

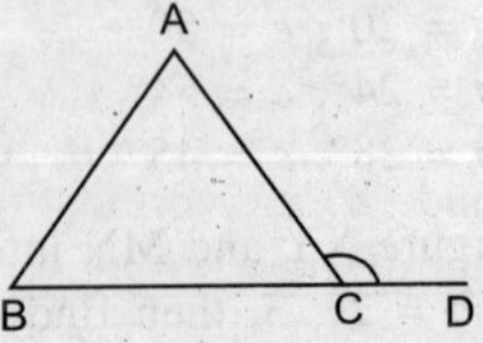

A. 40°　　B. 50°
C. 80°　　D. can't be determined

23. In the following figure ADBC, BD = CD = AC, ∠ABC = 27°, ∠ACD = Y. What is the value of y?

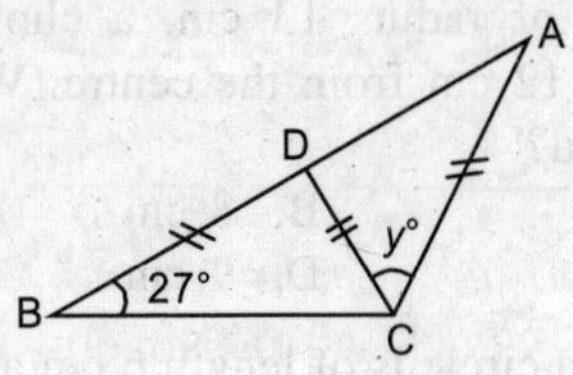

A. 27°　　B. 54°
C. 72°　　D. 58°

24. ABC is an isosceles triangle with AB = AC. Side BA is produced to D such that AB = AD. What is ∠BCD?
A. 60°　　B. 90°
C. 120°　　D. can't be determined

25. A, B, C are the three angles of a Δ. If A – B = 15° and B – C = 30°, then ∠A is equal to :
A. 65°　　B. 80°
C. 75°　　D. 85°

26. In a Δ ABC, if 2∠A = 3∠B = 6∠C, then ∠A is equal to :
A. 60°　　B. 30°
C. 90°　　D. 120°

27. In the given figure, the side BC of a Δ ABC is produced on both sides, then ∠1 + ∠2 is equal to :

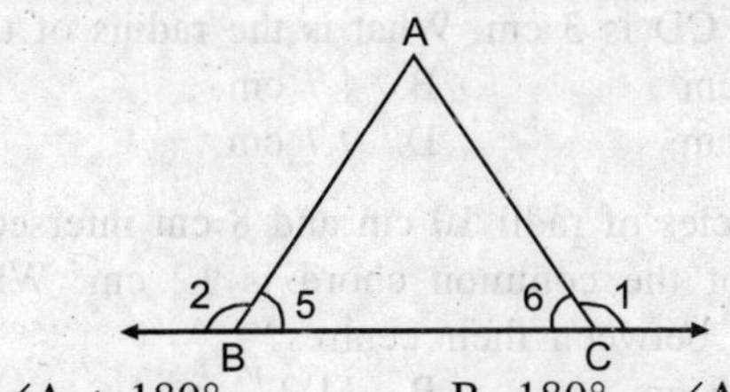

A. ∠A + 180°　　B. 180° – ∠A
C. $\frac{1}{2}$(∠A + 180°)　　D. ∠A + 90°

28. In a Δ ABC, ∠A = x°, ∠B = y° and ∠C = (y + 20)°. If 4x – y = 10, then the triangle is :
A. Right-angled　　B. Obtuse-angled
C. Equilateral-angled　　D. None of these

29. It is given that d° = 70°, b° = 120°, then :

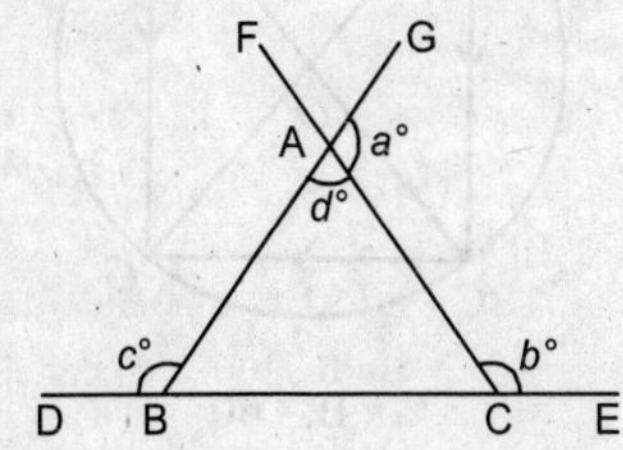

A. c° = 130°
B. a° = 110°
C. Both (A) and (B) are correct
D. Both (A) and (B) are wrong

30. It is given that AB ⊥ BC. Which one of the following is true?

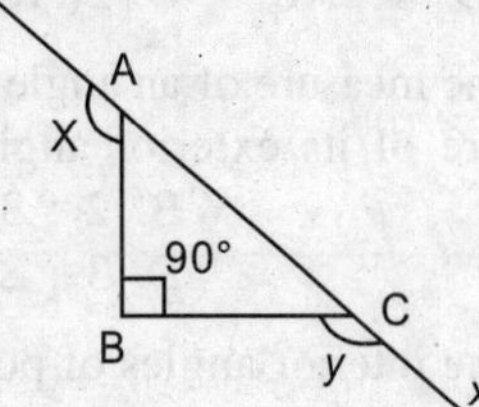

A. $x + y$ = 180°　　B. $x + y$ = 270°
C. $x + y$ = 300°　　D. can not be said

31. In which of the following is the lengths of diagonals equal?
A. Rhombus　　B. Rectangle
C. Parallelogram　　D. Trapezium

32. How many diagonals are there in a octagon?
A. 10　　B. 14
C. 18　　D. 20

33. A polygons has 44 diagonals. The number of sides of the polygon is:
A. 11　　B. 10
C. 13　　D. 12

34. The angles of a quadrilateral are in the ratio 1 : 2: 3 : 4, the largest angle is:
A. 120°　　B. 134°
C. 144°　　D. 150°

35. The sides BA and DC of a quadrilateral ABCD are produced as shown in figure. Then the true statement is:

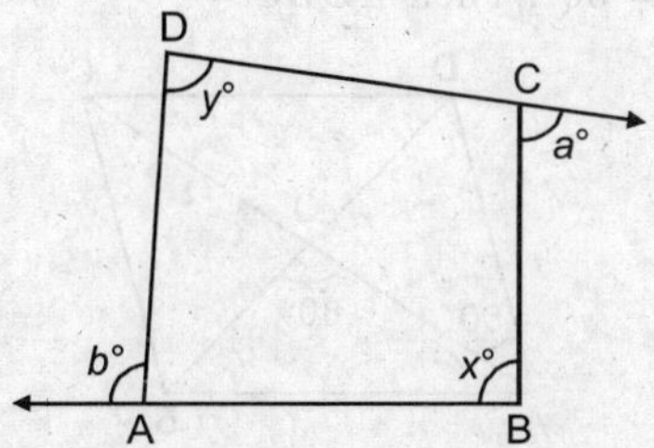

A. $x° + y° = a° + b°$　　B. $x° + a° = y° + b°$
C. $2x° + y° = a° + b°$　　D. $x + \frac{1}{2}y° = \frac{a° + b°}{2}$

36. Each interior angle of a regular polygon is 120°. The number of sides is:
A. 7　　B. 6
C. 5　　D. 8

37. Each interior angle of a regular octagon is:
A. 120°　　B. 90°
C. 135°　　D. None of these

38. □ABCD is a | | gm, AB = 14 cm, BC = 18 cm and AC = 16 cm. What is the length of the other diagonal?
A. 30 cm　　B. 32 cm
C. 26 cm　　D. 28 cm

39. If ABCD is a rhombus, then:
A. $AC^2 + BD^2 = 4AB^2$ B. $AC^2 + BD^2 = AB^2$
C. $AC^2 + BD^2 = 2AB^2$ D. $2(AC^2 + BD^2) = 3AB^2$

40. The ratio of the measure of an angle of a regular octagon to the measure of its exterior angle is:
A. 1 : 3 B. 2 : 3
C. 3 : 1 D. 3 : 2

41. The sum of the interior angles of polygon is 1440°. The number of sides of the polygon is:
A. 9 B. 10
C. 8 D. 12

42. Two parallelograms stand on equal bases and between the same parallels. The ratio of their areas is:
A. 1 : 1 B. $\sqrt{2}:1$
C. 1 : 3 D. 1 : 2

43. The length of a side of a rhombus is 13 cm and one of its diagonal is 24 cm. The length of the other diagonal is:
A. 14 cm B. 12 cm
C. 20 cm D. 10 cm

44. The sum of all exterior angles of a convex polygon of *n* sides is:
A. 4 right angle B. $\frac{2}{n}$ right angle
C. $(2n - 4)$ right angle D. $\frac{n}{2}$ right angle

45. The diagonals AC and BD of a || gm ABCD intersect each other at the point O such that ∠DAC = 50° and ∠AOB = 80°. Then ∠DBC = ?

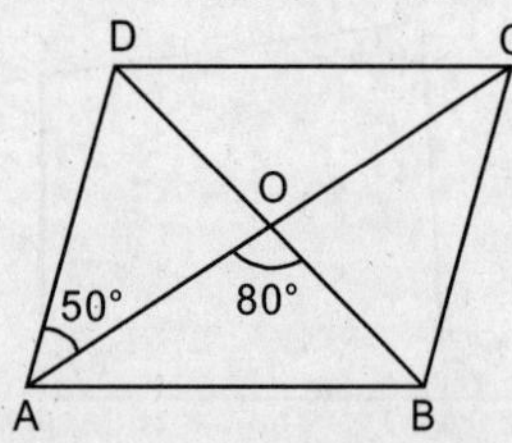

A. 50° B. 40°
C. 45° D. 30°

46. In a circle of radius 10 cm, a chord is at a distance 6 cm from the centre. What is the length of the chord?
A. 16 cm B. 12 cm
C. 9 cm D. 8 cm

47. AB is a chord of a circle of radius 5 cm with centre O. If OM ⊥ AB and AB = 8 cm. What is the length OM?
A. 4 cm B. 5 cm
C. 3 cm D. 2 cm

48. AB is a chord of the circle with centre O and radius 13 cm. If OM ⊥ AB and OM = 5 cm. What is the length of the chord AB?
A. 20 cm B. 24 cm
C. 15 cm D. 18 cm

49. A chord of a circle of radius 7.5 cm with centre O is of length 9 cm. What is its distance from the centre?
A. 3 cm B. 4 cm
C. 5 cm D. 6 cm

50. In a circle of radius 13 cm, a chord is drawn at a distance of 12 cm from the centre. What is the length of the chord?
A. 10 cm B. 8 cm
C. 11 cm D. 9 cm

51. A chord of a circle is of length 6 cm and is at a distance of 4 cm from the centre. What is the radius of the circle?
A. 3 cm B. 4 cm
C. 5 cm D. 2 cm

52. In a circle whose radius is 10 cm, a chord is at a distance of 6 cm from the centre. How long is the chord?
A. 12 cm B. 16 cm
C. 9 cm D. 20 cm

53. AB and CD are two parallel chords of a circle such that AB = 10 cm and CD = 24 cm. If the chords are on the opposite sides of the centre and the distance between them is 17 cm. What is the radius of the circle?
A. 9 cm B. 10 cm
C. 12 cm D. 13 cm

54. AB and CD are two chords of a circle such that AB = 6 cm, CD = 12 cm and AB || CD. If the distance between AB and CD is 3 cm. What is the radius of the circle?
A. 6.7 cm B. 4.7 cm
C. 5.7 cm D. 9.7 cm

55. Two circles of radii 10 cm and 8 cm intersect and the length of the common chord is 12 cm. What is the distance between their centres?
A. 10.25 cm B. 11.27 cm
C. 13.29 cm D. 12.24 cm

56. AB and CD are diameters of circle C (O, *r*) where AC || DB and DA || BC. If ∠OBD = 50°, the measure of ∠AOC is:

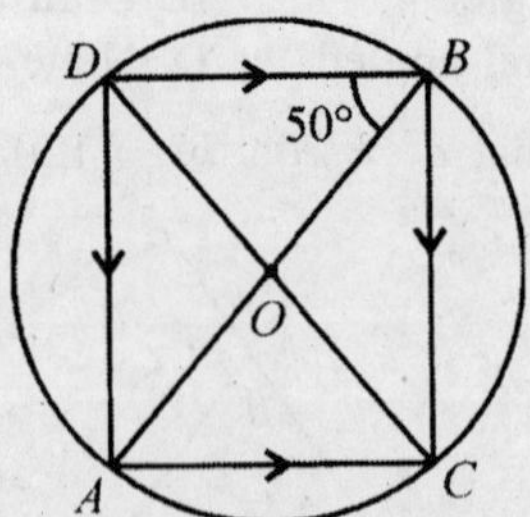

A. 50° B. 60°
C. 70° D. 80°

57. In two circles C(O, 5) and C(O′, 5), Chord PQ = Chord RS. If $m(\overparen{PQ}) = 80°$, then $m(\overparen{SR})$ is:

A. 80° B. 180°
C. 280° D. 300°

58. In adjacent figure, measure of ∠AOB is:

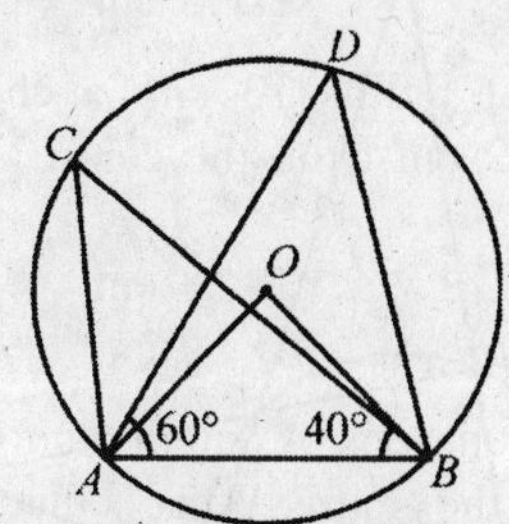

A. 110° B. 160°
C. 80° D. 90°

59. In the figure, the value of ∠PSY is:

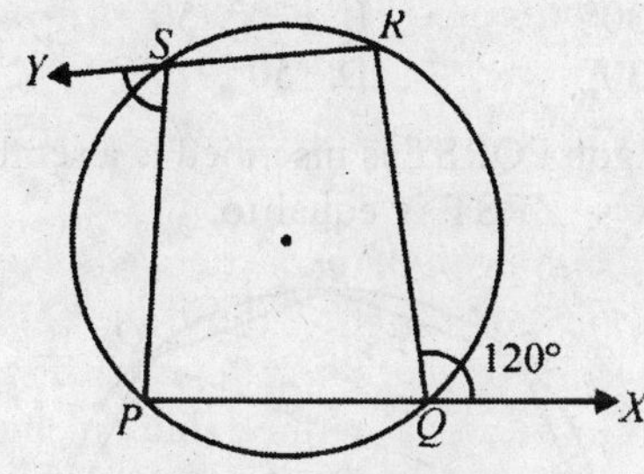

A. 45° B. 50°
C. 60° D. 80°

60. In adjoining figure, O is the centre of the circle, then measure of ∠x is:

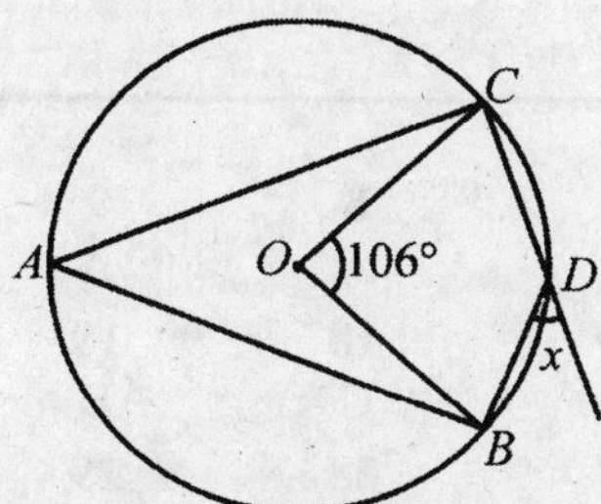

A. 106° B. 90°
C. 67° D. 53°

61. In adjacent figure, O is the centre of the circle ∠ABD = 28°, then measure of ∠y is:

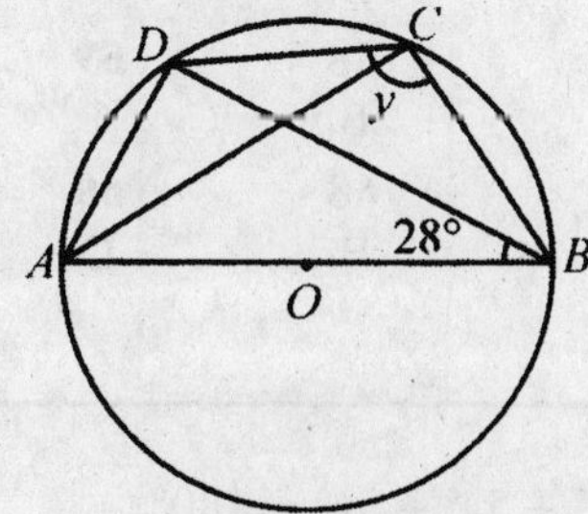

A. 106° B. 118°
C. 126° D. 132°

62. In the given figure, O is the centre of a circle and ABCO is a parallelogram, then values of x and y, respectively are:

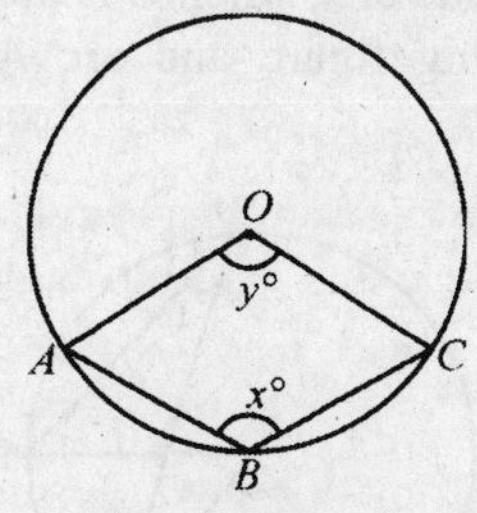

A. 80°, 100° B. 50°, 130°
C. 100°, 80° D. 120°, 120°

63. PQ is a diameter of a circle with centre O and radius OR is perpendicular on PQ. If S be any point in the arc QS, then ∠QPR and ∠PSR are:
A. 70°, 45° B. 60°, 50°
C. 50°, 70° D. 45°, 45°

64. If O is the centre of the circle, find the value of ∠ACB in the adjoining figure:

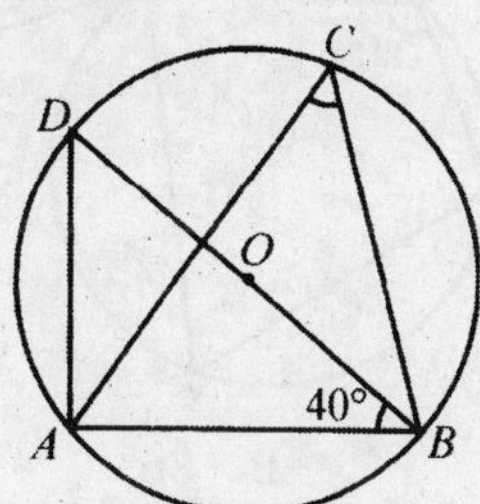

A. 40° B. 50°
C. 80° D. 160°

65. What is the value of x, O is the centre of the circle in the adjoining figure?

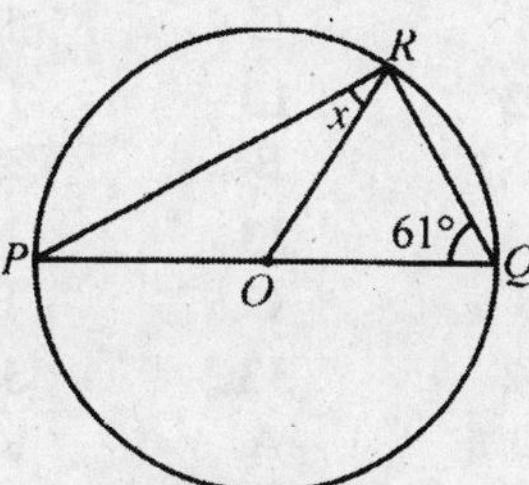

A. 16° B. 23°
C. 29° D. 30½°

66. What is the value of x, O is the centre of the circle?

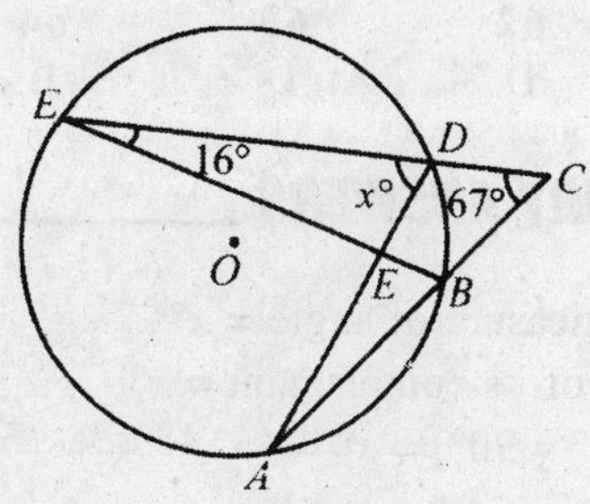

A. 36° B. 43°
C. 23° D. 83°

67. What is the value of x, when O is the centre of the circle in the adjoining figure and arc AB is equal to arc BC?

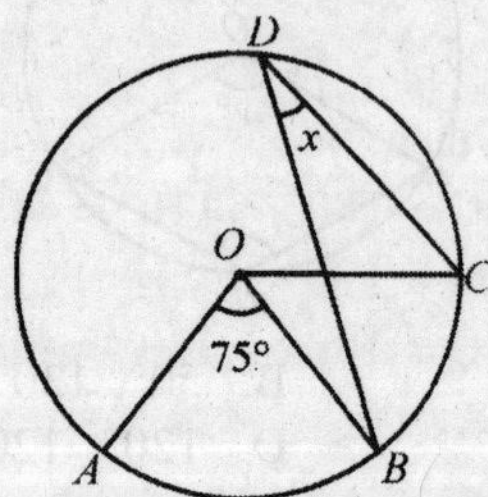

A. 15° B. 22½°
C. 28° D. 37½°

68. In the adjoining figure, ABCD is a cyclic quadrilateral. If CD || BE, ∠DAB = 115° and ∠EBF = 21°, then ∠ADC is equal to:

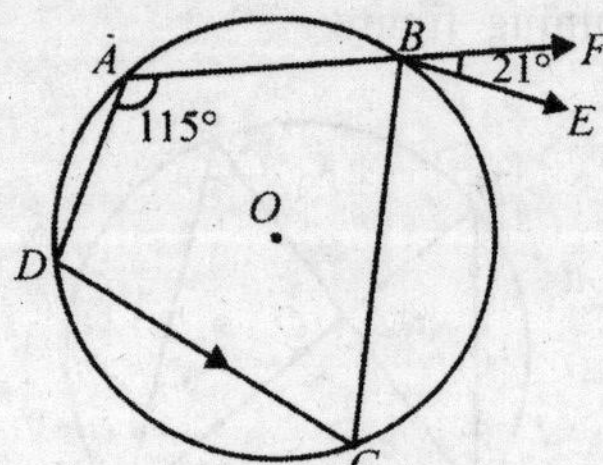

A. 73° B. 86°
C. 105° D. 110°

69. In the adjoining figure, the measure of ∠DPC and ∠BQC respectively is:

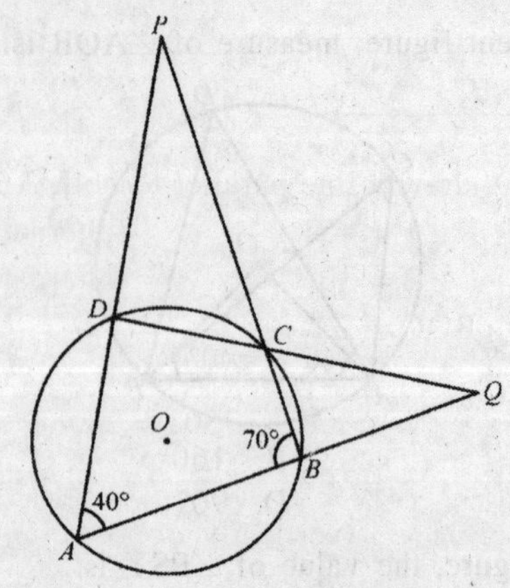

A. 50°, 30° B. 70°, 50°
C. 70°, 30° D. 50°, 70°

70. If a pentagon PQRST is inscribed is a semi-circle, value of ∠PQR + ∠RST is equal to:

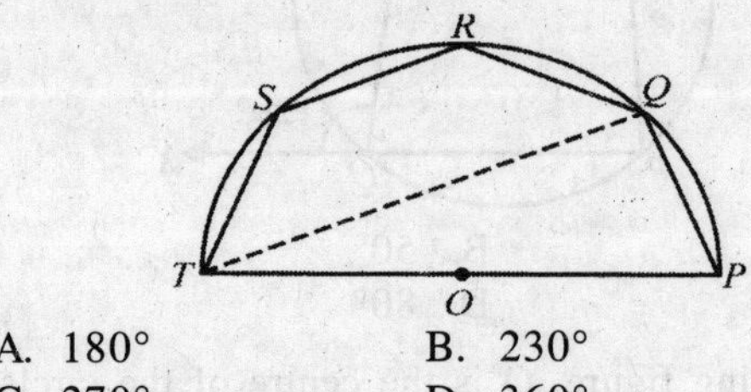

A. 180° B. 230°
C. 270° D. 360°

ANSWERS

1	2	3	4	5	6	7	8	9	10
C	B	C	D	A	C	A	A	A	C
11	**12**	**13**	**14**	**15**	**16**	**17**	**18**	**19**	**20**
A	C	B	A	B	A	C	C	B	A
21	**22**	**23**	**24**	**25**	**26**	**27**	**28**	**29**	**30**
C	B	C	B	B	C	A	A	C	B
31	**32**	**33**	**34**	**35**	**36**	**37**	**38**	**39**	**40**
B	D	A	A	A	B	C	D	A	C
41	**42**	**43**	**44**	**45**	**46**	**47**	**48**	**49**	**50**
B	A	D	A	D	A	C	B	D	A
51	**52**	**53**	**54**	**55**	**56**	**57**	**58**	**59**	**60**
C	B	D	A	C	D	C	B	C	D
61	**62**	**63**	**64**	**65**	**66**	**67**	**68**	**69**	**70**
B	D	D	B	C	D	D	B	C	C

EXPLANATORY ANSWERS

1. Let the measure of angle = $x°$
measure of its complement = $x°$
$\therefore x° + x° = 90° \Rightarrow x° = 45°$

2. ∠COD = ∠EOF = 5Y° (vertically opposite angle)
$\therefore$ ∠AOD + ∠DOC + ∠COB = 180°

$\Rightarrow \quad 2y° + 5y° + 5y° = 180°$

$\Rightarrow \quad 12y° = 180°$

$y = 15°$

3. ∠DGC = ∠DEF = ∠ABC = 70°
(corresponding angles).

4. 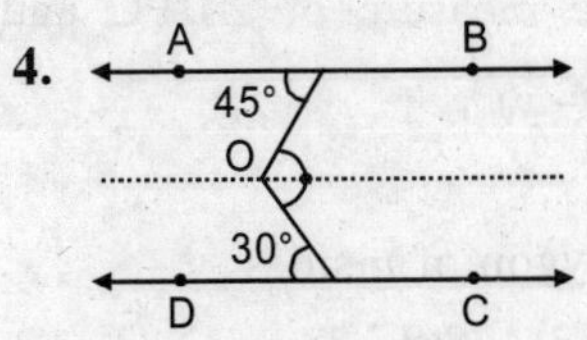

Through O, draw a line parallel to both AB & CD.

Then, $\angle 1 = 45°$ (alternative angle)

and $\angle 2 = 30°$ (alternative angle)

$\therefore$ $\angle BOC = \angle 1 + \angle 2$

$= 45° + 30° = 75°$

So, $x = 360° - 750° = 285°$

Hence, $x = 285°$

5. $\angle ROQ = \angle POS$ (vertically opposite angle)

$\therefore$ $a = 4b$

$75° + b + a = 180°$

$\Rightarrow$ $b + 4b = 180° - 75° = 105°$

$\Rightarrow$ $b = 21°$

$\therefore$ $a = 4b = 4 \times 21 = 84°$

$a + 2c = 180°$

$\Rightarrow$ $2c = 180° - 84° = 48°$

$\Rightarrow$ $c = 48°$

$\therefore$ $a = 84°, b = 21°, c = 48°$

6. $\angle POQ = 90°$

by line property – $\angle a + \angle b = 90°$

$a : b = 2 : 3$

So, $\angle a = 36°$ and $\angle b = 54°$

Here MN is a line so

$\Rightarrow$ $54° + \angle C = 180°$

$\Rightarrow$ $\angle C = 126°$

8. Let the measure of angle = $x°$

$\therefore$ its supplement = $(180 - x)°$

$x = \frac{1}{3}(180 - x) \Rightarrow x = 45°$

9. $60° + a = 180° \Rightarrow a = 120°$

$\therefore$ $\angle loq = 180° - a = 60°$

$\therefore$ $\angle c = \angle loq = 60°$ (Alternate angles)

and $\angle b = \angle c = 60°$

(Vertically opposite angles)

and $\angle d = 180° - \angle c = 120°$

$\therefore$ $a = 120°, b = 60°, c = 60°, d = 120°$

10. $\angle COE = \angle ABE = 75°$ (corresponding angles)

$\therefore$ $\angle DOE = 180° - \angle COE = 180° - 75°$

$= 105°$

in Δ DOE – $105° + 35° + \theta = 180°$

$\Rightarrow$ $\theta = 180° - 140° = 40°$

11. $\because$ BE || DF

$\therefore$ $\angle ACE = \angle CDF = 70°$

$\therefore$ $\angle ACB = 180° - \angle ACE = 110°$

$\therefore$ $\angle ABC = 180° - 20° - 110° = 50°$

12. 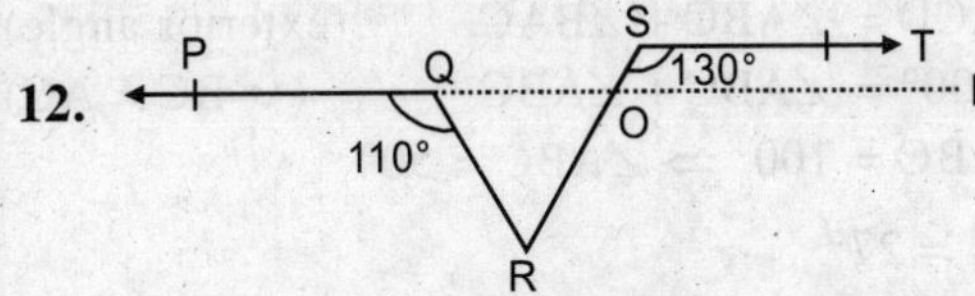

draw a line QI, then

$\angle RQO = 180° - 110° = 70°$

$\angle ROI = 130°$ (corresponding)

So, $\angle ROQ = 180° - 130° = 50°$

Now in Δ QRO

$\Rightarrow$ RQO + $\angle ROQ + \angle QRO = 180°$

$\Rightarrow$ $\angle QRO = 180° - (70° + 50°)$

$= 60° = \angle QRS$

13.

Draw EF parallel to both AB and CD

$\because$ AB || EF and AE transversal cuts them at A and E respectively.

$\therefore$ $\angle BAE + \angle FEA = 180°$

$\Rightarrow$ $112° + \angle 1 = 180°$

$\angle 1 = 68°$

again EF || CD and transversal cuts them at C and E.

$\therefore$ $\angle FEC + \angle ECD = 180°$

$\Rightarrow$ $\angle 2 + 108° = 180°$

$\Rightarrow$ $\angle 2 = 72°$

Now, $x = \angle 1 + \angle 2$

$\Rightarrow$ $x = 72° + 68° = 140°$

14. CD || AB $\therefore$ $\angle AED = \angle PDC = 34°$

$\therefore$ $\angle DEF = 180° - 78° - 34° = 68°$

$\because$ QD || EF

$\therefore$ $\angle PDQ = \angle DEF = 68°$ (corresponding)

15. $\angle PGH = 80° \Rightarrow \angle QGH = 100°$

$\angle QHD = 120° \Rightarrow \angle CHQ = 60°$

$\therefore$ $\angle x + 100° + 60° = 180° \Rightarrow x = 20°$

16. $\angle ACD = \angle B + \angle A = 90° + 30°$

$= 120°$ (exterior angle)

17. $y = 80°$ (vertically opposite angle)

$\therefore$ $x = 180° - 50° - 80° = 50°$

18. $\angle XYB = \angle YBC$ and $\angle XYB = \angle BYC$

$\Rightarrow$ $\angle YBC = \angle BYC$

20. $\angle B + \angle C < 90°$

$\because \angle A + \angle B + \angle C = 180°$

21. $x + 4x + 7x = 180° \Rightarrow x = 15°$

$\therefore$ $7x = 105°$

22. $\angle ACD = \angle ABC + \angle BAC$ (exterior angle)

$\Rightarrow$ $100° = \angle ABC + \angle ABC$ ($\because$ BC = AC)

$\Rightarrow$ $2\angle ABC = 100° \Rightarrow \angle ABC = 50°$

23. $\angle ABC = 27°$

$\angle BDC = 180° - (27° + 27°) = 126$

$\therefore$ $\angle ACD = 180° - (54° + 54°) = 72°$

24.

$\angle 1 = \angle 2$ $\because$ AB = AC

and $\angle 3 = \angle 4$ $\because$ AB = AC = AD

Now, $\angle B + \angle C + \angle D = 180°$

$\Rightarrow \angle 1 + \angle 2 + \angle 4 + \angle 3 = 180°$

$\Rightarrow \angle 2 + \angle 2 + \angle 4 + \angle 4 = 180°$

$\Rightarrow$ $2(\angle 2 + \angle 4) = 180°$

$\Rightarrow$ $\angle 2 + \angle 4 = 90° \Rightarrow \angle C = 90°$

25. Since A, B and C are the angles of a Δ.

$\therefore$ $\angle A + B + C = 180°$

Now, $A - B = 15°$, $B - C = 30°$,

$\therefore$ $B = C + 30°$

$\therefore$ $\angle A = B + 15° = C + 30° + 15° = C + 45°$

$\therefore$ $A + B + C = (C + 45°) + (C + 30°) + C = 180°$

$3C = 180° - 75° = 105°$

$\Rightarrow$ $C = 35°$

$\therefore$ $\angle A = 35° + 45° = 80°$

26. Let $2\angle A = 3\angle B = 6\angle C = K$

$\therefore$ $\angle A = \frac{K}{2}, \angle B = \frac{K}{3}, \angle C = \frac{K}{6}$

But $\angle A + \angle B + \angle C = 180°$

$\frac{K}{2} + \frac{K}{3} + \frac{K}{6} = 180° \Rightarrow K = 180°$

$\therefore$ $\angle A = \frac{180°}{2} = 90°$

27. $\angle 1 = \angle A + \angle 5$

and $\angle 2 = \angle A + \angle 6$ (exterior angle)

$\angle 1 + \angle 2 = \angle A + (\angle A + \angle 5 + \angle 6)$

$= \angle A + 180°$

28. $x + y + (y + 20) = 180°$

$\Rightarrow$ $x + 2y = 160$

$4x - y = 10 \Rightarrow y = 70, x = 20$

$\therefore$ The angles of the triangle are 20°, 70°, 90°.

29. $a° = 180° - d° = 180° - 70° = 110°$

and $C° = d° + \angle ACB$

$= 70° + (180° - b°)$

$= 70° + 60° = 130°$

30. $\angle BCA = 180° - Y$

$\therefore$ $x = 90° + (180° - y)$

$\Rightarrow$ $x + y = 270°$

32. No. of diagonals of a polygon of n sides

$= \frac{n(n-3)}{2} = \frac{8(8-3)}{2} = 20$

33. $\frac{n(n-3)}{2} = 44 \Rightarrow n(n-3) = 88 = 11 \times 8$

$\therefore$ $n = 11$

34. Angles be x, $2x$, $3x$, $4x$

$\therefore$ $x + 2x + 3x + 4x = 360°$

$\Rightarrow$ $10x = 360° \Rightarrow x = 36°$

$\therefore$ Largest angle = $4x = 144°$

35. $\angle DAB = 180° - b$ and $\angle BCD = 180° - a$

But, $\angle A + \angle B + \angle C + \angle D = 360°$

$\Rightarrow (180° - b°) + x° + (180° - a°) + y = 360°$

$\Rightarrow x° + y° = a° + b°$

36. Each interior angle = 120°

$\therefore$ Exterior angle = 180° − 120° = 60°

$\therefore$ No. of sides = $\frac{360°}{\text{exterior angle}} = \frac{360}{60} = 6$

37. Exterior angle of a regular octagon = $\frac{360}{8} = 45°$

$\therefore$ Interior angle = 180° − 45° = 135°

38.

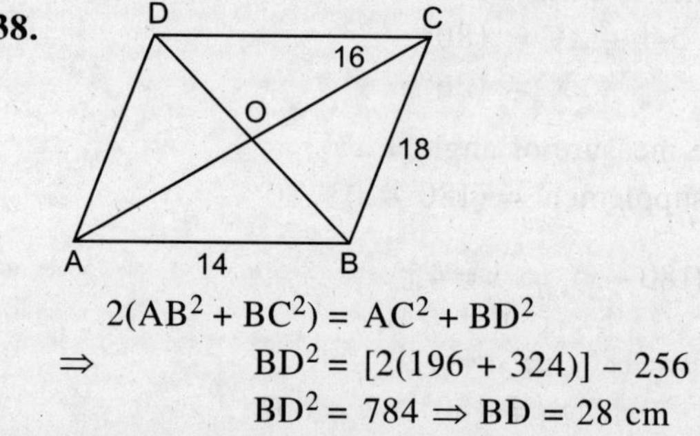

$2(AB^2 + BC^2) = AC^2 + BD^2$

$\Rightarrow$ $BD^2 = [2(196 + 324)] - 256$

$BD^2 = 784 \Rightarrow BD = 28$ cm

39. Since diagonals bisect each other at right angles and all sides are equal.

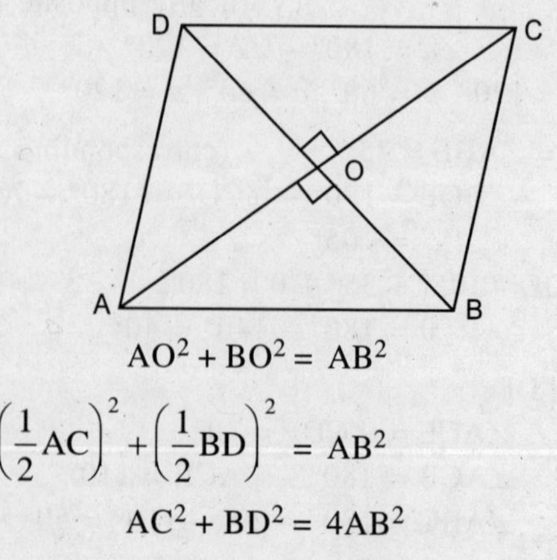

$AO^2 + BO^2 = AB^2$

$\left(\frac{1}{2}AC\right)^2 + \left(\frac{1}{2}BD\right)^2 = AB^2$

$AC^2 + BD^2 = 4AB^2$

40. Exterior angle = 360/8 = 45

Interior angle = 180 – 45 = 135

∴ Interior angle : exterior angle

= 135 : 45 = 3 : 1

41. Sum of all interior angles = $(n - 2) \times 180°$

$\Rightarrow \quad 1440 = (n - 2) \times 180$

$\Rightarrow \quad n = 10 (n \to \text{no. of sides})$

42. Since, their base and perpendicular heights are same.

43.

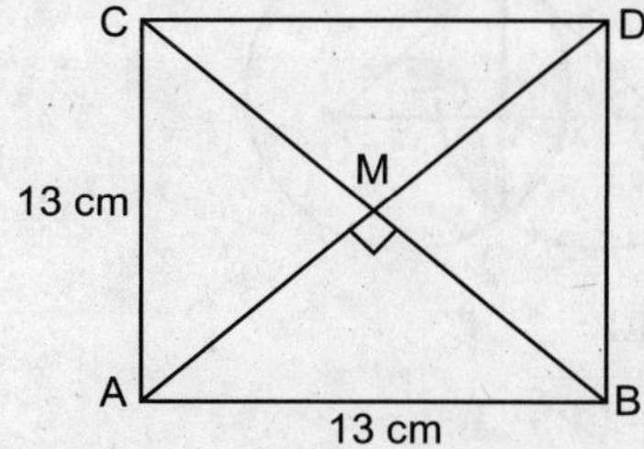

Let BD = 24 cm

∴ BM = 12 cm

$AM = \sqrt{13^2 - 12^2} = 5$ cm

∴ AD = 2AM = 10 cm

45. ∠ACB = ∠DAC = 50° (Alternate inerior ∠s)

∠BOC = 180° – 80° = 100°

∴ Now, in Δ BOC,

∠DBC = 180° – (100° + 50°) = 30°

46. In right angled Δ AOM

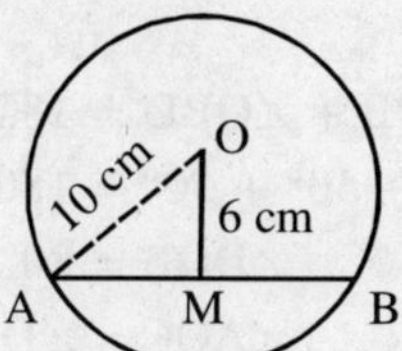

$AO^2 = OM^2 + AM^2$

$10^2 = 6^2 + AM^2$

$100 - 36 = AM^2$

$\Rightarrow AM^2 = 64$

$AM = \sqrt{64} = 8$ cm

AB = 2 AM = 2 × 8 = 16 cm.

47. In right angled Δ AOM.

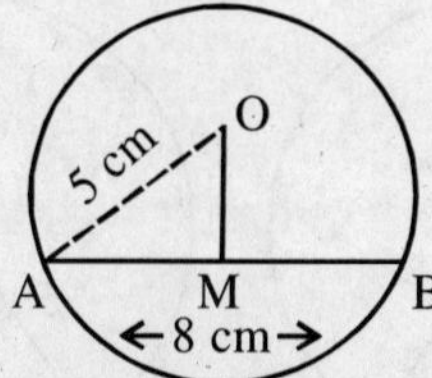

$AO^2 = OM^2 + AM^2$ AB = 8 cm

$5^2 = OM^2 + 4^2$ 2AM = 8

$25 - 16 = OM^2$ AM = 4 cm

$\Rightarrow OM = \sqrt{9} = 3$ cm.

48. In right angled Δ AOM.

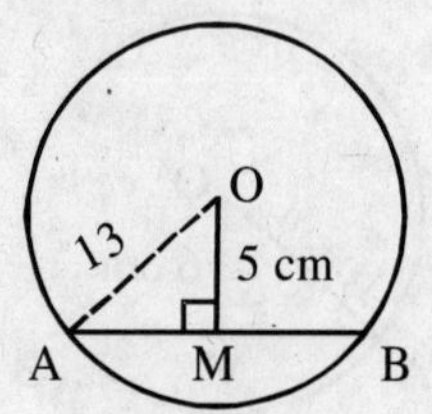

$AO^2 = OM^2 + AM^2$

$13^2 = 5^2 + AM^2$

$169 - 25 = AM^2$

$\Rightarrow AM = \sqrt{144} = 12$ cm.

AB = 2 AM = 2 × 12 = 24 cm.

49. In right angled Δ AOM.

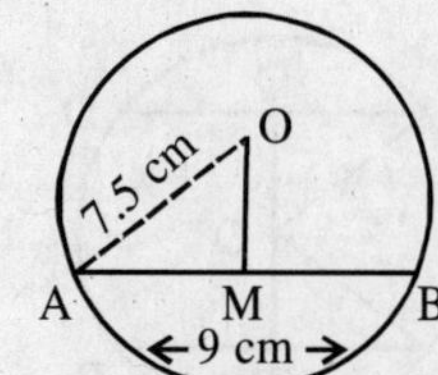

[AB = 9 cm, 2AM = 9 cm, AM = 4.5 cm]

$AO^2 = AM^2 + OM^2$

$(7.5)^2 = (4.5)^2 + OM^2$

$56.25 = 20.25 + OM^2$

$56.25 - 20.25 = OM^2$

$36.00 = OM^2$

$\Rightarrow OM = \sqrt{36} = 6$ cm

50. In right angled Δ AOM

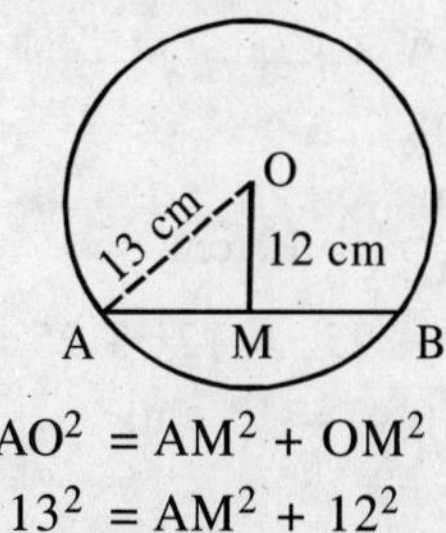

$AO^2 = AM^2 + OM^2$

$13^2 = AM^2 + 12^2$

$169 - 144 = AM^2$

$\Rightarrow AM = \sqrt{25} = 5$ cm

AB = 2AM = 5 × 2 = 10 cm.

51. In right angled Δ AOM

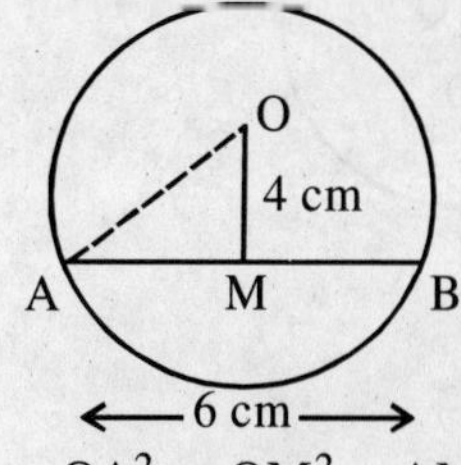

$\left[\because AB = 6 \text{ cm} \quad \therefore AM = \frac{6}{2} = 3 \text{ cm}\right]$

$OA^2 = OM^2 + AM^2$

$= 4^2 + 3^2 = 16 + 9 = 25$

$OA = \sqrt{25} = 5$ cm.

Radius of the circle = 5 cm.

52. In right angled Δ AOM.

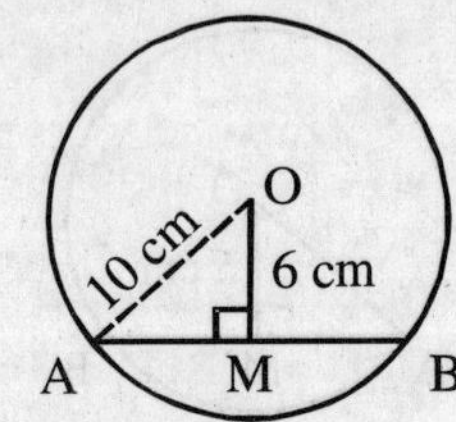

$$AO^2 = OM^2 + AM^2$$
$$10^2 = 6^2 + AM^2$$
$$100 - 36 = AM^2$$
$$\Rightarrow \quad AM = \sqrt{64} = 8 \text{ cm.}$$
$$AB = 2AM = 2 \times 8 = 16 \text{ cm.}$$

53. In right angle Δ OAP and OCQ.

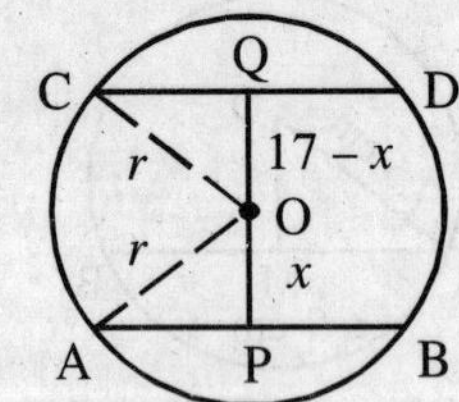

$$OA^2 = OP^2 + AP^2$$
$$r^2 = x^2 + 5^2 \quad \text{... }(i)$$
$$OC^2 = OQ^2 + CQ^2$$
$$r^2 = (17 - x)^2 + 12^2 \quad \text{... }(ii)$$

Eqn. (*i*) and (*ii*)

$$x^2 + 25 = (17 - x)^2 + 144$$
$$x^2 + 25 = 289 - 34x + x^2 + 144$$
$$34x = 289 + 144 - 25$$
$$34x = 408$$
$$x = \frac{408}{34} = 12 \text{ cm.}$$
$$r^2 = x^2 + 25 = 12^2 + 25 = 144 + 25.$$
$$r = \sqrt{169} = 13 \text{ cm.}$$

54. Let, $OQ = x$.

$$OP = 3 + x$$

In right angle Δ OAP and OCQ.

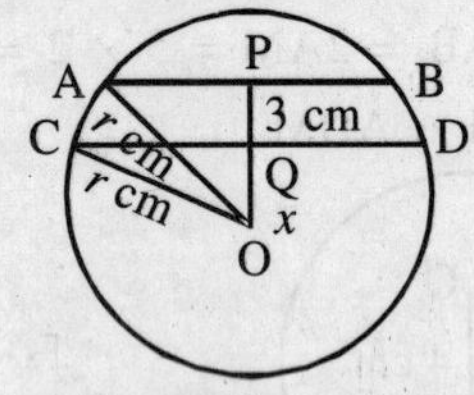

$$OA^2 = OP^2 + AP^2$$
$$r^2 = (x + 3)^2 + 3^2 \quad \text{... }(i)$$
$$OC^2 = OQ^2 + CQ^2$$
$$r^2 = x^2 + 6^2 \quad \text{... }(ii)$$

Eqn. (*i*) and (*ii*)

$$(x + 3)^2 + 3^2 = x^2 + 6^2$$
$$x^2 + 6x + 9 + 9 = x^2 + 36$$
$$6x = 18$$
$$x = 3 \text{ cm}$$
$$r^2 = x^2 + 6^2 = 9 + 36 = 45$$
$$r = \sqrt{45} = 6.7 \text{ cm.}$$

55. $PL = \frac{1}{2} PQ = \frac{1}{2} \times 12 = 6 \text{ cm.}$

In right triangle OLP.

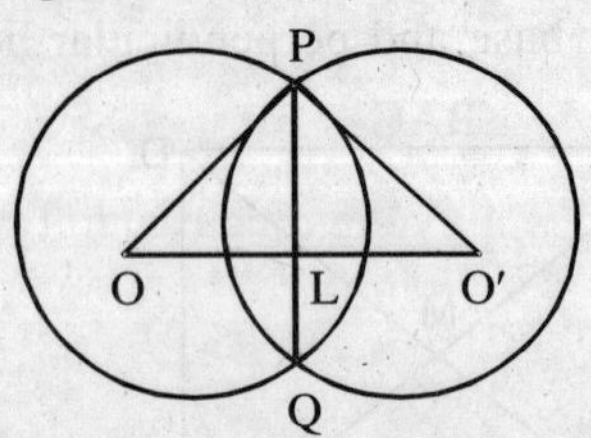

$$OP^2 = OL^2 + LP^2$$
$$OL = \sqrt{OP^2 - LP^2}$$
$$= \sqrt{10^2 - 6^2} = \sqrt{100 - 36} = \sqrt{64} = 8 \text{ cm.}$$

Again in right triangle O′LP

$$O'P^2 = O'L^2 + LP^2$$
$$O'L = \sqrt{O'P^2 - LP^2}$$
$$= \sqrt{8^2 - 6^2} = \sqrt{64 - 36} = \sqrt{28} = 5.29 \text{ cm}$$
$$OO' = OL + LO' = 8 + 5.29 = 13.29 \text{ cm.}$$

56. $OB = r \text{ (given)} = OD$

⇒ Δ OBD is an isosceles triangle

⇒ $\angle ODB = 50°$

From Δ ODB,

$$\angle DOB + \angle ODB + \angle OBD = 180°$$
$$\Rightarrow \quad \angle DOB + 50° + 50° = 180°$$
$$\Rightarrow \quad \angle DOB = 80°$$
$$\therefore \quad \angle AOC = \angle DOB = 80°$$

(Vertically opposite angles).

57. $m\left(\overset{\frown}{PQ}\right) = 80°$

$$\Rightarrow \quad m\left(\overset{\frown}{RS}\right) = 80°$$
$$\Rightarrow \quad m\left(\overset{\frown}{SR}\right) = 360° - 80° = 280°$$

58. From Δ ABC,

$\angle ACB = 180° - (60° + 40°) = 80°$, which is the angle subtended by $\overset{\frown}{AB}$ on the circle.

∴ angle subtended by $\overset{\frown}{AB}$ at the centre of the circle $= 2 \times \angle ACB = 2 \times 80° = 160°$.

59. $\angle PSR = \angle RQX = 120°$

(∵ exterior angle of a cyclic quadrilateral is equal to its opposite angle)

But XSR is a straight line.

So, $\angle YSP = 180° - 120° = 60°$.

60. $\angle BAC = \dfrac{106°}{2} = 53°$

∵ ABDC is a cyclic quadrilateral and x is its exterior angle,

$x = \angle BAC = 53°$.

61. $\angle ADB = 90°$ (angle in the semi-circle)

In Δ ADB, $\angle DAB = 180° - (28° + 90°) = 62°$

∵ ABCD is a cyclic quadrilateral,

$\angle DAB + y = 180°$

⇒ $y = 180° - \angle DAB$

$= 180° - 62° = 118°$.

62. Angle subtended by $\overset{\frown}{CA}$ at centre $= 2x°$

Now, $2x° + y° = 360°$ and opposite angles of parallelogram are equal,

∴ $x° = y°$

Thus, $3x° = 360°$

⇒ $x° = 120°$

⇒ $x° = y° = 120°$.

63. $\angle ROQ$ = angle made by $\overset{\frown}{RQ}$ at centre

$= 90°$

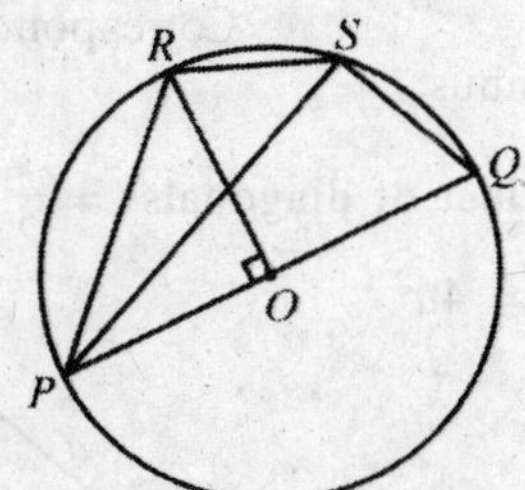

∴ $\angle QPR = \dfrac{90°}{2} = 45°$

$\angle ROP$ = angle made by chord PR at the centre

$= 90°$

∴ $\angle PSR = \dfrac{90°}{2} = 45°$.

64. $\angle BAD = 90°$

(∵ angle in a semi-circle is a right angle)

In Δ ABD,

$\angle ABD = 180° - (40° + 90°) = 50°$

∵ angles in the same segment of a circle are equal,

∴ $\angle ACB = 50°$.

65. $\angle ORQ = \angle OQR$ (since Δ OQR is an isoceles Δ)

∴ $\angle PRQ = 90°$ (angle in the semi-circle)

∴ $\angle PRO = x° = 90° - \angle ORQ$

$= 90° - 61° = 29°$.

66. ∵ Angle subtended by $\overset{\frown}{BD}$ are same,

$\angle BAD = \angle BFD = 16°$

$x°$ is exterior angle of Δ ADC,

∴ $x° = 67° + 16° = 83°$.

67. $\overset{\frown}{BC} = \overset{\frown}{AB}$

⇒ angle subtended by alternate segments by them are also equal.

∴ Angle subtended by $\overset{\frown}{BC}$ in the alternate segment

$x° = \dfrac{75°}{2} = 37½°$.

68. ∵ Sum of the opposite angles of a cyclic quadrilateral is 180°.

∴ $\angle A + \angle C = 180°$

⇒ $\angle C = 180° - 115° = 65°$

DC ∥ BE

⇒ $\angle DCB = \angle CBE = 65°$

∴ $\angle CBF = 65° + 21° = 86°$

Since exterior angle of a cyclic quadrilateral is equal to the interior opposite angle,

$\angle ADC = 86°$

69. ABCD is a cyclic quadrilateral,

$\angle B + \angle D = 180°$

⇒ $\angle D = 110°$

and $\angle A + \angle C = 180°$

⇒ $\angle C = 140°$

In Δ PDC, $\angle PDC = 180° - \angle D$

$= 180° - 110° = 70°$

and $\angle PCD = 180° - \angle C$

$= 180° - 140° = 40°$

∴ $\angle DPC = 180° - (70° + 40°) = 70°$

Similarly, in Δ QBC,

$\angle QBC = 180° - 70° = 110°$

and $\angle QCB = 180° - \angle C$

$= 180° - 140° = 40°$

∴ $\angle CQB = 180° - (110° + 40°) = 30°$

70. QRST is a cyclic quadrilateral,

$\angle TSR + \angle RQT = 180°$

$\angle TQP = 90°$

(since it is the angle in a semi-circle)

∴ $\angle TSR + \angle RQT + \angle TQP$

$= 180° + 90° = 270°$

⇒ $\angle RST + \angle PQR = 270°$.

□□□□□

11

Mensuration

PART–A
AREA OF PLANE FIGURES

AREA OF RECTILINEAR FIGURES

Points to Remember

Rectilinear Figure : A figure made up of some line segment is called a rectilinear figure and the line segments forming the figure are known as its sides.

Closed Rectilinear Figure : A rectilinear figure is said to be a closed rectilinear figure if it has no free ends.

Simple Rectilinear Figure : A rectilinear figure is said to be simple if no two sides of it intersect except at a common end-point.

Region : The part of the plane enclosed by a simple closed rectilinear figure is called the region enclosed by it.

Area : The magnitude of the plane region enclosed by a simple closed figure is called its area.

Various units of Measurement of Area

1 dm^2	= 10×10 cm^2	= 100 cm^2
1 m^2	= 10×10 dm^2	= 100 dm^2
1 m^2	= 100×100 cm^2	= 10000 cm^2
1 dam^2	= 10×10 m^2	= 100 m^2
1 arc	= 1 dam^2	= 100 m^2
1 hm^2	= 100×100 m^2	= 10000 m^2
1 hectare	= 10000 m^2	
1 hectare	= 100 acres	
1 km^2	= $(1000 \times 1000)m^2$	= $10^6 m^2$
1 km^2	= 100 hectares.	

Some Important Formula

(*i*) Area of rectangle = $l \times b$

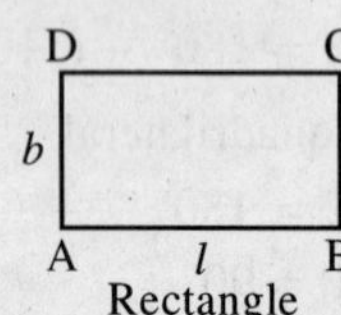

Rectangle

(*ii*) Length = $\dfrac{\text{Area}}{\text{Breadth}}$ (*iii*) Diagonal = $\sqrt{l^2 + b^2}$

(*iv*) Perimeter = $2(l + b)$

(*v*) Area of the square = a^2 sq units

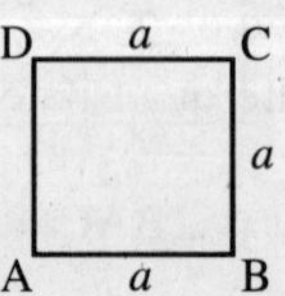

(*vi*) Diagonal of the square = $\sqrt{2}\,a$ units

(*vii*) Perimeter of the square = $4a$ units

(*viii*) Side of the square = $\dfrac{1}{\sqrt{2}}$ (diagonal)

(*ix*) Side of the square = $\sqrt{\text{Area}}$ units

(*x*) Area of parallelogram = Base × height = $a \times h$

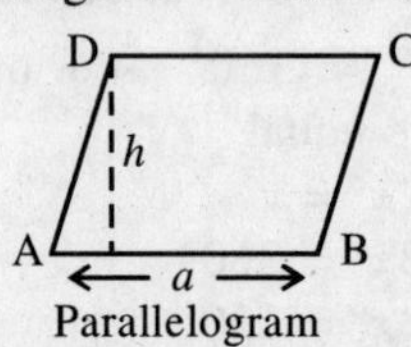

Parallelogram

(*xi*) Base of a parallelogram = $\dfrac{\text{Area}}{\text{Height}}$

(*xii*) Side of parallelogram = $\dfrac{\text{Area}}{\text{Corresponding altitude}}$

(*xiii*) Area of rhombus

$= \dfrac{1}{2}$ (product of diagonals) $= \dfrac{1}{2}(d_1 \times d_2)$

(*xiv*) $d_1^{\,2} + d_2^{\,2} = 4a^2$

or $a = \dfrac{1}{2}\sqrt{d_1^2 + d_2^2}$

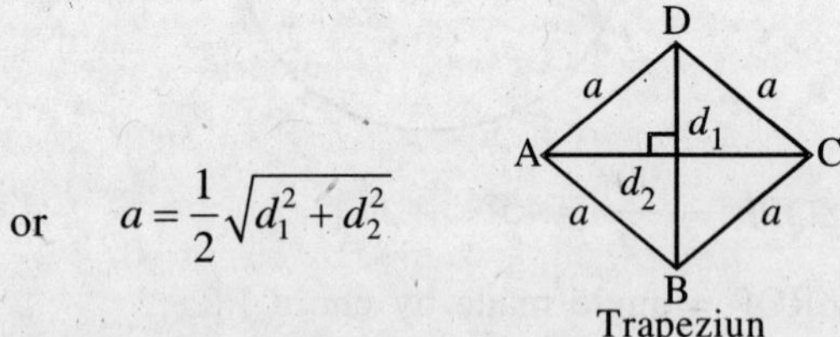

Trapeziun

(*xv*) Area of Trapezium

$= \dfrac{1}{2} \times$ (Sum of parallel sides) × height

(*xvi*) Area of quadrilateral

ABCD $= \dfrac{1}{2} \times d\,(h_1 + h_2)$

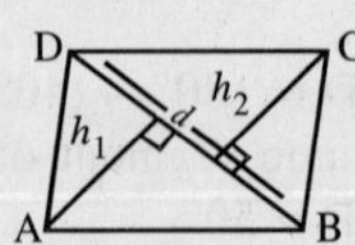

(*xvii*) Area of four walls = 2 (Length + Breadth) × Height

Triangle

(*i*) Area of right angle triangle.

$$= \frac{1}{2} \times \text{base} \times \text{height} = \frac{1}{2} \times a \times h$$

$$\text{inradius, } r = \frac{\text{Height} + \text{Base} - \text{Hypotenuse}}{2}$$

$$\text{Circum radius, } R = \frac{\text{Hypotenuse}}{2}$$

(*ii*) Area of triangle whose three sides are given.

$$s = \frac{a+b+c}{2}$$

$$\text{Area of } \Delta\, ABC = \sqrt{s(s-a)(s-b)(s-c)}$$

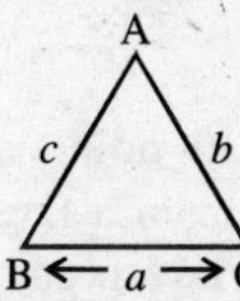

$$r = \frac{\Delta}{s},\ R = \frac{abc}{4\Delta}$$

(*iii*) Area of an equilateral triangle

$$ABC = \frac{\sqrt{3}}{4}(\text{side})^2 = \frac{\sqrt{3}}{4}(a)^2$$

$$r = \frac{a}{2\sqrt{3}},\ R = \frac{a}{\sqrt{3}},\ R : r = 2 : 1$$

(*iv*) Height of equilateral triangle

$$= \frac{\sqrt{3}}{2} \times \text{side} = \frac{\sqrt{3}}{2} \times a$$

(*v*) Area of an isosceles triangle

$$ABC = \frac{1}{2} \times \text{base} \times \sqrt{(\text{equal side})^2 - \frac{1}{4}(\text{base})^2}$$

$$= \frac{1}{2} a \times \sqrt{b^2 - \frac{1}{4}a^2}$$

(OR)

$$= (s-b)\ \sqrt{s(s-a)}$$

where s is semi-perimeter

$$s = \frac{b+b+a}{2} = \frac{2b+a}{2}$$

Circumference and Area of A Circle

Points To Remember:

- The perimeter of a circle is called its circumference.
- The ratio of the circumference of a circle to its diameter is the same for all circles. The constant ratio is denoted by π.

$$\pi = \frac{22}{7} \text{ or } 3.14 \qquad \frac{\text{Circumference}}{\text{Diameter}} = \pi$$

- Circumference of a circle = $2\pi r$
- Area of a circle of radius r is given by $A = \pi r^2$
- Radius of a circle = $\sqrt{\frac{A}{\pi}}$
- Length of arc $\overset{\frown}{AB}$
- $(l) = \frac{\pi r\theta}{180°}$

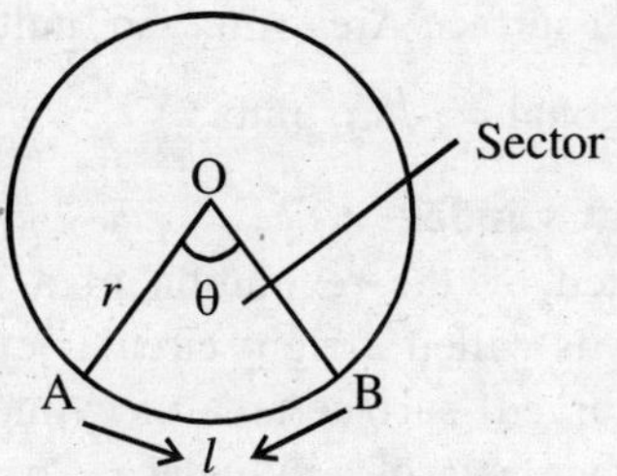

- Area of Sector AOB = $\frac{\pi r^2\theta}{360°} = \frac{1}{2}rl.$
- Area of segment = $\frac{\pi r^2\theta}{360°} - \frac{1}{2}r^2 \sin\theta$

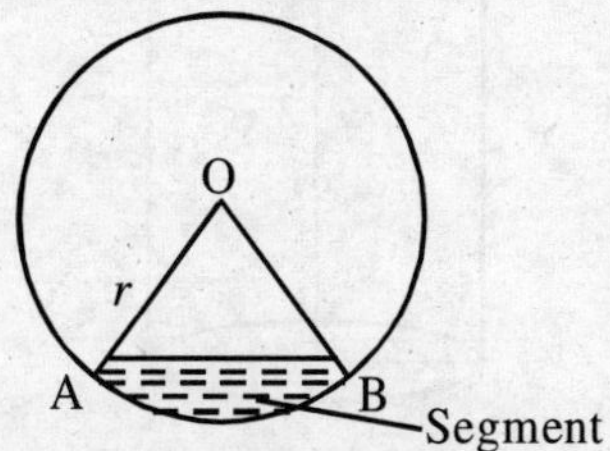

PART–B
SURFACE AREA AND VOLUME OF CUBE, CUBOIDS AND CYLINDER

Surface Area and Volume

(A) Cube and Cuboid

1. Cuboid : Let length = l, breadth = b and height = h units. Then,

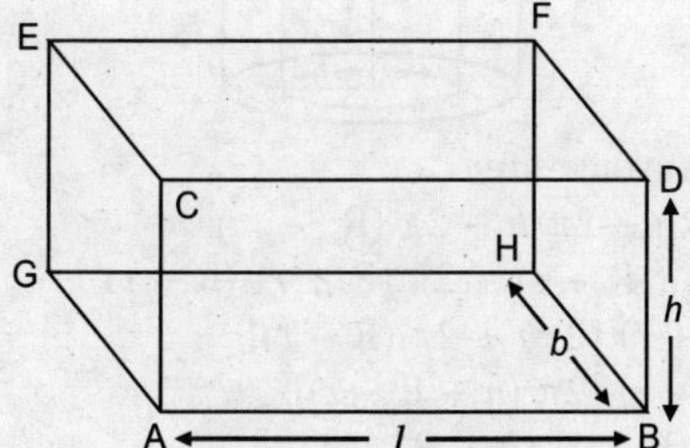

(1) Volume = $(l \times b \times h)$ cubic units
(2) Curved surface area = $2(l + b)h$ sq. units (area of four walls of a room)
(3) Total surface area = $2(lb + bh + hl)$ sq. units
(4) Diagonal = $\sqrt{l^2 + b^2 + h^2}$ units.

2. Cube : Let each edge of a cube be of length a. Then,

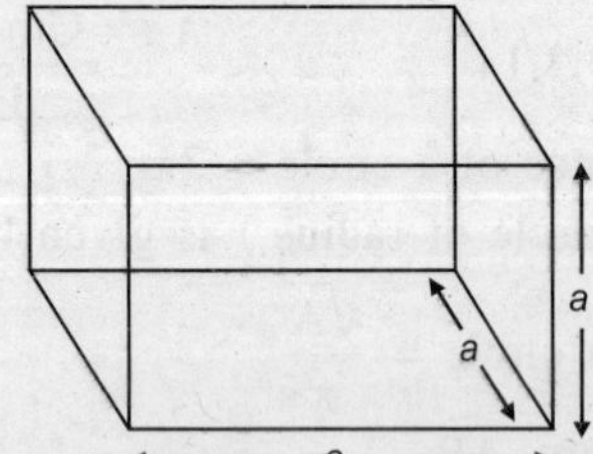

(1) Volume = a^3 cubic units
(2) Curved surface Area = $4a^2$ sq. units
(3) Total surface Area = $6a^2$ sq. units
(4) Diagonal = $\sqrt{3}a$ units

Right Circular Cylinder

A solid generated by the revolution of a rectangle about one of its sides is called a right circular cylinder.

(*i*) Lateral (curved) surface area of cylinder = $2\pi rh$
(*ii*) Total surface area of a cylinder = $2\pi rh + 2\pi r^2$
$= 2\pi r\ (h + r)$
(*iii*) Volume of a cylinder = $\pi r^2 h$

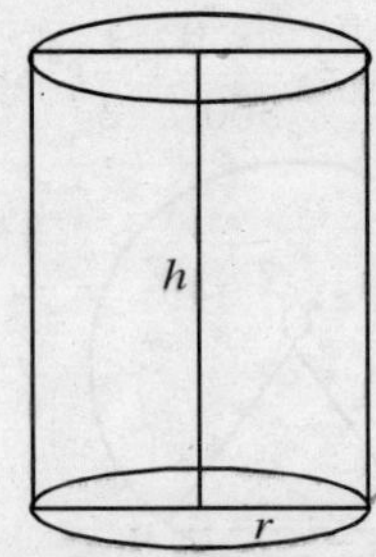

Hallow Cylinder

(*i*) Each base surface area = $\pi\ (R^2 - r^2)$
(*ii*) Curved surface area = External surface area + Internal surface area = $2\pi Rh + 2\pi rh = 2\pi h\ (R + r)$

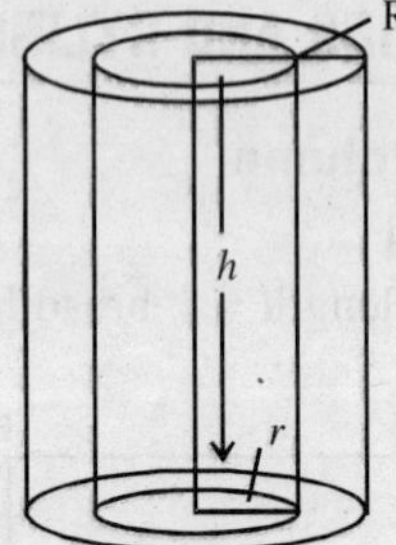

(*iii*) Total surface area
$= 2\pi Rh + 2\pi rh + 2\pi\ (R^2 - r^2)$
$= 2\pi h\ (R + r) + 2\pi\ (R + r)\ (R - r)$
$= (R + r)\ [2\pi h + 2\pi\ (R - r)]$
$= (R + r)\ [2\pi\ (h + R - r)]$
$= 2\pi\ (R + r)\ (h + R - r).$

(*iv*) Volume of the material
= Exterior volume – Interior volume
$= \pi R^2 h - \pi r^2 h = \pi h(R^2 - r^2)$

Right Circular Cone

A right circular cone is a solid generated by revolving a line segment which passes through a fixed point and which makes a constant angle with a fixed line.

(*i*) Curved surface area of a cone = πrl

Where $l = \sqrt{h^2 + r^2}$

(*ii*) Total surface area of a cone
$= \pi rl + \pi r^2 = \pi r\ (l + r)$

(*iii*) Volume of the cone = $\frac{1}{3}\pi r^2 h$

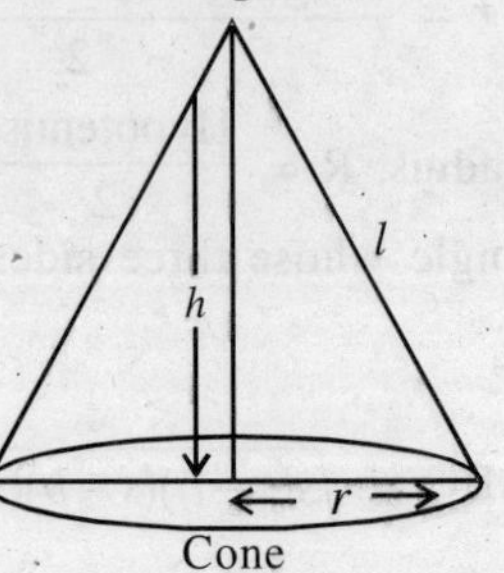

Cone

Sphere/Hemisphere

- **Sphere:** The set of all points in space which are equidistant from a fixed point, is called a *sphere*. The fixed point is called the *centre* of the sphere and constant distance is called its *radius*.

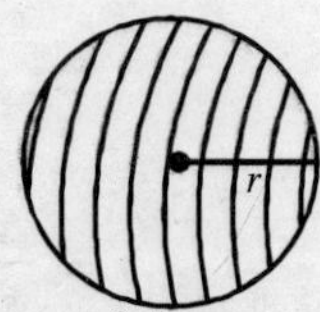

Sphere

- **Hemisphere :** A plane through the centre of a sphere divides the sphere into two equal parts, each of which is called a hemisphere.
- **Spherical shell :** The difference of two solid concentric spheres is called a spherical shell.

Important formula

(*i*) Surface area of the sphere = $4\pi r^2$
(*ii*) Volume of the sphere = $\frac{4}{3}\pi r^3$
(*iii*) Curved surface area of a hemisphere = $2\pi r^2$
(*iv*) Total surface area of a hemisphere = $3\pi r^2$
(*v*) Volume of a hemisphere = $\frac{2}{3}\pi r^3$

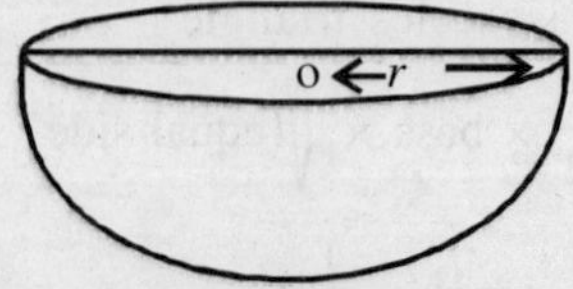

Hemisphere

(*vi*) Volume of a hemispherical Shell/Bowl

Volume = $\frac{2}{3}\pi(r_1^3 - r_2^3)$

Curved surface area
$= 3\pi r_1^2 + 3\pi r_2^2 = 3\pi(r_1^2 + r_2^2)$

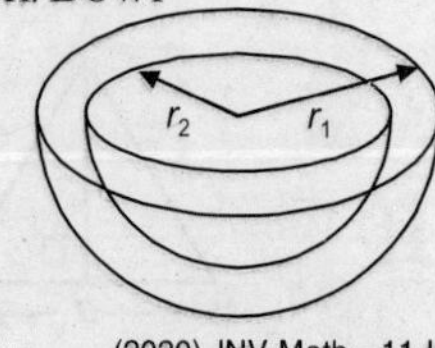

Multiple Choice Questions

1. The length of a rectangle is twice its breadth. What is the dimensions of the rectangle if its area is 288 cm^2?
A. 24 cm, 12 cm B. 16 cm, 10 cm
C. 20 cm, 16 cm D. 28 cm, 10 cm

2. The length and breadth of a rectangular field are in the ratio 3 : 2. If the area of the field is 3456 m^2. What is its dimensions?
A. 48 m, 60 m B. 72 m, 48 m
C. 40 m, 70 m D. 64 m, 52 m

3. What is the area of a rectangular plot if one side of it is 48 cm and its diagonal is 50 cm?
A. 560 cm^2 B. 620 cm^2
C. 672 cm^2 D. 682 cm^2

4. The area of square ABCD is 16 cm^2. What is the area of the square joining the mid-points of the sides?
A. 4 cm^2 B. 6 cm^2
C. 10 cm^2 D. 8 cm^2

5. The area of 4 walls of a room is 375 m^2. The breadth and height of the room are 10 m and 7.5 m respectively. What is the length of the room?
A. 15 m B. 16 m
C. 17 m D. 18 m

6. A room 5 m long and 4 m wide is surrounded by a verandah. What is the width of the verandah, if it occupies 22 m^2?
A. 1.5 m B. 1 m
C. 2.5 m D. 2 m

7. The cost of fencing a square field at 60 paise per metre is ₹ 1200. What is the cost of reaping the field at the rate of 50 paise per 100 sq metres?
A. ₹ 8 B. ₹ 12
C. ₹ 10 D. ₹ 9

8. What is the altitude of a rhombus whose area is 420 cm^2 and perimeter is 140 cm?
A. 12 cm B. 10 cm
C. 11 cm D. 13 cm

9. Two sides of a parallelogram are 20 cm. and 25 cm. If the altitude corresponding to the sides of length 25 cm. is 10 cm. What is the altitude corresponding to the other pair of sides?
A. 10.5 cm B. 12.5 cm
C. 11.5 cm D. 9.5 cm

10. The area of trapezium is 105 cm^2 and its height is 7 cm. If one of the parallel sides is longer than the other by 6 cm. What are the two parallel sides?
A. 12 cm, 18 cm B. 16 cm, 20 cm
C. 10 cm, 15 cm D. 11 cm, 20 cm

11. What is the circumference of a circle whose diameter is 35 cm?
A. 110 cm B. 112 cm
C. 115 cm D. 120 cm

12. What is the circumference of a cycle wheel whose radius is 3.7 dm?
A. 20.35 cm B. 23.24 cm
C. 22.34 cm D. 24.24 cm

13. The diameter of a coin is 2 cm. What is its circumference?
A. 5.28 cm B. 6.28 cm
C. 7.28 cm D. 5.25 cm

14. Two circles having the same centre have radii 350 m and 490 m. What is the difference in their circumferences?
A. 820 m B. 840 m
C. 880 m D. 860 m

15. The diameter of a cycle wheel is 70 cm. How many times the wheel will revolve in order to cover a distance of 110 m?
A. 50 B. 60
C. 40 D. 45

16. A water sprinkler in a lawn sprays water as far as 7 m in all directions. What is the length of the outer edge of wet grass?
A. 40 m B. 42 m
C. 48 m D. 44 m

17. An ox in a kolhu is tethered to a rope 3 m long. How much distance does it cover in 14 rounds?
A. 264 m B. 260 m
C. 262 m D. 268 m

18. A circular piece of thin wire is converted into a square of side 6.25 cm. If there is no loss or gain in its length, find the radius of the circular wire.
A. 3.75 cm B. 3.98 cm
C. 3.25 cm D. 4.25 cm

19. The ratio of the radii of two wheels is 3 : 4. What is the ratio of their circumferences?
A. 2 : 3 B. 2 : 5
C. 3 : 4 D. 4 : 5

20. A piece of thin wire in the form of an equilateral triangle of side 31.4 dm is bent into a ring with no loss in wire. What is the diameter of the ring?
A. 15 dm B. 10 dm
C. 12 dm D. 14 dm

21. What is the surface area of a 10 cm × 4 cm × 3 cm brick?
A. 84 sq. cm B. 124 sq. cm
C. 164 sq. cm D. 180 sq. cm

22. A cistern 6 m long and 4 m wide contains water up to a depth of 1 m 25 cm. The total area of the wet surface is:
A. 49 m^2 B. 50 m^2
C. 53.5 m^2 D. 55 m^2

23. The area of the base of a rectangular tank is 6500 cm^2 and the volume of water contained in it is 2.6 cubic metres. The depth of water in the tank is:

A. 3.5 m B. 4 m
C. 5 m D. 6 m

24. Half cubic metre of gold sheet is extended by hammering so as to cover an area of 1 hectare. The thickness of the sheet is:

A. 0.0005 cm B. 0.005 cm
C. 0.05 cm D. 0.5 cm

25. In a shower, 5 cm of rain falls. The volume of water that falls on 1.5 hectares of ground is:

A. 75 cu. m B. 750 cu. m
C. 7500 cu. m D. 75000 cu. m

26. The volume of a rectangular block of stone is 10368 dm^3. Its dimensions are in the ratio of 3 : 2 : 1. If its entire surface is polished at 2 paise per dm^2, then the total cost will be:

A. ₹ 31.50 B. ₹ 31.68
C. ₹ 63 D. ₹ 63.36

27. The edges of a cuboid are in the ratio 1 : 2 : 3 and its surface area is 88 cm^2. The volume of the cuboid is:

A. 24 cm^3 B. 48 cm^3
C. 64 cm^3 D. 12 cm^3

28. What is the length of the longest rod that can be placed in a room 16 m long, 12 m broad and $10\frac{2}{3}$ m high?

A. $22\frac{1}{3}$ m B. $22\frac{2}{3}$ m
C. 23 m D. 68 m

29. How many bricks, each measuring 25 cm × 11.25 cm × 6 cm, will be needed to build a wall 8 m × 6 m × 22.5 cm?

A. 5600 B. 6000
C. 6400 D. 7200

30. 50 men took a dip in a water tank 40 m long and 20 m broad on a religious day. If the average displacement of water by a man is 4 m^3, then the rise in the water level in the tank will be?

A. 20 cm B. 25 cm
C. 35 cm D. 50 cm

31. The curved surface area of a right circular cylinder of height 14 cm is 88 cm^2. What is the radius of the base of the cylinder?

A. 2 cm B. 3 cm
C. 1 cm D. 4 cm

32. It is required to make a closed cylinderical tank of height 1 m and base diameter 140 cm from a metal sheet. How many square metres of the metal sheet are required for the same?

A. 3.4 m^2 B. 4.4 m^2
C. 2.4 m^2 D. 5.4 m^2

33. Inner and outer radii of a metallic pipe are 3 cm and 3.5 cm respectively if the length of the pipe is 56 cm. What is its total surface area?

A. 2225 cm^2 B. 2244 cm^2
C. 2264 cm^2 D. 2288 cm^2

34. A right circular cylinder has base radius 8 cm and height 35 cm. What is the curved surface area of the cylinder?

A. 1760 cm^2 B. 1780 cm^2
C. 1750 cm^2 D. 1770 cm^2

35. The circumference of the base of a right circular cylinder is 176 cm. If the height of the cylinder is 1 m, what is the lateral surface area of the cylinder?

A. 17500 cm^2 B. 17400 cm^2
C. 17600 cm^2 D. 17800 cm^2

36. A closed circular cylinder has diameter 10 cm and height 15 cm. What is the total surface area of the cylinder?

A. 620 cm^2 B. 625 cm^2
C. 628 cm^2 D. 630 cm^2

37. The radius of the base of a closed right circular cylinder is 21 cm and its height is 1 m. What is the total surface area of the cylinder?

A. 15972 cm^2 B. 15827 cm^2
C. 15944 cm^2 D. 15895 cm^2

38. The diameter of a roller is 84 cm and its length is 120 cm. It takes 500 complete revolutions to move once over to level a playground. What is the area of the playground in m^2.

A. 1275 m^2 B. 1584 m^2
C. 1484 m^2 D. 1348 m^2

39. A cylindrical pillar is 50 cm in radius and 3.5 m in height. What is the cost of white washing the curved surface of the pillar at the rate of ₹ 12.50 per m^2?

A. ₹ 127.50 B. ₹ 227.50
C. ₹ 132.50 D. ₹ 137.50

40. Curved surface area of a right circular cylinder of height 35 cm is 121 cm^2. What is the radius of its base?

A. 0.25 cm B. 0.35 cm
C. 0.55 cm D. 0.45 cm

41. Diameter of the base of a cone is 10.5 cm and its slant height is 10 cm. What is the curved surface area of the cone?

A. 154 cm^2 B. 165 cm^2
C. 175 cm^2 D. 185 cm^2

42. The height of a cone is 16 cm and the radius of its base is 12 cm. What is the curved surface area and the total surface area of the cone?

A. 753.6 cm^2, 1205.76 cm^2
B. 853.6 cm^2, 1208.76 cm^2
C. 953.5 cm^2, 1212.76 cm^2
D. 764.6 cm^2, 1185.76 cm^2

43. Curved surface area of a cone is 308 cm^2 and its slant height is 14 cm. What is the radius of the base and total surface area of the cone?

A. 7 cm, 462 cm B. 5 cm, 460 cm^2
C. 6 cm, 452 cm^2 D. 4 cm, 475 cm^2

44. The radius of the base of a conical tent is 12 m. The tent is 9 m high. What is the cost of the canvas required to make the tent, if one square metre of canvas costs ₹ 120?

A. ₹ 67885.20 B. ₹ 68885.20
C. ₹ 66985.20 D. ₹ 68675.20

45. What is the curved surface area of a right circular cone whose slant height is 10 cm and base radius is 7 cm?

A. 210 cm^2 B. 220 cm^2
C. 230 cm^2 D. 215 cm^2

46. The diameter of a right circular cone is 14 cm and its slant height is 9 cm. What is its curved surface area and total surface area?

A. 190 cm^2, 341 cm^2 B. 195 cm^2, 348 cm^2
C. 198 cm^2, 352 cm^2 D. 196 cm^2, 350 cm^2

47. What is the curved surface area of a cone if its slant height is 60 cm and the radius of its base is 25 cm?

A. 4710 cm^2 B. 4690 cm^2
C. 4720 cm^2 D. 4725 cm^2

48. What is the total surface of a cone, if its slant height is 9 dm and diameter of its base is 24 dm?

A. 692 dm^2 B. 792 dm^2
C. 892 dm^2 D. 698 dm^2

49. The radius of the base of a cone is 9 cm and its height is 12 cm. What is the curved surface area of the cone?

A. 410.42 cm^2 B. 375.42 cm^2
C. 339.42 cm^2 D. 336.42 cm^2

50. A conical tent is 10 m high and the radius of its base is 24 m. What is slant height of the tent and cost of the canvas required to make the tent, if the cost of 1 m^2 canvas is ₹ 90?

A. 26 m, ₹ 176502.60
B. 24 m, ₹ 182408.60
C. 25 m, ₹ 196232.60
D. 10 m, ₹ 188402.60

51. Diameter of a sphere is 10 cm. What is its surface area?

A. 314.28 cm^2 B. 318.24 cm^2
C. 312.28 cm^2 D. 310.28 cm^2

52. The surface of a solid hemisphere with its circular base is to be painted. If the radius of the hemisphere is 28 cm, find the cost of painting the surface at the rate of ₹ 3 per 100 cm^2.

A. ₹ 220.76 B. ₹ 218.76
C. ₹ 221.76 D. ₹ 230.5

53. Assuming the earth to be a sphere of radius 6370 km. What is surface area of the earth?

A. 510109600 km^2 B. 410109600 km^2
C. 520109600 km^2 D. 490109600 km^2

54. What is the surface area of a sphere whose diameter is 14 cm?

A. 616 cm^2 B. 612 cm^2
C. 624 cm^2 D. 620 cm^2

55. The radius of a spherical balloon increases from 7 cm to 14 cm as air is being pumped into it. What is the ratio of surface areas of the balloon in the two cases?

A. 2 : 3 B. 1 : 4
C. 3 : 4 D. 4 : 5

56. A hemispherical bowl made of brass has inner diameter 10.5 cm. What is the cost of tin plating it on the inside at the rate of ₹ 16 per 100 cm^2?

A. ₹ 25.72 B. ₹ 28.72
C. ₹ 27.72 D. ₹ 26.72

57. The dome of a building is in the form of a hemisphere. Its radius is 6.3 m. What is the cost of painting it at the rate of ₹ 12 per m^2?

A. ₹ 2993.76 B. ₹ 2996.76
C. ₹ 2988.76 D. ₹ 2991.76

58. A solid sphere of radius 3 cm is melted and then cast into small spherical balls each of radius 0.6 cm. What is the number of balls?

A. 115 B. 118
C. 120 D. 125

59. How many spherical bullets can be made out of a solid cube of lead whose edge measures 44 cm, each bullet being 4 cm in diameter?

A. 2496 B. 2525
C. 2541 D. 2552

60. How many spherical lead shots each 4.2 cm in diameter can be obtained from a rectangular solid of lead with dimensions 66 cm, 42 cm, 21 cm?

A. 1200 B. 1500
C. 1400 D. 1300

ANSWERS

1	2	3	4	5	6	7	8	9	10
A	B	C	D	A	B	C	A	B	A
11	**12**	**13**	**14**	**15**	**16**	**17**	**18**	**19**	**20**
A	B	B	C	A	D	A	B	C	A
21	**22**	**23**	**24**	**25**	**26**	**27**	**28**	**29**	**30**
C	A	B	B	B	D	B	B	C	B

31	32	33	34	35	36	37	38	39	40
C	B	D	A	C	C	A	B	D	C
41	**42**	**43**	**44**	**45**	**46**	**47**	**48**	**49**	**50**
B	A	A	A	B	C	A	B	C	A
51	**52**	**53**	**54**	**55**	**56**	**57**	**58**	**59**	**60**
A	C	A	A	B	C	A	D	C	B

EXPLANATORY ANSWERS

1. Let length of rectangle = x cm.

$$\text{Breadth} = \frac{x}{2} \text{ cm.}$$

$$\text{Area of rectangle} = 288$$

$$l \times b = 288$$

$$x \times \frac{x}{2} = 288$$

$$x^2 = 288 \times 2 = 576$$

$$x = \sqrt{576} = \sqrt{24 \times 24} = 24 \text{ cm.}$$

$$\text{Length} = 24 \text{ cm.}$$

$$\text{Breadth} = \frac{24}{2} = 12 \text{ cm.}$$

2. Let length = $3x$ and breadth = $2x$

$$\text{Area of rectangular field} = 3456\ m^2$$

$$l \times b = 3456$$

$$3x \times 2x = 3456$$

$$x^2 = \frac{3456}{6}$$

$$x = \sqrt{576} = 24.$$

$$\text{Length} = 3x = 3 \times 24 = 72 \text{ m.}$$

$$\text{Breadth} = 2x = 2 \times 24 = 48 \text{ m.}$$

3. Area of rectangular plot = length × breadth

$$AD^2 = BD^2 - AB^2 = 50^2 - 48^2$$

$$= (50 + 48)(50 - 48)$$

$$= 98 \times 2 = 14 \times 7 \times 2$$

$$= 7 \times 2 \times 7 \times 2$$

$$AD = \sqrt{7 \times 2 \times 7 \times 2} = 7 \times 2 = 14 \text{ cm.}$$

$$\text{Area} = 48 \times 14 = 672 \text{ cm}^2.$$

D C
50 cm
A B
48 cm

4. Area of square = 16

$$\text{side}^2 = 16$$

$$\text{side} = \sqrt{16}$$

$$AB = 4$$

D R C
S Q
A P B

Diagonal of PQRS = 4 cm.

$$\sqrt{2}\ \text{side} = 4$$

$$2\ \text{side}^2 = 16$$

$$\text{Area} = \text{side}^2 = \frac{16}{2} = 8 \text{ cm}^2.$$

5. Area of four walls = $2(l + b) \times h$

$$2(l + b) \times h = 375.$$

$$2(l + 10) \times 7.5 = 375$$

$$l + 10 = \frac{375}{15}$$

$$l = 25 - 10 = 15 \text{ m.}$$

6. Area of room = $5 \times 4 = 20 \text{ m}^2$

$$(l + 2x)(b + 2x) = 20 + 22$$

$$(5 + 2x)(4 + 2x) = 42$$

$$20 + 10x + 8x + 4x^2 = 42$$

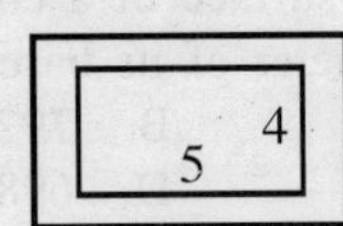

$$4x^2 + 18x - 22 = 0$$

$$2x^2 + 9x - 11 = 0$$

$$2x^2 + 11x - 2x - 11 = 0$$

$$x(2x + 11) - 1(2x + 11) = 0$$

$$\Rightarrow (x - 1)(2x + 11) = 0$$

$$x - 1 = 0,\ 2x + 11 = 0$$

$$x = 1,\ x = -11/2$$

Not possible

∴ Width of varandah = 1 m.

7. $\text{Area of square field} = \dfrac{\text{Total cost}}{\text{Per sq. m. cost}}$

$$= \frac{1200}{\frac{60}{100}} = \frac{1200 \times 100}{60} = 2000 \text{ m}^2.$$

$$\text{The cost of reaping} = \frac{\frac{50}{100} \times 2000}{100} = ₹\ 10.$$

8. $4a = 140,\ a = \dfrac{140}{4} = 35$

Side of rhombus = 35 cm.

$$\text{Altitude of rhombus} = \frac{\text{Area}}{\text{Side}} = \frac{420}{35} = 12 \text{ cm.}$$

9.

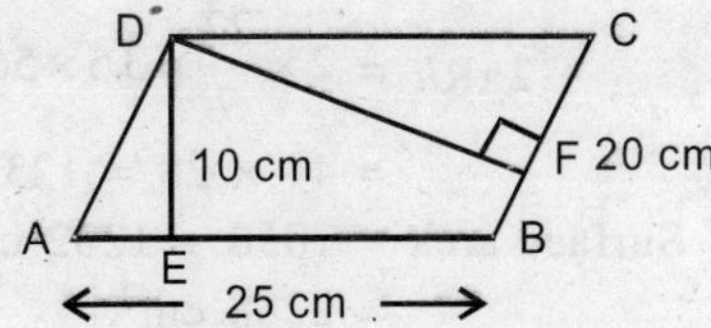

Area of parallelogram = base × height

$$BC \times DF = AB \times DE$$

$$20 \times DF = 25 \times 10$$

$$DF = \frac{25 \times 10}{20} = 12.5 \text{ cm.}$$

10. Let other side = x cm.

One side = $(x + 6)$ cm.

$$\frac{1}{2}(x + x + 6) \times 7 = 105$$

$$2x + 6 = \frac{105 \times 2}{7} = 30$$

$$2x = 24 \Rightarrow x = 12$$

Sides = 12 cm, 18 cm.

11. $d = 35$ cm.,

$$r = \frac{d}{2} = \frac{35}{2} \text{ cm.}$$

$$\text{Circumference} = 2\pi r = 2 \times \frac{22}{7} \times \frac{35}{2}$$

$$= 22 \times 5 = 110 \text{ cm.}$$

12. $r = 3.7$ dm

Circumference = $2\pi r$

$$= 2 \times \frac{22}{7} \times 3.7 = 2 \times 3.14 \times 3.7$$

$$= 23.236 \text{ cm} = 23.24 \text{ cm.}$$

13. $d = 2$ cm.

$$r = \frac{2}{2} = 1 \text{ cm}$$

$$\text{Circumference} = 2\pi r = 2 \times \frac{22}{7} \times 1$$

$$= 2 \times 3.14 = 6.28 \text{ cm.}$$

14. Difference in circumference = $2\pi R - 2\pi r$

$= 2\pi\,(R - r)$ R = 490 m

$= 2 \times \frac{22}{7}\,(490 - 350)$ r = 350 m

$$= 2 \times \frac{22}{7} \times 140 = 44 \times 20 = 880 \text{ m.}$$

15. Nos. of revolution

$$= \frac{110}{2 \times \pi \times \frac{70}{2} \times \frac{1}{100}} = \frac{110 \times 100 \times 2 \times 7}{2 \times 22 \times 70} = 50.$$

16. Circumference $= 2\pi r = 2 \times \frac{22}{7} \times 7 = 44$ m.

17. Distance covered $= 14 \times 2 \times \frac{22}{7} \times 3$

$$= 12 \times 22 = 264 \text{ m.}$$

18. Circumference of wire = Perimeter of square

$$2\pi r = 4 \times 6.25$$

$$2 \times \frac{22}{7} \times r = 25$$

$$r = \frac{25 \times 7}{44} = \frac{175}{44}$$

$$= 3.977 \text{ cm} = 3.98 \text{ cm.}$$

19. The ratio of circumference

$$= \frac{2\pi 3x}{2\pi 4x} = \frac{3}{4} = 3 : 4.$$

20. Circumference of circle

= Perimeter of Equilateral triangle = 3×31.4

$$2\pi r = 3 \times 31.4$$

$$2 \times 3.14 \times r = 3 \times 31.4$$

$$r = \frac{3 \times 31.4}{3.14 \times 2} = 15 \text{ dm.}$$

21. Surface area = $[2(10 \times 4 + 4 \times 3 + 10 \times 3)]$ cm^2

$= (2 \times 82)$ cm^2 = 164 cm^2.

22. Area of the wet surface = $[2(lb + bh + lh) - lb]$

$= 2(bh + lh) + lb$

$= [2(4 \times 1.25 + 6 \times 1.25) + 6 \times 4]$ m^2

$= 49$ m^2.

23. Volume = $(2.6 \times 100 \times 100 \times 100)$ cu. cm.

$$\text{Depth} = \frac{\text{Volume}}{\text{Area of the base}} = \left(\frac{2.6 \times 100 \times 100 \times 100}{6500}\right) \text{ cm}$$

= 400 cm = 4 m.

24. Volume of gold = $\left(\frac{1}{2} \times 100 \times 100 \times 100\right)$ cm^3.

Area of sheet = 10000 m^2 = $(10000 \times 100 \times 100)$ cm^2

$$\therefore \text{ Thickness of the sheet} = \left(\frac{1 \times 100 \times 100 \times 100}{2 \times 10000 \times 100 \times 100}\right) \text{ cm}$$

= 0.005 cm.

25. Area = (1.5×10000) m^2 = 15000 m^2.

$$\text{Depth} = \frac{5}{100}\text{ m} = \frac{1}{20}\text{ m}.$$

$\therefore$ Volume = (Area × Depth)

$$= \left(15000 \times \frac{1}{20}\right) \text{m}^3 = 750 \text{ m}^3.$$

26. Let the dimensions be $3x$, $2x$ and x respectively. Then,

$$3x \times 2x \times x = 10368 \Leftrightarrow x^3 = \left(\frac{10368}{6}\right) = 1728 \Leftrightarrow x = 12.$$

So, the dimensions of the block are 36 dm, 24 dm and 12 dm.

Surface area = $[2(36 \times 24 + 24 \times 12 + 36 \times 12)]$ dm^2

$= [2 \times 144\,(6 + 2 + 3)]$ dm^2

$= 3168$ dm^2

$\therefore$ Cost of polishing = ₹ $\left(\frac{2\times 3168}{100}\right)$ = ₹ 63.36.

27. Let the dimensions of the cuboid be x, $2x$ and $3x$.
Then, $2(x \times 2x + 2x \times 3x + x \times 3x) = 88$
$\Leftrightarrow 2x^2 + 6x^2 + 3x^2 = 44 \Leftrightarrow 11x^2 = 44$
$\Leftrightarrow x^2 = 4 \Leftrightarrow x = 2.$
$\therefore$ Volume of the cuboid = $(2 \times 4 \times 6)$ cm^3 = 48 cm^3.

28. Required length $= \sqrt{(16)^2+(12)^2+\left(\frac{32}{3}\right)^2}$ m

$= \sqrt{256+144+\frac{1024}{9}}$ m

$= \sqrt{\frac{4624}{9}}$ m $= \frac{68}{3}$ m $= 22\frac{2}{3}$ m.

29. Number of bricks $= \frac{\text{Volume of the wall}}{\text{Volume of 1 brick}}$

$= \left(\frac{800\times 600\times 22.5}{25\times 11.25\times 6}\right) = 6400.$

30. Total volume of water displaced = (4×50) m^3
= 200 m^3.

$\therefore$ Rise in water level $= \left(\frac{200}{40\times 20}\right)$ m
= 0.25 m = 25 cm.

31. Curved surface of right circular cylinder = 88 cm^2

$2\pi rh = 88$

$2\times\frac{22}{7}\times r\times 14 = 88$

$r = \frac{88}{88} = 1$ cm.

32. Area of cylinder = $2\pi rh$

$= 2\times\frac{22}{7}\times 100\times 70$

$= \frac{44\times 1000}{100\times 100}\text{m}^2 = 4.4 \text{ m}^2.$

33. h = 56 cm
r = 3 cm
R = 3.5 cm

3 cm
56
3.5 cm

$2\pi rh = 2\times\frac{22}{7}\times 3\times 56$
= 44 × 24 = 1056 cm^2

$2\pi Rh = 2\times\frac{22}{7}\times 3.5\times 56$
= 44 × 28 = 1232 cm^2

Surface area = 1056 + 1232 cm^2
= 2288 cm^2.

34. Curved surface of the cylinder
$= 2\pi rh$
$= 2\times\frac{22}{7}\times 8\times 35$
= 44 × 40 = 1760 cm^2.

35. $2\pi r = 176 = 2\times\frac{22}{7}\times r = 176$

$\Rightarrow r = \frac{176\times 7}{2\times 22} = 28$ cm

h = 1 m = 100 cm

Lateral surface of the cylinder
$= 2\pi rh$
$= 2\times\frac{22}{7}\times 28\times 100$
= 17600 cm^2.

36. r = 5 cm, h = 15 cm

Total surface area of the cylinder
$= 2\pi r(h + r)$
$= 2\times\frac{22}{7}\times 5(15+5)$
$= 2\times\frac{22}{7}\times 5\times 20$
= 2 × 3.14 × 100 = 628 cm^2.

37. h = 1 m = 100 cm, r = 21

Total surface area = $2\pi r(r + h)$
$= 2\times\frac{22}{7}\times 21(21+100)$
$= 2\times\frac{22}{7}\times 21\times 121$
= 132 × 121 = 15972 cm^2.

38. $r = \frac{84}{2} = 42\,\text{cm} = \frac{42}{100} = .42\,\text{m}$

$h = 120 \text{ cm} = \frac{120}{100} = 1.2\,\text{m}$

Area of playground = 500 × $2\pi rh$
$= 500\times 2\times\frac{22}{7}\times .42\times 1.2$
= 30 × 44 × 1.2 = 1584 m^2.

39. Curved surface of the pillar
$= 2\pi rh$
$= 2\times\frac{22}{7}\times\frac{50}{100}\times 3.5 = 11 \text{ m}^2$

The cost of white washing

$= 11\ m^2 \times 12.50 = ₹\ 137.50.$

40. Curved surface of the cylinder $= 121\ cm^2$

$2\pi rh = 121\ cm^2$

$2 \times \frac{22}{7} \times r \times 35 = 121$

$r = \frac{121}{2 \times 22 \times 5} = \frac{121}{220} cm$

$r = \frac{121}{220}\ cm = 0.55\ cm.$

41. Curved surface of the cone $= \pi rl$

$= \frac{22}{7} \times \frac{10.5}{2} \times 10$

$= 22 \times 7.5 = 165\ cm^2.$

42. Curved surface of the cone

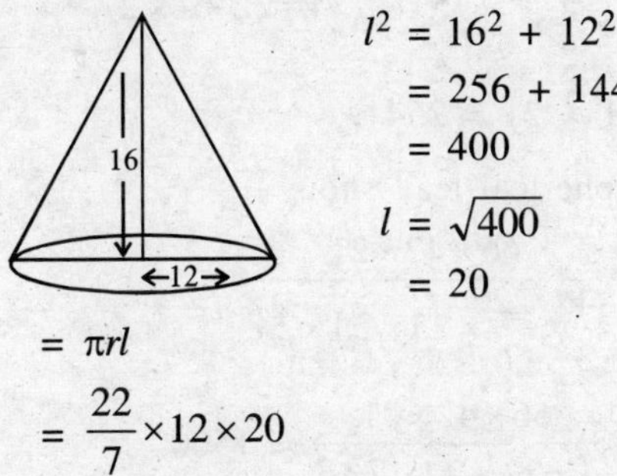

$l^2 = 16^2 + 12^2$

$= 256 + 144$

$= 400$

$l = \sqrt{400}$

$= 20$

$= \pi rl$

$= \frac{22}{7} \times 12 \times 20$

$= 3.14 \times 240 = 753.6\ cm^2.$

Total surface area

$= \pi rl + \pi r^2$

$= 753.6 + \frac{22}{7} \times 12 \times 12$

$= 753.6 + 3.14 \times 144$

$= 753.6 + 452.16 = 1205.76\ cm^2.$

43. Curved surface area of cone, $\pi rl = 308$

$\frac{22}{7} \times r \times 14 = 308 \Rightarrow r = \frac{308 \times 7}{22 \times 14}$

$r = 7\ cm.$

Total surface area of the cone $= \pi rl + \pi r^2$

$= 308 + \frac{22}{7} \times 7 \times 7$

$= 308 + 154 = 462\ cm^2.$

44. Curved surface area of the tent $= \pi rl$

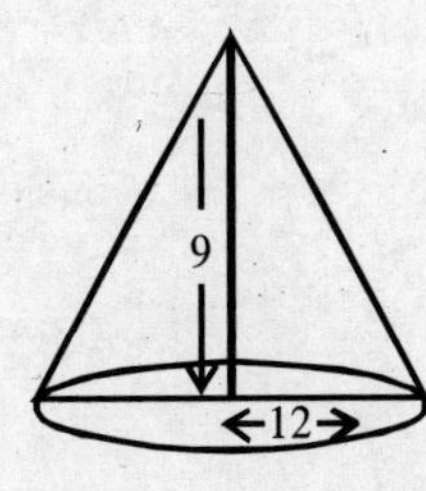

$l^2 = 12^2 + 9^2$

$= 144 + 81$

$= 225$

$l = \sqrt{225} = 15$

$= \frac{22}{7} \times 12 \times 15 = \frac{3960}{7}$

$= 565.71\ m^2$

The cost of canvas $= 565.71 \times 120$

$= ₹\ 67885.20.$

45. Curved surface of the cone $= \pi rl$

$= \frac{22}{7} \times 7 \times 10 = 220\ cm^2.$

46. Curved surface $= \pi rl$

$= \frac{22}{7} \times 7 \times 9 = 198\ cm^2$

Total surface $= \pi rl + \pi r^2$

$= 198 + \frac{22}{7} \times 7 \times 7$

$= 198 + 154 = 352\ cm^2.$

47. Curved surface $= \pi rl$

$= \frac{22}{7} \times 25 \times 60$

$= 3.14 \times 1500 = 4710\ cm^2.$

48. Total surface area of the cone

$= \pi rl + \pi r^2 = \pi r\ (l + r)$

$= \frac{22}{7} \times 12 \times (9+12) = \frac{22}{7} \times 12 \times 21$

$= 22 \times 36 = 792\ dm^2.$

49. Curved surface $= \pi rl$

$= \frac{22}{7} \times 9 \times 12 = \frac{2376}{7}$

$= 339.42\ cm^2.$

50. $l^2 = 10^2 + 24^2$

$= 100 + 576 = 676$

$l = \sqrt{676} = 26\, m.$

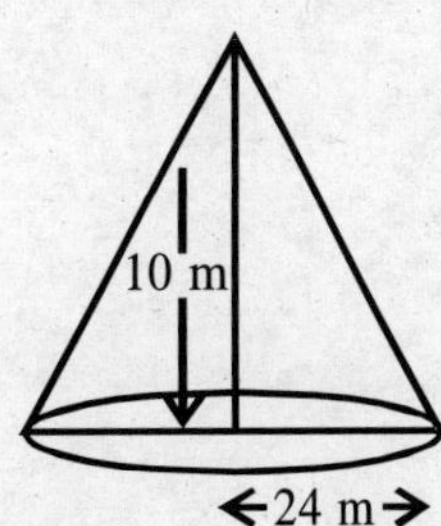

Curved surface $= \pi rl$

$= \frac{22}{7} \times 21 \times 26 = \frac{13728}{7}$

$= 1961.14\, m^2$

The cost of canvas

$= 1961.14 \times 90 = ₹\ 176502.60.$

51. $r = \frac{10}{2} = 5\ cm$

Surface area of the sphere $= 4\pi r^2$

$= 4 \times \frac{22}{7} \times 5 \times 5 = \frac{88 \times 25}{7} = \frac{2200}{7}$

$= 314.28\ cm^2.$

52. The cost of painting

$= 3\pi r^2 \times \frac{3}{100}$

$= 3 \times \frac{22}{7} \times 28 \times 28 \times \frac{3}{100}$

$= \frac{66 \times 84}{25} = \frac{5544}{25}$

= ₹ 221.76.

53. Surface area of the earth = $4\pi r^2$

$= 4 \times \frac{22}{7} \times 6370 \times 6370$

$= 88 \times 910 \times 6370 \text{ km}^2$

$= 510109600 \text{ km}^2$.

54. Surface area of sphere = $4\pi r^2$

$= 4\pi \times 7 \times 7$

$= 4 \times \frac{22}{7} \times 7 \times 7 = 4 \times 154 = 616 \text{ cm}^2$.

55. The ratio of Areas

$= \frac{4\pi \times 7 \times 7}{4\pi \times 14 \times 14} = \frac{1}{4} = 1 : 4.$

56. The cost of tin plating

$= 2 \times \frac{22}{7} \times \frac{10.5}{2} \times \frac{10.5}{2} \times \frac{16}{100}$

= 1.76 × 1.5 × 10.5 = ₹ 27.72.

57. Area of hemisphere

$= 2 \times \frac{22}{7} \times 6.3 \times 6.3$

$= 44 \times 0.9 \times 6.3$

The cost of painting

$= 12 \times 44 \times 0.9 \times 6.3$

= ₹ 2993.76.

58. The number of balls

$= \frac{\frac{4}{3}\pi \times 3 \times 3 \times 3}{\frac{4}{3}\pi \times .6 \times .6 \times .6} = \frac{1}{.008} = \frac{1000}{8} = 125.$

59. Nos. of bullets

$= \frac{44 \times 44 \times 44}{\frac{4}{3} \times \frac{22}{7} \times \frac{4}{2} \times \frac{4}{2} \times \frac{4}{2}} = \frac{44 \times 44 \times 44 \times 21}{4 \times 22 \times 4 \times 2}$

$= 11 \times 11 \times 21 = 2541.$

60. Nos. of spherical lead shots

$= \frac{66 \times 42 \times 21}{\frac{4}{3} \times \frac{22}{7} \times 2.1 \times 2.1 \times 2.1}$

$= \frac{66 \times 42 \times 21}{4 \times 22 \times 2.1 \times .7 \times .3} = 1500.$

□□□□□

12

Data Handling

Graphical Representation of Statistical Data

One of the most convincing and appearing ways in which statistical result may be presented is through diagrams and graphs. The impressions created by diagrams last much longer than those created by the figures presented in a tabular form.

> *Rather than present data numerically in the form of a table it can sometimes be better to illustrate the information through the use of graphs, charts, diagrams and so on.*

The frequency distribution of a discrete value is best represented by a bar diagram. The height of the bars is proportional to the frequency of each variate-value. The bars must be kept distinct to show that the variate-values are distinct.

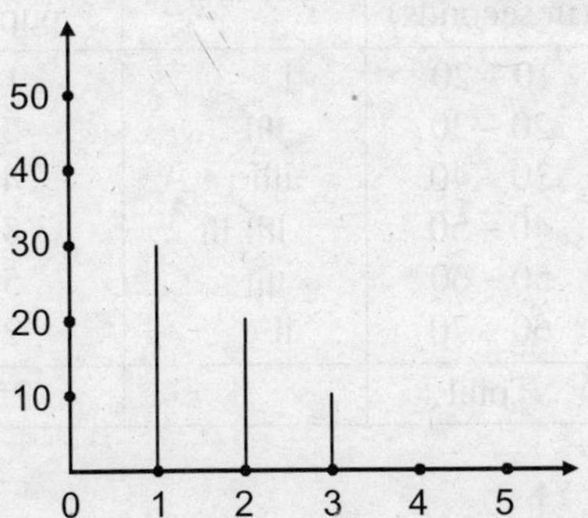

A simple bar chart is used to illustrate a frequency distribution. The lengths of the bars are proportional to the frequency and the bars are of equal width.

Some Important Types of Diagrams and Graphs

The different types of Diagrams and Graphs

(1) Bar diagram
(2) Histogram
(3) Frequency circle
(4) Cumulative frequency curve of the ogive
(5) Pie diagram.

Bar Diagram

Bar diagram is the easiest and most adaptable general purpose chart. In this, bars or rectangles of uniform width are drawn with equal spaces in between on the axis. Along the y-axis is shown, the scale of the height of the rectangles. Thickness of bars is not taken into account, they should be so constructed that they look attractive and beautiful. This can be done by colouring them or by preparing designs in them. However, the colour or designs of all bars representing one type of data should be identical. The bars may be vertical or horizontal. Some of the main bar diagrams are:

(*i*) Simple Bar-Diagram
(*ii*) Sub-divided Bar-Diagram
(*iii*) Multiple Bar-Diagram

The following Examples of Illustrate :

Example: The following table gives the population of India (in millions). Draw a bar diagram of the data:

Population (in million) of India 1931-1971

Year	Population (*in millions*)
1931	275.5
1941	312.1
1951	356.9
1961	439.9
1971	546.9

Solution: The above data is represented by a simple bar diagram as follows :

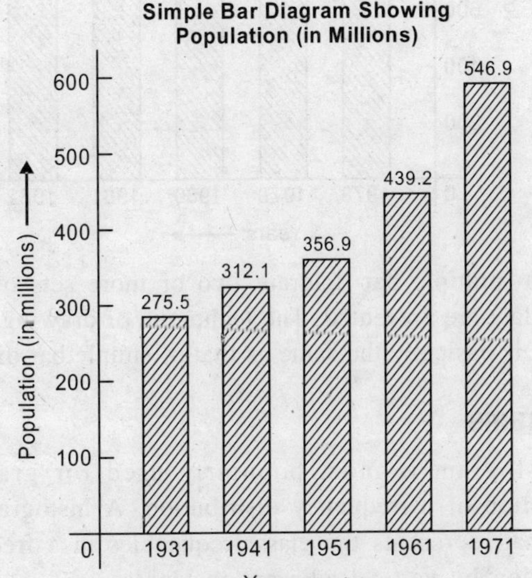

Here years are denoted on the x-axis and population (in millions) on the y-axis. The length of each bar corresponds to the number representing population on the y-axis.

Sub-Divided or Component Bar Diagram

The sub-divided bar diagram is used where the total magnitude of the given variable is to be divided into various parts or sub-classes. The bars are drawn proportional in length to the total and divided in the ratios of their components. Different colours, shades, designs, etc. are used to distinguish the various components.

Example: Represent the following data of sex-wise distribution of students in a school by a bar diagram.

Year	No. of Students		Total
	Male	*Female*	
1978	800	250	1050
1979	900	300	1200
1980	950	375	1325
1981	1000	400	1400
1982	1150	450	1600

Solution: The above data are represented by a sub-divided bar diagram, as follows.

Sub-Divided Bar Diagram showing Sex-wise Distribution of Students

Y
1600
1400
1200
1000
800
600
400
200
0
No. of Students
1050
250
1200
300
1325
375
1400
400
1600
450
1978
1979
1980
1981
1982
X
Years

In a multiple bar diagram two or more sets of inter-related data are presented. The technique of drawing such a diagram is basically the same as that of simple bar diagram.

Histograms

The histogram is most popularly used for graphical presentation of a frequency distribution. A histogram is a graph that represents the class frequencies in a frequency distribution by vertical adjacent rectangles.

After choosing a convenient scale on the axes, mark off the class intervals along *x*-axis and the frequencies of the respective class intervals along *y*-axis. Then construct rectangles with each class intervals as breadth and the respective frequency of the class interval as height. The set of the all adjacent rectangles so constructed form a histogram.

Note : A histogram is a development of the bar chart but remember when drawing a histogram it is the Area of each bar which is proportional to the frequency and there are no gaps between the bars because the classes are usually arranged so that there are no gaps.

The following Examples of Illustrates:

Example: The time taken, in seconds, to solve a problem by each of 25 pupils is as follows:

16, 20, 26, 27, 28, 30, 33, 37, 38, 40, 42, 42, 43, 46, 46, 48, 49, 50, 53, 58, 59, 60, 64, 52, 20.

(*a*) Construct a frequency distribution for these data, using a class interval of 10 seconds.

(*b*) Draw a histogram to represent the frequency distribution.

Solution:

(*a*) Lowest observation = 10

Highest observation = 64

Range = 64 – 10 = 54

We can have six classes, each of width 10.

Frequency Distribution Table

Time (in seconds)	Tally marks	Number of pupils
10 – 20	I	1
20 – 30	IIII̸	5
30 – 40	IIII	4
40 – 50	IIII̸ III	8
50 – 60	IIII̸	5
60 – 70	II	2
Total		25

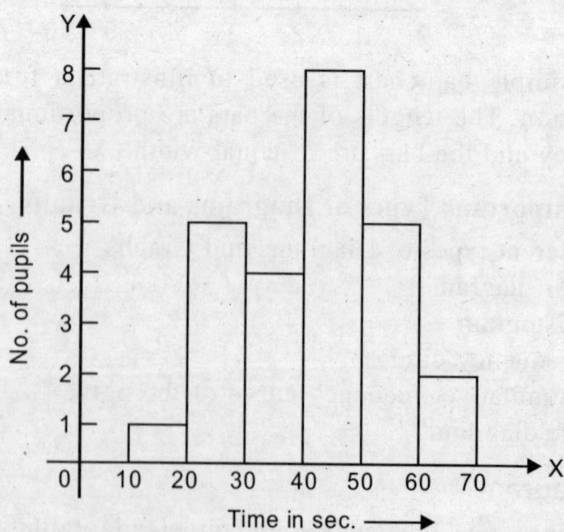

Frequency Polygon

A frequency polygon is a graph of frequency distribution. The steps constructing a frequency polygonal are:

1. Draw a suitable histogram keeping in view all the basic principles.
2. Get the mid-points of the upper horizontal side of each rectangle.
3. Join these mid-points of the adjacent rectangles of the histogram by straight lines taken in order, they form a polygon called frequency polygon.
4. End of frequency polygon preferably extended to the base line.

In a frequency polygon the variables or individuals of each class are assumed to be concentrated at the class-intervals.

Note: If only frequency polygon is to be drawn, first represent the class-marks (x_i) on the x-axis and corresponding frequencies (f_i) on y-axis. Plot all the points (x_i, f_i). Then join these points by line segments. The figure so obtained is known as the frequency polygon. The polygon should be brought down at the ends to the x-axis at each and of the drawn.

The following Examples of Illustrate:

Example: In a city the following weekly observations were made in a study on cost of Living Index for the year 1970–71.

Cost of Living Index	No. of weeks
140 – 150	5
150 – 160	10
160 – 170	20
170 – 180	9
180 – 190	6
190 – 200	2

Draw a histogram and frequency polygon on the same scale.

Solution:

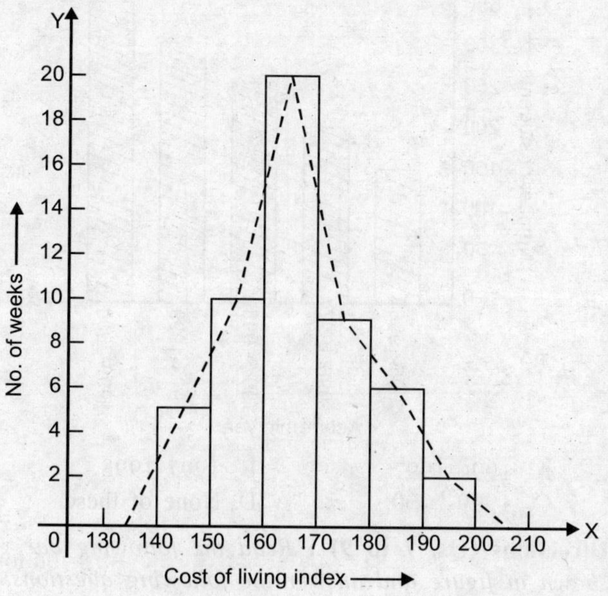

Pie Diagram

Pie-diagrams are used to represent a relative frequency distribution. A pie diagram consists of a circle divided into as many sectors as there are classes in a frequency distribution. The area of each sector is proportional to the relative frequency of the class.

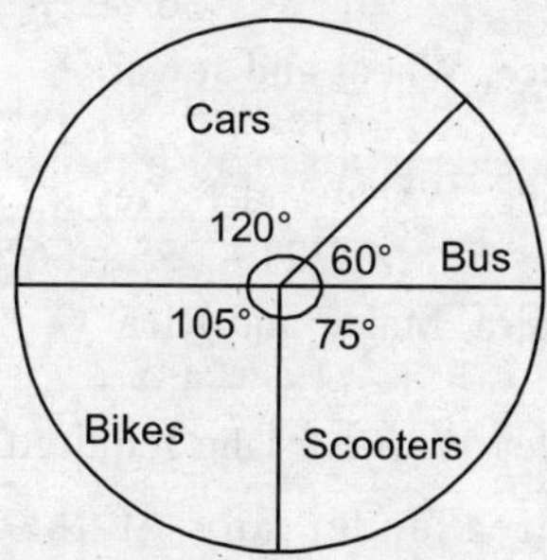

Now we make angles at the centre proportional to the relative frequencies. And in order to get the angles of the disired sectors, we divide 360° in the proportion of the various relative frequencies, *i.e.*,

$$\text{Central angle} = \left[\frac{\text{Frequency} \times 360°}{\text{Total frequency}}\right]$$

Example : The pie-chart provided below gives the distribution of land (in a village) under various food crops. Study the pie-chart carefully and answer the questions that follow.

Distribution of Areas (in Acre) Under various Food Crops

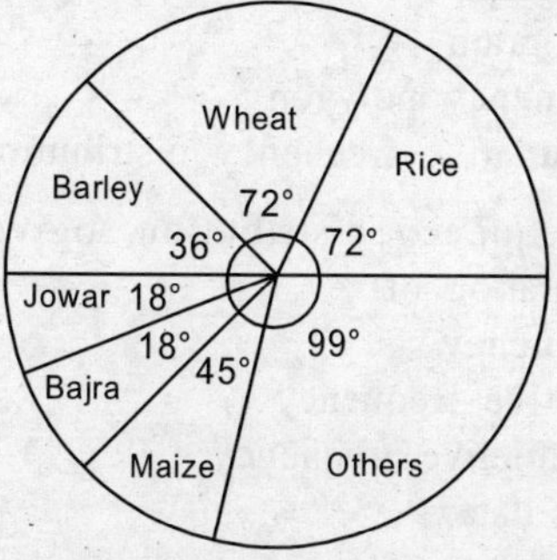

1. Which combination of three crops contribute to 50% of the total area under the food crops?
(*a*) Wheat, Barley and Jowar
(*b*) Rice, Wheat and Jowar
(*c*) Rice, Wheat and Barley
(*d*) Bajra, Maize and Rice

2. If the total area under jowar was 1.5 million acres, then what was the area (in million acres) under rice?
(*a*) 6 (*b*) 7.5
(*c*) 9 (*d*) 4.5

3. If the production of wheat is 6 times that of barley, then what is the ratio between the yield per acre of wheat and barley?
(*a*) 3 : 2 (*b*) 3 : 1
(*c*) 12 : 1 (*d*) 2 : 3

Solution:

1 (*c*): The total of the central angles corresponding to the three crops which cover 50% of the total area, should be 180°. Now, the total of the central angles for the given combinations are:

(*i*) Wheat, Barley and Jowar
$= (72° + 36° + 18°) = 126°$

(*ii*) Rice, Wheat and Jowar
$= (72° + 72° + 18°) = 162°$

(*iii*) Rice, Wheat and Barley
$= (72° + 72° + 36°) = 180°$

(*iv*) Bajra, Maize and Rice
$= (18° + 45° + 72°) = 135°$

Clearly, (*iii*) is the required combination.

2 (*a*): The area under any of the food crops is proportional to the central angle corresponding to that crop.

Let, the area under rice production be x million acres.

Then, $18 : 72 = 1.5 : x \Rightarrow x = \left(\frac{72 \times 1.5}{18}\right) = 6.$

Thus, the area under rice production = 6 million acress

3 (*b*): Let, the total production of barley be T tonnes and let Z acres of land be put under barley production.

Then, the total production of wheat = (6T) tonnes.

Also, area under wheat production = (2Z) areas.

$\left[\because \frac{\text{Area under Wheat production}}{\text{Area under Barley production}} = \frac{72°}{36°} = 2\right.$ and therefore, Area under wheat = 2× Area under barley = (2Z) acres $\left.\right]$

Now, yield per acre for wheat = $\left(\frac{6T}{2Z}\right)$ tonnes/acre = $\left(\frac{3T}{Z}\right)$ tonnes/acre and yield per acre for barley = $\left(\frac{T}{Z}\right)$ tonnes/acre.

$\therefore$ Required Ratio = $\left(\frac{3T/Z}{T/Z}\right) = 3:1.$

Multiple Choice Questions

1. Which one of the following is not the graphical representation of statistical data?
A. Bar graph
B. Histogram
C. Frequency polygon
D. Cumulative frequency distribution

2. In a frequency distribution, ogives are graphical representation of:
A. Frequency
B. Relative frequency
C. Cumulative frequency
D. Raw data

3. A frequency polygon is constructed by plotting frequency of the class interval and the:
A. upper limit of the class
B. lower limit of the class
C. mid value of the class
D. any values of the class

4. In a histogram the area of each rectangle is proportional to:
A. the class mark of the corresponding class interval
B. the class size of the corresponding class interval
C. frequency of the corresponding class interval
D. cumulative frequency of the corresponding class interval

5. In a histogram, each class rectangle is constructed with base as:
A. frequency
B. class-intervals
C. range
D. size of the class

6. Read the bar graph shown in figure and answer the following question:
In which year is the increase of students maximum?

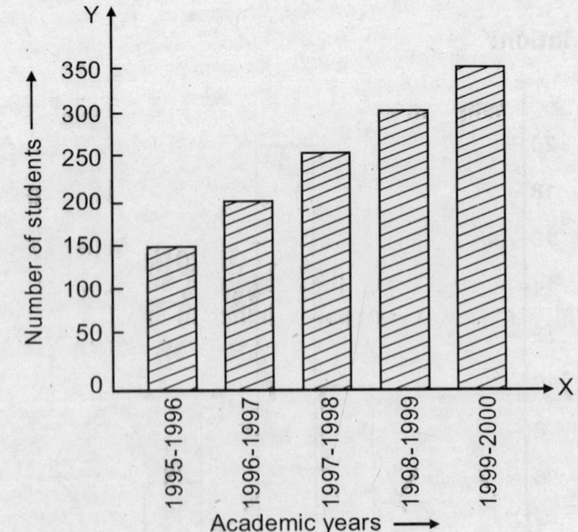

A. 1996-1997 B. 1997-1998
C. 1999-2000 D. None of these

Directions (Qs. 7 to 9) : *Read the following bar graph shown in figure and answer the following questions:*

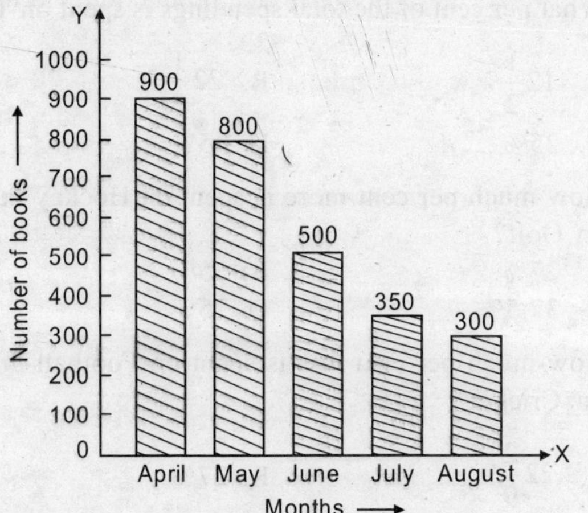

7. In which month was the sale of the books maximum?

A. April
B. May
C. June
D. August

8. In which month was the sale of the books minimum?

A. April
B. May
C. July
D. August

9. What is the total sale during these five months?

A. 3800 copies
B. 2850 copies
C. 2800 copies
D. 2950 copies

Directions (Qs. 10 to 12) : *Read the following bar graph given in figure and answer the following questions:*

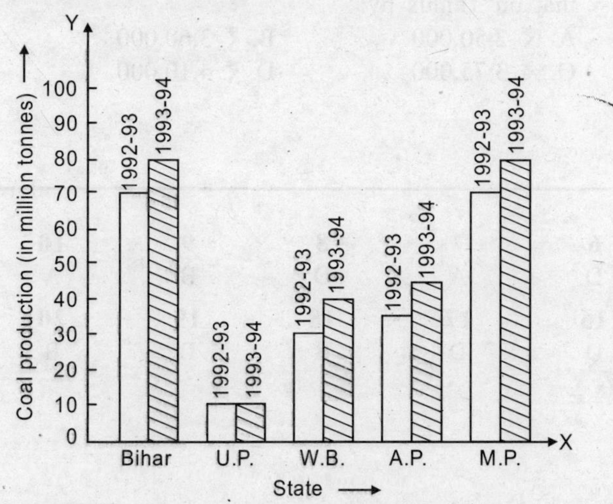

10. Which two states have same production in 1993-94?

A. M.P. and Bihar
B. M.P. and U.P.
C. U.P. and Bihar
D. W.B. and U.P.

11. Which state has same production in both the years?

A. M.P.
B. Bihar
C. U.P.
D. W.B.

12. Which state has minimum production?

A. M.P.
B. A.P.
C. W.B
D. U.P.

Directions (Qs. 13 to 15) : *The following bar graph shows the results of an annual examination in a secondary school. Read the bar graph and choose the correct alternative in each of the following.*

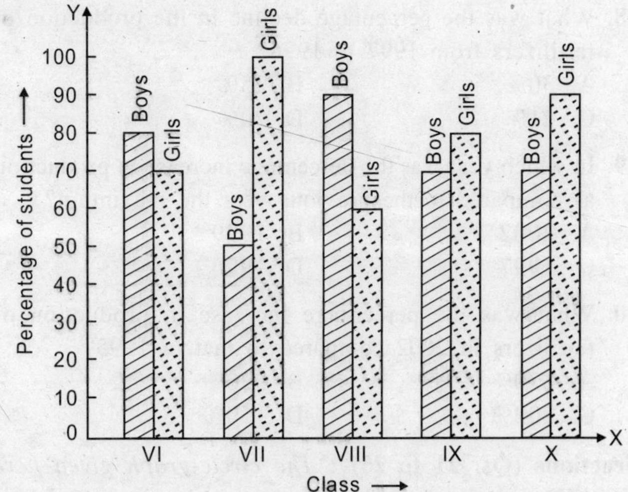

13. The pair of classes in which the results of boys and girls are inversely proportional are:

A. VI, VIII
B. VI, IX
C. VIII, IX
D. VIII, X

14. The class having the lowest failure rate of girls is:

A. VII
B. X
C. IX
D. VIII

15. The class having the lowest pass rate of boys is:

A. VI
B. VII
C. VIII
D. IX

Directions (Qs. 16 to 20) : *Study the following bar-graph and answer the questions given below.*

Production of Fertilizers by a Company (in 10000 tonnes) over the Years

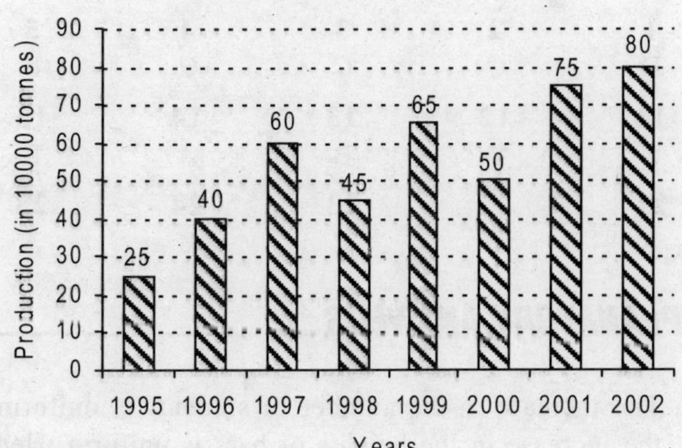

16. In how many of the given years was the production of fertilizers more than the average production of the given years?

A. 1
B. 2
C. 3
D. 4

17. The average production of 1996 and 1997 was exactly equal to the average production of which of the following pairs of years?

A. 2000 and 2001 B. 1999 and 2000
C. 1995 and 1999 D. 1995 and 2001

18. What was the percentage decline in the production of fertilizers from 1997 to 1998?
A. 30% B. 25%
C. 21% D. 20%

19. In which year was the percentage increase in production as compared to the previous year the maximum?
A. 2002 B. 1999
C. 1997 D. 1996

20. What was the percentage increase in production of fertilizers in 2002 compared to that in 1995?
A. 320% B. 220%
C. 200% D. 150%

Directions (Qs. 21 to 25) : *The circle-graph given here shows the spendings of a country on various sports during a particular year. Study the graph carefully and answer the questions given below it.*

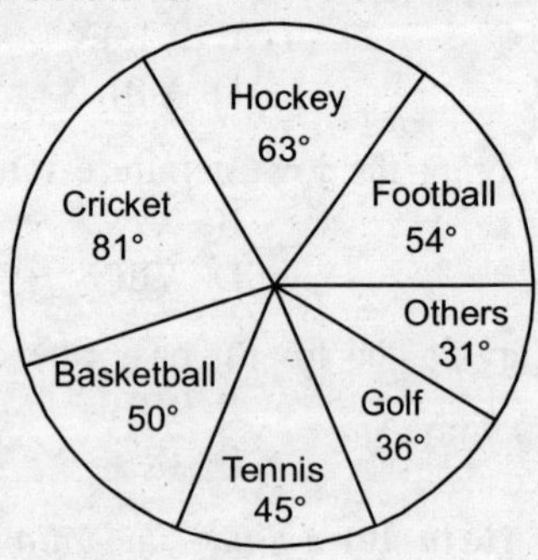

21. What per cent of the total spendings is spent on Tennis?
A. $12\frac{1}{2}\%$ B. $22\frac{1}{2}\%$
C. 25% D. 45%

22. How much per cent more is spent on Hockey than that on Golf?
A. 27% B. 35%
C. 37.5% D. 75%

23. How much per cent less is spent on Football than that on Cricket?
A. $22\frac{2}{9}\%$ B. 27%
C. $33\frac{1}{3}\%$ D. $37\frac{1}{2}\%$

24. If the total amount spent on sports during the year was ₹ 2 crores, the amount spent on Cricket and Hockey together was:
A. ₹ 8,00,000
B. ₹ 80,00,000
C. ₹ 1,20,00,000
D. ₹ 1,60,00,000

25. If the total amount spent on sports during the years be ₹ 1,80,00,000, the amount spent on Basketball exceeds that on Tennis by:
A. ₹ 2,50,000 B. ₹ 3,60,000
C. ₹ 3,75,000 D. ₹ 4,10,000

ANSWERS

1	2	3	4	5	6	7	8	9	10
D	C	C	C	B	D	A	D	B	A
11	**12**	**13**	**14**	**15**	**16**	**17**	**18**	**19**	**20**
C	D	B	A	B	D	D	B	D	B
21	**22**	**23**	**24**	**25**					
A	D	C	B	A					

EXPLANATORY ANSWERS

6. The increase in the number of students is uniform as the increase in the heights of bars is uniform. Hence, in this case the increase is not maximum in any of the year.

7. The sale of the books was maximum in the month of April as the height of the rectangle corresponding to April month is maximum.

8. The sale of the books was minimum in the month of August as the height of the corresponding rectangle is minimum.

9. Total sale of the books during 5 months.
(900 + 800 + 500 + 350 + 300) = 2850 copies.

10. M.P. and Bihar have same production in 1993-1994.

11. U.P. has the same production in both the years.

12. U.P.

16. Average production (in 10000 tonnes) over the given years

$= \frac{1}{8} \times (25 + 40 + 60 + 45 + 65 + 50 + 75 + 80) = 55$

$\therefore$ The productions during the years 1997, 1999, 2001 and 2002 are more than the average production.

17. Average production (in 10000 tonnes) of 1996 and 1997 $= \dfrac{40+60}{2} = 50.$

We shall find the average production (in 10000 tonnes) for each of the given alternative

(*a*) 2000 and 2001 $= \dfrac{50+75}{2} = 62.5$

(*b*) 1999 and 2000 $= \dfrac{65+50}{2} = 57.5$

(*c*) 1995 and 1999 $= \dfrac{25+65}{2} = 45$

(*d*) 1995 and 2001 $= \dfrac{25+75}{2} = 50$

$\therefore$ The average production of 1996 and 1997 is equal to the average production of 1995 and 2001.

18. Required percentage $= \left[\dfrac{(45-60)}{60}\times 100\right]\% = -25\%.$

$\therefore$ There is a decline of 25% in production from 1997 to 1998.

19. The percentage increase in production compared to previous year for different years are :

In 1996 $= \left[\dfrac{(40-25)}{25}\times 100\right]\% = 60\%$

In 1997 $= \left[\dfrac{(60-40)}{40}\times 100\right]\% = 50\%$

In 1999 $= \left[\dfrac{(65-45)}{45}\times 100\right]\% = 44.44\%$

In 2002 $= \left[\dfrac{(80-75)}{75}\times 100\right]\% = 6.67\%$

Clearly, there is maximum percentage increase in production in 1996.

20. Required percentage $= \left[\dfrac{(80-25)}{25}\times 100\right]\% = 220\%$

21. Percentage of money spent on Tennis

$= \left(\dfrac{45}{360}\times 100\right)\% = 12\dfrac{1}{2}\%$

22. Let the total spendings on sports be ₹ x. Then,

Amount spent on Golf = ₹ $\left(\dfrac{36}{360}\times x\right) =$ ₹ $\dfrac{x}{10}$

Amount spent on Hockey = ₹ $\left(\dfrac{63}{360}\times x\right) =$ ₹ $\dfrac{7}{40}x.$

Difference = ₹ $\left(\dfrac{7}{40}x - \dfrac{x}{10}\right) =$ ₹ $\dfrac{3x}{40}$

$\therefore$ Required Percentage $= \left[\left(\dfrac{3x/40}{x/10}\right)\times 100\right]\% = 75\%$

23. Let the total spendings on sports be ₹ x. Then,

Amount spent on Cricket = ₹ $\left(\dfrac{81}{360}\times x\right) =$ ₹ $\left(\dfrac{9}{40}x\right)$

Amount spent on Football = ₹ $\left(\dfrac{54}{360}\times x\right) =$ ₹ $\left(\dfrac{3}{20}x\right)$

Difference = ₹ $\left(\dfrac{9}{40}x - \dfrac{3}{20}x\right) =$ ₹ $\dfrac{3}{40}x$

$\therefore$ Required Percentage $= \left[\left(\dfrac{3x/40}{9x/40}\right)\times 100\right]\% = 33\dfrac{1}{3}\%$

24. Amount spent on Cricket and Hockey together

= ₹ $\left[\dfrac{(81+63)}{360}\times 2\right]$ crores = ₹ 0.8 crores = ₹ 8000000.

25. Amount spent on Basketball exceeds that on Tennis by :

₹ $\left[\dfrac{(50-45)}{360}\times 18000000\right]$ = ₹ 250000.

❑❑❑❑❑

13

Statistics

Statistics is defined as the mathematics of the collection, organisation and interpretation of numerical data, especially the analysis of population characteristics by inference from the sampling.

Points To Remember

- Observations gathered initially are called **Raw data**.
- The difference between the highest and the lowest values of the observations in given data is called the range.
- Mean of given data

$$= \frac{\text{Sum of all observations}}{\text{Total number of observation}}$$

- In given data, the number of times a particular observation occurs is called its **frequency**.
- A table showing the frequencies of various observations of data is called a frequency distribution table or simply a frequency table.
- When the number of observations is large, we make use of tally marks to count the frequencies.
- Tallies are usually marked in bunches of five for ease of counting.
- When the list of observations is very large, we organise the data into groups called classes or class interval. The data so obtained is called grouped data or a grouped frequency distribution.
- The lower value of a class interval called its lower class limit and the upper value of a class interval is called its upper class limit.
- The difference between the upper and lower values of a class interval is called its **width** or **size**.
- The mid-value of a class interval is called its class mark.
- The frequency of a class interval is called its class frequency.
- A histogram is a graphical representation of grouped data in which class intervals are taken along the horizontal axis and frequencies along the vertical axis.

Measures of Central Tendency

Generally, average value of a distribution in the middle part of the distribution, such type of values are known as measures of central tendency.

The following are the five measures of central tendency:

1. Arithmetic Mean
2. Geometric Mean
3. Harmonic Mean
4. Median
5. Mode

1. Arithmetic Mean : The arithmetic (or simple mean) of a set of observations is obtained by dividing the sum of the value of observations by the number of observations.

(i) **Arithmetic Mean for Unclassified (Ungrouped) Data:** If n observations, $x_1, x_2, x_3, ..., x_n$, then their arithmetic mean

$$\text{A or } \bar{x} = \frac{x_1 + x_2 + ... + x_n}{n} = \frac{\sum_{i=1}^{n} x_i}{n}$$

(ii) **Arithmetic Mean for Frequency Distribution :** Let $f_1, f_2, ... f_n$ be corresponding frequencies of $x_1, x_2, ..., x_n$. Then, arithmetic mean

$$\text{A} = \frac{x_1 f_1 + x_2 f_2 + ... + x_n f_n}{f_1 + f_2 + ... + f_n} = \frac{\sum_{i=1}^{n} x_i f_i}{\sum_{i=1}^{n} f_i}$$

(iii) **Arithmetic Mean for Classified (Grouped) Data :** For a classified data, we take the class marks $x_1, x_2, ..., x_n$ of the classes as variables, then arithmetic mean by

$$\text{Direct method is A} = \frac{\sum_{i=1}^{n} x_i f_i}{\sum_{i=1}^{n} f_i}$$

(iv) **Combined Mean :** If $A_1, A_2, ..., A_n$ are the n arithmetic mean having number of corresponding observations $n_1, n_2, ..., n_r$, then arithmetic mean of the combined group x is called the combined mean of the observation

$$\text{A} = \frac{n_1 A_1 + n_2 A_2 + ... + n_r A_r}{n_1 + n_2 + ... + n_r} = \frac{\sum_{i=1}^{r} n_i A_i}{\sum_{i=1}^{r} n_i}$$

(v) **Weighted Arithmetic Mean :** If $w_1, w_2, ..., w_n$ are the weights assigned to the values $x_1, x_2, ...,$

x_n respectively, then the weighted arithmetic mean is:

$$A_w = \frac{\sum_{i=1}^{n} w_i x_i}{\sum_{i=1}^{n} w_i}$$

Properties of Arithmetic Mean

(*i*) Mean is dependent of change of origin and change of scale.

(*ii*) Algebraic sum of the deviations of a set of values from their arithmetic mean is zero.

(*iii*) The sum of the squares of the deviations of a set of values is minimum when taken about mean.

2. Geometric Mean

(*i*) If $x_1, x_2, ..., x_n$ be *n* non-zero observations, then their geometric mean is defined as:

$$G = \sqrt[n]{x_1 x_2, ... x_n}$$

3. Harmonic Mean : The harmonic mean of *n* non-zero observations $x_1, x_2,..., x_n$ is defined as

$$HM = \frac{n}{\frac{1}{x_1}+\frac{1}{x_2}+...+\frac{1}{x_n}} = \frac{n}{\sum_{i=1}^{n}\frac{1}{x_i}}$$

4. Median : The median of a distribution is the value of the middle variable, when the variables are arranged in ascending or descending order.

Median (M_d) is an average of position of the numbes.

(*i*) **Median for Simple Distribution :** Firstly, arrange the data in ascending or descending order and then find the number of observations *n*.

(*a*) If *n* is odd, then $\left(\frac{n+1}{2}\right)$ th term is the median.

(*b*) If *n* is even, then there are two middle terms namely $\left(\frac{n}{2}\right)$ th and $\left(\frac{n}{2}+1\right)$ th terms. Hence,

Median = Mean of $\left(\frac{n}{2}\right)$ th and $\left(\frac{n}{2}+1\right)$ th observations

$$= \frac{1}{2}\left[\left(\frac{n}{2}\right)\text{th} + \left(\frac{n}{2}+1\right)\text{th}\right] \text{ of observations}$$

Properties

(*i*) The median can be calculated graphically, while mean cannot be.

(*ii*) The sum of the absolute deviations taken from the median is less than the sum of the absolute deviations taken from any other observation in the data.

(*iii*) Median is not affected by extreme values.

5. Mode : The mode (M_o) of a distribution is the value at the point about which the observations tend to be most heavily concentrated. It is generally the value of the variable which appears to occur most frequently in the distribution.

The value which is repeated maximum number of times, is the required mode.

e.g. Mode of the data 70, 80, 90, 96, 70, 96, 90 is 96 as 96 occurs maximum number of times.

Propperties

(*i*) It can be calculated graphically.

(*ii*) It is not affected by extreme values.

(*iii*) It can be used for open-ended distribution and qualitative data.

In a moderately symmetric distribution mean, median and mode are connected by the following formula

Mode = 3 Median − 2 Mean

Relation between Mean, Median and Mode

(*i*) Mean − Mode = 3(Mean − Median)

(*i*) Mode = 3 Median − 2 Mean

Effects of Average and Dispersion on Change of Origin and Scale

	Change of Origin	Change of Scale
Mean	Dependent	Dependent
Median	Not Dependent	Dependent
Mode	Not Dependent	Dependent

Note : (*i*) Change of origin means either subtract of add in observation

(*ii*) Change of scale means either multiply or divide in observations.

Multiple Choice Questions

1. The mean of *n* observations is $\overline{X}$. If *k* is added to each observation, then the new mean is:

A. $\overline{X}$ B. $\overline{X}+k$
C. $\overline{X}-k$ D. $k\overline{X}$

2. The mean of *n* observations is $\overline{X}$. If each observation is multiplied by *k*, the mean of new observations is:

A. $k\overline{X}$ B. $\frac{\overline{X}}{k}$
C. $\overline{X}+k$ D. $\overline{X}-k$

3. The mean of a set of seven numbers is 81. If one of the numbers is discarded, the mean of the remaining numbers is 78. The value of discarded number is:

A. 98 B. 99
C. 100 D. 101

4. For which set of numbers do the mean, median and mode all have the same value?
A. 2, 2, 2, 2, 4 B. 1, 3, 3, 3, 5
C. 1, 1, 2, 5, 6 D. 1, 1, 1, 2, 5

5. For the set of numbers 2, 2, 4, 5 and 12, which of the following statements is true?
A. Mean = Median B. Mean > Mode
C. Mean < Mode D. Mode = Median

6. The empirical relation between mean, mode and median is:
A. Mode = 3 Median – 2 Mean
B. Mode = 2 Median – 3 Mean
C. Median = 3 Mode – 2 Mean
D. Mean = 3 Median – 2 Mode

7. The mean of a, b, c, d and e is 28. If the mean of a, c, and e is 24, what is the mean of b and d?
A. 31 B. 32
C. 33 D. 34

8. Which of the following is dependent of the change of origin?
A. Mean B. Median
C. Mode D. Variance

9. What is the mean of first nine even natural numbers?
A. 10 B. 12
C. 11 D. 13

10. What is the median of first 15 odd numbers?
A. 15 B. 17
C. 19 D. 21

11. If the mean of a given data is 51 kg and its median is 50 kg. What is the mode of that data?
A. 52 kg B. 51 kg
C. 53 kg D. 54 kg

12. What is the mean of first 12 multiple of 7?
A. 45 B. 46
C. 45.5 D. 46.5

13. What is the mode of the given data :
16, 20, 8, 17, 27 34, 28, 32, 27, 15, 27, 54, 42.
A. 8 B. 27
C. 54 D. None of these

14. What is the mean of the following data?

Marks obtained	45	27	20	56	82	75	17
No. of students	5	3	8	7	2	4	12

A. 34.22 B. 36.22
C. 37.22 D. None of these

15. What is the median of the following data?

Marks obtained	72	47	62	57	42	52	67
No. of students	9	8	11	8	3	6	5

A. 56.5 B. 57.5
C. 58.5 D. 59.5

16. The ages in years of 15 teachers of a school are 41, 32, 51, 43, 24, 38, 49, 56, 42, 28, 37, 48, 45, 47, 50. What is the range of ages of teachers?
A. 32 years B. 30 years
C. 28 years D. None of these

17. Following are the margins of victory in the football matches of a league.
1, 3, 2, 5, 1, 4, 6, 2, 5, 2, 2, 2, 4, 1, 2, 3, 1, 1, 2, 3, 2, 6, 4, 3, 2, 1, 1, 4, 2, 1, 5, 3, 3, 2, 3, 2, 4, 2, 1, 2.
What is the mode of this data?
A. 1 B. 2
C. 3 D. 4

18. If the mean and mode of a given data is 51 and 48 respectively, what is the median?
A. 48 B. 49
C. 50 D. 52

19. What is mean of first 10-prime numbers?
A. 12.9 B. 12.7
C. 11.3 D. None of these

20. The mean of 6 observations was found to be 40. Later on, it was detected that one observation 82 was misread as 28. What is the correct mean?
A. 45 B. 46
C. 47 D. 49

21. The rainfall (in mm) in a city on 7 days of a certain week were recorded as follows?

Day	Mon	Tue	Wed	Thur	Fri	Sat	Sun
Rainfall (in mm)	2.2	21.3	25.6	0.0	4.9	0.0	5.5

What is the range of the rainfall in the above data?
A. 25.6 B. 24.4
C. 20.7 D. 20.1

22. The mean of marks scored by 100 students was found to be 40. Later on it was discovered that a score of 53 was misread as 83. What is the correct mean?
A. 39.7 B. 38.9
C. 39.4 D. 38.7

23. The median of the observations 11, 12, 14, 18, $x + 2$, $x + 4$, 30, 32, 35, 41 arranged in ascending order is 24. What is the value of x?
A. 18 B. 19
C. 20 D. 21

24. Calculate the median of the following data:
83, 37, 70, 29, 45, 63, 41, 70, 30, 54.
A. 46.5 B. 49.5
C. 47.5 D. 48.5

25. The median of the following observations, arranged in ascending order is 30. What is the x?
11, 12, 14, 18, $x + 2$, $x + 4$, 30, 32, 35, 41, 45.
A. 24 B. 25
C. 26 D. 28

26. Mean temperature of a certain week was 25°C. If mean temperature of Monday, Tuesday, Wednesday and Thursday was 23°C and that of Thursday, Friday, Saturday and Sunday was 28°C. What is the temperature of Thursday?

A. 25°C B. 27°C
C. 29°C D. 31°C

27. What is the arithmetic mean of the scores 8, 6, 10, 12, 1, 3, 4 and what is the range of the data?

A. 5, 8 B. 6, 11
C. 7, 10 D. 8, 9

28. Determine the median of the following data 24, 23, *a*, *a* – 1, 12, 16, where *a* is the mean of 10, 20, 30, 40, 50.

A. 23.5 B. 24.5
C. 22.5 D. 22.8

29. If the mean of the following distribution is 6. What is the value of P?

x	2	4	6	10	P + 5
f	3	2	3	1	2

A. 4 B. 5
C. 6 D. 7

30. Following are the ages (in years) of 10 teachers in a school:
32, 41, 28, 54, 35, 26, 23, 33, 38, 40.
What is the range of the age of the teachers?

A. 28 years B. 29 years
C. 30 years D. 31 years

ANSWERS

1	2	3	4	5	6	7	8	9	10
B	A	B	B	B	A	D	A	A	B
11	**12**	**13**	**14**	**15**	**16**	**17**	**18**	**19**	**20**
C	C	B	C	D	A	B	C	A	D
21	**22**	**23**	**24**	**25**	**26**	**27**	**28**	**29**	**30**
A	A	D	B	C	C	B	A	D	D

EXPLANATORY ANSWERS

9. Mean $= \dfrac{2+4+6+8+10+12+14+16+18}{9} = \dfrac{90}{9} = 10$

10. First 15 odd numbers are 3, 5, 7, 9, 11, 13, 15, 17, 19, 21, 23, 25, 27, 29, 31

$n = 15$, which is odd

Median $= \left(\dfrac{15+1}{2}\right)$th term = 8th term = 17

11. Mode = 3 × median – 2 × Mean
= 3(51) – 2(50) = 153 – 100 = 53 kg

12. Mean $= \dfrac{7+14+21+28+35+42+49+56+63+70+77+84}{12} = \dfrac{546}{12} = 45.5$

13. Mode = 27, as it occurs 3 times.

14.

Marks obtained (x_i)	No. of Students (f_i)	$x_i f_i$
45	5	225
27	3	81
20	8	160
56	7	392
82	2	164
75	4	300
17	12	204
	$\Sigma f_i = 41$	$\Sigma f_i x_i = 1526$

Mean $= \dfrac{\Sigma f_i x_i}{\Sigma f_i} = \dfrac{1526}{41} = 37.219 \approx 37.22$

15.

Marks obtained	No. of Students	Cumulative frequency
42	3	3
47	8	3 + 8 = 11
52	6	11 + 6 = 17
57	8	17 + 8 = 25
62	11	25 + 11 = 36
67	5	36 + 5 = 41
72	9	41 + 9 = 50

N = 50 (even)

$$\text{Median} = \frac{\left(\frac{50}{2}\right)\text{th term} + \left(\frac{50}{2}+1\right)\text{th term}}{2}$$

$$= \frac{\text{25th term + 26th term}}{2}$$

$$= \frac{57+62}{2} = \frac{119}{2} = 59.5$$

16. The age in the ascending order are
24, 28, 32, 37, 38, 41, 42, 43, 45, 47, 48, 49, 50, 51, 56
Range = 56 – 24 = 32
Maximum value – Minimum value

17. The frequency of 2 is highest

So, Mode = 2

18. Mode = 3 Median – 2 Mean

48 = 3 Median – 2 × 51

$\Rightarrow$ 3 Median = 102 + 48

$\Rightarrow$ 3 Median = 150

$\Rightarrow$ Median = $\frac{150}{3} = 50$

19. $\text{Mean} = \frac{2+3+5+7+11+13+17+19+23+29}{10}$

$= \frac{129}{10} = 12.9$

20. $\text{Correct Mean} = \frac{40 \times 6 + (82-28)}{6}$

$= \frac{240+54}{6} = \frac{294}{6} = 49.$

21. Range = 25.6 – 0 = 25.6 mm.

22. Total Marks by 100 students

= 100 × 40 = 4000

$\text{Correct Mean} = \frac{4000-(83-53)}{100} = \frac{3970}{100}$

= 39.7.

23. $n = 10$ (even)

$$\text{Median} = \frac{\frac{n}{2}\text{th term} + \left(\frac{n}{2}+1\text{th term}\right)}{2}$$

$$24 = \frac{\text{5th term} + \text{6th term}}{2}$$

$$24 = \frac{x+2+x+4}{2} = \frac{2x+6}{2}$$

$2x + 6 = 48$

$2x = 42$

$x = \frac{42}{2} = 21.$

24. Data in ascending order.

29, 30, 37, 41, 45, 54, 63, 70, 70, 83

$n = 10$ (even)

$$\text{Median} = \frac{\frac{n}{2}\text{th term} + \left(\frac{n}{2}+1\text{th}\right)\text{ term}}{2}$$

$$= \frac{\text{5th term} + \text{6th term}}{2}$$

$$= \frac{45+54}{2} = \frac{99}{2} = 49.5.$$

25. $n = 11$ (odd)

$\text{Median} = \frac{n+1}{2}\text{th term} = \text{6th term}$

$30 = x + 4$

$x = 30 - 4 = 26.$

26. Total temp. of a week = 7 × 25 = 175°

Total temp. of Mon, Tues, Wed, Thurs.

= 23 × 4 = 92°C

Total temp. of Thurs, Fri, Sat and Sunday

= 28 × 4 = 112°C

Temp. of Thursday = (112 + 92) – 175

= 204 – 175 = 29°C.

27. $\text{Mean} = \frac{8+6+10+12+1+3+4+4}{8}$

$= \frac{48}{8} = 6.$

Range = Maximum value – Minimum value

= 12 – 1 = 11.

28. $a = \frac{10+20+30+40+50}{5} = \frac{150}{5}$

= 30

The given data in ascending order

12, 16, 23, 24, 29, 30

$n = 6$ (even)

$$\text{Median} = \frac{\frac{n}{2}\text{th term} + \left(\frac{n}{2}+1\right)\text{th term}}{2}$$

$$= \frac{\text{3rd term} + \text{4th term}}{2}$$

$$= \frac{23+24}{2} = \frac{47}{2} = 23.5.$$

29.

x	f	fx
2	3	6
4	2	8
6	3	18
10	1	10
P + 5	2	2 (P + 5)
Total	11	42 + 2P + 10

= 2P + 52

$\text{Mean} = \frac{\Sigma fx}{\Sigma f} = \frac{2P+52}{11}$

$6 = \frac{2P+52}{11}$

2P = 66 – 52 = 14 $\Rightarrow$ P = 7.

30. 54 – 23 = 31 years.

□□□□□

14

Probability

Important Facts and Formulae

1. Experiment : An operation which can produce some well-defined outcomes is called an experiment.

2. Random Experiment : An experiment in which all possible outcomes are known and the exact output cannot be predicted in advance, is called a random experiment.

Examples of Performing a Random Experiment:

(*i*) Rolling an unbiased dice.

(*ii*) Tossing a fair coin.

(*iii*) Drawing a card from a pack of well-suffled cards.

(*iv*) Picking up a ball of certain colour from a bag containing balls of different colours.

Details:

(*i*) When we throw a coin. Then either a Head (H) or a Tail (T) appears

(*ii*) A dice is a solid cube, having 6 faces, marked, 1, 2, 3, 4, 5, 6 respectively. When we throw a die, the outcome is the number that appears on its upper face.

(*iii*) A pack of cards has 52 cards.
It has 13 cards of each suit, namely Spades, Clubs, Hearts and Diamonds.
Cards of spades and clubs are black cards.
Cards of hearts and diamonds are red cards.
There are 4 honours of each suit.
These are Aces, Kings, Queens and Jacks.
These are called face cards.

3. Sample Space : When we perform an experiment, then the set S of all possible outcomes is called the sample space.

Examples of Sample Spaces:

(*i*) In tossing a coin, S = {H, T}.

(*ii*) If two coins are tossed, then S = {HH, HT, TH, TT}.

(*iii*) In rolling a dice, we have, S = {1, 2, 3, 4, 5, 6}.

4. Event : Any subset of a sample space is called an event.

5. Probability of Occurrence of an Event:

Let S be the sample space and let E be an event. Then, $E \subseteq S$.

$$\therefore \quad P(E) = \frac{n(E)}{n(S)}$$

6. Results on Probability:

(*i*) $P(S) = 1$

(*ii*) $0 \le P(E) \le 1$

(*iii*) $P(\phi) = 0$

(*iv*) For any events A and B, we have:
$P(A \cup B) = P(A) + P(B) - P(A \cap B)$

(*v*) If $\bar{A}$ denotes (not-A), then $P(\bar{A}) = 1 - P(A)$.

Example 1 : Two unbiased coins are tossed. What is the probability of getting at most one head?

Solution: Here S = {HH, HT, TH, TT}.

Let E = event of getting at most one head.

$\therefore$ E = {T T, HT, TH}

$$\therefore \quad P(E) = \frac{n(E)}{n(S)} = \frac{3}{4}.$$

Example 2 : An unbiased die is tossed. Find the probability of getting a multiple of 3.

Solution : Here S = {1, 2, 3, 4, 5, 6}

Let E be the event of getting a multiple of 3.

Then, E = {3, 6}

$$\therefore \quad P(E) = \frac{n(E)}{n(S)} = \frac{2}{6} = \frac{1}{3}$$

Example 3 : A bag contains 6 white and 4 black balls. Two balls are drawn at random. Find the probability that they are of the same colour.

Solution : Let S be the sample space. Then,

$n(S)$ = Number of ways of drawing 2 balls out of (6 + 4)

$$= {}^{10}C_2 = \frac{(10 \times 9)}{(2 \times 1)} = 45.$$

Let E = Event of getting both balls of the same colur. Then,

$n(E)$ = Number of ways of drawing (2 balls out of 6) or (2 balls out of 4)

$= ({}^6C_2 + {}^4C_2) = \frac{(6\times5)}{(2\times1)} + \frac{(4\times3)}{(2\times1)} = (15+6) = 21$

$\therefore \quad P(E) = \frac{n(E)}{n(S)} = \frac{21}{45} = \frac{7}{15}.$

Example 4 : Two dice are thrown together. What is the probability that the sum of the numbers on the two faces is divisible by 4 or 6?

Solution : Clearly, $n(S) = 6 \times 6 = 36$.

Let E be the event that the sum of the numbers on the two faces is divisible by 4 or 6. Then

E = {(1, 3), (1, 5), (2, 2), (2, 4), (2, 6), (3, 1), (3, 3), (3, 5), (4, 2), (4, 4), (5, 1), (5, 3), (6, 2), (6, 6)}

$\therefore n(E) = 14.$

Hence, $P(E) = \frac{n(E)}{n(S)} = \frac{14}{36} = \frac{7}{18}.$

Multiple Choice Questions

1. Following table shows the marks scored by a group of 90 students in a mathematics test of 100 marks.

Marks	0-20	20-30	30-40	40-50	50-60	60-70	70-100
No. of students	7	10	10	20	20	15	8

What is the probability that a student obtained less then 20% marks?

A. $\frac{5}{90}$ B. $\frac{7}{90}$

C. $\frac{1}{10}$ D. None of these

2. A dice is rolled 600 times and the occurrence of the outcomes 1, 2, 3, 4, 5 and 6 are given below:

Outcome	1	2	3	4	5	6
Frequency	200	30	120	100	50	100

The probability of getting a prime numbers is:

A. $\frac{1}{3}$ B. $\frac{2}{3}$

C. $\frac{49}{60}$ D. $\frac{39}{125}$

3. A bag contains 50 coins and each coin is marked from 51 to 100. One coin is picked at random. The probability that the number on the coin is not a prime number, is

A. $\frac{1}{5}$ B. $\frac{3}{5}$

C. $\frac{2}{5}$ D. $\frac{4}{5}$

4. In a football match, a player makes 4 goals from 10 penalty kicks. The probability of converting a penalty kick into a goal by the player, is:

A. $\frac{1}{4}$ B. $\frac{1}{6}$

C. $\frac{1}{3}$ D. $\frac{2}{5}$

5. Three coins are tossed simultaneously 200 times with the following frequencies of different outcomes:

Outcome	3 heads	2 heads	1 head	No head
Frequency	23	72	77	28

What is the probability of getting at most two heads?

A. $\frac{177}{200}$ B. $\frac{172}{200}$

C. $\frac{19}{40}$ D. None of these

6. In Q. No. 5, what is the probability of getting at least two heads?

A. $\frac{13}{40}$ B. $\frac{19}{40}$

C. $\frac{23}{40}$ D. None of these

Directions (Qs. 7 to 10) : *1000 families with 2 children were selected randomly, and the following data were recorded:*

Number of boys in a family:	0	1	2
Number of families :	140	560	*300*

If a family is chosen at random, find the probability that it has:

7. No boy

A. 0.14 B. 0.56

C. 0.3 D. None of these

8. One boy

A. 0.56 B. 0.3

C. 0.14 D. None of these

9. At least one boy

A. 0.14 B. 0.56

C. 0.86 D. 0.7

10. At most one boy

A. 0.7 B. 0.56

C. 0.14 D. 0.86

11. In a simultaneous throw of two coins, the probability of getting at least one head is:

A. $\frac{1}{2}$ B. $\frac{1}{3}$

C. $\frac{2}{3}$ D. $\frac{3}{4}$

12. Three unbiased coins are tossed. What is the probability of getting at least 2 heads?

A. $\frac{3}{4}$ B. $\frac{1}{4}$

C. $\frac{3}{8}$ D. $\frac{7}{8}$

13. In a single throw of a die, what is the probability of getting a number greater than 4?

A. $\frac{1}{2}$ B. $\frac{1}{3}$

C. $\frac{2}{3}$ D. $\frac{1}{4}$

14. In a simultaneous throw of two dice, what is the probability of getting a total of 7?

A. $\frac{1}{6}$ B. $\frac{1}{4}$

C. $\frac{2}{3}$ D. $\frac{3}{4}$

15. What is the probability of getting a sum 9 from two throws of a dice?

A. $\frac{1}{6}$ B. $\frac{1}{8}$

C. $\frac{1}{9}$ D. $\frac{1}{12}$

16. In a simultaneous throw of two dice, what is the probability of getting a total of 10 or 11?

A. $\frac{1}{4}$ B. $\frac{1}{6}$

C. $\frac{7}{12}$ D. $\frac{5}{36}$

17. Two dice are thrown simultaneously. What is the probability of getting two numbers whose product is even?

A. $\frac{1}{2}$ B. $\frac{3}{4}$

C. $\frac{3}{8}$ D. $\frac{5}{16}$

18. Tickets numbered 1 to 20 are mixed up and then a ticket is drawn at random. What is the probability that the ticket drawn bears a number which is a multiple of 3?

A. $\frac{3}{10}$ B. $\frac{3}{20}$

C. $\frac{2}{5}$ D. $\frac{1}{2}$

19. From a pack of 52 cards, one card is drawn at random. What is the probability that the card drawn is a ten or a spade?

A. $\frac{4}{13}$ B. $\frac{1}{4}$

C. $\frac{1}{13}$ D. $\frac{1}{26}$

20. The probability that a card drawn from a pack of 52 cards will be a diamond or a king, is:

A. $\frac{2}{13}$ B. $\frac{4}{13}$

C. $\frac{1}{13}$ D. $\frac{1}{52}$

21. A bag contains 6 black and 8 white balls. One ball is drawn at random. What is the probability that the ball drawn is white?

A. $\frac{3}{4}$ B. $\frac{4}{7}$

C. $\frac{1}{8}$ D. $\frac{3}{7}$

22. A box contains 5 green, 4 yellow and 3 white marbles. Three marbles are drawn at random. What is the probability that they are not of the same colour?

A. $\frac{3}{44}$ B. $\frac{3}{55}$

C. $\frac{52}{55}$ D. $\frac{41}{44}$

23. A bag contains 4 white, 5 red and 6 blue balls. Three balls are drawn at random from the bag. The probability that all of them are red, is:

A. $\frac{1}{22}$ B. $\frac{3}{22}$

C. $\frac{2}{91}$ D. $\frac{2}{77}$

24. A box contains 10 black and 10 white balls. The probability of drawing two balls of the same colour, is:

A. $\frac{9}{19}$ B. $\frac{9}{38}$

C. $\frac{10}{19}$ D. $\frac{5}{19}$

25. Two dice are tossed. The probability that the total score is a prime number is:

A. $\frac{1}{6}$ B. $\frac{5}{12}$

C. $\frac{1}{2}$ D. $\frac{7}{9}$

ANSWERS

1	2	3	4	5	6	7	8	9	10
B	A	D	D	A	B	A	A	C	A
11	**12**	**13**	**14**	**15**	**16**	**17**	**18**	**19**	**20**
D	D	B	A	C	D	B	A	A	B
21	**22**	**23**	**24**	**25**					
B	D	C	A	B					

EXPLANATORY ANSWERS

1. Total No. of students = 90
No. of students scoring less than 20 marks = 7

Required probability = $\frac{7}{90}$

2. Total outcomes = 600
Total outcomes of getting prime numbers, (2, 3, 5) = 30 + 120 + 50 = 200

$\therefore$ Required probability = $\frac{200}{600} = \frac{1}{3}$

3. Total prime no. between 51 to 100 (53, 59, 61, 67, 71, 73, 79, 83. 89, 97) = 10

$\therefore$ Total Non-prime No = 50 − 10 = 40

$\therefore$ Required probability = $\frac{40}{50} = \frac{4}{5}$

4. Required probability = $\frac{4}{10} = \frac{2}{5}$

5. No. of coins getting at most two heads
= 28 + 77 + 72 = 177

Required probability = $\frac{177}{200}$

6. No. of coins getting at least two heads = 23 + 72 = 95

Required probability = $\frac{95}{200} = \frac{19}{40}$

7. Total number of families = 1000
Number of families having no boy child = 140.

$\therefore$ Probability that a family chosen at random does not have a boy child

$= \frac{140}{1000} = 0.14$

8. Total number of families = 1000
Number of families having one boy child = 560
$\therefore$ Probability that a family chosen at random has one boy child

$= \frac{560}{1000} = 0.56$

9. Total number of families = 1000
Number of families having at least one boy child
= 560 + 300 = 860

$= \frac{860}{1000} = 0.86$

10. Total number of families = 1000
Number of families having at most one boy child
= 140 + 560 = 700

$\therefore$ Probability that a family chosen at random has at most one boy child

$= \frac{700}{1000} = 0.7$

11. Here S = {HH, HT, TH, TT},
Let E = event of getting at least one head
= {HT, TH, HH}

$\therefore$ $P(E) = \frac{n(E)}{n(S)} = \frac{3}{4}.$

12. Here $S = \{TTT, TTH, THT, HTT, THH, HTH, HHT, HHH\}$.

Let E = event of getting at most two heads

Then, E = {TTT, TTH, THT, HTT, THH, HTH, HHT}

$$\therefore \ P(E) = \frac{n(E)}{n(S)} = \frac{7}{8}.$$

13. When a die is thrown, we have S = {1, 2, 3, 4, 5, 6}

Let E = event of getting a number greater than 4 = {5, 6}

$$\therefore \quad P(E) = \frac{n(E)}{n(S)} = \frac{2}{6} = \frac{1}{3}.$$

14. We know that in a simultaneous throw of two dice,

$n(S) = 6 \times 6 = 36$.

Let E = event of getting a total of 7 = {(1, 6), (2, 5), (3, 4), (4, 3), (5, 2), (6, 1)}

$$\therefore \quad P(E) = \frac{n(E)}{n(S)} = \frac{6}{36} = \frac{1}{6}.$$

15. In two throws of a die, $n(S) = (6 \times 6) = 36$.

Let E = event of getting a sum 9 = {(3, 6), (4, 5) (5, 4), (6, 3)}

$$\therefore \quad P(E) = \frac{n(E)}{n(S)} = \frac{4}{36} = \frac{1}{9}.$$

16. In a simultaneous throw of two dice, we have

$n(S) = (6 \times 6) = 36$

Let E = event of getting a total of 10 or 11 = {(4, 6), (5, 5), (6, 4), (5, 6), (6, 5)}

$$\therefore \quad P(E) = \frac{n(E)}{n(S)} = \frac{5}{36}.$$

17. In a simultaneous throw of two dice, we have

$n(S) = (6 \times 6) = 36$

Let E = event of getting two numbers whose product is even.

Then, E = {(1, 2), (1, 4), (1, 6), (2, 1), (2, 2), (2, 3), (2, 4), (2, 5), (2, 6), (3, 2), (3, 4), (3, 6), (4, 1), (4, 2), (4, 3), (4, 4), (4, 5), (4, 6), (5, 2), (5, 4), (5, 6), (6, 1), (6, 2), (6, 3), (6, 4), (6, 5), (6, 6)}.

$\therefore \quad n(E) = 27$.

$$\therefore \quad P(E) = \frac{n(E)}{n(S)} = \frac{27}{36} = \frac{3}{4}$$

18. Here, S = {1, 2, 3, 4, ..., 19, 20}

Let E = event of getting a multiple of 3 = {3, 6, 9, 12, 15, 18}

$$\therefore \quad P(E) = \frac{n(E)}{n(S)} = \frac{6}{20} = \frac{3}{10}.$$

19. Here, $n(S) = 52$

There are 13 spades (including one ten) and there are 3 more tens.

Let E = event of getting a ten or a spade.

Then, $n(E) = (13 + 3) = 16$

$$\therefore \quad P(E) = \frac{n(E)}{n(S)} = \frac{16}{52} = \frac{4}{13}.$$

20. Here, $n(S) = 52$

There are 13 cards of diamond (including one king) and there are 3 more kings.

Let E = event of getting a diamond or a king.

Then $n(E) = (13 + 3) = 16$

$$\therefore \quad P(E) = \frac{n(E)}{n(S)} = \frac{16}{52} = \frac{4}{13}.$$

21. Total number of balls = (6 + 8) = 14.

Number of white balls = 8.

$$P \text{ (drawing a white ball)} = \frac{8}{14} = \frac{4}{7}.$$

22. Let S be the sample space. Then,

$n(S)$ = number of ways of drawing 3 marbels out of 12

$$= {}^{12}C_3 = \frac{(12 \times 11 \times 10)}{(3 \times 2 \times 1)} = 220$$

Let E be the event of drawing 3 balls of the same colour.

Then, E = event of drawing (3 balls out of 5) or (3 balls out of 4) or (3 balls out of 3)

$$\Rightarrow \quad n(E) = ({}^5C_3 + {}^4C_3 + {}^3C_3) = ({}^5C_2 + {}^4C_1 + 1)$$

$$= \frac{(5 \times 4)}{(2 \times 1)} + 4 + 1 = 15$$

$$\Rightarrow \quad P(E) = \frac{n(E)}{n(S)} = \frac{15}{220} = \frac{3}{44}$$

$$\therefore \text{ Required probability } = \left(1 - \frac{3}{44}\right) = \frac{41}{44}.$$

23. Let S be the sample space. Then,

$n(S)$ = number of ways of drawing 3 balls out of 15

$$= {}^{15}C_3 = \frac{(15 \times 14 \times 13)}{(3 \times 2 \times 1)} = 455$$

Let E = event of getting all the 3 red balls.

$\therefore \quad n(E) = {}^5C_3 = {}^5C_2 = \frac{(5 \times 4)}{(2 \times 1)} = 10$

$\therefore \quad P(E) = \frac{n(E)}{n(S)} = \frac{10}{455} = \frac{2}{91}.$

24. Total number of balls = 20

Let S be the sample space. Then,

$n(S) =$ Number of ways of drawing 2 balls out of 20

$= {}^{20}C_2 = \frac{(20 \times 19)}{(2 \times 1)} = 190$

Let E = event of drawing 2 balls of the same colour

$n(E) = ({}^{10}C_2 + {}^{10}C_2)$

$= 2 \times \frac{(10 \times 9)}{(2 \times 1)} = 90$

$\therefore \quad P(E) = \frac{n(E)}{n(S)} = \frac{90}{190} = \frac{9}{19}.$

25. Clearly, $n(S) = (6 \times 6) = 36$.

Let E = Event that the sum is a prime number.

Then, E = {(1, 1), (1, 2), (1, 4), (1, 6), (2, 1), (2, 3), (2, 5), (3, 2), (3, 4), (4, 1), (4, 3), (5, 2), (5, 6), (6, 1), (6, 5)}

$\therefore \quad n(E) = 15$

$\therefore \quad P(E) = \frac{n(E)}{n(S)} = \frac{15}{36} = \frac{5}{12}.$

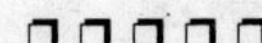

GENERAL SCIENCE

1

Food-Crop Production and Management; Microorganism; Food Preservation

CROP PRODUCTION AND MANAGEMENT

We all know that every living organism needs food to survive. Plants can synthesise their own food but, animals including human beings are dependent on others for food. So for providing food for large number of people we need proper management. So for this large scale demand of food for humans, they started agriculture practises.

AGRICULTURE: It is a human activity of cultivating crops and plantations for the large scale production of food and goods such as bio fuels, fibres, animal feed etc.

CROPS: When the plants of same types are cultivated at a place on a very large scale are known as crop.

Types of Crops in India

India is a vast country where diverse practices of farming are seen in different parts. But crops in India can be divided into two main types, which are basically:

Kharif (monsoon crops): These are sown in the beginning of rainy season. Ex-paddy, maize, cotton etc.

Rabi (winter crops): These are sown in the beginning of winter season. Ex—wheat, gram, pea etc.

Basic Practices of Crop Production

Cultivation of crop involves various activities and steps which are referred as agriculture practices. There are seven agriculture practices.

These activities are:

1. Preparation of soil
2. Sowing
3. Adding manure and fertilisers
4. Irrigation
5. Protection from weeds
6. Harvesting
7. Storage

Preparation of Soil

One of the most important steps in preparation of soil is to loosen it, which allows the microorganism and earthworm to enrich the soil. This helps the root to penetrate deep into the soil and also bring the nutrient rich soil on the top layer. The process of loosening or turning of soil is called tilling or ploughing.

Ploughing

- This is done with the help of plough.
- Ploughed field contains big pieces of soil called crumbs.
- Further it is levelled using a wooden or an iron leveller to prevent the soil from being eroded by wind or water.
- Next manure or fertilizer is added to increase the soil fertility.

Plough

- It is tool for ploughing in olden days.
- Made up of wood or iron.
- It contains triangular iron strip called as the plough-share.
- The main part is a rod of wood known as plough shaft.
- The last end is attached to the beam which is attached to the bull.

Hoe

- It helps in removing the weeds.
- It has long rod made up of wood or iron.
- A strong bent plate made up of iron is present at one end.
- This is pulled generally by ox.

Sowing

Seeds which are used for sowing should be of good quality, healthy and free from infections.

- Seeds must be planted at correct depth in the soil.
- Proper amount of water is needed for the seeds to germinate.

The gap between the seeds should be proper and at the right distance.

Traditional tool

- It is shaped like a funnel.
- Funnel's end is pierces into the soil.
- Funnel is passes through the funnel.

Seed drill

- Now days drills are used present in the tractors.
- It sows the seeds uniformly at proper distance and depth.
- It ensures that seeds are properly covered by the soil.

Adding Manure and Fertilizers

- Soil itself supplies necessary minerals and nutrients to the plant.
- In certain areas when farmer grows crops after crops it decrease the fertility of the soil.

Difference between Manure and Fertilizers

S.N.	Manure Fertilizers	Fertilizers
1.	Made up of animal and plants waste	Made up of chemicals in factories
2.	Provides mainly organic matter	Provides mainly nutrients
3.	No side effects as it is natural	Gives side effects
4.	Provides long term soil fertility	Not good for long term soil fertility
5.	It is cheaper	It is costlier than manures
6.	It gives slow result	Provides fast and effective result

Irrigation

- Supply of water to crops at different interval of time is known as IRRIGATION.
- Water is the basic and important requirement for growth and development of plants.
- Germination of seeds doesn't take place under dry conditions.
- Proper irrigation system will ensure the timely and adequate required water to crops. This will lead to more yield.

Sources of irrigation: wells, tube wells, ponds, lakes, rivers, dams and canals.

1. **Traditional method of irrigation:** The water available in wells, lakes and canals is lifted up by different regions, for taking it to the fields.
2. **Modern methods of irrigation:**

   (*a*) **Sprinkler system:**
   - Used where uneven land is present.
   - Perpendicular pipes, having rotating nozzles on top.
   - Joined to the main pipeline at regular intervals.

   (*b*) **Drip System:**
   - Water Falls drop by drop at the position of the roots.
   - Best technique for watering fruit plants, garden and trees.
   - Very less water wastage.

Protection from Weed

- Weeds are the undesirable plants which grow naturally along with the crops.
- Removal of weeds is called weeding.
- Weeding is important as they effect the growth of crop by compete with the crop plants.

Weed Control

- Tilling before sowing of crops helps in uprooting and killing of weeds.
- Manual removal includes physical removal of weeds by cutting them.
- Weeds are control by spraying weedicides.
- Weedicides are the chemical to kill the weed.

Harvesting

Cutting of crops after it is mature is called harvesting.

- Crops are pulled out or cut close to the ground.
- It can be done manually by sickle or by machine.
- The grain seed need to be separated from the chaff with the help of machine called "combined".

Storage

- Grains are kept for the longer time without getting spoiled is known as storage.
- Should be kept safe from moisture, insect, rats and microorganism.
- If grains are stored without drying they may get spoilt and lose their germination capacity.
- Small scale storage in jute bags and metallic bins.
- Large scale storage in silos and granaries.

Food from Animals

- Like plants, animals also provide us with different kinds of foods.
- People living in coastal areas consume fish as a major part of their diet.
- Just like crop production involve number of steps, similarly animals reared at home or in farm.
- When this is done on large scale it is known as animal husbandry.

MICROORGANISMS : AN INTRODUCTION

Microscopic organisms, commonly known as microorganisms or microbes, are found all around us and even inside our bodies. The category 'Microbes' includes a massive range of organisms including bacteria, fungi, viruses, algae, archaea and protozoa. Some of these, such as bacteria and fungi, are well known, but others such as archaea much less so.

Microorganisms, as their name implies, are so small that they usually require a microscope to see. The vast majority of microbes on the earth pose no real threat to humans, plants or animals; in fact they actually work alongside humans to make world go round, aiding decomposition, decay and even helping us to digest our food. However, there are some microorganisms which negatively impact our lives, causing illness, bad odours and damaging products and surfaces. Some of the names we regularly hear in the media are Salmonella, E.Coli, MRSA, Malaria and Bird flu.

We will briefly explore some major divisions within microorganisms, and hopefully highlight some interesting facts and differences within each group.

Bacteria

Bacteria, perhaps the most well-known microorganism, are a member of the prokaryotes; they have no nucleus within the cell and contain no organelles (specialised cellular 'organs'). Within bacteria there are two classes, Gram positive bacteria which have thicker cell wall and Gram negatives which have a thinner layer sandwiched between an inner and outer membrane.

Bacteria are extremely diverse and in terms of number are by far the most successful organism on Earth. Bacteria are the only microorganisms which can live harmlessly within the human body, often aiding bodily functions such as digestion. In fact there are more bacterial cells within the human body than humans cells, albeit much smaller in size.

Bacteria, of all the 'living' microorganisms, cause the most problems in terms of disease in humans, despite only relatively few bacteria being dangerous.

Fungi

Fungi are eukaryotes which means they have a defined nucleus and organelles. The cells are larger than prokaryotes such as bacteria. Fungal colonies can be visible to the human eye once they have achieved a certain level of growth, for example mould on bread. Fungi can be split into three main groups, 1) moulds which display thread-like (filamentous) growth and multicellular structures, 2) yeasts which are typically non-filamentous and can be single celled and 3) mushrooms which possess a fruiting body for production of spores.

Fungi can be problematic for the immuno compromised and contain significant pathogens which can cause disease in plants. However, we also recognise organisms from this group from widespread use in the food industry, for production of beer and other foodstuffs.

Viruses

Viruses are considered by many experts to not be living organisms. They essentially consist of nucleic acid (DNA or RNA,) and a protein coat. A virion (a virus particle) requires a host cell in order to replicate. Within the human anatomy a virus enters a human cell and hijacks the it, using the cell to replicate.

In many cases the immune system detects the presence of the virus and takes action leaving us with the symptoms of a common cold or influenza. Some viruses can cause permanent and irreversible damage to cells, for example HIV.

Algae

Algae are a more difficult to define group of organisms, containing both prokaryotes and eukaryotes by some definitions. Unlike other micro-organisms algae are typically photosynthesisers and are typically found in marine environments. Prokaryotic algae, or Cyanobacteria, are often called blue-green algae although some definition or opinions will state that algae are eukaryotes only (that they are essentially small aquatic plants). There are other groups such as **Archaea** and **Protozoa** which are generally less well known.

FOOD PRESERVATION

The term food preservation refers to any one of a number of techniques used to prevent food from spoiling. It includes methods such as canning, pickling, drying and freeze-drying, irradiation, pasteurization, smoking, and the addition of chemical additives. Food preservation has become an increasingly important component of the food industry as fewer people eat foods produced on their own lands, and as consumers expect to be able to purchase and consume foods that are out of season.

The vast majority of instances of food spoilage can be attributed to one of two major causes:

- The attack by pathogens (disease-causing micro-organisms) such as bacteria and molds, or
- Oxidation that causes the destruction of essential biochemical compounds and/or the destruction of plant and animal cells. The various methods that have been devised for preserving foods are all designed to reduce or eliminate one or the other (or both) of these causative agents.

Traditional techniques

Drying

Drying is one of the oldest techniques used to hamper the decomposition of food products.

Vegetables and fruits are naturally dried by the sun and wind, but "still houses" were built in areas that did not have enough sunlight to dry things. A fire would be built inside the building to provide the heat to dry the various fruits, vegetables, and herbs.

Cooling

Cooling preserves food by slowing down the growth and reproduction of microorganisms and the action of enzymes that cause food to rot.

Freezing

Freezing is also one of the most commonly used processes, both commercially and domestically, for preserving a very wide range of foods, including prepared foods that would not have required freezing in their unprepared state.

Boiling

Boiling liquid food items can kill any existing microbes. Milk and water are often boiled to kill any harmful microbes that may be present in them.

Heating

Heating to temperatures which are sufficient to kill microorganisms inside the food is a method used with perpetual stews. Milk is also boiled before storing to kill many microorganisms.

Salting

Salting or curing draws moisture from a substance through a process of osmosis. Substances are cured with salt or sugar, or a combination of the two. Nitrates and nitrites are also often used to cure meat and contribute the characteristic pink colour.

Sugaring

The earliest cultures have used sugar as a preservative, and it was commonplace to store fruit in honey. Similar to pickled foods, sugar cane was brought to Europe through the trade routes. In northern climates without sufficient sun to dry foods, preserves are made by heating the fruit with sugar.

Pickling

Pickling is a method of preserving food in an edible anti-microbial liquid. Pickling can be broadly classified into two categories: chemical pickling and fermentation pickling. In chemical pickling, the food is placed in an edible liquid that inhibits or kills bacteria and other micro-organisms. Typical pickling agents include brine (high in salt), vinegar, alcohol, and vegetable oil, especially olive oil but also many other oils.

Lye

Sodium hydroxide (lye) makes food too alkaline for bacterial growth. Lye will saponify fats in the food, which will change its flavour and texture. Lutefisk uses lye in its preparation, as do some olive recipes. Modern recipes for century eggs also call for lye.

Canning

Canning involves cooking food, sealing it in sterile cans or jars, and boiling the containers to kill or weaken any remaining bacteria as a form of sterilization. Foods have varying degrees of natural protection against spoilage and may require that the final step occur in a pressure cooker. High-acid fruits like strawberries require no preservatives to can and only a short boiling cycle, whereas marginal vegetables such as carrots require longer boiling and addition of other acidic elements. Low-acid foods, such as vegetables and meats, require pressure canning. Food preserved by canning or bottling is at immediate risk of spoilage once the can or bottle has been opened.

Jellying

Food may be preserved by cooking in a material that solidifies to form a gel. Such materials include gelatin, agar, maize flour, and arrow root flour. Some foods naturally form a protein gel, when cooked, such as eels and elvers, and sipunculid worms, which are a delicacy in Xiamen, in the Fujian province of the People's Republic of China.

Jugging

Meat can be preserved by jugging. Jugging is the process of stewing the meat (commonly game or fish) in a covered earthenware jug or casserole. The animal to be jugged is usually cut into pieces, placed into a tightly-sealed jug with brine or gravy, and stewed. Red wineand/or the animal's own blood is sometimes added to the cooking liquid. Jugging was a popular method of preserving meat up until the middle of the 20th century.

Modern industrial techniques

Pasteurization

Pasteurization is a process for preservation of liquid food. It was originally applied to combat the souring of young local wines. Today, the process is mainly applied to dairy products. In this method, milk is heated at about 70 °C (158 °F) for 15–30 seconds to kill the bacteria present in it and cooling it quickly to 10 °C (50 °F) to prevent the remaining bacteria from growing. The milk is then stored in sterilized bottles or pouches in cold places. This method was invented by Louis Pasteur, a French chemist, in 1862.

Vacuum packing

Vacuum packing stores food in a vacuum environment, usually in an air-tight bag or bottle. The vacuum environment strips bacteria of oxygen needed for survival. Vacuum packing is commonly used for storing nuts to reduce loss of flavour from oxidization. A major drawback to vacuum packaging, at the consumer level, is that vacuum sealing can deform contents and rob certain foods, such as cheese, of its flavour.

Freeze drying

Freeze drying, also known as lyophilisation, is a low temperature dehydration process which involves freezing the product, lowering pressure, then removing the ice by sublimation. This is in contrast to dehydration by most conventional methods that evaporate water using heat. Freeze drying results in a high quality product because of the low temperature used in processing.

Food irradiation

Food irradiation is the process of exposing food and food packaging to ionizing radiation. Ionizing radiation, such as from gamma rays, x-rays or electron beams, is energy that can be transmitted without direct contact to the source of the energy (radiation) capable of freeing electrons from their atomic bonds (ionization) in the targeted food.

Hurdle technology

Hurdle technology is a method of ensuring that pathogens in food products can be eliminated or controlled. This means the food products will be safe for consumption, and their shelf life will be extended.

MULTIPLE CHOICE QUESTIONS

1. Which one of the following condition is not essential to grow maize?
A. High temperature B. Humidity
C. Low temperature D. Rainfall

2. Propagation of ginger is generally done using
A. seed B. stem (rhizome)
C. root D. leaf

3. Which of the following statement is not true for organic manure?
A. It enhances water holding capacity of soil.
B. It has a balance of all plant nutrients.
C. It provides humus to soil.
D. It improves texture of soil.

4. The term used for the process of separation of grains from chaff is:
A. sieving B. threshing
C. winnowing D. hand picking

5. Read the statements given below.
(*i*) Seeds require moisture for germination.
(*ii*) Plants can absorb nutrients mostly in dissolved form.
(*iii*) Irrigation protects crops from both frost and hot air currents.
(*iv*) Irrigation improves soil texture.
Choose the combination of statements which indicate the need to irrigate crops.
A. (*i*) and (*ii*)
B. (*i*), (*ii*), (*iii*)
C. (*i*), (*ii*), (*iii*), (*iv*)
D. (*i*) and (*iii*)

6. Which of the following tools would a farmer use to remove weeds from the field?
A. Hoe B. Plough
C. Axe D. Cultivato

7. Which of the following is not true for fertilisers?
A. They increase the yield.
B. Their excessive use disturbs the balance of nutrients in soil.
C. They are generally used in small quantity.
D. They are environment friendly.

8. Given below are statements about the harmful effects of weeds on crop plants.
(*i*) They interfere in harvesting.
(*ii*) They help crop plants to grow healthily.
(*iii*) They compete with crop plants for water, nutrients, space and light.
(*iv*) They affect plant growth.
Choose the correct combination of statements.
A. (*i*), (*iii*), (*iv*) B. (*iii*) only
C. (*iii*), (*iv*) D. (*i*), (*ii*), (*iii*), (*iv*)

9. The process of loosening and turning of soil is called:
A. irrigation and manuring
B. digging and winnowing
C. tilling and ploughing
D. harvesting and storage

10. The monsoon season in our country is during the months:
A. April to December B. June to September
C. November to March D. January to May

11. The system of irrigation where in water is supplied drop by drop near the roots of plants, is called:
A. pulley system B. drip system
C. sprinkler system D. lever system

12. The process of loosening and turning the soil is called:
A. Broadcasting B. Irrigation
C. Ploughing D. Levelling

13. The organic substance obtained from dead plants and animal wastes is:
A. Manure B. Fertilizer
C. Irrigation D. Agriculture

14. In which of the following methods of irrigation rotating nozzles are used?
A. Moat B. Drip system
C. Chain Pump D. Sprinkler system

15. The management and care of farm animals by humans for profit is known as:
A. Granary B. Animal Husbandry
C. Poultry farm D. Warehouse

16. The process of separating grain from chaff is called:
A. Threshing B. Weeding
C. Sowing D. Winnowing

17. Weeds can be removed by using:
A. Pesticides B. Fungicides
C. Weedicides D. Bactericides

18. The conversion of nitrogen into nitrates is known as:
A. Nitrogen fixation B. Ammonification
C. Nitrate Assimilation D. Nitrogen cycle

19. Animals like horse, donkey that carries load are called:
A. Drought species B. Load carrying Animals
C. Dairy Animals D. Draught Animal

20. Raising of fish in inland waters and coastal waters are called:
A. Pisciculture B. Fishery
C. Fish culture D. Harvesting

21. The process of loosening and turning the soil is called ______.
A. broadcasting B. irrigation
C. tilling D. levelling

22. Which of the following is not a rabi crop?
A. Rice B. Mustard
C. Wheat D. Barley

23. In which of the following method of irrigation rotating nozzles are use:
A. Moat B. Drip System
C. Chain pump D. Sprinkler System

24. Which of the following nutrient replenish the soil after growing legum plants?
A. Nitrogen B. Oxygen
C. Phosphorus D. Potassium

25. The management of rearing animals for food and other products is *k* _______ .
A. Granaries B. Animal husbandry
C. Poultry D. Warehouse

26. The process of separating the grain from the chaff is:
A. Threshing B. Weeding
C. Sowing D. Tilling

27. Weeds can be removed by using?
A. Pesticides B. Fungicides
C. Weedicides D. Bactericides

28. Which leaves are used by farmers to protect their crops from weeds insects?
A. Peepal leaves B. Basil leaves
C. Neem leaves D. Mango leaves

29. Who discovered the fungus called Pencillium from which Pencillin is produced?
A. James D. Watson B. Louis Pasteur
C. Alexander Flemming D. Sir Ronald Ross

30. Fermentation is carried out by the yeast cells in the absence of:
A. Nitrogen B. Carbondioxide
C. Hydrogen D. Oxygen

31. Bacteria in the root nodules of the plant and the plant help each other for mutual benefit. This is called:
A. Combination B. Symbiosis
C. Adoption D. Amalgamation

32. Which of the following bacteria live in the root nodules of plants?
A. Azotobacter
B. Pencillium
C. Rhizobium legumino sarum
D. Mycobacterium leprae

33. Which of the following are damaged by the growth of Fungus?
A. Wood B. Clothes
C. Paper D. All the above

34. Antibiotic called penicillin is produced from fungus called:
A. Entamoeba B. Penicillium
C. Plasmodium D. Aspergillus

35. The fungi look like a group of fine threads called:
A. Flagella B. Fronds
C. Hyphae D. Calyx

36. The microorganism Fungi are found in:
A. Water
B. Decaying bodies of plants and animals
C. Rotting fruits, bread, pickles
D. All the above

37. Which of the following is true about Protozoans?
A. Some of the protozoans move with Pseudopodium
B. Some of the protozoans move with Cilia
C. Some of the protozoans do not move
D. All the above

38. The green Algae swims in water with the help of hair like projections called:
A. Diatoms B. Fronds
C. Flagella D. Corolla

39. Genera Science Which of the following are the kinds of the Algae?
A. Brown Algae B. Blue Green Algae
C. Green Algae D. All the above

40. The green Algae in oceans is called:
A. Flagella B. Diatoms
C. Fronds D. Stigma

41. Which of the following are formed by Bacteria when conditions are not suitable?
A. Fronds B. Corolla
C. Spores D. Flagella

42. In which of the following places Bacteria are found?
A. Air B. Water
C. Soil D. All the above

43. Which of the following is true about the bacteria?
A. They do not have nucleus
B. They are unicellular organisms
C. Some bacteria live in group
D. All the above

44. What is the shape of the Bacteria?
A. Rod shape B. Comma shape
C. Round shape D. All the above

45. The thread like structures of the bacteria are called:
A. Fronds B. Flagella
C. Spores D. Ranvier

46. Bacteria were first discovered by Leeuwenhoek in:
A. 1721 B. 1725
C. 1674 D. 1689

47. Which of the following diseases are caused by Viruses?
A. AIDS and Polio
B. Mumps, Common cold
C. Measles and Chicken pox
D. All the above

48. Viruses are transmitted from one organism to another through:
A. Insects
B. Dust particles in air
C. Body fluids of infected person
D. All the above

49. The virus which lives inside the cell is called:
A. Parasite B. Host Cell
C. Host D. Leucocyte

50. The cell in which viruses live is called:
A. Host cell B. Leucocyte
C. Erythrocyte D. Parasite

51. Viruses live inside the living cells of:
A. Animals B. Plants
C. Bacterium D. All the above

52. The study of disease condition is called:
A. Microbiology B. Bacteriology
C. Pathology D. Virology

53. The study of microorganisms is called:
A. Microbiology B. Bacteriology
C. Pathology D. Virology

54. The study of Bacteria is called:
A. Microbiology B. Bacteriology
C. Pathology D. Virology

55. The study of viruses is called:
A. Microbiology B. Bacteriology
C. Pathology D. Virology

56. The microorganisms which can prepare their food are called:
A. Eukaryotes
B. Prokaryotes
C. Autotrophic organisms
D. Heterotrophic organisms

57. The microorganisms that depend on other organisms for food are called
A. Heterotrophic organisms
B. Autotrophic organisms
C. Eukaryotes
D. Prokaryotes

58. The microorganisms which have a nucleus are called:
A. Autotrophic organisms
B. Heterotrophic organisms
C. Eukaryotes
D. Prokaryotes

59. Microorganisms which do not have a nucleus are called:
A. Prokaryotes
B. Eukaryotes
C. Heterotrophic organisms
D. Autotrophic organisms

60. Which of the following is true about microorganisms?
A. The cells contain small amount of protoplasm
B. They have either DNA or RNA
C. They are usually single celled organisms
D. All the above

61. Which of the following are the different types of microorganisms?
A. Viruses and Bacteria B. Protozoans
C. Algae and Fungi D. All the above

62. Antony Van Leeuwenhoek first discovered microorganisms in the year:
A. 1612 B. 1674
C. 1690 D. 1698

63. Amoeba belongs to:
A. Algae B. Fungi
C. Protozoa D. Virus

64. Pasteurization is the process of heating milk:
A. above 121 °C
B. above boiling point
C. below boiling point
D. above 150 °C

65. The process of preserving food by rapid freezing followed by dehydration under vacuum is called
A. Lyophilisation B. Sterilization
C. Cold Dehydration D. Cryopreservation

66. 'Cold sterilization' refers to the preservation of food by:
A. Refrigeration B. Radiation
C. Dehydration D. Lyophilisation

67. All the following techniques are household preservation technique except:
A. Smoking B. Lyophilisation
C. Dehydration D. Salting

68. What is the purpose for blanching (immersing food in hot water) vegetables during canning?
A. to soften products to fill better
B. to denature enzymes that change colour, texture
C. to reduce microbial population
D. All of the above

69. Who is regarded as the father of canning?
A. Nicolas Appert B. Louis Pasteur
C. John Hall D. Bryan Dokin

70. The method of preventing or reducing pathogens in food products by combining many methods like high temperature during processing, low temperature during storage, increasing the acidity etc is called:
A. Mixed preservation approach
B. High pressure food preservation
C. Hurdle technology
D. Stumbling technology

71. Which of the following methods dehydrates microbial cells by plasmolysis thereby killing them?
A. Sugaring B. Smoking
C. Heating D. Pasteurization

72. The reason for food spoilage is:
A. Growth of microorganisms like bacteria, fungus etc or insects
B. Autolysis
C. Oxidation by air that causes rancidity or colour changes
D. All of the above

73. The process of preserving meat by stewing in a covered earthenware jug:
A. burial B. curing
C. jugging D. all of these

ANSWERS

1	2	3	4	5	6	7	8	9	10
C	B	B	C	A	A	D	A	C	B
11	**12**	**13**	**14**	**15**	**16**	**17**	**18**	**19**	**20**
B	C	A	D	B	A	C	A	B	A
21	**22**	**23**	**24**	**25**	**26**	**27**	**28**	**29**	**30**
C	A	D	A	B	A	C	C	C	D
31	**32**	**33**	**34**	**35**	**36**	**37**	**38**	**39**	**40**
B	C	D	B	C	D	D	C	D	B
41	**42**	**43**	**44**	**45**	**46**	**47**	**48**	**49**	**50**
C	D	D	D	B	C	D	D	A	A
51	**52**	**53**	**54**	**55**	**56**	**57**	**58**	**59**	**60**
D	C	A	B	D	C	A	C	A	D
61	**62**	**63**	**64**	**65**	**66**	**67**	**68**	**69**	**70**
D	B	C	B	A	B	B	D	A	C
71	**72**	**73**							
A	D	C							

☆ ☆ ☆

2

Synthetic Fibres; Metals and Non-Metals; Coal and Petroleum; Fossil Fuels

CARBON AND ITS COMPOUNDS

Some Important Facts

- Carbon is a non-metallic element, represented by the symbol C.
- All living things contain carbon. All the things that support life, such as proteins, fats, carbohydrates and vitamins contain carbon.
- Carbon had a unique property that it can join with other carbon atoms to form carbon—carbon bonds.
- This can result in the formation of compounds with long chains. This property is called Catenation.
- The name carbon is derived from the Latin word *carbo,* which means *charcoal.*
- Carbon constitutes only 0.03% of the earth crust.
- Carbon is present in coal and petroleum wood, coke, charcoal, saw dust, kerosene, alcohol, petrol, Liquefied Petroleum Gas (LPG), Compressed Natural Gas (CNG) and Gobbar Gas (Biogas).
- Carbon is present in the form of calcium carbonate ($CaCO_3$) in minerals like chalk, marble and limestone.
- Carbon also occurs in the form of CO_2 (0.03%) in the atmosphere.
- The exchange of carbon between the living and the non-living things by the processes of respiration and photosynthesis.
- The process of heating wood or coal in the absence of air is known as **destructive distillation**.
- When an element can exist in more than one structural form in the same physical state is called **allotropy**.
- The different forms of the same element are known as **allotropes.**
- Allotropes of the same element possess the same chemical properties. Carbon, phosphorus, sulphur and oxygen shows the property of allotropy.
- Carbon exists mainly in two allotropic forms:
  — Crystalline form
  — Non-crystalline or amorphous form

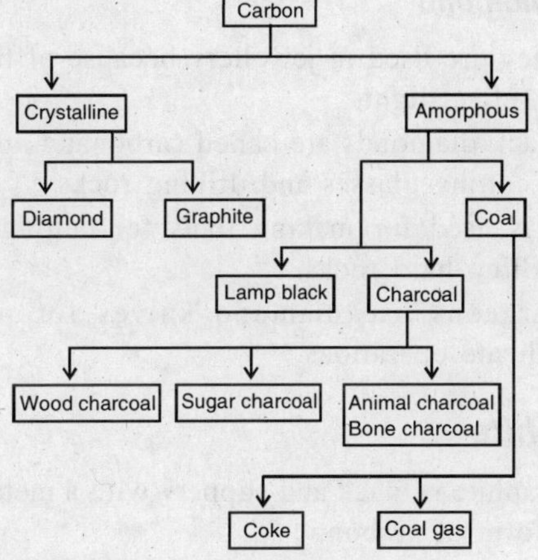

Crystalline forms of Carbon

Diamond and graphite are the two crystalline forms of carbon.

Diamond

It is one of the purest forms of carbon. Diamond crystals found in nature are generally **octahedral** (eight faced). In diamond, each carbon atom is attached to four other carbon atoms by strong forces. This results in a three-dimensional rigid structure which makes the **hardest substance**.

- The density of diamond is 3.5 gm per cubic centimetre (g/cm^3).
- The weight of diamond is expressed in **Carats**.
  1 Carat = 200 mg
- Melting and Boiling point of Diamond are 3550°C & 4827°C respectively.
- It does not conduct electricity.
- Diamonds are found in South Africa, Brazil, Congo, Angola, Tanzania and the USA.
- In India diamonds are found in **Panna** mines of Madhya Pradesh and Wajrakarur in Andhra Pradesh.
- The largest producer of diamonds in the world is South Africa.
- The famous diamonds in the world are **the Kohinoor**, **the Pitt** and **the Hope**.

Properties of Diamond

(*i*) It occurs naturally in free state and has octahedral shape.

(*ii*) It is the hardest known substances.

(*iii*) It has high specific gravity (3.5 g/cm^3)

(*iv*) It is transparent and has high refractive index (about 2.4).

(*v*) On heating of 800°C in the presence of oxygen it gives carbon dioxide.

$$\underset{\text{Diamond}}{C + O_2} \xrightarrow{800°C} CO_2$$

Uses of Diamond

(*i*) They are used in jewellery because of their ability to reflect light.

(*ii*) Black diamonds are called carbonado and are used in cutting glasses and drilling rocks.

(*iii*) It is used for making tools for cutting glass and drilling hard rocks.

(*iv*) Surgeons use diamond knives for performing delicate operations.

Graphite

- Graphite is black and slippery with a metallic lustre, a form of carbon.
- In graphite, each carbon is bonded to only three neighbouring carbon atoms in the same plane forming layers of hexagonal networks separated by larger distances.
- The different layers are held together by weak forces, called Vanderwaals forces.
- The layers can easily slide over one another. This makes graphite lubricating soft and greasy to touch.
- Graphite conducts electricity.
- The density of graphite ranges from 1.9 to 2.3 gram per cubic centimetre (g/cm^3).
- The melting and boiling point of graphite are 3697 °C and 4827 °C respectively.
- It is found in Sri Lanka, Mexico, Austria, North Korea, China and India.

In India, graphite is found in Andhra Pradesh, Bihar, Jammu and Kashmir, Odisha, Rajasthan, Tamil Nadu and Uttar Pradesh.

(*i*) It is soft and greasy to touch.

(*ii*) Its specific gravity is 2.3 g/cm^3.

(*iii*) It is greyish black and opaque.

(*iv*) It is a good conductor of heat and electricity.

(*v*) It occurs in hexagonal layers.

(*vi*) When heated at 700 °C in presence of oxygen it gives CO_2.

$$\underset{\text{graphite}}{C + O_2} \xrightarrow{700°C} CO_2$$

Uses of Graphite

(*i*) It is used for making pencil lead printer's ink, black point and artificial diamond.

(*ii*) It is used as dry lubricant for heavy machinery.

(*iii*) It is used in making crucibles for melting substances.

(*iv*) It is used as an electrode in batteries and electric furnaces.

(v) It is used in nuclear reactors as moderator to regulate nuclear reactions.

(*vi*) It is used in making pencil leads.

The graphite can transform into diamond by applying extremely high pressure more than 1 lakh times the atmospheric pressure at the sea level and temperature about 3700°C. High temperature and pressure make the carbon atoms in graphite to rearrange themselves into a diamond structure. About 90% of diamonds used in making tools are made from graphite.

Differences between properties of Diamond and Graphite

Property	*Diamond*	*Graphite*
Hardness	The hardest natural Substance	Very soft
Density	3.5 g/cm^3	2.4 g/cm^3
Tendency to conduct electric current	Bad conductor	Good conductor
Colour	Pure diamond is colourless	Black
Transparency	Transparent	Opaque
Occurrence	Rare	Abundant

Fullerenes

Fullerene is a naturally occurring allotrope of carbon in which 60 carbon atoms are linked to form a stable structure, called fullerenes.

American architect Buekminister Fuller, who designed such domes that had hexagons and pentagons to provide rigid structures with a three dimensional geometry. Fullerenes having C_{70}, C_{90} and C_{120} also have now been discovered. It forms compounds such as $Rb_3\ C_{60}$ are superconductors i.e. they can conduct electricity with no resistance. Fullerenes are the materials of the future.

Amorphous Carbon

Amorphous carbon has physical and chemical properties that may vary depending on its method of manufacture and conditions to which it is later subjected. Amorphous carbon burns relatively easily in air.

The important varieties of amorphous carbon are:

(*i*) Charcoal

(*ii*) Coke

(*iii*) Carbon Black

(i) Charcoal

Wood charcoal is obtained from wood by a process known as **destructive distillation** or **pyrolysis**, by heating it in the absence of air.

The various varieties of charcoal are: wood charcoal, animal charcoal and sugar charcoal.

Wood charcoal is a black porous solid and contains 35% carbon, density 1.5 g/cm^3. It floats over water and is a bad conductor of electricity.

It is used in gas masks. It is used as a fuel and also for filtration of water. It is also used in the manufacture of gun powder.

Animal charcoal or Bone charcoal: Contains about 10% carbon. It is obtained from the bones of animals. It absorbs coloured impurities mixed with water and some other liquids, such as cane sugar syrup. Bone charcoal is extensively used in the manufacturing of sugar to produce the **white crystals**.

Sugar charcoal: The sugar charcoal is obtained from sugar, is a pure form of carbon. It is obtained destructive distillation of sugar.

The following chemical reaction takes place in this process:

$$\text{Sugar} \xrightarrow[\text{- Water}]{\text{Conc. } H_2SO_4} \text{Carbon.}$$

Sugar charcoal is used as reducing agent in metallurgy.

$ZnO + C \rightarrow Zn + CO$

Zinc oxide Zinc Carbon monoxide

Lampblack

Carbon black is obtained by burning mustard oil, turpentine oil, petroleum and its several products form lampblack, also known as **carbon black**. Carbon black contains about 99% carbon. It is the purest form of carbon.

Uses of Carbon Black

(*i*) In making black printing ink.

(*ii*) As a filler in tyres to increase their durability.

(*iii*) In shoe polish and kajal.

(ii) Coke

Coke is obtained from coal by heating it in the absence of air. This process is called destructive distillation of coal.

Uses of Coke

(*i*) As a fuel

(*ii*) For making gaseous fuels

(*iii*) For reducing iron ore to iron in blast furnace

(*iv*) For making electrodes

Coal

Coal is a mixture of compounds of carbon, hydrogen, oxygen and some free carbon.

Coal is formed at the result of high temperature and pressure on the logs of wood and the remains of animals which got buried under the earth due to earthquakes and volcanoes millions of years ago. The different varieties of coal are obtained as a result of slow chemical conversion of wood into coal called carbonization.

Type of Coal	*% of Carbon*
Peat	11%
Lignite (Soft Coal)	38%
Bituminous Coal	65%
Anthrasite Coal	96%

The Unique Properties of Carbon

Carbon is a non-metal in Group IV of the Periodic Table. It forms covalent compounds. The uniqueness of carbon lies in the versatility of that bonding.

- The carbon atoms can join to each-other to form long chains.
- The carbon atoms in a chain can be linked by single, double or triple covalent bonds.
- Carbon atoms can also arrange themselves in rings.

Compounds of Carbon and Hydrogen

Hydrocarbons are compounds that contain only the elements of hydrogen and carbon.

There are two basic groups of hydrocarbon:

— Aliphatics &

— Aromatics

In aliphatics hydrocarbons, the carbon atoms are usually linked in chains.

Methane is an example of an aliphatic hydrocarbon. Its chemical formula is **CH_4**.

Aromatic hydrocarbons are made up of rings. Toluene is an example of an aromatic hydrocarbon. Its chemical formula is $C_6H_5CH_3$.

Structure formula —

```
        H
        |
      H—C—H
        |
        C
      /   \\
   H—C     C—H
     ||    |
   H—C     C—H
      \\   //
        C
        |
        H
```

Toluene ($C_6H_5CH_3$)

Methane

Chemical formula: CH_4

Structure formula:

```
    H
    |
  H—C—H
    |
    H
```

The first and the simplest hydrocarbon is methane. Saturated hydrocarbon, such as methane, ethane, propane, butane etc., are known as **Alkane**.

General formula of Alkane: $C_n H_{2n+2}$.

n = 1, CH_4 — (Methane)
n = 2, C_2H_6 — (Ethane)
n = 3, C_3H_8 — (Propane)
n = 4, C_4H_{10} — (Butane)
n = 5, C_5H_{12} — (Pentane)
n = 6, C_6H_{14} — (Hexane)
n = 7, C_7H_{16} — (Heptane)

Fuels: A fuel is a substance which burns in air to produce heat energy. The burning of fuel is an exothermic reaction. Carbon and compounds of carbon are used as domestic fuels. The chief property of a fuel is its **Calorific value**—is the amount of heat produced by complete combustion of a unit mass or volume of fuel.

There are three types of fuels:

(*i*) **Solid fuels:** Wood, charcoal, coal and coke are common example of solid fuels.

(*ii*) **Liquid Fuels:** The common liquid fuels are kerosene oil, petrol and diesel. They are all hydrocarbon and are obtained by **fractional distillation of Petroleum**.

Heat Value of Liquid Fuels

Name of Fuel	*Heat value Kj/Kg*
Petrol	47000
Kerosene	45000
Diesel	45000
Spirit (ethanol)	28000

The petroleum is dark oily liquid with unpleasant odour. It is insoluble in water and floats on it. Petroleum is usually formed in sedimentary rocks.

In India, petroleum is found in the states of Assam, Gujarat, and also near Bombay— Bombay High in the Arabian sea. Recently petroleum has also been discovered in Godavari and Cauveri basins.

Petroleum is refined by **fractional distillation** producing the fractions gasoline, kerosene, diesel oil, fuel oil, lubricating oil and asphalt.

Ethanol is an alcohol also used as a fuel in Spirit lamps. Alcohol when mixed with petrol is called **power alcohol**. A mixture of dimethyl hydrazine and nitric acid is now used in rockets and missiles.

Gaseous Fuels: Gaseous fuels are used for domestic as well as industrial heating. Natural gas, LPG, producer gas, water gas and coal gas.

The calorific value of a fuel is measured in a **Calorimeter**.

- **Biogas** is the mixture of CH_4, H_2, CO and H_2S.
- **Natural gas** mainly contains methane (CH_4) and small proportion of ethane (C_2H_6).
- The main components of **producer gas** are carbon monoxide (CO), hydrogen (H_2), nitrogen (N_2) and carbon dioxide (CO_2).
- The main components of **coal gas** are hydrogen (H_2), methane (CH_4), carbon monoxide (CO).
- The main components of **water gas** are carbon monoxide (CO), Hydrogen (H_2), carbon dioxide (CO_2) and Nitrogen (N_2).
- The main components of LPG (Liquified Petroleum Gas) are ethane (C_2H_6), propane (C_3H_8) and butane (C_4H_{10}). It has no own odour, a very small quantity of strong smelling ethyl mercaptan (C_2H_5SH) is added to it.
- The fuels which are used in rockets are called **propellants.** They are:

— Liquid hydrogen — Synthetic rubber
— Liquid Ammonia — Alcohol
— Hydrazine — Kerosene oil
— Paraffin wax and — Cellulose.

Points to Remember

- Carbon forms the largest number of compounds and about 85% of known compounds contain carbon.
- Carbon has a unique property that it can join with other carbon atoms to form carbon—carbon bonds. This property is called **Catenation**.
- Coal is a mixture of compounds of carbon hydrogen, oxygen and some free carbon.
- Allotropy is the property by virtue of which an element exists in more than one form and each form has different physical properties but identical chemical properties.
- Carbon occurs naturally in the form of graphite and diamond. Graphite and diamond are allotropes of carbon.
- Charcoal, coke and carbon black are amorphous forms of carbon.
- Carbon on burning in an insufficient supply of oxygen, forms carbon monoxide which is a poisonous gas.
- Carbon dioxide is an important constituent of air (0.03%). Carbon dioxide reacts with metal oxide to form metal carbonates.
- Diamond is very hard solid at room temperature with a melting point of 3550°C and boiling point of 4827°C.
- Diamond has a rigid structure. In graphite the carbon atoms are arranged in layers. These layers are loosely joined to each other i.e. the layer of carbon atoms in graphite can slip over each other.
- Graphite is soft, slippery solid at room temperature with a melting point of 3697°C and boiling point 4827°C.

- **Fullerenes** are one of the allotropic forms of carbon. They may have 60, 70,.90, or 120 carbon atoms in their molecules. Fullerenes are the materials of the future.
- In the laboratory, carbon dioxide is prepared by the action of dilute HCl on lime stone or marble chips.
- Hydrocarbon are the organic compounds which are made up of only two elements—hydrogen and carbon.
- There are two basic groups of hydrocarbons—aliphatics and aromatics.
- Carbon dioxide is an important greenhouse gas. It is useful for us in many ways.
- Carbon dioxide turns freshly prepared lime water into milky.
- Methane (CH_4) is the simplest hydrocarbon in which each carbon atom is attached to four hydrogen atoms.
- Methane is found inside coal mine and in marshy lands.
- Methane is a very useful gas. It is used as a clean fuel for heating. Compressed Natural Gas (CNG) consists mainly of methane. It is an important domestic and industrial fuel.
- **Propane** and **Butane** can be liquified under pressure, hence they are supplied in cylinder (LPG — Liquid Petroleum Gas) for domestic use.
- Petroleum and coal are fossil fuels.
- Anthracite is the oldest form of fossil coal having 95% carbon.
- The main solid fuels are wood, charcoal and coal.
- The main liquid fuels are kerosene, petrol and diesel.
- The main gaseous fuels are natural gas, biogas and bottled gas (LPG).
- Biogas is produce by animal faces and contains mainly methane.
- Combustion is a process of oxidation.
- Very rapid combustion occurs in an explosion.
- Charcoal is obtained by heating wood in the absence of air.
- Coke is obtained by the destructive distillation of coal.
- Bituminous coal is a solid fossil fuel of plant origin.
- Distillation is the process of converting liquid into vapour and then changing again to liquid.
- C^{12} (Carbon - 12) is used as a standard for atomic weights.
- C^{14} shows radioactive characters.
- Carbon shows a covalency of four.
- Coke and Coaltar are products of destructive distillation of coal.
- Fractional distillation of Coaltar produces Asphalt (Pitch) and **Creosote** a wood preservative.
- Synthetic graphite is produced by heating anthracite to 2500°C in an electrical furnance in the absence of air.
- Dry ice (Solid Carbon dioxide) is often used to create **artificial rain** and used for **refrigeration**. On warming Dry ice vaporises directly into a gas. It passes from the solid state straight to gaseous state without going through liquid state, hence it is called **Dry ice**.

METALS AND NON-METALS

Some Important Facts

Elements are pure form of substances. Chemical elements can be classified into: • metals, • metalloids and • non-metal

On the basis of their physical and chemical properties.

Out of the 92 naturally occurring elements, about 70 are metals and 22 are non-metals. Some example of metals are — iron, copper, aluminium, zinc, sodium, gold, sulphur, tungsten, cadmium, nickel, uranium and mercury etc.

Examples of non-metals are — sulphur, iodine, bromine, chlorine, helium, oxygen, carbon, fluorine etc. Metalloids have some chemical and physical properties of metals and other properties of non-metals.

Example of metalloids are — silicon, germanium, arsenic which are also semiconductors.

Semiconductor: is an element that does not conduct electricity as efficiently as metal, but does conduct slightly better than a non-metal.

Ore: An ore is a naturally occuring mineral from which one or more metals can be profitably extracted.

Metallurgy: is the science of extracting metals from their ores and purifying them. Metallurgical processes may contain three main operations:

Concentration of Ore: It is the primary treatment of the ore in which impurities are removed. The ore gets concentrated in this process.

Reduction: The metal compound is reduced to get free metal.

Refining of metal: The metal is purified. After refining, some substances are added to give the desired properties to the final product.

Physical Properties of Metals

- Metals have a shiny appearance.
- Metals are generally hard.
- Metals are malleable.
- Metals are ductile.
- Metals are good conductors of heat.
- Metals are good conductors of electricity.

- Metals in general have high melting points.
- Metals are sonorous.
- Metals have high densities.

Classification of Metals

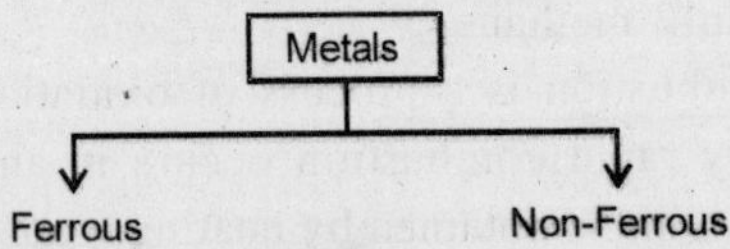

(*i*) Ferrous metals — Iron.

(*ii*) Non-ferrous metals are further divided into:

(*i*) Heavy metals — Pb, Hg, Cu, Ag, Au, Pt.

(*ii*) Light metals — Na, K, Mg, Al.

(*iii*) Noble metals — Au, Ag, Pt.

(*iv*) Rare metals — Li, Be, Sr.

(*v*) Radioactive metals — Ra, U, Th.

(*vi*) Protective metals — Cr, Ni, Zn, Sn.

Chemical Properties of Metals

(1) Reaction of metals with oxygen

Metals combine with oxygen to form basic oxides:

$2\,Mg + O_2 \rightarrow 2\,MgO$

$MgO + H_2O \rightarrow Mg\,(OH)_2$ (Basic oxide)

$Mg\,(OH)_2$ turns red litmus blue *i.e.*, $Mg(OH)_2$ is basic oxide.

$Zn + O_2 \rightarrow 2\,ZnO$

Zinc oxide (Basic oxide)

$4\,Na + O_2 \rightarrow 2\,Na_2O$ (burn with yellow light)

$2\,Cu + O_2 \rightarrow 2\,CuO$ (copper gets blackened but does not burn)

$S + O_2 \rightarrow SO_2$

Sulphur dioxide (Acidic oxide)

$SO_2 + H_2O \rightarrow H_2SO_3$ (Sulphurous acid)

(2) Reaction of metals with water

Metals react with water to form metal hdyroxide and evolve hydrogen gas:

$2\,Na + 2H_2O \rightarrow 2\,NaOH + H_2\uparrow$

This reaction takes places very vigorously so, sodium metal is stored in kerosene oil.

$Mg + H_2O \rightarrow MgO + H_2\uparrow$

$MgO + H_2O \rightarrow Mg(OH)_2$

Magnesium hydroxide

Magnesium oxide when dissolved in water forms a base.

$Zn + H_2O \rightarrow ZnO + H_2\uparrow$

$3\,Fe + 4\,H_2O \rightarrow Fe_3O_4 + 4\,H_2\uparrow$

Ag (silver), Au (Gold), Cu (Copper) do not react even with stream.

(3) Reaction of metals with dilute acids

Metals react with dilute acids to form metal salt and liberate hydrogen gas.

$Na + 2HCl \rightarrow 2NaCl + H_2\uparrow$

dilute Sodium chloride

$Mg + 2HCl \rightarrow MgCl_2 + H_2\uparrow$

dilute Magnesium chloride

$Zn + 2HCl \rightarrow ZnCl_2 + H_2\uparrow$

dilute Hydrogen gas

$Fe + 2HCl \rightarrow FeCl_2 + H_2\uparrow$

dilute Ferrous chloride

(4) Reaction of metals with Salt solutions

More reactive metal displaces a less reactive metal from its salt solution.

$Zn + CuSO_4 \rightarrow Cu + ZnSO_4$

Copper Sulphate Zinc Sulphate

Zinc displaces copper from copper sulphate solution.

$Fe + CuSO_4 \rightarrow Cu + FeSO_4$

Ferrous Sulphate

Iron metal displaces copper from copper sulphate solution.

$Mg + CuSO_4 \rightarrow Cu + MgSO_4$

Magnesium Sulphate

$2\,AgNO_3 + Cu \rightarrow Cu(NO_3)_2 + 2\,Ag$

(Silver nitrate) Copper nitrate Silver metal

Reactivity Series: The arrangement of metals in the order of decreasing reactivities is called reactivity series of metals. The most reactive metal is at the top and the least reactive metal is at the bottom of the series.

Reactivity Series of Metals

Metals		*Reactivity*
K	Potassium	Most reactive metal
Na	Sodium	
Ba	Barium	
Ca	Calcium	
Mg	Magnesium	
Al	Aluminium	
Zn	Zinc	
Cr	Chromium	
Fe	Iron	
Cd	Cadmium	
Co	Cobalt	
Ni	Nickel	
Sn	Tin	Least reactive metals
Pb	Lead	
H	Hydrogen —	[Hydrogen is a non metal although placed in the reactivity series of metal due to its nature of loses electron and form positive (H^+) ions.]
Cu	Copper	
Hg	Mercury	
Ag	Silver	
Au	Gold	
Pt	Platinum	Least reactive metal.

Physical Properties of Non-Metals

(i) Non-metals are brittle in nature, e.g. sulphur and phosphorus.

(ii) Non-metals are non-ductile.

(iii) Non-metals are bad conductor of heat and electricity except Graphite.

(iv) Non-metals are non-lustrous and cannot be polished.

(v) Non-metals are not strong and have low tensile strength.

(vi) Non-metals may be solid, liquid or gases at the room temperature.

Solid non-metals: Carbon, Sulphur, Phosphorus

Liquid non-metals: Bromine

Gaseous non-metals: hydrogen, nitrogen, oxygen, fluorine, chlorine, helium, argon, neon, xenon, krypton and radon.

(vii) Non-metals are soft *e.g.*, sulphur and phosphorus. Except Diamond.

(viii) Non-metals have low densities.

(ix) Non-metals are non-sonorous.

Chemical Properties of Non-Metals

(1) **Non-metals are electronegative in nature.**

(2) **Reaction of non-metals with oxygen.**

Non-metals form active or neutral oxides.

$C + O_2 \rightarrow CO_2$

$S + O_2 \rightarrow SO_2$

$4P + 5O_2 \rightarrow 2P_2O_5$

$2H_2 + O_2 \rightarrow 2H_2O$

$N_2 + 2O_2 \rightarrow 2NO_2$

$2C + O_2 \rightarrow 2CO$

(3) **Reaction of non-metals with water**

Non-metals do not react with water or steam to evolve hydrogen gas. It is due to the reason that non-metals cannot give electrons to hydrogen ions of water.

(4) Non-metals do not react with dilute acids.

(5) A more reactive non-metal displaces a less reactive non-metal from its salt solution.

$2NaBr(aq) + Cl_2(g) \rightarrow 2\ NaCl(aq) + Br_2(l)$

Bromine

Occurrence of Metals

Metals occur either in the native or free state or in the combined state. This is mainly due to the reason that different metals posses different chemical reactivities.

(i) **Free or nature state:** Metals which do not react with moisture, oxygen and CO_2 of air occur in the nature state. e.g. gold, platinum, copper, silver and mercury can occur in free as well as or combined states.

(ii) **Combined state:** These metals react with moisture, oxygen and CO_2 of the air and occur in the combined state in the form of compounds known as minerals.

Important Compounds of Metals (Ores)

Ore	*Formula*	*Ore of Metal*
1. Oxides Ore		
Zincite	ZnO	Zinc
Haematite	Fe_2O_3	Iron
Magnetite	Fe_3O_4	Iron
Corundum	Al_2O_3	Aluminium
Cuprite	Cu_2O	Copper
Calcia	CaO	Calcium
Cassiterite	SnO_2	Tin
Pyrolusite	MnO_2	Manganese
2. Hydrated oxides		
Bauxite	$Al_2O_3.\ 2H_2O$	Aluminium
Limonite	$2\ Fe_2O_3.\ 3H_2O$	Iron
3. Carbonates		
Calamine	$ZnCO_3$	Zinc
Siderite	$FeCO_3$	Iron
Malachite	$CuCO_3.\ Cu(OH)_2$	Copper
Marble or Lime Stone	$CaCO_3.$	Calcium
Azurite	$2\ CuCO_3.\ Cu(OH)_2$	Copper
Dolomite	$CaCO_3.\ MgCO_3$	Calcium, Magnesium
Magnesite	$MgCO_3$	Magnesium
Trona, Natron	$NaCO_3$	Sodium
4. Sulphides		
Zinc blends	ZnS	Zinc
Iron Pyrites	FeS_2	Iron
Copper Pyrites	$Cu_2S,\ Fe_2S$	Copper
Galena	PbS	Lead
Connabar	HgS	Mercury
Argentite	Ag_2S	Silver
Copper glance	Cu_2S	Copper
Greenockite	CdS	Cadmium
Pyragyrite	Ag_3SbS_3	Silver
5. Sulphates		
Gypsum	$CaSO_4.\ 2H_2O$	Calcium
Epsom salt	$MgSO_4.\ 7H_2O$	Magnesium
Anglesite	$PbSO_4$	Lead
Barytes	$BaSO_4$	Barium
Alunite	$K_2SO_4\ Al_2(SO_4)_3\ 4Al\ (OH)_3.$	Aluminium
Schonite	$K_2SO_4.\ MgSO_4.6H_2O$	Potassium

Ore	Formula	Ore of Metal
6. Chlorides/Fluorides		
Cryolite	$AlF_3 . 3NaF$	Aluminium
Common Salt or Rock Salt	$NaCl$	
Fluorspar	CaF_2	Calcium
Carnallite	$KCl\ MgCl_2 . 6H_2O$	Potassium and magnesium
Horn Silver	$AgCl$	Silver
Sylvine	KCl	Potassium
7. Nitrates		
Chili Saltpetre	$Na\ NO_3$	Sodium
Nitre	KNO_3	Potassium
Borax	$Na_2\ B_4O_7\ 10H_2O$	Boron.

Occurrence of Inert gas

Helium, Neon, Argon, Krypton, Radon and Xenon are found in the atmosphere. Helium is the second lightest gas after hydrogen and is found with natural gas deposits. All stars contain Helium. During the nuclear reaction hydrogen in stars are changed into helium and give enormous amount of energy. About 1 per cent air is Argon. Radon is found in associated radium bearing minerals, while Neon occurs in small amounts in the air. All of these inert gases are colourless and odourless.

Occurrence of the Halogens

The elements like fluorine, chlorine, bromine and iodine are commonly known as halogens. The halogens are so active, none of then is found free in Nature.

Element	Occurrence
Fluorine	The mineral fluorspar CaF_2 The mineral cryolite Na_3AlF_6
Chloride	In Sea water Rock Salt (NaCl), Salt beds of KCl, $MgCl_2$ and $CaCl_2$. In the human gastric juices as HCl (0.05%).
Bromine	As bromide ion (Br^-) in sea water (0.008%). As NaBr in salt beds.
Iodine	As iodine ion (I^-) in sea water (0.000004%). As sodium iodate $NaIO_3$

Fluorosis

If the concentration of fluorine increases to 3 parts per million in the drinking water than it leads to a diseases called **fluorosis** in which teeth became mottled with brown spots.

Noble Metals

The group is made up of the metals like gold, silver, platinum, iridium, rhodium, osmium, ruthenium and palladium. They are called noble because they are very unreactive.

Carats

The proportion of gold in an alloy is measured in carats. Pure gold is 24 carat gold. *e.g.* 20 carat gold contain 83.33 per cent of pure gold.

The weight of the diamond is measured in carats. One carat weight is 200 mg. This is not the same carat that is used in purity of gold.

Alloys

An alloy is generally a homogenous mixture of two or more metals prepared by mixing the components in the molten state. When one of the metals is mercury the alloy is called as **amalgam**.

Properties of Alloys

—Alloys are harder than the metals from which they are made.

—They are also more resistance to corrosion.

—Their melting point usually lower than those of the constituent metals.

Some important Alloys

Name of Alloys	Composition
Amalgam	Hg + any other metal
Alpax	Al + Si
Alnico	12% Al, 20% Ni and 5% Co
Bell metal	80% Cu, 20% Sn
Brass	Cu — 60 - 80% Zn — 40 - 20%
Bronze	Cu — 75% to 90% Sn — 25% to 10%
Constantan	60% Cu, 40% Ni
Common Solder	50% Pb, 50% Sn
Coinage Alloy	75% Cu and 25% Ni
Delto metal	Cu + Zn + Fe
Duralumin	Al — 94.4% Cu — 4% Mg — 1.6%
Dutch metal	Cu — 80% Zn — 20%
Fine Solder	Sn — 67% Pb — 33%
German Silver	Cu — 60% Zn — 25% Ni — 15%

Name of Alloys	Composition
Gun metal	Cu — 86%
	Sn — 10%
	Zn — 4%
Invar	Fe — 63%
	Ni — 36%
	C — 1%
Maganin	Cu — 84%
	Mn — 12%
	Ni — 4%
Magnelium	Al — 85% to 99%
	Mg — 15% to 1%
Monel metal	Cu — 30%
	Ni — 70%
Munz metal	Cu — 60%
	Zn — 40%
Newtons metal	Sn + Pb + Bi
Nichrome	Cr (15%) + Ni (60%) + Fe (25%)
Pewter	Sn — 75%
	Pb — 25%
Phosphor Bronze	Cu — 85%
	Sn — 13%
	P — 2%
Plumber's Solder	Pb — 70%
	Sn — 30%
Rolled Gold	Cu — 90%
	Al — 10%
Stainless Steel	Fe — 73%
	Cr — 18%
	Ni — 8%
	C — 1%

Corrosion and its prevention

Corrosion is the action of atmospheric oxygen, also of other gas, on metals to form a layer of oxides or other compounds. Dry corrosion involves atmospheric gases only. Wet corrosion involves water in addition to atmospheric gases. It results in loss of metals and the metal cannot be used further as it loses its strength.

The presence of air and water are necessary for corrosion to occur. Corrosion in case of iron is called **rusting**. Rusting is a slow oxidation process. The formula of rust is Fe_2O_3.

$2Fe(OH)_2$. (hydrated ferric oxide).

$4Fe + 3O_2 + 3H_2O \rightarrow Fe_2O_3 + 2\,Fe(OH)_3$

Iron (Moist air) (Rust)

Aluminium is more reactive than iron and starts corroding immediately as it comes in contact with moist air.

$4Al + 3O_2 \rightarrow 2Al_2O_3$

Aluminium oxide (protective coating)

A thin layer of aluminium oxide is deposited on aluminium articles by passing electric current. This method is called *anodising* and it protects aluminium from corrosion.

- Copper domes deposit a green coating on their surfaces when copper combines with water and carbon dioxide and makes coating of basic copper carbonate.

  $2Cu + CO_2 + H_2O + O_2 \rightarrow CuCO_3.\ Cu(OH)_2$

  green mass of basic copper carbonate.
- Silver farnishes because it readily combines with hydrogen sulphide present in air. It forms a black coating of silver sulphide.

  $2Ag + H_2S \rightarrow Ag_2S + H_2\uparrow$

  Silver sulphide

Titanium metal is highly resistant to corrosion.

Method of Preventing Corrosion

- By using oil and grease.
- By using paints.
- **Galvanisation:** It is a process of coating iron with zinc to prevent rusting. Zinc forms a protective layer of zinc oxide on exposure to air. A thin layer of zinc on the surface of iron protects iron from rusting. This process is called **galvanisation.**
- **Electroplating:** Iron and steel are protected from corrosion by coating them with a layer of tin or chromium metals which are resistant to corrosion.

Alloying: Some metals when alloyed with other metals become more resistant to corrosion. e.g. Alloy of Iron with chromium and nickel forms stainless steel, which is resistant to corrosion and does not rust at all.

Points to Remember

- Elements can be classified into metals and non-metals on the basis of their physical and chemical properties.
- Metals are generally hard, malleable ductile, lustrous and sonorous.
- Metals are good conductors of heat and electricity.
- Some metals as well as non-metals occur in a free state.
- Metals on combustion produce basic oxides.
- Non-metals on combustion produce acidic oxides.
- Non-metals exhibit a dull lustre. They are poor conductors of heat and electricity and are brittle.
- A semiconductor is an element that does not conduct electricity as efficiently as metal, but does conduct slightly better than a non-metal.
- Some metals react with acids and replace the hydrogen gas from the acids. Gold, copper and silver are not affected by dilute acids like HCl.
- Metals occur either in the native or free state or in the combined state. This is mainly due to the reason that different metals posses different chemical reactivities.

- The noble metals are a group of metallic elements. The group is made up of the metal like gold, silver, platinum, iridium, rhodium, osmium, ruthenium and palladium.
- The weight of the diamond is measured in carats. One carat weight is 200 mg.
- An alloy is generally a homogenous mixture of two or more metals prepared by mixing the components in the molten state.
- Eating away of metals by oxygen, water, acids or other chemicals is called corrosion.
- Corrosion can be prevented by oiling, painting, galvanizing, electroplating and anodizing.
- Some active metals like sodium react with water.
- Metals like aluminium, magnesium react with acids.
- Non-metals like sulphur reacts with concentrated acids.
- A metal higher in the activity series replaces metals that are lower in the activity series.
- Alloys are the homogenous mixtures of metals and non-metals.
- Rocks contain minerals.
- The average thickness of earth's crust is about 35 Km.
- The most common sedimentary rock is sandstone.
- Fossils are mostly formed in sedimentary rocks.
- Minerals show colour due to the presence of impurities.
- The red colour of ruby is due to the presence of chromium oxide.
- German Scientist Mohs devised the scale of hardness.
- Talc is softest mineral with hardness of 1, and diamond is hardest mineral with hardness of 10.
- Specific gravity of gold is 19.3 and of copper is 8.9.
- Ruby is also known as **red corrundum**.
- Titanium is said to be metal of future.
- Uraninite (pitch blende) is the ore of Uranium and found in Jaduguda (Jharkhand).
- Iron is mainly extracted from haematite.
- Copper is mainly extracted from copper pyrite.
- All metals are solid except mercury, which is **liquid**.
- Metals have mostly high melting point.
- Iodine is denser than many metals.
- Sodium is very soft and can be cut by a knife.
- Copper is non-magnetic while iron is magnetic.
- Most metals react with acids to form salts and hydrogen.
- Iron, magnesium and zinc are more reactive than copper.
- Air and water are necessary for corrosion to take place.

CHEMICAL REACTIONS AND EQUATIONS

Some Important Facts

Chemical Reaction is a process in which some known substances are changed into new substance or new substances. The starting substances are called **reactants**. The new substances formed are called products.

e.g.

Hydrogen (reactant) + Oxygen (reactant) → Water (product)

Zinc (reactant) + sulphuric acid (reactant) → Zinc sulphate (product) + Hydrogen (product)

Chemical Equation: A shorthand notation of describing an actual chemical reaction in terms of the symbols and formula along with the number of atoms and molecules of the reactant and products is called **chemical equation.**

e.g., $CH_4(g) + 2O_2(g) \rightarrow CO_2(g) + 2H_2O\ (l)$ + Heat

Balanced chemical equation: A chemical equation is said to be balanced when the number of atoms of each element on the reactant side is equal to the number of atoms of corresponding element on the product side,

e.g.,

$$CH_4(g) + 2O_2(g) \rightarrow CO_2(g) + 2H_2O(l) + \text{Heat}$$

Reactant Side		*Product Side*	
Element	***No. of atoms***	***Element***	***No. of atoms***
C	1	C	1
H	4	H	4
O	4	O	4

It is clear that the number of each element on the reactant side is equal to the number of atoms of the corresponding element on the product side. Therefore the chemical equation is balanced.

Rules to write a balanced chemical equation for a reaction

- It should represent an actual chemical change.
- The correct symbols and formula of reactants are written on left hand side. If there are two or more reactants then plus (+) sign is written between them.
- An arrow directing toward right (→) is written after the formulae of reactants.
- The number of atoms of different elements on the two sides of the equation must be equal.
- All the substances concerned could be expressed as molecules.

Information conveyed by chemical equation

- The formulae, symbol, names and physical states of the reactants and products.
- The relative number of atoms and molecules of the reactants that take part in the reaction.
- The relative number of atoms and molecules of the products formed in the reaction.
- The ratio of the moles of the reactants and products.
- The ratio of the masses of the reactants and product.
- The ratio of the volumes of the gaseous reactants and products.
- The energy change in the reaction.

Limitations of a chemical equations

It gives us no information about the followings:

- The physical state of the reactants
- The concentration of the reactants
- The time taken for the reaction to complete
- The rate at which the reaction proceeds
- The conditions necessary to start and carry on the reaction. What is the temperature needed to start and continue the reaction?
- Is the reaction exothermic or endothermic?

Some Chemical reactions and balanced chemical equations

(*i*) Phosphorous burns in oxygen to give phosphorus pentoxide.

$P_4(s) + 5O_2(g) \rightarrow 2P_2O_5$
Phosphorus pentoxide

(*ii*) Barium chloride reacts with zinc sulphate to give zinc chloride and barium sulphate.

$BaCl_2(aq) + ZnSO_4(aq) \rightarrow BaSO_4(s) + ZnCl_2(aq)$

(*iii*) Zinc metal reacts with hydrochloric acid to give hydrogen gas and an aqueous solution of zinc chloride:

$Zn(s) + 2HCl(aq) \rightarrow H_2(g) + ZnCl_2(aq)$
Zinc, Hydrochloric acid, Hydrogen, Zinc chloride

(*iv*) Solid mercury (II) oxide is heated to give liquid mercury and oxygen gas.

$2HgO(s) \rightarrow 2Hg(l) + O_2(g)$

(*v*) Carbon disulphide burns in air to give carbon dioxide and sulphur dioxide

$CS_2(l) + 3O_2(g) \rightarrow CO_2(g) + 2SO_2(g)$

(*vi*) Hydrogen gas combines with nitrogen gas to give ammonia gas.

$3H_2(g) + N_2(g) \rightarrow 2NH_3(g)$
Ammonia

(*vii*) Sodium metal reacts with water to give sodium hydroxide and hydrogen gas.

$2Na(s) + 2H_2O(l) \rightarrow 2NaOH(aq) + H_2(g)$

(*viii*) Hydrogen sulphide gas burns in air to give water and sulphur dioxide

$2H_2S(g) + 3O_2(g) \rightarrow 2H_2O(l) + 2SO_2(g)$

(*ix*) Phosphorus burns in chlorine to give phosphorus pentachloride.

$P_4(s) + 10Cl_2(g) \rightarrow 4PCl_5(g)$

(*x*) Aluminium metal replaces iron from oxide (Fe_2O_3) giving aluminium hydroxide and iron.

$Fe_2O_3 + 2Al \rightarrow Al_2O_3 + 2Fe$

(*xi*) Aqueous solutions of sulphuric acid and sodium hydroxide react to give sodium sulphate and water.

$H_2SO_4 (aq) + 2NaOH(aq) \rightarrow Na_2SO_4(aq) + H_2O$

Types of Chemical Equations

Based on the change the chemical reactions can be categorised as shown in the following chart:

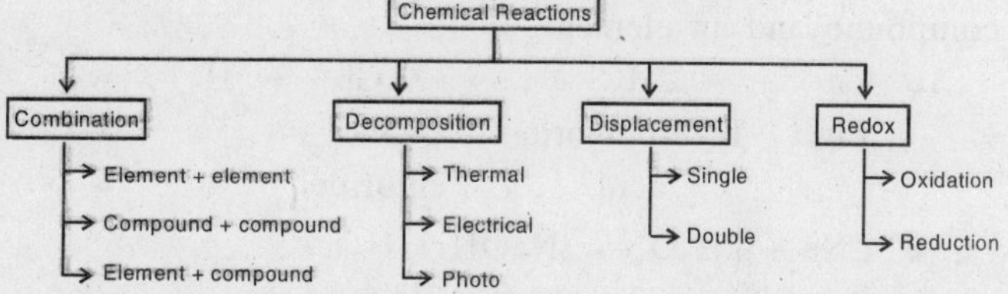

Combination Reactions

Combination reactions are those reactions in which two types of pure substances react and form a new single substances.

$$A + B \rightarrow AB.$$

Types of combination reactions

There are three types of combination reactions:

(*i*) Both A and B are two elements.
(*ii*) Both A and B are two compounds.
(*iii*) A is an element and B is a compound.

(I) Combination reaction between two elements

When hydrogen and oxygen combine water is formed.

$$2H_2(g) + O_2(g) \rightarrow 2H_2O(l)$$

Mercury and oxygen together form oxide of mercury.

$2Hg + O_2 \rightarrow 2HgO$
Mercury oxide

When magnesium is burnt it combines directly with the oxygen of the air to form magnesium oxide.

$$2Mg(s) + O_2(g) \rightarrow 2MgO(s)$$

(II) Combination reaction between two Compounds

The reaction between two compounds to form a third compound is also combination reaction.

When ammonia gas and hydrogen chloride gas combine to form solid ammonium chloride is an example of combination reaction between two compounds.

$$NH_3(g) + HCl(g) \rightarrow NH_4Cl(s).$$

Some other examples of combination reaction between two compounds as below:

$CaCO_3(s) + 2HCl \rightarrow CaCl_2 + H_2O + CO_2\uparrow$
Calcium chloride

$MgO(s) + H_2O(l) \rightarrow Mg(OH_2)$
Magnesium hydroxide

$CO_2(g) + H_2O(l) \rightarrow H_2CO_3$
Carbonic acid

(III) Combination reactions between a Compound and an element

Burning of carbon monoxide gas (CO) in oxygen gas (O_2) to form carbon dioxide gas (CO_2) is an example of combination reaction between a compound (CO) and an element (O_2).

$$2CO(g) + O_2(g) \rightarrow 2CO_2(g)$$

Other examples of combination reactions between a compound and an element

- $Zn + 2HCl \rightarrow ZnCl_2 + H_2\uparrow$
  Zinc, Hydrochloric acid, Zinc chloride
- $2Na + 2H_2O \rightarrow 2NaOH + H_2\uparrow$
- $Fe + H_2SO_4 \rightarrow FeSO_4 + H_2\uparrow$
- $Zn + 2NaOH \rightarrow Na_2ZNO_2 + H_2\uparrow$

Decomposition Reactions

Such reactions where two or more products are obtained from a single reactant are decomposition reactions.

e.g. In presence of manganese dioxide, hydrogen peroxide decomposes into water and oxygen

$2H_2O_2 \rightarrow 2H_2O + O_2$

$NH_4\,NO_3(s) \rightarrow N_2O(g) + 2H_2O$
Ammonium nitrate, Nitrous oxide, Water

$CaCO_3 \xrightarrow{heat} CaO + CO_2\uparrow$
Calcium carbonate, Calcium oxide, Carbon dioxide

Decomposition reactions are classified as follows:

— Thermal decomposition (caused by heat)
— Electric decomposition (caused by electricity)
— Photo decomposition (caused by light)

Examples of thermal decompositions

Mercury (II) oxide decomposes on heating to form mercury and oxygen.

$$2HgO(s) \xrightarrow{heat} 2Hg(l) + O_2(g)$$

- When potassium chlorate is heated it gives potassium chloride and oxygen gas.

$$2KClO_3 \xrightarrow{Heat} 2KCl(s) + 3O_2(g)$$

- $CaCO_3 \xrightarrow{Heat} CaO(s) + CO_2(g)$
  Calcium carbonate, Calcium oxide, Carbon oxide

Electric decomposition reaction

On passing electricity through acidified water it decomposed into hydrogen and oxygen.

$2H_2O \xrightarrow[Current]{Electric} 2H_2(g) + O_2(g)$
Water, Hydrogen, Oxygen

Photo decomposition reaction

In the presence of sunlight hypochlorous acid decomposes to give back oxygen and hydrochloric acid.

$2HClO(aq) \xrightarrow{Sunlight} 2HCl(aq) + O_2(g)$
Hypochlorous acid, Hydrochloric acid, Oxygen

Displacement Reactions

In this reaction one substance has replaced the other substance in a compound is called displacement reactions.

Displacement reactions are of two types:

(*i*) Single displacement reactions
(*ii*) Double displacement reactions

Single Displacement Reactions: When an iron nail is dipped in a copper sulphate solution, it is coated with copper.

$$Fe + CuSO_4 \rightarrow FeSO_4 + Cu.$$

Fe is more reactive metal than Cu.

When a piece of zinc metal is immersed in mercury II nitrate solution it coated with mercury.

$$Zn + Hg(NO_3)_2 \rightarrow Zn(NO_3)_2 + Hg$$

When zinc metal is dipped in a solution of copper sulphate, zinc reduces copper from copper sulphate.

$$Zn + CuSO_4 \rightarrow ZnSO_4 + Cu$$

When zinc reacts with sulphuric acid, hydrogen gas is liberated and zinc sulphate is formed.

$Zn(s) + H_2SO_4(aq) \rightarrow ZnSO_4 + H_2(g)$
Zinc sulphate

Zn is more reactive than hydrogen.

Double Displacement Reactions

Double displacement reactions are those reactions in which two compounds exchange ions to form two new compounds.

$$AB + CD \rightarrow AD + CB.$$

Here, A and C are cations of the two compounds, while B and D are their anions. The new compounds are AD and CB.

Types of double displacement reactions

— formation of precipitate
— evolution of gas
— change of colour

Double Displacement reaction with the formation of precipitate

When a solution of sodium chloride is mixed with a solution of silver nitrate a white precipitate of silver chloride is formed.

$NaCl$	+	$AgNO_3$	→	$AgCl$	+	$NaNO_3$
Sodium Chloride		Silver Nitrate		Silver chloride		Sodium Nitrate

$BaCl_2(aq)$	+	$Na_2SO_4(aq)$	→	$BaSO_4$	+	$2NaCl$
Barium Chloride		Sodium Sulphate		Barium Sulphate		

Double displacement with the evolution of gas

When Iron sulphide reacts with sulphuric acid the double displacement reaction takes place resulting into the formation of hydrogen sulphide gas and iron sulphate solution.

FeS	+	H_2SO_4	→	$FeSO_4$	+	$H_2S(g)$
Iron sulphide		Sulphuric acid		Iron sulphate		Hydrogen sulphide

Double displacement with the change of Colour

When hydrogen sulphide gas is passed through the blue solution of copper sulphate, a black precipitate of copper sulphide is formed.

$CuSO_4$	+	$H_2S(g)$	→	CuS	+	H_2SO_4
Copper sulphate (Blue)		Hydrogen sulphide		Copper sulphide (Black)		

Double decomposition and neutralization reaction

A reaction between an acid and a base is called neutralization reaction salt and water are formed and heat is liberated.

HCl	+	$NaOH$	→	$NaCl$	+	H_2O + Heat
Hydrochloric acid		Sodium hydroxide		Sodium chloride		

Oxidation and Reduction Reactions

Oxidation-reduction reactions are called **redox reactions.** In redox reaction one substance is reduced while other is oxidised.

Oxidation Reaction

(*i*) Oxidation is a process in which oxygen combines with a substance, e.g.,

$4Na$	+	O_2	→	$2Na_2O$
Sodium		Oxygen		Sodium Oxide
Mg	+	O_2	→	$2MgO$
Magnesium		Oxygen		Magnesium oxide
S	+	O_2	→	SO_2
Sulphur		Oxygen		Sulphur dioxide
C	+	O_2	→	CO_2
Carbon		Oxygen		Carbon dioxide

In these reactions Na, Mg, S and C are oxidised.

(*ii*) Oxidation is a process in which hydrogen is removed, e.g.,

$4\ HCl + MnO_2 \rightarrow MnCl_2 + 2H_2O + Cl_2$

$H_2S + Cl_2 \rightarrow 2HCl + S$

$8\ HCl + Pb_3O_4 \rightarrow 3\ PbCl_2 + 4H_2O + Cl_2$

(*iii*) Oxidation is the process of loss of electrons. It is represented by

Atom → Cations + Electrons

$A \rightarrow A^{n+} + ne^-$

Atom A loses n electrons to become a positively charged ion A^{n+}. The positively charged ion is called **cation.**

Reduction Reaction

(*i*) Reduction is a process of combination of hydrogen.

$2H_2(g) + O_2(g) \rightarrow 2H_2O(l)$

Reduction of oxygen.

$H_2(g) + Cl_2(g) \rightarrow 2HCl$ Hydrogen chloride

Reduction of chlorine

(*ii*) Reduction is a process of removal of oxygen.

$CuO(s) + H_2(g) \rightarrow Cu(s) + H_2O(l)$

$CuO(s) + CO(g) \rightarrow Cu(s) + CO_2(g)$

In this reaction CuO reduces to Cu.

(*iii*) The gain of electrons by an atom or ion is called reduction. It is represented as

$B + ne^- \rightarrow B^{n-}$

The atom B gain n electrons to become negatively charged ion B^{n-}. The negatively charged ion is called **anion**.

Redox Reaction: Oxidation and reduction occur simultaneously, is called redox reaction. Only oxidation or only reduction is called half reaction.

Thus

$A \rightarrow A^{n+} + ne^-$ oxidation

$B + ne^- \rightarrow B^{n-}$ Reduction on Adding

$A + B \rightarrow A^{n+} + B^{n-} \rightarrow AB$ Redox

e.g. gain of electron is reduction

$Na + Cl \rightarrow \overset{+\ -}{NaCl} \rightarrow NaCl$

2,8,1 2,8,7 2,8 2,8,8

loss of electron is oxidation

$Zn + CuSO_4 \rightarrow ZnSO_4 + Cu$

is example of redox reaction

$Zn + Zn^{2+} + 2e^-$ loss of electron is oxidation

$Cu^{2+} + 2e^- \rightarrow Cu$ gain of electron is reduction

gain of $2e^-$ electron

$Zn + Cu^{2+} \rightarrow Zn^{2+} + Cu$

loss of $2e^-$ (electron)

The redox reaction is called displacement reaction also.

Oxidising agent: The atom which oxidises another atom or ion is called **oxidising agent**. An oxidising agent itself is reduced.

$Na + \frac{1}{2}\ Cl_2 \rightarrow Na^+\ Cl^-$

Here Cl_2 is an oxidising agent. It oxidies Na into Na^+ and Cl_2 is reduced to Cl^-.

Reducing agent: Reducing agent is that which oxidises itself and reduces others. *e.g.* Na reduces Cl_2 but Na itself is oxidised. So Na is reducing agent.

The oxidation number is defined as the charge which an atom appears to have when electrons are counted in ion, molecules or compounds.

For counting the oxidation number some points are more useful to you.

These are:

(*i*) In the elementary or uncombined state, the atoms having **zero** oxidation number.

(*ii*) In compounds the oxidation number of fluorine is always –1.

(*iii*) In compounds, the group IA elements having oxidation number +1 and the group IIA element having an oxidation number +2.

(*iv*) Oxidation number of hydrogen in compounds is generally +1 except in metalic hydrides wherein its oxidation number is –1.

(*v*) In compounds, the oxidation number of oxygen is generally –2 except in F_2O wherein oxidation number of fluorine is –1 and that of oxygen is +2.

(*vi*) In neutral molecules, the sum of the oxidation numbers of all the atoms is zero.

(*vii*) The sum of the oxidation numbers of all the atoms is equal to the net charge on the ion.

e.g., What is the oxidation number of S in

(*a*) H_2SO_4 (*b*) H_2S

(*c*) $H_2S_2O_7$ (*d*) $Na_2S_2O_3$.

Sol.: Let oxidation number of S be x.

(*a*) $2 \times (+1) + x + 4 \times (-2) = 0 \Rightarrow x = +6$

(*b*) Let oxidation number of S be x

$$2 \times (+1) + x = 0$$

$$x = -2$$

Oxidation of S = –2.

(*c*) Let oxidation number of S be x

$$2 \times (+1) + 2x + 7 \times (-2) = 0$$

$$2 + 2x - 14 = 0$$

$$2x = +12$$

$$x = +6.$$

Oxidation number of S = +6.

(*d*) Let oxidation number of S be x

$$2 \times (+1) + 2x + 3(-2) = 0$$

$$2 + 2x - 6 = 0$$

$$2x = 4$$

$$x = 2$$

Oxidation number of S in $Na_2S_2O_3$ = +2.

Oxidation and Reduction in Terms of Oxidation Numbers

Oxidation refers to any chemical change involving **increase** in oxidation number where as the **reduction** refers to any chemical change involving **decrease** in oxidation number, e.g.,

$$2\overset{0}{H_2} + \overset{0}{O_2} \rightarrow 2\overset{+4}{H_2}\overset{-4}{O}$$

Here, oxidation number of hydrogen changes from zero to +1 i.e. oxidation of hydrogen.

Oxidation number of oxygen changes from zero to –2 i.e. reduction of oxygen.

Points to Remember

- Atoms are the building blocks of matter.
- Atom is composed of subatomic particles **electron, proton** and **neutron**.
- Mass of the entire atom is concentrated in its centre known as **nucleus**.
- Loss or gains of electron from or to an atom leads to the formation of ions.
- Atomic number is the characteristic property of an element. It gives the number of protons, which is also equal to the number of electrons in the neutral atom. (Z = P).
- The number of protons together with the number of neutrons give us the mass number of that atom. *i.e.* mass number, A = $n + p$.
- Atoms of an element having the same atomic number but different mass number are called isotopes.
- Each element has a specific combining capacity is called its **valence**.
- Formula of a compound can be obtained using the valence of combining elements.
- Chemical equation is a symbolic representation of a chemical reaction.
- Removal of unwanted components leads to the purification of the substances.
- Purity of a given sample of a substances can be tested by determining its melting point or boiling point or both.
- Chemical reactions are characterised by the evolution of a gas, change of colour, formation of precipitate, change of energy or change of state.
- Chemical reactions are different types. They can be classified as .... combination, decomposition, displacement, neutralisation and redox reactions.
- Matter exists in three states .... solid, liquid and gas.
- All matter is made up of tiny particles. These tiny particles are known as atoms or molecules.
- In solid, state, atoms or molecules are fixed in their positions.
- The liquid state is not rigid because atoms or molecules can move around.
- In gaseous state, atoms or molecules can move freely and randomly.
- Solid substances are hard because the atoms or molecules in them are held very close to one another

by strong attractive forces. That is why solids have definite shape and volume.

- Liquids take the shape of the container in which they are kept. The liquids can be compressed slightly because molecules in them are held together less firmly.
- In gases, the force of attraction between molecules is negligible as compared to solids or even liquids. They therefore assume the shape and even volume of the container and can be compressed easily.
- Irregular or haphazard movement of solid particles in a gas or a liquid is called **Brownian movement**.
- The process by which different substances mix also a result of the haphazard or random motions of their particles is called **diffusion**.
- The substances, which contain only one kind of atoms having same atomic number is called **element**.
- A compound is a substance composed of two or more elements that are chemically combined in definite proportions.
- A mixture could contain several elements or compounds or both in any proportions.
- The components of a mixture can be separated easily by applying appropriate physical methods.
- The components of a compound can be separated only by applying chemical methods.
- Symbols and groups of symbol are used to represent elements and compounds.
- Symbol of a chemical element denotes one atom of that element.
- Molecules of mono atomic elements contain only one atom.
- Molecules of diatomic elements contain two atoms.
- Some elements exist in the form of aggregates of their atoms.
- The chemical formula of a substance represents its one molecule.
- In a molecule of a compound, the atoms are present in whole numbers.
- A balanced chemical equation shows the fact that atoms are neither created nor destroyed during a chemical reaction.
- A chemical equation provides us the following information:
  — Substances that take part in the chemical reaction and those that are produced.
  — Number of atoms or molecules of different reactants taking part in a chemical reaction and the number of atoms or molecules of the products formed.
- Major component of the solution is called **Solvent** while its other components are called **Solute**.
- The concentration of a solution is expressed as mass per cent, mole per cent molarity or normality.
- Mass per cent of a component is equal to its mass in 100 mass units of solution.
- **Suspension** is a heterogeneous mixture in which the suspended particles are visible.
- **Atomic mass unit (amu)**: $\frac{1}{12}$th of mass of an atom of ^{12}C is called atomic mass unit. Its value is 1.6603×10^{-24} grams.
- **Relative atomic mass:** The mass of an atom of a substances relative to $\frac{1}{12}$th of the mass of a ^{12}C atom whose atomic mass is exactly 12 amu.

  Mole: Collection of 6.023×10^{23} particles of definite formula/symbol is called **mole**. It is the unit to represent the amount of a substance.

  Molar mass: The mass of 6.023×10^{23} particles of a substance is called molar mass.

  Empirical formula: The simplest ratio of the atoms of the constituent elements of a compound is called its empirical formula.

  Molecular formula: Actual number of all types of atoms of the constituent elements of a molecule is called its molecular formula.

  Molecular formula = (Empirical formula) × n
- Characteristics of a chemical reaction are:
  — Evolution of gas
  — Change of colour
  — Formation of precipitate
  — Energy change
  — Change of state
- The process of converting a liquid into its vapours by heating and then condensing the vapours back into original liquid is called **distillation**.
- There are two methods which can be used to check the purity of a substance. These methods are:
  — Chromatography method
  — Measuring melting and boiling point of a substance.
- Temperature does not rise while a substance is melting or boiling.
- The fixed temperature at which solid starts melting is called its **melting point**.
- The constant temperature at which the pressure of the vapours leaving the surface of the liquid equals the atmospheric pressure is called boiling point of the liquid.
- Some materials may change directly form a solid to a gas. This is called sublimation.
- Condensation is the reverse of evaporation.
- A reaction in which an atom loses electrons is called an **oxidation reaction**.
- A reaction in which an atom gains one or more electrons is called **reduction reaction**.
- The reactions in which both oxidation and reduction takes place together are called as **redox reactions**.

- Oxidizing agent is that which reduces itself and oxidizes others while reducing agent oxidises itself and reduces others.
- John Dalton's invented symbols for the atoms of the elements. He also made first table of atomic weights.
- J.J. Thomson discovered negatively charged particles *i.e.,* electrons which is a fundamental part of an atom.
- Goldstein discovered positively charged rays, known as **Canal rays** which later, known as **protons**.
- **Chadwick** discovered the presence of neutral particles inside the atoms and called them as **neutrons**.
- Ernest Rutherford preformed gold foil experiment for the discovery of **nucleus**.
- An ion is a particle with an electric charge on it. Metals form positive ions and non-metals form negative ions.
- Atoms of an element that have the same numbers of protons but different numbers of neutrons are called **isotopes**.
- A group of atoms may also have a valency. Such a group is called a **ralical**.
- Chemical reactions are described as interactions between particles (Atoms molecules or ions) which involved the breaking and making of chemical bonds.

Acids, Bases and Salts

Acid: According to Arrhenius's theory an acid was a compound which dissolved in water to give hydrogen ions (H^+).

All Acids contain Hydrogen.

The oxides of non-metals, when dissolved in water form acids, *e.g.,*

$CO_2 + H_2O \rightarrow H_2CO_3$
Carbon dioxide — Carbonic acid

$SO_2 + H_2O \rightarrow H_2SO_3$
Sulphur dioxide — Sulphurous acid

The formation of acids in these reactions can be tested by dipping **blue** litmus paper in these solutions. It turns **red**.

Uses of Acids

— Hydrochloric acid (HCl) is used in cleaning kitchen sink and sanitarywares.

— Nitric acid (HNO_3) is used by goldsmiths for cleaning gold and silver ornaments.

— Sulphuric acid (H_2SO_4) is used in batteries for cars, buses, trucks, tractors and inverters. These acids are called mineral acids.

Some acids are found in animals and plants are called organic acids.

Example of organic acids are:

Lactic acid	(in soured milk)
Citric acid	(in citrus fruits)
Tartaric acid	(Tamarind)
Acetic acid	(Vinegar)
Formic acid	(Ants)
Ascorbic acid	(Vitamin C).

The Chemical formulas of some important Acids

Name of the Acid	*Chemical Formula*
Hydrochloric acid	HCl
Nitric acid	HNO_3
Sulphuric acid	H_2SO_4
Carbonic acid	H_2CO_3
Acetic acid	CH_3COOH
Formic acid	HCOOH
Sulphurous acid	H_2SO_3
Nitrous acid	HNO_2
Phosphoric acid	H_2PO_4
Boric acid	H_3BO_3
Hydrobromic acid	HBr
Hydroiodic acid	HI
Chloric acid	$HClO_3$
Tetraboric acid	$H_2B_4O_7$
Hydrocyanic acid	HCN
Oxalic acid	$H_2C_2O_4$
Chromic acid	H_2CrO_4
Dichromic acid	$H_2Cr_2O_7$
Thiosulfuric acid	$H_2S_2O_3$
Pyro-sulphuric acid	$H_2S_2O_7$
Per sulphuric	$H_2S_2O_8$

Base: A base is a compound which dissolved in water to give hydroxide ions (OH^-).

Some metal oxides on reacting with water is formed hydroxides of that metal oxide.

Some metal oxides on reacting with water to form hydroxides.

MgO	+ H_2O →		$Mg(OH)_2$
Magnesium oxide	water		Magnesium hydroxide
Na_2O	+ H_2O →		2 NaOH
Sodium oxide	water		Sodium hydroxide
K_2O	+ H_2O →		2KOH
Potassium oxide	water		Potassium hydroxide
CaO	+ H_2O →		$Ca(OH)_2$
Calcium oxide	water		Calcium hydroxide

The hydroxides of metals which dissolve in water are known as **alkalies**. Thus all soluble hydroxides are **alkalies**.

Neutralisation reactions: Acid and base react with one another neutralising each other's characteristic properties

Salt and water are formed as products in the neutralisation reactions. e.g.,

HCl	+	NaOH	→	NaCl	+	H_2O
Hydrochloric acid		Sodium hydroxide		Sodium chloride (Salt)		
HNO_3	+	NaOH	→	$NaNO_3$	+	H_2O
Nitric acid		Sodium hydroxide		Sodium nitrate (Salt)		
H_2SO_4	+	2NaOH	→	Na_2SO_4	+	H_2O
Sulphuric acid		Sodium hydroxide		Sodium sulphate (Salt)		

Indicators of Testing Acids and Bases

Indications	*Acid*	*Base*
Litmus paper	turns blue to red	turns red to blue
Methyl orange	pinkish red	yellow
Phenolphthalein	Colourless	Pink

Salts: A salt is a compound made from an acid when a metal takes the place of the hydrogen in the acid. e.g.,

HCl	+	NaOH	→	NaCl	+	H_2O
Hydrochloric acid		Sodium hydroxide		Sodium chloride (Salt)		
HNO_3	+	NH_4OH	→	NH_4NO_3	+	H_2O
		Ammonium hydroxide		Ammonium nitrate		
H_2SO_4	+	$Ca(OH)_2$	→	$CaSO_4$	+	$2H_2O$
Sulphuric acid		Calcium hydroxide		Calcium Sulphate		

In these reactions, the hydrogen atom of the acid has been replaced by a sodium/calcium atom or a group of atoms (NH_4).

Some Salts in Common Use

Name of Salt	*Chemical Formula*	*Uses*
Calcium carbonate (marble, chalk, lime)	$CaCO_3$	Building materials, lime, cement, iron.
Calcium Sulphate gypsum, plaster of Paris	$CaSO_4$	Wall plaster Statue, Surgery
Sodium Carbonate Washing soda	Na_2CO_3	Water softening making glass
Magnesium Sulphate' (epsom salt)	$MgSO_4$	Health salts laxative
Copper Sulphate (Blue Vitriol)	$CuSO_4$	Fungicides
Calcium phosphate	$Ca_3(PO_4)_2$	Fertilizers
Ammonium chloride	NH_4Cl	Fertilizer, dry cell
Ammonium nitrate	NH_4NO_3	Fertilizers explosives
Ammonium sulphate	$(NH_4)_2SO_4$	Fertilizers

Some Hydrated Salts

Name of Hydrated Salt	*Chemical Formula*	*Colour*
Copper Sulphate	$CuSO_4 . 5H_2O$	Blue
Iron sulphate	$FeSO_4 . 6H_2O$	Green
Magnesium sulphate	$MgSO_4 . 7H_2O$	White
Sodium carbonate	$Na_2CO_3 . 10H_2O$	White
Barium chloride	$BaCl_2 . 2H_2O$	White

Uses of Salts

Some of its important uses are given below:

- As table Salt.
- In the manufacture of butter and cheese.
- In leather industry for taming of leather.
- For manufacturing washing soda and baking soda.
- For preparing sodium hydroxide by electrolysis of brine.
- Rock salt is spread on ice roads to melt ice in cold countries.

Points to Remember

- The oxides of non-metals mainly form acidic solutions and the oxides of metals if soluble, mainly form alkaline solutions.
- All bases are not alkalies. Some bases are soluble in water. They are called alkalies.
- Acid and alkali solutions conduct electricity.
- All acids contain hydrogen and dissolve in water.
- Acids turn blue litmus into red. Whereas alkalies turn red litmus into blue.
- Acids neutralise bases and bases neutralise acids. Salt and water are formed in these neutralisation reactions. Acids also react with metals to form salt and hydrogen gas. They also react with metal carbonates to give salt, water and carbon dioxide gas.
- Acids and alkalies can be weak or strong.
- Salts are substances, which are produced from acids by reactions in which the hydrogen in the acid is replaced by a metal.
- Some salts have the tendency to absorb water from air and turn into a solution. Such substances are called **deliquescent**.
- The crystals, which have lost their water of crystallisation, are called **anhydrous**.
- The crystals of some salts have some water molecules associated with them. These water molecules are known as **water of crystallisation**.
- **Neutral salts** are formed by the neutralisation of a strong acid with a strong base.
  $HCl + NaOH \rightarrow NaCl + H_2O$
- **Acidic Salts** are formed when a strong acid is neutralised by a weak base.
  $HCl + NH_4OH \rightarrow NH_4Cl + H_2O$
- **Basic Salts** are formed by the neutralisation of a weak acid by a strong base.
  $CH_3COOH + NaOH \rightarrow CH_3COONa + H_2O$.

MULTIPLE CHOICE QUESTIONS

1. The isomeric pair is:
   A. ethane and propane
   B. propane and butane
   C. ethane and ethane
   D. butane and 2-methyl propane

2. Which of the following is used to oxidise ethanol to ethanoic acid?
   A. Alkaline $KMnO_4$ B. Conc. H_2SO_4
   C. Acidified $K_2Cr_2O_7$ D. All of above

3. Which is denatured spirit?
   A. ethanol only
   B. ethanol and methanol (50%)
   C. ethanol and methanol (5%)
   D. methanol only

4. Tertiary butane gets oxidised with oxidising agents like alkaline $KMNO_4$ to:
   A. Isobutane
   B. Ter-butyl alcohol
   C. Seconadary-propyl alcohol
   D. All of above

5. The substance not responsible for the hardness of water is:
   A. Sodium nitrate
   B. Calcium hydrogen carbonate
   C. Calcium carbonate
   D. Magnesium carbonate

6. The by product of soap is:
   A. isoprene B. glycerol
   C. butene D. ethylene glycol

7. Covalent compounds:
   A. (a) have high melting and boiling point
   B. are mostly soluble in water
   C. are formed between atoms of metals and non-metals
   D. are formed by the sharing of electrons in the bonding atoms.

8. Which of the following can be used for the denaturation of ethyl alcohol?
   A. Methyl alcohol B. Pyridines
   C. Copper sulphate D. All of above

9. Soaps are formed by saponification of:
   A. alcohols B. glycosides
   C. simple esters D. carboxylic acids

10. What is the common name of ethanoic acid?
    A. Acetic acid B. Formic acid
    C. Propionic acid D. Butanoic acid

11. What type of flame is produced when the oxygen supply is sufficient?
    A. Yellow flame B. Blue flame
    C. Orange flame D. None of the above

12. Which of the following is the chemical property of carbon compounds?
    A. Combustion reactions B. Substitution reactions
    C. Addition reactions D. All of the above

13. The cooking gas (LPG) mainly consists of:
    A. Butane B. Ethene
    C. Ethyne D. Propene

14. The reaction in which an unsaturated hydrocarbon combines with another substance to give a single product is called:
    A. Addition reaction B. Combustion reaction
    C. Combination reaction D. Substitution reaction

15. What is the boiling point of ethanol?
    A. 100 °C B. 50 °C
    C. 88 °C D. 78 °C

16. Which of the following is used as a fuel in cars along with petrol?
    A. Methane B. Ethane
    C. Butane D. Ethanol

17. What is formed when ethanol reacts with ethanoic acid on warming in the presence of a few drops of concentrated sulphuric acid?
    A. Ester B. Ethene
    C. Sodium Ethoxide D. Ethane

18. Which of the following is a use of ethanol?
    A. Manufacturing paints
    B. In cough syrups
    C. In alcoholic drinks
    D. All of the above

19. What is used as an antiseptic to sterilise wounds and syringes in hospitals?
    A. Propanol B. Ethyl alcohol
    C. Butanol D. Methanol

20. Carbon exists in the atmosphere in the form of
    A. Only carbon monoxide
    B. Carbon monoxide in traces and carbon dioxide
    C. Only carbon dioxide
    D. Coal

21. Which of the following statements are usually correct for carbon compounds? These
    (*i*) Are good conductors of electricity.
    (*ii*) Are poor conductors of electricity.
    (*iii*) Have strong forces of attraction between their molecules.
    (*iv*) Do not have strong forces of attraction between their molecules.
    A. (*i*) and (*iii*) B. (*ii*) and (*iii*)
    C. (*i*) and (*iv*) D. (*ii*) and (*iv*)

22. A molecule of ammonia (NH_3) has:
A. Only single bonds
B. Only double bonds
C. Only triple bonds
D. Two double bonds and one single bond

23. Buckminsterfullerene is an allotropic form of:
A. Phosphorus B. Sulphur
C. Carbon D. Tin

24. Oils on treating with hydrogen in the presence of palladium or nickel catalyst form fats. This is an example of:
A. Addition reaction
B. Substitution reaction
C. Displacement reaction
D. Oxidation reaction

25. In which of the following compounds -OH is the functional group?
A. Butanone B. Butanol
C. Butanoic D. Butanal

26. The soap molecule has a:
A. Hydrophilic head and a hydrophobic tail
B. Hydrophobic head and a hydrophilic tail
C. Hydrophobic head and a hydrophobic tail
D. Hydrophilic head and a hydrophilic tail

27. Chlorine reacts with saturated hydrocarbons at room temperature in the:
A. absence of sunlight
B. presence of sunlight
C. presence of water
D. presence of hydrochloric acid

28. Ethanol reacts with sodium and forms two products. These are:
A. Sodium ethanoate and hydrogen
B. Sodium ethanoate and oxygen
C. Sodium ethoxide and hydrogen
D. Sodium ethoxide and oxygen

29. Which of the following is a noble gas?
A. Carbon B. Argon
C. Nitrogen D. Hydrogen

30. How many electrons are there in the outermost shell of carbon?
A. 1 B. 2
C. 3 D. 4

31. Which allotrope of carbon is in the form of the geodesic globe?
A. Graphite B. Diamond
C. Fullerene D. Carbon nanotube

32. Which of the following has a triple bond?
A. Hydrogen molecule B. Oxygen molecule
C. Nitrogen molecule D. Ammonia molecule

33. Which of the following has a double bond?
A. Hydrogen molecule B. Oxygen molecule
C. Nitrogen molecule D. Methane molecule

34. Which of the following is not a saturated hydrocarbon?
A. cyclohexane B. benzene
C. butane D. isobutene

35. The bond between two identical non metallic atom has a pair of electron?
A. un equally shared between two atoms.
B. transferd completely from one atom to another.
C. with identical spins
D. equally shared between them.

36. Covalent compounds are generally:
A. soluble in water B. insoluble in water
C. ionize in water D. hydrolyse in water

37. Propane with the molecular formula C_3H_8 has
A. 7 covalent bonds B. 8 covalent bonds
C. 9 covalent bonds D. 10 covalent bonds

38. A hydrocarbon reacts with ammonical cuprous chloride solution to form a red precipitate. The hydrocarbon is:
A. ethane B. ethene
C. butane D. 1-propyne

39. Which of the following substance is added to denature Ethanol?
A. methanol B. pyridine
C. copper sulphate D. all of them

40. Which of the following is not an allotropic form of carbon?
A. fluorine B. fullerene
C. diamond D. graphite

41. Which of the following represents the correct decreasing order of hydrogen atoms?
A. alkanes, alkenes, alkynes
B. alkanes, alkaynes, alkenes
C. alkenes, alkynes, alkanes
D. alkynes, alkanes, alkenes

42. Detergents are sodium or potassium salts of long chain of:
A. aldehydes B. ketones
C. carboxylic acid D. sulphonic acid

43. Which of the following represents the structure of N_2 molecule?
A. $N \equiv N$ B. $N = N$
C. N - N D. None of the above

44. In double covalent bond there is sharing of:
A. 2 electrons B. 4 electrons
C. 6 electrons D. 3 electrons

45. Cation is formed when:
A. atom gains electrons
B. atom loses electrons
C. proton is lost by the atom
D. atom shared by electrons

46. The total no. of electrons that take part in forming a bond in N_2 is:
A. 2 B. 4
C. 6 D. 10

47. Which of the following has the weakest carbon-carbon strength?
A. C_2H_2
B. C_2H_4
C. C_2H_6
D. all have the same bond strength

48. Which of the following salt when dissolved in water produces hard water.
A. Calcium sulphate
B. Magnesium bicarbonate
C. Calcium chloride
D. Any of the above

49. The most reactive metal is:
A. Iron B. Gold
C. Zinc D. Potassium.

50. The liquid metal at room temperature
A. Mercury B. Bromine
C. Sodium D. Gold

51. Non-metals are:
A. generally liquids
B. generally gases
C. generally solids and gases
D. generally gases and liquids.

52. The metal which is stored in kerosene:
A. Phosphorus B. Magnesium
C. Sodium D. None of these

53. The non-metal which is liquid at room temperature is:
A. Carbon B. Iodine
C. Bromine D. Chlorine.

54. Materials around us can be classified into:
A. Elements and compounds
B. Metals and non-metals
C. Acids and bases
D. None of these.

55. All metals are solids except:
A. Sodium B. Calcium
C. Mercury D. Hydrogen.

56. Metal oxides are of nature:
A. Acidic B. Basic
C. Neutral D. All of these

57. The metal which can be cut with a knife:
A. Sodium and potassium
B. Barium and calcium
C. Sodium and mercury
D. Potassium and calcium

58. When non-metals react with water then:
A. Hydrogen gas is formed
B. Carbon dioxide gas is formed
C. Non-metals do not react with water
D. None of these

59. The property of metals by which they can be beaten in to thin sheets is called:
A. Malleability B. Ductility
C. Conduction D. Expansion

60. Which one of the following is metal?
A. C B. N
C. Na D. O

61. Which one of the following is non metal?
A. Zn B. Al
C. Fe D. N

62. All materials shown property of malleability expect:
A. Iron B. Graphite
C. Aluminium D. Silver

63. Which one of the following is a good conductor of electricity?
A. Iron B. Plastic
C. Wood D. Glass

64. The property of metal by which it can be drawn into wires is called:
A. Conductivity B. malleability
C. Ductility D. Decorating

65. The metals that produce ringing sounds, are said to be:
A. malleable B. sonorous
C. Lustrous D. hard

66. Which metal is found in liquid state at room temperature?
A. Fe B. Zn
C. Hg D. Al

67. The solution of ash of magnesium ribbon is:
A. Acidic B. Basic
C. Neutral D. All of these

68. What is the product when sulphur reacts with oxygen?
A. Sulphuric acid B. Sulphur trioxide
C. Sulphurous acid D. Sulphur dioxide

69. When sulphur dioxide is dissolve in water then:
A. Sulphur is formed
B. Sulphur trioxide is formed
C. Sulphuric acid is formed
D. Sulphurous acid is formed

70. What is the chemical formula of sulphurous acid?
A. H_2SO_4 B. SO_2
C. SO_3 D. H_2SO_3

71. The sulphuric acid turns blue litmus paper into:
A. Red B. Green
C. Yellow D. Dark blue

72. Oxides of non metals are _______ in nature.
A. Basic B. Acidic
C. Neutral D. All of these

73. Sodium metal is stored in:
A. Water B. Alcohol
C. Kerosene D. Ether

74. Which one of the following metal reacts vigorously with oxygen and water?
A. Sodium B. Potassium
C. Calcium D. Magnesium

75. Which metal is present in Calcium Hydroxide?
A. C B. O
C. Ca D. H

76. Which non-metal catches fire if the exposed to air?
A. Sodium B. Phosphorous
C. Calcium D. Uranium

77. What is the chemical formula of copper sulphate?
A. $CuSO_4$ B. $CuCO_3$
C. $CuCl_2$ D. CuO

78. Which gas are produced when metal react with acids?
A. Oxygen B. Nitrogen
C. Hydrogen D. Carbon dioxide

79. Which one of the following does not react with acids?
A. Cu B. Ni
C. Cr D. O

80. Which one of the following gas burns with the "pop" sound?
A. Oxygen B. Hydrogen
C. Chlorine D. Hydrogen sulphide

81. Which of the following can be beaten in to thin sheets?
A. Zinc B. Phosphorus
C. Sulphur D. Oxygen

82. Which of the following statements are correct?
A. All metals are ductile
B. All non metals are ductile
C. Generally metals are ductile
D. some metals are ductile

83. What happens when dilute sulphuric acid is poured on a copper plate?
A. Copper sulphate formed
B. Zinc sulphate formed
C. Copper chloride formed
D. Zinc sulphate formed.

84. On burning metals react with oxygen to produce:
A. Metal hydroxide B. Metal chloride
C. Metal oxide D. Metal sulphate

85. Which gas produced by piece of burning charcoal?
A. CO_2 B. CO
C. H_2S D. O_2

86. Which non metal is essential for our life and inhale during breathing?
A. H B. O
C. C D. N

87. Non metals used in:
A. Aeroplanes B. making machinery
C. Water boilers D. Fertilisers

88. Which one of the following is applied on wounds as an antiseptic?
A. Metals B. Non metals
C. Metalloids D. All of these

89. Which metal is found in plants?
A. Fe B. Cr
C. Mg D. CO

90. Copper sulphate ($CuSO_4$) possesses:
A. Red colour B. Blue colour
C. Green colour D. Yellow colour

91. Which one of the following are very reactive non metals?
A. Sodium B. Potassium
C. Carbon D. Phosphorous

92. Which one of the following is the good conducter of electricity?
A. Iron rod B. Sulphur
C. Coal piece D. Wood

93. Which material show shiny appearance?
A. Coal B. Sulphur
C. Aluminium D. Carbon

94. Which material is hard in nature?
A. Iron B. Coal
C. Oxygen D. Wood

95. Gold is used in:
A. Thermometers B. Fuel
C. Jewellery D. Machinery

96. Which one of the following metal is used thermometers?
A. Copper B. Mercury
C. Aluminium D. Iron

97. Which one of the following can't be drawn into wires?
A. Fe B. Al
C. Cu D. Coal

98. Which substance is present in fuel?
A. Copper B. Iron
C. Gold D. Carbon

99. Zinc replaces copper from:
A. Zinc sulphate B. Copper sulphate
C. Sulphuric acid D. Copper oxide

100. Metallic oxides are:
A. Acidic is nature B. Neutral
C. Basic in nature D. Either acidic or basic

101. Aluminium foil used for wrapping:
A. Food B. Clothes
C. Plastic D. Wires

102. Which one of the following is used for decorating sweets?
A. Aluminium foil B. Copper foil
C. Silver foil D. All of these

103. Which one of the following enhances the growth of plants?
A. Industrial gadgets B. Fertilisers
C. Automobiles D. Water boilers

104. Which one of the following is in crackers?
A. metals B. Semi metals
C. Non-metal D. All of these

105. Hydrogen gas produce when metal react with:
A. Acid B. Base
C. Salt D. Both acid & base

106. Which of the following can't be beaten into sheets?
A. Zinc B. Iron
C. Aluminium D. Sulphur

107. Heat conduction is the property of:
A. Non-metal B. Metal
C. Metalloids D. All of these

108. Moist air is the combination of:
A. $H_2O + CO_2 + O_2$ B. $H_2O + CO + O_2$
C. $H_2O + CO_2 + H_2$ D. $H_2O + O_2 + H_2$

109. Which of the following product is formed when calcium oxide reacts with water?
A. Slaked lime B. Carbon dioxide
C. Calcium oxide D. Oxygen gas

110. What is the another name of quick lime?
A. Calcium hydroxide B. Calcium oxide
C. Carbon dioxide D. Sodium oxide

111. What is the chemical name for slaked lime?
A. Calcium carbonate B. Calcium oxide
C. Calcium hydroxide D. Carbon monoxide

112. Heating of ferrous sulphate gives which of the following product?
A. Ferric oxide B. Sulphur dioxide
C. Sulphur trioxide D. All of the above

113. In which of the following category will you put the reaction of heating of ferrous sulphate?
A. Decomposition reaction
B. Combination Reaction
C. Displacement reaction
D. All of the above

114. In which of the following category will you put the reaction of heating of calcium carbonate?
A. Decomposition reaction
B. Thermal decomposition reaction
C. Endothermic reaction
D. All of the above

115. Which of the following product is formed after heating of limestone?
A. Calcium oxide
B. Calcium carbonate
C. Hydrogen gas
D. All of the above

116. What happens when silver chloride is put unde sunlight?
A. Silver metal and chlorine gas are formed
B. Silver metal and hydrogen gas are formed
C. Only silver metal is formed
D. Only hydrogen gas is formed

117. Which of the following is formed when lead nitrate i put under thermal decomposition?
A. Lead oxide B. Nitrogen dioxide
C. Oxygen gas D. All of the above

118. What happens when carbon dioxide is passed in lim water?
A. Lime water turns milky because of formation o calcium carbonate
B. Lime water turns milky because of formation o water
C. Lime water turns red because of formatio permanganate
D. Lime water turns red because of formation o copper sulphate

119. What happens when silver bromide is exposed t sunlight?
A. Hydrogen gas is formed
B. Bromine gas is formed
C. Chlorine gas is formed
D. Iodine gas is formed

120. Which metal is displaced when lead is put in th solution of copper chloride?
A. Lead B. Copper
C. Chlorine D. All of the above.

121. Which of the following is formed when lead meta reacts with the solution of copper chloride?
A. No reaction takes place
B. Copper chlorine
C. Lead chloride
D. Copper-lead chloride

122. Which metal is displaced when zinc metal is put in th solution of copper sulphate?
A. Copper B. Zinc
C. Sulphate D. All of the above

123. What happens when sodium sulphate solution is mixe with the solution of barium chloride?
A. Barium sulphate is formed
B. Sodium sulphate is formed
C. Sulphur dioxide gas is formed
D. No reaction takes place

124. What happens when Copper metal is dipped in the solution of zinc sulphate?
A. Copper sulphate is formed
B. Oxygen gas is formed
C. Zinc metal is separated
D. No reaction takes place

125. What happens when zinc metal is dipped in the solution of copper sulphate?
A. Zinc sulphate is formed
B. Zinc oxide is formed
C. Zinc sulphide is formed
D. No reaction takes place

126. Why are articles made of iron painted to prevent rust?
A. Paint makes articles made of iron beautiful
B. Paint prevents iron articles to come in contact with moisture present in air.
C. Paint prevents iron articles to getting sticky
D. All of the above

127. Which of the following is termed as rancidity?
A. Reduction of oxygen present in food
B. Oxidation of oil present in food
C. Oxidation of sugar present in food
D. All of the above

128. How rancidity can be prevented?
A. By adding antioxidants in food
B. By adding more oxygen to food
C. By keeping food items in open
D. All of the above

129. Which of the following product is formed when calcium oxide reacts with water?
A. Slaked lime B. Carbon dioxide
C. Calcium oxide D. Oxygen gas

130. What is the another name of quick lime?
A. Calcium hydroxide B. Calcium oxide
C. Carbon dioxide D. Sodium oxide

131. What is the chemical name for slaked lime?
A. Calcium carbonate
B. Calcium oxide
C. Calcium hydroxide
D. Carbon monoxide

132. Heating of ferrous sulphate gives which of the following product?
A. Ferric oxide
B. Sulphur dioxide
C. Sulphur trioxide
D. All of the above

133. In which of the following category will you put the reaction of heating of ferrous sulphate?
A. Decomposition reaction
B. Combination Reaction
C. Displacement reaction
D. All of the above

134. In which of the following category will you put the reaction of heating of calcium carbonate?
A. Decomposition reaction
B. Thermal decomposition reaction
C. Endothermic reaction
D. All of the above.

135. Which of the following product is formed after heating of limestone?
A. Calcium oxide B. Calcium carbonate
C. Hydrogen gas D. All of the above

136. What happens when silver chloride is put under sunlight?
A. Silver metal and chlorine gas are formed
B. Silver metal and hydrogen gas are formed
C. Only silver metal is formed
D. Only hydrogen gas is formed

137. Which of the following is formed when lead nitrate is put under thermal decomposition?
A. Lead oxide B. Nitrogen dioxide
C. Oxygen gas D. All of the above

138. What happens when carbon dioxide is passed in lime water?
A. Lime water turns milky because of formation of calcium carbonate
B. Lime water turns milky because of formation of water
C. Lime water turns red because of formation permanganate
D. Lime water turns red because of formation of copper sulphate

139. Which of the following is termed as exothermic reaction?
A. Reaction in which heat is evolved
B. Reaction in which heat is absorbed
C. Reaction in which there is loss of oxygen
D. Reaction in which there is gain of hydrogen

140. Which of the following is termed as endothermic reaction?
A. Reaction in which heat is evolved
B. Reaction in which heat is absorbed
C. Reaction in which there is loss of oxygen
D. Reaction in which there is gain of hydrogen

141. What is the name of reaction which decomposes after supply of heat?
A. Combination reaction
B. Thermal decomposition
C. Displacement reaction
D. Redox reaction

142. What is the name of reaction in which both oxidation and reduction takes place?
A. Combination reaction
B. Thermal decomposition
C. Displacement reaction
D. Redox reaction

143. What is the name of substance which does get deposited over iron because of moisture present in air?
A. Sulphide B. Rust
C. Carbonate D. Oxygen

144. Why magnesium ribbon is cleaned before burning?
A. To remove dust
B. To remove magnesium oxide
C. To remove ribbon oxide
D. All of the above

145. On the basis of evolution or absorption of heat, chemical reactions can be divided in how many types?
A. Two B. Three
C. Four D. One

146. Which of the following gas is produced when carbon is burnt in air?
A. Carbon dioxide B. Sulphur dioxide
C. Oxygen D. Hydrogen

147. Which of the following gives energy while respiration?
A. Burning of coal B. Burning of natural gas
C. Burning of oxygen D. Burning of glucose

148. What happens when hydrogen reacts with oxygen?
A. Carbon dioxide is formed
B. Water is formed
C. Hydrogen carbonate is formed
D. All of the above

149. The chemical formula of lead sulphate is:
A. Pb_2SO_4 B. $Pb(SO_4)_2$
C. $PbSO_4$ D. $Pb_2(SO_4)_3$

150. Which information is not conveyed by a balanced chemical equation?
A. Physical states of reactants and products
B. Symbols and formulae of all the substances involved in a particular reaction
C. Number of atoms/molecules of the reactants and products formed
D. Whether a particular reaction is actually feasible or not

151. Chemically rust is:
A. hydrated ferrous oxide
B. only ferric oxide
C. hydrated ferric oxide
D. none of these

152. Both CO_2 and H_2 gases are:
A. heavier than air B. colourless
C. acidic in nature D. soluble in water

153. Which of the following gases can be used for storage of fresh sampel of an oil for a long time?
A. Carbon dioxide or oxygen
B. Nitrogen or helium
C. Helium or oxygen
D. Nitrogen or oxygen

154. The electrolytic decomposition of water gives H_2 and O_2 in the ratio of:
A. 1: 2 by volume B. 2: 1 by volume
C. 8: 1 by mass D. 1: 2 by mass

155. In the decomposition of lead (II) nitrate to give lead (II) oxide, nitrogen dioxide and oxygen gas, the coefficient of nitrogen dioxide (in the balanced equation) is:
A. 1 B. 2
C. 3 D. 4

156. Fatty foods become rancid due to the process of:
A. oxidation B. corrosion
C. reduction D. hydrogenation

157. We store silver chloride in a dark coloured bottle because it is:
A. a white solid
B. undergoes redoc reaction
C. to avoid action by sunlight
D. none of the above

158. Silver article turns black when kept in the open for a few days due to formation of
A. H_2S B. AgS
C. $AgSO_4$ D. Ag_2S

159. When crystals of lead nitrate are heated strongly in a dry test tube
A. crystals immediately melt
B. a brown residue is left
C. white fumes appear in the tube
D. a yellow residue is left

160. Dilute hydrochloric acid is added to granulated zinc taken in a test tube. The following observations are recorded. Point out the correct observation.
A. The surface of metal becomes shining
B. The reaction mixture turns milky
C. Odour of a pungent smelling gas is recorded
D. A colourless and odourless gas is evolved

161. When carbon dioxide is passed through lime water,
A. calcium hydroxide is formed
B. white precipitate of CaO is formed
C. lime water turns milky
D. colour of lime water disappears.

162. When a magnesium ribbon is burnt in air, the ash formed is:
A. black B. white
C. yellow D. pink

163. In which of the following, heat energy will be evolved?
A. Electrolysis of water
B. Dissolution of NH_4Cl in water
C. Burning of LPG
D. Decomposition of AgBr in the presence of sunlight

164. Rancidity can be prevented by:
A. adding antioxidants
B. storing food away from light
C. keeping food in refrigerator
D. all of these

165. The reaction of H_2 gas with oxygen gas to form water is an example of
A. combination reaction
B. redox reaction
C. exothermic reaction
D. all of these reactions

166. The reaction in which two compound exchange their ions to form two new compounds is called:
A. displacement reaction
B. combination reaction
C. double displacement reaction
D. redox reaction

167. On immersing an iron nail in $CuSO_4$ solution for few minutes, you will observe
A. no reaction takes place
B. the colour of solution fades away
C. the surface of iron nails acquire a black coating
D. the colour of solution changes to green

168. An element X on exposure to moist air turns reddish-brown and a new compound Y is formed. The substance X and Y are:
A. X = Fe, Y = Fe_2O_3
B. X = Ag, Y = Ag_2S
C. X = Cu, Y = CuO
D. X = Al, Y = Al_2O_3

169. A chain of small chemical units combined to form a large single units is called _______.
A. Polymer B. Poly
C. Polythene D. None of the above

170. Polythene and PVC are examples of:
A. Bio degradable substance
B. Thermosetting plastics
C. Thermoplastics
D. Rayon

171. Plastics which when moulded once, cannot be softened by heating. Such plastics are called ______.
A. Polythene B. Thermoplastics
C. Polyster D. Thermosetting plastics

172. Polycot is made by mixing two types of fibres namely:
A. Silk + Cotton B. Polythene + Cotton
C. Silk + Polyester D. Polyester + Cotton

173. The 4R Principle is:
A. Reduce, Reuse, Recycle, Recover
B. Remember, Reduce, Recycle, Rejoice
C. Repeat, Rejoice, Recycle, Reduce
D. None of the above

174. _____ is an example of natural polymer.
A. Rayon B. Cellulose
C. Nylon D. All of the above

175. Which of the following is Non-biodegradable?
A. Woolen clothes B. Plastic bag
C. Cotton cloth D. Wood

176. Bakelite and Melamine are examples of:
A. Thermosetting plastics
B. Silk
C. Nylon
D. Rayon

177. Fire proof plastic uniform worn by fire fighters has a coating of ______ to make it fire resistant.
A. Nylon B. Rayon
C. Melamine Plastic D. Silk

178. The coating on modern non-stick cookware and electric iron is of:
A. Terrycot B. Rayon
C. Polyester D. Teflon

179. The property of metals by which they can be beaten into thin sheets is called ______.
A. Ductility B. Sheetability
C. Metallic D. Malleability

180. The property of metal by which it can be drawn into wires is called ______.
A. Ductility B. Sheetability
C. Metallic D. Malleability

181. The metal found in liquid state is:
A. Iron B. Aluminium
C. Mercury D. Gold

182. When a copper vessel is exposed to moist air for long, it acquires a dull green coating. The green material is a mixture of:
A. Copper oxide and Copper Nitrate
B. Copper hydroxide and Copper Carbonate
C. Copper carbonate and Copper sulfate
D. Copper hydroxide and Copper Nitrate

183. When sulphur dioxide is dissolved in water _______ is formed.
A. Sulphuric acid
B. Sulphoxy acid
C. Sulphurous acid
D. Sulphur trioxide

184. Sodium metal is stored in:
A. Water
B. Kept under open air
C. Alcohol
D. Kerosene

185. Phosphorus is stored in:
A. Water B. Kept under open air
C. Alcohol D. Kerosene

ANSWERS

1	2	3	4	5	6	7	8	9	10
D	D	C	B	A	B	D	D	C	A
11	**12**	**13**	**14**	**15**	**16**	**17**	**18**	**19**	**20**
B	D	A	A	D	D	A	D	B	C
21	**22**	**23**	**24**	**25**	**26**	**27**	**28**	**29**	**30**
D	A	C	A	B	A	B	C	B	D
31	**32**	**33**	**34**	**35**	**36**	**37**	**38**	**39**	**40**
C	C	B	B	D	B	D	D	D	A
41	**42**	**43**	**44**	**45**	**46**	**47**	**48**	**49**	**50**
A	D	A	B	B	C	A	D	D	A
51	**52**	**53**	**54**	**55**	**56**	**57**	**58**	**59**	**60**
C	C	C	B	C	B	A	C	A	C
61	**62**	**63**	**64**	**65**	**66**	**67**	**68**	**69**	**70**
D	B	A	C	B	C	B	D	C	D
71	**72**	**73**	**74**	**75**	**76**	**77**	**78**	**79**	**80**
A	B	C	A	C	B	B	C	D	B
81	**82**	**83**	**84**	**85**	**86**	**87**	**88**	**89**	**90**
A	C	A	C	B	B	D	B	C	B
91	**92**	**93**	**94**	**95**	**96**	**97**	**98**	**99**	**100**
D	A	C	A	C	B	D	D	B	C
101	**102**	**103**	**104**	**105**	**106**	**107**	**108**	**109**	**110**
A	C	B	C	B	D	B	A	A	B
111	**112**	**113**	**114**	**115**	**116**	**117**	**118**	**119**	**120**
C	D	A	D	A	A	D	A	B	B
121	**122**	**123**	**124**	**125**	**126**	**127**	**128**	**129**	**130**
C	A	A	D	A	B	B	A	A	B
131	**132**	**133**	**134**	**135**	**136**	**137**	**138**	**139**	**140**
C	D	A	D	A	A	D	A	A	B
141	**142**	**143**	**144**	**145**	**146**	**147**	**148**	**149**	**150**
B	D	B	B	A	A	D	B	C	D
151	**152**	**153**	**154**	**155**	**156**	**157**	**158**	**159**	**160**
C	B	B	B	D	A	C	D	B	D
161	**162**	**163**	**164**	**165**	**166**	**167**	**168**	**169**	**170**
C	B	C	D	A	C	D	A	A	C
171	**172**	**173**	**174**	**175**	**176**	**177**	**178**	**179**	**180**
B	D	A	B	B	A	C	D	B	A
181	**182**	**183**	**184**	**185**					
C	B	C	D	A					

★ ★ ★

3

Living/Non-Living; Cell Structure and Function; Conservation of Plants and Animals

FUNDAMENTAL UNITS OF LIFE

Some Important Facts

- The cell is the basic structural and functional unit of living organisms.
- A cell is made of life giving substance called **protoplasm**.
- A single cell may constitute a whole organism. Such organisms are called unicellular organisms and include bacteria, Amoeba, Euglena, Paramecium, Yeast.
- Non-cellular organisms which do not contain any cell in their body organisation, e.g., Viruses.
- Cellular organisms which contain either one or many cells in their bodies e.g. bacteria, plants and animals.
- All the living beings are made up of cells.
- The structure of plants and animals is different, they perform basic functions of life.
- In spite of variations in structure, shape and the size, all organisms are made up of basic units called cells. These were first observed by **Robert Hooke**.
- The smallest cell observed is that of a bacteria. Ostrich egg represents the largest cell visible to unaided eye.
- Each cell has smaller components called cell organelles. These are common to all cells. Each organelles performs a specific function.
- There are some differences between plant and animal cells.
- The word **cell** is derived from the Latin word **cellula** which means **"a little room"**. An English botanist **Robert Hooke** (1635-1703) who in 1665 discovered and named the **cells.**
- **Adenosine triphosphate (ATP):** An energy rich compound that is found in all cells and serves as an energy source for various cellular functions.
- **Amino Acid:** The basic building block of protein.
- **Bacterium:** An unicellular organisms which lacks an organised nucleus.
- **Carbohydrates:** Organic molecules containing carbon, hydrogen and oxygen in the ratio of CH_2O, e.g., glucose, starch, glycogen, sugar, cellulose.
- **Centromere:** It is the point of attachment of sister chromatids and site of chromosomes attachment to the spindle fibres.
- **Chlorophyll:** Green photosynthetic, light capturing pigment of plant cells, typically located in the grana of chloroplasts.
- **Chromosomes:** Thread-like stainable condensed chromatin, visible at cell division and containing hereditary information in the form of genes.
- **Cytology:** The study of cells and their parts using microscope.
- **Cytoplasm:** The living matter in a cell, outside the nucleus.
- **Deoxyribonucleic acid (DNA):** Genetic material deoxyribose containing nucleic acid that stores hereditary informations in the form of code words and makes chromosomes and genes.
- **Differentiation:** Specialisation of cells to perform different specific functions in the organism.
- **Diploid:** An individual or cell with two complete sets of chromosomes symbolised as 2n characteristic of somatic cells.
- **Enzymes:** An organic catalyst, usually a protein which modifies the rate of chemical reaction without being consumed or permanently modified in the process.
- **Genes:** Hereditary units, specific functional units along chromosomes responsible for given traits of an organism.
- **Homologous chromosomes:** A pair of chromo somes of the same size and shape bearing corres-ponding genes governing the same set of traits. One member of such a pair is derived from each of two parents.
- **Leucoplast:** A colourless plastid which stores proteins, lipids and starch.
- **Lipid:** A type of a fatty organic compound, e.g. fats, oils and steriods.
- **Lysosome:** A membrane-bounded cytoplasmic organelle having various hydrolytic enzymes.

- **Matrix:** The essentially unstructured colloidal ground substance of a cell or organelle consisting of a suspension of particles and molecules in a watery medium.
- **Osmosis:** The tendency of water to move across a differentially permeable membrane from a dilute to a concentrated solution.
- **Plasma Membrane:** Membrane surrounding the cell.
- **Prokaryote:** Organisms lacking nucleus and membrane-bounded organelles in their cells.
- **Protein:** A specific chain of amino acids. Essential in producing cell structure and a variety of enzymes.
- **Ribonucleic acid (RNA):** A nucleic acid containing phosphate, ribose sugar and the nitrogen base, uracil besides adenine, guanine and cytosine. Functions in protein synthesis.
- **Ribosome:** A grainy structure having RNA and proteins and acts as the site of protein synthesis.
- **Stroma:** The granular matrix of the chloroplast.
- **Virus:** An infections, submicroscopic cellular parasite that consists of a RNA or DNA core with a protein coat.
- **Xanthophyll:** The yellow, red or orange pigments of green plants.

Prokaryotic and Eukaryotic Cells

- **Prokaryotic Cell:** These have primitive and incomplete cells. It has all three basic structures of a typical cell but lack nuclear membranes around their genetic substances (DNA). *e.g.* bacteria, blue-green algae.
- **Eukaryotic Cell:** These cells contain membrane bound cellular organelles and are called eukaryotic cells. e.g. plants and animals cells.

Differences between Prokaryotic Cells and Eukaryotic Cells

Prokaryotic Cell	*Eukaryotic Cell*
(*i*) Size of the cell is generally small.	(*i*) Size of cell is generally large.
(*ii*) Nucleus is absent.	(*ii*) Nucleus is present.
(*iii*) It contains single chromosomes.	(*iii*) It contains more than one chromosomes.
(*iv*) Membrane bound cell organelles are absent.	(*iv*) Cell organelles are present.
(*v*) Cell division takes place by fission or budding.	(*v*) Cell division occurs by miotic and miosis.

- Cells were discovered in 1665 by **Robert Hooke**.
- **Anton Von Leeuwenhoek** discovered in 1674 the free cells in the form of bacteria. He also discovered sperm in 1678 and discovered the sperm cells of human, dogs, frogs and insects.
- **Robert Brown** discovered and named the **nucleus** in plant cells.
- **J.E. Purkinje** gave the term **protoplasm** for the living fluid substance present inside the cell.
- In 1883, **Jakob Matthias Schleiden** a German botanist and **Theodor Schwann**, a German zoologist gave the **cell theory**.

The basis of the cell theory are given below:

(*i*) All organisms are composed of cells and cell products.

(*ii*) All metabolic reactions take place in cells. Thus, cells are structured and functional units of life.

(*iii*) All cells arise from pre-existing cells only.

(*iv*) Every organism starts its life as a single cell.

Characteristics of Cells

(*i*) All cells are covered by a cell membrane.

(*ii*) Cell membrane encloses a jelly like substance—the cytoplasm.

(*iii*) A round ball—like nucleus is present in the centre of the cell which controls all the activities of the cell.

(*iv*) Mitochondria helps in respiration.

(*v*) Chloroplasts help in photosynthesis.

(*vi*) Endoplasmic Reticulum helps in transport of substances within the cell.

(*vii*) Plant cells posses an outer cell wall surrounding the cell membrane. It provides rigid shape to the cell and prevents it from bursting.

Structure of Cell

Cell Shape: Cells may have diverse shapes such as polyhedral, spherical, spindle shaped, elongated, branched, discoidal.

Cell Size: The size of different cells ranges between broad limits. Some plant and animals cells are visible to the naked eye.

Most cells, however, are visible only with a microscope.

Average Size of Different Cells in the Living Organisms

S.No.	Type of Cell	Size $1\mu = 10^{-6}$ m
1.	Living red blood cell	9μm [9×10^{-6} m]
2.	Nerve cell	more than a metre long
3.	Green algae	10 cm
4.	Ostrich egg	170 mm in diameter

- **Cell organelles, their location and shape and their main functions:** Plant and animal cells have the same basic structure, sharing many features. Cell contain smaller units called **organelles**.

Cell organelle	*Location and shape*	*Main Function*
1. Plasma Membrane	Outermost covering of each cells that provides and maintains shape of the cell. It is a living, thin, delicate, elastic, selectively, permeable membrane. It encloses a liquid substance known as protoplasm.	• Provides and maintains shape of the cell. Regulates the transportation of materials in and out of the cell.
2. Cell Wall	Present in plant cell only. It is present outer to the cell membrane. It is made up of non-living cellulose.	• Provides mechanical support, protection and rigidity to the plant cells. • Helps the plant cells to bear unfavourable conditions. • Provides shape. • Prevent osmotic bursting of the cell.
3. Cytoplasm	The part of the cell which occurs between the plasma membrane and nuclear envelop is called the cytoplasm. It is an aggregation of carbohydrates, proteins, fats, vitamin and minerals dissolved in water.	• Physical basis of all metabolic activities. • It acts as a store of vital chemicals such as amino acids, glucose vitamins, irons etc. • Living cytoplasm is always in a stable of movement.
4. Endoplasmic Reticulum (ER)	Irregular, interconnected network of flattened sacs made up of double membrane. It is connected with cell membrane nuclear membrane golgi bodies. ER is of two types: (*i*) Rough endoplasmic reticulum (RER) (*ii*) Smooth endoplasmic reticulum (SER). The ER is absent in the red blood cells of mammals.	• It forms cytoskeleton. • It forms intracellular transporting system. • It provides space for cellular secretions, storage and helps in transportation. • It forms many cell organelles. • It is site of lipid and steroid synthesis.
5. Ribosomes	Ribosomes are dense, spherical and grannular particles which occur freely in the matrix, Ribosomes are made up of RNA and proteins.	• Ribosomes play an important part in the synthesis of protein.
6. Golgi Apparatus	It consists of a set of membrane-bounded, fluid filled vesicles, vacuoles and flattened sacs. Golgi apparatus is absent in bacteria, blue green algae, nature sperm and red blood cells of mammals and other animals.	• Its main function is secretory. • It forms internal processing and transport system. • It helps in the formation of lysosomes and cell wall. • It acts as a way-station of assembly area for the storage, packaging of various cellular secretions.
7. Lysosomes	Lysosomes are simple tiny spherical Sac—like structures evenly distributed in the cytoplasm. It contain powerful enzymes.	• Intracellular digestion. • Digestion of worn-out cell organelles. • Destroy foreign substances.
8. Mitochondria	Double membrane bag like structure whose outer membrane is smooth whereas inner membrane is thrown into finger like structure, called **cristae**. Contain enzymes needed for aerobic oxidation of glucose.	• Sites of cellular respiration. • The energy released is stored in the form of ATP and is used by the cell. They are known as power house of the cell.
9. Plastids	Present in plant cells and absent in animal cells. They have the green pigment called chlorophyll. Trap solar energy for the process of photo-synthesis. So chloroplasts are known as **kitchens of the cells**.	• Chloroplasts trap solar energy and utilise it to manufacture food for the plant. • Provide bright colours to fruits and flowers. • Leucoplasts store food in the from of carbo.

Cell organelle	Location and shape	Main Function
10. Centrosome	Centrosome is found only in animal cells. It is present near the nucleus.	• Initiates and regulates cell division. • Produces basal bodies from which cilia and flagella.
11. Vacuoles	Vacuoles are fluid filled and membrane bounded spaces. The vacuole is covered from outside by a covering called tonoplast. In plant cells, the vacuoles are large and permanent.	• To maintain the osmotic pressure in a cell. • They store toxic metabolic by products.
12. Granules	These are also nonliving cytoplasmic inclusions. These are small particles crystals or droplets.	• Starch grains, fat droplets, help in the storage of food in cells.
13. Nucleus	The nucleus is a major, centrally located spherical cellular component. It is bounded by two nuclear membranes both forming a nuclear envelops. Nucleus contain chromosomes. It contain many segments called genes.	• Controls all the functions of a cell directly or indirectly. • Helps in the transmission of characters from parents to offspring. • Control cell division. • Variations help in evolution.

Chromosome Number of Some Organisms

Organism	*Chromosome number in each body cell*
Round Worm	2
Mosquito	6
Frog	26
Rat	42
Human beings	46
Guinea pig	64
Gold fish	100
Sunflower	34
Garden pea	14
Maize	20
Rice	24
Onion	16

Differences between Animal and Plant Cells

Animal Cell	*Plant Cell*
(*i*) Animal cells are generally small in size.	(*i*) Plant cells are larger than animal cells.
(*ii*) Cell wall is absent.	(*ii*) Cell wall made up of cellulose is present around the cell membrane. It is non living.
(*iii*) Chloroplasts are absent.	(*iii*) Chloroplasts are present.
(*iv*) Vacuoles are many but small in size.	(*iv*) Vacuoles are fewer but large in size.
(*v*) Animal cells have centrosome and centrioles.	(*v*) Plant cells lack centrosome and centrioles.

Chemical Constituents of the Cytoplasm

S.No.	*Chemical*	*Percentage*
1.	Oxygen	64.00
2.	Carbon	18.00
3.	Hydrogen	10.00
4.	Nitrogen	03.00
5.	Trace elements (Ca, P, Cl, S, K, Na, Mg, I, Fe)	05.00

Comparison of Plant and Animal Cells

S.No.	*Component organelle*	*Planet cell*	*Animal cell*
1.	Cell wall	Present	Absent
2.	Plasma Membrane	Present	Present
3.	Plastids	Present	Absent
4.	Vacuoles	Large size	Small size
5.	Nucleus	Present	Present
6.	Mitochondria	Present	Present

Cell Division

The process through which multiplication is achieved is called cell division. Cells multiplies by dividing itself again and again. Cells divide in two different ways:

— Mitosis and

— Meiosis.

- **Mitosis** is the kind of cell division that occurs in the somatic (body) cells of all plants and animals during growth and asexual reproduction.
- **Meiosis** takes place in the germinal cells of organisms during gametogenesis or formation of gametes—eggs and sperms.

NATURAL RESOURCES, AGRICULTURE AND ENVIRONMENT

The Natural Resources

The assets of nature, which are useful to mankind, are called natural resources.

Natural resources are two types:

(*i*) **Inexhaustible natural resources:** These resources are present in unlimited quantity in the nature and they are not likely to be exhausted by human activities. *e.g.* Solar radiation, air, water, precipitation and atomic power.

(*ii*) **Exhaustible natural resources:** These natural resources are liable to be degraded in quantity and quality by the human activities. *e.g.* Soil, minerals, fossil fuels etc.

Management and Replacement of Natural Resources

Management and conservation means scientific utilisation of resources while maintaining their sustained yield and quality.

Conservation of forests

Afforestation of deforested areas becomes necessary to get sufficient rainfall for the conservation of soil, for the conservation of rare forest plants and for conservation of unique wild life of the area.

The conservation of forest includes the following methods: (*i*) Afforestation (*ii*) Ex-situ conservation.

Afforestation

Afforestation is the process of transforming an area into forest.

(*i*) **Conservation of reserve forests:** Reserve forests are areas where water regimes are located. *e.g.* Himalayas and Western and Eastern Ghats. In reserve forests no commercial exploitation is allowed.

(*ii*) **Commercial forestry:** The basic aim of commercial forestry is to supply goods and services to meet the needs of local people for firewood, fodder, food fertiliser etc. It includes two main types of forestry:

- **Social forestry:** In social forestry those forest trees are planted on community lands, individuals holdings and other public lands which are needed by local rural and tribal populations.

  Social forestry has the following objectives:

(*i*) To use public and common land to produce fire wood, fodder and timber.

(*ii*) To manage soil and water conservation.

(*iii*) To relieve pressure from conservation forests.

(*iv*) To improve the environment of denuded or degraded wasteland by social forestry.

- **Ex-situ Conservation:** It involves plantation of trees of aesthetic value and ornamental trees in the botanical gardens.

Conservation of wildlife

The International Union for Conservation of Nature (IUCN) and Natural Resources, has made five main conservation categories of wild animals and plants.

(*i*) **Extinct species:** A species is considered extinct when there is no reasonable doubt that its last individual has died. *e.g.* Mountain quail, pink headed duck, Lesser one horned rhino, cheetah. Extinct plant species—Sarpgandha, Brahmkamal etc.

(*ii*) **Endangered species:** It is the species which is in danger of extinction and whose survival is causal factor continue to operate. *e.g.* Brow antlered deer, Hispid hare, Lion-tailed macaque, Asiatic lion, Great Indian bustard, Crocodile, Musk deer, Blue whale etc.

(*iii*) **Vulnerable species:** Such a species contains sufficient number of individuals in its habitat, but in near future, it may represent the category of endangered species. *e.g.* Crab-eating macaque, Golden langur, Chinkara deer etc.

(*iv*) **Rare species:** Such a species contains small world population that are not presently endangered or vulnerable, but are at risk. *e.g.* Indian egg-eating snake, Olive Ridley turtle, Golden cat etc.

(*v*) **Insufficiently known species:** Such a species requires more information for its conservation.

Some of the important measures for the conservation of Indian wildlife are following:

The protection of natural habitat and maintenance of endangered and other important species by certain protected areas such as national parks, wildlife or bird sanctuaries. In India, there are 104 national parks 544 sanctuaries and 18 biosphere reserves.

Biosphere Reserves: Biosphere reserves are multi-purpose protected areas with following major objectives:

(*i*) to conserve diversity and integrity of plants, animals and micro-organisms.

(*ii*) to promote ecological conservation.

(*iii*) to educate, train and create awareness about environmental aspects and eco-friendly living.

In India, 18 biospheres have been set up to year 2018.

1. Nilgiri (1986)	2. Nandadevi (1988)
3. Nokrok (1988)	4. Great Nicobar (1989)
5. Gulf of Mannar (1989)	6. Manas (1989)
7. Sunderbans (1989)	8. Simplipal (1994)
9. Dibrusaikhowa (1997)	10. Debong-Debang (1998)
11. Panchmarhi (1999)	12. Kanchanjangha (2000)
13. Agasthyamalai (2001)	14. Achanakmar–Amarkantak (2005)
15. Kachchh (2008)	16. Cold Desert (2009)
17. Seshachalom (2010)	18. Panna (2011)

MULTIPLE CHOICE QUESTIONS

1. The largest cell in the human body is:
A. Nerve cell B. Muscle cell
C. Liver cell D. Kidney cell

2. The barrier between the protoplasm and the other environment in an animal cells:
A. Cell wall B. Nuclear membrane
C. Tonoplast D. Plasma membrane

3. The term 'Cell' was given by:
A. Leeuwenhoek B. Robert hooke
C. Flemming D. Robert Brown

4. Who proposed the cell theory?
A. Schleiden and Schwann
B. Watson and Crick
C. Darwin and Wallace
D. Mendel and Morgan

5. A plant cell differs from an animal cell in the absence of:
A. Endoplasmic Reticulum
B. Mitochondria
C. Ribosome
D. Centriole

6. Centrosome is found in:
A. Cytoplasm B. Nucleus
C. Chromosomes D. Nucleolus

7. The power house of a cell is:
A. Chloroplast B. Mitochondrion
C. Golgi apparatus D. Nucleolus

8. Within a cell the site of respiration (oxidation) is the:
A. Ribosome
B. Golgi apparatus
C. Mitochondrion
D. Endoplasmic Reticulum

9. Which is called 'Suicidal Bag'?
A. Centrosome B. Lysosome
C. Mesosome D. Chromosome

10. Ribosomes are the center for:
A. Respiration B. Photosynthesis
C. Protein synthesis D. Fat synthesis

11. Double membrane is absent in:
A. Mitochondrion B. Chloroplast
C. Nucleus D. Lysosome

12. Cell organelle found only in Plant is:
A. Golgi apparatus B. Mitochondria
C. Plastids D. Ribosomes

13. Organisms lacking nucleus and membrane bound organelle are:
A. Diploids B. Prokaryotes
C. Haploids D. Eukaryotes

14. Animal cell is limited by:
A. Plasma membrane B. Shell membrane
C. Cell wall D. Basement membrane

15. The network of Endoplasmic Reticulum is present in the:
A. Nucleus B. Nucleolus
C. Cytoplasm D. Chromosomes

16. Lysosome are reservoirs of:
A. Fat
B. RNA
C. Secretary Glycoprotein
D. Hydrolytic Enzymes

17. The membrane surrounding the vacuole of a plant cell is called:
A. Tonoplast B. Plasma membrane
C. Nuclear membrane D. Cell wall

18. Cell secretion is done by:
A. Plastids B. ER
C. Golgi apparatus D. Nucleolus

19. Centrioles are associated with:
A. DNA synthesis B. Reproduction
C. Spindle formation D. Respiration

20. Main difference between animal cell and plant cell is:
A. Chromosome
B. Ribosome
C. Lysosome
D. Endoplasmic Reticulum

21. Animal cell lacking nuclei would also lack in:
A. Chromosome B. Ribosome
C. Lysosome D. Endoplasmic Reticulum

22. Plasmolysis occurs due to:
A. Absorption B. Endosmosis
C. Osmosis D. Exosmosis

23. A plant cell becomes turgid due to:
A. Plasmolysis B. Exosmosis
C. Endosmosis D. Electrolysis

24. Solute concentration is higher in the external solution:
A. Hypotonic B. Isotonic
C. Hypertonic D. None of the above

25. A cell placed in hypertonic solution will:
A. Shrink
B. Show Plasmolysis
C. Swell up
D. No change in shape or size

26. The radiant energy of sunlight is converted to chemical energy and is stored as:
A. AMP B. ADP
C. ATP D. APP

27. Which of the following organelle does not have membrane?
A. Ribosome B. Nucleus
C. Chloroplast D. Mitochondria

28. Root hair absorbs water from soil through:
A. Osmosis B. Active transport
C. Diffusion D. Endocytosis

29. The number of lenses in compound light microscope is:
A. 2 B. 3
C. 4 D. 1

30. The history of the cell began in 1665 with the publication of Micrographia in London by:
A. Robert Hooke B. Robert Brown
C. Strasburger D. Dujardin

31. Cell inclusions are:
A. Non-living materials present in the cytoplasm
B. Another name of cell organelle
C. Cytoskeletal framework of cell
D. Combined name for cell wall and plasma membrane

32. Which cell organelle is not bounded by a membrane?
A. Ribosome B. Lysosome
C. ER D. Nucleus

33. Which of the following cellular part possess a double membrane?
A. Nucleus B. Chloroplast
C. Mitochondrion D. All of the above

34. Cristae and Oxysomes are associated with:
A. Mitochondria B. Plastids
C. Golgi apparatus D. Plasma membrane

35. Karyotheca is another name of:
A. Nuclear envelope B. Nucleus
C. Nuclear pores D. Nucleolus

36. Cell organelle that acts as supporting skeletal framework of the cell is:
A. Golgi apparatus B. Nucleus
C. Mitochondria D. ER

37. Plastids are present in:
A. Animal cell only
B. Plant cells only
C. Both animal cells and Plant cells
D. Neither animal nor plant cells

38. Cell wall of plant is chiefly composed of:
A. Hemicellulose B. Cellulose
C. Phospholipids D. Proteins

39. Intercellular connections of plant cells are called:
A. Middle lamella B. Micro fibrils
C. Matrix D. Plasmodesmata

40. Genes are located on the:
A. Chromosomes B. Nucleolus
C. Nuclear membrane D. Plasma membrane

41. Chromatin consists of:
A. RNA
B. DNA
C. RNA and histones (proteins)
D. DNA and histones (proteins)

42. Different types of chromosomes can be recognized by the positions of the following separating the two arms:
A. Centromere B. Genes
C. Spindle D. Nucleus

43. Name of the process that requires energy provided by ATP:
A. Diffusion B. Osmosis
C. Active transport D. Plasmolysis

44. Mitochondria are found:
A. in all type of living cells
B. only in animal cells
C. only in plant cells
D. in eukaryote cells only

45. Who discovered the first living cell?
A. Robert Hooke B. Leeuwenhoek
C. Purkinje D. Robert Brown

46. Which of the following can be made into crystal?
A. A bacterium B. An Amoeba
C. A virus D. A sperm

47. Who used the word 'protoplasm first time for living cells?
A. Robert Hooke B. Leeuwenhoek
C. Purkinje D. Robert Brow

48. The main constituent of cell-wall is:
A. Starch B. cellulose
C. protein D. none of these

49. Function of centriole is:
A. formation of spindle fibre
B. nucleolus formationation
C. cell wall formation
D. cell division initiation

50. Which organelle is the power house of the cells?
A. Plastids B. Mitochondria
C. Golgi D. Nucleus

51. Chromosomes are made up of nucleic acid and ________ .
A. Phosphorus B. Protein
C. Sugar D. Calcium

52. Which organelle is considered as a suicide bag?
A. Centrosome B. Mesosomes
C. Lysosomes D. Chromosome

53. Plastids which are responsible for giving colors to fruits and flowers are:
A. chloroplasts B. leucoplasts
C. protoplasts D. chromoplasts

54. Which of the following organelle is present onion cells but not in human cheek cells?
A. cell wall B. cytoplasm
C. nucleus D. plasma membrane

55. Which cell organelle plays a crucial role in detoxifying many poisons and drugs?
A. Golgi Apparatus
B. Lysosomes
C. Smooth Endoplasmic Reticulum
D. Vacuoles

56. Projections of different lengths protruding out of the body of Amoeba is called:
A. Walking legs B. Legs
C. Pseudopodia D. Needle

57. Which of the following cells can change its shape?
A. White blood cell B. Egg cell
C. Red blood cell D. All of the above

58. One millionth of a metre is:
A. Millimetre B. Micrometre
C. Nanometre D. Centimetre

59. Which of the following combinations are present in plant cell but not in animal cell?
A. Cell Wall & Plastid
B. Cell wall and Cell membrane
C. Plastid and Nucleus
D. Cell Membrane and Cytoplasm

60. Nucleus is separated from cytoplasm by:
A. Protoplasm
B. Cell membrane
C. Cell Wall
D. Nuclear membrane

61. Deforestation means:
A. Planting more trees
B. Designing a forest
C. Demanding a forest
D. Clearing of forests and using that land for other purposes

62. Species of plants and animals which are found exclusively in a particular area are called:
A. Exotic species B. Local species
C. Specific species D. Endemic species

63. Increased level of carbon dioxide in the atmosphere traps the heat rays reflected by the earth causing an increase in the temperature on the earth. This is:
A. Local warming B. House warming
C. Global warming D. Country warming

64. Part of the earth which supports life where living beings exists is called ______
A. Atmosphere B. Biosphere
C. Biology D. Biodiversity

65. Variety of organisms existing on the earth, their inter-relationships and their relationship with the environment is called:
A. Diversity B. Biosphere
C. Biology D. Biodiversity

ANSWERS

1	2	3	4	5	6	7	8	9	10
A	D	B	A	D	A	B	C	B	C
11	**12**	**13**	**14**	**15**	**16**	**17**	**18**	**19**	**20**
D	C	B	A	C	D	A	C	C	A
21	**22**	**23**	**24**	**25**	**26**	**27**	**28**	**29**	**30**
A	D	C	C	C	C	A	A	A	A
31	**32**	**33**	**34**	**35**	**36**	**37**	**38**	**39**	**40**
A	A	D	A	A	D	B	B	D	A
41	**42**	**43**	**44**	**45**	**46**	**47**	**48**	**49**	**50**
D	A	C	D	B	C	C	B	A	B
51	**52**	**53**	**54**	**55**	**56**	**57**	**58**	**59**	**60**
B	C	D	A	C	C	A	B	A	D
61	**62**	**63**	**64**	**65**					
D	D	C	B	D					

★★★

4

Reproduction–Asexual and Sexual Reproduction, Reaching the Age of Adolescence

Some Important Facts

- The production of new organisms from the existing organisms of the same species is known as reproduction.
- Reproduction is essential for the survival of a species on this earth.
- The process of reproduction ensures continuity of life on earth.
- Reproduction by human beings ensures that the human species will continue to exist on this earth for all the time to come.
- Reproduction gives rise to more organisms with the same basic characteristics as their parents.
- Reproduction multiplies organisms while development builds up the body structures.
- The methods of reproduction show much diversity offspring may arise
  (*i*) from a single individual or
  (*ii*) by the participation of two individuals.
- There are two main methods of reproduction in living organisms:
  (*i*) Asexual reproduction and
  (*ii*) Sexual reproduction.
- **Asexual Reproduction:** The production of a new organism from a single parent without the involvement of sex cells is called asexual reproduction.

Some of the examples of asexual reproduction are: Binary fission in Amoeba, budding in hydra, spore formation in Rhizopus fungus, regeneration in Spirogyra and Planaria and vegetative propagation in flowering plants.

Asexual reproduction takes place by five different methods. These are:

(*i*) Fission
(*ii*) Budding
(*iii*) Spore formation
(*iv*) Regeneration and
(*v*) Vegetative propagation.

1. Fission

When the individual cell is fully mature, it divides into two. This is called fission.

Fission are two types: (*i*) Binary fission and (*ii*) Multiple fission.

(*i*) **Binary Fission:** When two individuals are formed during fission, the process is called **binary fission**. *e.g.*, The unicellular organisms like Amoeba, Paramecium, bacteria etc. reproduce by binary fission.

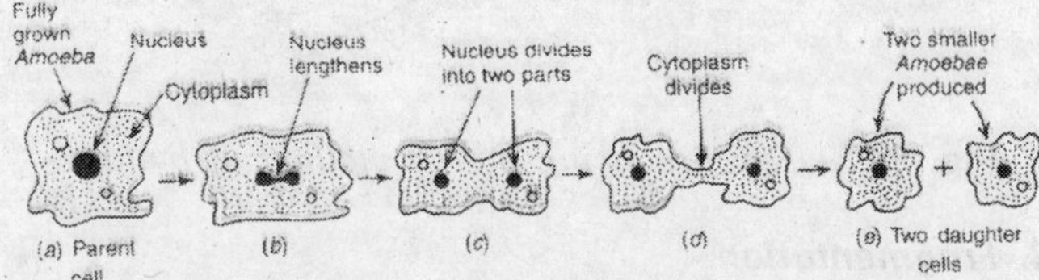

Fig. 1. *Amoeba reproducing by binary fission*

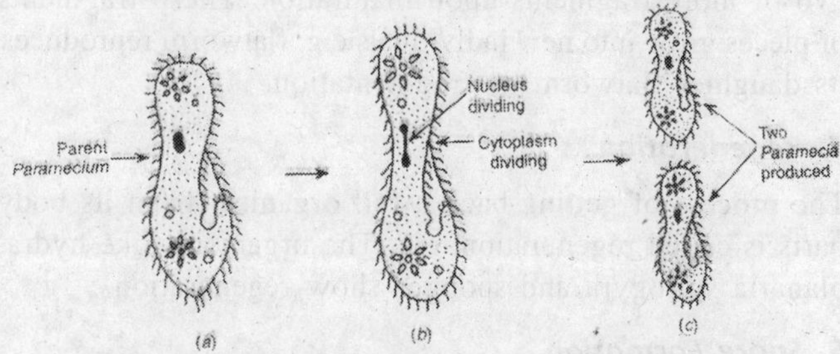

Fig. 2. *Paramecium reproducing by binary fission*

(*ii*) **Multiple Fission:** The cell divides many times within the cyst to produce many daughter cells. This is called **multiple fission**. *e.g.* Plasmodium is a protozoan which reproduces by the asexual method of multiple fission. About 1000 daughter cells are produced by the multiple fission of one plasmodium cell.

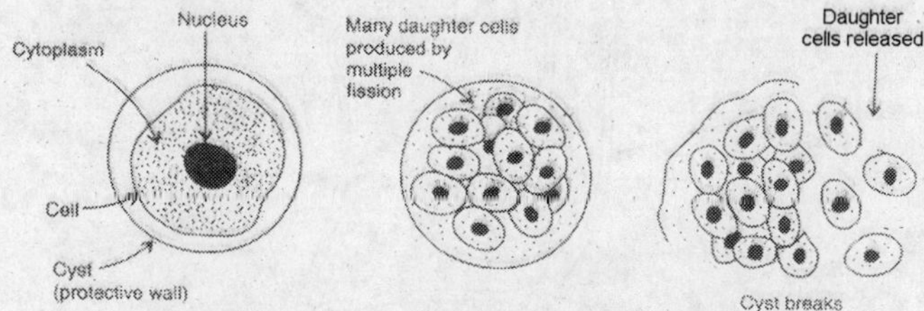

Fig. 3. *Reproduction by multiple fission*

2. Budding

A bulb—like projection formed on the body is known as the **bud**. The nucleus of the body divides into two and one of the nuclei passes into the bud. The bud detaches itself from the parent body, grows to full size and becomes a new individual. e.g. Yeast and Hydra.

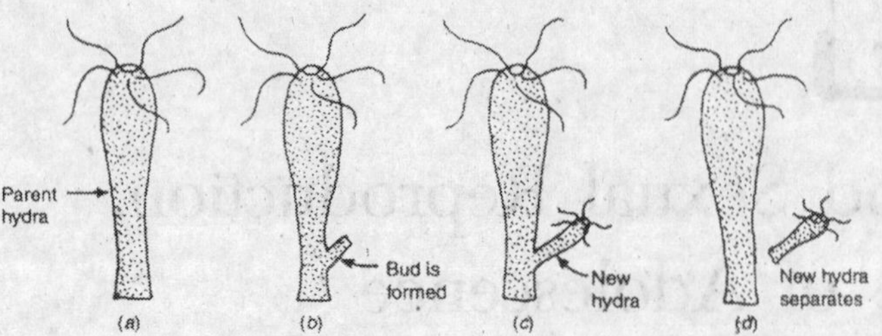

Fig. 4. *Hydra reproducing by the method of budding*

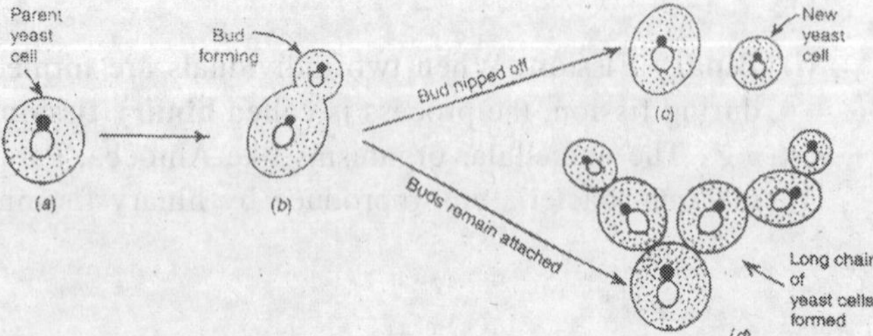

Fig. 5. *Yeast reproducing by the method of budding*

3. Fragmentation

Some organisms such as spirogyra (algae) break up into two or more fragments upon maturation. These fragments or pieces grow into new individuals e.g. flatworm reproduces its daughter flatworm by fragmentation.

4. Regeneration

The process of getting back a full organism from its body parts is called regeneration. e.g. The organisms like hydra, planaria spirogyra and sponges show regeneration.

5. Spore Formation

Some bacteria and lower forms of life form spores. It is a resting state in which the cell is protected by a thick wall during unfavourable conditions of heat or dryness. On return of favourable conditions, the thick wall breaks open and the bacteria reproduce and grow. e.g. Most of the fungi and bacteria reproduce by the method of spore formation.

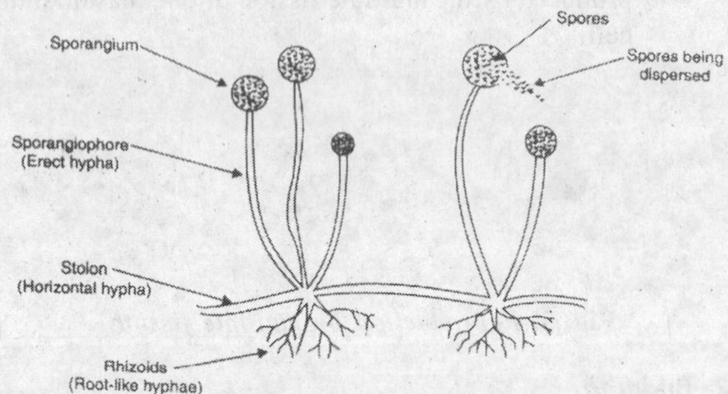

Fig. 6. *Rhizopus fungus plant (or bread mould) reproduces by forming spores.*

Vegetative Propagation

- Vegetative propagation is an asexual method of propagation in some higher plants.
- In vegetative propagation some plants can reproduced by growing new plants from the single parent plant are obtained from the parts of old plants (like stems, roots and leaves) without the help of any reproductive organs. *e.g.* Strawberry, iris, potato and rose plants can reproduce by this method.

There are many other plants which can grow by vegetative propagation.

(*i*) **Strawberry runners:** Shoots have buds which grow into new plants.

(*ii*) **Potato tubers:** A potato is an underground stem of a potato plant. The eyes on the potato sprout into new plants.

(*iii*) **Rhizomes (ginger):** Rhizomes are stems that grow and produce new plants.

(*iv*) **Gladiolus corms:** A corm is a short stem and form new plants.

(*v*) **Leaves:** The leaves of some plants. *e.g.* Bryophyllum.

A number of methods of artificial propagation of plants are used in agriculture and horticulture.

The common methods for the artificial vegetative propagation are:

(*i*) Grafting (*ii*) Cutting (*iii*) Layering.

(*i*) **Grafting:** Grafting is a method in which the cut stems of two different plants (one with roots and the other without roots) are joined together in such a way that the two plant stems join and grow as a single plant. The cut stem of a plant having roots is called **stock**. The cut stem of another plant without root is called **scion**. Using their practice plants of desired quality and fruits are obtained. Many varieties.

(*ii*) **Cutting:** A part of the plant which is a removed by cutting it, is called a cutting. A cutting may be a piece of stem, root or leaf. The cutting mode of propagation can be used to grow bougainvillea, sugarcane and cactus. Cutting allows to produce many new plants from one plant, without waiting for flowers and seeds.

(*iii*) **Layering:** In this method, a branch of the plant bends towards the ground and gets covered with moist soil. After some time, new roots emerge from the branch and produce new plantlets. These plantlets can be separated from the parent plant and made to grow as new individual plants.

e.g. Jasmine, roses and bougainvillea.

Advantages of Artificial Vegetative Propagation

The artificial vegetative propagation has the following advantages:

(*i*) The new plants produced by artificial vegetative propagation will be exactly like the parent plants.

(ii) Fruit trees grown from seeds may take many years before they start to bear fruits. Fruit trees grown from cutting or by grafting start to bear fruits after only a few growing seasons.

(iii) The plants grown by vegetative propagation usually need less attention in their early years than the plants grown for seeds.

Tissue Culture

The production of new plants from isolated plant cells or small pieces of plant tissue in a synthetic medium is called micropropagation or tissue culture.

The plant material is grown in special synthetic medium called culture solution it contains various plant nutrients and plant hormones. Which are necessary for plant growth.

Tissue culture for producing new plants is as follows:

(i) Some plant cells is taken from the tip of the plant and put into a suitable synthetic medium under sterile conditions.

(ii) The callus is then transferred to another medium containing suitable plant hormones which stimulus the callus to develop roots.

(iii) The callus with developed roots is then put into a yet another medium containing a different set of hormones which stimulate the development of shoots.

(iv) The callus having roots and shoots separate into tiny plantlets.

(v) The plantlets thus produced are transplanted into pots or soil where they can grow to form mature plants. Orchids, chrysanthemums, asparagus and many other plants are now grown using plant tissue culture.

Sexual Reproduction in Plants

The function of a flower is to make male and female gametes and to ensure that fertilisation will take place to make new seeds for the reproduction of plants.

Sexual reproduction is the most common method of reproduction in flowering plants.

The sexual reproduction in plants takes place in the following steps:

(i) The male organ of flower called **Stamen** makes the male gametes of the plant. These male sex cells are present in pollen grains.

(ii) The female organ of a flower called carpel or pistil makes the female gametes of the plant. These female sex cells are presented in ovules.

(iii) The male gametes present in pollen grains fertilise the female gametes present in ovules.

(iv) The fertilised ovules grow and become seeds.

(v) The seeds produce new plants.

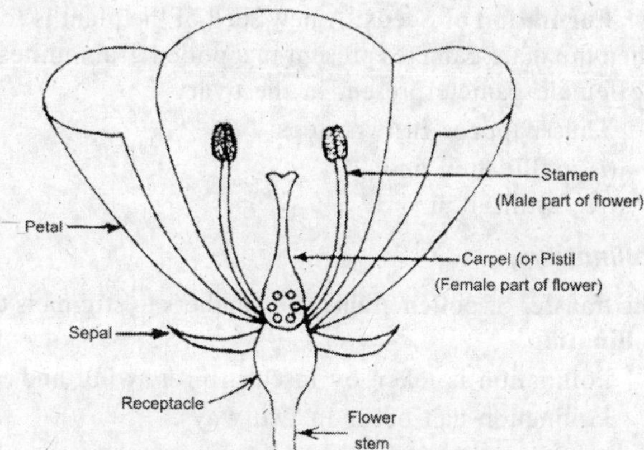

Fig. 7. *The parts of a flower.*

The main parts of a flower are: Receptacle, Sepals, Petals, Stamen and Carpel or Pistil.

Receptacle: The base of a flower to which all the parts of a flower are attached is called receptacle.

Sepals: The green, leaf-like parts in the outermost circle of a flower are called sepals. All the sepals taken together are called calyx.

Petals: The colourful parts of a flower are called **petals**. The petals lie inside the sepals. All the petals taken together are called corolla. The petals are usually scented. The function of petals is to attract insect for pollination.

Stamen: Stamen is the male reproduction organ of the plant. The stamen is made of two parts:

(i) a filament and

(ii) an anther

The Stalk of Stamen is called filament and the swollen top of stamen is called anther. Anther makes the pollen grains and stores them. Pollen grains contain the male gametes of the plant. Each pollen grain contains two male gametes of the plant.

Carpel or pistil: Carpel is the female reproductive organ of the plant. A carpel is made of three parts:

(i) Stigma (ii) Style and (iii) Ovary.

The top part of carpel is called **stigma**. Stigma is for receiving the pollen grains from the anther of stamen. The middle part of carpel is called **style**. Style is a tube which connects stigma to the ovary. The swollen part at the bottom of a carpel is called **ovary**. The ovary makes ovules and stores them. Ovules contain the female gametes of the plant. Each ovule contains only one female gametes of the plant.

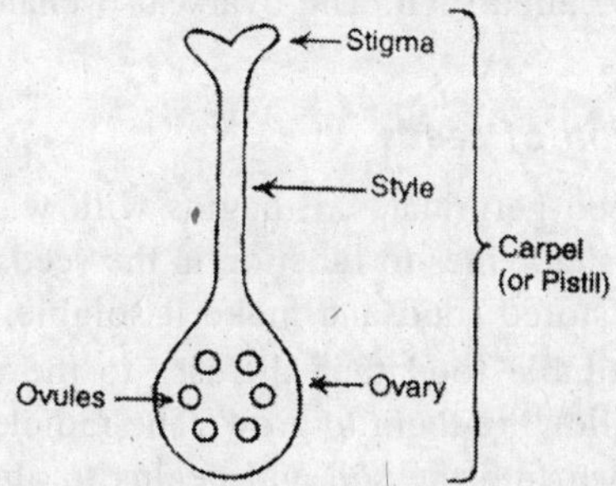

Fig. 8. *Carpel or pistil: Female reproductive organ of plant*

Formation of Seeds: A new seed of the plant is formed when the male gametes present in a pollen grain unites with the female gamete present in the ovary.

Thus happens in two steps:

(*i*) pollination and

(*ii*) fertilisation.

Pollination

The transfer of pollen grains from anthers to stigma is called **pollination**.

Pollination is taken by insects, birds, wind and water. Pollination can occur in two ways:

(*i*) Self-pollination and

(*ii*) Cross-pollination.

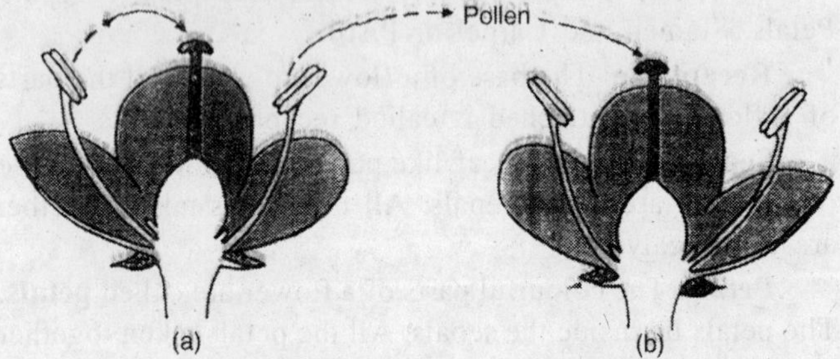

Fig. 9. *(a) Self-pollination and (b) cross-pollination*

Self-pollination: When the pollen grains from the anther of a flower are transferred to the stigma of the same flower is called self-pollination.

Cross-pollination: When the pollen grains from the anther of a flower on one plant are transferred to the stigma of a flower on another plant, it is called cross pollination.

Fertilisation

During pollination, pollen grains are carried from the anther to the stigma. The stigma secretes a liquid, containing sugar. If the stigma belongs to the right species of flower, the pollen grain responds to this liquid by beginning to form a tube. The tube grows out of the pollen grain and reaches one of the ovules.

The male gamete leaves the pollen grain and makes its way along the tube. When it reaches the ovule, it goes inside and fuses with the female gamete. Fertilisation has taken place. The fertilised egg cell is known as a **zygote**.

The fertilised and developed ovule, which contain embryo, is called **seed**. The ovary also changes to become a **fruit**.

Germination of seeds

When a seed germinates, it begins with water intake. The water helps enzymes to function in the seeds. The enzymes digest the stored food and make it soluble.

The soluble food then diffuses to the radicle and the plumule, allowing them to grow. The radicle grows first. It pushes down into the soil and begins to absorb water and minerals. The plumule pushes upwards. When it breaks out above the soil into the light, it becomes green and begins to photosynthesis.

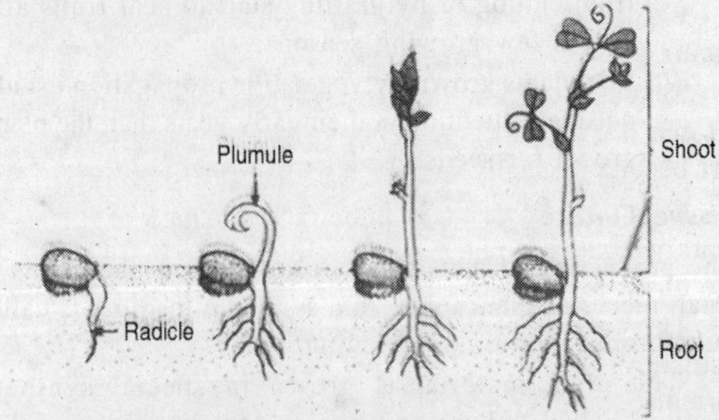

Fig. 10. *Germination of seed*

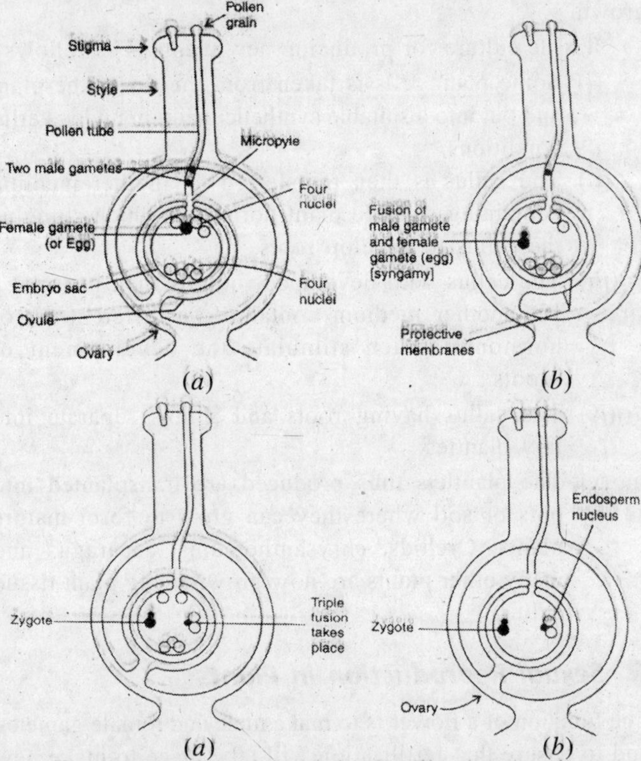

Fig. 11. *Explanation of the fertilisation in plants (including syngamy and triple fussion).*

Reproduction in Animals

Reproduction takes place in animal in two ways:

(*i*) Asexual and

(*ii*) Sexual.

Sexual Reproduction in Animals: The fusion of a male gamete with a female gamete to form a zygote during the sexual reproduction, is called **fertilisation**.

The stage of development between the zygote and the newly formed body is called **embryo**.

The fertilisation which occurs inside the female body is called **internal fertilisation**.

e.g., In mammals, birds and reptiles the fertilisation occurs inside the female body.

The fertilisation which occurs outside the female body is called **external fertilisation**.

e.g., Frogs, toads and fishes the fertilisation of eggs occurs outside the female body.

Sexual Reproduction in Humans: The age at which the sex hormones begin to be produced and the boy and girl become sexually mature is called **puberty**.

Generally boys attain puberty at the age of 13 to 14 years which girls reach puberty at a comparatively lower age of 10 to 12 years.

The testes produce the male sex hormone called testosterone and the ovaries produce two female sex hormones estrogen and progesterone. The sex hormons play an important role in the process of reproduction.

The various function of sex hormone are given below:

(*i*) The sex hormones control the process of gametogenesis.

(*ii*) The sex hormones maintain the structure and functions of accessory sex organs.

(*iii*) The sex hormones develop the secondary sex characteristics.

The Male Reproductive System

The human male reproductive system consists of the following organs:

(*i*) Testes

(*ii*) Scrotum and

(*iii*) Epididymis.

Testes are the primary reproductive organs in man. The function of testes is to make the male sex cells called sperms and also to make the male sex hormone called testosterone.

The sperms formed in testes come out and go into a coiled tube called epididymis. The sperms get stored temporarily in epididymics.

The Female Reproductive System

The human female reproductive system consists of the following organs:

(*i*) Ovaries

(*ii*) Fallopian tubes

(*iii*) Uterus

(*iv*) Vagina.

Ovaries are the oval shaped organs which are inside the abdominal cavity of a woman near the kidneys. The function of ovaries is to make the female sex cells called ova or eggs and also make the female sex hormones called estrogen and progesterone.

The fallopian tubes are not directly connected to ovaries but have funnel shaped openings which almost cover the ovaries. The fertilisation of egg by a sperm takes place in the fallopian tube.

The two fallopian tubes connect to a bag like organ called uterus. The growth and development of a fertilised ovum into a body takes place in the uterus. The embedding of embryo in the thick lining of the uterus is called implantation. The exchange of nutrients, oxygen and waste products between the embryo and the mother takes place through the placenta.

The time period from the fertilisation upto the birth of the body is called **gestation**. The average gestation period in humans is about 40 weeks or 280 days. The average weight of a new born baby is about 3.5 kilograms.

MULTIPLE CHOICE QUESTIONS

1. The two oviducts in a human female unite into an elastic bag like is known as:

A. Vagina B. Uterus
C. Fallopian tube D. Cervix

2. Which of the following disease is transmitted sexually?

A. Kala azar B. Jaundice
C. Cholera D. Syphilis

3. Which of the following is a contraceptive?

A. Copper-T B. Condom
C. Diaphragm D. All of these

4. When a animal is cut into pieces and each piece grows into a complex organism. What is the process?

A. Budding B. Fragmentation
C. Spore formation D. Regeneration

5. Which is the portion on which grafting is done it provides the roots?

A. Stock B. Scion
C. Both A and B D. None of these

6. Where does fertilization occur in human females?

A. Uterus B. Cervix
C. Oviduct D. None of these

7. Growing foetus derive nutrition from mother's blood through:

A. Uterus B. Fallopian tube
C. Placenta D. Cervix

8. What is the puberty age in human males?

A. 8-10 B. 10-12
C. 12-14 D. 14-16

9. Fruits are formed from:

A. Stamen B. Stigma
C. Ovary D. Ovule

10. IUCD is for:

A. Vegetative propagation
B. Contraception
C. Increasing fertility
D. Avoiding miscarriage

11. The male hormone testesterone is produced by ______.
A. Leydig cells B. Seminiferous tubules
C. Epididymis D. Vas deferens

12. Male gonads are called ______.
A. testes B. ovaries
C. scrotal sacs D. sperm duct

13. The fertilized egg is called ______
A. ovum B. blastocyst
C. diploid cell D. zygote

14. The ultimate stoppage of menstrual cycle is called ______.
A. puberty B. menarche
C. menopause D. old age

15. The process by which the sperms are produced is known as ______.
A. ovulation B. spermatogenesis
C. oogenesis D. gestation

16. The tube that carries the sperms out of the testes is the ______
A. vasa efferentia B. vas deferens
C. oviduct D. epididymis

17. The process by which the sperms are released is called ______.
A. spermatogenesis B. oogenesis
C. ovulation D. ejaculation

18. The external genitalia in females is called ______
A. pubis B. vagina
C. vulva D. clitoris

19. Sterilisation in males is called as ______.
A. tubectomy B. vasectomy
C. IVF D. GIFT

20. Binary fission is seen in ______.
A. plasmodium B. hydra
C. amoeba D. mucor

21. The endosperm nucleus is ______.
A. haploid B. diploid
C. triploid D. tetraploid

22. The fertilization of human egg by the sperms takes place in ______.
A. ovary B. oviduct
C. vagina D. uterus

23. Pollen tube contains ______.
A. one male nucleus B. two male nuclei
C. three male nuclei D. four male nuclei

24. If the pollen is transferred to the stigma of the same flower, it is called ______.
A. allogamy B. autogamy
C. cross pollination D. double fertilization

25. Pollen grains are produced by ______.
A. ovary B. filament
C. stigma D. anther

26. The collective name for sepals is ______.
A. androecium B. gynoecium
C. corolla D. calyx

27. The individual units of corolla are called ______.
A. petals B. sepals
C. stamens D. pistils

28. The attachment of the embryo to the uterus is called ______.
A. gestation B. fertilisation
C. implantation D. menstruation

29. The onset of the reproductive age is called ______.
A. menstruation B. menarche
C. menopause D. puberty

30. The first time that the monthly bleeding occurs is called ______.
A. maturity B. menarche
C. menopause D. puberty

31. The most important part of the plant for continuation of the life of the species is______.
A. stem B. root
C. flower D. leaf

32. The type of vegetative propagation seen in chrysanthemum is ______.
A. runner B. sucker
C. stolon D. offset

33. Successfully grafted plants bear the flowers and fruits characteristic of the ______.
A. scion
B. stock
C. either scion or stock
D. a mixture of scion and stock

34. Sugarcane is normally grown by ______.
A. cutting B. grafting
C. layering D. seeds

35. Unequal daughter cells are produced in ______.
A. fragmentation B. sporulation
C. fission D. budding

36. Vegetative propogation in sweet potato is by ______.
A. stem B. root
C. leaf D. none of the above

37. Vegetative propogation in *Bryophyllum* is by ______.
A. stem B. root
C. leaf D. none of the above

38. An example of a hermaphrodite is ______.
A. frog B. fish
C. earthworm D. hydra

39. Multiple fission is seen in __________.
A. yeast
B. paramoecium
C. plasmodium
D. rhizopus

40. Progesterone is secreted by __________.
A. Ovarian follicle
B. Graffian follicle
C. Corpus luteum
D. Corpus albicans

41. The hormone secreted by the pituitary to start the ovulation process is __________.
A. FSH
B. Luteinizing hormone
C. Oestrogen
D. Progesterone

42. Sperms are produced at a temperature that is ______ the body temperature.
A. same as
B. lower than
C. higher than
D. immaterial to

43. The part of the sperm that contains the lytic enzymes is __________.
A. acrosome
B. nucleus
C. mid-piece
D. tail

44. The life span of the sperm is __________.
A. 2 days
B. 1-3 days
C. 1-3 weeks
D. 7 days

45. The sperms are temporarily stored in __________.
A. vas deferens
B. vas efferens
C. epididymis
D. bladder

46. Identical gametes are also known as:
A. heterogametes
B. isogametes
C. anisogamete
D. hypogametes

47. Placenta passes out through vagina:
A. 10-20 minutes after birth
B. 10-15 minutes after birth
C. 10-30 minutes after birth
D. 10-45 minutes after birth

48. Germinating pollen grain is a rich source of:
A. cytokinin
B. gibberellin
C. auxin
D. rennin

49. Secondary spermatocytes and spermatids are formed by meiotic division in:
A. primary spermatocytes
B. spermatogonia
C. primary oocytes
D. polar body

50. Multiple fission is a characteristic reproduction mechanism in:
A. plant like protoctists
B. animal like protoctists
C. hydra
D. earthworm

ANSWERS

1	2	3	4	5	6	7	8	9	10
B	D	D	D	A	D	C	C	C	B
11	**12**	**13**	**14**	**15**	**16**	**17**	**18**	**19**	**20**
A	A	D	C	B	B	D	C	B	C
21	**22**	**23**	**24**	**25**	**26**	**27**	**28**	**29**	**30**
C	B	B	B	D	D	A	C	D	B
31	**32**	**33**	**34**	**35**	**36**	**37**	**38**	**39**	**40**
C	B	A	A	D	B	C	C	C	C
41	**42**	**43**	**44**	**45**	**46**	**47**	**48**	**49**	**50**
B	B	A	B	C	B	D	C	A	B

★ ★ ★

Force–Frictional Force; Gravitational Force; Thrust and Pressure

Physical Quantities

- Physical quantities may be divided in two classes:
  (*i*) Scalar Quantities
  (*ii*) Vector Quantities
- A scalar quantity is one which has only magnitude.
- A vector quantity has both magnitude and direction.
- Force, Velocity, Momentum, Acceleration are examples of vector quantities.
- Mass, length, time, volume, speed, energy, work are examples of scalar quantities.

Units

- All measurements in physics require standard units.
- In 1960, the General Conference of Weights and Measures recommended that a metric system of measurements called the International System of Units, abbreviated as SI units, be used.

Some Important Units

S. No.	Units	Quantity
1.	Metre	Length
2.	Kilogram	Mass
3.	Second	Time
4.	Ampere	Electric Current
5.	Candela	Luminous Intensity
6.	Newton	Force
7.	Joule	Workdone
8.	Watt	Power
9.	Coulomb	Quantity of Electricity
10.	Volt	Potential Difference
11.	Ohm	Electrical Resistance
12.	Farad	Capacitance
13.	Henry	Inductance
14.	Lumen	Luminous Flux

- Very small distances are measured in micrometers or (microns) (μm), angstroms (Å), nanometers (nm) and femtometers (fm).
- 1 m = 10^6 μm = 10^9 nm = 10^{10} Å = 10^{15} fm
- 1 micron (1μ) = 10^{-4} cm = 10^{-6} m
- 1 Angstrom (1 Å) = 10^{-8} cm = 10^{-10} m
- 1 Fermi (1F) = 10^{-13} cm = 10^{-15} m

Motion

- When a body changes its position with respect to something else as time goes on, we say the body is in motion.
- There are two types of motion— translational (linear) and rotational (spin).
- The motion of a car on a road is translational whereas the motion of a top, spinning on its axis is rotational.

Speed

- It is a scalar form of velocity and is defined as the distance travelled irrespective of direction in one second.
- Speed = $\dfrac{\text{distance travelled}}{\text{time required}}$
- SI unit of speed is meters per second (m/s).

Velocity

- The distance covered by an object in a specified direction in unit time interval is called velocity.
- The SI unit of velocity is m/s.
- Velocity is a vector quantity.

Acceleration

- The velocity of a body changes due to change in its speed or direction or both. The rate of change of the velocity of a body is called its acceleration.
- Acceleration = $\dfrac{\text{change in velocity}}{\text{time}}$
- Negative acceleration is known as retardation. It indicates that the velocity of the object is decreasing with respect to time.
- Acceleration is uniform when neither its direction nor magnitude changes with respect to time.

Acceleration Due to Gravity

- When a body falls freely, then the increase in velocity per second is called acceleration due to gravity. It is represented by '*g*'.

$$g = \frac{GMe}{Re^2}$$

where G = Universal Gravitational Constant
Me = Mass of Earth
Re = Radius of the Earth

- Value of 'g' depends upon the radius of the earth as $g \propto \frac{1}{R}$
- Value of 'g' is maximum at poles and minimum at equator.

Equations of Motion

1. $V = u + at$
2. $S = ut + \frac{1}{2}at^2$
3. $V^2 = u^2 + 2as$

where u is initial velocity; V is final velocity; t is time; a is acceleration; s is distance

Force

Gravitational Force

- It is the force of attraction between two masses.
- The gravitational force exists between all bodies, even between two apples lying on a table.
- It is gravitational force that holds the moon in its orbit round the earth and the earth in its orbit round the sun.
- **Newton's Law of Universal Gravitation** states that every particle in the universe attracts every other particle with a force that is directly proportional to the product of their masses and inversely proportional to the square of the distance between them.
- In equation form, the gravitational force

$$F = G\frac{m_1 m_2}{r^2}$$

where r is the distance between two particles of masses m_1 and m_2 and G the universal gravitational constant.
- The value of G is 6.67×10^{-11} SI units.

Centripetal Force

- The force acting towards the centre on a particle executing uniform circular motion is called centripetal force and is given by

$$F = \frac{mv^2}{r}$$

where m = Mass of the object
v = Speed
r = Radius of the Circular Path
- In case of the moon, gravitational force between the earth and the moon acts as the centripetal force.
- When a stone tied at one end of a string is whirled in a circle, the pull in the string provides the centripetal force.
- Without centripetal force there can be no circular motion.
- Centripetal force always acts on the particle performing circular motion.

Centrifugal Force

- The pseudo force that balances the centripetal force in uniform circular motion is called centrifugal force.
- Centrifugal force is directed away from the centre along the radius.
- The centrifugal force is zero exactly at the poles and maximum at the equator.

Weight

- The weight of a body is the force with which the earth attracts the body towards its centre.
- The weight of a body should not be confused with its mass, which is a measure of the quantity of matter contained in it. When we say that a person weighs 60 kg, we are actually describing his mass and not weight.
- The mass of a body is a constant quantity whereas its weight varies slightly from place-to-place on the earth.
- The weight of a body is maximum at the poles and minimum at the equator. This variation in weight is due to:
  1. The shape of the earth.
  2. The rotation of the earth about its axis.
- The weight of an object is less at high elevations them at sea level.
- At the centre of the earth, the weight of a body would be zero.
- The weight of a body can also be expressed in terms of the acceleration due to gravity (g). The weight (w) of a body of mass m is given by the product of m and g, *i.e.*, $w = mg$
- On the surface of the moon the value of the acceleration due to gravity is nearly one-sixth of that on earth and, therefore, an object on the moon would weigh only one-sixth its weight on the earth. The mass of an object on the moon would be the same as on earth.
- The weight of a body would be more if the earth stopped rotating. Conversely, if the speed of rotation were higher, the weight would be lesser.
- A person weighs more in a lift, which is accelerating upward.
- An astronaut feels weightlessness in a spaceship because he is not pushing against anything.

Friction

- Friction is the force which opposes the relative motion of two surfaces in contact.
- It is friction between the ground and the soles of our shoes that makes walking possible and it is lack of friction that makes our feet slip on highly polished surfaces.

- The force of friction that acts when a body is moving (sliding) on a surface is called sliding friction.
- When a cylindrical or spherical body rolls over a surface, the force opposing the motion is called rolling fric.ion. For the same pair of materials rolling friction is much smaller than sliding friction.
- Friction in machines wastes energy and also causes wear and tear. This friction is reduced by using (1) lubricants, and (2) ball bearings.
- Rolling friction is always lesser than the sliding friction and hence it is easier to move a heavy object on rollers rather than to slide it. This property can be attributed to the fact that in case of rolling friction, the area of contact between the two surfaces is far less.

Newton's Laws of Motion

First Law

- Every object continues in its state of rest or of uniform motion in a straight line if no net force acts upon it. It is also known as **law of inertia.**
- **Examples:**
  1. An unwary passenger in a fast-moving bus falls forward when it stops suddenly. This happens because the feet of the passenger come to rest suddenly whereas his body continues to be in motion.
  2. A person getting down from a moving bus has to run some distance, in the direction of the bus, before stopping. If he does not run he is bound to fall because his feet come to rest whereas his body continues to be in motion.

Momentum

- The momentum of a body is defined as the product of its mass and velocity.

Second Law

- This law states that "the rate of change of momentum of a body is proportional to the applied force and takes place in the direction of the force".
- If we express force (F) in Newtons, mass (*m*) in kilograms and acceleration (*a*) in metres per second squared, we can write the second law as

$$F = ma$$

- In travelling the same distance, a car consumes more fuel on a crowded road than on a free road. This happens because the car has to stop and start quite often on a crowded road. The repeated acceleration requires a force (second law), which ultimately comes from the fuel. On a free road the car runs at almost uniform speed requiring fewer accelerations and hence less fuel consumption.

Third Law

- This law states that "to every action there is an equal and opposite reaction". The statement means that if body A exerts a force on body B, then B exerts an equal and opposite force on A along the same line of action.
- When a bullet is fired from a gun, equal and opposite forces are exerted on the bullet and the gun.
- A rocket contains solid chemicals which burn to produce a high velocity blast of hot gases. Space rockets have liquid fuel together with a supply of liquid oxygen to enable the fuel to burn. In either case, the large force created by chemical reaction propels out hot gases through the tail nozzle with a very high velocity. The reaction to this force propels the rocket forward.
- The engine in a jet aeroplane works on the same principle as a rocket but there is a difference in the method of obtaining the high velocity gas jet.
- The fuel used in a jet engine in Kerosene (paraffin).

Impulse

- If a force acts on a body for a very short time, then the product of force and time is called the impulse.

Impulse = Change in momentum

= Force × Time

Application of Impulse

1. A cricket player draws his hand back while catching.
2. A person jumping on hard cement floor receives more injuries than a person jumping on muddy or sandy floor.

Work, Power and Energy

Work

- Whenever a force acting on a body displaces it, work is said to be done.

  Work = Force × Distance moved in the direction of force.
- Work is a scalar quantity and its SI unit is Joule (J).

Power

- Power is defined as the rate of doing work.

$$\text{Power} = \frac{\text{Work done}}{\text{Time taken}}$$

- The SI unit of power is Watt (W) and is also measured in horse power.

1 HP = 746 W

Energy

- Energy is defined as the capacity to do work.
- The SI unit of energy is Joule (J).
- There are two forms of mechanical energy—Kinetic and Potential.

Kinetic Energy

- The energy possessed by an object due to its motion is called kinetic energy and is described by the expression

$$KE = \frac{1}{2}mv^2$$

where m = mass of the object

v = speed

Potential Energy

- Potential energy is the energy possessed by the body by virtue of its position, configuration or any condition of stress or strain.
- One of the commonest forms of potential energy is that possessed by an object when it is above the level of the earth's surface. This is called gravitational potential energy and is described by the expression

$$PE = mgh$$

where m is the mass of the object, g the acceleration due to gravity and h the height of the object above the earth's surface.
- There are many examples of potential energy. A stone held at some height above the ground has potential energy. Water in an elevated reservoir possesses potential energy.

Conservation of Energy

- Energy can neither be created nor destroyed; it can only be transformed from one form into another, but the total amount of energy remains constant.

Transformation of Energy

S.No.	Equipment	Transformation
1.	Dynamo	Mechanical energy into electrical energy
2.	Microphone	Sound energy into electrical energy
3.	Loud Speaker	Electrical energy into sound energy
4.	Electric Bulb	Electrical energy into light and heat energy
5.	Battery	Chemical energy into electrical energy
6.	Electrical Motor	Electrical energy into mechanical energy

Einstein Relation

- According to Einstein, mass can be converted into energy and energy can be converted into mass. One can be obtained at the cost of the other. The equivalence between mass and energy is expressed in terms of Einstein Relations:

$$E = mc^2$$

where m is the mass that disappears, E is the energy that appears and c is the velocity of light in vacuum ($c = 3 \times 10^8$ m/s)

Centre of Gravity

- The centre of gravity of a body is the point where the whole weight of the body can be considered to act.
- The centre of gravity of a body may even lie outside the actual material of the body. For example, the centre of gravity of a ring lies at its centre, which is outside its material.
- The stability of an object is connected with the position of its centre of gravity (CG).
- If the vertical through the CG passes through the base of an object, then it is stable, otherwise it is unstable and topples down.
- Racing cars are built low and with wide wheel bases to reduce the risk of overturning at sharp bends.
- While crossing a river in a boat, passengers are not allowed to stand. This keeps the CG of the system (boat and passengers) low and ensures stability.
- A porter carrying a load on his back leans forward to keep the vertical line passing through the CG of the system between his feet.

Artificial Satellites

- In the case of a satellite, the centripetal force is provided by the gravitational pull of the earth.
- The speed of the satellite does not depend on its mass. It means that at a particular distance from the earth, all objects would have the same speed of revolution. If a satellite moves from a higher orbit to a lower orbit, its speed increases.
- If the speed of a satellite is more than 11.2 km/s or 25,000 miles/hour, the satellite would escape the earth entirely and would never come back. This is called escape velocity.
- The existence of gaseous atmosphere on the earth is due to the high value of its escape velocity.
- On the moon the value of the escape velocity is 1.9 km/s (nearly one-sixth of that on earth). If any gases are formed on the moon, the molecules would have velocities greater than 1.9 km/s and would therefore escape, leaving the moon bare.
- The value of escape velocity does not depend upon the mass of the projected body, instead it depends on the mass and radius of the planet from which it is being projected.
- The value of escape velocity does not depend on the angle and direction of projection.
- The root mean square velocity of hydrogen is more than that of the escape velocity of earth, therefore, hydrogen is not found in earth's lower atmosphere.

Geostationary Satellites

- Geostationary satellites are stationary with respect to an observer on the earth. Their time period is 24-hour. There height above the surface of earth is 36,000 km. They are always in equatorial plane and their orbits are circular. They are also called parking orbits.

Density and Relative Density

- The mass per unit volume of a substance is called its density.

$$\text{Density} = \frac{\text{Mass}}{\text{Volume}}$$

- The SI unit of density is kilogram per metre cubed (kg/m^3).

Densities of Some Common Substances

Sr. No.	*Substance*	*Density in kg/m^3*
1.	Alcohol	790
2.	Water	1,000
3.	Aluminium	2,700
4.	Steel (vories)	7,800
5.	Copper	8,900
6.	Lead	11,300
7.	Mercury	13,600
8.	Gold	19,300
9.	Platinum	21,500

- The relative density of a substance is the ratio of the density of the substance to the density of water.
- Relative density has no unit.

Pressure

- Pressure is defined as force acting per unit area.

$$\text{Pressure} = \frac{\text{Force}}{\text{Area}}$$

- The SI unit of pressure is newton per metre square or pascal.
- There is a inverse relationship between magnitude of pressure and area of contact.
- It is much easier to cut fruit with a sharp knife than with a blunt one. In the case of a sharp knife the blade makes such a small area of contact with the fruit that the pressure below it, is very high and easily cuts the fruit.
- Broad wooden sleepers are placed below the rails to reduce the pressure exerted by the weight of a train.
- The pressure of water increases with depth, therefore bottom of a dam is made much thicken than the top.
- The pressure exerted on an enclosed liquid at one place is transmitted equally throughout the liquid. This is called Pascal's Principle.
- Hydraulic presses, hydraulic brakes, hydraulic door closers, etc. are applications of the Pascal's Principle.
- At high attitudes where atmosphere pressure is less nose bleeding may occur due to the greater pressure of blood.
- It is due to the pressure of the atmosphere that ink rises in the tube of a fountain pen or liquid rises in a syringe when the piston is pulled.
- In an aircraft flying at high altitude, normal atmospheric pressure is maintained by the use of air pumps. If this were not done, the crew and passengers would experience difficulty in breathing and consequently face dangers.
- Atmospheric pressure is measured with an instrument called the **Barometer.**
- Aneroid barometer does not use any liquid.
- If the barometric height falls suddenly, it indicates the coming of a storm. A gradual fall in the barometric height indicates the possibility of rain. A gradual increase in the barometric height indicates fair weather.

Archimede's Principle

- This principle states that when a body is wholly or partially immersed in a fluid, it experiences an upthrust (upward force) equal to the weight of the fluid displaced.
- When an object is immersed in a fluid, two forces act on it: (*i*) the weight of the object acting downward, and (*ii*) upthrust acting upward.
- It is due to upthrust that objects apparently weightless when immersed in fluids.

Law of Floatation

- When a body is immersed in a fluid then if—
  1. The weight of body is equal to upthrust, the body floats with whole of its volume inside the liquid.
  2. The weight of body is more than the upthrust, the body will sink.
  3. The weight of body is less than the upthrust, the body will float with some of its part outside the liquid.
- An iron nail sinks in water whereas a ship made of iron and steel floats. This is due to the fact that a ship is hollow and contains air and, therefore, its density is less than that of water.
- The density of sea water is more than that of river water, due to this a ship sinks less in sea water. It is for this reason that a ship rises a little when it enters a sea from a river.
- It is because of the higher density of sea water that it is easier to swim in the sea.
- A solid chunk of iron will sink in the water but float in mercury because the density of iron is more than that of water but less than that of mercury.
- A balloon filled with a light gas, such as hydrogen, rises because the average density of the balloon and the gas is less than that of air. The balloon cannot rise indefinitely because the density of the air decreases with increasing altitude. At a certain height, where the density of air is equal to the average density of the balloon, it ceases to rise and drifts sideways with the wind.

- When an ice block floats in water the water level will remain the same when all the ice melts into water.
- A **hydrometer** is an instrument used for measuring the relative density of liquids.
- A special type of a hydrometer called **Lactometer** is used for testing milk by measuring its density.

Surface Tension

- Surface tension is that property of liquids owing to which they tend to acquire minimum surface area.
- Surface tension is caused by molecular attractions.
- When a paint brush is dipped in water all its hair spread out but when it is taken out it is covered with a thin film of water which contracts due to surface tension and pulls the hair together.
- Liquid drops, such as raindrops, oildrops, drops of molten metals, dewdrops etc. are all spherical because their surface tend to contract in order to have minimum surface area. For a given volume, a sphere has the minimum surface area.
- Soaps and detergents lower the surface tension of water. This increases the wetting power of water or its ability to detach dirt particles from clothes and untensils.
- Cohesive forces are the forces of attraction acting between molecules of same substance. The liquids for which cohesive forces are large do not wet the walls of the vessel, *e.g.*, mercury. Surface tension forces arise due to cohesive forces.
- Adhesive forces are the forces of attraction acting between the molecules of different substances. If adhesive forces are greater than cohesive force then the liquid wets the walls of the vessel, *e.g.*, water wets the walls of a glass-capillary.
- The force of attraction between unlike molecules is called **adhesion** and that between like molecules **cohesion.**
- The melted wax of a candle is drawn up into the wick by capillary action. Oil rises up a lamp wick for the same reason.
- If one end of a sugar cube is dipped into tea, the entire cube is quickly wet on account of capillary action.
- The fine pores of a blotting paper act as tiny capillary tubes. The ink rises into the blotting paper through these pores.

Viscosity

- The force which opposes the relative motion between different layers of liquid or gases is called viscous force.
- Viscosity is the property of liquids and gases both.
- The viscosity of a liquid is due to cohesive force between its molecules.
- The viscosity of a gas is due to diffusion of its molecules from one layer to other layer.

Bernoulli's Theorem

- According to Bernoulli's theorem, in case of streamline flow of incompressible and non-viscous fluid (ideal fluid) through a tube, total energy (sum of pressure energy, potential energy and kinetic energy) per unit volume of fluid is same at all points.
- An important corollary of this theorem is: pressure in a fluid decreases with increased velocity of the fluid. Examples:
  1. When a bowler spins a ball, it changes its direction (swings) in the air due to unequal pressure acting on it.
  2. The shape of the wings of an aeroplane is such that wind velocity above the wings is higher than that below them. Consequently, there is higher pressure below the wings and this lifts the aeroplane.
  3. When the piston of a sprayer is pushed, air is forced past the upper end of a tube, whose lower end dips in the liquid to be sprayed. Due to the increased velocity of air, the pressure near the upper end of the tube is reduced. The atmospheric pressure in the container, therefore, pushes the liquid to the top, from where it is carried away by the stream of air.

Heat

- Heat is that form of energy which flows from one body to other body due to difference in temperature between the bodies. The amount of heat contained in a body depends upon the mass of the body.

Temperature and Heat

- The temperature of a body is the quantity that tells how hot or cold it is with respect to some standard body.
- Heat is the internal energy transferred from one body to another due to temperature difference.

Measurement of Temperature

- Temperature is measured by a thermometer.
- To measure temperature two fixed points are taken on each thermometer. One of the fixed points is the freezing point of water or ice point as lower fixed point (LFP). The other fixed point is the boiling point of water or steam point as upper fixed point.
- A thermometer may be graduated in following scales—
  1. The upper and lower points of centigrade scale are 100°C and 0°C.

2. The upper and lower points of Fahrenheit scale are 212°F and 32°F.
3. The upper and lower points of Reaumur scale are 80°R and 0°R.
4. The upper and lower points of Kelvin scale are 373K and 273K.
5. The upper and lower points of Rankine scale are 672° Ra and 460° Ra.

- Relation between different temperature scales

$$\frac{C}{100} = \frac{F-32}{180} = \frac{R}{80} = \frac{K-273}{100} = \frac{Ra-460}{212}.$$

- At – 40 degrees both celsius and Fahrenheit scales will show identical readings.
- **Pyrometer** is a instrument for measuring high temperatures.
- Weather reports in newspapers carry the maximum and the minimum temperatures recorded during the last 24 hours.
- Mercury is used in thermometers because—
  1. It is opaque and shining and, therefore, temperature can be read conveniently.
  2. It is a good conductor of heat, and, therefore, records temperatures rapidly.
  3. It does not stick to glass and also does not vapourise much and therefore yields correct readings.
- Water cannot be used in a thermometer because it freezes at 0°C and also because of its irregular expansion.
- In cold countries where winter temperatures of –40°C are not uncommon, mercury thermometers cannot be used because mercury freezes at –39°C. In such countries, alcohol thermometers are useful, since alcohol freezes at –115°C.

Thermal Expansion

- Solids, liquids and gases generally expand when heated and contract when cooled.
- Gaps have to be left in railway tracks to make allowance for expansion, otherwise the rails will buckle. Allowance is made for the expansion of long steel bridges. One end of such bridge is fixed while the other rests on rollers.
- Telephone wires sag more in summer than in winter due to thermal expansion.

Expansion of Water

- Water has its minimum volume and maximum density at 4°C.
- Water shows unusual expansion. If we take a cube of ice at –5°C and heat it, it expands till ice starts melting. During melting its temperature remains 0°C but its volume decreases. If heat is continuously supplied to water at 0°C, it further contracts up to 4°C and then it starts expanding.
- Anomalous expansion of water helps preserve aquatic life during very cold weather. When temperature falls, the top layer of water in a pond contracts, becomes denser and sinks to the bottom. A circulation is thus set up until the entire water in the pond reaches maximum density at 4°C. If the temperature falls further, the top layer expands and remains on top till it freezes. Thus, even though the upper layers are frozen the water near the bottom is at 4°C and the fishes etc., can survive in it easily.

Transmission of Heat

- There are three ways of heat transmission:
  1. Conduction
  2. Convection
  3. Radiation

Conduction

- In this process, heat is transferred from one place to other place by the successive vibration of the particles of the medium without bodily movement of the particles of the medium.
- Conduction takes place mainly in solids.
- Air is a very bad conductor of heat. The good insulating properties of wool, cotton, etc. are mainly due to the air spaces they contain.
- Sawdust is a bad conductor of heat. Therefore, ice slabs are covered with sawdust to minimise melting.
- On a cold night two thin blankets are preferred to a single thick blanket because the layer of air between the two blankets serves as a better insulator.

Convection

- In this process, heat is transferred by the actual movement of particles of the medium from one place to other place.
- In liquids and gases heat is transmitted by convection.

Radiation

- It is the fastest means of heat transfer.
- In this mode of heat transmission heat is transferred from one place to another without effecting the intervening medium.
- Both conduction and convection require a material medium for conveying heat from one part to another. Radiation, on the other hand, does not require any medium.

Newton's Law of Cooling

- This law states that the rate of which a hot body loses heat is directly proportional to the difference between its temperature and the surrounding temperature.
- **Example:** Hot water takes much less time in cooling from 90°C to 80°C than in cooling from 40°C to 30°C.

Kirchhoff's Law

- According to Kirchhoff's law, the ratio of emissive power to absorptive power is same for all surfaces at the same temperature and is equal to emissive power of black body at that temperature.

Greenhouse Effect

- A greenhouse acts like a radiation trap.
- In a greenhouse, heat radiation from the sun passes through the glass and keeps the plants and the air inside warm. The glass prevents warm air from escaping.
- A car parked in the sun with its windows closed gets terribly warm due to the greenhouse effect.

Heat Capacity

- The heat capacity of a body is defined as the heat required to raise the temperature of the body by 1 K. Its SI unit is J/K.

Specific Heat Capacity

- The specific heat capacity of a substance is the heat required to raise the temperature of a unit mass of the substance by 1 K.
- Its SI unit is J/kg K.
- Water has a very high specific heat capacity.
- It is because of its high specific heat capacity that water is used as a cooling liquid in car engine.

Latent Heat

- It is defined as the amount of heat absorbed or given out by a body during the change of state.
- The latent heat of fusion of a substance is defined as the heat required to convert a unit mass of the substance from the solid to the liquid state without change of temperature.
- The latent heat of vapourization of a substance is the heat required to change a unit mass of the substance from liquid to the vapour state without change of temperature.
- The latent heat of steam is 2260000 J/kg or 2260 J/g.
- Each gram of ice that melts absorbs 336 J of heat.
- Scalding (burning) with steam is more severe than that caused by boiling water because steam contains more energy than boiling water at the same temperature.
- Latent heat of vapourisation is maximum at 0°C and decreases on increasing temperature.
- Melting point decreases on adding impurity.
- Boiling point increases on adding impurity.
- Boiling point increases on increasing pressure.
- Bottled drinks are cooled more effectively when surrounded with lumps of ice than with iced water because ice absorbs more heat than does the same amount of iced water.

Evaporation

- Water can change into the vapour state either by boiling or by evaporation at lower temperatures.
- When evaporation takes place at room temperature, the energy required for evaporation is taken from the liquid itself, which cools as a consequence.
- When sweat evaporates from the skin it draws much heat from the body and produces a cooling sensation.
- In summer, water is stored in pitchers for cooling. Water oozes out of the pores of the pitchers and cools on evaporation.
- The rate of evaporation increases with increase in temperature.
- Evaporation increases with increase in surface area.

Refrigerator

- In a refrigerator, cooling is produced by the evaporation of a volatile liquid, freon, inside a copper coil (evaporator), which surrounds the freezer.
- The cooling unit (freezer) in a refrigerator is fitted near the top to cool the whole of the interior.
- A thermostat switch regulates the temperature inside the refrigerator by switching the pump on and off at intervals.

Relative Humidity

- Relative humidity is defined as the ratio of the mass of water vapour in a given volume of air to the mass required for saturating the same volume of air at the same temperature.
- The weather report in newspapers expresses relative humidity as percentage.
- Relative humidity is measured with an instrument called the hygrometer.

Pressure Cooker

- The boiling point of a liquid depends on external pressure.
- When the atmospheric pressure is 76 cm of mercury, water boils at 100°C. But when the pressure is increased, the boiling point of water is raised.
- In a pressure cooker, water boils at temperatures higher than 100°C due to increased pressure. The increased boiling temperature allows water to hold more heat which cooks food faster.
- At higher altitudes, atmospheric pressure is reduced. This lowers the boiling point of water and food takes much longer to cook.

MULTIPLE CHOICE QUESTIONS

1. What is force?
A. pull B. push
C. push and push both D. none of these

2. What is state of motion?
A. position of rest
B. position of motion
C. both by the state of rest or motion
D. none of these

3. The strength of force is expressed by:
A. weight B. mass
C. magnitude D. longitudinal force

4. The force between two charged bodies is called:
A. muscular force B. gravitational force
C. magnetic force D. electrostatic force

5. When two forces act in opposite directions, then net force acting two forces:
A. sum of two factors
B. difference bwteen two factors
C. both of these
D. none of these

6. Magnetic force is:
A. contact force B. non-contact force
C. both A and B D. none of these

7. Force acts on an object may change:
A. direction B. shape
C. speed D. all of above

8. Leaves or fruits fall on the ground due to:
A. magnetic force B. gravitational force
C. electrostatic force D. muscular force

9. Displacement is a:
A. Scalar quantity B. Vector quantity
C. Base quantity D. Derived quantity

10. SI unit for force is:
A. Kilograms B. Newton
C. Joules D. Acceleration

11. Adding of two vectors to get a single vector is termed as:
A. Final vector B. Resultant vector
C. Dominant vector D. Recessive vector

12. The __________ forces are used are used in the method of sections for the calculation of the internal forces.
A. Internal rotational B. Couple rotational
C. Translational D. External

13. Twisting moment is also called as __________.
A. Moment of line B. Moment of section
C. Moment of plane D. Torsional moment

14. The loading generally act upon the __________ of the body.
A. Centroid B. Symmetrical centre
C. Rotational centre D. Chiral centre

15. Torsional moment is applied at the __________ part of the beam.
A. The centroid
B. The left end
C. The right end
D. The axis beyond the body of the beam

16. If the normal force creates a tension then the force is said to be __________ .
A. Positive B. Negative
C. Rotational D. Collinear

17. If the bending of the beam is concave upwards then the bending moment developed is called __________ moment.
A. Positive B. Negative
C. Rotational D. Collinear

18. The force of friction acts in a direction ____ to the direction of motion of object.
A. Same B. Opposite
C. Perpendicular D. Downwards

19. The force of friction depends upon:
A. Nature of surface of contact
B. Material of objects in contact
C. Both 'A' and 'B'
D. None of the above

20. The body will move only when:
A. Force of friction = applied force
B. Force of friction < applied force
C. Force of friction > applied force
D. All of the above

21. The ratio of the limiting force of friction (F) to the normal reaction (R) is known as:
A. Coefficient of friction B. Force of friction
C. Angle of friction D. None of the above

22. When the two surfaces in contact have a thick layer of lubricant in between them, it is known as:
A. Solid friction B. Rolling friction
C. Greasy friction D. Film friction

23. Which motion has magnitude of static frictional force directly proportional to normal reaction?
A. Actual motion B. Impending motion
C. Both A and B D. None of the above

24. Frictional force depends on ________.
A. surface area in contact B. roughness of surface
C. both A and B D. none of the above

25. Which of the following statements is true for flat belts?
A. They are used for short distances between the pulleys
B. They have high efficiency
C. They are used in lathe machines
D. All of the above

26. There will be a great distance in stopping a vehicle which is moving?
A. slowly B. steady
C. fast D. continuously

27. A bowling ball on a bowling lane is an example of what type of friction?
A. Dry friction B. Rolling friction
C. Fluid friction D. Static Friction

28. Whenever the surfaces in contact tend to move or move with respect to each other, the force of friction comes into play:
A. only if the objects are solid.
B. only if one of the two objects is liquid.
C. only if one of the two objects is gaseous.
D. irrespective of whether the objects are solid, liquid or gaseous

29. To sharpen the blade of a knife by rubbing it against a surface, which of the following will be most suitable?
A. stone B. plastic block
C. wooden block D. glass block

30. A toy car released with the same initial speed will travel farthest on:
A. muddy surface B. polished marble surface
C. cemented surface D. brick surface

31. If we apply oil on door hinges, the friction will:
A. increase
B. decrease
C. disappear altogether
D. will remain unchanged

32. Which of the following statements is incorrect?
A. Friction acts on a ball rolling along the ground.
B. Friction acts on a boat moving on water.
C. Friction acts on a bicycle moving on a smooth road.
D. Friction does not act on a ball moving through air

33. A boy rolls a rubber ball on a wooden surface. The ball travels a short distance before coming to rest. To make the same ball travel longer distance before coming to rest, he may
A. spread a carpet on the wooden surface.
B. cover the ball with a piece of cloth.
C. sprinkle talcum powder on the wooden surface.
D. sprinkle sand on the wooden surface.

34. Complete the sentence. Friction always ___________
A. helps the motion B. opposes the motion
C. both of these D. none of these

35. Which one of these characteristics does a smooth surface has?
A. Less frictional force
B. More frictional force
C. Sometimes less and sometimes more force
D. All of above

36. Friction is a ___________.
A. Contact force B. Non-contact force
C. Magnetic force D. None of these

37. What kind of substances are known as lubricants?
A. Increase friction
B. Decrease friction
C. Increase or decrease friction
D. None of these

38. Fluid are ____.
A. Gases B. Liquids
C. Gases and liquids both D. None of these

39. On what force of friction depends?
A. Smoothness of surface
B. Roughness of surface
C. Inclination of surface
D. All of above

40. Friction is a /an_______.
A. Evil B. Foe
C. Both A and B D. None

41. Lubricants ________.
A. Increase friction B. Reduce friction
C. Both A and B D. None

42. Rolling friction is smaller than?
A. Sliding friction B. Static friction
C. Fluid friction D. All of the above

43. The shape of the airplane is like a:
A. Bird B. Car
C. Dog D. All

44. If the displacement is measured with strain gauge then the number of strain gauge normally required are:
A. One B. Two
C. Three D. Four

45. The instruments used for the measurement of pressure is/are:
A. Bellows
B. Diaphragms
C. Fiber optic pressure sensors
D. All of these

46. Bourdon tube is used for the measurement of gauge pressure of:
A. Gas B. Liquid fluid
C. Solid D. Both A and B

47. The ionization gauge an instrument used for the measurement of:
A. Very low pressure B. Medium pressure
C. High pressure D. Very high pressure

48. When visual indication of pressure level is required then the instrument generally used is:
A. Monometers B. Diaphragm sensors
C. Bourdon tube D. Resonant wire device

49. Advantage of passive instrument is:
A. It does not need power supply
B. Cheap
C. Sensitive
D. Accurate

50. Which of the following statements is false? The pressure at a given depth in a fluid:
A. is equal in all directions
B. is independent of the shape of the container
C. acts at right angles to the surface containing the fluid
D. depends on the area of the surface

51. Which of the following devices does not measure pressure?
A. barometer B. McLeod gauge
C. thermocouple D. manometer

52. The universal law of gravitation was propounded by:
A. Kepler B. Galileo
C. Newton D. Copernicus

53. The gravitational force with which the sun attracts the earth:
A. is less than the force with which the earth attracts the sun
B. is the same as the force with which earth attracts the sun
C. is more than the force with which the earth attracts the sun
D. is constant throughout the year

54. The mass of a body is different from its weight because:
A. mass is a variable quantity whereas weight is constant
B. mass varies very little at different places whereas weight varies a lot
C. mass is constant but weight increases as the body moves from the poles to the equator
D. mass is a measure of the quantity of matter whereas weight is a force

55. The weight of a body is:
A. the same everywhere on the surface of the earth
B. maximum at the poles
C. maximum at the equator
D. more on the hills than in the plains

56. A person weighs more in a lift, which is:
A. moving up with a constant velocity
B. moving down with a constant velocity
C. accelerating upward
D. accelerating downward

57. Atmospheric pressure is measured with a:
A. hydrometer B. barometer
C. hygrometer D. altimeter

58. The atmosphere exerts enormous pressure on us. But we do not feel it because:
A. we are used to it
B. our bones are very strong and can withstand this pressure
C. the surface area of our head is very small
D. our blood exerts a pressure slightly more than that of the atmosphere

59. In a barometer, mercury is preferred over water because:
A. mercury is a good conductor of heat
B. mercury is shining and therefore its level can be read easily
C. mercury is available in pure form
D. mercury has high density and low vapour pressure

60. Raindrops are spherical due to:
A. viscosity of water
B. surface tension
C. continuous evaporation
D. air friction

ANSWERS

1	2	3	4	5	6	7	8	9	10
C	C	C	D	B	B	D	B	B	B
11	**12**	**13**	**14**	**15**	**16**	**17**	**18**	**19**	**20**
B	D	D	A	A	A	A	B	C	B
21	**22**	**23**	**24**	**25**	**26**	**27**	**28**	**29**	**30**
A	D	B	B	A	C	B	D	A	C
31	**32**	**33**	**34**	**35**	**36**	**37**	**38**	**39**	**40**
B	D	C	B	A	A	B	C	D	C
41	**42**	**43**	**44**	**45**	**46**	**47**	**48**	**49**	**50**
B	D	A	D	D	D	A	A	A	D
51	**52**	**53**	**54**	**55**	**56**	**57**	**58**	**59**	**60**
C	C	B	D	B	C	B	D	D	B

★ ★ ★

6

Light and Sound

LIGHT

- **Source of light:** An object, which emits light, is called a source of light.
- **Scattering of light:** The process in which objects spreads the light in all directions is called scattering of light.
- **Rectilinear propagation of light:** Light travels in a straight line. This property of light is called rectilinear propagation of light.
- **Speed of light** is 3,00,000 km per second. Light takes about 8 mintues to travel from the sun to the earth.
- When light or a ray of light falls on an object, three things can happen:
  (*i*) It may be transmitted through the object almost completely.
  (*ii*) Only part of it may be transmitted and the rest absorbed or spread out.
  (*iii*) It may not be allowed to pass through at all.
- **Transparent:** Such materials absorb or spread out only a small part of light falling on them and transmit the remaining of it. Which completely transmit light rays through them are called transparent, e.g., air, pure water, glass, some plastics.
- **Translucent:** Materials which transmit only a small part of the light rays are called translucent. Translucent materials absorb and scatter the remaining light. e.g. butter paper, gelatin sheet, smoked glass, muddy water.
- **Opaque:** Such materials which allow very little or no light to pass through them. These materials are called Opaque. e.g. wood, coaltar, paints, metal sheets.
- Object Scatter the light falling on than from the source and make then visible to our eyes.
- Rectilinear propogation of light explains the formation of the image of an object in a pin hole camera.
- The materials through which we are able to see clearly because light passes through them almost completely are called transparent.
- The materials which do not allow light to pass through them at all are called opaque.
- The materials which allow only part of the incident light to pass through them are called translucent.
- In the presence of a source of light, opaque objects act as obstacles to propagation of light and form shadows beyond them in the form of Umbra and Penumbra.
- The region of the space where the light from the source does not reach and hence is the darkest, is called Umbra.
- The region where the light does not reach from all parts of the source is called Penumbra.
- Eclipses of the Moon and the Sun occur due to the shadows cast by the Earth and the Moon respectively.
- When light rays fall on polished surface they change their direction in a well-defined manner. This is called regular reflection.
- Light falling on non-polished surfaces does not change the direction in a well-defined manner. This is called diffuse reflection.
- There are two laws of reflection:
  (*i*) The incident ray, the normal at the point of incidence and the reflected rays are in the same plane.
  (*ii*) The angle of incidence and the angle of reflection are equal.
- In a plane mirror, the reflected rays appear to come from some object kept behind the mirror. This is called a virtual image of the object.
- Laws of reflection are also applicable to polished curved surfaces.
- In case of curved reflecting surfaces the normal at different points of incidence have different directions.
- Part of a spherical surface, when polished, gives rise to spherical mirrors.
- Spherical mirrors are two types:
  (*i*) Concave mirror
  (*ii*) Convex mirror
  depanding upon the surface that us polished/silvered to allow regular reflection.
- The centre of the sphere of which the spherical mirror is a part, is called the centre of curvature of the mirror.

- Any straight line joining the centre of curvature with any point on the spherical mirror is normal to the mirror at that point.
- The point through which the incident rays parallel to the principal axis, after reflection from the mirror, pass through or appers to pass through is called focus of the spherical mirror.
- When the reflected rays meet in front of the mirror, they are supposed to form a real image.
- A real image can be obtained on a screen.
- Any ray passing through the focus or appearing to pass through the focus becomes parallel to the principal axis after reflection.
- Any ray passing through or appearing to pass through the centre of curvature is reflected back along the same path.
- Concave mirrors are used by dentists and in optical instruments.
- Concave mirror forms a real and inverted image of the object when it is kept beyond the focus and a virtual, erect but magnified image is formed when an object us kept in between the mirror and the focus.
- Convex mirrors are used as rear view mirrors in cars and for viewing images of larger areas.
- Convex mirror always forms a smaller and virtual image.
- Light affects plants and animals.
- **Incident ray:** The light ray striking a surface is called the incident ray.
- **Point of incidence:** The point at which the incident ray strikes the surface is called the point of incidence.
- **Reflected ray:** The light ray obtained after reflection from the surface, in the medium in which the incident ray is coming, is called the reflected ray.
- **Normal:** The perpandicular drawn to the surface at the point of incidence is called the normal.
- **Angle of incidence:** The angle which the incident ray makes with the normal at the point of incidence, is called angle of incidence.
- **Angle of reflection:** The angle which the reflected ray makes with the normal at the point of incidence, is called angle of refleciton.
- **Plane of incidence:** The plane containing the incident ray and the normal is called the plane of incidence.
- **Plane of refleciton:** The plane containing the reflected ray and the normal is called the plane of refleciton.
- **Real and Virtual image:** An image which can be obtained on a screen is called a real image. It is formed when the light rays after reflection actually intersect.
- The image which can not be obtained on a screen is called a *virtual image.* It is formed when the light rays after reflection do not actually intersect but appear to diverge from it.
- Light is a form of radiant energy.
- Light may be regarded as a form of electromagnetic radiation.
- Light can travel without a medium.
- In a homogeneous medium light travels in a straight line.
- The velocity of light is different in different medium.
- A ray of light bends towards the normal as it passes from a rarer medium to denser medium and bends away from the normal when it travels from a denser medium to a rarer medium.
- A convex lens converges a parallel beam of light as its focal point and a concave lens diverges a parallel beam of light.
- The distance between the lens and its focal point is called the *focal length* of the lens.
- The image of an object formed by a convex lens when the object is placed beyond the focal length is real and inverted.
- The image of an object formed by a convex lens when the object is placed between the lens and the focal point is virtual and magnified.
- The term eclipse literally means the act of disappearing or becoming invisible.
- An object can become invisible to an observer under the following conditions:
  (*i*) Objects itself is not a source of light and light from any other source is not falling on it.
  (*ii*) View of the object is blocked completely by an obstacle started between the object and the observer.
- The lunar eclipse occurs due to the first of the above conditions. The solar eclipse occurs due to the second condition.

The Lunar Eclipse

On a certain full-moon night, the shadow of the Earth falls on the moon's surface. When this happens a part or whole of the Moon is not visible to us for some time from some parts on the Earth. This phenomena is known as *Lunar Eclipse*. A lunar eclipse does not occur on every full moon day. Thus happens because the centres of the Sun, the Earth and the Moon do not lie on a straight line on every full-moon day.

This diagram shows the various positions of the Moon as it passes through the penumbra and the Umbra of the earth during a lunar eclipse. At position A, the Moon is yet to enter the penumbro and it looks bright as usual. At position B, it has entered the penumbro. At this position, the Moon looks pale, as if it has gone behind the clouds. After some time, a part of the Moon enters the Umbro. This part is then not visible from the Earth, but the remaining part of the Moon is still visible. This is called a *partial lunar eclipse.* At positon C, the Moon has completely enterd the Umbra and is not visible from the Earth. This is called total lunar eclipse. During the total lunar eclipse, the Moon completely disappears from the sight. The Moon than moves again to position D, the perumbra and finally emerges out of the shadow of the Earth, position E. Thus a total lunar eclipse is again followed by a partial lunar eclipse. Finally, the Moon becomes as bright as before the beginning of the eclipse.

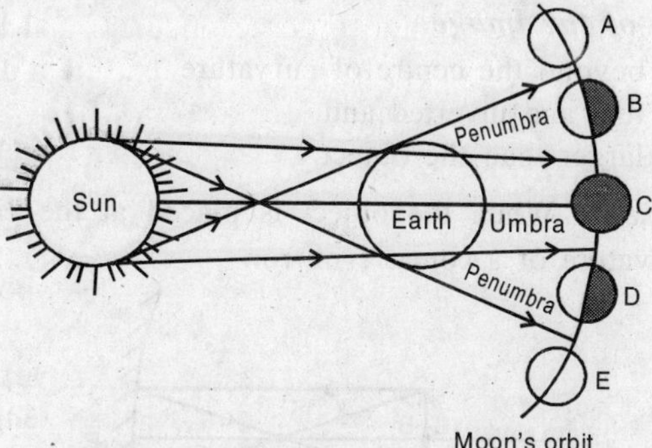

Fig. *Occurence of Lunar Eclipse*

The Solar Eclipse

On a new-moon day, the Moon lies in between the Earth and the Sun. Sometimes, their centres may lie on the same straight line. When this happens, the moon's shadow may fall on the Earth. This event occurs only on certain new-moon days and not on all new-moon days. Thus event is known as *solar eclipse.*

Occurrence of the solar eclipse can be explained with the help of figures given below:

A Solar eclipse may be partial or total. The type of Solar eclipse that would be visible from a given place on the earth depends whether it lies in the Umbro or the Penumbro of the moon. The sun cannot be seen from that region on the earth where the Umbra of the moon falls. This is because the Moon blocks the view of the Sun.

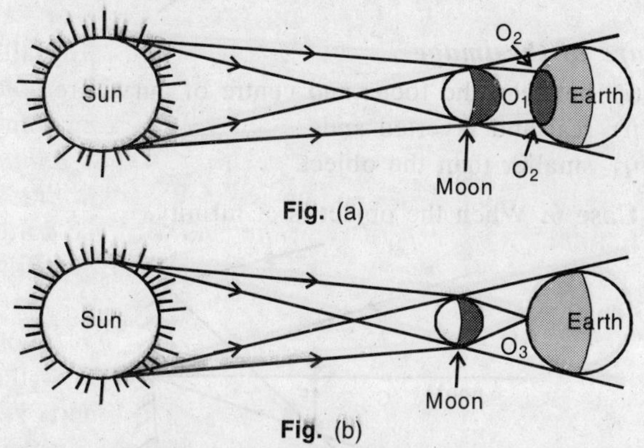

Fig. *(a, b) Occurence of different types of solar eclipse*

From the given Fig.(a), point O_1 on the earth, the Sun is completely blocked by the Moon. This is called a total Solar eclipse. The point O_2 in the penumbro the Sun is only partly visible, a *partial Solar eclipse* occurs when this happens. As *annular solar eclipse* occurs when only the tip of the Umbra of the Moon falls on the earth, the point O_3 lies the view of the Sun would be completely blocked by the Moon. The outer rim of the Sun is known as *Corona* is visible for a very short period, a very bright ring, known as *diamond ring*, appears in the sky. A total Solar eclipse is a rare event.

Lateral inversion: The image in a plane mirror formed the left side appears on the right and the right side appears on the left in the mirror. This phenomenon is called *Lateral inversion.*

Kaleidoscope: Is an device fased on the principle of multiple reflections in inclined mirrors. It is called *Kaleidoscope.* It consists of three plane mirrors inclined at an angle of 60° to each other.

Periscope: Is a device, used to see objects which are not in the direct line of sight. e.g. it is used to see ships on the surface of water from a submarine.

Spherical mirror: Is a part of a sphere. It has two surfaces or faces. The inner face is called *Concave* and outer face is known as *Convex.*

There are two type of spherical mirrors:

(*i*) Concave mirror and

(*ii*) Convex mirror.

Concave mirror: The central point (P) is called the pole of the mirror, which is denoted by P.

Centre of curvature: The centre of the sphere, of which the given spherical mirror is a part is called its centre of Curvature. It is denoted by C. The centre of Curvature of a Concave mirror is in front of the mirror where as that of a Convex mirror is behind the mirror.

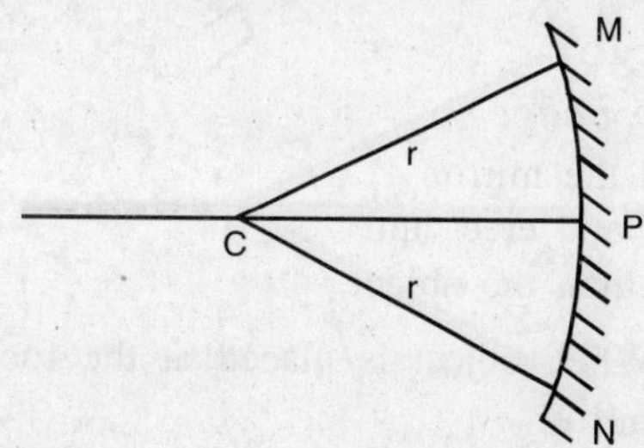

Concave mirror

Principal axis: The straight line, joining the points C and P, is called the principal axis of the mirror. The steps to draw a ray diagram for the formation of image by a spherical mirror as follows:

- A ray of light parallel to the principal axis passes through the focus of the mirror after reflection.

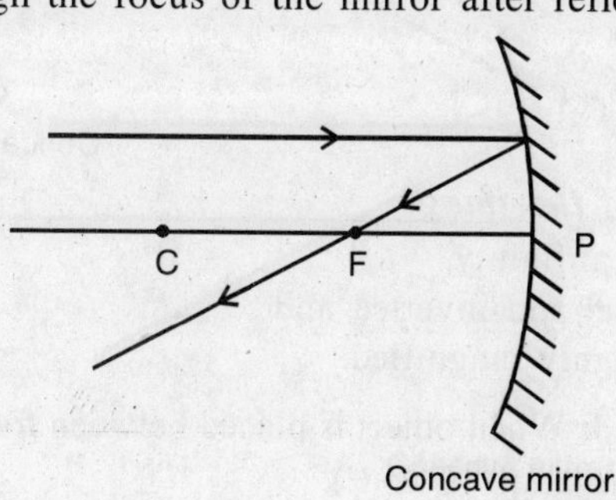

Concave mirror

- A ray of light that passes through the focus of the mirror becomes parallel to its principal axis after reflection.
- A ray of light passing through the centre of curvature of the mirror returns along the same path after reflection from the mirror.

The images formed by a Concave mirror

The type of image formed by a Concave mirror depends on the position of object in front of the mirror.

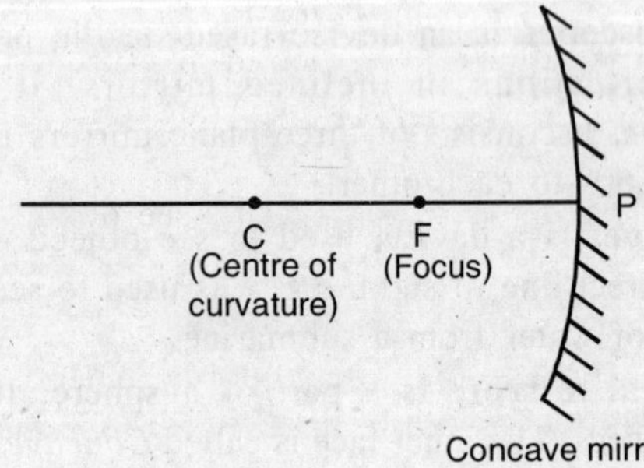

☛ **Case 1:** Image formed by a Concave mirror when the object is placed between pole and focus of the mirror.

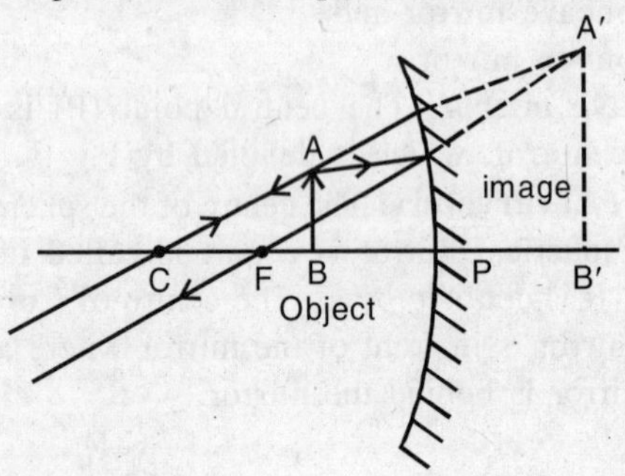

Nature of the image

(*i*) behind the mirror
(*ii*) virtual and erect and
(*iii*) larger than the object.

☛ **Case 2:** When object is placed at the focus (f) of a Concave mirror.

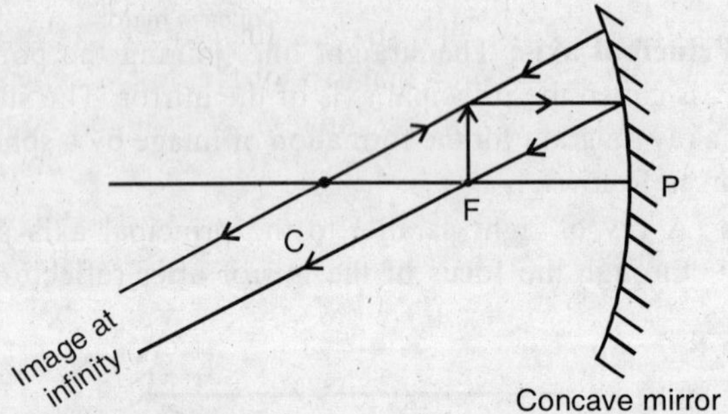

Nature of the image

(*i*) at infininty
(*ii*) real and inverted and
(*iii*) highly magnified.

☛ **Case 3:** When object is placed between focus and centre of Curvature (F & C).

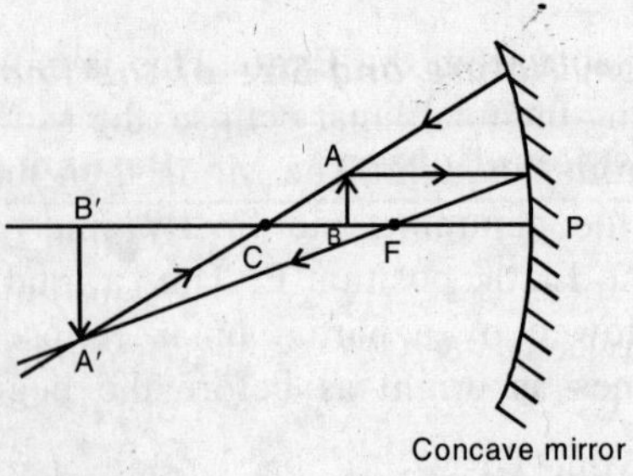

Nature of the image

(*i*) beyond the centre of curvature
(*ii*) real and inverted and
(*iii*) larger than the object.

☛ **Case 4:** When the object is placed at the centre of curvature of a concave mirror.

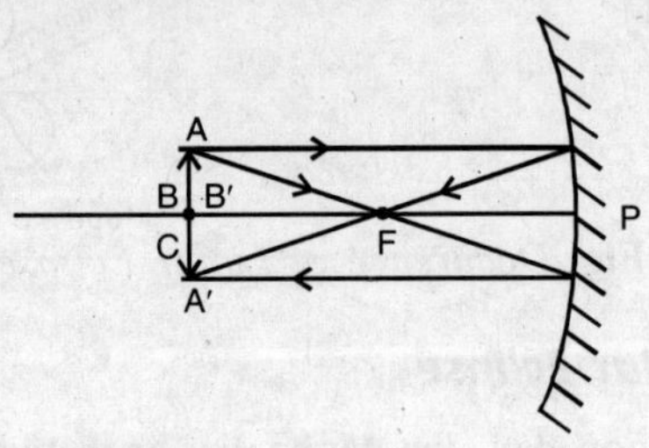

Nature of the image

(*i*) at the centre of curvature C
(*ii*) real and inverted, and
(*iii*) same size as the object.

☛ **Case 5:** When the object is beyond the centre of curvature of the concave mirror.

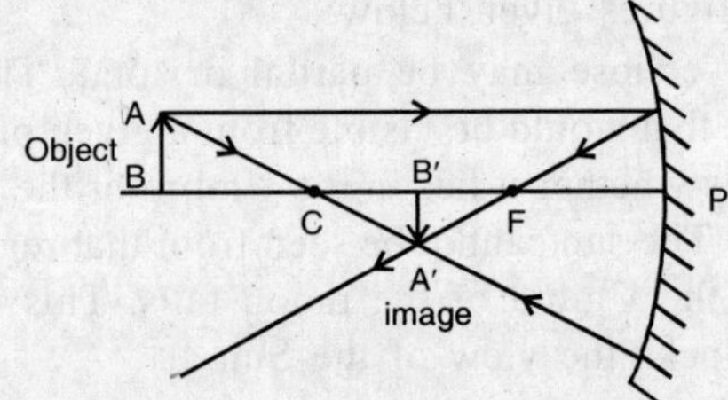

Nature of the image

(*i*) between the focus and centre of curvature
(*ii*) real and inverted and
(*iii*) smaller than the object.

☛ **Case 6:** When the object is at infinity.

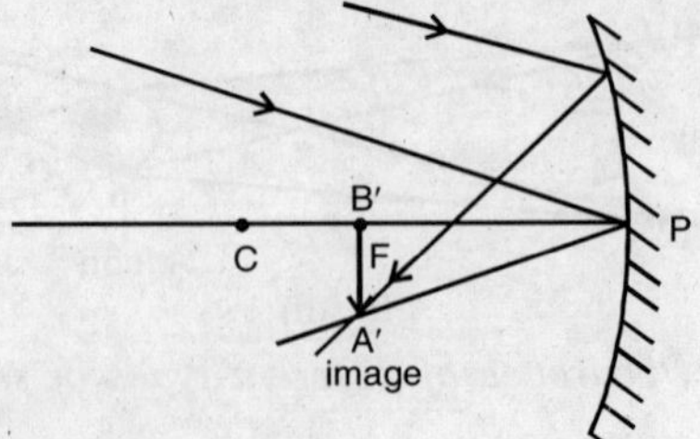

Nature of the image

(*i*) at the focus (F)
(*ii*) real and inverted and
(*iii*) highly diminished.

Position, Nature and Size of the image of an object formed by Concave mirror.

Position of object	Position of image	Size of image	Nature of image
Between P and F	Behind the mirror	Enlarged	Vital and erect
At focus (F)	At infinity	Highly enlarged	Real and inverted
Between F & C	Beyond C	Enlarged	Real and inverted
At C	at C	Equal to object	Real and inverted
Beyond C	Between F & C	Diminished	Real and inverted
At infinity	At focus (F)	Highly diminished	Real and inverted

Sign Convention for Spherical Mirrors

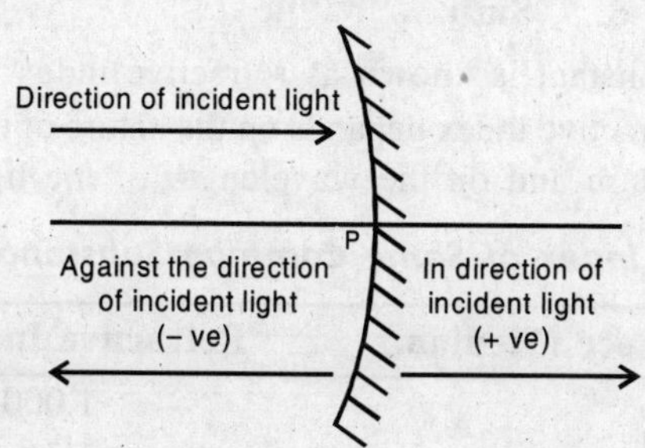

According to the new Cartesion Sign Convention:

(*i*) All the distances are measured from pole of the mirror as origin.

(*ii*) Distance measured in the same direction as that of incident light are taken as positive (+ve).

(*iii*) Distances measured against the direction of incident light are taken as negative.

(*iv*) Distances measured upward and perpendicular to the principal axis are taken as positive.

(*v*) Distances measured downward and perpendicular to the principal axis are taken as negative.

Mirror Formula

A formula which gives the relationship between image distance (v), object distance (u) and focal length (f) of a mirrror is known as the mirror formula as given below.

$$\frac{1}{v} + \frac{1}{u} = \frac{1}{f}$$

where v = distance of image from mirror.

u = distance of object from mirror.

f = focal length of the mirror.

Magnification Produced by Mirrors

The ratio of the height of image to the height of object is known as magnification.

i.e. $$m = \frac{h_2}{h_1}$$

where h_2 = height of image.

h_1 = height of object.

The magnification produced by a mirror is equal to the ratio of the image distance to the object distance with a minus sign.

i.e. $$m = -\frac{v}{u}$$

where v = image distance

u = object distance.

$$m = \frac{h_2}{h_1} = -\frac{v}{u}$$

Formation of image by a Convex Mirror

☛ **Case 1:** When object is placed any where between pole P and infinity.

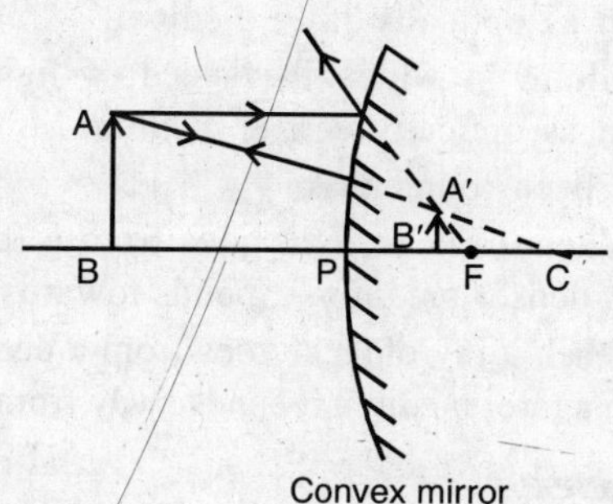

Convex mirror

Nature of the image

(*i*) behind the mirror between pole (P) and focus (F)

(*ii*) virtual and erect and

(*iii*) diminished.

☛ **Case 2:** When the object is at infinity.

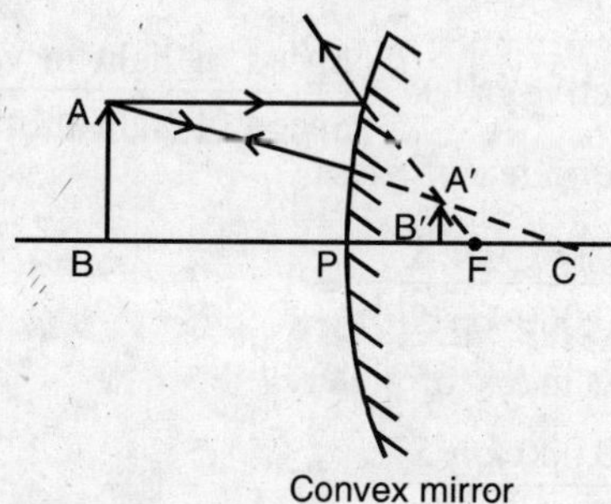

Convex mirror

Nature of the image

(*i*) behind the mirror at focus (F)

(*ii*) virtual and erect and

(*iii*) highly diminished.

Refraction of Light

The change in direction of light when it passes from one medium to another, is called refraction of light.

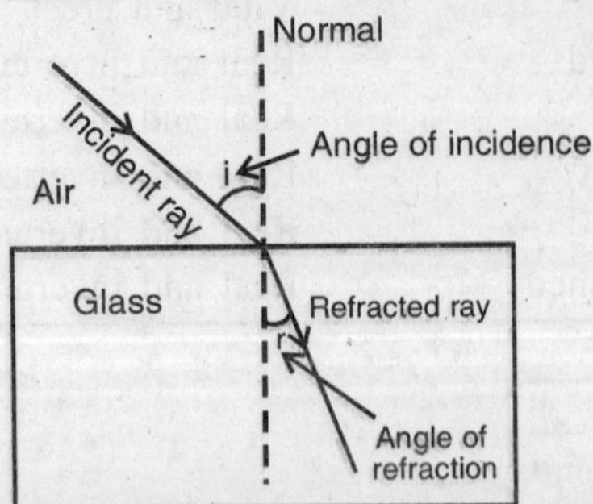

The angle between incident ray and normal is called the *angle of incidence.*

The angle between the refracted ray and the normal is called the *angle of refraction.*

Case of Refraction

The refraction of light takes place on going from one medium to another because the speed of light is different in the two media.

- A medium in which the speed of light is more is known as optically rarer medium.
- A medium in which the speed of light is less, is known as optically denser medium

It has been found that:

(*i*) When a ray of light goes from a rarer medium to denser medium, it bends towards the normal.

(*ii*) When a ray of light goes from a denser medium to a rarer medium it bends away from the normal.

Refractive Index

Refractive Index of a medium is defined as the ratio of the velocity of light in free space to the velocity of light in that medium. i.e. The refractive index of a medium gives an indication of the light-bending ability of that medium.

The ratio of speed of light in vacuum to the speed of light in a medium, is called the refractive index of that medium.

$$i.e.\ \text{Refractive index} = \frac{\text{Speed of light in vacuum}}{\text{Speed of light in medium}}$$

Refractive index of glass

$$= \frac{3,00,000\ km\ S^{-1}}{2,00,000\ km\ S^{-1}} = 1.5.$$

Refractive index of water

$$= \frac{3,00,000\ km\ S^{-1}}{2,25,000\ km\ S^{-1}} = \frac{300}{225} = 1.33.$$

Laws of Refraction of Light

There are two laws of refraction of light. These are:

(*i*) The incident ray, the refracted ray and the normal at the point of incidence, all lie in the same plane.

(*ii*) The ratio of sine of the angle of incidence to the sine of angle of refraction is a constant for the two given media.

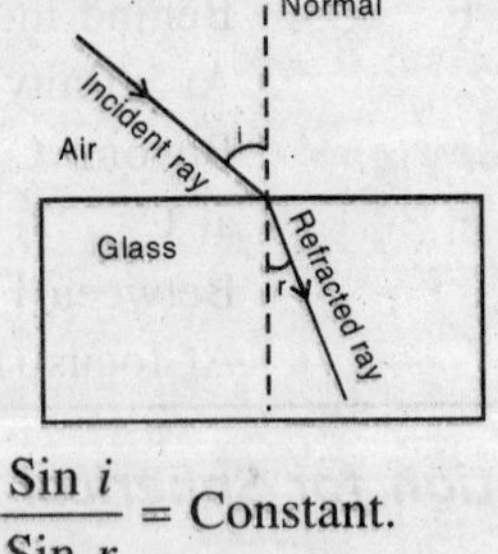

$$\text{i..e} \quad \frac{\text{Sin } i}{\text{Sin } r} = \text{Constant.}$$

This constant is known as refractive index.

The refractive index depands on the nature of the material of the medium and on the wavelength of the light used.

Refractive Index of Some Common Substances

Substance (Medium)	Refractive Index (n)
Air	1.0003
Ice	1.31
Water	1.33
Alcohal	1.36
Sulphuric Acid	1.43
Kerosene	1.44
Turpentine Oil	1.47
Benzene	1.50
Crown Glass	1.52
Carbon Disulphide	1.63
Dense Flint Glass	1.65
Ruby	1.71
Sappire	1.77
Diamond	2.42
Glycerine	1.47

Dispersion of Light

The phenomenon of splitting of light into its constituent colours is known as *dispersion of light.* The band of seven colours formed on a white screen, when a beam of white light is passed through a glass prism, is called spectrum of white light.

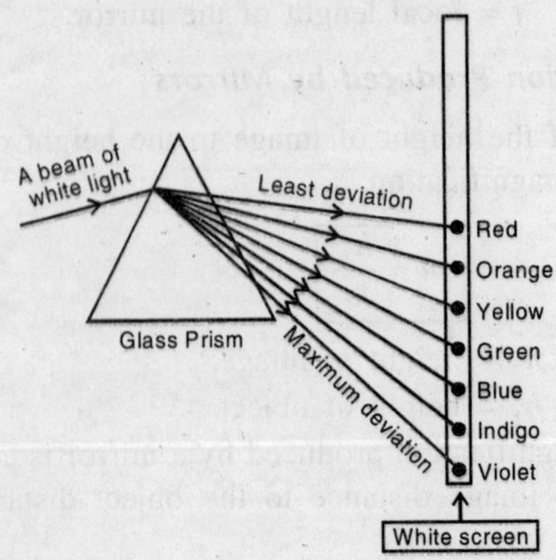

White light is made from seven colours: red, orange, yellow, green, blue, indigo and violet.

The dispersion of white light occurs because the angle of refraction of different colours is different when passing through the glass prism.

Primary Colours of Light

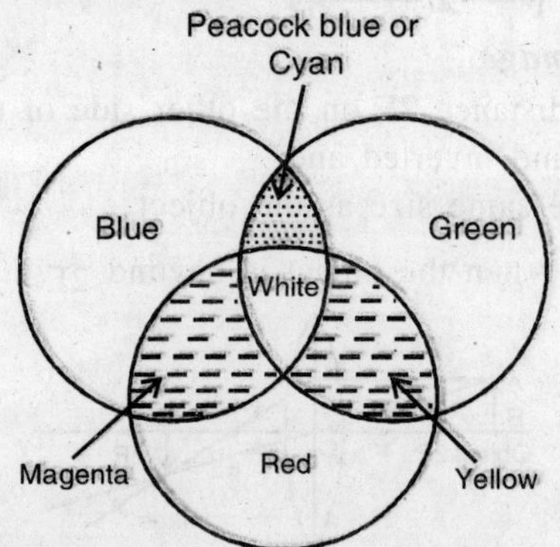

Red, Green and Blue are called primary colours of light, because all the other colours can be obtained by mixing these three colours in suitable proportions.

These results can be written as:

(*i*)	Red	+	Blue	=	Magenta.
(*ii*)	Blue	+	Green	=	Pecock Blue.
(*iii*)	Red	+	Green	=	Yellow.

Refraction of Light by Spherical Lenses

Any transparent material bound with two surface of different curvature form a lens. There are two type of lenses:

- Convex lens and
- Concave lens.

Convex Lens: A convex lens is thick at the centre but thinner at the edges.

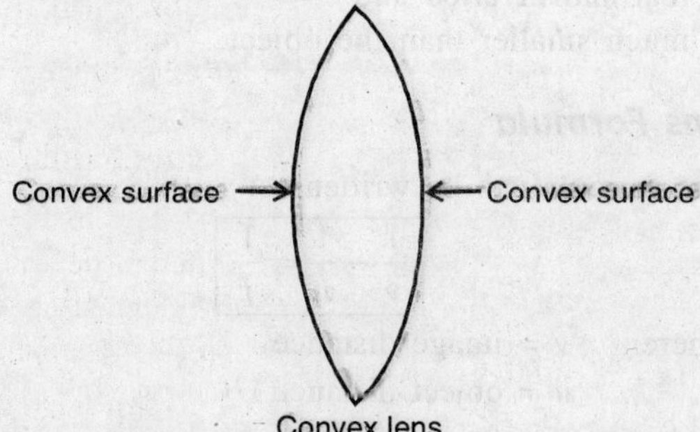

Convex lens

Concave Lens: A concave lens is thin in the middle but thicker at the edges.

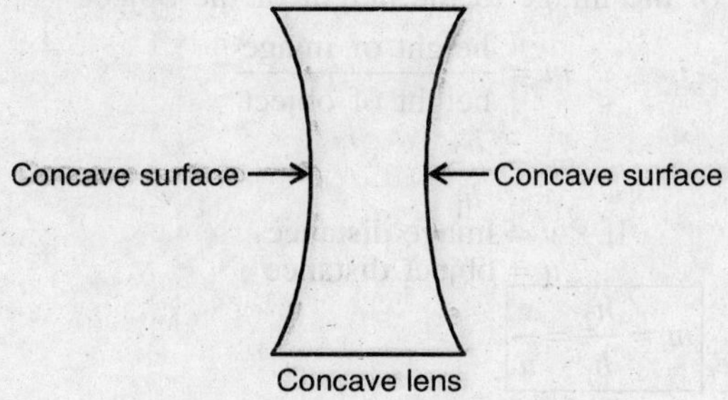

Concave lens

Principal Focus and Focal length of a Convex Lens

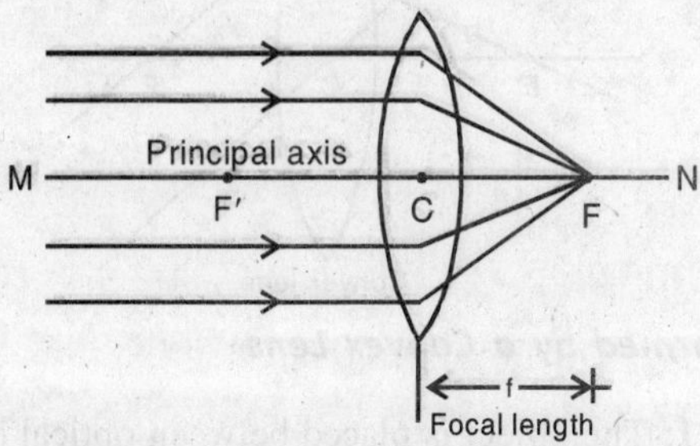

The principal focus of a convex lens is a point on its principal axis to which light rays parallel to the principal axis converge after passing through the lens. MN is called principal axis of the lens. The point C is called the centre or the optical centre of the lens.

The point F is called principal focus or the foucs of the lens.

The distance between the centre of the lens and its focus is known as the *focal length* of the lens.

A convex lens is also known as a *converging lens* because it converges a parallel beam of light rays.

Principal Focus and Focal length of the Concave Lens

The point F is the principal focus of the concave lens. A concave lens is also known as a diverging lens because it diverges a parallel beam of light rays. A concave lens has a virtual focus.

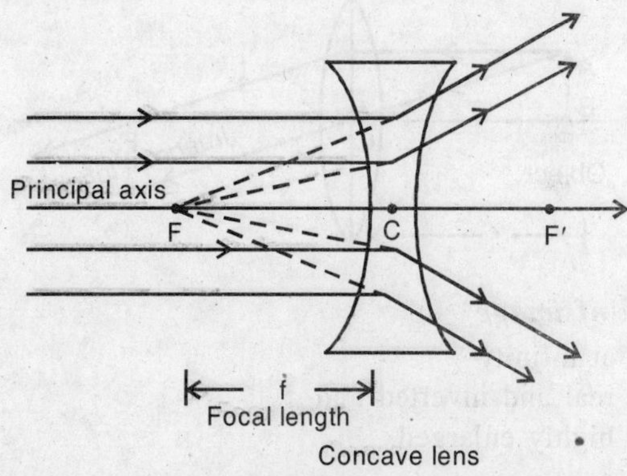

Concave lens

Rules for obtaining images Formed by Convex Lenses

There are three rules for obtaining images by convex lenses. These are:

(*i*) An incident ray parallel to the principal axis of a convex lens passes through the focus of the lens after refraction.

(*ii*) An incident ray passing through the optical centre of a convex lens goes straight after refraction through the lens. It does not get deviated.

(*iii*) An incident ray passing through the foucs of a convex lens, becomes parallel to the principal axis after refraction through the lens.

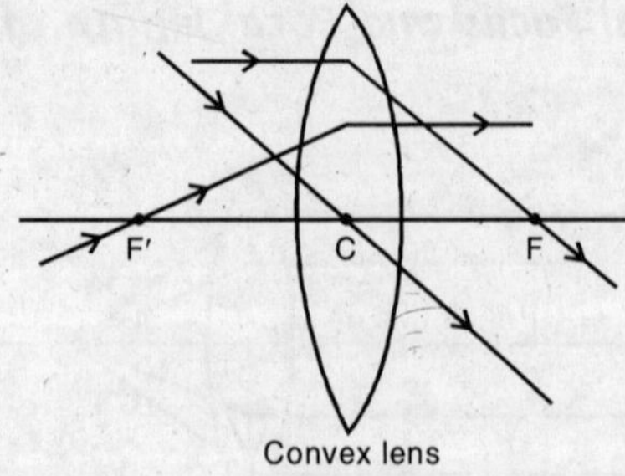

Convex lens

Image Formed by a Convex Lens

☛ **Case 1:** The object is placed between optical centre and focus.

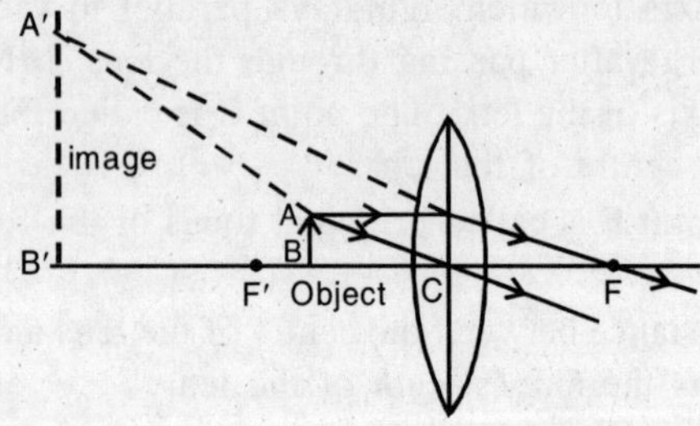

Nature of image

(*i*) behind the object
(*ii*) virtual and erect and
(*iii*) larger than the object.

☛ **Case 2:** When the object is placed at the focus of a convex lens.

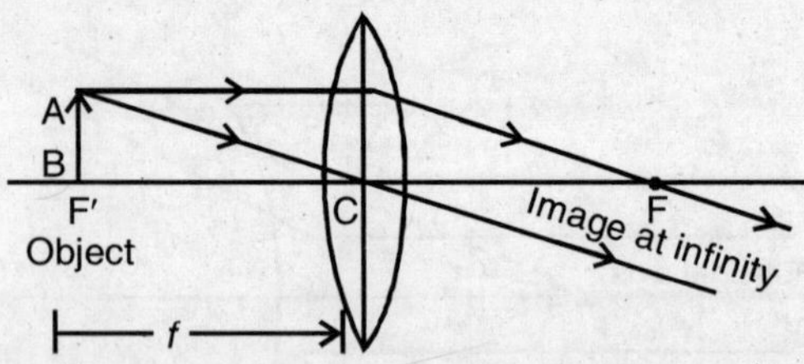

Nature of image

(*i*) at infinity
(*ii*) real and inverted and
(*iii*) highly enlarged.

☛ **Case 3:** When the object is between F′ & 2F′.

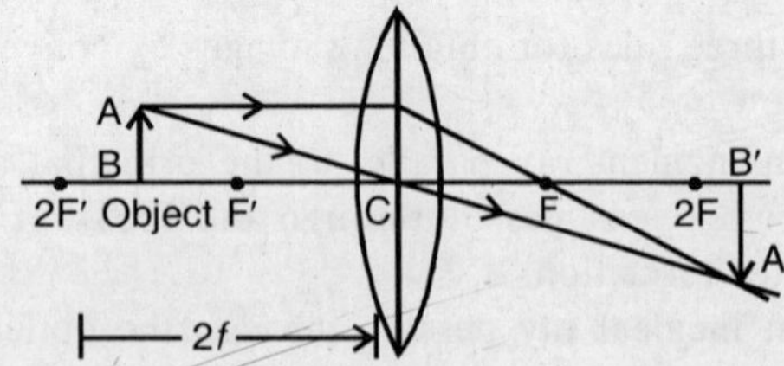

Nature of image

(*i*) beyond 2F
(*ii*) real and inverted and
(*iii*) larger than the object.

☛ **Case 4:** When the object is at 2F′.

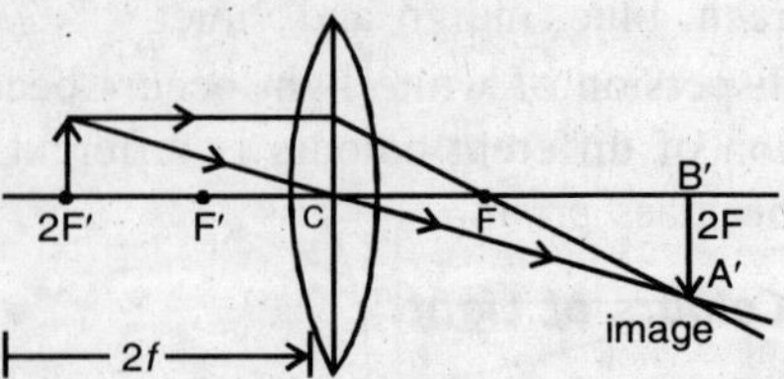

Nature of image

(*i*) at a distance 2F on the other side of the lens
(*ii*) real and inverted and
(*iii*) of the same size as the object.

☛ **Case 5:** When the object is beyond 2F′.

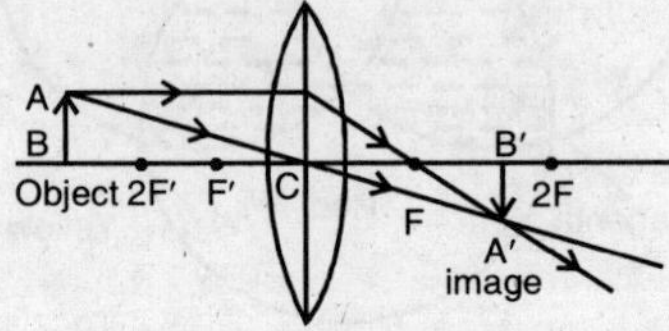

Nature of image

(*i*) between F and 2F on the other side of the lens.
(*ii*) real and inverted and
(*iii*) smaller than the object.

☛ **Case 6:** When the object is at infinity.

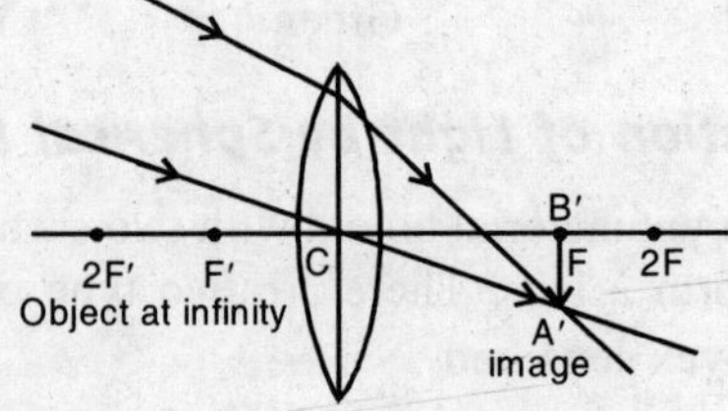

Nature of image

(*i*) at the focus
(*ii*) real and inverted and
(*iii*) much smaller than the object.

Lens Formula

The lens formula can be written as:

$$\frac{1}{v} - \frac{1}{u} = \frac{1}{f}$$

Where v = image distance
u = object distance
f = focal length.

Magnification: The magnification is the ratio of the height of the image to the height of the object.

i.e. $m = \dfrac{\text{height of image}}{\text{height of object}}$

$$m = \frac{h_2}{h_1}$$

If v = image distance
u = object distance

$$m = \frac{h_2}{h_1} = \frac{v}{u}$$

Formation of Image by a Concave Lens

☛ **Case 1:** When an object is placed anywhere between optical centre (C) and infinity.

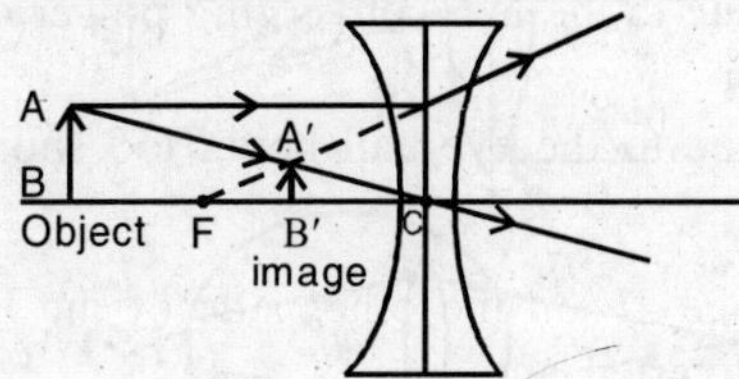

Nature of image

(*i*) between optical centre (C) and focus (F)

(*ii*) virtual and erect and

(*iii*) smaller than the object.

☛ **Case 2:** When an object is at infinity.

Nature of image

(*i*) at focus F

(*ii*) virtual and erect

(*iii*) highly diminished.

Power of a Lens

The power of a lens is a measure of the degree of convergence or divergence of light rays falling on it. The power of a lens is defined as the reciprocal of its focal length in metres.

$$\text{Power of lens} = \frac{1}{\text{focal length of the lens in (metres)}}$$

$$\boxed{P = \frac{1}{f}}$$

where P = power of the lens.

f = focal length of the lens.

The S.I. unit of the power of a lens is **dioptre**. Which is denoted by the letter D. One dioptre is the power of a lens whose focal length is 1 metre.

Total Internal Reflection

The critical angle for a medium is the angle of incidence in the medium for which the angle of refraction in air is 90°. When the angle of incidence of a beam of light travelling in a denser medium is greater than the critical angle of the medium, then, there is no refraction of light into the rarer medium, all the light is reflected back into the denser medium. This phenomenon is called total internal reflection of light.

Condition for Total Internal Reflection

(*i*) The incident light must pass from a denser medium into a rarer medium.

(*ii*) The angle of incidence in denser medium must be greater than the critical angle of the medium.

The Human Eye: A Living Lens

The main parts of human eye are: Cornea (C), iris (I), pupil (P), ciliary muscles (M), convex lens (called eye lens) (L), retina (R) and optic nerve (N).

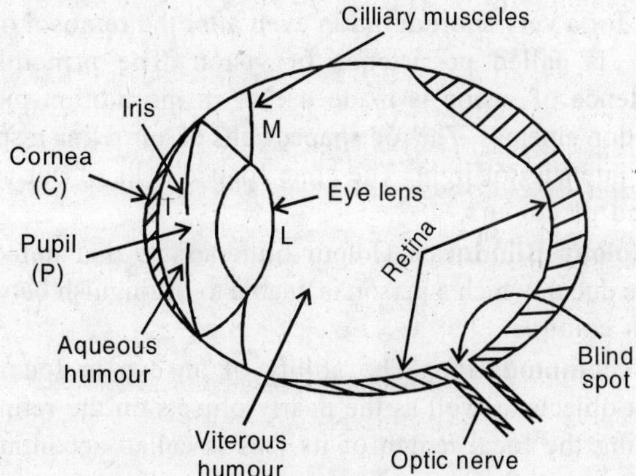

Fig. Structure of human eye

Construction of Eye: The front part of the eye is called cornea. It is made of a transparent substance and it is bulging outwards. The light coming from objects enters the eye through cornea. Just behind the cornea is the **iris**. There is a hole in the middle of the iris which is called pupil of the eye. The pupil appears black because no light is reflected from it.

The eye-lens is a convex lens made of a transparent and flexible material like jelly made of proteins. The eye-lens is held in position by ciliary muscles. The focal length of eye-lens can be changed by the action of ciliary muscles. The screen on which the image is formed in the eye is called **retina**. The retina is behind the eye-lens and at the back part of the eye. The retina of an eye is just like the film in a camera. The retina has a large number of light sensitive cells called rods and cones. Which respond to the intensity of light and colour of objects respectively, by generating electrical signals. The space between cornea and eye-lens is filled with a viscous liquid called **aqueous humour** and the space between eye-lens and retina is filled with another liquid called **vitreous humour**.

Working: The eye-lens in the front of the eyeball makes a real and inverted image of the objects on the retina, which is located behind it. The retina is a thin tissue that has many layers of cells. The most important layer of the retina consists of nerve cells that are sensitive to the brightness as well as to the colours of light. The nerve cells carry the message about the image from the retina to the brain in the form of special signals. The brain then interprets these signals and enables us to see the objects we are looking at. The ciliary muscles contract or tighten up when looking at close things. The eye-lens because thicker and shortens its focal length. This enables eyes to form image on the retina of the objects close to you. The relaxing of muscles makes the eye-lens thinner and increases its focal length to focus the image of distant objects on the retina.

Persistence of Vision: The image of an object seen by our eyes persists. On the retina for about $\frac{1}{16}$th of a second even after we have stopped seeing the object.

The ability of an eye to continue to see the image of an object for a very short duration even after the removal of the object, is called persistence of vision. The principle of persistence of vision is made use of in the motion picture projection cinemas. The rod shaped cells of our retina respond to the intensity of light. The cone shaped cells of our retina respond of colours.

Colour Blindness: Colour blindness is that defect of the eye due to which a person is unable to distinguish between certain colours.

Accommodation: The ability of an eye to focus the distant objects as well as the nearly objects on the retina by changing the focal length of its lens is called accommodation.

A normal eye has a power of accommodation which enables objects as far as infinity and as close as 25 cm to be focused on the retina.

Least Distance of Distinct Vision: The minimum distance at which a object must be placed so that a normal eye may see it clearly, is called the least distance of distinct vision. The least distance of distinct vision for a normal human eye is about 25 cm.

Defects of Vision

There are four defects of vision which can be corrected by using suitable eye glasses or spectacles. These are:

I. Myopia (Short-Sightedness or Near-Sightedness)

II. Hypermetropia (Long-Sightedness or Far-Sightedness)

III. Presbyopia and

IV. Astigmatism

I. Myopia or Short-Sightedness: Myopia is that defect of the eye due to which an eye cannot see the distant objects clearly. This defect of eye is caused:

— due to the high converging power of the eye-lens

or

— due to the eye-ball being too long.

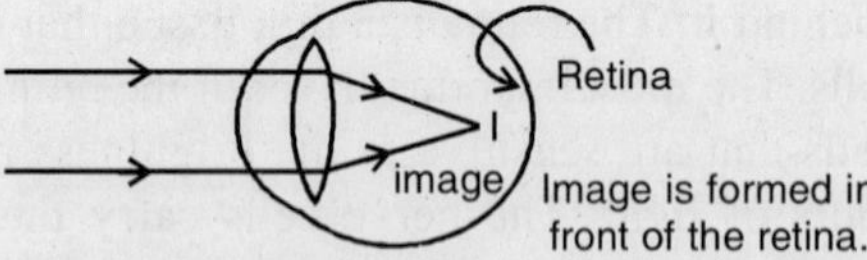

Fig. An eye suffering from myopia.

Myopia or short-sightedness is corrected by using concave lenses.

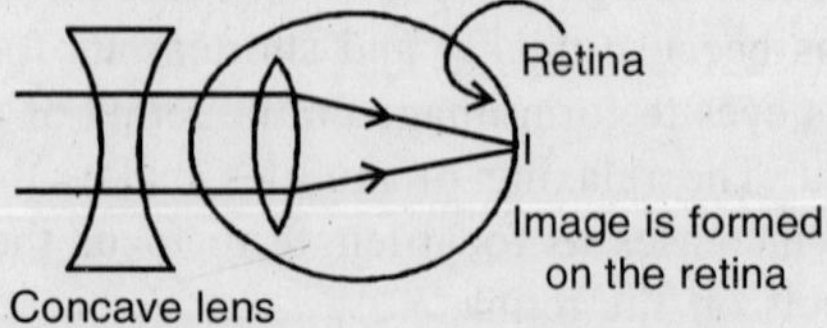

II. Hypermetropia or Long-Sightedness: Hypermetropia or long-sightedness is that defect of the eye due to which an eye cannot see the nearby objects clearly. This defect of eye is caused:

— due to the low converging power of the eye-lens

or

— due to the eye-ball being too short.

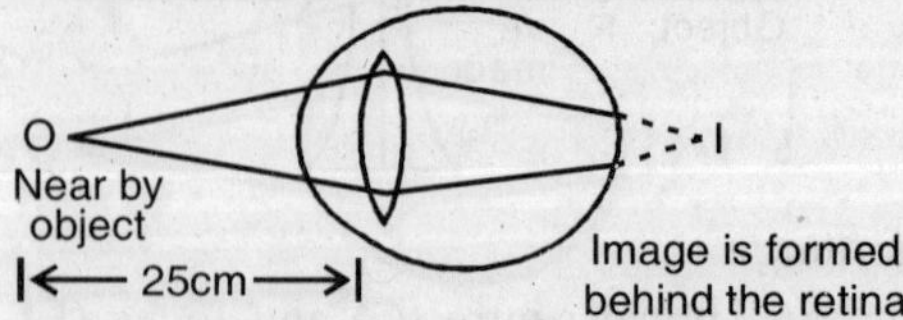

Fig. An eye suffering from hypermetropia.

Hypermetropia or long-sightedness is corrected by using spectacles containing **convex lenses**.

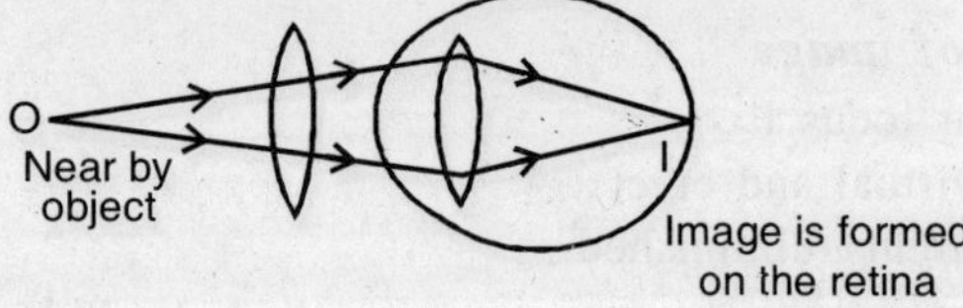

III. Presbyopia: Presbyopia is that defect of the eye due to which an old person cannot read comfortably and clearly without spectacles.

Presbyopia occurs in old age due to the gradual weakening of the ciliary muscles and diminishing flexibility of the eye-lens.

Presbyopia defect is corrected by using spectacles having **bifocal lenses**.

IV. Astigmatism is that defect of the eye due to which a person cannot focus on both horizontal and vertical lines simultaneously. This defect arises due to the irregularities in the surface of **cornea**.

Astigmatism can be corrected by superimposing cylindrical lenses upon the spherical shape of spectacle lenses. **Contract** develops when the eye-lens of a person becomes opaque due to the formation of a membrane over it.

Applications of Lenses

Magnifying Glass or Simple Microscope: The simple microscope is a convex lens of short focal length. It is also called magnifying glass. It is used to get magnified and erect image of small objects. A watchmaker's glass is also a magnifying lens.

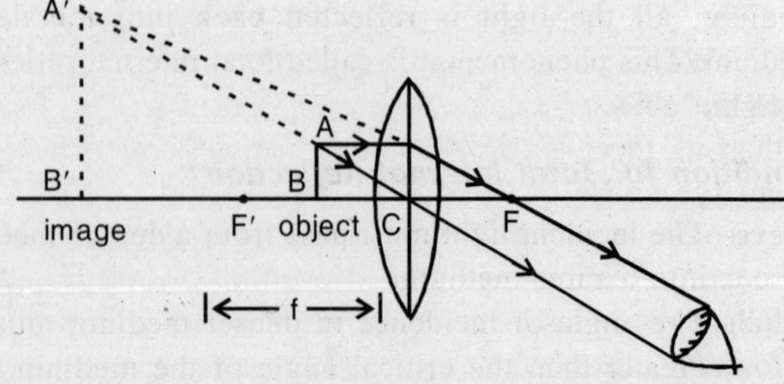

Magnification produced by a Simple Microscope

Magnification, $m = \dfrac{\text{size of image}}{\text{size of object}}$

The magnification of a simple microscope is given by

$$m = 1 + \frac{D}{f}$$

where D = Least distance of distinct vision (25 cm.)

f = Focal length of the convex lens.

e.g. A magnifying glass is of 5.0 cm focal length then the magnification produced by it is:

Sol. Magnification of simple microscope is given by

$$m = 1 + \frac{D}{f}$$

$$D = 25 \text{ cm.}$$

$$f = 5.0 \text{ cm.}$$

$$m = 1 + \frac{25}{5} = 1 + 5 = 6.$$

This means that the object will appear 6 times larger with this magnifying glass.

Compound Microscope

The most commonly used microscope has two convex lenses fixed at two ends of a small cylindrical tube. Such a microscope is known as a compound microscope.

Anton Van Leeuwenhoek (1632-1723) invented the compound microscope. The lens fixed at viewing or the upper end of the microscope, which is used to took at enlarged image of the object, is known as its **eye-piece lens.** The object is kept in front of the lens at the other end, which is known as the **objective lens** of the microscope. The objective and eye-piece of a compound microscope are convex lenses of very short focal lengths.

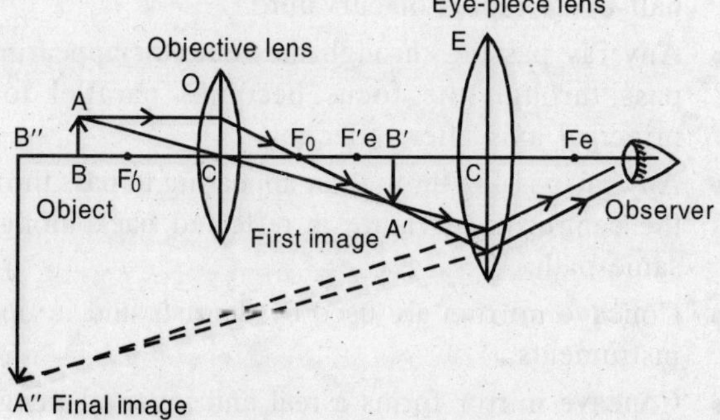

Fig. Ray-diagram of a compound microscope.

Working of a Compound Microscope: The distance of the object from the objective lens is kept slightly more than its focal length. This lens forms a real, inverted and enlarge image of the object. This acts as an object for the eye-piece lens. The distance between the two lenses of microscope is so adjusted that the image formed by the objective falls between the eye-piece and its focus. The eye-piece, formed a further enlarged but virtual image of the object.

Magnification Produced by a Compound Microscope is given by

$$m = \frac{v_o}{u_o}\left(1 + \frac{D}{f_e}\right)$$

where, D = Least distance of distinct vision (25 cm)

v_o = Image distance for the objective lens (in cm.)

u_o = Object distance for the objective lens (in cm.)

f_e = Focal length of eye-piece lens (in cm.)

Telescope

A telescope is an optical instrument which is used for viewing distant objective such as the moon, stars, planets etc.

There are two types of telescope:

— Astronomical telescope and

— Terrestrial telescope.

Astronomical Telescope: An astronomical telescope is used to see the details of celestial bodies like stars, planets and satellite. This telescope produces a virtual, inverted and magnified image of the distance object. It was invented by **Kepler in 1611**.

Construction: This telescope consists of two convex lenses.

— Objective, which is towards the object and

— Eye-piece, which is towards the eye.

The objective is of larger focal length (50-100 cm.), while the eye-piece is of shorter focal length (2-5 cm.).

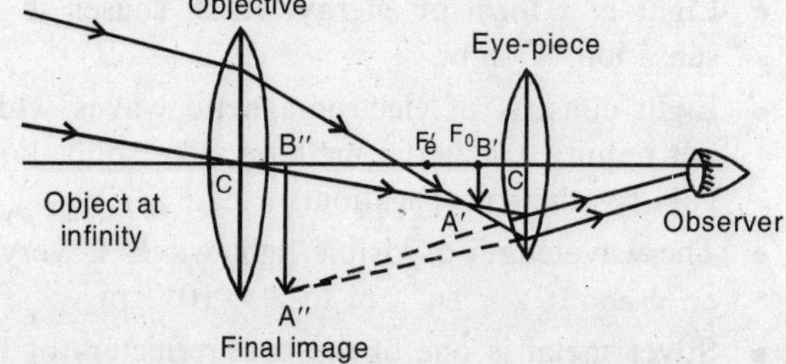

Fig. Ray-diagram for an astronomical telescope.

Working: The objective forms a real and very small image of the distant object near its focus. The real image formed by the objective is inverted and acts as an object for the eye-piece. The distance between the objective and the eye-piece in a telescope is so adjusted that the image formed by the objective lies between the eye-piece and its focus. Therefore the final image formed by the eye-piece is enlarged and virtual. The final image of the object seen through the telescope is inverted with respect to the object.

Magnification: The magnification of a telescope is given by

$$m = \frac{f_o}{f_e}$$

where f_o = focal length of objective of the telescope

f_e = focal length of eye-piece of the telescope

Points to Remember

- An object, which has its own light is called a source of light.
- Source of light are natural as well as man-made.
- Objects scatter the light falling on them from the source and make them visible to our eyes.
- Light travels in straight line. It is called rectilinear propagation of light.
- Rectilinear propagation of light explains the formation of the image of an object in a pinhole camera.
- The materials through which we are able to see clearly because light passes through them almost completely are called **transparent**.
- The materials which do not allow light to pass through them at all are called **opaque**.
- The materials which allow only part of the incident light to pass through them are called **translucent**.
- In the presence of a source of light, opaque objects act as obstacles to propagation of light and form shadows beyond them in the form of Umbra and Penumbra.
- The region of the space where the light from the source does not reach and hence is the darkest, is called **Umbra**.
- The region where the light does not reach from all parts of the source is called penumbra.
- Eclipses of the Moon and the Sun occur due to the shadows cast by the Earth and the Moon respectively.
- Light is a form of energy which causes in us the sensation of sight.
- Light consists of electromagnetic waves which do not require a material medium (like solid, liquid or gas) for their propagation.
- The wavelength of visible light waves is very small only about 4×10^{-7} m to 8×10^{-7} m.
- Silver metal is one of the best reflectors of light.
- A bundle of light rays is called a beam of light.
- When light rays fall on polished surfaces, they change their direction in a well-defined manner. This is called regular reflection.
- Light falling on non-polished surfaces does not change the direction in a well-defined manner. This is called **diffuse reflection**.
- There are two laws of reflection:
  (*i*) The incident ray, the normal at the point of incidence and the reflected rays are in the same plane.
  (*ii*) The angle of incidence and the angle of reflection are equal.
- In a plane mirror, the reflected rays appear to come from some object kept behind the mirror. This is called a **virtual image** of the object.
- The image which can be obtained on a screen is called a **real image**.
- The image which cannot be obtained on a screen is called a virtual image. A virtual image can be seen only by looking into a mirror or a lens.
- Laws of reflection are also applicable to polished curved surfaces.
- In case of curved reflecting surfaces the normal at different points of incidence have different directions.
- The image formed in a plane mirror is laterally inverted with respect to the object.
- A spherical mirror is that mirror whose reflecting surface is the part of a hollow sphere of glass.
- Spherical mirrors are two types:
  — concave mirror and
  — convex mirror.
- The centre of curvature of a concave mirror is in front of it but the centre of curvature of a concave mirror is behind it.
- The centre of the sphere of which the spherical mirror is a part, is called the centre of curvature of the mirror.
- Any straight line joining the centre of curvature with any point of the spherical mirror is normal to the mirror at that point.
- The centre of a spherical mirror is called its pole.
- The point through which the incident rays parallel to the principal axis, after reflection from the mirror, pass through or appear to pass through, is called focus of the spherical mirror.
- When the reflection rays meet in front of the mirror, they are to form a **real image**.
- The focal length of a spherical mirror is equal to half of its radius of curvature.
- Any ray passing through the focus or appearing to pass through the focus becomes parallel to the principal axis after reflection.
- Any ray passing through or appearing to pass through the centre of curvature is reflected back along the same path.
- Concave mirrors are used by dentists and in optical instruments.
- Concave mirror forms a real and inverted image of the object when it is kept beyond the focus and a virtual, erect but magnified image is formed when the object is kept in between the mirror and the focus.
- Convex mirrors are used as rear view mirrors in care and for viewing images of larger areas.
- Convex mirror always forms a smaller and virtual image.
- Refraction takes place when light enters from one transparent medium to another.

- Objects kept partly in a transparent liquid, like water, appear to bend at the surface.
- The speed of light is different in different transparent media. Light travels with maximum speed in vacuum.
- The ratio of speed of light in two media is expressed as refractive index of one medium with respect to the other.
- The angle of incidence is larger than the angle of refraction, when light travels from an optically rarer to an optically denser medium.
- A ray incident obliquely on a rectangular glass slab and the emergent ray corresponding to it are parallel but laterally displaced with respect to each other.
- Refraction of Sunlight through a glass prism splits in into a band of seven colours.
- The seven colours in the spectrum of white light are Violet, Indigo, Blue, Green, Yellow, Orange and Red. These are often represented by the acronym **"VIBGYOR"**.
- Lenses could be divergent or convergent depending on the nature of the curvature of their surfaces.
- A convex lens is a converging lens, which can produce a real or virtual image of an object depending on its position with respect to it.
- A concave lens is a divergent lens, which always produces a virtual image of the object irrespective of where it is placed.
- Convex lenses are used as a magnifying glass and also in making telescope and microscopes.
- The most important component of a photographic camera is its lens, which forms a real image of the objects on the film.
- Our eyes have a convex lens whose focal length can be changed at will with the action of **ciliary muscles**.
- The reciprocal of the focal length expressed in metres is called the power of lens.
- The phenomenon of splitting of white light into its constituent seven colours is called dispersion and the coloured band obtained on a screen is called a **spectrum.**
- The magnifying glass is also called a **simple microscope.**
- The magnification of an object can be described as the increase in apparent area of the object.
- A microscope that has more than one lens is called a compound microscope.
- The focal length of the objective lens is short and that of eye-piece is comparatively more in a compound microscope.
- A telescope is an optical instrument which is used for viewing distance object such as the moon, stars, planets etc.
- Astronomical telescope forms inverted image while terrestrial telescope form erect images.
- In a telescope the objective lens is larger focal length, while the eye-peace lens is of shorter focal length.
- A camera is an optical instrument based on the principal of formation of a real, inverted and usually diminished image of the object by a **convex lens**.
- A person suffering from myopia can see near objects distinctly. It can be corrected with diverging lenses.
- A person suffering from hypermetropia can see distant objects clearly but cannot see near objects distinctly. It can be corrected with converging lens.

SOUND

Sound Waves

emerges from a source—a voice, an instrument or an gine which gives the sensation of hearing. It begins with bration. Everything which is in the state of vibration must oducc a sound and it travels in a medium as a wave otion.

In solid and liquid sound travels as a transverse wave otion and in a gas sound travels as a longitudinal wave otion.

ansmission of Sound

unds are always transmitted through a definite medium. e speed of sound depends upon the medium through ich it travels.

Mathematically, $v = n\lambda$

where v is the frequency, λ is the wavelength.

Wavelength

It is defined as the distance transversed by a wave during the time a particle of the medium vibrating about its mean position, completes one vibration.

Frequency

It is defined as the number of vibration made per second.

Phase

It is defined as the fraction of time period or the angle 2π which has elapsed since the particle last passed through the mean position in the +ve direction.

Newton's Formula

The velocity of sound in air is given by $v = \sqrt{\frac{P}{d}}$

where P is the pressure, d is the density of the medium.

Laplace's Correction

$v = \sqrt{\lambda p / d}$

where γ is the ratio of two specific heats of a gas.

Speed of Sound

The speed of sound depends on the following factors:

(*a*) **Effect of temperature:** It increases with the increase in temperature as $v \propto \sqrt{t}$

(*b*) **Effect of pressure:** It is independent of the pressure at the same temperature.

(c) **Effect of humidity:** It decreases with increase in density $v \propto \frac{1}{\sqrt{d}}$.

Characteristics of Sound

There are three characteristics of sound

(*a*) **Loudness or intensity of sound:** It depends on the amplitude of vibration of the sound-walling object and on the distance from the object to the ear.

(*b*) **Pitch or Frequency:** It is the highness or loudness of sound. It depends upon the speed vibration of the sounding object.

(*c*) **Quality of Timbre:** It makes sound distinctive.

Reflection of Sound

- **Echo:** When the reflected sound is heard separately it is called an echo.
- **Refraction of sound:** When waves pass through a different medium they are refracted.
- **Resonance of sound:** It is a phenomenon of forced vibration due to which sound waves can be produced with a large amplitude or intensity.
- **Musical sound:** The sound which produces pleasing effect upon the ear is called a musical sound and which produces displeasing effect upon the ear is called noise.
- **Beats:** When two notes of nearly the same frequency are produced together, alternate loud and low sounds are heard.

  This phenomenon is called beats.

  No. of beats = difference in their frequency

  $= (n_1 - n_2)$
- **Melody and Harmony:** It is important to establish a relationship between tones of different pitch. This holds true for the tones that follow each other in a melody as well as for those which are sounded together in a chord. When two combined tones have a whole number ratio, they are called consonant. If they do not, they are called dissonant.

Sonar

- Sonar stands for Sound Navigation and Ranging
- The SONAR technique is used to determine the dep of sea and to locate under water hills, valley icebergs, submarines, sunken ships etc.
- A beam of ultrasonic sound is produced a transmitted by the transducer (it is a device th produces ultrasonic sound) of the SONAR, whi travels through sea water. Ultrasound is reflected seawater. The echo produced by the reflection this ultrasonic sound is detected and recorded the detector, which is converted into electric signals. Using the time taken for echo to come bac we can find the depth of sea.
- The distance (*d*) of the under-water object is calcul ted from the time (*t*) taken by the echo to return wi speed (*v*) is given by $2d = v \times t$. This method measuring distance is also known as 'echo-ranging
- Echo ranging is the process of finding distanc using process of ultrasound.

Human Ear

Structure of Human Ear

- The human ear can be divided into three main par viz. outer ear, middle ear and internal ear.
- **Outer Ear:** The outer ear is outside the body a is also called pinna. It extends into the ear can Ear canal is filled with air.
- **Middle Ear:** The middle ear is composed of the e drum or tympanum (it is an elastic membra circular in shape) and the bone ossicles. There a three bone ossicles, namely, the hammer, the an and the strirrup.
- **Internal/inner Ear:** The internal ear is compos of a cochlea and three semi-circular canals. T cochlea is filled with liquid. The cochlea makes t hearing apparatus and the auditory nerve from goes to the brain.
- Eardrum is the intersection of the outer and midc ear.
- Oval Window is the intersection of middle and inn ear.

Working of Human Ear

The outer ear called pinna collects the sound waves. T sound waves passes through the ear canal to a thin membra called eardrum. The eardrum vibrates. The vibrations a amplified by the three bones of the middle ear cal hammer, anvil and stirrup. The middle ear then transm the sound waves to the inner ear. In the inner ear the sou waves are converted into electrical signals by the coch and sent to the brain through the auditory nerves. The bra then interprets the signals as sound.

MULTIPLE CHOICE QUESTIONS

1. Focal length of plane mirror is................ .
A. Infinity B. Zero
C. Negative D. None of these

2. Image formed by plane mirror is:
A. Real and erect B. Real and inverted
C. Virtual and erect D. Virtual and inverted

3. A concave mirror gives real, inverted and same size image if the object is placed:
A. At F B. At infinity
C. At C D. Beyond C

4. Power of the lens is –40, its focal length is:
A. 4 m B. –40 m
C. –0.25 m D. –25 m

5. A concave mirror gives virtual, refract and enlarged image of the object but image of smaller size than the size of the object is:
A. At infinity B. Between F and C
C. Between P and F D. At E

6. In optics an object which has higher refractive index is called:
A. Optically rarer B. Optically denser
C. Optical density D. Refractive index

7. The optical phenomena, twinkling of stars, is due to:
A. Atmospheric reflection
B. Total reflection
C. Atmospheric refraction
D. Total refraction

8. Convex lens focus a real, point sized image at focus, the object is placed:
A. At focus B. Between F and 2F
C. At infinity D. At 2F

9. The unit of power of lens is:
A. Metre B. Centimeter
C. Diopter D. None of these

10. The radius of curvature of a mirror is 20 cm the focal length is:
A. 20 cm B. 10 cm
C. 40 cm D. 5 cm

11. The end product of alcoholic fermentation is:
A. pyruvic acid B. acetaldehyde
C. ethyl alcohol D. formic acid

12. Light wave is a:
A. Transverse wave B. Longitudinal wave
C. Any of both D. None of these

13. Protons and neutrons are bound in a nucleus by the:
A. short range 'weak interaction'
B. short range 'strong interaction'
C. long range 'electromagnetic interaction'
D. long range 'gravitational interaction'

14. To an astronaut in space, the sky will appear to be:
A. violet B. red
C. blue D. black

15. On a rainy day, small oily films on water show brilliant colours. This is due to:
A. scattering B. interference
C. polarisation D. none of these

16. Rainbow formation is due to:
A. absorption of sunlight by water droplets
B. diffusion of sunlight through water droplets
C. ionisation of water droplets
D. refraction and reflection of sunlight by water droplets

17. Golden view of sea shell is due to:
A. diffraction B. dispersion
C. polarisation D. reflection

18. A star appears twinkling in the sky because of:
A. scattering of light by atmosphere
B. reflection of light by atmosphere
C. refraction of light by atmosphere
D. diffraction of light by atmosphere

19. When a strong beam of light is passed through a colloidal solution, the light will:
A. be scattered B. pass unchanged
C. be absorbed D. be reflected

20. Persons suffering from myopia are advised to use:
A. convex lens B. concave lens
C. plano-convex lens D. plano-concave lens

21. The primary colours in photography are:
A. red, blue, yellow B. red, yellow, green
C. red, blue, green D. blue, yellow, green

22. Mirage is an example:
A. refraction of light only
B. total internal, reflection of light only
C. refraction and total internal reflection of light
D. dispersion of light only

23. Optical fibres are based on the phenomenon of:
A. interference B. dispersion
C. diffraction D. total internal reflection

24. The phenomenon of light associated with the appearance of blue colour of the sky is:
A. interference B. reflection
C. refraction D. scattering

25. Lens in made up of:
A. pyrex glass B. flint glass
C. ordinary glass D. cobalt glass

26. Lambert's law is related to:
A. reflection B. refraction
C. interference D. illumination

27. A water tank appears shallower when it is viewed from top due to:
A. rectilinear propagation of light
B. reflection
C. total internal reflection
D. refraction

28. To draw maximum current from a combination of cells, how should the cells be grouped?
A. Series
B. Parallel
C. Mixed
D. Depends upon the relative values of external and internal resistance

29. The image formed by retina of human eye is:
A. Virtual and erect B. Real and inverted
C. Virtual and inverted D. Real and erect

30. The change in the focal length of human eye is caused due to:
A. Ciliary muscles B. Pupil
C. Cornea D. Iris

31. The least distance of distinct vision for a young adult with normal vision is:
A. 25 m B. 20 m
C. 25 cm D. 20 cm

32. The persistence of vision for human eye is:
A. 1/10th of a second B. 1/16th of a second
C. 1/6th of the second D. 1/18th of a second

33. The light sensitive cell present on retina and is sensitive to the intensity of light is:
A. Cones B. Rods
C. Both rods and cones D. None of these

34. The phenomena of light responsible for the working of the human eye is:
A. Reflection
B. Refraction
C. Power of accommodation
D. Persistence of vision

35. Which of the following colors is least scattered by fog, dust of smoke?
A. Violet B. Blue
C. Red D. Yellow

36. The colored light that refracts most while passing through a prism is:
A. Yellow B. Violet
C. Blue D. Red

37. The amount of light entering the human eye is controlled by:
A. Ciliary muscles B. Pupil
C. Cornea D. Iris

38. The part of the eyes refracts light entering the e from external objects?
A. Lens B. Cornea
C. Iris D. Pupil

39. Variation of focal length to form a sharp image retina is called:
A. accommodation B. aperture
C. retina control D. sutter

40. In human eye, image is formed:
A. behind retina
B. in front of retina
C. on retina
D. in between lens and retina

41. Eardrum is a part of:
A. Sound producing organ
B. Skeletal system
C. Hearing organ
D. Reproductive organ

42. The hearing range of human ear is:
A. 20 Hz to 20,000 Hz B. Less than 20 Hz
C. More than 20,000 Hz D. 20 Hz to 25,000 Hz

43. The voice box is called:
A. Stomach B. Heart
C. Larynx D. Mouth

44. Large amplitude of sound vibrations will produce:
A. Loud sound B. Meak sound
C. Slow sound D. Shreak

45. The pitch of sound depends on:
A. frequency B. amplitude
C. both of these D. none of these

46. Sound is kind of:
A. Work B. Energy
C. Force D. None

47. To an fro motion of an object is called:
A. Waves B. Amplitude
C. Vibration D. All of the above

48. Voice box or larynx of human process:
A. Sound B. Wind
C. Loudness D. None

49. Sound propagates maximum in:
A. Gas B. Liquid
C. Solid D. All

50. Noise pollution is harmful for:
A. Human B. Cat
C. Bird D. All

51. Which of the following connects the external ear wi the inner structures?
A. Cornea
B. Iris
C. External Auditory Meatus
D. Cornea

52. Which of the following bones contain in the Middle Ear?
A. Malleus B. Incus
C. Stapes D. All the above

53. Old people cannot hear sounds even above:
A. 5,000 Hz B. 15,000 Hz
C. 10,000 Hz D. 8,000 Hz

54. A normal human ear can hear a sound only if its frequency lies between:
A. 30 Hz to 30,000 Hz B. 50 Hz to 50,000 Hz
C. 20 Hz to 20,000 Hz D. 10 Hz to 10,000 Hz

55. When frequency of sound increases, wavelength and period:
A. becomes negative B. remains constant
C. also increases D. decreases

56. Middle ear consists of:
A. Malleus, incus and stapes
B. Vestibule, semicircular canals and cochlea
C. Pinna, auditory canal and ear drum
D. None of these

57. External ear consists of:
A. Malleus, incus and stapes
B. Vestibule, semicircular canals and cochlea
C. Pinna, auditory canal and ear drum
D. Eustachian tube and oval window

58. Ear drum is also called:
A. Tympanum B. Pinna
C. Auditory canal D. Vestibule

59. Characteristic of sound by which we can distinguish between two sounds of same loudness and pitch is known as:
A. loudness B. pitch
C. quality D. intensity

60. Range of frequencies which a human ear can hear is called:
A. pitch of sound
B. loudness of sound
C. audible frequency range
D. quality of sound

61. Decibel scale is a logarithm measure of amplitude of:
A. sound waves B. light waves
C. heat waves D. electric current

62. Soft materials absorb large amount of:
A. heat energy
B. light energy
C. electromagnetic waves
D. sound energy

63. Louder sound can cause damage to:
A. hearing B. sight
C. skin D. brain

64. Sound having frequencies above 20000 Hz are called:
A. infrasound B. ultrasound
C. mega sound D. micro sound

65. If we tighten strings of instrument pitch will be:
A. higher B. lower
C. constant D. no pitch

ANSWERS

1	2	3	4	5	6	7	8	9	10
A	C	C	C	C	B	C	C	C	B
11	**12**	**13**	**14**	**15**	**16**	**17**	**18**	**19**	**20**
C	A	B	D	B	D	A	C	A	B
21	**22**	**23**	**24**	**25**	**26**	**27**	**28**	**29**	**30**
C	C	D	D	B	D	D	D	B	A
31	**32**	**33**	**34**	**35**	**36**	**37**	**38**	**39**	**40**
C	B	B	B	C	B	B	B	A	C
41	**42**	**43**	**44**	**45**	**46**	**47**	**48**	**49**	**50**
C	A	C	A	A	B	C	A	C	D
51	**52**	**53**	**54**	**55**	**56**	**57**	**58**	**59**	**60**
C	D	B	C	D	A	C	A	C	C
61	**62**	**63**	**64**	**65**					
A	D	A	B	A					

★★★

7

Chemical Effects of Electric Current; Electroplating

Electrolysis

Electrolysis is the process by which ionic substances are decomposed into simpler substances when an electric current is passed through them.

Electrolysis Process

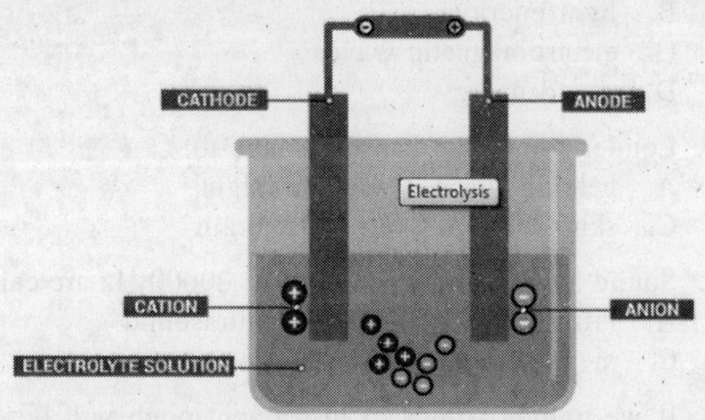

ELECTROLYSIS

- Ionic compounds contain charged particles called ions. For example, Sodium Chloride contains positively charged Sodium ions and negatively charged Chlorine ions.
- The ions must be free to move in order to start the electrolysis process. When an ionic substance is dissolved in water or melted then the ions are free to move. During electrolysis, positively charged ions move to the negative electrode and negatively charged ions move to the positive electrode. Then positively charged ions receive electrons and negatively charged ions lose electrons. Both the products of the dissociation get collected at the electrodes.
- For instance, if electricity is passed through molten sodium chloride, the sodium chloride is broken into sodium and chlorine and they collect at their respective electrodes. The metals get precipitated and the gases escape. This ability to break down substance with current is used in many ways.
- Electrolysis is widely used for Electroplating.

Implementation of Electrolysis

In the medieval times, aluminium was almost as precious as silver. Its extraction was not known and pure aluminium was extremely hard to come by. The application of electrolysis turned aluminium from a precious metal to one of the most largely used metals by humans. Aluminium is extracted from its ore by the process of electrolytic decomposition and deposition.

Uses of Electrolysis

- Electrolysis is done for coating one metal on another.
- The industrial use includes various metals such as aluminium, magnesium, chlorine, and fluorine.

Electroplating

Electroplating is basically the process of plating a metal onto the other by hydrolysis mostly to prevent corrosion of metal or for decorative purposes. The process uses an electric current to reduce dissolved metal cations to develop a lean coherent metal coating on the electrode. Electroplating is often applied in the electrical oxidation of anions on a solid substrate like the formation of silver chloride on a silver wire to form silver chloride electrodes.

Electroplating is majorly applied to modify the surface features of an object (e.g corrosion protection, lubricity, abrasion), but the process can also be used to build thickness or make objects by electroforming.

To understand the concept further, let's take an example of gold coating. In this instance, a layer of gold is to be electrodeposited on a metallic jewellery to enhance its appearance.

Usually, the gold plating is connected to the anode (+ve charged electrode) of the circuit and the jewellery is kept at the cathode (–ve charged electrode). Both are kept immersed in a highly developed electrolytic bat (solution). At this stage, a DC current is supplied to the anode that oxidizes the gold atoms and dissolves them into the solution.

The dissolved ions of gold are reduced at the cathode and plated on the jewellery. However, there are major factors that influence the last plating. These include:

- The voltage level of current.
- The temperature and chemical composition of the bath.
- The current length of time.
- The distance between the cathode and the anode.

Uses of Electroplating

Talking about the uses of electroplating, apart from enhancing the appearance of the substrate it is used in various other purposes as well. The major application is to optimize a material's resistance towards corrosion. The plated layer often serves as a sacrificial coating which reveals that it dissolves before the base substance. Some of the other common applications of electroplating involve:

- Improving wear resistance.
- Improving the thickness of metal surface.
- Enhancing the electrical conductivity like plating a copper layer on an electrical component.
- Minimizing Friction.
- Improving surface uniformity.

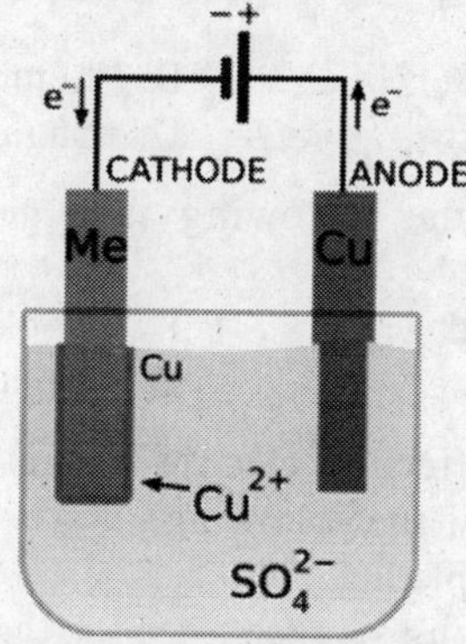

How does Electroplating work?

The positive electrode should be the metal that you want to coat the object with. The negative electrode will be the object that should receive the deposit of the electroplating metal. The electrolyte should be a solution of the coating metal, as it is a metal nitrate or sulphate. We can examine this better with few examples;

Silver Plating

The object that is to be plated is connected to the negative terminal of the power supply. A piece of silver is connected to the positive terminal. The electrolyte is a silver nitrate solution. This process can also be used to purify silver. We can take an impure block at the positive terminal and a strip of pure silver to the negative. The pure silver is deposited via electrolysis at the negative terminal leaving behind the impurities.

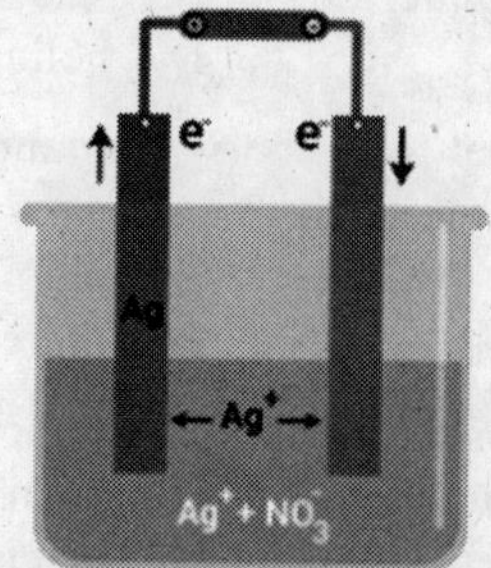

$Ag(s) \rightarrow Ag(s)^{+} + e^{-}$ $Ag^{+} + e^{-} \rightarrow Ag(s)$

Copper Plating

The object that is to be plated is connected to the negative terminal of the power supply. A piece of copper is connected to the positive terminal. The electrolyte is copper Sulphate solution.

Like with silver plating, copper deposition can be used to purify copper. In this case, both the electrodes are made from copper. As the impure positive electrode gradually disappears leaving the impurities behind the negative electrode gradually gets coated with pure copper.

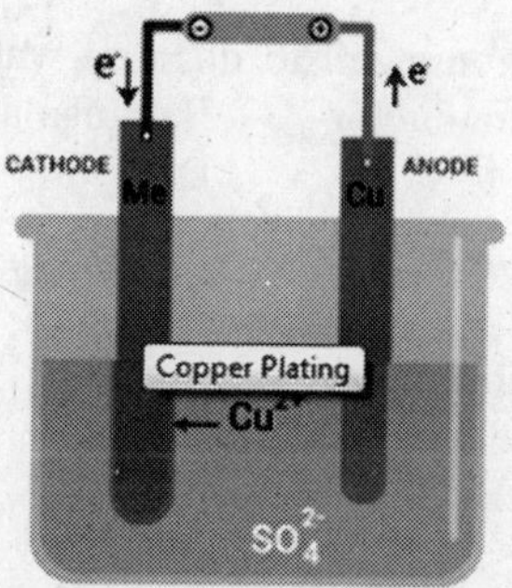

Some Important Facts:

- The materials which allow electric current to pass through are called good conductors of electricity. For example, metals like copper and aluminium.
- The materials which do not allow electric current to pass through them easily are called poor conductor of electricity. For example, rubber, plastic and wood.
- Due to the heating effect of current, the filament of the bulb of the tester gets heated to a high temperature and it starts glowing.
- If the current through a circuit is too weak, the filament does not get heated sufficiently and it does not glow.
- LED (Light Emitting Diodes) can be used in place of the electric bulb in the tester, LED glows even when a weak electric current flows through it.
- Electric current produces magnetic current, a tester can be prepared by using a compass needle. The deflection of the magnetic needle can be seen, even when current is small.
- Distilled water is poor conductor of electricity. Water collected from taps, hand pumps, wells and ponds is not pure contain dissolved salts so it is good conductor of electricity.
- Most liquids that conduct electricity are solutions of acids, bases and salts.
- Chromium has a shiny appearance, does not corrode and is resistant to scratches. But, chromium is expensive and it is not economical to make the whole object out of chromium. So, the objects, such as taps, car parts, wheel rims etc. made from a cheaper metal and electroplated with chromium.

MULTIPLE CHOICE QUESTIONS

1. Plastic wire is:
A. An insulator B. A conductor
C. Both of these D. None of these

2. Electroplating is based on:
A. Magnetic effect of electricity
B. Chemical effect of electricity
C. Heating effect of electricity
D. Physical effect of electricity

3. Adding common salt to distilled water makes it:
A. Good conductor B. Insulator
C. No D. Both A and B

4. An electrolyte is:
A. a metal
B. a solution
C. a liquid that conducts current
D. all of above

5. Copper wire is a:
A. Good conductor B. Poor conductor
C. Both A and B D. None of these

6. Poor conductors are:
A. Plastics B. Clothes
C. Wood D. All of these

7. Distilled water is:
A. Poor conductor B. Good conductor
C. Both A and B D. None

8. Flow of electron is called:
A. Electroplating B. Electric current
C. Electrodes D. Electrolyte

9. Electroplating prevents:
A. Current B. Chemical effect
C. Rusting D. All

10. An electric lamp glows due to:
A. Chemical effect B. Magnetic effect
C. Heating effect D. None

11. Steel cans are made of:
A. lead B. tinplate
C. tungsten D. cobalt

12. Pure piece of metal which is used to be plated, is made the:
A. anode B. cathode
C. nematode D. posit rode

13. Shiny objects are often made by electroplating steel with:
A. nickel B. titanium
C. chromium D. zinc

14. In our daily life, we find most of compounds contain:
A. sodium B. chlorine
C. oxygen D. hydrogen

15. A sheet of pure copper is used as:
A. cathode B. anode
C. positrode D. negatrode

16. Electric poles are coated with a layer of which metal?
A. Chromium B. Zinc
C. Silver D. Aluminium

17. Sanitary fitings are generally coated with a layer of which metal?
A. Chromium B. Zinc
C. Silver D. Aluminium

18. Which of the following is a bad conductor of electricity?
A. Tap water B. Lemon juice
C. Vinegar D. Sugar solution

19. Which of the following is a good conductor of electricity?
A. Distilled water B. Cooking oil
C. Tap water D. Sugar solution

20. Chemical effect of electric current is primarily used for which of the following?
A. Electroplating
B. Separating oxygen
C. Separating hydrogen
D. Separating gold

21. Which of the following will work best as a tester for electric current?
A. Bulb B. LED
C. CFL D. Magnetic compass

22. Which material is used for making the central rod in an electric cell?
A. Copper B. Carbon
C. Aluminium D. Iron

23. Which scientist was the first to show electrolysis of water?
A. Oersted B. William Nicholson
C. Michael Faraday D. Galileo

24. The liquid will conduct electric current in a circuit when the vessel is with ______.
A. distilled water B. salt solution
C. air D. helium

25. Which of the following substance is not a good conductor of electricity?
A. copper B. aluminium
C. rubber D. mercury

26. The decomposition of liquid compound on passing an electric current though it is known as ______ .
A. electroplating B. electrolysis
C. magnetic effect D. electro-resistivity

27. The glowing of filament bulb is due to:
A. heating effect of electric current
B. physical effect of electric current
C. magnetic effect of electric current
D. chemical effect of electric current

28. In a LED, the longer lead/leg is connected to ______.
A. positive terminal of the battery
B. negative terminal of the battery
C. either positive of negative terminal of the battery
D. none of these

29. Most liquids that conduct electricity are solutions of ______.
A. acids B. bases
C. salts D. all of these

30. Name the chemist who showed bubbles of oxygen and hydrogen are when electric current passes through water.
A. William Nicholson B. William Harvey
C. Luigi Galvani D. Alessandro Volt

31. To prevent iron from corrosion it is electroplated with ______.
A. aluminium B. copper
C. oxygen D. zinc

32. The whole apparatus of electrodes, electrolytes and vessel container is called ______.
A. thermometer B. electrometer
C. voltameter D. ammeter

33. What is current?
A. The flow of matter B. The flow of electrons
C. The flow of protons D. The flow of charge

34. In electrolytic solutions, which of the following acts as carrier of charge?
A. Protons B. Electrons
C. Neutrons D. Ions

35. What are insulators?
A. Materials that conduct electricity
B. Materials that do not conduct electricity
C. Materials that conduct electricity only at low temperatures
D. Materials that conduct electricity at room temperature

36. Which of the following is an insulator?
A. Wood B. Iron
C. Graphite D. Silver

37. Which of the following energy conversions takes place in a cell?
A. Electrical energy into chemical energy
B. Chemical energy into electrical energy
C. Magnetic energy into electrical energy
D. Electrical energy into mechanical energy

38. Which of the following are the characteristics of an electrolyte?
A. It has a positive charge.
B. It has a negative charge.
C. It conducts charge without dissociating.
D. It forms positive and negative ions.

39. Which acid is present in lemon juice that acts as an electrolyte?
A. Sulphuric acid B. Nitric acid
C. Hydrochloric acid D. Citric acid

40. Which of the following is the electrolyte in a dry cell?
A. Copper sulphate B. Zinc sulphate
C. Sulphuric acid D. Ammonium chloride

41. In a dry cell, which of the following acts as the positive terminal?
A. Carbon rod
B. Manganese dioxide
C. Manganese dioxide and powdered carbon
D. A metal cap on the carbon rod

42. What is the common voltage produced by a dry cell?
A. 1.5 V B. 30 V
C. 60 V D. 3 V

43. What happens when electric current is made to flow through a conductor?
A. Some amount of electrical energy is converted into heat energy.
B. Some amount of electrical energy is converted into mechanical energy.
C. Some amount of mechanical energy is converted into electrical energy.
D. Some amount of heat energy is converted into electrical energy.

44. Nichrome is an alloy. Which of the following metals make up this alloy?
A. Nickel and chromium
B. Nitrogen and chromium
C. Nitrogen, chlorine and chromium
D. Nickel, chromium and manganese

45. What is the splitting of a compound using electricity called?
A. Electrolysis B. Electrolyte
C. Electrokinesis D. Electrochemistry

46. What is the principle involved in the glowing of an electric bulb?
A. Magnetic effect of current
B. Heating effect of current
C. Chemical effect
D. Conduction of current

47. Which of the following is the best conductor of electricity?
A. Tap water B. Distilled water
C. Sea water D. Rain water

48. Which of the following effects of current is responsible for the deflection of a compass needle in an electric field?
A. Heating effect of current
B. Magnetic effect of current
C. Conducting effect of heat
D. Chemical effect of current

49. Which of these is the industrial applications of the chemical effects of electric current?
A. Electroplating B. Galvanizing
C. Anodizing D. All of the above

50. Which of the following liquids is a bad conductor of electricity?
A. Lemon juice B. Vinegar
C. Sea water D. Distilled water

51. A positively charged ion is called:
A. Atom B. Anion
C. Cation D. Neutral Ion

52. The instrument needed to measure the current flowing through a circuit is:
A. voltmeter B. voltameter
C. galvanometer D. ammeter

53. The process in which any electrolyte gets decomposed when electricity is passed through it, is called
A. electrolysis B. decomposition
C. dissociation D. splitting

54. The process of depositing a thin layer of any superior metal over an object of a cheaper metal with the help of electricity is called
A. electrorefining B. electrometallurgy
C. electroplating D. electrowinning

55. Which of the following is the most essential for an electric circuit to work?
A. A switch B. An electric current
C. A switch board D. None of these

56. In LEDs, the longer lead (wire) is always connected to the ______ terminal:
A. negative B. neutral
C. positive D. Any terminal

57. Tap water is a good conductor of electricity while distilled water is not because:
A. Tap water contain salts
B. Distilled water do not contain salt
C. Only A is correct
D. Both A and B is correct

58. When electrodes are immersed in water and electricity passed, the bubbles formed on the positive terminal is actually ______ gas.
A. Hydrogen B. Carbon dioxide
C. Oxygen D. Nitrogen

59. Some liquids are good conductors of electricity and some are poor conductors. Which one is a poor conductor?
A. Distilled water
B. Alkaline solution
C. Common salt solution
D. Acidic solution

60. Why do we add little dilute sulphuric acid to copper sulphate solution during electroplating?
A. To inerease acidity
B. To increase conductivity
C. So that the colour becomes more prominent
D. To burn copper sulphate

ANSWERS

1	2	3	4	5	6	7	8	9	10
A	B	A	C	A	D	A	B	C	C
11	**12**	**13**	**14**	**15**	**16**	**17**	**18**	**19**	**20**
B	A	C	A	A	B	A	D	C	A
21	**22**	**23**	**24**	**25**	**26**	**27**	**28**	**29**	**30**
D	B	B	B	C	B	A	A	D	A
31	**32**	**33**	**34**	**35**	**36**	**37**	**38**	**39**	**40**
D	C	D	D	B	A	B	B	D	D
41	**42**	**43**	**44**	**45**	**46**	**47**	**48**	**49**	**50**
D	A	A	A	A	B	C	B	D	D
51	**52**	**53**	**54**	**55**	**56**	**57**	**58**	**59**	**60**
C	D	A	C	B	C	D	C	A	B

★ ★ ★

8

Natural Phenomena–Lightning; Earthquakes, Pollution of Air and Water

Lightning

Lightning, the visible discharge of electricity that occurs when a region of a cloud acquires an excess electrical charge, either positive or negative, that is sufficient to break down the resistance of air.

Lightning is a sudden electrostatic discharge that occurs typically during a thunderstorm. This discharge occurs between electrically charged regions of a cloud (called intra-cloud lightning or IC), between two clouds (CC lightning), or between a cloud and the ground (CG lightning).

The charged regions in the atmosphere temporarily equalize themselves through this discharge referred to as a flash. A lightning flash can also be a strike if it involves an object on the ground. Lightning creates light in the form of black body radiation from the very hot plasma created by the electron flow, and sound in the form of thunder. Lightning may be seen and not heard when it occurs at a distance too great for the sound to carry as far as the light from the strike or flash.

Causes of Lightning

Lightning is an electric current. Within a thundercloud many small bits of ice (frozen raindrops) bump into each other or collide as they move around in the air. Those collisions create an electric charge.

After a period of time, the whole cloud fills up with electrical charges. The positive charges, or protons, form at the top of the cloud and the negative charges, or electrons, form at the bottom of the cloud. Since opposites attract, that causes a positive charge to build up on the ground beneath the cloud. The ground's electrical charge concentrates around anything that sticks up, such as mountains, people, or single trees. The charge coming up from these points eventually connects with a charge reaching down from the thundercloud and lightning strikes!

As storms develop, clouds become charged with electricity. Scientists are still not sure exactly what causes this, but they do know that when the voltage becomes high enough for the electricity to leap across the air from one place to another, lightning flashes!

Lightning can strike within a cloud, from one cloud to another, from a cloud to the ground, or from the ground to a cloud.

Lightning protection systems

Hundreds of devices, including lightning rods and charge transfer systems, are used to mitigate lightning damage and influence the path of a lightning flash.

A lightning rod (or lightning protector) is a metal strip or rod connected to earth through conductors and a grounding system, used to provide a preferred pathway to ground if lightning terminates on a structure. The class of these products are often called a 'finial' or 'air terminal'. A lightning rod or 'Franklin rod' in honor of its famous inventor, Benjamin Franklin, is simply a metal rod, and without being connected to the lightning protection system, as was sometimes the case in the old days, will provide no added protection to a structure. Other names include 'lightning conductor', 'arrester', and 'discharger'; however, over the years these names have been incorporated into other products or industries with a stake in lightning protection. Lightning arrester, for example, often refers to fused links that explode when a strike occurs to a high voltage overhead power line to protect the more expensive transformers down the line by opening the circuit. In reality, it was an early form of a heavy duty surge protection device (SPD). Modern arresters, constructed with metal oxides, are capable of safely shunting abnormally high voltage surges to ground while preventing normal system voltages from being shorted to ground.

Earthquake

An earthquake is a natural occurrence, like rain. Earthquakes affect almost every part of the Earth and like rain they can be either mild or catastrophic. Over the course of geological time, earthquakes, floods, and other natural events have helped to shape the surface of our planet. An earthquake may last only a few seconds, but the processes that cause earthquakes have operated within the Earth for millions and millions of years.

Why does the earth shake?

The release of energy occurs along a fault. A fault is a sharp break in the crustal rocks. Rocks along a fault tend to move in opposite directions. As the overlying rock strata press them, the friction locks them together. However, their tendency to move apart at some point of time overcomes the friction. As a result, the blocks get deformed and eventually, they slide past one another abruptly. This causes a release of energy, and the energy waves travel in all directions. The point where the energy is released is called the focus of an earthquake, alternatively, it is called the hypocentre. The energy waves travelling in different directions reach the surface. The point on the surface, nearest to the focus, is called epicentre. It is the first one to experience the waves. It is a point directly above the focus.

Earthquake Waves

All natural earthquakes take place in the lithosphere. An instrument called 'seismograph' records the waves reaching the surface. A curve of earthquake waves recorded on the seismograph is given in figure. Note that the curve shows three distinct sections each representing different types of wave patterns. Earthquake waves are basically of two types - body waves and surface waves. Body waves are generated due to the release of energy at the focus and move in all directions travelling through the body of the earth. Hence, the name body waves. The body waves interact with the surface rocks and generate new set of waves called surface waves. These waves move along the surface. The velocity of waves changes as they travel through materials with different densities. The denser the material, the higher is the velocity. Their direction also changes as they reflect or refract when coming across materials with different densities.

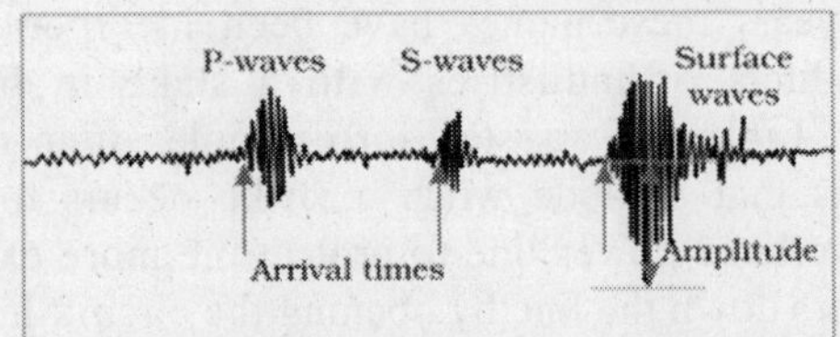

Figure: *Earthquake wave*

There are two types of body waves. They are called P and S-waves. P-waves move faster and are the first to arrive at the surface. These are also called 'primary waves'. The P-waves are similar to sound waves. They travel through gaseous, liquid and solid materials. S-waves arrive at the surface with some time lag. These are called secondary waves. An important fact about S-waves is that they can travel only through solid materials. This characteristic of the S-waves is quite important. It has helped scientists to understand the structure of the interior of the earth.

Types of Earthquakes

- The most common ones are the tectonic earthquakes. These are generated due to sliding of rocks along a fault plane.
- A special class of tectonic earthquake is sometimes recognised as volcanic earthquake. However, these are confined to areas of active volcanoes.
- In the areas of intense mining activity, sometimes the roofs of underground mines collapse causing minor tremors. These are called collapse earthquakes.
- Ground shaking may also occur due to the explosion of chemical or nuclear devices. Such tremors are called explosion earthquakes.
- The earthquakes that occur in the areas of large reservoirs are referred to as reservoir induced earthquakes.

Measuring Earthquakes

The earthquake events are scaled either according to the magnitude or intensity of the shock. The magnitude scale is known as the Richter scale. The magnitude relates to the energy released during the quake. The magnitude is expressed in numbers, 0-10. The intensity scale is named after Mercalli, an Italian seismologist. The intensity scale takes into account the visible damage caused by the event. The range of intensity scale is from 1-12.

Effects of Earthquake

Earthquake is a natural hazard. The following are the immediate hazardous effects of earthquake:

(*i*) Ground Shaking
(*ii*) Differential ground settlement
(*iii*) Land and mud slides
(*iv*) Soil liquefaction
(*v*) Ground lurching
(*vi*) Avalanches
(*vii*) Ground displacement
(*viii*) Floods from dam and levee failures
(*ix*) Fires
(*x*) Structural collapse
(*xi*) Falling objects
(*xii*) Tsunami

MULTIPLE CHOICE QUESTIONS

1. Name the resin which produces spark is:
A. Gum B. Amber
C. Both A and B D. None of these

2. The like charges:
A. Repel each other
B. Attract each other
C. No interaction takes place
D. All of these

3. The shaking of earth is called:
A. Tsunami B. Volcano
C. Earthquake D. All of these

4. Lightening occurs due to:
A. Electric discharge
B. Rain
C. Wind
D. None of these

5. Interaction of charges is called:
A. Lightening B. Electrical discharge
C. Earthing D. Electricity

6. Sparkers can be seen on electric pole. Which wires become?
A. Loose B. Tight
C. Wrinkle D. None

7. Benjamen Franklin showed lightening in:
A. 1725 B. 1527
C. 1752 D. 1572

8. The charge acquired by a glass rod when it is rubbed with silk is:
A. Negative B. Positive
C. Both D. None

9. As per convention, what is the charge on a glass rod when it is rubbed with silk cloth?
A. Positive B. Negative
C. Either 'A' or 'B' D. No charge

10. As per convention, what is the charge on silk cloth when a glass rod is rubbed with silk cloth?
A. Positive B. Negative
C. Either 'A' or 'B' D. No charge

11. Transfer of which atomic particle produces charge in a body?
A. Neutron B. Proton
C. Electron D. All of the above

12. A place where an earthquake originates is called the __________.
A. Focus B. Tsunami
C. Fault Line D. Epicenter

13. As the magnitude of natural disasters increases their frequency of occurrence _________.
A. increases B. decreases
C. remains the same D. varies over time

14. Which natural hazard has resulted in the greatest monetary losses in a single even for the period of time listed?
A. earthquake B. hurricane
C. fire D. flood

15. The largest wave during a tsunami event is______.
A. the first
B. the third
C. the fifth
D. unpredictable, it could be any of them

16. The destructive powers of tsunami result mainly from their ___________________.
A. incredible height
B. unpredictability
C. cold water
D. momentum and long wavelength

17. Which event produces the biggest tsunami?
A. Earthquake
B. Underwater landslides
C. Hurricanes
D. Impacts of asteroids and comets

18. Powerful tsunami are most frequently produced by __________.
A. volcanoes B. underwater landslides
C. earthquakes D. impacts of asteroids

19. Which device is used to protect building from lightning conductor?
A. Seismograph B. Lightning Conductor
C. Barometer D. Thermal Conductor

20. Name the scientist who showed that lightning and the spark from your clothes are essentially the same phenomena?
A. Thomas Alva Edison
B. Benjamin Franklin
C. Franklin D. Roosevelt
D. Isaac Newton

21. Two objects with like charges will ______.
A. attract each other
B. repel each other
C. either attract or repel
D. neither attract nor repel

22. Two objects with unlike charges will _______.
A. attract each other
B. repel each other
C. either attract or repel
D. neither attract nor rep

23. The charge acquired by a glass rod when it is rubbed with silk is considered as _______.
A. neutral
B. either positive or negative
C. positive
D. negative

24. When charges move, they constitute an _______ .
A. electric current B. magnetic effect
C. heating effect D. all of the above

25. Device can which be used to test whether an object is carrying charge or not is known as ______ .
A. Electroscope B. Microscope
C. Periscope D. Telescope

26. In thunderstorm, the charges accumulate near the upper edges of clouds are ________ .
A. negatively charged B. positively charged
C. neutral D. none of these

27. Which scale is used to measure the magnitude of earth quake?
A. Celsius B. Kelvin
C. Richter D. Pascal

28. During lightning which of the following is a NOT a safe place?
A. Open field B. Inside a house
C. Bus Stop D. Elevated Ridge

29. Using science and technology damaged caused by natural disasters like hurricane, earthquakes can be:
A. prevented B. reduced
C. enhanced D. raised

30. Catastrophic natural disaster losses in developed countries involve which of the following?
A. large numbers of deaths
B. large financial costs to individuals and companies
C. primarily losses borne by insurance companies
D. large numbers of deaths and large financial costs

31. Areas of cities that are subjected to significant natural hazards should be used for which of the following?
A. office buildings because they can withstand the effects of the hazard
B. inexpensive single-family houses
C. parks and golf courses
D. shopping malls

32. What kind of natural hazards are not normally insurable?
A. earthquakes B. volcanoes
C. landslides D. floods

33. Which of the following is not part of geological disaster?
A. Volcanoes B. Earthquakes
C. Tsunami D. Sea Surge

34. What is the rank of India in the world for natural disasters after China as per UNISDR?
A. Third B. Second
C. Seventh D. Eighth

35. Which of the following types of volcanic eruptions associated with Lacroix?
A. Hawaii Eruption
B. Strombolian Eruption
C. Vulcanian
D. All of the above

36. The volcanic eruption in Iceland falls under which volcanic belt in the World?
A. Belts of Convergent boundaries
B. Divergent Plate Boundaries
C. Hot Spots
D. None of the above

37. A geophysicist who studies earthquakes and the mechanical characteristics of the Earth is called ___________.
A. Seismologist B. Geologist
C. Geographer D. Archaeologist

38. What causes Tsunami?
A. Sudden vertical movement of the Earth
B. Convergence of destructive plates in the ocean floor
C. Explosive volcanic eruptions in the seas/oceans.
D. All of the above

39. An earthquake of magnitude 8-9 is:
A. strong B. very strong
C. mild D. not felt

40. Which of the following is the leading cause of death and diseases worldwide?
A. water pollution B. radioactive pollution
C. air pollution D. soil pollution

41. All the following are notorious oil spills except:
A. Deepwater Horizon, 2010
B. Love canal disaster
C. Exxon Valdes, 1991
D. Gulf War, 1991

42. Eutrophication by sewage pollution refers to the:
A. nutrient enrichment of freshwater bodies
B. nutrient depletion of freshwater bodies
C. toxic chemical accumulation in freshwater bodies
D. Heavy metal accumulation in freshwater bodies

43. Which of the following is the major reason for algal bloom?
A. Presence of heavy metals
B. Contamination by pathogens
C. Eutrophication
D. Soil erosion

44. Which of the following is the major cause of biomagnifications?
A. Eutrophication B. Detergent pollution
C. Pesticide pollution D. Industrial pollution

45. Which of the following is an indicator of organic water pollution?
A. BOD B. pH
C. Salinity D. Eutrophication

46. Blue baby syndrome is due to the presence of:
A. excess sulphate in drinking water
B. excess chlorine in drinking water
C. excess heavy metals in drinking water
D. excess nitrates in drinking water

47. Mercury poisoning in water is the reason for:
A. Pellegra B. Minimata disease
C. Itai-Itai disease D. Scurvy

48. Itai-itai disease is caused by:
A. Pb poisoning B. Cd poisoning
C. Hg poisoning D. Cu poisoning

49. Which of the following is not a green house gas?
A. carbon dioxide B. nitrous oxide
C. methane D. nitrogen

50. Which of the following air pollutant reduces the oxygen-carrying capacity of a blood to a large extent?
A. carbon dioxide B. nitrogen monoxide
C. carbon monoxide D. sulphur dioxide

51. The constituent of polluted air which contributes in producing acid rain is:
A. nitrogen B. sulphur dioxide
C. oxygen D. argon

52. Which of the following will be reduced in air in a city forest where lot of dust and fly ash is emitted by a coal based factory in the vicinity?
A. nitrogen B. carbon dioxide
C. oxygen D. water vapour

53. Which of the following disease cannot be caused by drinking of river water contaminated with untreated sewage?
A. cholera B. typhoid
C. tuberculosis D. diarrhoea

54. Drinking water can be made absolutely safe by adding some:
A. aspirin tablets B. iodine tablets
C. chlorine tablets D. cholorophyll tablets

55. Which of the following are used in electric water filters to kill all the harmful microrganisms present in tap water and make it absolutely safe for drinking?
A. infrared radiation B. gamma radiation
C. visible radiation D. ultraviolet radiation

56. Which of the following will reach the earth in greater amounts, if the amount of chlorofluorocarbons released into the air increases?
A. infrared rays B. X-rays
C. gamma rays D. ultraviolet rays

57. Highest percentage of air consists of:
A. Oxygen B. Carbon dioxide
C. Nitrogen D. Argon

58. The Taj Mahal is being affected by:
A. Noise pollution B. Air pollution
C. Water pollution D. None of these

59. Most polluted river in the world is:
A. Yamuna B. Cavery
C. Chenab D. Ganga

60. Air pollution causes:
A. Global warming B. Respiratory problems
C. Soil erosion D. None of these

61. Green House gas is:
A. Nitrogen B. Oxygen
C. Methane D. Carbon dioxide

62. The percentage of nitrogen is:
A. 21% B. 78%
C. 12% D. 87%

63. What causes pollution?
A. Human activities B. Trees
C. Both of these D. None of these

64. CNG is a:
A. Polluted fuel B. Clean fuel
C. Harmful fuel D. None

65. Pollution of water is responsible for:
A. Oil refineries B. Paper factories
C. Sugar mills D. All

66. Chlorofluorocarbon is used in:
A. Refrigerators B. Air conditioners
C. Perfumes D. All

ANSWERS

1	2	3	4	5	6	7	8	9	10
B	A	C	A	A	A	C	B	A	B
11	**12**	**13**	**14**	**15**	**16**	**17**	**18**	**19**	**20**
C	A	B	B	D	D	D	C	B	B
21	**22**	**23**	**24**	**25**	**26**	**27**	**28**	**29**	**30**
B	A	C	D	A	B	C	D	B	B
31	**32**	**33**	**34**	**35**	**36**	**37**	**38**	**39**	**40**
C	C	D	B	D	B	A	D	B	A
41	**42**	**43**	**44**	**45**	**46**	**47**	**48**	**49**	**50**
B	A	C	C	A	D	B	B	D	C
51	**52**	**53**	**54**	**55**	**56**	**57**	**58**	**59**	**60**
B	B	C	C	D	D	C	B	D	B
61	**62**	**63**	**64**	**65**	**66**				
D	B	A	B	D	D				

★ ★ ★

9

Solar System; Stars and Constellations

OUR SOLAR SYSTEM

For thousands of years, from our small world, we have looked upon the cosmic ocean. Early star watchers thought that the Earth was in the middle of the solar system and that the sun and all the other stars spun around the Earth. Copernicus showed that Earth and the other planets in our solar system revolved around our sun. Early astronomers perceived dots of light that seemed to move in the midst of the stars. They called these objects "planets," meaning nomads, and titled them after Ancient Roman holy beings Jupiter, ruler of the divinities; Mercury, an emissary of the gods; Venus, the deity of love and beauty, Mars, the god of war and Saturn, dad of Jupiter and god of cultivation. The astronomers also detected Comets with twinkling tails, and meteors or shooting stars seemingly falling from the heavens.

Subsequently, the telescope was invented, and three more planets were revealed in our solar system: Uranus in 1781, Neptune in 1846, and now demoted to a dwarf planet, Pluto was discovered in 1930. Moreover, there are thousands of smaller bodies such as comets and asteroids. Almost all asteroids orbit in a section sandwiched between the orbits of Mars and Jupiter while the comets lie in the Oort Cloud, outside the orbit of Pluto.

Mercury, Venus, Earth and Mars are closest to the sun and are termed as the terrestrial planets because they have compact stony surfaces. Saturn, Jupiter, Neptune and Uranus are the four huge planets (Jovian Planets) past the trajectory of Mars and are called gas giants. Petite, distant, Pluto has a hard but frostier surface than the other planets.

Just about every planet and even some of the moons have an atmosphere. Our world's atmosphere is mainly made up of oxygen and nitrogen. Venus has a thick atmosphere of carbon dioxide, with hints of poisonous gases, for instance, sulphur dioxide. Mars has a carbon dioxide atmosphere which is very thin. Jupiter, Saturn, Uranus, and Neptune are mainly helium and hydrogen.

Let us know about some members of the solar family:

The Sun

The Sun is the nearest star from us. It is continuously emitting huge amounts of heat and light. The Sun is the source of almost all energy on the Earth. In fact, the Sun is the main source of heat and light for all the planets.

The Planets

The planets look like stars, but they do not have light of their own. They merely reflect the sunlight that falls on them. Can you distinguish between planets and stars? The simplest method of identifying planets from stars is that stars twinkle, whereas planets do not. Also the planets keep changing their positions with respect to the stars. A planet has a definite path in which it revolves around the Sun. This path is called an orbit. The time taken by a planet to complete one revolution is called its period of revolution.

The period of revolution increases as the distance of the planet increases from the sun. Besides revolving around the Sun, a planet also rotates on its own axis like a top. The time taken by a planet to complete one rotation is called its period of rotation.

Some planets are known to have moons/satellites revolving round them. Any celestial body revolving around another celestial body is called its satellite.

The Earth can be said to be a satellite of the Sun, though generally we call it a planet of the Sun. We use the term satellite for the bodies revolving around planets. Moon is a satellite of the Earth. There are many man-made satellites

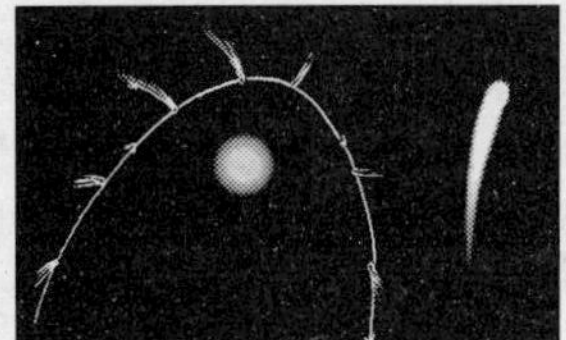

Fig. 3: *Different position of a Comet*

Meteors and Meteorites

At night, when the sky is clear and the moon is not there, you may sometimes see bright streaks of light in the sky (Fig. 4). These are commonly known as shooting stars, although they are not stars. They are called meteors. A meteor is usually a small object that occasionally enters the earth's atmosphere. At that time it has a very high speed. The friction due to the atmosphere heats it up. It glows and evaporates quickly. That is why the bright steak lasts for a very short time. Some meteors are large and so they can reach the Earth before they evaporate completely. The body that reaches the Earth is called a meteorite.

Fig. 4: *Streak of a Meteor*

Artificial Satellites

You must have heard that there are a number of artificial satellites which are orbiting the Earth. You might wonder how artificial satellites are different from natural satellites. Artificial satellites are man-made. They are launched from the Earth. They revolve around the Earth much closer than earth's natural satellite, the moon. India has built and launched several artificial satellites. Aryabhata was the first Indian satellite. Some other Indian satellites are INSAT, IRS, Kalpana-1, EDUSAT, etc.

Constellations and Constellations of Stars

On a clear moonless night we can see thousands upon thousands of stars dotting the night sky. If we are a little creative, we can imagine shapes and patterns these stars can make. Some of these patterns made up of groups of bright stars are easy to recognize and we call such groups as a constellations.

The ancients named many of these recognizable constellation after the objects or animals they resembled. They built stories around them too. For example, the constellation Perseus, Andromeda, Cetus, Cassiopeia and Pegasus are all linked to the mythology of the Greeks. Common constellation names are similar across cultures such as Pisces - the fish in Greek is also called Meena (also meaning fish) in Sanskrit.

All the constellations appear to move in the sky from west to east because the earth rotates from west to east. Moreover, all constellations in the southern hemisphere are not visible in the northern hemisphere and vice versa. This is because the earth is round and some constellations do not fall in the line of sight. A person in the equator can see almost all the constellations.

Zodiac constellations

There are 12 major constellations that line up along the sun's path along the sky (called the ecliptic). These are the Zodiac constellations: Aries (Mesha), Taurus (Vrushabha), Gemini (Mithuna), Crab/Cancer (Karka), Leo (Simha), Virgo (Kanya), Libra (Tula), Scorpion (Vruschika), Saggitarius (Dhanusha), Capricorn (Makara), Aquarius (Kumbha), Pisces (Meena). These constellations were used to track the movement of the sun and track time in ancient times.

Big Dipper

The big dipper also called as Saptarishi in India is a group of seven stars visible in the northern hemisphere. The constellation looks like a big ladle or like a wheel barrow and is part of a bigger constellation called Ursa Major (The great Bear). Two of the stars on this constellation appear to point to the pole star (Polaris/Dhruva). The pole star is the only star in the night sky that does not appear to move east to west but appears fixed. This is because it is directly above the earth's axis.

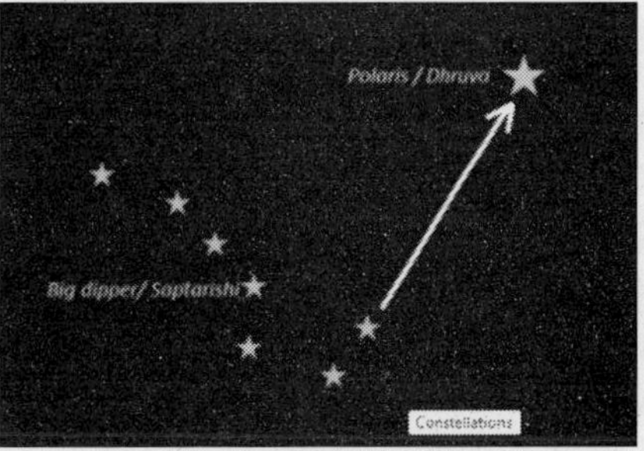

Orion

This is a constellation known as 'the hunter' or Mriga in India. It has a large number of bright stars in it. Three bright stars that are in line make up the 'belt' of the hunter. These three stars point to the brightest star in the night sky —Sirius.

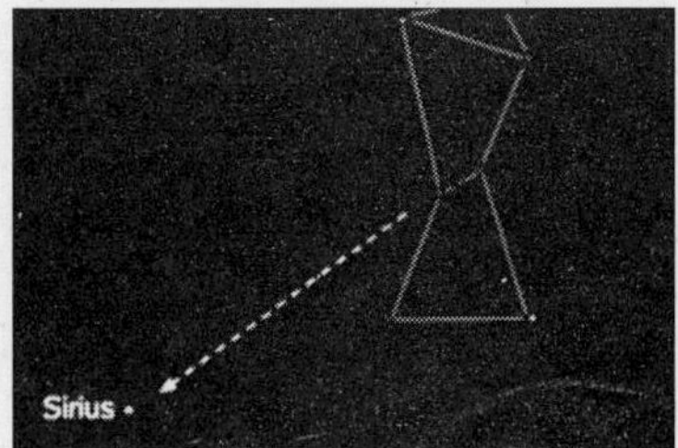

MULTIPLE CHOICE QUESTIONS

1. Which is the brightest planet in the universe?
A. Mercury B. Venus
C. Earth D. Saturn

2. Which is the nearest planet to the sun?
A. Neptune B. Mars
C. Mercury D. Earth

3. On which planet the life exists?
A. Earth B. Moon
C. Jupiter D. None

4. Which planet appears to be yellowish?
A. Asteroids B. Mars
C. Uranus D. Saturn

5. Which is the farthest planet of solar system?
A. Neptune B. Jupiter
C. Mercury D. Earth

6. The first outside orbit of the earth planet is:
A. Jupiter B. Mars
C. Saturn D. Uranus

7. Which is the largest planet in solar system?
A. Mercury B. Mars
C. Jupiter D. Saturn

8. What is the gap between the orbit of mars and Jupiter called?
A. Asteroids B. Comets
C. Meteor D. Meteorite

9. Stars appear to move from:
A. West to east
B. East to west
C. North to south
D. South to west

10. The tilting of the earth is responsible for:
A. Change of days
B. Change of the sun's rays
C. Change of the season
D. None

11. Largest Planet of the Inner Planets of Solar system is:
A. Mercury B. Venus
C. Earth D. Mars

12. Galileo discovered 4 moons in 1660 of which planet?
A. Earth B. Venus
C. Saturn D. Jupiter

13. The exact time taken by the earth to rotate one of its own axis is:
A. 24 hours
B. 23 hours 51 minutes
C. 23 hours 48 minutes 46 seconds
D. 23 hours 56 minutes 4 seconds

14. What is the black hole?
A. Star that has no atmosphere
B. Star with high temperature
C. Contracted Star that has high gravitational pull.
D. Pulsating star

15. What is great bear?
A. Constellation B. planet
C. Neutron Star D. Sun

16. What type of orbit planets have while revolving around the sun?
A. Parabolic and Hyperbolic
B. Circular and Parabolic
C. Elliptical and circular
D. Elliptical and Hyperbolic

17. What is the colour of lunar sky during day time from moon?
A. Blue B. Black
C. Red D. White

18. What is the distance between Earth and Sun?
A. 149 million B. 136 million
C. 159 million D. 196 million

19. The Brightest star in the sky observed from earth is:
A. Sun B. Alfa Centauri
C. Proxima Centauri D. Sirius

20. Sun Spots are:
A. The opposite surface of moon where no light reaches.
B. Dark patches of sun surface where temperature fall below 4050 K.
C. Black spot on moon
D. Polar region of Sun

21. Why pole star always seen at the one point in the sky?
A. pole star rotate with the same period of the Earth
B. pole star has opposite to the sun from earth
C. This is one another star from our galaxy.
D. pole star lies in the axis of spin of the earth

22. Parsec is a unit of:
A. Measurement of density of star
B. Astronomical unit of Distance
C. Brightness of Star
D. Unit of magnetic moment

23. What idea we get from the light coming from stars?
A. Density of Stars B. Temperature of Stars
C. Mass of the Stars D. Size of the stars

24. The time period of sun revolve around the galaxy is known as:
A. light years B. Astronomical year
C. Cosmic Year D. Parsec

25. What is supernova?
A. A dying star
B. A worm hole
C. A special type of comet
D. A bright asteroid of size equal to sun

26. Laws of planetary motion discovered by:
A. Galileo B. Copernicus
C. Kepler D. Newton

27. Twelve constellations or Zodiac are referred to which of the following?
A. A group of stars
B. All planet of solar system
C. It is the symbol of Roman God
D. None of these

28. What is the evidence that comets are the member of our solar system?
A. Their properties of compositions
B. Their Shape and size
C. Their shape of the orbit
D. Their structure of tails

29. We can see Full moon once a month and that night is called as _______.
A. Half Poornima B. Amavasya
C. Poornima D. Half Amavasya

30. Poornima is also called as _______.
A. Half Moon Night B. New Moon Night
C. Full Moon Night D. Old Moon Light

31. The sun, the moon and all those objects shining in the night sky are called _________.
A. Shining Satellites
B. Shining Earth
C. Astrological Satellites
D. Celestial Bodies

32. Celestial Bodies that have their own heat and which emit light in large amounts is called as _______.
A. Android B. Planets
C. Constellations D. Stars

33. Which of the following is considered as Star?
A. Earth B. Sun
C. Moon D. Galaxy

34. While watching the night sky, various patterns formed by different groups of stars are called as ________.
A. Star Patterns B. Pole Star
C. Android D. Constellations

35. Most easily recognisable Constellation is _________.
A. Capricornus B. Saptarshi
C. Norma D. Chamaeleon

36. Saptarishi is a group of ______ stars.
A. 8 B. 10
C. 9 D. 7

37. In ancient times, people used to determine directions during the night with the help of ______.
A. Pole B. Stars
C. Planets D. Constellations

38. The North Star which indicates the north direction is also called the ________.
A. Constellations B. Pole Star
C. Asteroids D. Androids

39. Which of the star remains in the same position in the sky?
A. Vega B. Sirius
C. Pole Star D. Aldebaran

40. Position of the Pole Star with can be easily find with the help of the ________.
A. Norma B. Saptarishi
C. Reticulum D. Phoenix

41. Some celestial bodies do not have their own heat and light are called as ________.
A. Planets B. Galaxy
C. Universe D. Stars

42. The word planet came from ________ language.
A. English B. Greek
C. Sanskrit D. Roman

43. Planets are depends on __________ for getting light and heat.
A. Constellations B. Stars
C. Galaxy D. Satellite

44. Planet on which we are living is called as _________.
A. Pluto B. Mars
C. Jupitor D. Earth

45. Which is nearest star of the Earth?
A. Spica B. Sirius
C. Sun D. Deneb

46. Asteroids and Meteoroids consists of ____.
A. Satellites B. Nine planets
C. All of these D. The sun

47. How many days it takes to complete one revolution around sun for Planet Mercury?
A. 88 days B. 255 days
C. 155 days D. 365 days

48. How many days Mercury took to complete one spin around own axis?
A. 12 days B. 59 days
C. 365 days D. 1 day

49. Venus took ____ days to spin around sun and ______ days to spin around own axis.
A. 255 and 243
B. 255 and 1
C. 687 and 243
D. 365 and 1

50. To complete one revolution around sun, Mars took ________ days.

A. 155 B. 365
C. 687 D. 255

51. Arrange the following planets in increase order of time require to complete one rotation around sun:

(*a*) Earth (*b*) Uranus
(*c*) Mars (*d*) Jupiter

A. (*a*) (*c*) (*b*) (*d*) B. (*c*) (*a*) (*d*) (*b*)
C. (*c*) (*a*) (*b*) (*d*) D. (*a*) (*c*) (*d*) (*b*)

52. Arrange following planets in the increasing order of number of moons:

(*a*) Uranus (*b*) Jupiter
(*c*) Earth (*d*) Saturn

A. (*c*) (*d*) (*a*) (*b*) B. (*c*) (*a*) (*b*) (*d*)
C. (*c*) (*a*) (*d*) (*b*) D. (*c*) (*b*) (*a*) (*d*)

53. Which is nearest known planet to Sun?

A. Saturn B. Mars
C. Mercury D. Earth

54. Which is farthest planet to a sun?

A. Pluto B. Uranus
C. Mercury D. Neptune

55. Sun provides pulling force to a solar system that binds complete solar system in one unit:

A. True B. False
C. Cant Say D. None of these

56. Which of the following is ultimate source of light and heat on earth?

A. Satellite B. Constellations
C. Sun D. Moon

57. Planets revolves around the sun in ________ path.

A. Elongated B. Circular
C. Rectangular D. Semi Circular

58. Earth is the ______ nearest planet to the Sun.

A. Second B. Fourth
C. First D. Third

59. Earth is slightly flattened at the poles and so its shape is described as ________.

A. Diamond B. Ellipsoid
C. Asteroid D. Geoid

60. Conditions favourable to support life are probably found on ________ planet.

A. Mars B. Jupiter
C. Earth D. Pluto

ANSWERS

1	2	3	4	5	6	7	8	9	10
B	C	A	D	A	B	C	A	B	C
11	**12**	**13**	**14**	**15**	**16**	**17**	**18**	**19**	**20**
C	D	D	C	A	C	B	A	D	B
21	**22**	**23**	**24**	**25**	**26**	**27**	**28**	**29**	**30**
D	B	B	C	A	B	A	C	C	C
31	**32**	**33**	**34**	**35**	**36**	**37**	**38**	**39**	**40**
D	D	B	D	B	D	B	B	C	B
41	**42**	**43**	**44**	**45**	**46**	**47**	**48**	**49**	**50**
A	B	B	D	C	C	A	B	A	C
51	**52**	**53**	**54**	**55**	**56**	**57**	**58**	**59**	**60**
D	D	C	A	A	C	A	D	D	C

★ ★ ★

ENGLISH

1

Verb Patterns

The *Pattern* of a verb shows the various forms it assumes, either by inflection or by combination with parts of other verbs, in order to mark voice, tense, number, person and mood.

The following are the principal parts of a verb in the English language:

(*a*) The Present Tense

(*b*) The Past Tense

(*c*) The Past Participle

The verbs are of two kinds. They are:

(*a*) Strong Verbs

(*b*) Weak Verbs

Verbs that form their past tense and past participle by a change of the inside vowel in the present are called *strong verbs. e.g.,*

Present Tense	***Past Tense***	***Past Participle***
Come	Came	Come
Do	Did	Done
Fall	Fell	Fallen
Write	Wrote	Written
Speak	Spoke	Spoken

Verbs that form their past tense and past participle by adding *-ed, -d* or *-t* to the present, with or without change of the inside vowel are called *weak verbs. e.g.,*

Present Tense	***Past Tense***	***Past Participle***
Believe	Believed	Believed
Burn	Burnt	Burnt
Talk	Talked	Talked
Sleep	Slept	Slept
Walk	Walked	Walked

The following is a list of *strong verbs* and *weak verbs*:

Present Tense	***Past Tense***	***Past Participle***
Abet	Abetted	Abetted
Abide	Abode	Abode
Am/Be	Was	Been
Are	Were	Been
Aver	Averred	Averred
Abhor	Abhorred	Abhorred
Arise	Arose	Arisen
Awake	Awoke	Awoken
Beat	Beat	Beaten
Befall	Befell	Befallen
Bandy	Bandied	Bandied
Bed	Bedded	Bedded
Behold	Beheld	Beheld
Believe	Believed	Believed
Beseech	Besought	Besought
Behave	Behaved	Behaved
Bethink	Bethought	Bethought
Bind	Bound	Bound
Bleed	Bled	Bled
Bless	Blessed	Blessed
Win	Won	Won
Withstand	Withstood	Withstood
Work	Worked	Worked
Welcome	Welcomed	Welcomed
Will	Would	—
Write	Wrote	Written
Wake	Woke	Woken
Wear	Wore	Worn
Withdraw	Withdrew	Withdrawn
Withhold	Withheld	Withheld
Wed	Wedded	Wedded
Whip	Whipped	Whipped
Worry	Worried	Worried
Wrong	Wronged	Wronged
Yell	Yelled	Yelled
Yield	Yielded	Yielded
Zigzag	Zigzagged	Zigzagged

Each of the following verbs has exactly the same form in present tense, past tense and past participle:

Present Tense	*Past Tense*	*Past Participle*	*Present Tense*	*Past Tense*	*Past Participle*
Beset	Beset	Beset	Outbid	Outbid	Outbid
Bet	Bet	Bet	Put	Put	Put
Bid	Bid	Bid	Quit	Quit	Quit
Burst	Burst	Burst	Read	Read	Read
Broadcast	Broadcast	Broadcast	Recast	Recast	Recast
Cast	Cast	Cast	Reset	Reset	Reset
Cost	Cost	Cost	Rid	Rid	Rid
Cut	Cut	Cut	Set	Set	Set
Forecast	Forecast	Forecast	Shed	Shed	Shed
Hit	Hit	Hit	Slit	Slit	Slit
Hurt	Hurt	Hurt	Split	Split	Split
Knit	Knit	Knit	Spread	Spread	Spread
Let	Let	Let	Thrust	Thrust	Thrust
Miscast	Miscast	Miscast	Underbid	Underbid	Underbid
			Upset	Upset	Upset

Note 1: The past tense and the past participle of *bid*, when used in the sense of *order* or *tell,* are *bade* and *bidden* respectively.

2: The past tense as well as the participle of *Knit,* when used in the sense of *make (a garment, etc) by forming wool, silk etc, yarn into connecting loops; make a plain stitch, is knitted.*

AGREEMENT OF SUBJECTS AND VERBS

It is very important that the verb in a sentence should obey the subject, otherwise the sentence will be considered wrong. The rules are:

1. When the Subject is a Singular Noun it takes a singular verb, *e.g.,*

(*i*) Mohit **makes** a noise in the class.

(*ii*) The child is **crying** for a cake.

2. When two singular nouns are joined with 'and' and they refer to two different persons, the plural verb should be used, *e.g.,*

(*i*) The novelist and the poet **were** honoured by the government.

(*ii*) The black and the white dogs **bark** at the strangers.

☛ Article 'the' is used with both the subjects.

If article is used only once, singular verb should be used.

(*i*) The painter and singer **is** going abroad.

(*ii*) The white and black dog **has** a bushy tail.

3. When the subjects together give a single idea, singular verb is used.

(*i*) Slow and steady **wins** the race.

(*ii*) Rice and curry **is** my favourite dish.

4. A collective noun takes a singular verb when it acts as a whole, but it takes a plural verb when the individual, of which it is composed are considered separately.

(*i*) The committee **was** unanimous on imposing the new law.

(*ii*) The committee **have** given their separate opinions in the matter.

5. When the subjects are joined by neither . . . nor, either . . . or, and 'or', the verb should obey the last subject.

(*i*) Rakesh or his friends **have** been selected for the match.

(*ii*) His friends or Rakesh **has** been selected for the match.

(*iii*) Neither Rohit nor his brothers **are** going abroad.

(*iv*) Neither his brothers nor Rohit **is** going abroad.

(*v*) Either Sohan or his sisters **were** dancing at the function.

(*vi*) Either his sisters or Sohan **was** dancing at the function.

6. Either, neither, either of, neither of, take singular verb.

(*i*) Either boy **was** honest.

(*ii*) Neither girl **was** allowed to leave the premises.

(*iii*) Either of the boys **was** ready to help the old man.

(*iv*) Neither of the girls **was** asked to join the extra classes.

7. Some nouns are always used as plurals so, they take plural verbs.

(*i*) Where **are** your glasses?

(*ii*) His pants are attractive.

(*iii*) Cattle **are** grazing in the field.

(*iv*) Whose scissors **are** these?

8. Some nouns are always used as singulars, so, they take singular verbs.
   (*i*) What **is** the latest news?
   (*ii*) The furniture in the house **is** of a poor quality.
   (*iii*) Mumps **is** not a fatal disease.
   (*iv*) Physics **is** a tough subject.

9. Nouns formed by alongwith, as well as, together with, accompanied by, etc., take verb according to the first subject.
   (*i*) I, as well as you, **am** to blame.
   (*ii*) You, as well as I, **are** going to see a movie.
   (*iii*) John, accompanied by his parents, **is** going to visit the Taj.
   (*iv*) His parents, accompanied by John, **are** going to visit the Taj.
   (*v*) His brothers, together with Vivek, **are** ready to whitewash the fence.

10. To indicate something hypothetical or not factually true, plural verb 'were' with *as if* is used.
   (*i*) He talks as if he **were** a king.
   (*ii*) She dresses herself as if she **were** a princess.

MULTIPLE CHOICE QUESTIONS

Directions: *In the following questions choose the correct options to fill in the blanks.*

1. The bus with all its passengers .... lost.
   A. were B. was
   C. are D. would

2. You as well as I .... responsible for this work.
   A. am B. are
   C. was D. is

3. Raghava like all his companions .... a spoiled child.
   A. are B. were
   C. is D. will be

4. Pen and ink .... required for me.
   A. are B. were
   C. is D. has required

5. Every girl and every boy .... attended the seminar.
   A. have B. has
   C. is D. are

6. Not only she but all her sisters ...... been married.
   A. has B. have
   C. is D. are

7. There .... nothing but miseries in life.
   A. is B. are
   C. were D. will be

8. Neither prose nor poem .... given.
   A. were B. was
   C. has D. have

9. Either he or I .... wrong.
   A. is B. are
   C. am D. were

10. Either Sulekha or Rekha .... coming here.
   A. are B. is
   C. were D. have

11. .... the child or his parents to blame?
   A. Is B. Are
   C. Were D. Has

12. You and I .... neighbours.
   A. am B. are
   C. was D. has

13. The house with all its belongings ..... sold away.
   A. were B. are
   C. was D. must

14. Either water or juice .... required.
   A. is B. are
   C. were D. has

15. There were not as many tables as .... required.
   A. was B. were
   C. is D. are

16. They each .... a book.
   A. have B. are
   C. has D. is

17. He and I .... close friends.
   A. is B. am
   C. was D. are

18. She as well as I .... guilty.
   A. is B. are
   C. am D. must be

19. Rohan .... not read more on this chapter.
   A. needs B. has been need
   C. need D. had been need

20. He came .... to his aunt.
   A. run B. running
   C. to run D. in run

21. She dislikes .... meat.
   A. eat to B. to eat
   C. eating D. to eating

22. He likes ....
   A. sing to B. singing
   C. to sing D. to singing

23. We are ready .... the match.
A. play to B. to playing
C. playing D. to play

24. .... is injurious to health.
A. Smoking B. To smoke
C. To smoking D. Smoke to

25. He loves .... raw vegetables.
A. eaten B. eating
C. to eating D. eat to

26. He seemed .... finished his homework.
A. have to B. to have
C. having D. to having

27. Either Arpan or his friends .... asked to pay a visit to the university.
A. has been B. have been
C. has D. have

28. Where .... your spectacles?
A. is B. are
C. were D. have

29. Measles .... not a fatal disease.
A. is B. are
C. has D. have

30. He walks as if he .... a prince.
A. was B. were
C. have been D. has been

31. The captain alongwith his team mates .... reached the ground.
A. have B. has
C. is D. are

32. The jury ..... given its opinion.
A. has B. have
C. is D. are

33. Slow and steady .... the race.
A. win B. wins
C. has wins D. have win

34. The poet and the novelist .... invited by the PM.
A. is B. are
C. has D. have

35. Mathematics .... a tough subject.
A. is B. are
C. has D. have

36. Either girl .... in a sad mood.
A. was B. were
C. has D. have

37. They will .... performed on the stage.
A. had B. has
C. have D. be

38. Ravi is .... to railway station.
A. went B. going
C. goes D. to

39. We will .... playing this match at Green Park Stadium.
A. be B. being
C. have D. has

40. He will .... a glass of water.
A. drank B. drink
C. drunk D. drinks

ANSWERS

1	2	3	4	5	6	7	8	9	10
B	B	C	C	B	B	A	B	C	B
11	**12**	**13**	**14**	**15**	**16**	**17**	**18**	**19**	**20**
A	B	C	A	B	A	D	A	C	B
21	**22**	**23**	**24**	**25**	**26**	**27**	**28**	**29**	**30**
C	B	D	A	B	B	B	B	A	B
31	**32**	**33**	**34**	**35**	**36**	**37**	**38**	**39**	**40**
B	A	B	B	A	A	C	B	A	B

★★★

2

Sequence of Tenses

1. Tense indicates a point in time or period of time in the past, present, or future tense.

2. Tense is related to the form of verb. The verb may consist of a single word, or a main verb and one or more auxiliary words. There are normally three forms of the verb, say, V_1, V_2, V_3 and for convenience a fourth form V_4 as 'verb + ing' may be assumed.

Forms of Verb

V_1	V_2	V_3	V_4
Write	Wrote	Written	Writing
Read	Read	Read	Reading
Go	Went	Gone	Going
...	...	...	...

A Comparative Chart Regarding Tenses and Verbs

Simple Present	Simple Past	Simple Future
V_1	V_2	shall/will + V_1
Present Continuous	**Past Continuous**	**Future Continuous**
is/am/are + V_4	was/were + V_4	shall/will + be + V_4
Present Perfect	**Past Perfect**	**Future Perfect**
has/have + V_3	had + V_3	shall/will + have + V_3
Present Perfect Cont.	**Past Perfect Cont.**	**Future Perfect Cont.**
has/have + been + V_4	had + been + V_4	shall/will + have been + V_4

Tenses, their application and examples:

SIMPLE PRESENT

A. A present state of affairs.
B. A general fact.
C. Habitual actions.
D. Future time-tables.

A. My sister lives in Kashmir.
B. The sun rises in the east.
C. I listen to the radio in the mornings.
D. My flight leaves at 10:00.

PRESENT CONTINUOUS

A. A specific action that is occurring.
B. A general activity that takes place.
C. Future arrangements.

A. Arvind is watching TV (right now).
B. These days, I'm taking it easy.
C. I'm inviting Hari to the party on Friday.

SIMPLE PAST

A. An action that began and ended at a particular time in the past.
B. An action that occurred over a period of time but was completed in the past.
C. An activity that took place regularly in the past.

A. The mail came early this morning.
B. Dad worked in advertising in the past.
C. We jogged every morning before class.

PAST CONTINUOUS

A. Interrupted Actions. — A. I was sewing when the telephone rang.

B. A continuous state over a period of time but was completed in the past. — B. She was looking very ill, I was meeting lots of people at that time.

C. Events planned in the past. — C. Neetu was leaving for Jammu but had to make a last minute change

D. Expressing a future intent. — D. Jyoti is going to bring her sister tonight.

E. Predicting an event. — E. You are going to pass the test, don't worry.

SIMPLE FUTURE

A. Making a future decision. — A. I will call you after lunch.

B. Predicting a future event. — B. You will pass the test, don't worry.

C. Indicating willingness to do something. — C. If I don't feel better soon, I will go to the doctor.

FUTURE CONTINUOUS

A. An action that will be going at a particular time in the future. — A. At noon tomorrow, I will be taking the children to their piano lessons.

B. Future actions which have already been decided. — B. I will be wearing my black dress to the dinner.

PRESENT PERFECT

A. An action that happened at an unspecified time. — A. She has never climbed a mountain. I'm sorry, I have forgotten your Name.

B. An action that has recently occurred. — B. He has just gone to sleep.

C. An action that began in the past and continues up to the present (often used with "for" or "since"). — C. Jack has lived in Shri Nagar all his life. I have been here since Monday. He has known her for two weeks.

D. An action that happened repeatedly before now. — D. We have flown across the Pacific four times. I've failed my driver's test twice.

PRESENT PERFECT CONTINUOUS

A. An action that began in the past and has just recently ended. — A. Have you been ringing the Bell?

B. An action that began in the past and continues in the present. — B. Lokesh has been studying for two hours.

C. An action repeated over a period of time in the past and continuing in present. — C. Suresh has been playing since he was fifteen.

PAST PERFECT

A. An action that occurred before another past action. — A. Tarun had left hours beforewe got there.

B. An action that was expected to occur in the past. — B. I had hoped to know about the job before now.

PAST PERFECT CONTINUOUS

A. An action that occurred before another past action. — A. His eyes hurt because he had been reading for eight hours.

B. An action that was expected to occur in the past. — B. I had been expecting a change in his attitude.

FUTURE PERFECT

A. An action that will be completed before a particular time in the future. — A. By next July, my parents will have been married for fifty years.

FUTURE PERFECT CONTINUOUS

A. Emphasizing the length of time that has occurred before a specific time in the future. — A. By May, my father will have been working at the same job for thirty years.

MULTIPLE CHOICE QUESTIONS

Directions: *Find the correct word(s) that completes the sentence according to tenses.*

1. The manner in which bombs ...... in five trains within a short span of time suggests that it is a part of a conspiracy.
A. explode B. exploding
C. exploded D. has been exploding

2. What ..... the postage for an airletter?
A. are B. am
C. is D. be

3. I don't really know how to ..... the problem.
A. tackle B. tackling
C. do tackle D. did tackle

4. ...... a two-inch margin on each page for the teacher's remarks.
A. Leave B. Has left
C. Leaves D. Left

5. We ..... such a wonderful time at the party last night.
A. has B. have
C. had D. are having

6. Due to a failure of some traffic lights, traffic ...... very slowly.
A. move B. is moving
C. has moved D. had moved

7. ...... the earlier train will give us the chance to do some shopping.
A. Catch B. To catch
C. Having caught D. Catching

8. 'Please' and 'Thank you' are the little courtesies by which we ...... the machine of life oiled and running smoothly.
A. keep B. keeps
C. keeping D. were keeping

9. The French ..... reputed to have a very good sense of humour.
A. is B. was
C. are D. will be

10. Life ...... to death as pleasure is to pain.
A. is B. was
C. are D. will be

11. Do you know ..... ?
A. where she comes from
B. where does she come from
C. where from she comes
D. from where does she come

12. Few works of reference ..... so valuable as the Encyclopaedia Britannica.
A. is B. was
C. are D. will be

13. The paths of glory ..... but to the grave.
A. leads B. lead
C. leading D. have lead

14. ..... at three o'clock, I heard the rumble of thunder.
A. Walk B. Walks
C. Walking D. Walked

15. The thief ..... all the money.
A. made up B. made off with
C. made do with D. made good

16. Pakistan lost a crucial wicket just when they ..... to be doing so well, and that led to their eventual defeat.
A. seem B. seems
C. have seemed D. seemed

17. In high school many of us never realised the importance that grammar would ..... in later life.
A. plays B. played
C. play D. have played

18. I was ...... at his colossal lack of knowledge about the Continent of Africa.
A. astounded B. astounding
C. have astounded D. had astounded

19. The veracity of the Minister's statement cannot be ...... by people who have no access to official records.
A. verify B. verifies
C. verified D. have verified

20. You haven't had your lunch yet, ... you?
A. are B. aren't
C. have D. haven't

21. A woman came in with a baby who, she said, ... a safety pin.
A. was just swallowing B. swallowed
C. had just swallowed D. just swallowed

22. The telephone ..... several times before I answered it.
A. was ringing B. has rung
C. had rung D. would ring

23. An employment advertisement should ..... the number of vacancies.
A. specifies B. specify
C. be specifying D. have specified

24. A crescendo of metallic thuds arose from the market, where the iron-smiths were ..... the pieces of metals.
A. hammers B. to hammer
C. hammering D. having hammered

25. Ambition is one of those passions which are never ..... .
A. satisfy B. satisfies
C. satisfying D. satisfied

26. Like any other country India ...... its fair share of superstitions.
A. has B. have
C. had D. having

27. The miser ..... avidly at the pile of gold coins in front of him.
A. gaze B. gazes
C. gazed D. has gazed

28. The pilot ..... about the storm before he took off.
A. has been warned B. have been warned
C. had been warned D. was warned

29. On account of the dearth of grass on the arid plains the cattle became ..... .
A. amaciated B. amaciating
C. amaciate D. amaciates

30. I ..... a herd of cows in the field.
A. sees B. saw
C. seeing D. has seen

31. Besides other provisions, that shopkeeper ..... in cosmetics too.
A. deals B. deal
C. dealing D. has deal

32. That rule ..... applicable to everyone.
A. be B. were
C. is D. are

33. I ...... revenge on you.
A. take B. taking
C. shall take D. takes

34. The ruling party ..... its own house in order.
A. put B. shall have to put
C. will have to put D. have to put

35. To all intents and purposes, the manager ..... the master of the firm.
A. be B. is
C. are D. were

36. He ...... to prison for his crime.
A. sent B. send
C. has sent D. was sent

37. Restoration of old paintings .... a job for the experts.
A. is B. are
C. has D. have

38. Once he ..... the agreement, he won't be able to back out.
A. sign B. signing
C. has signed D. had signed

39. She ..... a brief appearance at the end of the party.
A. put on B. put in
C. put across D. put up

40. The battalion operating from the mountain was able to ..... three enemy divisions.
A. tie up B. tie down
C. tie on D. tie with

ANSWERS

1	2	3	4	5	6	7	8	9	10
C	C	A	A	C	B	D	A	C	A
11	**12**	**13**	**14**	**15**	**16**	**17**	**18**	**19**	**20**
A	C	B	C	B	D	C	A	C	C
21	**22**	**23**	**24**	**25**	**26**	**27**	**28**	**29**	**30**
C	C	B	C	D	A	C	C	A	B
31	**32**	**33**	**34**	**35**	**36**	**37**	**38**	**39**	**40**
A	C	C	C	B	D	A	C	B	B

★ ★ ★

3

Articles and Determiners

ARTICLES

The family of the articles has only three members. They are : A, An and The. However, they fall under two groups :

(a) Definite Article

(b) Indefinite Article

'The' is known as definite article whereas 'a' and 'an' are known as indefinite articles.

Use of the Definite Article 'The'

'The' is used before:

1. The superlative degree, *e.g.,*
   He is the ablest man of the town.
   (ablest is a superlative degree)
2. The name of states, countries etc. having a descriptive name, *e.g.,*
   (*i*) The J & K is a small state. (J & K is a descriptive name)
   (*ii*) He lives in the U.S.A. (U.S.A. is a descriptive name)
   (But 'the Delhi' and 'the America' are wrong because neither Delhi nor America is a descriptive name)
3. The names of the scriptures, *e.g.,*
   The Gita is a holy book. (Gita is a scripture)
4. Name of newspapers, *e.g.,*
   The Tribune is published from Chandigarh.
5. Name of rivers, canals, seas, oceans, bays, gulfs, groups of islands etc., *e.g.,*
   (*i*) The Ganga is a holy river.
   (*ii*) The Indian Ocean is the deepest ocean.
   (*iii*) The Persian Gulf is a narrow gulf.
6. The name of famous buildings, *e.g.,*
   The Taj is one of the best buildings in India.
7. The names of nationals, sects and communities, *e.g.,*
   (*i*) The English defeated the Germans in the World War.
   (*ii*) The rich should help the poor.
   (*iii*) The Hindus believe in the caste system.
8. Proper nouns used as common nouns, *e.g.,*
   (*i*) Kalidas is the Shakespeare of India.
   (*ii*) Delhi is the London of India.
9. Famous historical events, *e.g.,*
   The Industrial Revolution changed the face of England.
10. The directions and the celestial bodies, *e.g.,*
    The sun rises in the east.
11. Titles, *e.g.,*
    Akbar, the Great was loved by his subjects.

Do not use 'the':

1. Before languages :
   The English is an international language. (Incorrect)
   English is an international language. (Correct)
2. Before the names of games, *e.g.,*
   The hockey is a popular game. (Incorrect)
   Hockey is a popular game. (Correct)

Use of the Indefinite Articles 'A' and 'An'

'A' is used before:

1. All singular common nouns beginning with a consonant, *e.g.,*
   (*i*) A boy sings a song.
   (*ii*) A black and a white cow were grazing in the field.
2. If a word begins with a vowel but gives the sound of a consonant, 'a' should be used before it, *e.g.,*
   (*i*) He was helped in his work by a European.
   (*ii*) He is a one-eyed man.
   (*iii*) It is a useful work.

'An' is used as follows:

1. All singular common nouns beginning with a vowel (*i.e.*, a, e, i, o, u), *e.g.*,
   (*i*) He is an artist.
   (*ii*) He is an old man.
   (*iii*) I intend to buy an umbrella.
2. If a word starts with a consonant but gives the soun of a vowel, 'an' should be used before it, *e.g.*,
   (*i*) Brutus is an honourable man.
   (*ii*) He is an honour to his profession.
   (*iii*) He is an L.L.B.
   (*iv*) He is an M.A.
   (*v*) You will reach there in an hour.

DETERMINERS

Determiners are actually Adjectives. They are always followed by nouns.

Determiners are of the following kinds:

1. Demonstrative Determiners
e.g., this, that, these, those

2. Possessive Determiners
e.g., my, our, your, his, her, its, their

3. Quantitative Determiners
e.g., some, any, much, enough, sufficient, whole, a littl the little, little, all, both

4. Numerical Determiners
e.g., a few, some, few, the few, any, several, many, no, et
One, two, three ... (Cardinals)
First, second, third ... (Ordinals)

5. Distributive Determiners
e.g., either, neither

MULTIPLE CHOICE QUESTIONS

Directions (Q. No. 1-20): *Fill in the blanks with suitable articles. If no article is required, choose option 'D'.*

1. Please give me .... orange.
A. a B. an
C. the D. No article

2. ...... boyhood of Rahul was full of happy events.
A. A B. An
C. The D. No article

3. I daily read .... Indian Express.
A. a B. an
C. the D. No article

4. My brother bought .... new car yesterday.
A. a B. an
C. the D. No article

5. Many valuable herbs are found on ..... Himalayas.
A. a B. an
C. the D. No article

6. .... Ganga is a sacred river.
A. A B. An
C. The D. No article

7. .... Mahabharata is the longest epic.
A. A B. An
C. The D. No article

8. ...... rich should help the poor.
A. A B. An
C. The D. No article

9. .... more you sing, the happier we feel.
A. A B. An
C. The D. No article

10. The countries which lie near ...... equator keep hig temperature.
A. a B. an
C. the D. No article

11. My friend plays .... violin perfectly well.
A. a B. an
C. the D. No article

12. My uncle is ..... MA.
A. a B. an
C. the D. No article

13. I shall board ...... Flying Mail.
A. a B. an
C. the D. No article

14. John is ...... Newton of our class.
A. a B. an
C. the D. No article

15. Rohit daily eats ...... egg.
A. a B. an
C. the D. No article

16. I have ...... white and a black cow.
A. a B. an
C. the D. No article

17. What ...... beautiful bird it is!
A. a B. an
C. the D. No article

18. She is ...... best player of tennis in our school.
A. a B. an
C. the D. No article

19. ......Yamuna passes through Delhi.
A. A B. An
C. The D. No article

20. ...... Nile is the longest river.
A. A B. An
C. The D. No article

Directions (Q. No. 21-40): *In the following questions choose the correct options to fill in the blanks.*

21. .... dogs were barking at the strangers.
A. Some B. Any
C. Much D. Less

22. The girl bought her father .... juice.
A. few B. some
C. any D. many

23. You should take .... honey everyday.
A. any B. many
C. a little D. a few

24. .... boy was punished by the teacher.
A. Either B. All
C. Any D. Many

25. .... girl was asked to join the army.
A. None B. Neither
C. All D. Any

26. .... water in the jug has been drunk by Mohan.
A. The little B. The few
C. A few D. Few

27. I shall play .... piano at the party.
A. some B. any
C. the D. few

28. .... labourers were found dead in the mine.
A. Any B. Fewer
C. Many D. Less

29. Could I borrow .... umbrella?
A. our B. your
C. yours D. my

30. My brother is standing in the .... row.
A. any B. many
C. some D. first

31. Give me .... rice.
A. some B. few
C. a few D. any

32. .... sheep grazing on the slope of the hill had gone away.
A. Any B. The few
C. This D. Much

33. Have you got .... magazines to read?
A. all B. much
C. some D. little

34. I have .... money that I want to invest in shares.
A. any B. much
C. less D. some

35. There is .... owl on the branch of the tree.
A. a B. the
C. an D. some

36. My brother is .... MBA.
A. a B. an
C. the D. any

37. Have you got .... cheese?
A. some B. many
C. a few D. few

38. No, I have not got .... cheese.
A. many B. few
C. any D. some

39. There is only .... milk left in the bottle.
A. enough B. few
C. much D. a little

40. There is .... hope of his recovery.
A. any B. little
C. many D. few

ANSWERS

1	2	3	4	5	6	7	8	9	10
B	C	C	A	C	C	C	C	C	C
11	12	13	14	15	16	17	18	19	20
C	B	C	C	B	A	A	C	C	C
21	22	23	24	25	26	27	28	29	30
A	B	C	A	B	A	C	C	B	D
31	32	33	34	35	36	37	38	39	40
A	B	C	D	C	B	A	C	D	B

★★★

4

Prepositions

A *Preposition* is a word which is placed before a noun or a pronoun to show its relation to some other word in the sentence.

(*i*) I saw a goat *in* the field.
(*ii*) I am fond *of* hot coffee.

In sentence (*i*), the word *in* shows the relation between two things—*goat* and *field.*

In sentence (*ii*), the word *of* shows the relation between the attribute expressed by the adjective *fond* and *tea.*

The words *in* and *of* are here used as prepositions.

Use of Important Prepositions

1. Among, Between

'**Among**' is used for more than two persons or things; '**Between**' is used only for two.

Examples:

(*i*) Distribute these sweets *among* the poor students of the class.
(*ii*) Distribute these books *between* Ram and Shyam.

2. Among, In

'**Among**' is used before collective plural nouns. '**In**' is used before collective singular nouns.

Examples:

(*i*) I found him standing *among* the crowd.
(*ii*) I saw him in the crowd.

3. Beside, Besides

'**Beside**' means 'by the side of'; '**Besides**' means 'in addition to'.

Examples:

(*i*) The daughter was sitting *beside* her mother.
(*ii*) *Besides* his relatives, he invited his friends also.

4. In, Within

'**In**' means at the expiry of a period of time in future, '**Within**' means before the expiry of a period of time in any tense.

Examples:

(*i*) She will return *in* a week.
(*ii*) I shall finish my work *within* a weak.

5. On, Upon

'**On**' is used for things at rest; '**Upon**' is used for things in motion.

Examples:

(*i*) He is sitting *on* the floor.
(*ii*) The dog sprang *upon* the table.

6. By, With

'**By**' denotes the agent or doer; '**With**' denotes the instrument with which anything is done.

Examples:

(*i*) The bird was killed *by* the hunter with an arrow.
(*ii*) He beat the dog *with* a stick.
(*iii*) I shall reach here *by* five o'clock.

7. After, In

'**After**' means at the end of a period of time in the past '**In**' means at the end of a period of time in future.

Examples:

(*i*) I shall return your book *in* a week.
(*ii*) He returned the book *after* a week.

8. For, From, Since

'**For**' is used before a noun denoting a period of time with all the tenses. '**From**' is used before a noun or phrase denoting a point of time, it is used in all the tenses. '**Since**' is used before a noun or phrase denoting some point of time and is always preceded by a verb in the perfect continuous tense or third form of a verb

Examples:

(*i*) We have been playing cards *for* two hours.
(*ii*) She stayed with her uncle *from* the 15th of March to the 15th of May.
(*iii*) I have been reading this book *since* morning.

9. Above, Over

'**Above**' means 'higher from'; **Over** is used in the following four senses:

(*i*) In the sense of 'above', *e.g.,*
At noon, the sun is *over* our heads.
(*ii*) In the sense of 'beyond', *e.g.,*
I cannot get *over* my disappointment.

(*iii*) In the sense of 'Superiority', *e.g.,*
God *over* all blesses for ever more.

(*iv*) In the sense of 'Conclusion', *e.g.,*
It is all *over* with me.

10. At, Towards

'**At**' denotes the idea of aim; '**Towards**' denotes the idea of destination.

Examples:

(*i*) He threw the stone *at* the cat.

(*ii*) He went *towards* the house.

11. At, In, On

(*i*) '**At**' is used with small towns and villages.

Examples :

(*a*) He was born *at* Sonepat.

(*b*) He lives *at* village Bangra.

(*ii*) '**At**' is used before a noun denoting a definite point of time.

Example:

He called on me *at* 9 p.m. yesterday.

(*iii*) '**In**' is used with the names of big cities, provinces and countries.

Examples:

(*a*) His father lives *in* England.

(*b*) His younger brother lives *in* Lucknow.

(*iv*) '**In**' is used before the names of months and years.

Example:

His elder sister was born *in* 1972 *in* the month of May.

(*v*) '**On**' is used with dates and names of days.

Examples :

(*a*) I joined college *on* the 26th April.

(*b*) He will leave for Kolkata *on* Wednesday next.

Important Information

1. '**In**' is also used in the following phrases :
In the morning; In the evening, In winter, In summer.

2. '**In**' also denotes a place inside anything, *e.g.,*
He travelled *in* a crowded bus.

3. '**At**' is used in the following phrases :
At home, *At* the station, *At* work, *At* play.

12. Below, Beneath

'**Below**' means 'of lower level in position, dignity and expectation' etc. '**Beneath**' means 'under'.

Examples:

(*i*) It is *below* my dignity to talk to her.

(*ii*) They rested *beneath* the shade of a tree.

13. In, Into, To

'**In**' expresses Rest or Motion inside anything. '**Into**' expresses Motion towards the inside of anything or change from one medium to another. '**To**' denotes motion from one place to another.

Examples:

(*i*) The boys are *in* the room.

(*ii*) Translate this passage from English *into* Hindi.

(*iii*) Every morning he goes *to* the temple.

14. Till, By, Of, Off

'**Till**' means upto or not earlier than.

'**By**' means not later than.

'**Of**' shows cause, source, separation, quality, contents, possession, apposition, point of reference, space in time etc.

'**Off**' shows separation at a near distance, and detached condition.

Consider the following examples:

(*i*) I shall work *till* 5 a.m.

(*ii*) Asha died *of* cancer.

(*iii*) The nib *of* the pen is made *of* gold.

(*iv*) He presented me a bottle *of* perfume.

(*v*) Our principal is a man *of* principles.

(*vi*) He lived in the house *of* his friend.

(*vii*) *By* this time tomorrow, I'll have finished my job.

(*viii*) My house is *off* the road.

(*ix*) The book fell *off* the table.

MULTIPLE CHOICE QUESTIONS

Directions: *Tick the correct preposition for the blank in each of the following sentences.*

1. He applied ...... the manager.
A. for B. to
C. with D. by

2. Trust ...... God and do the right.
A. in B. for
C. to D. with

3. She is worthy ...... a prize.
A. with B. for
C. to D. of

4. Mr. Gomes has no taste ...... music.
A. of B. for
C. with D. to

5. You are hard ...... hearing.
A. at B. of
C. with D. for

6. He is sure ...... his success.
A. for B. with
C. on D. of

7. Preeti was warned ...... the danger ahead.
A. for B. at
C. of D. about

8. I am thankful ...... you for a good advice.
A. for B. with
C. to D. of

9. Deepak would not surrender .... the police.
A. with B. to
C. for D. on

10. The small plant in your lawn is very sensitive .... touch.
A. on B. with
C. to D. about

11. Divya was sure to succeed ..... the examination.
A. for B. in
C. to D. with

12. Geeta was jealous ...... Ravina's beauty.
A. to B. with
C. for D. of

13. He was ignorant ..... what was happening there.
A. for B. of
C. to D. with

14. Your pen is inferior ..... mine.
A. than B. with
C. from D. to

15. Reenu is no match ...... Meenu.
A. to B. for
C. with D. upon

16. It is necessary ...... you to apply for this job.
A. on B. with
C. for D. to

17. Be loyal ...... your country.
A. for B. to
C. on D. with

18. Mukesh is junior ...... me.
A. than B. to
C. from D. of

19. Deepika was innocent ...... the crime.
A. of B. with
C. from D. to

20. I am desirous.... joining the Indian cricket team.
A. for B. of
C. to D. on

21. Pradeep is not eligible ...... the post.
A. to B. on
C. upon D. for

22. Does she believe ...... God?
A. to B. for
C. in D. over

23. Mr. Posh was charged..... the murder of his aunt.
A. for B. with
C. on D. to

24. Tagore is famous (or popular) ...... Indians.
A. for B. with
C. to D. towards

25. Kalidasa is famous ...... his drama the *Shakuntalam*.
A. for B. with
C. on D. about

26. He applied ...... the post of a teacher.
A. to B. on
C. for D. at

27. I differ ...... you in this matter.
A. from B. with
C. for D. above

28. My pen differs ...... yours.
A. with B. from
C. for D. upon

29. The air escaped out ...... the balloon.
A. from B. of
C. to D. under

30. I am confident ...... success.
A. of B. to
C. from D. about

ANSWERS

1	2	3	4	5	6	7	8	9	10
B	A	D	B	B	D	D	D	B	D
11	**12**	**13**	**14**	**15**	**16**	**17**	**18**	**19**	**20**
B	D	B	D	B	D	B	B	A	B
21	**22**	**23**	**24**	**25**	**26**	**27**	**28**	**29**	**30**
D	C	B	B	A	C	B	B	A	A

★★★

5

Synonyms & Antonyms

SYNONYMS

Ardent	eager, avid
Arduous	difficult, troublesome, tough
Aspire	hope, wish
Astonish	amaze, confound
Authentic	genuine, actual
Awesome	astonishing, amazing, fearful
Ban	bar, debar
Bare	denuded exposed
Bear	carry, bring
Beautiful	attractive, charming
Becoming	attractive, graceful
Benchmark	model, example
Benevolent	bountiful, benign
Bewitch	attract, captivate
Boisterous	noisy, clamorous
Bonny	handsome, attractive, healthy
Brave	bold, courageous
Break	crack, separate
Brief	laconic, curt
Bright	shining, flashing
Brisk	active, lively
Broad	generous, capacious
Build	assemble, construct
Busy	brisk, active
Cajole	coax, dupe
Call	announce, shout
Calm	peaceful, mild
Candid	fair, frank
Capacious	spacious, roomy
Care	anxiety, concern
Catchy	attractive, captivating
Charming	attractive, appealing
Chief	main, key
Clean	pure, spotless
Clever	apt, intelligent
Clumsy	bungling, awkward
Colossal	giant, enormous
Compact	dense, condensed
Conspicuous	clear, apparent
Cordial	agreeable, cheerful
Credulous	trustful, unsuspicious
Cruel	atrocious, barbarous
Dangerous	alarming, hazardous
Dazzling	glorious, radiant
Deceive	cheat, betray
Deep	profound, bottomless
Delicate	fragile, weak, tender
Delight	ecstasy, happiness
Deny	disprove, rebuf
Eager	ardent, avid
Effective	active, capable
Elegant	beautiful, artistic
Emerge	arise, appear
Encouraging	cheerful, promising
Enormous	colossal, gigantic
Faded	dim, dull
Fair	clean, honest
Fascinating	attractive, bewitching
Foolish	imprudent, senseless
Frank	candid, ingenuous
Garrulous	chattering, gossiping
Generous	liberal, benevolent
Genuine	bonafide, authentic
Gloomy	dark, sad
Glorious	magnificent, excellent
Great	colossal, enormous
Haughty	assuming, arrogant
Hefty	big, robust

Humane	benign, gentle
Humble	modest, meek
Idle	lazy, inactive
Illogical	faulty, incorrect
Immense	enormous, colossal
Impudent	bold, brazen
Indolent	lazy, sluggish
Intelligent	clever, bright
Keen	ardent, avid
Kind	benevolent, benign
Laconic	brief, curt
Leading	dominating, chief
Lively	agile, active
Lucid	evident, clear
Magnificent	excellent, glorious
Morose	gloomy, sad
Neglect	disdain, ignore
Obedient	submissive, amenable
Obscure	cloudy, vague
Obstinate	stubborn, firm
Opulent	lavish, affluent
Overnight	fault, mistake
Peaceful	harmonious, friendly
Polite	humble, civil
Prolific	teeming, bountiful
Radiant	bright, glorious
Rejoicing	delight, cheer
Sad	gloomy, depressed
Select	choose, opt
Silence	calm, peace

ANTONYMS

Abhor	Admire, love, adore
Adore	hate, abhor
Alert	listless, careless
Annex	remove, unfasten
Apex	bottom, nadir
Ban	allow, permit
Beautiful	awful, ugly
Benign	stern, harsh
Boisterous	quiet, peaceful
Brief	lengthy, extensive
Calm	stir, agitate
Careful	careless, unconcerned
Clear	cloudy, vague
Clever	clumsy, boring
Colossal	diminutive, small
Compatible	incompatible, inapt
Courageous	cowardly, timid
Damaging	useful, advantageous
Dangerous	safe, harmless
Deceit	honesty, candour
Delicate	harsh, indelicate
Deny	admit, accept
Dim	bright, clear
Eager	impassive, lazy
Efficient	inefficient, inept
Emerge	enter, fall
Encourage	deter, depress
Engaging	repulsive, unattractive
Fair	unfair, prejudiced
Fake	genuine, bonafide
Fascinating	unattractive, disgusting
Ferocious	mild, gentle
Gallant	cowardly, fearful
Gentle	aggressive, harsh
Gigantic	tiny, puny
Glorious	dull, dim
Handy	clumsy, inept
Happy	unhappy, gloomy
Hard	soft, flexible
Honest	dishonest, unfair
Huge	minute, puny
Idle	active, busy
Illogical	logical, coherent
Incorrect	correct, accurate
Indecent	decent, modest
Innocent	cunning, dishonest
Kind	unkind, cruel
Lazy	active, diligent
Like	unlike, diverse
Lovable	hateful, abhorrent
Major	minor, unimportant
Meek	arrogant, stubborn
Merry	sad, gloomy
Morose	happy, delightful
Nadir	apex, Zenith
Nonsense	sense, wisdom
Object	admire, accept
Obscure	clear, vivid
Overbearing	humble, modest
Peaceful	agitated, disturbed
Playful	gloomy, morose
Polite	impolite, ill-mannered

Proficient	incompetent, unskilled	Tempting	untempting, unattractive
Promising	unpromising, discouraging	Tepid	zealous, eager
Realistic	unrealistic, fanciful	Timid	arrogant, bold
Refined	unrefined, boorish	True	untrue, false
Reject	accept, select	Ungainly	elegant, attractive
Robust	feeble, frail	Unmannerly	mannerly, polite
Secure	insecure, unsafe	Valid	invalid, illegal
Sensible	senseless, stupid	Verbose	curt, brief
Sluggish	energetic, brisk	Violent	calm, quiet

MULTIPLE CHOICE QUESTIONS

Directions (Qs. No. 1 to 40): *In the following questions, each word is followed by four options A, B, C & D. Select the option which best expresses the meaning of the given word.*

1. ABSURD
A. Foolish B. Simple
C. Courageous D. Silly

2. ABANDON
A. Lose B. Profit
C. Vacate D. Foil

3. CAJOLE
A. Pause B. Lenient
C. Blast D. Lure

4. COMBAT
A. Fight B. Conflict
C. Shoot D. Quarrel

5. LAMENT
A. Condone B. Console
C. Complain D. Contribution

6. DEBACLE
A. Disgrace B. Defeat
C. Collapse D. Decline

7. SHIVER
A. Fear B. Tremble
C. Shake D. Ache

8. TORTURE
A. Terror B. Harassment
C. Torment D. Tranquility

9. LAUDABLE
A. Lovable B. Commendable
C. Profitable D. Oblivious

10. FIXED
A. Sterile B. Static
C. Stubborn D. Parennial

11. QUEER
A. Unfamiliar B. Cute
C. Curious D. Strange

12. SUFFICIENT
A. Fit B. Proper
C. Adequate D. Vast

13. GLOSS
A. Brightness B. Soothing
C. Rubbing D. Miracle

14. LONGING
A. Prune B. Apathy
C. Curtail D. Craving

15. JEER
A. Applaud B. Magnanimity
C. Avoid D. Scoff

16. ZENITH
A. Minimum B. Nadir
C. Plant D. Peak

17. GARB
A. Distort B. Dress
C. Trivial D. Rage

18. ABHOR
A. Rude B. Reconcile
C. Crave D. Detest

19. YIELD
A. Shun B. Incisive
C. Retain D. Surrender

20. YOKE
A. Twist B. Release
C. Link D. Extra

21. VENT
A. End B. Strode
C. Opening D. Cure

22. INDICT
A. Allege B. Condemn
C. Warn D. Accuse

23. VENUE
A. Agenda B. Time
C. Distance D. Place

24. FAKE
A. Loyal
B. Original
C. Trustworthy
D. Imitation

25. PONDER
A. Pollution
B. Evaluation
C. Anticipation
D. Think

26. BRIEF
A. Limited
B. Small
C. Little
D. Short

27. GARRULITY
A. Credulity
B. Senility
C. Loquaciousness
D. Speciousness

28. FURORE
A. Excitement
B. Worry
C. Flux
D. Anteroom

29. NEUTRAL
A. Unbiased
B. Non-aligned
C. Undecided
D. Indifferent

30. LAMENT
A. Complain
B. Comment
C. Condone
D. Console

31. ADVERSITY
A. Failure
B. Helplessness
C. Misfortune
D. Crisis

32. TURNUP
A. Land up
B. Show up
C. Crop up
D. Come up

33. DEIFY
A. Flatter
B. Challenge
C. Worship
D. Face

34. ERROR
A. Misadventure
B. Misgiving
C. Ambiguity
D. Blunder

35. SHALLOW
A. Artificial
B. Superficial
C. Foolish
D. Worthless

36. MASSACRE
A. Murder
B. Stab
C. Assassinate
D. Slaughter

37. COMBAT
A. Conflict
B. Quarrel
C. Feud
D. Fight

38. VORACIOUS
A. Wild
B. Hungry
C. Angry
D. Quick

39. IMPROMPTU
A. Offhand
B. Unimportant
C. Unreal
D. Effective

40. RABBLE
A. Mob
B. Noise
C. Roar
D. Rubbish

Directions (Qs. Nos. 41 to 75): *In the following questions, each word is followed by four options A, B, C and D. Select the option which looks like the antonym of the given word.*

41. TRAGIC
A. Dramatic
B. Strong
C. Gentle
D. Comic

42. ORAL
A. Verbal
B. Sane
C. Minor
D. Written

43. ADMIRE
A. Hate
B. Unlike
C. Dislike
D. Enough

44. VIOLENT
A. Gentle
B. Savage
C. Haughty
D. Decline

45. ADVERSITY
A. Windfall
B. Inprosperity
C. Prosperity
D. Slave

46. GENUINE
A. Spurious
B. Obscure
C. Countless
D. Apathetic

47. GRUDGE
A. Essence
B. Guile
C. Goodwill
D. Ill-will

48. STIFF
A. Soft
B. Courteous
C. Lively
D. Flexible

49. VANITY
A. Conceit
B. Pride
C. Ostentious
D. Humility

50. FRONT
A. Upper
B. Unusual
C. Back
D. Rear

51. TANGIBLE
A. Solid
B. Actual
C. Concrete
D. Ethereal

52. ATTRACT
A. Lured
B. Longing
C. Repel
D. Disguise

53. COMFORT
A. Discomfort
B. Discontent
C. Uncomfort
D. Miscomfort

54. WELCOME
A. Repel
B. Accept
C. Resist
D. Fight

55. TACTFUL
A. Naive
B. Loose
C. Strict
D. Uncivilized

56. DUTIFUL
A. Harmful
B. Watchful
C. Forgetful
D. Remiss

57. RIGID
A. Flux
B. Adoptable
C. Yielding
D. Adaptable

58. RARE
A. Petty
B. Poor
C. Small
D. Common

59. ZEAL
A. Despair
B. Calmness
C. Passiveness
D. Indifference

60. FAMILIAR
A. Dangerous
B. Strange
C. Friendly
D. Unpleasant

61. AMUSED
A. Abused
B. Astonished
C. Saddened
D. Jolted

62. SHRINK
A. Spoil
B. Expand
C. Stretch
D. Contract

63. GENUINE
A. Fraudulent
B. Direct
C. Candid
D. Forthright

64. VIOLENT
A. Tame
B. Harmless
C. Humble
D. Gentle

65. PATCHY
A. Clear
B. Simple
C. Attractive
D. Uniform

66. STRINGENT
A. General
B. Vehement
C. Lenient
D. Magnanimous

67. FLIMSY
A. Frail
B. Filthy
C. Firm
D. Flippant

68. BUSY
A. Occupied
B. Engrossed
C. Relaxed
D. Engaged

69. ADAPTABLE
A. Adoptable
B. Flexible
C. Yielding
D. Rigid

70. LOVE
A. Villainy
B. Hatred
C. Compulsion
D. Force

71. BALANCE
A. Disbalance
B. Misbalance
C. Debalance
D. Imbalance

72. RELINQUISH
A. Abdicate
B. Renounce
C. Possess
D. Deny

73. MOUNTAIN
A. Plain
B. Plateau
C. Precipice
D. Valley

74. FICKLE
A. Courageous
B. Sincere
C. Steadfast
D. Humble

75. PERENNIAL
A. Frequent
B. Regular
C. Lasting
D. Rare

ANSWERS

1	2	3	4	5	6	7	8	9	10
D	C	D	A	C	C	B	C	B	B
11	**12**	**13**	**14**	**15**	**16**	**17**	**18**	**19**	**20**
D	C	A	D	D	D	B	D	D	C
21	**22**	**23**	**24**	**25**	**26**	**27**	**28**	**29**	**30**
C	C	D	D	D	D	C	A	A	A
31	**32**	**33**	**34**	**35**	**36**	**37**	**38**	**39**	**40**
C	B	C	D	B	D	D	B	A	A
41	**42**	**43**	**44**	**45**	**46**	**47**	**48**	**49**	**50**
D	D	C	A	C	A	C	D	D	D
51	**52**	**53**	**54**	**55**	**56**	**57**	**58**	**59**	**60**
D	C	A	C	A	D	D	D	D	B
61	**62**	**63**	**64**	**65**	**66**	**67**	**68**	**69**	**70**
C	C	A	D	D	C	C	C	D	B
71	**72**	**73**	**74**	**75**					
D	C	D	C	D					

★★★

6

Comprehension Passages

Directions: *Read the following passages and answer the questions given below each.*

PASSAGE-1

There is no general agreement about how the planets were formed. The most widely accepted theory is that about 5000 millions years ago swirling clouds of matter began to condense. Through the action of centrifugal force, the heavier molecules were concentrated near the centre of the eddies and the lighter, gaseous material was thrown out towards the periphery. Such is the theory. What is known is that nine satellites began orbiting round the sun. These are the planets.

The planet on which man lives is the third closest to the sun, with the third shortest orbit. It also has something none of the others has—an atmosphere that can support life in all the manifold forms that exist on our planet. There may be satellites circling other stars in other parts of the universe that have the right ingredients for some sort of life to evolve, but the earth is the only one in the solar system.

1. According to the passage, the planets are
A. nothing but condensed clouds
B. a collection of gaseous material
C. a collection of condensed swirling material
D. a collection of centrifugal forces

2. The theory of the formation of the planets
A. is generally agreed upon by everyone
B. is a debatable one
C. covers a very wide area
D. is fairly well-known

3. A planet is a 'heavenly body' which moves round
A. the sun
B. a star
C. a satellite of the solar system
D. the universe

4. One essential difference between the earth and the other planets is that
A. the atmosphere of the earth makes possible the presence of life on it
B. the earth draws the heavier molecules into its centre through the action of centrifugal force
C. only the earth is on the periphery of the solar system
D. the earth has the capacity to come into closer contact with the sun

5. The writer claims that the life-supporting atmosphere
A. is there on other planets in the solar system
B. may be there on the other satellites in the universe
C. may evolve on other satellite circling other stars in the universe
D. cannot evolve anywhere outside the earth

PASSAGE-2

Through the break between the trees, she looked into one of the lighted windows above the shop. She could see the cartons of biscuits neatly piled near the far wall. Against her conscious wishes Cissy's saliva glands started pumping the fluid into her mouth. She felt her heart beating strongly from the top of her throat into the back of her mouth. There is nobody, she thought. I can dash in and take a box and dash out again. I know it is a sin but the Lord will not punish us if we are so hungry.

1. The whole passage is a description of
A. Cissy's courage for stealing
B. Cissy's plans before stealing
C. Cissy's temptation before stealing
D. Cissy's greed for stealing

2. How do you know that Cissy felt guilty?
A. She knew what she was doing was morally wrong
B. She felt her heart pounding inside her chest
C. She was saying her prayers before she went to steal
D. She knew that she was about to do something selfish

3. Why did her heart beat strongly?
A. She thought nobody was watching her
B. She was thinking of stealing the biscuits
C. She was eager to taste the biscuits
D. She was ill and was running temperature

4. How was Cissy able to see the cartons of biscuits?
   A. She had very good eyesight
   B. She was able to smell the biscuits
   C. She saw another child eating biscuits
   D. She was aided by a light in the room
5. What was Cissy's reaction when she saw the biscuit cartons?
   A. She wanted to eat all the biscuits
   B. She felt like vomiting
   C. Her mouth started watering
   D. She thought of all the toffees she had eaten

PASSAGE-3

A certain Ameer was on a voyage in his ship when a great storm arose. One of the slaves on board, who had never been to sea, began to wail and cry out in fear. This went on for sometime and no one could silence him. In anger the Ameer asked, 'Is there no one here who can silence this wretched coward?'

A philosopher, who happened to be a passenger, said, 'I think I can quiet this man, Sir, if you give me full permission to do as I please with him.'

'Go ahead,' said the Ameer, 'you have my permission'.

1. What kind of prose is used in this extract?
   A. Informative B. Argumentative
   C. Lyrical D. Narrative
2. The verb 'to wail' means
   A. to smile B. to call
   C. to weep D. to speak
3. The word 'voyage' means
   A. travelling by sea
   B. walking on foot
   C. riding a horse
   D. swimming in sea
4. The slave was afraid because
   A. the Ameer was about to beat him
   B. there was a storm in the sea
   C. he was about to be thrown into the sea
   D. the journey was not coming to an end
5. The philosopher volunteered to
   A. throw off the slave
   B. persuade the slave
   C. silence the slave
   D. kill the slave

PASSAGE-4

We stand poised precariously and challengingly on the razor's edge of destiny. We are now at the mercy of atom bombs and the like which would destroy us completely if we fail to control them wisely. And wisdom in this crisis means sensitiveness to the basic values of life; it means a vivid realisation that we are literally living in one world where we must either swim together or sink together. We cannot afford to tamper with man's single-minded loyalty to peace and international understanding. Anyone who does it is a traitor not only to man's past and present, but also to his future, because he is mortgaging the destiny of unborn generations.

1. Form the tone and style of the passage it appears that the writer is
   A. unware of the global power situation
   B. a humanist with a clear foresight
   C. a prose writer with a fascination for images and metaphors
   D. a traitor who wishes to mortgage the destiny of future generations
2. The phrase "razor's edge of destiny" stands for
   A. an enigma that cuts through the pattern of life like the edge of a razor
   B. a critical situation that foreordains the future
   C. a sharp line of division that marks the alternative courses of action in the future
   D. destiny having sharp edges
3. According to the writer "wisdom" in the present crisis means
   A. responsibility to the "unborn generations"
   B. awareness that we stand poised precariously on the razor's edge of destiny
   C. awareness of the basic values of life
   D. determination to ban nuclear weapons
4. The author is so concerned about the threat of nuclear weapons because he feels that
   A. his country is threatened by a nuclear power
   B. a nuclear war will destroy human civilisation
   C. all countries are interlinked and one cannot escape the consequences of what happens to another country
   D. the world is on the brink of disaster
5. The best way to escape complete annihilation is an atomic war is
   A. to ban nuclear weapons
   B. to turn to religion
   C. to work for international understanding and harmony
   D. to invent more powerful weapons

PASSAGE-5

The editorial policy of a popular daily is controlled by two chief factors. The first is the interest of the advertisers from whom it gets the money which enables it to keep up its large circulation. No widely circulated newspaper dare support a public policy, howsoever much in the national interest, that might conflict with the vested interests of its advertisers. On the other hand, any product that refuses to pay the advertising rates of a powerful national organ will be denounced, smashed and driven off the market. You are not allowed to use any product that dissociates itself from the advertising ring. All this is understandable, since big circulation spells bankruptcy if the paper has to depend on its sales for its revenue.

1. According to this passage, one of the chief factors that controls the editorial policy of a newspaper is
A. the interest of the nation
B. the interest of the reader
C. the interest of the advertisers
D. its cost of production

2. Big circulation spells bankruptcy if the paper depends on its sale for its revenue because
A. to retain its big circulation, it will have to be sold far below the cost of its production
B. the advertisers will not be there to support its cost production
C. the advertisers would drive it out of circulation
D. it will not be able to pursue the policy that would be in the interest of the nation

3. A widely circulated newspaper cannot support a public policy
A. if it is not in the national interest
B. even if it is in the national interest
C. if it supports the interest of the advertiser
D. unless it supports the interest of the advertiser

4. If a producer refuses to pay high rates of advertisement in a widely circulated newspaper
A. the circulation of the newspaper will decrease
B. the rival producers/advertisers will come forward with advertisements against that producer
C. the newspaper will see to it that the product of that producer is driven off the market
D. the newspaper will cut its number of pages to reduce its cost of production

5. The expression *"vested interests of its advertisers"* means
A. selfish motives of the advertisers
B. concerns securely possessed by the advertisers
C. something from which the advertisers get interest
D. something by which the advertisers interests are enhanced

PASSAGE-6

It was very hot. Suddenly at about 3 o'clock in the afternoon, there fell such an abundance of rain that 150 men of the grand guard, in order not to be submerged, were obliged to leave a large depression in which they were hidden. Much to their amazement there began to fall on the ground all about a considerable number of toads, the size of hazelnuts, which began to jump about in every direction. M. Gayet (the soldier who provided this information), who could not believe that these myriad reptiles fell with the rain, stretched out his handkerchief at the height of a man, his comrades holding the corners; they caught a considerable number of toads, most of which had the posterior part elongated into a tail, that is to say, in the tadpole state. During this rain storm, which lasted about half an hour, the men of the grand guard felt very distinctly on their hats and on their clothing the blows struck by falling toads. As a final proof of the reality of this phenomenon, M. Gayet reports that after the storm the three-cornered hats of the men of the guard held in their folds some of the reptiles.

1. A suitable title for this passage would be
A. A Mystery
B. A Rain of Toads
C. Long Time Ago
D. M. Gayet's Report

2. What proof does M. Gayet give to prove that what happened was real?
A. Toads were found in the depression
B. Soldiers felt the toads striking blows as they fell
C. 150 men of the grand guard swore it rained toads
D. Toads, were found in the guards' hats after the rain stopped

3. From where could this account have been taken?
A. A novel
B. A weather report
C. A newspaper
D. A pamphlet

4. The soldiers left their hiding places because they
A. were scared of toads
B. were ordered to
C. were getting wet
D. might have drowned there

5. M. Gayet and his friends caught the toads in
A. a handkerchief
B. their hats
C. their clothing
D. the depression

PASSAGE-7

Workers who repeat the same operation day after day can take no pleasure or pride in their work. Their chief pleasure in life is outside the factory. Their work is dull, and they spend their time with one eye on the clock. It is realised that modern work is often dull, and in some factories wireless set or a gramophone is turned on to provide music for the workers. The title of a common programme given by the British Broadcasting Corporation is "Music while you work". The provision of entertainment while the factory wheels are turning does not cause the work-people to neglect their duty; on the contrary, it increases output. In spite of various attempts to brighten the lives of workers, however, the average man in a factory is rather to be pitied than envied. The dullness of his life is one of the drawbacks of mass production.

1. The workers pass their time in the factory looking at the clock because
A. their work is dreary and uninteresting
B. their pleasure lies outside the factory
C. they wish to deceive the management
D. they want to get their salary without working

2. Some modern factories play radio or gramophone music for workers to
A. distract them from their work
B. reduce the dull nature of their work
C. make them forget the clock
D. cheer them up while working

3. Labourers doing only one type of work throughout their service
A. become experts in that type of work
B. are proud of their ability to do one type of work
C. do not like their work
D. take a lot of interest in their work

4. The modern system of mass production is responsible for
A. the dismal condition of labourers
B. the dullness of the life of the workers
C. the comfortable life of the labourers
D. the miserable condition of the labourers

5. Providing entertainment facilities to the workers when the factory work is going on may cause
A. the labourers to neglect their work
B. rise in the production quantity
C. the labourers to forget the monotony of work
D. a great fall in the output

PASSAGE-8

S.N. Bose is the only physicist whose name is linked with Einstein in all the textbooks of Physics. This is because he hit on a brilliant method whose value Einstein immediately recognised and proclaimed to the scientific world with all the prestige of his great name. In retrospect, it is now clear that even Einstein could not foresee the full power and application range of Bose's idea. Bose's work, along with its subsequent development by Fermi, provides the basis for dividing all the elementary particles of nuclear Physics into two categories—the *bosons* (after Bose) and the *fermions* after Fermi.

1. What Einstein really did for Bose was that
A. he allowed his name to be linked with S.N. Bose in all the textbooks of Physics
B. he fully recognised and proclaimed to the scientific world the importance of Bose's discovery
C. he eventually recognised and proclaimed to the scientific world the importance of Bose's discovery
D. he immediately, though not fully, recognised and proclaimed to the scientific world the importance of Bose's discovery

2. Bose and Fermi worked in the same field; Fermi's work
A. came before that of Bose
B. was published after that of Bose
C. came at the same time as that of Bose
D. led directly to Bose's discovery

3. The main contribution of S.N. Bose was that, he
A. alone divided the elementary particles into two new categories
B. in collaboration with Fermi, divided the elementary particles into two new categories
C. evolved a theory which was further developed by Fermi, and their research led to the division of the elementary particles into two new categories
D. discovered nuclear energy

4. The correct definition of 'Nuclear Physics' is that it is a branch of Physics that
A. involves the study of nuclear weapons
B. studies the application of nuclear energy
C. deals with atoms, their nuclear structure and behaviour
D. studies the nucleus or central part of all particles

5. Einstein endorsed the research done by Bose because he knew
A. it was an original work
B. it would bring about revolutionary changes in Nuclear Physics
C. it would have a powerful impact on other scientists
D. Bose was a dedicated scientist

PASSAGE-9

We are tempted to assume that technological progress is real progress and that material success is the criterion of civilisation. If the Eastern people become fascinated by machines and techniques and use them, as Western nations do, to build huge industrial organisations and large military establishments, they will get involved in power politics and drift into the danger of death. Scientific and technological civilisation brings great opportunities and great rewards but also great risks and temptations. Science and technology are neither good nor bad. They are not to be tabooed but tamed and assigned their proper place. They become dangerous only if they become idols.

1. According to the author, people think that real progress lies in
   A. material success and technological growth
   B. worshipping idols and having faith in them
   C. having large industries and political power
   D. taking risks and facing temptations
2. From the passage one gathers that the Eastern people must
   A. appreciate scientific achievements
   B. build huge industrial organisations
   C. avoid being controlled by machines and techniques of industrial production
   D. be fascinated by machines
3. According to the author, science and technology should be
   A. tabooed and eliminated from life
   B. used in a controlled and careful manner
   C. encouraged and liberally used
   D. made compulsory in education
4. According to the author, science and technology will bring benefits to
   A. only Western nations
   B. only Eastern countries
   C. nobody
   D. all, if tamed properly
5. According to the author, science and technology are
   A. totally harmless
   B. extremely dangerous
   C. to be treated as idols
   D. are useful, if they are not worshipped blindly

PASSAGE-10

The awareness of equal corruption will be a better emotional basis for the so-called multi-racial Commonwealth, of which much is made than its professed principle—the pursuit of common aims in world politics, aims which are so rarefied that a large volume of artificial political oxygen is needed to keep that body-politic breathing. After all, it cannot be denied that even the United States and the Russia are pursuing common aims in world affairs, such as peace, disarmament, democracy, technological progress, as well as freedom as understood by each. But that is not preventing them from doing things which might lead to the destruction or near destruction of mankind. Thus, common aims would seem to be very undependable as guarantees for goodwill and cooperation among nations. On the contrary, a frank admission of being equal sinners would at least encourage charity and discourage moral arrogance. That would be a better foundation for integration for international and multi-racial cooperation.

1. The Superpowers may claim to have the same laudable objectives, but
   A. do not work earnestly to achieve them
   B. undo each other's efforts
   C. still act against the interests of mankind
   D. do not see them in the right perspective
2. The Commonwealth is characterised by
   A. the failure of the constituents to
   B. the racial nature of its membership work for the same goals
   C. uniform lack of moral standards
   D. constant redefining of objectives
3. The thrust of the author's argument is that
   A. the Commonwealth has outlived its utility
   B. membership of the Commonwealth be restricted to the superpowers
   C. members are equally responsible for the present state of world politics
   D. international peace and cooperation are unattainable
4. International cooperation can come about, if
   A. nations become aware of their own failings and discard pride
   B. charitable organizations are encouraged
   C. different races are treated on the basis of equality
   D. nations guilty of immoral actions are exposed
5. Common goals are desirable, but these
   A. do not ensure international co-operation
   B. lead to unnecessary tensions
   C. encourage rivalry between superpowers
   D. lead to destruction of mankind

PASSAGE-11

There was a marked difference of quality between the personages who haunted the near bridge of brick and the personages who haunted the far one of stone. Those of lowest character preferred the former, adjoining the town; they did not mind the glare of the public eye. They had been of no account during their successes; and though they might feel dispirited, they had no sense of shame in their ruin. Instead of sighing at their adversaries they spat, and instead of saying the iron had entered into their souls they said they were down on their luck. The miserables, who would pause on the remoter bridge were of a politer stamp—persons who did not know how to get rid of the weary time. The eyes of this species were mostly directed over the parapet upon the running water below. While one on the downward bridge did not mind who saw him so and kept his back to the parapet to survey the passer-by, one on this never faced the road, never turned his head at coming footsteps, but, sensitive to his own condition, watched the current whenever a stranger approached, as if some strange fish interested him, though every finned thing had been poached out of the river years before.

1. People belonging to the lower strata, in their moments of distress
   A. remembered their days of glory
   B. dressed shabbily to earn sympathy
   C. visited the brick-made bridge
   D. felt ashamed of their failures

2. The two bridges were known
   A. for their similar design
   B. for being equi-distant from town
   C. for being haunted places
   D. for attracting dejected people to them

3. In this passage, the author is trying to
   A. explain the differences between the construction of two bridges
   B. describe the way different sections of people like to dress
   C. explain the variety of ways in which strangers can be treated
   D. describe how people of different classes behaved when unhappy

4. The attitude of the lowly and genteel towards strangers was
   A. virtually the same
   B. entirely different
   C. completely indifferent
   D. virulently hostile

5. The bridge of stone was frequented by
   A. all the sections of society
   B. those fond of fishing
   C. the sophisticated but luckless
   D. None of these

PASSAGE-12

When talking to a reporter early in the season, a coach tends to talk down the abilities of his new man. He does not want his team to become known as a favourite because, if the team loses, he will be criticised for not making the most of his material. Even when he knows he has a great team, a coach avoids favourable publicity. He realises that over-confidence, injuries, an error on the field or the better luck of his opponent may wreck any season.

1. When talking to a reporter, a coach usually
   A. praises his team
   B. highlights the qualities of the new members of the team
   C. does not acquaint him with the full potentialities of the new players
   D. derides his rival teams

2. If a favourite team loses the game, its fans
   A. feel let down
   B. accuse its members of lack of commitment
   C. blame the coach for not providing necessary training
   D. want to coach to be fired

3. If his team is elevated to the position of a favourite, it may
   A. become over-confident
   B. feel obliged to win the game
   C. have enthusiastic fans in the field
   D. easily intimidate its rivals

4. In spite of everything being favourite, a team may lose the game if its opponents
   A. are smarter
   B. have just as good material
   C. are favoured by chance and circumstances
   D. are more relaxed than it is

5. In spite of good players, a team may lose the game if
   A. there is no coordination among its members
   B. a few players get injured in the field
   C. its morale is not high
   D. it cannot understand the strategies of its opponents

PASSAGE-13

Though it may be inessential to the imagination, travelling is necessary for an understanding of men. Only with long experience and the opening of his wares on many a beach where his language is not spoken, will the merchant come to know the worth of what he carries and what is parochial and what is universal in his choice. Such delicate goods as justice, love and honour, courtesy and indeed all the things we care for, are valid everywhere but they are variously moulded and often differently handled and sometimes nearly unrecognisable if you meet them in a foreign land and the art of learning fundamental common values is perhaps the greatest gain of travelling to those who wish to live at ease among their fellows.

1. Travelling helps those who
   A. wish to make money
   B. want to learn foreign languages
   C. wish to learn fundamental common values
   D. want to resolve differences amongst people

2. When we meet other people while we travel, we learn to differentiate between
   A. friends and foes
   B. local and universal values
   C. imagination and understanding
   D. communities and nationalities

3. The things we care for are available in foreign lands in
   A. some form or the other
   B. unrecognisable forms
   C. plenty
   D. easily recognisable forms

4. The author terms justice, love, honour and courtesy as delicate goods because they are
A. fragile
B. perishable
C. desirable
D. important

5. According to the passage, travelling leads to
A. selling our wares to the others
B. establishing our superiority over foreigners
C. exploiting foreign lands
D. understanding human nature

PASSAGE-14

The first word-book to embody the ideals of the age was Nathaniel Bailey's *Universal Etymological Dictionary of the English Language,* originally published in 1721 and then, in a beautiful volume with illustrations by Flaxman, in 1731. This edition was the basis of Samuel Johnson's *Dictionary* of 1755; through Johnson, it influenced all subsequent lexicographical practice. The position of dictionary pioneer, commonly granted to Johnson or to Noah Webster, belongs in reality to one of the few geniuses lexicography ever produced: Nathaniel Bailey. Johnson extended Bailey's technique and also revised Bailey's crude etymologies on the basis of Francis Junius' book. Most Englishmen used the word *dictionary* as a mere synonym for Johnson's *Dictionary.* Being regarded as the ideal word-book, it continued in common use until 1990.

1. Nathaniel Bailey's *Dictionary* had
A. no influence on later dictionaries
B. a direct influence on later dictionaries
C. an indirect influence on later dictionaries
D. an influence on Francis Junius' *dictionary* only

2. Johnson's Dictionary was
A. an improvement upon Bailey's *Dictionary*
B. a simplified version of Bailey's *Dictionary*
C. nothing but a copy of Bailey's *Dictionary*
D. fundamentally different from Bailey's *Dictionary*

3. The publication of Johnson's dictionary was separated from the Flaxman edition of Bailey's dictionary by
A. 24 years
B. 10 years
C. 125 years
D. 34 years

4. In the 19th century most Englishmen used the word "dictionary" as a synonym for Johnson's *Dictionary* probably because
A. it was the oldest English dictionary
B. it was the only English dictionary published till then
C. it was more convenient for them to use this shortened form
D. it was the ideal and most commonly used dictionary

5. According to the author, the real pioneer of lexicography was
A. Noah Webster
B. Samuel Johnson
C. Flaxman
D. Nathaniel Bailey

PASSAGE-15

We stumbled slowly along in the darkness, with the black loom of the craggy hills around us, and the yellow speck of light burning steadily in front. There is nothing so deceptive as the distance of a light upon the pitch-dark night and sometimes the glimmer seemed to be far away upon the horizon and sometimes it might have been within a few yards from us. But at last we could see whence it came and then we knew that we were very close.

1. The passage as a whole indicates that the mission of the author and his companion was
A. to investigate the nature of the countryside
B. to detect the movements of suspicious characters
C. to study supernatural phenomena
D. to trace the light to its place of origin

2. The word "stumbled" in the first line suggests that the narrator and his friend
A. had very poor sight
B. were walking on an uneven road
C. had their attention fixed on the distant light
D. were trying to keep their movements secret

3. The last sentence suggests that when they discovered the source of the light,
A. they were surprised by its closeness
B. they were greatly relieved
C. they were very pleased
D. they were utterly disappointed

4. The author and his friend were walking
A. across a dark, bushy stretch
B. along a lonely, winding road
C. across a lonely, hilly countryside
D. along an ill-lit and ill-maintained forest road

5. For the narrator and his friend, the effect of the dim light was
A. to create confusion with regard to distance
B. to brighten an otherwise hopeless situation
C. to indicate divine intervention
D. to lessen the difficulty of their mission

PASSAGE-16

We started pitching the highest camp that has ever been made. Everything took five times as long as it would have taken in a place where there was enough air to breathe; but at last we got the, tent up and when we crawled in, it was not too bad. There was only a light wind, and inside it was not too cold for us to take off our gloves. At night most climbers take off their boots; but I prefer to keep them on. Hillary, on the other hand, took his off and laid them next to his sleeping bag.

1. The narrator of the story is
A. an airline pilot B. a mountaineer
C. a traveller D. a tourist

2. In this passage, 'we' refers to
A. the author and his friends
B. the author and his friend
C. the author and his wife
D. None of the above

3. They crawled into the tent because
A. they must have been too tired to work
B. the entrance to the tent must have been low
C. they had heavy loads on their back
D. they wanted to hide from enemies

4. They took a long time to finish the work because
A. they were very tired
B. it was very cold
C. there was not enough air to breathe
D. it was very dark

5. When they crawled into the tent
A. they took off their gloves because it was not very cold
B. they could not take off their gloves because it was very cold
C. they took off their gloves though it was very cold
D. they did not take off their gloves though it was not cold

PASSAGE-17

All sources of energy upon which industry depends are wasted when they are employed, and industry is expending them at a continually increasing rate. Already coal has been largely replaced by oil and oil is being used up so fast that the East and the West alike consider it to be necessary for their prosperity. And what is true of oil is equally true of other natural resources. Everyday, in fact, many miles of forests are turned into newspapers, but there is no known process by which newspapers can be turned into forests. You will say that this need not worry us, since newspapers will be replaced by radio, but radio requires electricity, electricity requires power and power requires raw materials.

1. The central contention of the passage is that
A. industries should be closed down, since they expend all sources of energy
B. newspapers should not be allowed to destroy forests
C. an all-out effort is necessary for the preservation of natural resources that ultimately supply power
D. power should be generated in abundance

2. The 'and' in the first sentence has the force of
A. as well as B. besides
C. still D. though

3. The statement 'many miles of forests are turned into newspapers' means
A. many miles of forests have become as dry as newspapers
B. devastation of vast areas of forests is a newsworthy item
C. a good part of forests has been felled and converted into newsprint
D. large numbers of trees in forests are converted into raw materials to supply power for the machines that print newspapers

4. According to this passage, oil has become necessary for the prosperity of a nation because
A. it is cheaper than coal
B. it is more useful than coal
C. the East and the West think so
D. it is now the chief source of energy

5. According to this passage, the most indispensable item for an industrialised society is
A. the radio
B. raw materials
C. power
D. electricity

PASSAGE-18

Democratic societies from the earliest times have expected their governments to protect the weak against the strong. No "era of good feeling" can justify discharging the police force or giving up the idea of public control over concentrated private wealth. On the other hand, it is obvious that a spirit of self-denial and moderation on the part of those who hold economic power will greatly soften the demand for absolute equality. Men are more interested in freedom and security than in an equal distribution of wealth. The extent to which Government must interfere with business, therefore, is not exactly measured by the extent to which economic power is concentrated into a few hands. The required degree of government interference depends mainly on whether economic powers are oppressively used, and on the necessity of keeping economic factors in a 'tolerable state of balance.'

But with the necessity of meeting all these dangers and threats to liberty, the powers of government are unavoidably increased, whichever political party may be in office. The growth of government is a necessary result of the growth of technology and of the problems that go with the use of machines and science. Since the government in our nation, as well as in all civilised nations, must take on more powers to meet its problems, there is no way to preserve freedom except by making democracy more powerful.

1. 'Era of good feeling' in second sentence can mean
   A. time of prosperity
   B. time of adversity
   C. time without government
   D. time of police atrocities
2. 'Tolerable state of balance' in the last sentence of the first paragraph may mean
   A. a reasonable amount of government interference
   B. an adequate level of police force
   C. a reasonable check on economic power
   D. a reasonable level of economic equality
3. A spirit of moderation on the part of the economically sound people would make the less-privileged
   A. unhappy with their lot
   B. clamourless for absolute equality
   C. unhappy the rich people
   D. more interested in freedom and security
4. The advent of science and technology has
   A. increased the chances of economic inequality
   B. increased the freedom of people
   C. increased the powers of the government
   D. increased the tyranny of the political parties
5. The growth of government is necessitated
   A. to curb the accumulation of wealth in a few hands
   B. to deploy the police force wisely
   C. to monitor science and technology
   D. to make the rich and the poor happy

PASSAGE-19

Youth today do not realise that one is modern only when his thoughts and actions bring out something new, which can set an example to the rest of the world. Imitating only the Western outlook in life-style, leaving aside their values, is not what modernism is. Should we consider a youth modern if he opts for a dozen girlfriends and then pretends to be ignorant when dowry in marriage is concerned?

The family also plays a vital role in shaping one's life. If the urban population in India is divided into two broad divisions, the elite and the middle class, we will find that youths belonging to both these classes suffer from severe frustrations. The parents in the higher society are so busy with their work that their children are left neglected. Loneliness, tensions arising out of parent's unhappy relations and family feuds result in psychiatric depression in the youth.

The case is similar in the middle class families, though with a difference. Lack of attention at home ruins them. The situation is not so grave with the girls as they generally prefer to stay at home, whatever its conditions be. But young men, desperate to find some refuge; quite often come in contact with drugs, alcohol and other illegal activities. Neither are they happy with the society nor is the society happy with them.

1. The passage is concerned with
   A. the urban youth
   B. the elite class youth
   C. the middle class youth
   D. the modern girls
2. Youths in the elite class families are
   A. lonely and depressed
   B. prone to drug-addiction
   C. desperate for revenge
   D. angry and defiant
3. Being truly modern means
   A. imitating the West
   B. opting for a dozen girl-friend
   C. accepting dowry in marriage
   D. doing something exemplary
4. The situation in case of the girls is
   A. desperate B. menacing
   C. not so serious D. gloomy
5. Young men seek refuge in
   A. dozen girl-friends
   B. modernism
   C. drugs, alcohol, etc.
   D. dowry in marriage

PASSAGE-20

In the evening we decided to pitch camp as the weather was not encouraging. The wind was high and gathering storm clouds predicted a wild wet night. Moreover, we had arrived at a spot which looked promising for a camp. A level expanse in the lee of a high hill afforded some shelter from the wind; fresh water was near at hand in a stream which flowed across the plain; a copse of trees provided adequate supplies of fuel; and the dry grasses which abounded on the hillside would enhance the comfort of our beds.

Each member of the party was allotted a task. Some erected the tents; others prepared a scanty meal; yet others attended to the needs of the ponies that were now exhausted after a very strenuous day. As the angry sun sank, the bustle of activity was hushed into silence and each man settled down to sleep.

1. As the weather was not encouraging we decided to
   A. set up the camp
   B. pack up the camp
   C. extend the camp
   D. shift the camp

2. The camp site looked encouraging because
A. it was sheltered by some trees
B. the dry grass would provide fuel
C. we had been promised that spot
D. it was level and sheltered

3. The day had been very
A. exciting
B. tiring
C. boring
D. comfortable

4. The task given to some members was to
A. pitch the tents
B. prepare a hot meal
C. walk the ponies
D. allot the tasks

5. This passage is about the selection of
A. a suitable home
B. a suitable place for animals
C. a suitable place to camp
D. a suitable route for trekking

ANSWERS

PASSAGE-1

1	2	3	4	5
A	C	A	A	C

PASSAGE-2

1	2	3	4	5
C	A	B	D	C

PASSAGE-3

1	2	3	4	5
D	C	A	B	C

PASSAGE-4

1	2	3	4	5
B	C	C	B	C

PASSAGE-5

1	2	3	4	5
C	B	D	C	B

PASSAGE-6

1	2	3	4	5
B	D	B	D	A

PASSAGE-7

1	2	3	4	5
A	D	C	B	B

PASSAGE-8

1	2	3	4	5
D	B	C	C	B

PASSAGE-9

1	2	3	4	5
A	C	B	D	D

PASSAGE-10

1	2	3	4	5
C	C	C	A	A

PASSAGE-11

1	2	3	4	5
C	D	D	B	C

PASSAGE-12

1	2	3	4	5
C	C	A	C	D

PASSAGE-13

1	2	3	4	5
C	C	B	D	D

PASSAGE-14

1	2	3	4	5
B	A	A	D	D

PASSAGE-15

1	2	3	4	5
D	B	A	C	A

PASSAGE-16

1	2	3	4	5
B	B	B	C	A

PASSAGE-17

1	2	3	4	5
C	C	C	C	B

PASSAGE-18

1	2	3	4	5
A	A	B	C	D

PASSAGE-19

1	2	3	4	5
A	A	D	C	C

PASSAGE-20

1	2	3	4	5
A	D	B	A	C

★ ★ ★

7

Phrases and Clauses

PHRASES

The Phrase

A group of words which does not have a finite verb and does not make a complete sense on its own, is known as a Phrase, *e.g.*,

(*i*) We'll play hockey **in the evening**.

(*ii*) **It being a hot day**, we decided not to go out for a picnic.

(*iii*) She ran away **to escape punishment**.

The three kinds of phrases are:

I. Noun Phrases: The phrase which does the function of a Noun is called a Noun Phrase.

(*i*) He likes **oranges**. (Noun)

(*ii*) He likes **to eat oranges**. (Noun Phrase)

The word 'oranges' is a noun and it can be replaced with the phrase 'to eat oranges'. In other words the said phrase acts like a noun therefore, it is a noun phrase.

II. Adverb Phrases: A phrase which does the function of an Adverb is called an Adverb Phrase. Most of the Adverb Phrases refer to the manner, place, time, *e.g.*,

1. (*i*) She knocked at/on the door **gently**. (Adverb of Manner)

   (*ii*) She knocked the door **in a gentle way**. (Adverb Phrase showing Manner)

2. (*i*) I found a coin **here**. (Adverb of Place)

   (*ii*) I found a coin **on this spot.** (Adverb Phrase referring to Place)

3. (*i*) You shall do it **now**. (Adverb of Time)

   (*ii*) You shall do it **at the very moment**. (Adverb Phrase referring to Time)

III. Adjective Phrases: A phrase which does the function of an Adjective is called an Adjective Phrase. Most often an Adjective can be replaced with an adjective phrase.

1. (*i*) Tagore was **a famous man**. (Adjective)

   (*ii*) Tagore was **a man of fame** (Adjective Phrase)

2. (*i*) She is **a cunning lady**. (Adjective)

   (*ii*) She is **a lady full of cunningness**. (Adjective Phrase)

3. (*i*) It is **a round stone**. (Adjective)

   (*ii*) It is **a stone of round shape**. (Adjective Phrase)

CLAUSES

The Clause

A group of words which has a subject and a finite verb but which still does not convey the full sense is known as a clause. Broadly speaking there are three kinds of clauses.

1. The Principal Clause.
2. The Coordinate Clause.
3. The Subordinate Clause.

When we just talk of a clause, we mean most often a subordinate clause which is also known as a dependent clause. A subordinate clause together with a principal clause conveys the full sense. *e.g.*,

(*i*) I know that he likes mangoes best.

(*ii*) Although he was well prepared he could not make an impressive speech.

(*iii*) The boy who scored a century is my classmate.

The three kinds of subordinate clauses are:

I. Adjective Clause: A clause which acts as an adjective is known as Adjectives clause. Most often it can replace an adjective or adjective phrase *e.g.*,

1. Mrs Sharma has a **black** purse. (Adjective)
2. Mrs Sharma has a purse of **black colour.** (Adjective Phrase)
3. Mrs Sharma has a purse **which is black in colour**. (Adjective clause)

Relative Pronouns which make Adjective clauses

• who • whose • whom • which • that
• as • what • whatsoever

Relative Adverbs which make Adjective clauses

• when • why • how • whenever
• where • wherever

Adjective clauses which are made by Relative Pronouns

1. This is the cat **that has sharp claws.**
2. Gopal is the boy **who lives at outskirts of our town.**
3. Jack **whom we met at the toy shop** is a good singer.
4. The boy **whose father is a doctor** was not allowed to go inside the operation theatre.
5. The chef **who prepared meal for us** belongs to France.
6. He is such a boy **as I like.**
7. **What I am looking for** is a post in the army.

Adjective clauses which are made by Relative Adverbs

1. I do not know the place **where she saw a snake.**
2. You may go to the place **wherever you like.**
3. I do not know the time **when the storm started.**
4. I do not know the reason **why he resigned his job.**

II. Adverb Clause: An Adverb clause is the clause which does the function of an Adverb. Most often it replaces an Adverb or an Adverb Phrase. It may modify a verb, an adjective or another adverb, *e.g.*,

1. Amar is taller **than you** (are).
2. **As soon as the boy saw the snake**, he cried loudly.
3. **If you work hard**, you'll get good marks.

III. Noun Clauses: The clause which does the function of a Noun is known as a Noun clause. The noun clause can act in the following ways:

1. As the Subject to a Verb:
   - **Why you are crying** we fail to understand.
   - **Where he will go,** nobody cares.
   - **How he earned money** is known to all.
   - **When he will wake up** is not sure.
2. As Object to a Participle:
   - **Knowing that his father will not rebuke him,** he starts disturbing his sister.
   - **Finding that the necklace lying on the ground** was of gold, he picked it up.
   - **Saying that he did not know French** he started singing English songs.
   - They started playing in the ground **thinking that nobody will object to it.**
3. As Object to an Infinitive:
   - I would like to know **whether you are going to the USA or Russia.**
   - He wants to say **whether his brother will come back or not.**
   - She wants to inform **why she did not attend the meeting.**
4. As Object to a Preposition:
   - He stuck to **what he believed.**
   - Listen to **what she says.**
   - She objected to **what you said.**
5. As Object to a Verb:
   - I do not understand **why he behaves like this.**
6. As Complement to a Verb:
   - His fear is **that he will be asked about the murder.**
   - It seems **that he would catch the train.**
7. Case in Apposition to a Noun or a Pronoun:
   - The fact **that he is honest is known to all.**
   - The reason **why he failed in the examination is not far to seek.**

MULTIPLE CHOICE QUESTIONS

Directions (Q.No. 1-5): *Rewrite each of the following sentences, replacing the adjectives in italics with adjective phrases of the same meaning:*

1. It was a *spacious* room.
A. It was a room of much space.
B. It was a room of long length.
C. It was a room of more width.
D. It was a room of great height.

2. They spent a *sleepless* night.
A. They spent a night with less sleep.
B. They spent a night without much sleep.
C. They spent a night without sleep.
D. They spent a night unsleep.

3. She is a *professional* singer.
A. She is a singer professional.
B. She follows/has the profession of singing.

C. She is a professor of singing.
D. She is a professional of singing.

4. That was a *cowardly* act.
A. That was a coward act.
B. That was a cowardice act.
C. That was an act of coward.
D. That was an act of cowardice.

5. That was a *courageous* act.
A. That was a courage action.
B. That was an act of courage.
C. That was an action of courage.
D. That was an encouraging act.

Directions (Q.No. 6-10): *Rewrite each of the following sentences, replacing the adjective phrases in italics with adjectives of the same meaning:*

6. He is a man *with a bad temper.*
A. He is a bad-tempered man.
B. He is a low-tempered man.
C. He is a high-tempered man.
D. He is a sharp-tempered man.

7. An elephant *with a white skin* is considered sacred by some people.
A. An elephant with a fair skin is considered sacred by some people.
B. An elephant with a fair complexion is considered sacred by some people.
C. A white elephant is considered sacred by some people.
D. A sacred elephant is considered white by some people.

8. His diary contained many pages *with no writing on them.*
A. His diary contained many white pages.
B. His diary contained many unwritten pages.
C. His diary contained many dry pages.
D. His diary contained many wet pages.

9. Everyone will admit that you are a man *of sense.*
A. Everyone will admit that you are a sense man.
B. Everyone will admit that you are a sensuous man.
C. Everyone will admit that you are a man-sensible.
D. Everyone will admit that you are a sensible man.

10. Gandhiji was a leader of *great fame.*
A. Gandhiji was a great famous leader.
B. Gandhiji was a famous leader.
C. Gandhiji was a famous great leader.
D. Gandhiji was a great leader of fame.

Directions (Q.No. 11-15): *Rewrite each of the following sentences, replacing the adverb in italics with an adverb phrase of the same meaning:*

11. Pitch the tent just *here.*
A. Pitch the tent just there.
B. Pitch the tent just at this place.
C. Pitch the tent just anywhere.
D. Pitch the tent just now.

12. Don't talk *impudently.*
A. Don't talk in an impudent way/manner.
B. Don't talk in impudent.
C. Don't talk impudence.
D. Don't talk impudicity.

13. I answered the question *promptly.*
A. I answered the question prompt.
B. I answered the question promptness.
C. I answered the question prompitude.
D. I answered the question with promptness or in a prompt way/manner.

14. They were hurrying *homeward.*
A. They were hurrying towards the home.
B. They were hurrying forward the home.
C. They were hurrying ahead the home.
D. They were hurrying into the home.

15. He thanked me *profoundly.*
A. He thanked me profundity.
B. He thanked me profound way.
C. He thanked me with profundity or in a profound way.
D. He thanked me profoundness.

Directions (Q.No. 16-20): *Rewrite each of the following sentences, replacing the adverb phrase in italics with an adverb of the same meaning:*

16. The boy went near the tiger *without any fear.*
A. The boy went near the tiger fearlessly.
B. The boy went near the tiger fearless.
C. The boy went near the tiger fearlessness.
D. The boy went near the tiger fearsome.

17. He answered my question *with great reservation.*
A. He answered my question reserved.
B. He answered my question reservedness.
C. He answered my question reservedly.
D. He answered my question reservoir.

18. I hope he will come *at a very early date.*
A. I hope he will come earlier.
B. I hope he will come soon.
C. I hope he will come earliest.
D. I hope he will come fast.

19. You will succeed *in the long run.*
A. You will succeed soon.
B. You will succeed running long.
C. You will succeed running longer.
D. You will succeed finally.

20. The chief guest arrived *at that moment.*
A. The chief guest arrived late.
B. The chief guest arrived then.
C. The chief guest arrived earlier.
D. The chief guest arrived momentarily.

Directions (Q.No. 21-30): *Complete each of the following sentences by adding an adjective clause:*

21. Jack is the boy ....
A. who won the first prize.
B. whom won the first prize.
C. which won the first prize.
D. this won the first prize.

22. The bird .... was a parrot.
A. who was green in colour
B. which was green in colour
C. whom was green in colour
D. it was green in colour

23. The thing .... was a knife.
A. who you saw on the road
B. whom you saw on the road
C. which you saw on the road
D. it you saw on the road

24. I do not exactly know the place .... this coin.
A. where he found this coin
B. there he found the coin
C. here he found the coin
D. that he found the coin

25. I do not know the time ....
A. then he left for the bus stop.
B. now he left for the bus stop.
C. when he left for the bus stop.
D. since he left for the bus stop.

26. Do you know the reason ....
A. because he does not help you.
B. since he does not help you.
C. as he does not help you.
D. why he does not help you.

27. The man .... was an army officer.
A. whose was tall and strong
B. who was tall and strong
C. whom was tall and strong
D. which was tall and strong

28. He .... was caught by the police.
A. it was a thief
B. this was a thief
C. that was a thief
D. who was a thief

29. That object .... is actually a purse.
A. which looks like a book
B. that looks like a book
C. who looks like a book
D. what looks like a book

30. You may go to the place ....
A. what you want.
B. whom you want.
C. where you want.
D. whose you want.

Directions (Q.No. 31-40): *Complete each of the following sentences by adding a noun clause:*

31. I do not know ....
A. who broke the windowpane.
B. which broke the windowpane.
C. whom broke the windowpane.
D. why broke the windowpane.

32. I am not sure ....
A. if he will come to see you or not.
B. about he will come to see you or not.
C. whether he will come to see you or not.
D. that he will come to see you or not.

33. Saying .... he began to sing.
A. which he was a good singer
B. that he was a good singer
C. this he was a good singer
D. it he was a good singer

34. Listen to ....
A. it she says.
B. this she says.
C. which she says.
D. what she says.

35. Please allow him to say ....
A. what he wants.
B. which he wants.
C. that he wants.
D. this he wants.

36. He guessed ....
A. it he could not climb up the hill.
B. this he could not climb up the hill.
C. that he could not climb up the hill.
D. which he could not climb up the hill.

37. Knowing .... he decided to go to England.
A. that he had no relatives in India
B. it he had no relatives in India
C. this he had no relatives in India
D. which he had no relatives in India

38. I wanted to know ....
A. what she would deliver her maiden speech.
B. who she would deliver her maiden speech.
C. which she would deliver her maiden speech.
D. when she would deliver her maiden speech.

39. He asserted ....
A. it he was honest.
B. this he was honest.
C. that he was honest.
D. which he was honest.

40. I cannot say ....
A. what she looks like.
B. why she looks like.
C. when she looks like.
D. where she looks like.

Directions (Q.No. 41-50): *Complete each of the following sentences by adding an adverb clause using the conjunction given in brackets:*

41. Stay here (until) ....
A. until he come back.
B. until I come back.
C. until you come back.
D. until she come back.

42. (As soon as) .... we'll go to see a movie.
A. As soon as she've finished
B. As soon as he've finished
C. As soon as I've finished
D. As soon as mother've finished

43. My brother is reading a novel (while) ....
A. while my sister is colouring the pictures.
B. while my sister was colouring the pictures.
C. while my sister has been colouring the pictures.
D. while my sister have been colouring the pictures.

44. Do (as) ....
A. as you instruct.
B. as you were instruct.
C. as you have been instruct.
D. as you are instructed.

45. He sits (as if) ....
A. as if he were a king.
B. as if he was a king.
C. as if he is a king.
D. as if he will be a king.

46. (As soon as) .... he began to smile.
A. As soon as the boy found his lost coin
B. As soon as the boy find his lost coin
C. As soon as the boy will find his lost coin
D. As soon as the boy founded his lost coin

47. He is thinner (than) ....
A. than himself.
B. than you.
C. than hisself.
D. than yourself.

48. I can lend you a hundred rupee note (provided that) ....
A. provided that you returns it to me by the end of this month.
B. provided that you returned it to me by the end of this month.
C. provided that you will return it to me by the end of this month.
D. provided that you return it to me by the end of this month.

49. (Since) .... we should postpone our tour to India.
A. Since we can't catch the flight now,
B. Since we shouldn't catch the flight now,
C. Since we couldn't catch the flight now,
D. Since we wouldn't catch the flight now,

50. (As long as) .... you need not worry about anything.
A. As long as I were here,
B. As long as I am here,
C. As long as I was here,
D. As long as I have been here,

ANSWERS

1	**2**	**3**	**4**	**5**	**6**	**7**	**8**	**9**	**10**
A	C	B	D	B	A	C	B	D	B
11	**12**	**13**	**14**	**15**	**16**	**17**	**18**	**19**	**20**
B	A	D	A	C	A	C	B	D	B
21	**22**	**23**	**24**	**25**	**26**	**27**	**28**	**29**	**30**
A	B	C	A	C	D	B	D	A	C
31	**32**	**33**	**34**	**35**	**36**	**37**	**38**	**39**	**40**
A	C	B	D	A	C	A	D	C	A
41	**42**	**43**	**44**	**45**	**46**	**47**	**48**	**49**	**50**
B	C	A	D	A	A	B	D	A	B

★ ★ ★

8

Active and Passive Voice

A sentence in active voice focuses on the person or thing doing the action.

A sentence in passive voice focuses on the person or thing affected by the action. e.g.,

The idol was built. (Active voice)

Someone built the idol. (Passive voice)

Transformation of voice

- *Voice and Tense are closely associated with each other.*
- *Tense remains the same while transforming the voice.*

MULTIPLE CHOICE QUESTIONS

Directions (Qs. 1 to 30): *In each of the following questions, a sentence is given in Active Voice. Below it are given four alternatives suggesting the Passive Voice form of the given sentence. Choose the correct alternative.*

1. They will have helped you.
A. You will have helped by them.
B. You will have been helped by them.
C. You will be helped by them.
D. You will be helped by them.

2. Open the door.
A. Door may be opened.
B. Let the door be open.
C. Let the door be opened.
D. Door be opened.

3. I am reading a book.
A. A book is read by me.
B. A book is being read by me.
C. A book has been read by me.
D. A book is been read by me.

4. Why did your brother write such a letter?
A. Why your brother wrote such a letter?
B. Why was by brother written such a letter?
C. Why was such a letter written by your brother?
D. Why was written such a letter by your brother?

5. Did you run a great risk?
A. Was a great risk run by you?
B. Was run a great risk by you?
C. Was by you run a great risk?
D. Had you run a great risk?

6. Was he knocking at the door?
A. Was the door being knocked at by him?
B. Was the door being knocked by him?
C. Was the door knocked by him?
D. Was the door knocking at him?

7. What was Rani doing?
A. What was done by Rani?
B. What was Rani being done?
C. What was being done by Rani?
D. What was being doing Rani?

8. Why were you wasting your Time?
A. Why was your time being wasted?
B. Why was your time being wasted by you?
C. Why was your time wasted by you?
D. Why was your time wasted?

9. She has laid out a small garden.
A. A small garden has been laid by her.
B. A small garden has laid out her.
C. A small garden being laid by her.
D. A small garden has been laid out by her.

10. She had already solved all the sums.
A. All the sums had already been solved by her.
B. All the sums have already been solved by her.
C. All the sums have been solved by her.
D. All the sums are solved by her.

11. He will have posted the letter.
A. The letter has been posted by him.
B. The letter will be posted by him.
C. The letter will have been posted by him.
D. The letter is posted by him.

12. They will have sold all the books by 4 P.M.
A. All the books will be sold by 4 P.M.
B. All the books will have been sold by 4 P.M.
C. All the books were being sold by 4 P.M.
D. All the books must be sold by 4 P.M.

13. Do you speak English?
A. Is English spoken by you?
B. Does English spoken by you?
C. Is English being spoken by you?
D. Does English being spoken by you?

14. Had they seen me before?
A. Had myself been seen by them before?
B. Had me being seen by them before?
C. Had I been seen by them before?
D. Had I being seen by them before?

15. May I take this pen?
A. May this pen will be taken by me?
B. May this pen shall be taken by me?
C. May this pen should be taken by me?
D. May this pen be taken by me?

16. Can we send it by air?
A. Can this be sent by air?
B. Can it be sent by air?
C. Can it go by air?
D. Can it be send by air?

17. Who wrote this book?
A. By whom was this book written?
B. By whom is this book written?
C. By whom was this book being written?
D. By whom is this book being written?

18. What did you buy?
A. What is bought by you?
B. What is being bought by you?
C. What was bought by you?
D. What was being bought by you?

19. Whom do you want?
A. Who is wanted by you?
B. Who is being wanted by you?
C. You are wanted by whom?
D. You are being wanted by whom?

20. When will you raise this question?
A. When this question will be raised by you?
B. When will this question be raised by you?
C. When this question is being raised by you?
D. When is this question being raised by you?

21. Who did this?
A. This was done by whom?
B. By whom was this done?
C. Who has done this?
D. By whom this was done?

22. One should keep one's promises.
A. Promises should be kept.
B. One's promises should be kept by one.
C. Promises must be kept.
D. One's promises one should keep.

23. Give the order.
A. Order given.
B. Order be given.
C. Let the order be given.
D. Order may be given by you.

24. You will have to do it.
A. It will be done by you.
B. It will have to be done by you.
C. It has to be done by you.
D. It would have to be done by you.

25. Keep to the left.
A. You are ordered to keep to the left.
B. You ought to keep to the left.
C. You are advised to keep to the left.
D. You must keep to the left.

26. They will arrange a party.
A. A party will have to be arranged by them.
B. A party they will have to arrange.
C. A party will be arranged by them.
D. A party by them will be arranged.

27. Someone has picked my pocket.
A. My pocket is picked.
B. My pocket has picked.
C. My pocket has been picked.
D. My pocket was picked.

28. He kept me waiting.
A. I kept waiting for him.
B. I kept waiting by him.
C. I was waiting for him.
D. I was kept waiting by him.

29. Why do you tell a lie?
A. Why is a lie told by you?
B. Why is told a lie by you?
C. Why is told by you a lie?
D. Why has a lie been told by you?

30. I have written a letter.
A. A letter is written by me.
B. A letter has been written by me.
C. A letter was written by me.
D. A letter had been written by me.

Directions (Qs. 31 to 35): *In the following questions, a sentence has been given in Active/Passive Voice. Out of the four alternatives suggested, select the one that Best Expresses the same sentence in Passive/Active Voice.*

31. Circumstances will oblige me to go.
A. I will oblige the circumstances and go.
B. I shall be obliged to go by the circumstances.
C. Under the circumstances, I should go.
D. I shall be obliged by the circumstances to go.

32. We waste much time on trifles.
A. Much time was wasted on trifles.
B. Much time will be wasted on trifles.
C. Much time is wasted by us on trifles.
D. Much time is wasted on trifles.

33. Mohan gave the beggar an old shirt.
A. An old shirt was given to Mohan by the beggar.
B. An old shirt was given to the beggar by Mohan.
C. The beggar is given an old shirt by Mohan.
D. An old shirt is given to the beggar by Mohan.

34. They have made him a king.
A. A king has been made by him.
B. He was made a king by them.
C. They have been made king by him.
D. He has been made a king by them.

35. Who taught you English?
A. By whom English was taught to you?
B. By whom you were taught English?
C. By whom was English taught to you?
D. By whom are you taught English?

Directions (Qs. 36 to 45): *In each of the following questions, a sentence is given in Passive Voice. Below it are given four alternatives suggesting the Active Voice form of the given sentence. Choose the correct alternative.*

36. He was made a king.
A. He became a king.
B. They made him a king.
C. They had made him a king.
D. He has been made a king.

37. Good news is expected by us.
A. We are expecting good news.
B. We have been expecting good news.
C. We had expected good news.
D. We expect good news.

38. The child must be looked after.
A. The child you must look after.
B. You must look after the child.
C. You must look the child after.
D. You may look after the child.

39. What is wanted by you?
A. What you want? B. What did you want?
C. What do you want? D. What you do want?

40. Your father is known to me.
A. I am known to your father.
B. I know your father.
C. I have known your father.
D. I knew your father.

41. She may be told the story by you.
A. The story may be told by you to her.
B. You may tell the story to her.
C. You may tell her the story.
D. You may tell to her the story.

42. Duty ought to be done.
A. Let duty be done.
B. One ought to do one's duty.
C. One should do his duty.
D. Do your duty.

43. Is English spoken by you?
A. Did you speak English?
B. Do you speak English?
C. Have you spoken English?
D. Do you know how to speak English?

44. Gold coins are contained in this box.
A. This box contains gold coins.
B. This box has contained gold coins.
C. This box is containing gold coins.
D. This box has gold coins.

45. Character is revealed by manners.
A. Manners revealed character.
B. Manners reveal character.
C. Manners have revealed character.
D. Manners do reveal character.

ANSWERS

1	2	3	4	5	6	7	8	9	10
B	C	B	C	A	A	C	B	D	A
11	**12**	**13**	**14**	**15**	**16**	**17**	**18**	**19**	**20**
C	B	A	C	D	B	A	C	A	B
21	**22**	**23**	**24**	**25**	**26**	**27**	**28**	**29**	**30**
B	A	C	B	C	C	C	D	A	B
31	**32**	**33**	**34**	**35**	**36**	**37**	**38**	**39**	**40**
D	C	B	D	C	B	D	B	C	B
41	**42**	**43**	**44**	**45**					
C	B	B	A	B					

★ ★ ★

9

Direct and Indirect Narration

The words spoken by a speaker are known to be in Direct Speech.

The words spoken by somebody and expressed by someone else with some modification are known as Indirect Speech. e.g.,

(a) Rohit says to me, "You do not understand me." *(Direct Speech)*

(b) Rohit tells me that I do not understand him. *(Indirect Speech)*

MULTIPLE CHOICE QUESTIONS

Directions (Qs. 1 to 13): *Select the correct indirect speech for the following sentences:*

1. I said to him, "I shall help you."

A. I told him that I can help him.
B. I told him that I would help him.
C. I told him that I will help him.
D. I told him that I shall be helping him.

2. My Teacher said to me, "The earth revolves round the sun."

A. My teacher told me that the earth revolves round the sun.
B. My teacher told me that the earth revolve round the sun.
C. My teacher told me that the earth had been revolving round the sun.
D. My teacher told me that the earth has been revolving round the sun.

3. I said to my friend, "My father daily goes for a walk."

A. I told my friend that my father daily goes for a walk.
B. I told my friend that my father daily went for a walk.
C. I told my friend that my father has to go for a walk.
D. I told my friend that my father had gone for a walk.

4. He said to me, "May God bless you!"

A. He requested that God can bless me.
B. He prayed that God can bless me.
C. He prayed that God might bless me.
D. He prayed that God will bless me.

5. The patient said, "Thank you, doctor."

A. The patient thanked the doctor.
B. The patient requested the doctor with thanks.
C. The patient told the doctor thanks.
D. The patient suggested the doctor thanks.

6. Satish said, "No, I shall not talk to him."

A. Satish told that he should not talk to him.
B. Satish suggested that he would not have talked to him.
C. Satish exclaimed with sorrow that he would not talk with him.
D. Satish refused to talk to him.

7. The child said, "What a lovely place!"

A. The child exclaimed with sorrow that it was a lovely place.
B. The child thought that the place was lovely.
C. The child exclaimed with joy that the place was very lovely.
D. The child suggested that the place was lovely.

8. He said, "What a fool I have been!"
   A. He told himself with sorrow that he was a fool.
   B. He confessed with regret that he had been a great fool.
   C. He said himself a fool.
   D. He suggested that he could be a fool.

9. He said, "Alas! I am ruined."
   A. He told me that he had been ruined.
   B. He exclaimed with joy that he had been ruined.
   C. He exclaimed with sorrow that he was ruined.
   D. He told me that he should not be ruined.

10. The accused said, "I am not guilty."
   A. The accused exclaimed with sorrow that I am not guilty.
   B. The accused exclaimed with joy that he was not guilty.
   C. The accused stated that he was not guilty.
   D. The accused told me that he has not been guilty.

1. My teacher said, "The earth is round".
   A. My teacher said that the earth was round.
   B. My teacher says that the earth is round.
   C. My teacher said that the earth is round.
   D. My teacher ordered that the earth is round.

12. He said, "What a place it is!"
   A. He said that it was a very fine place.
   B. He said that is a very fine place.
   C. He said that the place is fine.
   D. He exclaimed with joy/surprise that it was a very fine place.

13. Ria said, "Shall I thread the needle?"
   A. Ria asked if she should thread the needle.
   B. Ria asked if she shall thread the needle.
   C. Ria ordered if she should thread the needle.
   D. Ria says that if she would thread the needle.

rections (Qs. 14 to 33): *Pick out the correct alternative at completes the incomplete sentence which is changed o indirect narration.*

14. She said to me, "I shall see you as soon as I get time."

   She told me:
   A. that she will see me as soon as she will get time.
   B. that she would see me as soon as she would get time.
   C. she would see me whenever she got time.
   D. that she would see me whenever she gets time.

15. My secretary said to me, "Your plane will leave if you do not go at once."

   My secretary told me that:
   A. her plane would leave if she did not go at that time.
   B. her plane would leave if I do not go at once.
   C. my plane would leave if I did not go at that very time.
   D. my plane will leave if I did not go at that time.

16. My mother said to me, "Don't quarrel among yourselves".

   My mother:
   A. forbade me to quarrel among ourselves.
   B. asked me not to quarrel among ourselves.
   C. asked me that not to quarrel among ourselves.
   D. asked me to quarrel not among ourselves.

17. Her father said to her mother, "Excuse the daughter."

   Her father:
   A. requested her mother to excuse the daughter.
   B. asked her mother to excuse the daughter.
   C. asked her mother to have excused the daughter.
   D. asked her mother to have been excused.

18. He said to his friend, "Wait here till father comes."

   He requested his friend:
   A. to wait here till father had come.
   B. that to wait there till his friend came.
   C. to wait there till father came.
   D. to wait here until his friend came.

19. She said to her maid, "Run and catch the thief."

   She ordered her maid:
   A. ran and catch the thief.
   B. that to run and to catch the thief.
   C. ran and caught the thief.
   D. to run and catch the thief.

20. Anita said to Sunita, "What are you doing?"

   Anita asked Sunita:
   A. what she will be doing.
   B. that what she is doing.
   C. that what she was doing.
   D. what she was doing.

21. She said to me, "Are you meeting me today?"

   She enquired of me:
   A. whether I am meeting her that day.
   B. whether I was meeting her today.
   C. whether I was meeting her that day.
   D. I was meeting her that day.

22. Nitish said to me, "When did you buy this pen?"

   Nitish asked me:
   A. when I was to buy that pen.
   B. when I would buy that pen.
   C. when I had bought that pen.
   D. when I was buying that pen.

23. She said to me, "Are you going to market?"

She enquired of me:
A. I am going to market.
B. I was going to market.
C. if I was going to market.
D. if I had been going to the market.

24. Damini said, "Why did not you change your clothes?"

Damini asked me:
A. why I had not changed my clothes.
B. why I did not change my clothes.
C. why I would not change my clothes.
D. why I have not been changing my clothes.

25. Umesh said to me, "Have you read that novel?"

Umesh asked me:
A. if he was reading that novel.
B. if he had read that novel.
C. if I had read that novel.
D. if I was reading that novel.

26. She said to me, "I shall forgive you."

She told me:
A. that she will forgive me.
B. that she was going to forgive me.
C. that she will not forgive me.
D. that she would forgive me.

27. I said to her, "It was very hot last night."

I told her:
A. that it had been very hot the previous night.
B. that it was very hot the previous night.
C. that it has been very hot the last night.
D. that it had been very hot this night.

28. She said to me, "I thank you for the help you have given."

She:
A. told me that she thanked me for the help I had given.
B. thanked me for the help I have given.
C. thanked to me for the help I have given.
D. thanked me for the help I had given.

29. Mohini said to me, "Trust in God."

Mohini advised me:
A. that I should trust in God.
B. should trust in God.
C. trusted in God.
D. to trust in God.

30. I said to him, "Let us go to school."

I told him:
A. we would go to school.
B. we shall go to school.
C. that we would go to school.
D. that we should go to school.

31. Rajni said, "May God bless you?"

Rajni:
A. exclaimed with wish that God might bless me
B. expressed a wish that God might bless me.
C. asked God to bless me.
D. shouted with joy to bless me.

32. My mother said to me, "Do not have so many friend

My mother forbade me:
A. to have so many friends.
B. not to have so many friends.
C. to have been so many friends.
D. to possess so many friends.

33. Ram said, "Pay attention to me."

Ram asked:
A. pay attention to him.
B. paid attention to him.
C. having paid attention to him.
D. to pay attention to him.

Directions (Qs. 34 to 50): *In questions below, the senten have been given in Direct/Indirect Speech. Out of the fo alternatives suggested select the one which best expres the given sentence in Indirect/Direct Speech.*

34. She said that her brother was getting married.
A. She said, "Her brother is getting married."
B. She told, "My brother is getting married."
C. She said, "My brother is getting married."
D. She said, "My brother was married."

35. "Please don't go away", she said.
A. She said to please her and not go away.
B. She told me to go away.
C. She begged me not to go away.
D. She begged that I not go away.

36. "If you don't keep quiet I shall shoot you", he s to her in a calm voice.
A. He warned her to shoot if she didn't keep qu calmly.
B. He said calmly that I shall shoot you if you do be quiet.
C. He warned her calmly that he would shoot he she didn't keep quiet.
D. Calmly he warned her that be quiet or else he w have to shoot her.

37. I told him that he was not working hard.
A. I said to him, "You are not working hard."
B. I told him, "You are not working hard."
C. I said, "You are not working hard."
D. I said to him, "He is not working hard."

38. She said that she would finish the work the next day.
A. She said, "I will finish the work the next day."
B. She said, "I will finish the work tomorrow."
C. She said, "You will finish the work tomorrow."
D. She said, "I finished the work."

39. She said to him, "Why don't you go today?"
A. She asked him why he did not go that day.
B. She said to him that why he don't go today.
C. She asked him not to go today.
D. She asked him why he did not go today.

40. "Are you alone, my son?" asked a soft voice close behind me.
A. A soft voice asked that what I was doing there alone.
B. A soft voice said to me are you alone son.
C. A soft voice from my back asked if I was alone.
D. A soft voice close behind me asked if I was alone.

41. My cousin said, "My room-mate had snored throughout the night."
A. My cousin said that her room-mate snored throughout the night.
B. My cousin told me that her room-mate snored throughout the night.
C. My cousin complained to me that her room-mate is snoring throughout the night.
D. My cousin felt that her room-mate may be snoring throughout the night.

42. He asked Rama if he needed his help then.
A. He said to Rama, "Do you need my help?"
B. He told Rama, "Tell me if you need help."
C. He asked Rama, "Do I need your help?"
D. He said to Rama, "Do you need my help now?"

43. Nita ordered her servant to bring her a cup of tea.
A. Nita told her servant, "Bring a cup of tea."
B. Nita said, "Bring me a cup of tea."
C. Nita said to her servant, "Bring me a cup of tea."
D. Nita said to her servant, "Bring her that cup of tea."

44. He exclaimed with joy that India had won the Sahara Cup.
A. He said, "India has won the Sahara Cup."
B. He said, "India won the Sahara Cup."
C. He said, "How! India will win the Sahara Cup."
D. He said, "Hurrah! India has won the Sahara Cup."

45. The boy said, "Who dare call you a thief?"
A. The boy enquired who dared call him a thief.
B. The boy asked who called him a thief.
C. The boy told that who dared call him a thief.
D. The boy wondered who dared call a thief.

ANSWERS

1	2	3	4	5	6	7	8	9	10
B	A	A	C	A	D	C	B	C	C
11	**12**	**13**	**14**	**15**	**16**	**17**	**18**	**19**	**20**
C	D	A	B	C	A	B	C	D	D
21	**22**	**23**	**24**	**25**	**26**	**27**	**28**	**29**	**30**
C	C	C	A	C	D	A	A	A	D
31	**32**	**33**	**34**	**35**	**36**	**37**	**38**	**39**	**40**
B	A	D	C	C	C	A	B	A	D
41	**42**	**43**	**44**	**45**					
A	D	C	B	A					

★ ★ ★

10

One Word Substitution

There are many single words in English language which can be perfectly used for a number of words. These words help in expressing ideas in a short and correct manner for the right occasion. Such words not only increase the vocabulary but also enable you to economise in the use of words to a great extent.

Multiple Word Expression	*Substitution*
One who always looks towards the bright side of things	*Optimist*
One who always looks towards the dark side of things	*Pessimist*
The time when one develops from a child into an adult	*Adolescence*
The process of growing more plants in order to form a forest	*Afforestation*
The science which deals with farming	*Agriculture*
From some other country or place etc.	*Alien*
A term, etc. giving more than one meaning	*Ambiguous*
A vehicle which is used to carry sick persons	*Ambulance*
An animal which can live both in water and on land	*Amphibian*
A lawless situation when there is no government	*Anarchy*
Belonging to the history of thousands of years old	*Ancient*
Something happening once a year	*Annual*
A very old object but still valuable	*Antique*
Words of opposite meanings	*Antonyms*
Words of similar meanings	*Synonyms*
Signatures of a famous person	*Autograph*
A government led by one person with absolute authority	*Autocracy*
A written work of one's own life history	*Autobiography*
A person who has never been married	*Bachelor*
A person usually having no hair on his head	*Bald*
A place where one can deposit money and get interest	*Bank*
A person who cuts our hair	*Barber*
A building/group of buildings where soldiers live	*Barracks*
A person who makes buns and biscuits	*Baker*
A person who lives by asking people for food and money without doing any useful job	*Beggar*
The crime of having married to two persons at the same time	*Bigamy*
The branch of science which deals with the study of plants	*Botany*
Able to speak two languages	*Bilingual*
Able to speak more than two languages	*Polyglot*
The branch of science which deals with the living organisms	*Biology*
A powerful snow storm	*Blizzard*
A great successful book or movie	*Blockbuster*
A short news on the radio or TV	*Bulletin*

Multiple Word Expression	*Substitution*
A system in which the most important works are organised by the government officials	*Bureaucracy*
A person who has no vision in his eyes	*Blind*
A page or a series of pages on which the information of days, weeks, months, etc. is given	*Calendar*
A person who eats human flesh	*Cannibal*
A complete list of items often arranged alphabetically	*Catalogue*
A sudden disaster	*Catastrophe*
A period of 100 years	*Century*
A branch of science which deals with chemicals	*Chemistry*
A printed leaf usually issued by banks that we sign to carry certain financial deal	*Cheque*
A person who makes or mends shoes	*Cobbler*
A group of people who has been chosen by others to make decisions on their own	*Committee*
A building in which nuns live	*Convent*
An animal which feeds on other animals	*Carnivorous*
A person who does criticism	*Critic*
A person who cannot hear	*Deaf*
A condition in which one loses a lot of water from one's body because of vomiting, etc.	*Dehydration*
A system of government in which the people cast their votes to elect their leaders	*Democracy*
The study of skin problems	*Dermatology*
A large stretch of land covered with sand	*Desert*
The art of managing relationships between countries	*Diplomacy*
A piece of information about the words in a book form	*Dictionary*
A piece of information about the telephone numbers of the people in a book form	*Directory*
A person in charge of a newspaper, magazine etc.	*Editor*
A person who thinks he is better than others	*Egoist*
To leave your country and settle in some other country	*Emigrate*
A book or series of books giving almost all knowledge about an area or some persons, etc.	*Encyclopaedia*
Study of insects	*Entomology*
Time when day and night are of the same duration	*Equinox*
To sell things out of the country	*Export*
To purchase things from some other country	*Import*
A plant or animal no longer in existence	*Extinct*
A situation when there is a shortage of food for a long period of time	*Famine*
An amount of money that we pay for some action or services	*Fee*
Something related to women	*Feminine*
An animal strong and aggressive	*Ferocious*
A piece of land where plants grow easily from the soil that is favourable to them	*Fertile*
A work of literature having some imaginary events	*Fiction*
A large amount of water covering certain area	*Flood*
A person who sells flowers	*Florist*
A religious ceremony for burying or cremating a dead person	*Funeral*
A substance which kills fungus	*Fungicide*
A person studying or having studied the diseases and the related things of female reproductory system	*Gynaecologist*
The murder of the people of the same group, race or country	*Genocide*
A substance which kills germs	*Germicide*
A situation in which many people die because of fire during war	*Holocaust*
The act of killing a person deliberately	*Homicide*
A word having the pronunciation as the other one does but differing in meaning	*Homophone*
A word having the same spelling as the other one does but it is pronounced in some other way	*Homonym*
A person who is attracted towards the person of the same sex	*Homosexual*
Go across and parallel to the ground	*Horizontal*

Multiple Word Expression	*Substitution*
A substance which kills the insects	*Insecticide*
That cannot be corrected	*Incorrigible*
That cannot be defeated	*Invincible*
That cannot be eaten	*Inedible*
That cannot be seen	*Invisible*
A place in a school or college where books are kept for the benefit of students, teachers etc.	*Library*
A place in a school or college where scientific experiments are performed	*Laboratory*
An official who is a judge in the lowest court	*Magistrate*
A piece of music or a book before it is printed	*Manuscript*
Something related to men	*Masculine*
One who believes in the existence of God	*Theist*
One who does not believe in the existence of good	*Atheist*
That can be believed	*Credible*
That cannot be believed	*Incredible*
That which dissolves in a solvent	*Soluble*
That which does not dissolve in a solvent	*Insoluble*
Handwriting that can be read	*Legible*
Handwriting that cannot be read	*Illegible*
A person who does jobs beneficial to mankind	*Philanthropist*
A person who goes on foot	*Pedestrian*
A person who fights for his own country	*Patriot*
An act of killing oneself	*Suicide*
A woman whose husband is dead	*Widow*
A man whose wife is dead	*Widower*
A person who eats both vegetarian and non-vegetarian food	*Omnivorous*
Something which is present everywhere at the same time	*Omnipresent*
One who knows everything	*Omniscient*
A child who does not have parents	*Orphan*
An award, etc. given after the death of the recipient	*Posthumous*
The place where animals are kept for amusement and for the knowledge of the public	*Zoo*
The science which deals with the study of animals	*Zoology*

MULTIPLE CHOICE QUESTIONS

Directions: *In questions given below, out of the four alternatives, choose the one which can be substituted for the given words/sentences.*

1. Something that relates to everyone in the world
A. General B. Common
C. Usual D. Universal

2. An expression of mild disapproval
A. Warning B. Denigration
C. Impertinence D. Reproof

3. One who is not easily pleased by anything
A. Maiden B. Medieval
C. Precarious D. Fastidious

4. Murder of a king
A. Infanticide B. Matricide
C. Genocide D. Regicide

5. A remedy for all diseases
A. Stoic B. Marvel
C. Panacea D. Recompense

6. A dramatic performance
A. Mask B. Mosque
C. Masque D. Mascot

7. Study of birds
A. Orology B. Optology
C. Ophthalmology D. Ornithology

8. Ready to believe
A. Credulous B. Credible
C. Creditable D. Incredible

9. Incapable of being seen through
A. Ductile B. Opaque
C. Obsolete D. Potable

10. One who eats everything
A. Omnivorous B. Omniscient
C. Irresistible D. Insolvent

11. A place where bees are kept is called
A. An apiary B. A mole
C. A hive D. A sanctuary

12. One who cannot be corrected
A. Incurable B. Incorrigible
C. Hardened D. Invulnerable

13. One who is in charge of a museum
A. Curator B. Supervisor
C. Caretaker D. Warden

14. Continuing fight between parties, families, clans, etc.
A. Enmity B. Feud
C. Quarrel D. Skirmish

15. A voice loud enough to be heard
A. Audible B. Applaudable
C. Laudable D. Oral

16. A paper written by hand
A. Handicraft B. Manuscript
C. Handiwork D. Thesis

17. Habitually silent or talking little
A. Servile B. Unequivocal
C. Taciturn D. Synoptic

18. To slap with a flat object
A. Chop B. Hew
C. Gnaw D. Swat

19. A person who speaks many languages
A. Linguist B. Monolingual
C. Polyglot D. Bilingual

20. A light sailing-boat built specially for racing
A. Canoe B. Yacht
C. Frigate D. Dinghy

21. A fixed orbit in space in relation to earth
A. Geological B. Geo-synchronous
C. Geo-centric D. Geo-stationary

22. A style in which a writer makes a display of his knowledge
A. Pedantic B. Verbose
C. Pompous D. Ornate

23. A religious discourse
A. Preach B. Stanza
C. Sanctorum D. Sermon

24. A place that provides refuge
A. Asylum B. Sanatorium
C. Shelter D. Orphanage

25. Detailed plan of a journey
A. Travelogue B. Travelkit
C. Schedule D. Itinerary

26. A person who insists on something
A. Disciplinarian B. Stickler
C. Instantaneous D. Boaster

27. A drawing on transparent paper
A. Red print B. Blue print
C. Negative D. Transparency

28. One who believes that all things and events in life are predeter-mined is a
A. Fatalist B. Puritan
C. Egoist D. Tyrant

29. A school boy who cuts classes frequently is a
A. Defeatist B. Sycophant
C. Truant D. Martinet

30. The act of violating the sanctity of the church is
A. Blasphemy B. Heresy
C. Sacrilege D. Desecration

31. A place where monks live as a secluded community
A. Cathedral B. Diocese
C. Convent D. Monastery

32. One who is fond of fighting
A. Bellicose B. Aggressive
C. Belligerent D. Militant

33. Tending to move away from the centre or axis
A. Centrifugal B. Centripetal
C. Axiomatic D. Awry

34. Words inscribed on tomb
A. Epitome B. Epistle
C. Epilogue D. Epitaph

35. Leave or remove from a place considered dangerous
A. Evade B. Evacuate
C. Avoid D. Exterminate

36. Original inhabitants of a country
A. Aborge B. Aborger
C. Aborgory D. Aborigins

37. Government by the officials
A. Theocracy B. Plutocracy
C. Bureaucracy D. Democracy

38. Incapable of being exhausted
A. Inexhaustible B. Unexhaustible
C. Exhaustable D. Non-tired

39. A person of good understanding, knowledge and reasoning power
A. Expert B. Intellectual
C. Snob D. Literate

40. One absorbed in his own thoughts and feelings rather than in things outside
A. Scholar B. Recluse
C. Introvert D. Intellectual

41. One who is indifferent to pains and pleasure of life
A. stoic B. metaphysical
C. pessimist D. sceptic

42. List of names of persons showing duties to be performed by each in turn
A. notice B. bulletin
C. roster D. ågenda

43. Long angry speech of criticism or accusation
A. track record B. tirade
C. taut D. outburst

44. One who is in favour of never drinking alcoholic drinks
A. idealist B. uxorious
C. teetotaller D. unalcoholic

45. Trying to win favour by flattery and charm
A. smarmy B. shrewish
C. toady D. loquacious

46. A decision on which one cannot go back
A. incorrigible B. irrevocable
C. rigid D. invulnerable

47. The science that studies the varieties of human race
A. phrenology B. physiology
C. sociology D. ethnology

48. A person who hates women
A. philogynist B. philatelist
C. misogamist D. misogynist

49. A group of people in a particular grade in an organisation
A. colleague B. staff
C. echelon D. commission

50. Honourably discharged from service
A. emeritus B. latitudinarian
C. infallible D. meritorious

51. One who does not believe in the existence of God
A. atheist B. altruist
C. agnostic D. flippant

52. The large money paid for an early retirement
A. goldmine B. golden handshake
C. gratuity D. lion's share

53. A hater of learning and knowledge
A. misologist B. misogynist
C. philologist D. philanthropist

54. One who lives and acts for the welfare of others
A. misanthrope B. credulous
C. altruist D. gregarious

55. Mental weariness for want of occupation
A. desperate B. depression
C. fatigue D. ennui

56. That which makes it difficult to recognise the presen in real of somebody or something .
A. cover B. mask
C. make-up D. camouflage

57. To bear a hand in one's new business
A. partnership B. interfere
C. assist D. join

58. One who renounces the world and practices self-discipli in order to attain salvation
A. devotee B. ascetic
C. theist D. parsimonious

59. A place where gambling is practiced
A. hotel B. motel
C. casino D. stadium

60. A sad song is a
A. dirge B. elegy
C. ditty D. knell

ANSWERS

1	2	3	4	5	6	7	8	9	10
D	D	D	D	C	C	D	A	B	A
11	**12**	**13**	**14**	**15**	**16**	**17**	**18**	**19**	**20**
A	B	A	B	A	B	C	D	A	B
21	**22**	**23**	**24**	**25**	**26**	**27**	**28**	**29**	**30**
D	A	D	A	D	B	D	A	C	C
31	**32**	**33**	**34**	**35**	**36**	**37**	**38**	**39**	**40**
D	A	A	D	B	B	C	A	B	C
41	**42**	**43**	**44**	**45**	**46**	**47**	**48**	**49**	**50**
A	C	B	C	A	B	D	D	C	A
51	**52**	**53**	**54**	**55**	**56**	**57**	**58**	**59**	**60**
A	B	A	C	D	D	C	B	C	A

★ ★ ★

हिन्दी

(क) भाषिक अनुप्रयोग और व्याकरणिक कुशलताएँ

1

वर्ण विचार

वर्ण

वर्ण वह मूल ध्वनि है जिसका खण्ड नहीं किया जा सकता है। जैसे—अ, आ, क्, ख्, ग्, च्, ट् आदि।

वर्ण को लिखने के लिए जिन चिह्नों का प्रयोग किया जाता है, उसे अक्षर कहते हैं। अक्षर का अर्थ है, जिसका क्षर न हो अर्थात् जो नष्ट न हो।

वर्णमाला : वर्णों के समूह को वर्णमाला कहते हैं। अंग्रेजी में इसे ही Alphabet कहते हैं। हिन्दी वर्णमाला को दो भागों में विभक्त किया जा सकता है—(*i*) स्वर (*ii*) व्यंजन

स्वर (Vowel)

स्वर उन मूल ध्वनियों या वर्णों को कहा जाता है जिनका उच्चारण बिना किसी अवरोध के होता है। वस्तुतः इनका उच्चारण अबाध एवं स्वतंत्रतापूर्वक होता है। हिन्दी के भाषा-वैज्ञानिकों ने स्वर वर्णों की संख्या ग्यारह निर्धारित की है। स्वर निम्नलिखित हैं :—अ, आ, इ, ई, उ, ऊ, ए, ऐ, ओ, औ, ऋ।

विद्वानों का एक वर्ग 'ऋ' को अब हिन्दी वर्णमाला के अन्तर्गत नहीं रखता है। क्योंकि इसका प्रयोग मात्र तत्सम शब्दों में ही होता है। वास्तव में 'ऋ' के प्रयोग की अपनी सीमाएँ हैं।

स्वरों का वर्गीकरण : सामान्यतः स्वरों का वर्गीकरण चार आधारों पर किया जाता है—

(*i*) उच्चारण काल
(*ii*) उत्पत्ति
(*iii*) जाति
(*iv*) उच्चारण स्थान।

उच्चारण-काल का आधार : उच्चारण-काल का आधार स्वर के उच्चारण में लगे हुए समय से है। कुछ स्वर ऐसे हैं जिनके उच्चारण में कम समय लगता है और कुछ ऐसे हैं जिनके उच्चारण में अधिक। उच्चारण में लगे समय का मापन मात्रा से किया जाता है। उच्चारण के काल-मान को मात्रा कहते हैं। उच्चारण-काल के आधार पर स्वरों के दो भेद किये जाते हैं :

(क) ह्रस्व स्वर (Short Vowel)
(ख) दीर्घ स्वर (Long Vowel)

(क) **ह्रस्व स्वर** : जिनके उच्चारण में समय कम लगता है उन स्वरों को ह्रस्व स्वर कहते हैं। जैसे—अ, इ, उ, ए, ऋ।

(ख) **दीर्घ स्वर** : जिनके उच्चारण में अधिक समय लगता है, उन्हें दीर्घ स्वर कहते हैं। जैसे—आ, ई, ऊ, ऐ, औ।

उत्पत्ति का आधार : उत्पत्ति को आधार मानकर भी स्वरों का वर्गीकरण दो रूपों में किया गया है—(i) मूल स्वर (ii) संधि स्वर

(*i*) **मूल स्वर** : मूल स्वर उन स्वरों को कहते हैं जिनकी उत्पत्ति में दूसरे स्वरों की आवश्यकता नहीं होती है। जैसे—अ, इ, उ, ऋ।

(*ii*) **संधि स्वर** : संधि स्वर उन स्वरों को कहते हैं जिनकी उत्पत्ति मूल स्वरों के योग से होती है। संधि स्वर के भी दो भेद हैं—(अ) दीर्घ संधि स्वर (ब) संयुक्त संधि स्वर

(अ) **दीर्घ संधि स्वर** : किसी एक मूल स्वर में उसी मूल स्वर के योग से बने स्वर को दीर्घ संधि कहते हैं। जैसे : आ, ई, ऊ।

(ब) **संयुक्त संधि स्वर** : दो भिन्न स्वरों के मेल से निर्मित स्वर संयुक्त संधि स्वर कहे जाते हैं। जैसे—अ + इ = ए, अ + उ = ओ, आ + ए = ऐ, आ + ओ = औ। इस प्रकार—ए, ऐ, ओ, औ—संयुक्त संधि स्वर हैं।

जाति का आधार : जाति के आधार पर स्वरों को निम्नलिखित वर्गों में विभक्त किया गया है—

(*i*) सवर्ण स्वर (*ii*) असवर्ण स्वर

(*i*) **सवर्ण स्वर** : सवर्ण स्वर वे हैं जिनका उच्चारण समान स्थान तथा प्रयत्न से होता है। इन्हें सजातीय स्वर भी कहते हैं। जैसे : अ, आ, इ, ई, उ, ऊ।

(*ii*) **असवर्ण स्वर** : असवर्ण स्वर वे हैं जिनका उच्चारण अलग-अलग स्थानों तथा असमान प्रयत्नों से होता है। इसे विजातीय स्वर भी कहते हैं। जैसे : अ + इ = ए, आ + ए = ऐ, अ + उ = ओ, अ + ओ = औ।

उच्चारण-स्थान का आधार

स्वरों के उच्चारण में जिह्वा तथा ओष्ठ की विशेष भूमिका है। अतएव इनको आधार मानकर स्वरों के अनेक भेद किये गये हैं।

जिह्वा के भागों के आधार पर

स्वरों के उच्चारण में कभी जिह्वा का अग्रभाग काम करता है तो कभी पश्चभाग और कभी मध्यभाग। अतः इस दृष्टि से स्वरों के निम्नलिखित भेद हो सकते हैं:

(*i*) **अग्रस्वर :** ये वे स्वर हैं जिनके उच्चारण में जिह्वा का अग्रभाग कार्य करता है। जैसे—इ, ई, ए, ऐ।

(*ii*) **मध्य स्वर :** यह स्वर जिह्वा के मध्य भाग से उच्चरित होता है। जैसे—अ।

(*iii*) **पश्च स्वर :** पश्च स्वर वे स्वर हैं जिनका उच्चारण जिह्वा के पश्चभाग से होता है। जैसे—आ, उ, ऊ, ओ, औ।

जिह्वा की ऊँचाई के आधार पर : तालु और जिह्वा के मध्य की ऊँचाई के अनुसार स्वरों के निम्नलिखित चार भेद हैं :-

(*i*) **संवृत :** संवृत स्वरों के उच्चारण में जिह्वा तालु से नीचे सटी रहती है। जैसे—इ, ई, उ, ऊ।

(*ii*) **अर्द्ध संवृत :** अर्द्ध संवृत स्वरों के उच्चारण करते समय जिह्वा अपेक्षाकृत कम सटी रहती है। जैसे—ए, ओ।

(*iii*) **विवृत :** विवृत स्वर के उच्चारण में जिह्वा ऊपर उठी रहती है। जैसे :—आ।

(*iv*) **अर्द्ध विवृत :** अर्द्ध विवृत स्वर के उच्चारण में जिह्वा विवृत की अपेक्षा कुछ समय ऊपर जाती है। जैसे—ऐ, औ।

ओष्ठ की स्थिति के आधार पर

इसके अनुसार स्वरों के तीन भेद किये गए हैं :

(*i*) **वर्तुल :** वर्तुल स्वर वे हैं जिनके उच्चारण में ओष्ठ की स्थिति गोलाकार हो जाती है। जैसे—उ, ऊ।

(*ii*) **अर्द्ध वर्तुल :** इन स्वरों के उच्चारण में ओष्ठ वर्तुल स्वरों की अपेक्षा कुछ कम गोल होते हैं। जैसे—ओ, औ।

(*iii*) **अवर्तुल :** ऐसे स्वर जिनके उच्चारण में ओष्ठ फैले रहते हैं, अवर्तुल कहे जाते हैं। जैसे—इ, ई, ए, ऐ, अ, आ।

व्यंजन (Consonant)

व्यंजन : वे ध्वनियाँ जिनके उच्चारण में बाहर निकलती हुई वायु मुख विवर में किसी न किसी स्थान पर बाधित होती है, व्यंजन कहलाती हैं। व्यंजन ध्वनि का उच्चारण स्वतंत्र रूप से नहीं होता है। अर्थात् इनके उच्चारण में स्वर की सहायता की आवश्यकता पड़ती है। जैसे—क, च, ट, त, प, आदि। हिन्दी में व्यंजन ध्वनियों की संख्या 33 है।

व्यंजन की परिभाषा दूसरे प्रकार से भी दी जा सकती है। जिन वर्णों का उच्चारण किसी दूसरे वर्ण की सहायता से (स्वर की सहायता से) होता है या स्वरों की सहायता के बिना नहीं हो सकता—उन्हें व्यंजन वर्ण कहते हैं। 'अ' के बिना व्यंजन का उच्चारण संभव नहीं है। उदाहरण—क् + अ = क, ग् + अ = ग आदि।

व्यंजनों को निम्नलिखित वर्गों में रखा जाता है :

क वर्ग	क ख ग घ ङ
च वर्ग	च छ ज झ ञ
ट वर्ग	ट ठ ड ढ ण
त वर्ग	त थ द ध न
प वर्ग	प फ ब भ म
अन्तस्थ	य र ल व
उष्म	श ष स ह
संयुक्त व्यंजन	क्ष त्र ज्ञ
द्विगुण व्यंजन	ड़ ढ़
अनुस्वार	(ं)
विसर्ग	(:)

हिन्दी व्यंजन ध्वनियों का उच्चारण निम्नलिखित आधार पर किया जाता है—

(*i*) उच्चारण स्थान के आधार पर

(*ii*) उच्चारण प्रयत्न के आधार पर

उच्चारण स्थान के आधार पर

ध्वनि का उच्चारण मुख के जिस स्थान विशेष से होता है उसको उस ध्वनि विशेष का उच्चारण स्थान कहा जाता है। उच्चारण स्थान को दृष्टि में रखकर व्यंजन के निम्नलिखित भेद किये गये हैं :

(क) कंठ्य (ख) तालव्य (ग) मूर्धन्य (घ) दन्त्य (ङ) ओष्ठ्य (च) दन्तोष्ठ्य (छ) नासिक्य (ज) कण्ठ तालव्य (झ) कण्ठोष्ठ्य

(क) **कंठ्य :** कंठ से उच्चरित ध्वनियों को कंठ्य ध्वनियाँ कहते हैं। जैसे—क, ख, ग, घ, ङ। अ, आ, और विसर्ग भी।

(ख) **तालव्य :** तालु से उच्चारण की जाने वाली ध्वनियाँ तालव्य ध्वनियाँ कही जाती हैं। जैसे—च, छ, ज, झ, ञ, श, य। इ, ई भी।

(ग) **मूर्धन्य :** मूर्धा का स्थान कठोर तालु और कोमल तालु के मध्य है। जैसे :.ट, ठ, ड, ढ, ण।

(घ) **दन्त्य :** दन्त्य ध्वनियाँ वे हैं जिनके उच्चारण में जिह्वा ऊपर की दन्तावली का स्पर्श करती है। जैसे—त, थ, द, ध, न, ल, स।

(ङ) **ओष्ठ्य :** वे ध्वनियाँ जिनका उच्चारण दोनों ओष्ठों के सम्पर्क में आने से होता है ओष्ठ्य कहलाती हैं। जैसे—प, फ, ब, भ, म। उ, ऊ भी।

(च) **दन्तोष्ठ्य :** दन्तोष्ठ्य वे ध्वनियाँ हैं जिनका उच्चारण ऊपर की दन्तावली और अधरोष्ठ के सम्पर्क से होता है।

(छ) **नासिक्य :** जिन ध्वनियों के उच्चारण में नासिका की सहायता लेनी पड़ती है उन्हें नासिक्य या आनुनासिक ध्वनियाँ कहते हैं। जैसे—ङ, ञ, ण, न, य।

(ज) **कण्ठ तालव्य :** जिन ध्वनियों के उच्चारण में तालु और कण्ठ दोनों को सहयोग करना पड़ता है, उन्हें कण्ठ तालव्य ध्वनियाँ कहते हैं। जैसे—ए, ऐ।

(झ) **कण्ठोष्ठ्य :** वे ध्वनियाँ कण्ठोष्ठ्य हैं जिनका उच्चारण कण्ठ और ओष्ठ्य के मिले-जुले प्रयत्न से होता है। जैसे—ओ, औ।

उच्चारण प्रयत्न के आधार पर

व्यंजन ध्वनियों के उच्चारण-काल में उनमें स्पष्टता लाने के लिए जो क्रिया करनी पड़ती है उसे 'प्रयत्न' कहते हैं।

उच्चारण-प्रयत्न की दृष्टि से हिन्दी के व्यंजनों का वर्गीकरण निम्नलिखित है—

(क) **स्पर्श :** इन व्यंजनों के उच्चारण के समय वागेन्द्रिय विभिन्न उच्चारण अवयवों को संस्पर्शित करती है। वस्तुतः इनके उच्चारण-काल में वायु बाहर निकलते समय अवरुद्ध होती है। तदुन्तर वायु वेग से बाहर निकलती है और उसी समय व्यंजन ध्वनि का निर्माण करती है। इस प्रक्रिया से उत्पन्न व्यंजन को स्पर्श व्यंजन कहते हैं। क वर्ग, च वर्ग, ट वर्ग, तथा प वर्ग की व्यंजन ध्वनियाँ स्पर्श हैं।

(ख) **उष्म :** कुछ ध्वनियों के उच्चारण के समय वायु पूर्ण रूप से अवरुद्ध नहीं होती वरन् आंशिक रूप में अवरुद्ध होती है। इस समय वायु मुख-विवर से संकीर्ण मार्ग से बाहर निकलती है जिससे उसका संघर्षण होता है। इस संघर्षण की क्रिया से उत्पन्न ध्वनि को उष्म कहते हैं। श, ष, स, ह उष्म व्यंजन ध्वनियाँ हैं।

(ग) **पार्श्विक :** पार्श्विक ध्वनि के उच्चारण में जिह्वा का अगला हिस्सा मसूड़े को स्पर्श करता है और वायु जिह्वा के दाहिने तथा बायें पार्श्व से बाहर निकल जाती है। केवल 'ल' ध्वनि पार्श्विक है।

(घ) **लुण्ठित :** लुण्ठित ध्वनि वह है जिसके उच्चारण में जिह्वा का अग्रांश दन्त मूल को छूता है और छूते समय उसमें कम्पन उत्पन्न होता है। केवल 'र' लुण्ठित व्यंजन ध्वनि है।

(ङ) **उत्क्षिप्त :** इन ध्वनियों को उच्चारित करते समय जिह्वा का निचला हिस्सा कठोर तालु को ताड़ित करता है अर्थात् उसमें ठोकर मारता है और तेजी से सामान्य स्थिति में लौट आता है। ड़, ढ़ उत्क्षिप्त ध्वनियाँ हैं।

(च) **अल्पप्राण :** जिन वर्णों के उच्चारण में अल्पप्राण अर्थात् कम वायु की आवश्यकता पड़ती है, उन्हें अल्पप्राण कहते हैं। प्रत्येक वर्ण की प्रथम, तृतीय, पंचम ध्वनियाँ अल्पप्राण होती हैं। जैसे—क, ग, ङ, च, ज, ञ, ट, ड, ण, त, द, न, प, ब, म तथा य, र, ल, व अल्पप्राण हैं।

(छ) **महाप्राण :** महाप्राण ध्वनियाँ वे हैं जिनके उच्चारण में अधिक वायु की जरूरत होती है। इन ध्वनियों के उच्चारण में हकार की ध्वनि सुनाई देती पड़ती है। प्रत्येक वर्ग के द्वितीय, और चतुर्थ व्यंजन महाप्राण हैं। जैसे—ख, घ, छ, झ, ठ, ढ़, थ, ध, फ, भ, तथा श, ष, ह।

(ज) **घोष व्यंजन :** घोष व्यंजन वे हैं जिनके उच्चारण में स्वर यंत्रों में प्रकम्पन होते हैं। इन्हें नाद ध्वनियाँ भी कहते हैं। प्रत्येक वर्ग का तीसरा, चौथा और पाँचवा व्यंजन घोष या नाद वर्ण है। जैसे—ग, घ, ङ, ज, झ, ञ, द, ध, न, ब, भ, म।

(झ) **अघोष व्यंजन :** अघोष व्यंजन के उच्चरित होने में स्वर यंत्रों में कम्पन नहीं होता है। प्रत्येक वर्ग का प्रथम और द्वितीय वर्ण अघोष होता है। जैसे—क, ख, च, छ, त, थ, प, फ।

(ञ) **अन्तस्थ वर्ण :** य और व को अंतस्थ माना जाता है।

नवागत ध्वनियाँ

हिन्दी में कुछ विदेशी ध्वनियों का आगम हुआ है। ये ध्वनियाँ मूलतः अरबी-फारसी की हैं जो उर्दू के माध्यम से हिन्दी में पहुँची हैं। इन ध्वनियों को हिन्दी ने आत्मसात् कर लिया है। जैसे—क़, ख़, ग़, ज़, फ़।

अनुस्वार और विसर्ग

अनुस्वार और विसर्ग भी व्यंजन वर्ण हैं। अनुस्वार के लिए एक बिन्दु तथा विसर्ग के लिए दो बिन्दुओं का प्रयोग किया जाता है। अनुस्वार का प्रयोग स्वर/व्यंजन के ऊपर तथा विसर्ग का स्वर/व्यंजन के बाद किया जाता है। जैसे—अं, अः, पं, तः।

वर्तनी विवेक

अशुद्ध	शुद्ध	अशुद्ध	शुद्ध
आर्दश	आदर्श	अत्योक्ति	अत्युक्ति
आसीस	आशीष	अद्यपि	यद्यपि
आवश्यक्ता	आवश्यकता	तथापी	तथापि
आल्हाद	आह्लाद	असाढ़	आषाढ़
आशिर्वाद	आशीर्वाद	अध्यात्मिक	आध्यात्मिक
आमिश	आमिष	ऐतिहासज्ञ	इतिहासज्ञ
आधीन	अधीन	इतिहासिक	ऐतिहासिक
अधीनस्त	अधीनस्थ	संसारिक	सांसारिक
गृहस्त	गृहस्थ	समाजिक	सामाजिक
आरोग्यता	आरोग्य	अभीष्ठ	अभीष्ट
निरोग	नीरोग	इक्षा	इच्छा
अंधेर	अँधेरा	अस्थान	स्थान
आंख	आँख	अतिथी	अतिथि

अशुद्ध	शुद्ध	अशुद्ध	शुद्ध
अर्थात	अर्थात्	समीती	समिति
भगवान	भगवान्	इकठ्ठा	इकट्ठा
श्रीमान	श्रीमान्	इक्षुक	इच्छुक
श्रीमति	श्रीमती	स्वक्ष	स्वच्छ
अवकास	अवकाश	महत्व	महत्त्व
अर्ध	अर्द्ध	उद्येश	उद्देश्य
अहिल्या	अहल्या	उज्वल	उज्ज्वल
द्रोपती	द्रौपदी	उंगली	उँगली
द्वारिका	द्वारका	उलटा	उल्टा
इसाई	ईसाई	चिन्ह	चिह्न
ईर्षा	ईर्ष्या	एश्वर्य	ऐश्वर्य
आनाथ	अनाथ	उपलक्ष	उपलक्ष्य
असहनीय	असह्य	उलंघन	उल्लंघन

अशुद्ध	शुद्ध	अशुद्ध	शुद्ध	अशुद्ध	शुद्ध	अशुद्ध	शुद्ध
अपरान्ह	अपराह्न	उँषा	उषा	श्रृजन	सृजन	वनिक	वणिक्
पूर्वान्ह	पूर्वाह्न	अहसास	एहसास	द्वैवार्षिक	द्विवार्षिक	विधिवत	विधिवत्
मध्यान्ह	मध्याह्न	कवियित्रि	कवयित्री	द्रविभूत	द्रवीभूत	विरहणी	विरहिणी
स्वास्थ	स्वास्थ्य	कौशिल्या	कौशल्या	पृष्ट	पृष्ठ	वैमनस्यता	वैमनस्य
कार्यकर्म	कार्यक्रम	धूआं	धुआँ	पत्नि	पत्नी	विद्यार्थि	विद्यार्थी
कार्रवाही	कार्यवाही	नारायन	नारायण	निछावर	न्यौछावर	वापिस	वापस
कार्यबाई	कार्रवाई	रामायन	रामायण	निरपराधी	निरपराध	वक्तागण	वक्तृगण
केन्द्रीयकरण	केन्द्रीकरण	अर्चणा	अर्चना	भागिरथी	भागीरथी	श्राप	शाप
औद्योगीकरण	उद्योगीकरण	नबाब	नवाब	मिश्रदेश	मिस्रदेश	शुद्धीकरण	शुद्धिकरण
गूंगा	गूँगा	जबाब	जवाब	महाराजा	महाराज	शक्ती	शक्ति
कैलाश	कैलास	नुपुर	नूपुर	मृन्मय	मृण्मय	शाहस	साहस
कनिष्ट	कनिष्ठ	नैपुण्यता	नैपुण्य, निपुणता	मूर्छा	मूर्च्छा	विभूती	विभूति
कौतुहल	कौतूहल	निर्गुणी	निर्गुण	मूहुर्त	मुहूर्त्त	श्रीयुत्	श्रीयुत
कोमलांगिनी	कोमलांगी	निछावर	न्यौछावर	यथेष्ठ	यथेष्ट	श्री युक्त	श्री युत
गरदन	गर्दन	निरिह	निरीह	मुंह	मुँह	संग्रहीत	संगृहीत
गरिष्ट	गरिष्ठ	परिशिष्ठ	परिशिष्ट	महानतम	महत्तम	श्रेष्ट	श्रेष्ठ
गर्द्धव	गर्दभ	प्राप्ती	प्राप्ति	मंत्रीवर	मंत्रिवर	सदृश्य	सदृश
चर्मोत्कर्ष	चरमोत्कर्ष	पूज्यनीय	पूज्य, पूजनीय	मंत्रीमण्डल	मंत्रिमण्डल	सप्ताहिक	साप्ताहिक
चांद	चाँद	प्रमाणिक	प्रामाणिक	यशलाभ	यशोलाभ	विहंगिनी	विहंगी
चक्षूरोग	चक्षुरोग	प्रदर्शिनी	प्रदर्शनी	राजागण	राजगण	स्थायीत्व	स्थायित्व
चारदीवारी	चहारदीवारी	प्रज्ज्वलित	प्रज्वलित	लिपी	लिपि	समुद्रिक	सामुद्रिक
ज्योत्सना	ज्योत्स्ना	प्रसंशा	प्रशंसा	रूग्न	रुग्ण	स्वामी भक्ति	स्वामिभक्ति
जगत	जगत्	परिस्थिती	परिस्थिति	ललायित	लालायित	हितैशी	हितैषी
ज्येष्ट	ज्येष्ठ	पौरुषत्व	पौरुष, पुरुषत्व	रूपया	रुपया	सैना	सेना
जगबन्धु	जगद्बन्धु	पाठार	पठार	मैथली	मैथिली	सेनिक	सैनिक
तिलांजली	तिलांजलि	पक्षीगण	पक्षिगण	महान	महान्	पृथवी	पृथ्वी
तत्कालिक	तात्कालिक	बाल्मिकी	वाल्मीकि	याज्ञवल्क	याज्ञवल्य	दयालू	दयालु
तत्व	तत्त्व	ब्रम्ह	ब्रह्म	रुक्मणी	रुक्मिणी	इन्दू	इन्दु
तलाब	तालाब	बृज	ब्रज	धूली	धूलि	हिन्दु	हिन्दू
त्रिवार्षिक	त्रैवार्षिक	बृजभाषा	ब्रजभाषा	अंजली	अंजलि	गुरू	गुरु
तरुछाया	तरुच्छाया	बांस	बाँस	शशी भूषण	शशिभूषण	रितु	ऋतु
त्रितीय	तृतीय	बारात	बरात	जागरन	जागरण	व्यंग	व्यंग्य
तदोपरान्त	तदुपरान्त	बंगला	बँगला	अन्तरराष्ट्रीय	अन्तर्राष्ट्रीय	बधू	वधू
द्वन्द	द्वन्द्व	बुद्धिवान	बुद्धिमान	सन्यासी	संन्यासी	बृहस्पति	वृहस्पति
दूकान	दुकान	भष्म	भस्म	बन्दना	वन्दना	बुद्धवार	बुधवार
दाइत्व	दायित्व	भीस्म	भीष्म	परिनाम	परिणाम	तृया	त्रिया
दिवारात्रि	दिवारात्र	भाग्यमान	भाग्यवान	लक्षमण	लक्ष्मण	स्त्रीयाँ	स्त्रियाँ
धोका	धोखा	पाठान	पठान	नदीयाँ	नदियाँ	महीलाएँ	महिलाएँ
पुरष्कार	पुरस्कार	विकाश	विकास	भूगोलिक	भौगोलिक	ऐतिहासिक	ऐतिहासिक
श्रृंगार	शृंगार	व्यवहारिक	व्यावहारिक	ऐनक	ऐनक	जै	जय
श्रृष्टि	सृष्टि	बीणा	वीणा	पाठान	पठान	प्रतिक्षा	प्रतीक्षा
सूचि	सूची	बिमार	बीमार	छिपकिली	छिपकली	गीतांजली	गीतांजलि
संसारिक	सांसारिक	संपत्ती	संपत्ति	एंपायर	अंपायर	अगामी	आगामी
बजाए	बजाय	शिखिर	शिखर	महाबलि	महाबली	सूनसान	सुनसान

वस्तुनिष्ठ प्रश्नोत्तर

1. व्याकरण–
A. भाषा की लिपि निर्धारित करता है
B. भाषा को सुबोध बनाता है
C. भाषा का रूप निर्धारित करता है
D. भाषा के वर्णो का अध्ययन करता है

2. वर्ण–
A. स्वर हैं B. व्यंजन हैं
C. ध्वनियाँ हैं D. उच्चारण हैं

3. हिन्दी में कितने वर्ण हैं?
A. 56 B. 26
C. 44 D. 36

4. स्वर/स्वरों–
A. मूल ध्वनियाँ हैं
B. को किसी अन्य ध्वनि की सहायता के बिना उच्चरित किया जा सकता है
C. की संख्या 11 है
D. उपरोक्त सभी

5. जिन स्वरों के उच्चारण में 'अ' के उच्चारण के बराबर समय लगता है, उन्हें क्या कहते हैं?
A. दीर्घ स्वर B. ह्रस्व स्वर
C. प्लुत स्वर D. पूर्ण स्वर

6. क् + ष =
A. श B. क्ष
C. ष D. उपर्युक्त में से कोई नहीं

7. व्यंजन तीन प्रकार के होते हैं–(*i*) स्पर्श, (*ii*) अन्तर्स्थ और (*iii*)....
A. ऊष्म B. कन्ठ्य
C. दन्तोष्ठ D. नासिका

8. त, थ, द, ध, का उच्चारण–
A. दाँतों के साथ जिह्वा के मेल से होता है
B. कंठ और ओठों के मेल से होता है
C. केवल ओठों से होता है
D. जीभ के प्रयोग के बिना होता है

9. एक या एक से अधिक वर्णों के संयोग से बनी ध्वनियों को क्या कहते हैं?
A. स्वर B. व्यंजन
C. शब्द D. रूढ़ि

10. 'पाठशाला' शब्द किस वर्ग का है?
A. यौगिक
B. रूढ़ि
C. योगरूढ़ि
D. उपर्युक्त में से कोई नहीं

निर्देश (प्रश्न संख्या 11 से 25 तक): *इन प्रश्नों में स्वर या मात्रा की दृष्टि से शब्द को अशुद्ध रूप में लिया गया है। नीचे दिए गए चार विकल्पों में से शुद्ध रूप चुनिए।*

11. A. निलिप्त B. निर्लप्त
C. निर्लिप्त D. निर्लीप्त

12. A. इच्छादुम B. इच्छाद्रम
C. इच्छाद्रुम D. इच्छादम

13. A. द्विरूक्ति B. दिरुक्ति
C. द्विरक्ती D. द्विरुकती

14. A. विसमृति B. विसमरती
C. विस्मती D. विस्मृति

15. A. जगतापाण B. जगतप्राण
C. जगत्प्राण D. जगर्त्पाण

16. A. आर्शीवाद B. आशिर्वाद
C. आशीर्वाद D. आर्शिवाद

17. A. सास्टांग B. साष्टांग
C. सस्टांग D. शाष्टांग

18. A. परिस्थती B. परीस्थिति
C. परिस्थिति D. परिस्थिती

19. A. पृक्रति B. प्रकृती
C. प्रिकृति D. प्रकृति

20. A. वाँक्षनीय B. वाँछनीय
C. वाँछनिय D. वान्छनीय

21. A. स्वर्गिय B. स्वर्गीय
C. स्वर्गीय D. स्वर्गीअ

22. A. विस्वास B. विश्वास
C. वीश्वास D. विष्वास

23. A. प्रज्वलित B. प्रज्जलित
C. प्रज्जवलित D. प्रजलित

24. A. कौशल्या B. कोशल्या
C. कौसल्या D. कोसल्या

25. A. पूज्यनीय B. पूजनीय
C. पुजनीय D. पूजनिय

निर्देश (प्रश्न संख्या 26 से 40 तक): *नीचे दिए गए वाक्यों में गहरे काले शब्दों की वर्तनी के लिए चार-चार विकल्प दिए गए हैं। इनमें से एक विकल्प में शब्द की वर्तनी शुद्ध है। उस विकल्प को चुनिए–*

26. चारों ओर **उजज्वल** चाँदनी फैली थी
A. उज्वल B. उज्ज्वल
C. उज्जवल D. उजज्वल

27. हमें नियमों का **उलंल्घन** नहीं करना चाहिए
A. उल्लंघन B. उलंल्घन
C. उलंघन D. ऊल्लंघन

28. हम **जान्तंत्रिक** पद्धति में विश्वास करते हैं
A. जानतांत्रिक B. जनतांत्रिक
C. जनतांत्रीक D. जनतंत्रिक

29. इस पुस्तक के अन्त में दो **परिशिष्ठ** दिए गए हैं
A. परिशिष्ठ B. प्ररिशिष्ट
C. परिशिष्ट D. प्रशिष्ट

30. आपके दर्शन कर मैं स्वयं को **कृत्यकृत्य** अनुभव करता हूँ
A. कृत्यकृत B. कृत्यक्रत्य
C. कृत्कृत्य D. कृतकृत्य

31. यदि आप **विद्वेशपूर्ण** अफवाहें फैलाते हैं तो आपके साथी भी यही करने लगेंगे
A. विद्धेषपूर्ण B. विद्वेशपूर्ण
C. वीद्वेशपूर्ण D. विद्वेषपूर्ण

32. अपने **तात्कालीक** कर्त्तव्य के अतिरिक्त अन्य किसी भी बात पर विचार न कीजिए
A. तत्कालिक B. तात्कालिक
C. तातकालिक D. तात्कालीक

33. आइए पढ़-लिखकर स्वयं को **लाभान्वीत** करें
A. लाभान्वित B. लाभानिवित
C. लाभान्वीत D. लाभन्वित

34. कानपुर एक महत्वपूर्ण **व्यावसाइक** केन्द्र है
A. व्यावसायक B. व्यावसाइक
C. व्यावसाईक D. व्यावसायिक

35. प्रगति मैदान **प्रदर्शिनी** के लिए उपयुक्त स्थान है
A. पृदर्शनी B. प्रदर्शनी
C. प्रदर्शिनी D. प्रियदर्शिनी

36. अपने पूर्वजों के **पदचिन्हों** पर चलना हमारा कर्त्तव्य है
A. पादचिह्नों B. पदचिह्नों
C. पदचिह्नों D. पदचिण्हों

37. कल **साँयंकाल** का मौसम बड़ा ही सुहावना था
A. सायंकाल B. सांयकाल
C. साँयकाल D. सायमकाल

38. विक्रमी **संवत** ईसवी सन् से 57 वर्ष आगे रहता है
A. संवत् B. संबत
C. सम्वत D. समवत्

39. **युधिस्टिर** सबसे बड़े पाण्डव थे
A. युधिस्थिर B. युधिस्टिर
C. युधिष्ठिर D. युधष्ठिर

40. प्रधानमंत्री ने **मंत्रिमण्डल** के बैठक की अध्यक्षता की
A. मन्त्रिमन्डल B. मन्त्रिमण्डल
C. मन्त्रीमण्डल D. मंत्रीमण्डल

41. क्ष, त्र, ज्ञ वर्ण है :
A. संयुक्त व्यंजन B. उष्म व्यंजन
C. स्पर्श व्यंजन D. अंतःस्थ व्यंजन

42. फ, ब किस प्रकार के वर्ण हैं?
A. दंतोष्ठ्य B. मूर्धन्य
C. तालव्य D. ओष्ठ्य

43. ध्वनि किसकी लघुत्तम इकाई है?
A. शब्द B. भाषा
C. वाक्य D. अक्षर

44. बिना अवरोध के उच्चारित होने वाले वर्ण कहलाते हैं :
A. घोष B. स्पर्श
C. स्वर D. व्यंजन

45. इनमें से कौन स्पर्श व्यंजन है?
A. क–वर्ग B. च–वर्ग
C. त–वर्ग D. ये सभी

उत्तरमाला

1	2	3	4	5	6	7	8	9	10
C	C	C	D	B	B	A	A	C	A
11	**12**	**13**	**14**	**15**	**16**	**17**	**18**	**19**	**20**
C	C	A	D	C	C	B	C	D	A
21	**22**	**23**	**24**	**25**	**26**	**27**	**28**	**29**	**30**
C	B	C	A	B	B	A	B	C	D
31	**32**	**33**	**34**	**35**	**36**	**37**	**38**	**39**	**40**
D	B	A	D	B	B	A	A	C	B
41	**42**	**43**	**44**	**45**					
A	D	B	C	D					

★ ★ ★

2

शब्दभेद (स्रोत/उत्पत्ति)

शब्द

ध्वनियों के मेल से बने सार्थक वर्ण समुदाय को 'शब्द' कहते हैं। दूसरे शब्दों में—एक अक्षर या एक से अधिक अक्षरों का समूह, जिसका कुछ अर्थ होता है, शब्द कहा जाता है।

जैसे—पुष्प, पहाड़, लड़का, मैं, तुम आदि।

शब्दों का वर्गीकरण

साधारणतः शब्दों का वर्गीकरण चार आधारों पर किया जाता है। ये आधार निम्नलिखित हैं :

(1) व्युत्पत्ति के आधार पर
(2) उत्पत्ति के आधार पर
(3) अर्थ के आधार पर
(4) विकार के आधार पर

व्युत्पत्ति के आधार पर

व्युत्पत्ति के आधार पर शब्दों के तीन भेद होते हैं :-

(क) रूढ़ (ख) यौगिक (ग) योगरूढ़

(क) रूढ़ : रूढ़ वे शब्द हैं जिनका खण्ड नहीं हो सकता। यदि इन शब्दों को खण्डित कर दिया जाता है तो उनके खण्डों का कोई अर्थ नहीं होता। जैसे—नाक, कान, घर, जल, फल, शीला, सीता, राम, हल, रात आदि।

(ख) यौगिक : वे शब्द जिनका निर्माण अन्य शब्दों के या प्रत्ययों के जोड़ से होता है, यौगिक कहे जाते हैं। जैसे—पाठशाला, दहीवाली, नाकवाला, शक्तिवान, पानीवाला आदि।

(ग) योगरूढ़ : योगरूढ़ शब्द दूसरे शब्दों के योग से निर्मित होते हैं। खण्ड करने पर इनके प्रत्येक खण्ड या योग का अपना अर्थ होता है। परन्तु जब दोनों खण्डों को एक कर दिया जाता है तो उस शब्द का अपना एक विशेष अर्थ होता है। इस प्रकार, योगरूढ़ वे शब्द हैं जो दूसरे शब्दों के योग से बनते हैं और प्रत्येक योग का अपना अर्थ होता है तथापि उनका एक विशेष अर्थ होता है।

उदाहरणतः जलज में जल का अर्थ है पानी और 'ज' का अर्थ है—जन्म लेने वाला। इस प्रकार दोनों का अर्थ हुआ जल में जन्म लेने वाला। परन्तु यह शब्द जल में उत्पन्न होने वाले सेवार आदि अन्य पदार्थों के लिए व्यवहृत नहीं होता है, वरन् कमल के लिए रूढ़ हो गया है और उससे मात्र कमल का बोध होता है। इसी प्रकार जलद, कुशल, पीताम्बर, लम्बोदर आदि शब्द हैं।

उत्पत्ति के आधार पर

उत्पत्ति के अनुसार शब्दों का वर्गीकरण निम्नलिखित है : (क) तत्सम (ख) तद्‌भव (ग) देशज (घ) विदेशज

(क) तत्सम : तत्सम मूलतः संस्कृत के शब्द हैं। संस्कृत के इन शब्दों के प्रयोग हिन्दी में ज्यों-के-त्यों होते हैं। जैसेः—कवि, घृत, अग्नि, रवि, माता, भ्राता, पिता, अमृत, महान् आदि।

(ख) तद्‌भव : तद्‌भव वे शब्द हैं जिनका विकास संस्कृत के शब्दों से हुआ है। तद्‌भव का अर्थ है—'तत्' (तस्य) = उसके अर्थात् 'संस्कृत से' और 'भव' अर्थात् उत्पन्न। जैसे—घृतः = घी, अग्नि = आग, कर्म = काम, दाद्य = दही, अमृत = अमरित, कार्य = कारज, दुग्ध = दूध, जन्म = जनम, धर्म = धरम आदि।

(ग) देशज : देशज का अर्थ है—देश में उत्पन्न। हिन्दी भाषा के वे शब्द जो भारत की विभिन्न बोलियों एवं भाषाओं से आए हैं, देशज कहे जाते हैं। जैसे—कटोरी, थाली, पेट, पैर, पेड़, लोटा, डोरी आदि।

(घ) विदेशज : हिन्दी भाषा के वे शब्द जिनका आगम विदेशी भाषाओं से हुआ है, विदेशज शब्द कहे जाते हैं। जैसे—चाकू, मोटर, ट्रेन, स्टेशन, आदमी, अमीर, फालतू, किताब, तारीख़, तकिया, गवाह, देहात, जहर, बाल्टी, चेहरा, लगाम, कालीन, कैंची, बेग़म, तम्बाकू, बहादुर, प्रेस, पार्टी, स्टेशन, गजट, डायरी, रेडियो, नम्बर, नोटिस आदि।

अर्थ के आधार पर

अर्थ के अनुसार शब्दों के दो भेद हैं :

(क) सार्थक (ख) निरर्थक

(क) सार्थक : सार्थक शब्द वे हैं, जिनका कुछ अर्थ होता है। जैसे—घर, घोड़ा, कमल, कलम, पुस्तक आदि। ये सभी शब्द सार्थक हैं, क्योंकि इन शब्दों के कहने से किसी परिचित पदार्थ का बिम्ब बनता है। जैसे—पुस्तक कहने से पढ़ने के काम में आने वाली किताब का बोध होता है। इस प्रकार ऊपर सभी शब्द सार्थक हैं।

(ख) निरर्थक : निरर्थक शब्द वे हैं जिनका कुछ भी अर्थ नहीं होता है। जैसे–अल्ल, बल्ल, गर्र, फर्र, मलक, नीपा, धदू आदि।

विकार के आधार पर

विकार के अनुसार सार्थक शब्दों के दो भेद किए गए हैं : (क) विकारी (ख) अविकारी

(क) विकारी शब्द

विकारी शब्द वे शब्द हैं, जिनके रूप में विकार या परिवर्तन होता है। यह विकार लिंग, वचन और कारक में होता है। जैसे–घोड़ा।

लिंग के कारण परिवर्तन	घोड़ा से घोड़ी।
वचन के कारण परिवर्तन	घोड़ा से घोड़े, घोड़ों।
कारक के कारण परिवर्तन	घोड़ा से घोड़ों ने, घोड़े से आदि।

विकारी शब्दों के भेद

विकारी शब्दों के चार भेद हैं : (*i*) संज्ञा (*ii*) सर्वनाम (*iii*) विशेषण (*iv*) क्रिया

(*i*) **संज्ञा :** संज्ञा का अर्थ है नाम। किसी वस्तु, व्यक्ति, स्थान आदि के नाम को संज्ञा कहते हैं। जैसे–घर, पटना, कलम, बुढ़ापा आदि।

(*ii*) **सर्वनाम :** सर्वनाम उन शब्दों को कहते हैं जिनका प्रयोग संज्ञा के स्थान पर होता है। जैसे–वह, मैं, तुम, उस, आप, वे आदि।

(*iii*) **विशेषण :** संज्ञा अथवा सर्वनाम की विशेषता प्रकट करने वाले शब्द को विशेषण कहते हैं। जैसे–सुन्दर, मोटा, लाल, काला, दुबला आदि।

(*iv*) **क्रिया :** क्रिया उन शब्दों को कहते हैं जिनसे किसी काम का होना या करना प्रकट हो, जैसे–खाना, रोना, हँसना, लिखना आदि।

(ख) अविकारी शब्द

वे शब्द जिनके रूप में विकार अथवा परिवर्तन नहीं होता है, अविकारी शब्द कहलाते हैं, अर्थात लिंग, वचन और कारक की दृष्टि से कोई परिवर्तन या विकार नहीं होता है। अविकारी शब्द 'अव्यय' भी कहलाते हैं।

अविकारी शब्दों के चार भेद हैं–

(*i*) क्रिया विशेषण (*ii*) समुच्चय बोधक (*iii*) सम्बन्ध बोधक (*iv*) विस्मयादि बोधक

(*i*) **क्रिया विशेषण :** क्रिया की विशेषता प्रकट करने वाले शब्द क्रिया विशेषण कहलाते हैं। जैसे–धीरे-धीरे, जल्दी-जल्दी आदि।

(*ii*) **समुच्चय बोधक :** समुच्चय बोधक शब्द वे हैं जो दो शब्दों, वाक्यों या वाक्यांशों को परस्पर जोड़ते हैं। जैसे–परन्तु, किन्तु, तथा और आदि।

(*iii*) **सम्बन्ध बोधक :** सम्बन्ध बोधक वे अव्यय हैं जो एक शब्द का दूसरे शब्द से सम्बन्ध स्थापित करते हैं। जैसे–ऊपर, नीचे, समीप, पास, निकट आदि।

(*iv*) **विस्मयादि बोधक :** विस्मय, हर्ष, शोक, घृणा, आदि भावों व प्रकट करने के लिए जिन शब्दों का प्रयोग किया जाता है, उ विस्मयादि बोधक अव्यय कहते हैं। जैसे–हाय! छिः! अरे! आदि।

प्रमुख विदेशी शब्द

अंग्रेजी भाषा के शब्द

अफसर, अपील, अस्पताल, ऑर्डर, ऑर्डरली, इंच, इंजन, इन्जीनिय इन्सपेक्टर, एजेन्ट, एजेन्सी, कप्तान, कम्पनी, कमिश्नर, कमीशन, कै कोर्ट, क्वार्टर, क्रिकेट, केबिन, गार्ड, गजट, गवर्नर, गारंटी, जेलर, जे डॉक्टर, डायरी, डेयरी, डिप्टी, डिस्ट्रिक्ट, ट्यूशन, टीचर, पेन, पेंसि पॉकेट, नोटिस, नर्स, नम्बर, पार्टी, पार्सल, प्लेट, पाउडर, मीटिंग, मिनिस्ट मोनीटर, मेनेजमेंट, मार्केट, म्युनिस्पेलटी, पार्लियामेंट, क्वालिटी, कॉले कस्टमर, टिकट, चेन, चैलेंज, टेलीविजन, रेडियो, कम्प्यूटर, मीडि मेम्बर, ट्राफिक, ट्रेन, प्लेटफार्म, ड्रेस, ड्रामा, कार्बन, हेलिकॉप्टर, कॉर्पोरेश आदि।

अरबी भाषा के शब्द

अमीर, अजीब, अजब, अहमियत, आखिर, आदमी, अक्ल, असर, आद इनाम, इज्जत, इमारत, इलाज, ईनाम, औरत, औलाद, कसूर, कद कर्ज, किस्त, किस्मत, कसम, कीमत, कसरत, कुर्सी, किताब, खबर, खत खराब, गरीब, जवाब, तकदीर, तारीख, तकिया, तमाशा, तरक्की, दिमा दवा, दावा, दावत, दावात, दफ्तर, दुकान, दौलत, नतीजा, नशा, नक नकल, नहर, फकीर, फैसला, बहस, मुहावरा, माल, मालूम, मल्लाह, मवा मौसम, मुसाफिर, लिफाफा, लायक, वकील, शराब, हिम्मत, हैजा, कै हक, हुक्म, हाल, हवालात, हाकिम आदि।

तुर्की भाषा के शब्द

उर्दू, कालीन, कैंची, कुली, कुर्की, चेचक, चमचा, चुगली, चकमक, तमग तलाश, तोप, बहादुर, बेगम, लफंगा, लाश, सुराग, कुर्ता, खच्चर, दारोग बारूद आदि।

पुर्तगाली भाषा के शब्द

अलकतरा, अनन्नास, आया, आलपीन, आलमारी, इंसान, इस्तिरी, कमी किरानी, कमरा, काजू, गमला, गोदाम, गोभी, चाभी, तम्बाकू, तौलिय नीलाम, पादरी, पिस्तौल, फीता, मेज, लबादा, साया आदि।

फारसी भाषा के शब्द

आराम, आमदनी, अफसोस, आतिशबाजी, आवारा, आफत, आवाज, आई उम्मीद, कबूतर, कमीना, कुश्ती, किशमिश, कमरबन्द, किनारा, खा खुद, खामोश, खरगोश, खुश, खुराक, खूब, गल्ला, गवाह, गिरफ्त गरम, गुलाब, चाबुक, चिराग, चश्मा, चर्खा, चूंकि, चेहरा, जहर, जिन्द जादू, जान, जुर्माना, जोश, तमाशा, तेज, तीर, ताक, ताजा, दीवार, देहा दुकान, दरबान, दंगल, दिल, दवा, नाव, पलंग, पैदावार, पलक, पु पारा, पेशा, बहरा, बीमार, मुफ्त, मोर्चा, मुर्गा, मरहम, याद, यार, र रात, लेकिन, शादी, शोर, सितारा, सरदार, सरकार, सूद, सौदागर आदि

तत्सम-तद्भव शब्द

तत्सम	तद्भव	तत्सम	तद्भव	तत्सम	तद्भव	तत्सम	तद्भव
आम्र	आम	अग्नि	आग	दंश	डंक	धान्य	धान
उष्ट्र	ऊँट	वत्स	बच्चा	नव्य	नया	मुक्ता	मोती
नव	नौ	मध्य	में	पौत्र	पोता	मित्र	मीत
शलाका	सलाई	गृह	घर	दूर्वा	दूब	मृत्यु	मौत
पुष्प	फूल	मयूर	मोर	दृष्टि	दीठि	रिक्त	रीता
नारिकेल	नारियल	हरिद्रा	हल्दी	धरित्री	धरती	रक्षिका	राखी
कर्पूर	कपूर	घृत	घी	स्थाल	थाली	पंक्ति	पाँत
सक्तु	सत्तू	हस्त	हाथ	प्रस्तर	पत्थर	पाद	पाँव
चतुर्दश	चौदह	क्षीर	खीर	ग्रन्थि	गाँठ	ज्येष्ठ	जेठ
घोटक	घोड़ा	दुग्ध	दूध	क्षुद्र	छोटा	यम	जम
चंचु	चोंच	मेघ	मेह	द्यूत	जुआ	त्वरित	तुरत
शत	सौ	कार्य	काज	तादृश	तैसा	स्थल	थल
क्षेत्र	खेत	कर्ण	कान	रात्रि	रात	नृत्य	नाच
हस्ति	हाथी	दन्त	दाँत	वारिद	बादल	नासिका	नाक
तिक्त	तीता	वधू	बहू	विद्युत	बिजली	पूप	पूआ
कर्म	काम	स्वर्णकार	सोनार	वंशी	बाँसुरी	ध्वनि	धुन
चत्वारि	चार	अक्षि	आँख	भद्र	भला	गर्दभ	गदहा
पर्यंक	पलंग	कच्छप	कछुआ	भ्रातृ	भाई	निर्झर	झरना
अग्रणी	अगाड़ी	उपवास	उपास	भिक्षा	भीख	दण्ड	डण्डा
अक्षर	आखर	उच्च	ऊँचा	भ्रू	भौंह	तृण	तिनका
अट्टालिका	अटारी	कोटि	करोड़	भक्त	भगत	निर्वाह	निबाह
अगणित	अनगिनत	चित्रक	चीता	वंश	बाँस	ताम्र	ताम्बा
आमसक	आँवला	चतुष्पाद	चौपाया	लवण	नोन	योद्धा	जोधा
आलस्य	आलस	चतुर्वेदी	चौबे	यज्ञोपवीत	जनेऊ	युवक	जवान
कपाट	किवाड़	चैत्र	चैत	निमंत्रण	न्योता	शर्करा	शक्कर
कुम्भकार	कुम्हार	चतुर्थ	चौथा	श्वसुर	ससुर	शून्य	सूना
चन्द्रिका	चाँदनी	क्षुर	छुरा	शृंगार	सिंगार	श्रावण	सावन
कोकिल	कोयल	छिद्र	छेद	सर्व	सब	उल्लास	हुलास
कंकण	कंगन	कुपुत्र	कपूत	हरित	हरा	सूर्य	सूरज
कुष्ठ	कोढ़	चणक	चना	शृंगाल	सियार	शिंशपा	शीशम
काक	कौआ	चर्मकार	चमार	स्रोत	सोत	भ्रमर	भौंरा
कार्तिक	कातिक	घट	घड़ा	स्वर्ण	सोना	महिषी	भैंस
आश्चर्य	अचरज	चक्रवाक	चकवा	स्वामी	साईं	श्मशान	मसान
आदित्यवार	इतवार	तीक्ष्ण	तीखा	शृंग	सींग	मत्स्य	मछली
दधि	दही	पुस्तिका	पोथी	संध्या	सांझ	मस्तक	माथा
घृणा	घिन	पाषाण	पाहन	श्वाँस	साँस	मशक	मच्छर
गृहणी	घरनी	मिष्ट	मीठा	स्वजन	साजन	शूचि	सूई
ग्राहक	गाहक	पृष्ठ	पीठ	शिक्षा	सीख	शूकर	सूअर
ग्राम	गाँव	पूर्ण	पूरा	सूत्र	सूत	सर्प	साँप
गंभीर	गहरा	प्रतिच्छाया	परछाई	शय्या	सेज	हट्ट	हाट
गर्त	गड्ढ़ा	पश्चाताप	पछतावा	हरिण	हिरन	ओष्ठ	होंठ
युक्ति	जुगत	पर्पट	पापड़	हीरक	हीरा	शाक	साग
जंघा	जाँघ	पार्श्व	पास	श्रेणी	सीढ़ी	स्वप्न	सपना

वस्तुनिष्ठ प्रश्नोत्तर

1. उत्पत्ति की दृष्टि से शब्दों के कितने भेद हैं?
A. चार B. छह
C. आठ D. दस

2. तद्भव शब्द के कितने भेद बताए गए हैं?
A. दो B. चार
C. आठ D. दस

3. हिन्दी में 'अल्ला' किस विदेशी शब्द का रूपांतर है?
A. तुर्की B. फारसी
C. अरबी D. उपर्युक्त में से कोई नहीं

4. रचना/बनावट के अनुसार शब्दों के कितने भेद हैं?
A. एक B. दो
C. तीन D. चार

5. 'पीला-पान' निम्न में से किस प्रकार का शब्द है?
A. रूढ़ B. यौगिक
C. योगरूढ़ D. इनमें से कोई नहीं

6. निम्न में से कौन-सा शब्द योगरूढ़ है?
A. लम्बोद्रर B. पंकज
C. चक्रपाणि D. इनमें से सभी

7. 'आलपीन' किस विदेशी शब्द का हिन्दी रूप है?
A. पुर्तगाली B. तुर्की
C. अंग्रेजी D. इनमें से कोई नहीं

8. निम्न में से कौन-सा शब्द असंगत है?
A. अफसोस B. आतिशबाजी
C. आमदनी D. किताब

9. निम्न में से कौन योगरूढ़ है?
A. आग-बबूला B. दूध-वाला
C. छल-छंद D. पंकज

10. निम्न में से कौन संस्कृत का तत्सम रूप नहीं है?
A. गोमल B. घोटक
C. हरिद्रा D. आग

11. निम्न शब्दों में से कौन-सा मूल शब्द है?
A. नाक B. कान
C. मुंह D. इनमें से सभी

12. 'अपील' निम्न में से किसका तत्सम रूप है?
A. पुर्तगाली B. अंग्रेजी
C. अरबी D. फारसी

13. 'अधिकरण' शब्द रूप में कौन-सा शब्द रूप असंगत है?
A. अ B. करण
C. अधि D. इनमें से सभी

14. 'लालिमा' शब्द में कौन-सा प्रत्यय है?
A. इमा B. एमा
C. ईमा D. इनमें से कोई नहीं

15. 'इत' प्रत्यय से निर्मित शब्दों में कौन असंगत है?
A. पंचाइत B. संगीत
C. गोराइत D. रंगत

16. 'आई' प्रत्यय से बने शब्दों में कौन सही है?
A. चतुराई B. भलाई
C. बुराई D. इनमें से सभी

17. 'निपटारा' शब्द में कौन-सा प्रत्यय है?
A. आरा B. अरा
C. रा D. इनमें से कोई नहीं

18. 'पौरूषेय' में कौन-सा प्रत्यय है?
A. एय B. ए
C. ऐं D. इनमें से कोई नहीं

19. 'शौकीन' शब्द रूप से मूल शब्द को अलग कर प्रत्यय बताएं?
A. ईन B. कीन
C. ई D. इनमें से कोई नहीं

20. 'बांसुरी' शब्द रूप में कौन-सा प्रत्यय है?
A. सुरी B. री
C. बाँ D. इनमें से कोई नहीं

21. 'उमस' शब्द रूप से मूल शब्द और प्रत्यय को अलग कर मूल शब्द को लिखें?
A. मस B. उम
C. स D. इनमें से सभी

22. 'जमींदार' शब्द रूप में से प्रत्यय को अलग कर प्रत्यय को लिखें?
A. दार B. र
C. मींदा D. इनमें से कोई नहीं

23. नीचे दिए गए शब्दों में से कौन तत्सम रूप है?
A. गोबर B. घोड़ा
C. शत D. खीर

24. 'तम्बाकू' निम्न में से किस विदेशी शब्द का हिन्दी रूप है?
A. अरबी B. फारसी
C. पुर्तगाली D. अंग्रेजी

25. 'चक्रपाणि' निम्न में से किस तरह का शब्द है?
A. रूढ़ B. यौगिक
C. योगरूढ़ D. इनमें से कोई नहीं

26. 'लालटेन' निम्न में से किस विदेशी शब्द का तद्भव रूप है?
A. पुर्तगाली B. अंग्रेजी
C. अरबी D. तुर्की

27. दिए गए रूढ़ शब्दों में से कौन-सा असंगत है?
A. नाक B. कान
C. पीला D. पंकज

28. 'अधि' उपसर्ग से बने शब्दों में से कौन-सा असंगत है?
A. अधिपति B. अधिकार
C. अधिपाठक D. अत्यधिक

29. 'निपटारा' शब्द में कौन-सा प्रत्यय लगा है?
A. टारा B. आरा
C. पिटारा D. इनमें से कोई नहीं

30. 'आना' प्रत्यय से निर्मित शब्द-रूपों में से कौन-सा असंगत है?
A. मिलाना B. उठाना
C. सिरहाना D. इनमें से कोई नहीं

31. 'सुहावना' शब्द-रूप में से प्रत्यय को छाटिए?
A. हावना B. आवना
C. अवना D. वना

32. 'आहट' प्रत्यय से निर्मित शब्द रूपों में से कौन-सा असंगत है?
A. गड़गड़ाहट B. गुर्राहठ
C. चिकनाहट D. कड़वाहट

33. निम्न में से कौन-सा देशज प्रत्यय का उदाहरण है?
A. आहट B. इयल
C. ओड़ा D. उपरोक्त में सभी

34. 'प्यास' शब्द-रूप में कौन-सा प्रत्यय लगा है?
A. आश B. आष
C. आस D. इनमें से सभी

35. 'न' प्रत्यय से निर्मित शब्द रूपों में से कौन-सा असंगत है?
A. चलन B. कथन
C. प्रतन D. इनमें से कोई नहीं

36. 'धुंधला' शब्द-रूप में से प्रत्यय को अलग करें?
A. ल B. अला
C. ला D. आला

37. 'लालसा' शब्द-रूप में से प्रत्यय को अलग छांटिए?
A. स B. सा
C. आसा D. लसा

38. 'पीहर' शब्द-रूप में से प्रत्यय से मूल शब्द को छांटिए?
A. पीह B. हर
C. पहर D. इनमें से कोई नहीं

39. 'मेहनताना' मूल शब्द से प्रत्यय को अलग करें?
A. आना B. मेहनत
C. ताना D. इनमें से कोई नहीं

40. निम्न में से कौन-सा शब्द यौगिक का उदाहरण नहीं है?
A. विद्यालय B. हिमालय
C. आग-बबूला D. झट

41. 'जलज' निम्न में से किस तरह का शब्द है?
A. रूढ़ B. यौगिक
C. योगरूढ़ D. उपरोक्त में से सभी

42. 'चाबी' निम्न में से किस विदेशी शब्द का हिन्दी रूप है?
A. अंग्रेजी B. पुर्तगाली
C. अरबी D. फारसी

43. 'कुली' किस विदेशी भाषा का शब्द है?
A. तुर्की B. अरबी
C. पुर्तगाली D. अंग्रेजी

44. निम्न में से कौन-सा विदेशी उपसर्ग का उदाहरण है?
A. हर B. कम
C. बद D. इनमें से सभी

45. निम्न में से किस शब्द में अंग्रेजी उपसर्ग हैं?
A. हैड ऑफिस
B. सब-इंस्पेक्टर
C. को-ऑपरेटिव
D. उपरोक्त सभी में

उत्तरमाला

1	2	3	4	5	6	7	8	9	10
A	A	C	C	B	A	A	D	D	D
11	**12**	**13**	**14**	**15**	**16**	**17**	**18**	**19**	**20**
D	B	C	A	D	D	A	A	A	B
21	**22**	**23**	**24**	**25**	**26**	**27**	**28**	**29**	**30**
B	B	C	C	C	B	D	D	B	D
31	**32**	**33**	**34**	**35**	**36**	**37**	**38**	**39**	**40**
B	B	D	C	D	C	B	B	A	D
41	**42**	**43**	**44**	**45**					
C	B	A	D	D					

★ ★ ★

3

पर्याय/विलोम

पर्यायवाची शब्द

किसी शब्द के समान अर्थ के लिए जिन शब्दों को प्रयोग में लाया जाता है उन्हें पर्यायवाची शब्द कहा जाता है। आशय यह है कि पर्याय का अभिप्राय 'बदले में आने वाला' से लिया गया है। पर्यायवाची शब्द को 'प्रतिशब्द' भी कहते हैं। हिन्दी के कुछ पर्यायवाची शब्द निम्नांकित हैं—

अग्नि — पावक, आग, दहन, हुताशन, ज्वलन, कृशानु।

अमृत — सुधा, अमिय, पीयूष, मधु, जीवनोदक।

अधम — नीच, दुष्ट, पामर, खल, दुर्जन।

अन्न — अनाज, राशि, धान्य, दाना।

नदी — सरिता, नद, पयश्विनी, आपगा, तरंगिणी।

नरक — यमपुर, यमलोक, यमालय, कृतान्तगेह।

पवित्र — निर्मल, विमल, पावन, शुद्ध, विशुद्ध।

पर्वत — नग, पहाड़, भूधर, गिरि, तुंग, अंद्रि।

पण्डित — सुधी, विद्वान, मनीषी, प्रबुद्ध, कोविद।

पेड़ — पादप, वृक्ष, तरू, विटप, द्रुय, गाछ।

पुत्र — सुत, बेटा, तनय, आत्मज, लड़का, तनुज।

पुत्री — सुता, बेटी, तनया, आत्मजा, लड़की, तनुजा।

पृथ्वी — भू, धरा, वसुधा, वसुन्धरा, अवनि, मही।

भूपति — नृप, नरेश, राजा, नरपति, भूपाल।

हवा — वायु, समीर, पवन, अनिल, समीरण।

सरस्वती — वीणापाणि, शारदा, माहश्वेता, पद्मासना, वाणी, भारती।

साँप — सर्प, अहि, नाग, विषधर, भुजंग, व्याल, पन्नग।

समुद्र — सागर, उदधि, पयोधि, नदीस, सिन्धु, रत्नाकर, जलधि।

दुःख — पीड़ा, कष्ट, व्यथा, वेदना, यातना, खेद, सन्ताप।

विष्णु — वज्रपाणि, विश्वम्भर, माधव, दामोदर, लक्ष्मीपति, गोविन्द, नारायण।

तालाब — सरोवर, सर, जलाशय, पोखर, पुष्कर, पद्माकर, ताल, तड़ाग।

बाण — तीर, शर, नाराच, विशिख, शिलीमुख।

वाटिका — बाग, उपवन, बगीचा, उद्यान, आराम।

समूह — समुदाय, वृन्द, दज, झुण्ड, मण्डली, टोली, जत्था।

फूल — पुष्प, पुहुप, प्रसून, सुमन, कुसुम, सारंग।

ब्रह्मा — विधि, स्वयंभू, चतुरानन, प्रजापति, विधाता, पितामह

भौंरा — मधुप, भ्रमर, भृंग, मधुकर, षट्पद, भँवरा।

शिव — महेश्वर, शंकर, चन्द्रशेखर, नीलकण्ठ, त्रिलोचन, शंभु पशुपति, महादेव, त्रिनेत्र।

मुनि — संन्यासी, अवधूत, साधु, सन्त, योगी, वैरागी।

यमुना — कालिन्दी, तरणि-तनुजा, सूर्य-सुता, जमुना, रवि-तनया।

बादल — मेघ, घन, घटा, अम्बुद, नीरद, पयोधर, जलधर, वारिद, जलद।

बिजली — विद्युत, क्षणदा, चपला, चंचला, दामिनी, क्षणप्रभा, तड़ित, सौदामिनी।

इच्छा — वांछा, अभिलाषा, कामना, स्पृहा, मनोरथ।

आम — रसाल, आम्र, अमृतफल, सहकार।

गाय — गौ, धेनु, सुरभि, गौरी, दोग्धी, सौरमेयी।

चन्द्रमा — चाँद, शशि, रजनीश, राकेश, राकापति, सुधाकर मयंक, चन्द्र।

दूध — गोरस, दुग्ध, पय, क्षीर।

देवता — सुर, अमर, देव, निर्जर, विवुध।

धन — अर्थ, द्रव्य, वित्त, सम्पदा, सम्पत्ति, दौलत, विभूति

पक्षी — खग, विहग, विहंग, परिन्दा, पखेरू, चिड़िया, द्विज अण्डज।

गणेश — गणपति, गजानन, विनायक, एकदंत, लम्बोदर मोदकप्रिय।

गदहा — खर, गर्दभ, रासभ, वैशाखनन्दन, धूसर, वेशर।

गंगा — भागीरथी, जाह्नवी, त्रिपथगा, मंदाकिनी, देवापमा देवनदी, सुरसरि।

कुवेर — यक्षराज, धनपति, किन्नरेश, धनराज, धनद यक्षपति।

किरण — रश्मि, अंशु, कर, मरीचि, मयूख, गो, प्रभा, अर्चि

किनारा — कूल, तट, कगार, तीर, छोर।

इन्द्र — सुरपति, देवेन्द्र, देवराज, मधवा, पुरन्दर, वासव शचीपति, बिड़ौजा।

ईश्वर — परमात्मा, प्रभु, ईश, ब्रह्मा, भगवान्, जगदीश, परमपिता।

आँख — लोचन, दृग, नेत्र, नयन, चक्षु, दृष्टि, अक्षि।

घोड़ा — अश्व, घोटक, वाजि, हय, तुरंग, सैन्धव, हरी।

आकाश — गगन, अम्बर, व्योम, नभ, आसमान, अनन्त।

राक्षस — दैत्य, दनुज, दानव, यातुधान, निशाचर, रजनीचर।

कपड़ा — वस्त्र, पट, अम्बर, वसन, चीर, परिधान।

कामदेव — मदन, मन्मथ, अनंग, पुष्पधन्वा, पंचशर।

चतुर — निपुण, दक्ष, कुशल, चालाक, होशियार, विज्ञ, नागर।

अनुपम — अनूठा, अद्वितीय, अद्भुत, अपूर्व, अनूप, विलक्षण।

अहंकार — घमण्ड, दर्प, अभिमान, दंभ।

मछली — मीन, मत्स्य, झख, शफरी, नस-जीवन।

माता — माँ, जननी, अम्बा, अम्मा।

पत्थर — पाहन, पाथर, पाषाण, अश्म, उपस, प्रस्तर।

नाव — नौका, पतंग, बेड़ा, जलयान, डोंगी, तरी, तरणी।

रात — निशा, रजनी, विभावरी, रात्रि, यामिनी, रैन, शर्वरी, राका।

पत्नी — वधू, भार्या, दारा, कलय, प्राणप्रिय, अर्द्धांगिनी।

सोना — कंचन, कनक, हेम, सुवर्ण, कसधौत, हाटक, हिरण्य।

हाथी — गज, द्विप, करी, कुंजर, द्विरद, नाग।

हाथ — कर, हस्त, पाणि।

स्त्री — महिला, नारी, कान्ता, कामिनी, वनिता, रमणी।

सूर्य — दिनकर, दिवाकर, भास्कर, मार्तण्ड, दिनेश, दिनमान, अंशुमाली, भानु, रवि।

सिंह — शेर, मृगराज, शार्दूल, मृगेन्द्र, केशरी, व्याघ्र, वनराज, पंचानन, पंचमुख।

सुन्दर — सलिल, रुचिर, चारु, मनोहर, रमणीय, कमनीय, अभिराम।

सेवक — भृत्य, नौकर, अनुचर, चाकर, किंकर, दास, परिचारक।

विपरीतार्थक शब्द

परीतार्थक शब्द वे हैं जो दिए गए किसी शब्द का विलोम या उल्टा अर्थ बताते हैं।

शब्द	विपरीतार्थक शब्द	शब्द	विपरीतार्थक शब्द
उत्तम	अधम	आभ्यंतर	बाध्य
अन्तर्मुखी	बहिर्मुखी	आस्तिक	नास्तिक
सुगम	अगम	आर्द्र	शुष्क
सुलभ	दुर्लभ	आत्मा	परमात्मा
सुबोध	दुर्बोध	आयात	निर्यात
सरस	नीरस	आसक्त	अनासक्त
अन्तर्द्वन्द्व	बहिर्द्वन्द्व	अन्धकार	प्रकाश
अल्पायु	दीर्घायु	अथ	इति
अग्रज	अनुज	अवनि	अम्बर
आगमन	प्रस्थान	अधिक	न्यून
आदि	अन्त	अज्ञ	विज्ञ
अनुलोम	प्रतिलोम	अतिवृष्टि	अनावृष्टि
अति	अल्प	अँधेरा	उजाला
अमर	मर्त्य	अनुकूल	प्रतिकूल
अमावस्या	पूर्णिमा	अनिवार्य	वैकल्पिक
अनुरक्ति	विरक्ति	अल्पमत	बहुमत
आकाश	पाताल	अनुगामी	अग्रगामी
आगामी	गत/विगत	अपव्ययी	मितव्ययी
आदर	निरादर	अपमान	सम्मान
आय	व्यय	अपना	पराया
आशा	निराशा	अनुराग	विराग

शब्द	विपरीतार्थक शब्द	शब्द	विपरीतार्थक शब्द
आविर्भाव	तिरोभाव	अपेक्षा	उपेक्षा
अन्तर्धान	तिरोधान	अल्पसंख्यक	बहुसंख्यक
आकर्षण	विकर्षण	अमृत	विष
उत्कर्ष	अपकर्ष	अरुचि	सुरुचि
उत्थान	पतन	अभिशाप	वरदान
उन्नत	अवनत	आवृत्त	अनावृत्त
उन्नति	अवनति	इहलोक	परलोक
जय	पराजय	कटु	मधु
इच्छा	अनिच्छा	कठोर	कोमल
इष्ट	अनिष्ट	कपट	निष्कपट
उपकार	अपकार	कनिष्ठ	ज्येष्ठ
उत्साह	निरुत्साह	कर्मण्य	अकर्मण्य
उर्वर	उरुसर	कीर्ति	अपकीर्ति
उऋण	ऋणी	वक्र	सरल
उग्र	शान्त	सुन्दर	कुरूप
शान्त	अशान्त	क्रय	विक्रय
उतार	चढ़ाव	खरीद	फरोख्त
उच्च	निम्न	कृत्रिम	प्राकृतिक
उदय	अस्त	कृतज्ञ	कृतघ्न
उँच	नीच	कृष्ण	शुक्ल
उद्याचल	अस्ताचल	खण्डन	मण्डन

शब्द	विपरीतार्थक शब्द	शब्द	विपरीतार्थक शब्द	शब्द	विपरीतार्थक शब्द	शब्द	विपरीतार्थक शब्द
उदार	कृपण	गणतन्त्र	राजतन्त्र	नागरिक	ग्रामीण	लिप्त	निर्लिप्त
उत्कृष्ट	निकृष्ट	गरल	सुधा	नाम	अनाम	लोभी	निर्लोभी
उत्तीर्ण	अनुत्तीर्ण	स्वर्ग	नरक	नाथ	अनाथ	लौकिक	अलौकिक
उपयुक्त	अनुपयुक्त	गुण	दोष	निरर्थक	सार्थक	विमुख	सम्मुख
उपसर्ग	प्रत्यय	गुप्त	प्रकट	निरामिष	सामिष	विधवा	सधवा
उपयोग	अनुपयोग	गुरु	लघु	निर्लज्ज	सलज्ज	विशिष्ट	साधारण
सदुपयोग	दुरूपयोग	विपन्न	सम्पन्न	नैसर्गिक	कृत्रिम	विस्तृत	संक्षिप्त
उधार	नकद	राजा	रंक	परमार्थ	स्वार्थ	विधि	निषेध
हर्ष	विषाद	अमीर	गरीब	पक्ष	विपक्ष	विवेक	अविवेक
एक	अनेक	धनी	निर्धन	पराजय	जय/विजय	वीर	कायर
एड़ी	चोटी	दुर्बल	सबल	पण्डित	मूर्ख	वृद्धि	ह्रास
एकत्र	विकीर्ण	घर	बाहर	परतन्त्र	स्वतन्त्र	व्यावहारिक	अव्यावहारिक
ग्राह्य	त्याज्य	चर	अचर	आजाद	गुलाम	आसक्ति	अनासक्ति
गृहस्थ	संन्यासी	चिरन्तन	नश्वर	पाप	पुण्य	वैतनिक	अवैतनिक
आद्य	अन्त्य	चोर/असाधु	साधु	पुरस्कार	तिरस्कार	सदाचारी	दुराचारी
आम	खास	छूत	अछूत	प्रधान	गौण	समास	व्यास
ऐश्वर्य	अनैश्वर्य	जागरण	निद्रा	सम	विषम	सदय	निर्दय
ऐतिहासिक	अनैतिहासिक	जंगम	स्थावर	सक्रिय	निष्क्रिय	समष्टि	व्यष्टि
करुण	निष्ठुर	जीवित	मृत	सगुण	निर्गुण	सम्मुख	विमुख
झूठ	सच	जंगली	पालतू	सहयोगी	प्रतियोगी	समूल	निर्मूल
मिथ्या	सत्य	प्राचीन	नवीन/अर्वाचीन	सखा/मित्र	शत्रु	सार्थक	निरर्थक
ताप	शीत	प्रत्यक्ष	परोक्ष	सशंक	निस्संक	सात्विक	तामसिक
तीव्र	मन्द	प्रवृत्ति	निवृत्ति	सापेक्ष	निरपेक्ष	साकार	निराकार
तुच्छ	महान्	प्रशंसा	निन्दा	साक्षर	निरक्षर	सुपात्र	कुपात्र
तुकान्त	अतुकान्त	प्रसिद्ध	अप्रसिद्ध	सुगन्ध	दुर्गन्ध	सुपथ	कुपथ
दक्षिण	उत्तर	प्रेम	घृणा	सुशील	दुःशील	सुमति	कुमति
पूरब	पश्चिम	पूर्णता	अपूर्णता	सुकर्म	कुकर्म	स्तुत्य	निंद्य
प्रलय	सृष्टि	पूर्ण	अपूर्ण	स्थूल	सूक्ष्म	क्षम्य	अक्षम्य
दुर्जन	सज्जन	बन्धन	मोक्ष/मुक्ति	मूर्त	अमूर्त	श्री गणेश	इति श्री
स्वच्छ	अस्वच्छ	पूर्ववर्ती	परवर्ती	सुर	असुर	श्लील	अश्लील
संश्लिष्ट	विश्लेषित	सफल	असफल/निष्फल	सुकाल	अकाल	शोषक	पोषक
स्वामी	सेवक	पुरातन	नूतन	सुदूर	सन्निकट	शासक	शासित
देशज	विदेशज	पुराना	नया	सुसंगति	कुसंगति	स्तुति	निन्दा
देव	दानव	बर्बर/असभ्य	सभ्य	सौभाग्य	दुर्भाग्य	शिक्षित	अशिक्षित
देवता	राक्षस	अन्तरंग	बहिरंग	सम्पन्न	विपन्न	श्वेत	श्याम
धर्म	अधर्म	बलवान	बलहीन	संकल्प	विकल्प	श्रव्य	दृश्य
धैर्य	अधैर्य	भद्र	अभद्र	सन्धि	विच्छेद	हास	रुदन
नश्वर	शाश्वत	भेद	अभेद	सन्तोष	असन्तोष	हित	अहित
नगर	ग्राम	लघुता	गुरुता	संघटन	विघटन	हिंसा	अहिंसा

वस्तुनिष्ठ प्रश्नोत्तर

निर्देश (प्रश्न संख्या 1 से 15 तक): *नीचे एक शब्द दिया गया है। दिए गए चार विकल्पों में से पर्यायवाची शब्द ज्ञात करना है।*

1. अनन्त
A. विष्णु B. अतिशय
C. असंख्य D. आकाश

2. आडम्बर
A. ढोंग B. तम्बू
C. दर्प D. आवाज

3. कपाल
A. अदृष्ट B. खप्पर
C. भाग्य D. माथा

4. छंद
A. आवरण B. पद
C. बंधन D. आचरण

5. ऐश्वर्य
A. बड़ाई B. विलास
C. सुख D. सम्पदा

6. खर
A. रावण B. कुंठित
C. गधा D. मूर्ख

7. पक्षी
A. नीरज B. नभ
C. विहग D. सरसिज

8. कमल
A. कुसुम B. पुष्प
C. प्रसून D. पुंडरीक

9. चतुरानन
A. ब्रह्मा B. इन्द्र
C. विष्णु D. देवता

10. जल
A. घटा B. नीर
C. दिनकर D. सुधाकर

11. अमृत
A. सुधा B. कौमुदी
C. मन्मथ D. सुधाकर

12. इच्छा
A. अमिय B. हर्ष
C. आकांक्षा D. रश्मि

13. उद्यान
A. धाम B. कुसुमाकर
C. आलय D. वाटिका

14. अन्त्य
A. समाप्त B. अन्तिम
C. नीच D. कुलीन

15. घर
A. सदन B. उपवन
C. पंचशर D. हुताशन

निर्देश (प्रश्न संख्या 16 से 25 तक): *निम्नलिखित वाक्यों में गहरे काले शब्दों के लिए पर्यायवाची जोड़ों का चयन कीजिए।*

16. **मछली** का चित्र किसने बनाया है?
A. मीन–मत्स्य B. सफरी–धात्री
C. जलनिगग्नि–मकर D. भामा–मत्स्य

17. **नारी** स्वभावतः कोमल होती है
A. त्रिया–भामिनी B. कामिनी–दामिनी
C. रमणी–कालिन्दी D. कान्ता–निशा

18. सूर्य का **प्रकाश** सम्पूर्ण धरा को आलोकित करता है
A. दिनकर–ज्योति B. छवि–प्रभाकर
C. ज्योति–दीप्ति D. प्रस्तर–अचला

19. कितना सुन्दर **घर** है?
A. शान्ति–निकेतन B. गृह–वाटिका
C. पंकज–भवन D. धाम–आलय

20. समुद्र मंथन में निकले **अमृत** के लिए देव–दानव में युद्ध शुरू हो गया
A. सुधा–मधु B. सोम–मंगल
C. रसाल–पियूष D. दृग–सुरभोग

21. **तालाब** का जल सूख गया है
A. झील–सरोवर B. तड़ाग–खड़ग
C. ताल–अवयव D. जलाशय–सरिता

22. कितना सुन्दर **पुष्प** है
A. सुमन–भ्रमर B. सुता–सुमन
C. सुमन–कुसम D. उर्पी–प्रसून

23. **आसमान** में तारे हैं
A. व्योम–गगन B. अम्बर–लोचन
C. भवन–सैन्धव D. अम्बु–अम्बर

24. सुगन्धित **पवन** बह रही है
A. समीर–अनिल B. मारुत–अनल
C. वात–शैल D. वायु–प्रवाह

25. **घोड़ा** सड़क पर अड़कर भड़क गया
A. हय–मुकुल B. तुरंग–घोटक
C. वाजि–अम्बुज D. गदह–तुरंग

निर्देश (प्रश्न संख्या 26 से 30 तक): *निम्नलिखित विकल्पों में से कौन-सा दिए गए शब्द का सही पर्यायवाची नहीं है?*

26. देवता

A. सुर B. असुर
C. अमर D. निर्जर

27. तारा

A. अम्बु B. तारक
C. नक्षत्र D. नखत

28. बेटा

A. पुत्र B. सुत
C. आत्मज D. अग्रज

29. मनुष्य

A. नर B. महीपाल
C. मनुज D. मानव

30. गणेश

A. गणपति B. गौरीसुत
C. मतंग D. गजानन

निर्देश (प्रश्न संख्या 31 से 45 तक): *नीचे दिए गए शब्दों के विलोम के लिए चार-चार विकल्प दिए गए हैं। उनमें से उचित विकल्प का चयन कीजिए।*

31. कृपण

A. अधम B. दानी
C. कृतघ्न D. कनिष्ठ

32. क्षणिक

A. शाश्वत B. संक्षेप
C. विरह D. क्षुद्र

33. स्वदेश

A. गाँव B. नगर
C. परदेश D. स्वर्ग

34. स्तुति

A. सेवक B. निवेदन
C. प्रार्थना D. निन्दा

35. सर्दी

A. गर्मी B. धूप
C. उष्ण D. शीतल

36. शान्त

A. लघु B. चंचल
C. डरपोक D. बहादुर

37. भीगा

A. सूखा B. नरम
C. उष्ण D. गरम

38. कुसुम

A. वज्र B. नारी
C. खिन्न D. ठंडा

39. तम

A. सम B. कृश
C. नम D. प्रकाश

40. नख

A. शिख B. अनित्य
C. श्याम D. निन्दा

41. भौतिक

A. पाश्चात्य B. दैविक
C. दैहिक D. आध्यात्मिक

42. अवनि

A. आकाश B. अम्बर
C. गगन D. आसमान

43. कर्कशा

A. कोमल B. निर्मल
C. विह्वल D. व्याकुल

44. अवनत

A. बढ़ना B. उत्कर्ष
C. ऊँचा D. उन्नत

45. अति

A. न्यून B. कम
C. अल्प D. नगण्य

उत्तरमाला

1	2	3	4	5	6	7	8	9	10
C	A	D	B	D	C	C	D	A	B
11	**12**	**13**	**14**	**15**	**16**	**17**	**18**	**19**	**20**
A	C	D	C	A	A	A	C	D	A
21	**22**	**23**	**24**	**25**	**26**	**27**	**28**	**29**	**30**
A	C	A	A	B	B	A	D	B	C
31	**32**	**33**	**34**	**35**	**36**	**37**	**38**	**39**	**40**
B	A	C	D	A	B	A	A	D	A
41	**42**	**43**	**44**	**45**					
D	B	A	D	C					

★ ★ ★

4

शब्द विवेक (शब्द प्रयोग में सूक्ष्म अंतर)

युग्म शब्द को श्रुतिसम भिन्नार्थक या समोच्चरित शब्द भी कहा जाता है। इस प्रकार के दो शब्दों में मामूली-सा अन्तर होता है। वह अन्तर मात्रागत या वर्णगत होता है। फलतः ऐसे शब्द सुनने में एक समान तो लगते हैं लेकिन अर्थ भिन्न-भिन्न होते हैं। हिन्दी में ऐसे शब्दों की संख्या अत्यधिक है। नीचे वैसे प्रमुख शब्द युग्मों को अर्थ सहित प्रस्तुत किया जा रहा है—

1. अंश = भाग/हिस्सा
   अंस = कन्धा
2. अपेक्षा = आवश्यकता/उम्मीद
   उपेक्षा = अवहेलना
3. अभिराम = सुन्दर
   अविराम = लगातार
4. अनल = आग
   अनिल = हवा
5. अवलम्ब = आश्रय/सहारा
   अविलम्ब = शीघ्र
6. अन्त = समाप्त/खत्म
   अन्त्य = अन्तिम
7. अभिहित = कथित
   अविहित = अनुचित
8. अम्बुज = कमल
   अम्बुद = बादल
9. अलि = भ्रमर
   अली = सखी
10. उपकार = भलाई
    अपकार = बुराई
11. अजिक = ललाट
    अलीक = झूठ
12. अभिनय = स्वांग
    अविनय = उद्‌दण्डता
13. अतल = तलहीन
    अतुल = जिसकी तुलना न हो सके
14. अकथ = जो कहा नहीं जाय
    अथक = बिना थके हुए।
15. अन्न = अनाज
    अन्य = दूसरा
16. आदि = आरम्भ/शुरू
    आदी = अभ्यस्त, अदरक
17. अभय = निर्भय
    उभय = दोनों
18. अर्जन = संग्रह
    अर्चन = पूजा
19. अमित = अत्यधिक
    अमीत = शत्रु
20. अणु = सूक्ष्म कण
    अनु = पीछे
21. अशक्त = असमर्थ
    असक्त = विरक्त
22. अब्ज = कमल
    अब्द = बादल
23. अवधि = समय
    अवधी = अवध की भाषा
24. अभ्यास = अनुशीलन
    अभ्याश = पड़ोस
25. आभरण = आभूषण
    आमरण = मरण तक
26. आकर = खान
    आकार = आकृति
27. आयत = चतुर्भुज
    आयात = बाहर से लाना
28. आर्त = दुःखी
    आर्द्र = गीला
29. आवास = वास स्थान
    आभास = झलक
30. आवृत्त = घिरा हुआ
    आवृत्ति = दुहराना
31. इत्र = सुगन्धित पदार्थ
    इतर = दूसरा
32. स्त्री = महिला
    इस्त्री = कपड़े पर कलप करना
33. अरि = दुश्मन
    अरी = स्त्री के लिए सम्बोधन

34. उद्यत = तैयार, तत्पर
उद्धत = उद्दण्ड
35. ऋतु = मौसम
ऋत = सत्य
36. कश = चाबुक
कष = कसौटी
37. कुल = वंश
कूल = किनारा
38. कलि = कलियुग
कली = अधखिला फूल
39. कपिश = मटमैला
कपीश = बन्दरों का राजा
40. कर्म = कार्य
क्रम = सिलसिला
41. कंगाल = दरिद्र
कंकाल = ठठरी (मानव की)
42. कटिबद्ध = तैयार
कटिबन्ध = कमर बन्द
43. करोड़ = सौ लाख की संख्या
क्रोड़ = गोद
44. कृत = किया हुआ
क्रीत = खरीदा हुआ
45. कृपण = कंजूस
कृपाण = कटार
46. कृषाण = किसान
कृशानु = आम
47. क्रान्ति = उलटफेर, आन्दोलन
कांति = चमक
48. कुट = किला
कूट = पहाड़ की चोटी
49. कुजन = दुर्जन
कूजन = पक्षियों का कलरव
50. केशर = सिंह की गर्दन के बाल
केसर = कुमकुम
51. कोष = खजाना
कोश = शब्द-संग्रह
कोस = दो मील दूरी
52. खाद = उर्वरक
खाद्य = खाने की सामग्री
53. खोया = भूल गया
खोआ = दूध से निर्मित खाद्य पदार्थ
54. गिरि = पर्वत
गिरी = बीज/गूदा
55. चषक = प्याला
चसक = आदत
56. चरण = पैर
चारण = भाट
57. चिर = पुराना
चीर = वस्त्र
58. चिता = शव जलाने के लिए लकड़ियों की शय्या
चीता = एक हिंसक पशु
59. गृह = घर
ग्रह = नक्षत्र
60. करण = इन्द्रियाँ, करण कारक
कर्ण = कान
61. कुच = स्तर
कूच = प्रस्थान
62. कौर = ग्रास
कोर = किनारा
63. चतुष्पद = चौपाया
चतुष्पथ = चौराहा
64. चक्रवात = बवंडर
चक्रवाक = चकवा पक्षी
65. छत्र = छाता
छात्र = विद्यार्थी
66. क्षति = हानि
क्षिति = पृथ्वी
67. जलज = कमल
जलद = बादल
68. नीरज = कमल
नीरद = बादल
69. जघन्य = गर्हित
जघन = जाँघ
70. जगत् = संसार
जगत = कुएँ का चबूतरा
71. जामन = दूध जमाने के लिए प्रयुक्त पदार्थ
जामुन = एक फल
72. जेठ = वर्ष का एक महीना
ज्येष्ठ = बड़ा (उम्र में)
73. टुक = थोड़ा
टूक = टुकड़ा
74. टोटा = घाटा
टोंटा = बन्दूक का कारतूस
75. तरणि = सूर्य
तरणी = नाव
76. दाई = धामी, नौकरानी
दायी = जवाबदेह
77. दारु = लकड़ी
दारू = शराब

78. दिवा = दिन
दीया = दीपक
79. दिन = दिवस
दीन = गरीब
80. द्विप = हाथी
द्वीप = टापू
81. दुर्ग = गढ़
दुर्गा = एक देवी
82. दमन = दबाना
दामन = आँचल
83. तक्र = मट्ठा
तर्क = बहस
84. द्रव्य = धन
द्रव = तरल पदार्थ
85. देव = देवता
दैव = भाग्य
86. नहर = कृत्रिम नदी
नाहर = सिंह
87. नग = पहाड़
नाग = सर्प
88. नगर = शहर
नागर = चतुर व्यक्ति
89. नाश = ध्वंस
नास = सुंघनी
90. नारी = स्त्री
नाड़ी = नब्ज
91. निसान = झण्डा
निशान = चिह्न, प्रतीक
92. निर्जर = देवता
निर्झर = झरना
93. निहित = छिपा हुआ
निहत = मरा हुआ
94. नियत = निश्चित
नीयत = इरादा
नियति = भाग्य
95. नमित = नत
निमित्त = कारण
96. नीर = जल
नीड़ = घोंसला
97. निर्माण = बनाना
निर्वाण = मोक्ष
98. नकल = अनुकरण
नकुल = नेवला, पाण्डवों में एक
99. निधन = मृत्यु
निर्धन = गरीब

100. नित = प्रतिदिन
नीत = लाया हुआ
101. नीम = एक पेड़
नींव = आधार
102. नेत्र = आँख
नेतृ = नेता
103. पुरुष = मर्द
परुष = कठोर
104. परिधान = वस्त्र
प्रधान = मुख्य
105. पवन = हवा
पावन = पवित्र
106. पाहन = पत्थर
पाहुन = अतिथि
107. परवाह = चिन्ता
प्रवाह = बहाव
108. प्रहर = समय
प्रहार = चोट
109. परिताप = दुःख
प्रताप = पराक्रम
110. पथ = मार्ग
पथ्य = रोगी का भोजन
111. पट्ट = तख्ता
पट = वस्त्र
112. प्रमाण = सबूत
प्रणाम = नमस्कार
113. परिणाम = फल
परिमाण = मात्रा
114. प्रणय = प्रेम
परिणय = विवाह
115. परदेश = दूसरा देश
प्रदेश = प्रान्त, राज्य
116. परीक्षा = इम्तहान
परिक्षा = कीचड़
117. प्रदीप = दीपक
प्रतीप = उल्टा
118. पानी = जल
पाणि = हाथ
119. पास = निकट
पाश = बन्धन
120. पिक = कोयल
पीक = पान का थूक
121. प्रेषित = भेजा हुआ
प्रोषित = प्रवासी
122. फन = कला
फण = साँप का फण

123. बलि = बलिदान
बली = वीर
124. बहन = भगिनी
वहन = ढोना
125. बहु = बहुत
बहू = पुत्रवधू
126. बार = दफा
वार = दिन
127. वाण = तीर
बान = आदत
128. बात = वचन
वात = हवा
129. भवन = घर
भुवन = संसार
130. भट = योद्धा
भट्ट = पण्डित
131. भाल = ललाट
भार = वजन
132. मल = गन्दगी
मल्ल = पहलवान
133. मणि = रत्न
मणी = सर्प
134. मद = अहंकार
मद्य = शराब
135. मनुज = मनुष्य
मनोज = कामदेव
136. मांस = गोश्त
मास = महीना
137. मात्र = केवल
मातृ = माता
138. मेध = यज्ञ
मेघ = बादल
139. मेदा = पेट
मैदा = बारीक आटा
140. रत = तल्लीन
रक्त = खून
141. रेचक = दस्तावर
रोचक = रुचिकर
142. लक्ष = लाख
लक्ष्य = उद्देश्य
143. लवण = नमक
लवन = खेत की फसल की कटाई
144. वस्तु = चीज
वास्तु = इमारत, भवन

145. अकुल = बिना कुल के
आकुल = व्याकुल
146. वरद = वर देने वाला
विरद = यश
147. वरण = चुनना
वरन् = बल्कि
148. वाद = विचार/सिद्धान्त
वाद्य = बाजा
149. वदन = मुख
बदन = शरीर
150. विस्मृत = भूला हुआ
विस्मित = आश्चर्य में पड़ा हुआ
151. विपिन = जंगल
विपन्न = दुःखी, निर्धन
152. वित्त = धन
वृत्त = गोलाकार
153. विष = जहर
विस = कमल का डण्ठल
बीस = उन्नीस से एक अधिक संख्या
154. सम = समान
शय = संचय
155. सहर = सबेरा
शहर = नगर
156. शव = लाश
शब = रात
157. सिता = चीनी
सीता = जानकी
158. शस्त्र = हथियार
शास्त्र = ग्रन्थ
159. सर = तालाब
शर = बाण
160. सुर = देवता
सूर = अंधा
शूर = वीर
161. सुत = बेटा
सूत = सारथी, धागा
162. सप्त = सात
शप्त = शाप ग्रस्त
163. शंकर = शिव
संकर = दोगला
164. सर्ग = काव्य का अध्याय
स्वर्ग = कल्पित लोक
165. स्वपच = स्वयंवाकी
श्वपच = चाण्डाल
166. सत्व = सार
स्वत्व = अधिकार

167.	समिति	=	सभा
	सम्मति	=	सलाह
168.	शय्या	=	बिछावन
	सज्जा	=	सजावट
169.	संग	=	साथ
	संघ	=	समिति, संगठन
170.	शाला	=	घर
	साला	=	पत्नी का भाई
171.	सबल	=	ताकतवर
	शवल	=	चितकबरा
172.	सर्व	=	सभी
	शर्व	=	शंकर
173.	सुगन्ध	=	खुशबू
	सौगन्ध	=	कसम
174.	शुक्ति	=	सीप
	सूक्ति	=	अच्छी उक्ति
175.	शीशा	=	काँच
	सीसा	=	एक धातु
176.	सती	=	पतिव्रता नारी
	शती	=	शताब्दी
177.	श्वेत	=	सफेद
	श्वेद	=	पसीना
178.	शुक	=	सुग्गा
	शूक	=	जौ
179.	शिखर	=	चोटी (पर्वत की)
	शेखर	=	सिर
180.	शक्ल	=	चेहरा
	सकल	=	सम्पूर्ण
181.	हरि	=	विष्णु
	हरी	=	हरे रंग की
182.	सुमन	=	फूल
	सुअन	=	पुत्र
183.	संदेह	=	शक
	सदेह	=	सशरीर
184.	स्व	=	अपना
	श्व	=	आने वाला दिन
185.	शुचि	=	पवित्र
	सूची	=	विषय क्रम
186.	सुधि	=	स्मरण
	सुधी	=	समझदार, विद्वान्
187.	हल	=	जोतने का यंत्र
	हल्	=	शुद्ध व्यंजन
188.	भंगि	=	लहर
	भंगी	=	मेहतर
189.	दूत	=	संवाददाता
	द्यूत	=	जुआ का खेल
190.	देश	=	राज्य
	द्वेष	=	शत्रुता
191.	तरंग	=	लहर
	तुरंग	=	घोड़ा
192.	चालक	=	ड्राइवर
	चालाक	=	चतुर
193.	लोम	=	रोवाँ
	लोभ	=	लालच
194.	बिना	=	रहित, अभाव
	वीणा	=	एक वाद्य यंत्र
195.	प्रसाद	=	कृपा
	प्रासाद	=	महल
196.	भित्ति	=	दीवार
	भीति	=	डर
197.	मूल	=	जड़
	मूल्य	=	दाम
198.	अक्ष	=	धुरी
	यक्ष	=	एक देव योनि
199.	अश्व	=	घोड़ा
	अश्म	=	पत्थर
200.	आसन	=	बैठने की वस्तु
	अशन	=	भोजन
201.	अह	=	दिन
	अहि	=	साँप
202.	अणि	=	सूई की नोक
	अनी	=	फौज
203.	दारा	=	पत्नी
	द्वार	=	दरवाजा
204.	पृथा	=	कुन्ती
	प्रथा	=	रीति
205.	श्रवण	=	कान
	स्रवन	=	बहना
206.	श्याग	=	श्री कृष्ण
	स्याम	=	एक देश
207.	वृन्द	=	समूह
	वृन्त	=	डण्ठल
208.	मित	=	थोड़ा
	मित्र	=	दोस्त
209.	दुरति	=	पाप
	दुरत	=	छिपा
210.	चार	=	चार की संख्या
	चारु	=	सुन्दर

वस्तुनिष्ठ प्रश्नोत्तर

निर्देश (प्रश्न संख्या 1 से 40 तक): *अधोलिखित प्रश्नों में दिए गए शब्द युग्मों के सही अर्थभेद का विकल्प चयन कीजिए।*

1. अंश - अंस ....
A. भाग - संख्या B. भाग - कंधा
C. कंधा - भाग D. संख्या - कंधा

2. अंत्य - अंत
A. अंतिम - समाप्त होना B. समाप्त होना - अंत्यज
C. अनंतिम - समाप्त D. समाप्त - अनंतिम

3. अनल - अनिल ....
A. जल - वायु B. वायु - जल
C. अग्नि - वायु D. वायु - धूप

4. अंगना, अँगना ....
A. लक्ष्मी - दरवाजा B. आँगन - दुवार
C. स्त्री - आँगन D. आँगन - लक्ष्मी

5. अन्न - अन्य ....
A. गेहूँ - चावल B. अनाज - दूसरा
C. धान - कोई D. धान - कण

6. आसन - असन ....
A. बैठने की वस्तु - भोजन B. गद्दी - मिठाई
C. फूल - फल D. गद्दी - कुर्सी

7. उपेक्षा - अपेक्षा ....
A. अपमान - सम्मान B. निरादर - आवश्यकता
C. आवश्यकता - अपमान D. अपमान - तिरस्कार

8. असक्त - अशक्त ....
A. बली - निर्बल B. निर्बल - आसक्त
C. विरक्त - शक्तिहीन D. योगी - बीमार

9. आगम - अगम ....
A. पुराण - समुद्र B. शास्त्र - अथाह
C. महाकाव्य - फुटकर काव्य D. वेद पुराण - अज्ञात

10. उभय - अभय ....
A. सब - निर्भीक B. निर्भीक - सब
C. दोनों - निर्भय D. सभी - साहसी

11. अकथ - अथक ....
A. अवर्णनीय - बिना थके, लगातार
B. अद्वितीय - उत्साह का भाव
C. अलौकिक - बहादुरीपूर्वक
D. इनमें से कोई नहीं

12. अरी!, अरि ....
A. हे माई, भयानक
B. किसी नारी को संबोधन - शत्रु
C. प्रिय को संबोधन - अमित्र
D. प्रिय को उलाहना - भयंकर व्यक्ति

13. यक्ष - अक्ष ....
A. यायावर - घुमंतू B. किन्नर देवजाति - धुरी
C. पार्वत्य - मौलिक D. गंधर्व - चक्कर

14. आदी - आदि ....
A. साग - पुराना B. अदरक - आरंभ, वगैरह
C. भूमिज - क्षितिज D. कोई नहीं

15. इतर - इत्र ....
A. दूसरा - तेल B. सुगंधि - रस
C. दूसरा - सुगंध D. सुगंध - खुशबू

16. ऋतु - ऋत ....
A. मौसम - सत्य B. जलवायु - जगत्
C. जलवायु - ईश्वर D. जगत - ईश्वर

17. कृती - कृति ....
A. रचयिता - पुस्तक B. निपुण - कर्मकर्ता - रचना
C. बहादुर - सुलेख D. चतुर - कहानी

18. क्रीत - कृत ....
A. बाजार - वस्तु B. वस्तु - खरीद
C. खरीदा हुआ - किया हुआ D. पाया हुआ - बेचा हुआ

19. कर्ण - कारण ....
A. श्रवण - क्रिया
B. कान - तृतीया विभक्ति करण कारक
C. शरीर का अंग - व्याकरण का अंग
D. भाषा का अंग - शरीर का अंग

20. कपिश - कपीश ....
A. कड़ुआ - जानवर
B. मलिन, मटमैला - हनुमान, सुग्रीव
C. गंदा - वीर
D. मैला - शक्तिशाली

21. कर्कट - करकट ....
A. कठोर - गंदा B. केकड़ा - कूड़ा
C. जीव - गंदगी D. जलचर - भूमिस्थ

22. कपि - कपी ....
A. बंदर - घिरनी B. जीव - रहट
C. फलभक्षी - जल प्रदायी D. कोई नहीं

23. क्षात्र - छात्र ....
A. क्षत्रिय संबंधी - विद्यार्थी
B. योद्धा - शिक्षार्थी
C. युद्ध में जाने वाला - विद्यालय जाने वाला
D. विजेता - सुशिक्षित

24. चीता - चिता ....
A. शेर - श्मशान
B. मृत्यु - चिंता
C. श्मशान - मृत्यु
D. एक जानवर - शवदाह हेतु लकड़ी का ढेर

25. चारु - चार ....
A. सुंदर - आदमी B. गिनती - खूबसूरत
C. सुंदर - चार (गिनती का) D. अलौकिक - असंख्य

26. जगत् - जगत ....
A. दुनिया - मैदान B. संसार - कुएँ का चबूतरा
C. विस्तार - संकोच D. चबूतरा - विश्व

27. टूक - टुक ....
A. लकड़ी - आवाज B. स्पष्ट - ठक, ठक
C. टुकड़ा - थोड़ा D. एक हिस्सा - आधा हिस्सा

28. तरि - तरी ....
A. नाव - तलछट, गीलापन B. नदी - तलहटी
C. किनारा - कीचड़ D. तालाब - सड़ा कीचड़

29. तर्क - तक्र ....
A. बहस - रस B. वाद विवाद - पेय
C. बहस, विवाद - मट्ठा D. बातचीत - गोरस

30. दात - दाँत ....
A. दाता - एक अंग B. दाता - एक दाँत
C. दान - मुँह के दाँत D. पुण्य - याचक

31. दाई - दायी ....
A. दासी, (पालिका) - दाता, जवाबदेह
B. नौकरानी - अधिकारी
C. सेवक - दानी
D. सहायिका - नौकरानी

32. दैव - देव ....
A. सत्कर्य - देवता B. देवता - धर्मात्मा
C. मान - सुर D. भाग्य - देवता

33. दारू - दारु ....
A. तरल - ठोस B. पेय - जलाऊ
C. शराब - लकड़ी D. मूल्यवान् - सूखा काठ

34. दीवा - दिवा ....
A. अँधेरा - उजाला B. दीपक - दिन
C. प्रकाश - अंधकार D. ज्योति - प्रकाश

35. नाई - नांई ....
A. बाल बनाने वाला - तरल, भाँति
B. व्यवसायी - समान
C. प्रजा - दाता
D. श्रमजीवी - तरह-तरह से

36. चीर - चिर ....
A. धोठी - पुरानी B. साड़ी - प्राचीन
C. पहनावा - बीता समय D. कोई ठीक नहीं

37. निर्जर - निर्झर ....
A. न जलने वाला - प्रवाह
B. देवता - झरना
C. मानव - नदी
D. नदी - सड़क

38. नंदी - नांदी ....
A. देव - वाचाल
B. देवगो - सिफारिश
C. शिव का बैल - मंगलाचरण
D. कोई ठीक नही

39. प्रसाद - प्रासाद
A. भोग, (कृपा) - महल B. पकवान - देवालय
C. देवालय - अनुकंपा D. कोई भी सही नहीं

40. परिक्षा - परीक्षा ....
A. जल - खोज B. कीचड़ - इम्तहान
C. तलछट - आविष्कार D. परिणाम - असहाय

उत्तरमाला

1	2	3	4	5	6	7	8	9	10
B	A	C	C	B	A	B	C	B	C
11	12	13	14	15	16	17	18	19	20
A	B	B	B	C	A	B	C	B	B
21	22	23	24	25	26	27	28	29	30
B	A	A	D	C	B	C	A	C	C
31	32	33	34	35	36	37	38	39	40
A	D	C	B	A	B	B	C	A	B

★★★

5

पद परिचय एवं पद भेद की पहचान

संज्ञा (Noun)

क़िसी व्यक्ति, वस्तु, स्थान, व्यापार तथा भाव आदि के नाम को संज्ञा कहते हैं। जैसे–हिमालय, गंगा, कोलकाता, वेद, आकाश, सुख, दुःख, खेती आदि। संज्ञा एक विकारी शब्द है।

संज्ञा के भेद

संज्ञा का वर्गीकरण जीवन्तता, गणना, व्युत्पत्ति, एवं अर्थ के आधार पर किया गया है। लेकिन जीवन्तता, गणना, व्युत्पत्ति का आधार मानकर किया गया वर्गीकरण विशेष महत्त्वपूर्ण नहीं है। अर्थ के आधार पर किया गया वर्गीकरण ही परम्परागत है। अधिकांशतः विद्वानों ने संज्ञा के पाँच भेद माने हैं :

(*i*) व्यक्तिवाचक संज्ञा (*ii*) जातिवाचक संज्ञा (*iii*) द्रव्यवाचक संज्ञा (*iv*) समूहवाचक संज्ञा (*v*) भाववाचक संज्ञा।

(*i*) **व्यक्तिवाचक संज्ञा :** किसी विशेष व्यक्ति या स्थान का नाम बोध कराने वाली संज्ञा को व्यक्तिवाचक संज्ञा कहते हैं। जैसे–शीला, राकेश, कानपुर, इलाहाबाद, भारत, यमुना आदि।
व्यक्तिवाचक संज्ञा के अन्तर्गत निम्नलिखित नामों का समावेश होता है :-
व्यक्तियों के नाम–रमेश, शीला, ज्ञानप्रकाश, बिहारी, कालिदास।
दिशाओं के नाम–पूर्व, पश्चिम, उत्तर, दक्षिण।
नदियों के नाम–यमुना, महानन्दा, गंगा, सिन्धु, गोमती आदि।
गाँवों के नाम–कल्याणपुर, रामपुर, लालगँज आदि।
देशों के नाम–भारत, रूस, चीन, जापान आदि।
वस्तुओं के नाम–रामायण (ग्रंथ), महाभारत (ग्रंथ), टाइटन (घड़ी), फिलिप्स (रेडियो), ओनीडा (टेलीविजन) आदि।
समुद्रों के नाम–प्रशान्त महासागर, भूमध्य सागर, हिन्द महासागर, आदि।
इसी प्रकार त्योहारों एवं उत्सवों के नाम, पुस्तकों एवं समाचार-पत्रों के नाम, चौराहों तथा सड़कों के नाम, पर्वतों के नाम, राज्यों के नाम, ग्रह तथा नक्षत्रों के नाम, भाषाओं के नाम, वस्तुओं आदि के नाम भी व्यक्तिवाचक संज्ञा में समाविष्ट होते हैं।

(*ii*) **जातिवाचक संज्ञा :** जिस संज्ञा से एक ही प्रकार की वस्तुओं या प्राणी की पूरी जाति का बोध होता है, उसे जातिवाचक संज्ञा कहते हैं। जैसे–घोड़ा, गाय, बाघ, स्त्री, लड़का, पुस्तक, सड़क, विद्यालय आदि।
जातिवाचक संज्ञा के अन्तर्गत आगत शब्दों को अधोलिखित कोटियों में बाँटा जा सकता है–
जानवरों के नाम–बैल, ऊँट, भैंस, शेर, हिरण आदि।
स्थानों के नाम–मैदान, पाठशाला, औषधालय आदि।
वस्तुओं के नाम–घड़ी, आलमारी, पंखा, किताब, आदि।
सम्बन्धियों के नाम–चाचा, मामा, मौसी, भाई आदि।
व्यवसायों एवं पदों के नाम–लोहार, कुम्हार, मोची, अध्यापक, धोबी आदि।
प्राकृतिक तत्त्वों के नाम–वर्षा, गर्मी, भूकम्प, तूफान आदि।

(*iii*) **द्रव्यवाचक संज्ञा :** द्रव्यवाचक संज्ञा से धातु या किसी द्रव्य का बोध होता है, जिसे तौला या नापा जा सकता है तथा जिससे अन्य वस्तुओं का निर्माण होता है। जैसे–सोना, चाँदी, ताँबा, लोहा, पीतल, दूध, पानी, तेजाब, तेल, पारा, घी आदि।

(*iv*) **समूहवाचक संज्ञा :** समूहवाचक संज्ञा को समुदायवाचक संज्ञा भी कहते हैं। वस्तुतः जिस संज्ञा से पदार्थ या प्राणियों के समूह का बोध होता है, उसे समूहवाचक संज्ञा कहते हैं। जैसे–सेना, सभा, कक्षा, मेला, दल, गुच्छा, कुञ्ज, भीड़ आदि।

(*v*) **भाववाचक संज्ञा :** भाववाचक संज्ञा वह संज्ञा है, जिससे किसी वस्तु या प्राणी के स्वभाव, गुण, धर्म, व्यापार एवं दशा का बोध होता है। जैसे–वीरता, चतुराई, मिठास, बुढ़ापा, बचपन, चाल, खेल, दौड़ आदि।

भाववाचक संज्ञा का निर्माण

भाववाचक संज्ञाओं का निर्माण तद्धित और कृदन्त प्रत्ययों को विभिन्न शब्द भेदों में लगाकर किया जाता है। उदाहरणार्थ–

जातिवाचक संज्ञा से

जातिवाचक संज्ञा	भाववाचक संज्ञा	जातिवाचक संज्ञा	भाववाचक संज्ञा
पशु	पशुता	स्त्री	स्त्रीत्व
मनुष्य	मनुष्यता	विद्वान्	विद्वता
पंडित	पांडित्य/पंडिताई	शत्रु	शत्रुता
लड़का	लड़कपन	बूढ़ा	बुढ़ापा
दास	दासत्व	बंधु	बंधुत्व
ग्राम	ग्रामीण	शहर	शहरी

देहात	देहाती	मित्र	मित्रता
भ्राता	भ्रातृत्व	साधु	साधुता
देह	दैहिक	माता	मातृत्व
जाति	जातीयता	घर	घरेलू
समाज	सामाजिकता	मूर्ख	मूर्खता

विशेषण से–

विशेषण	भाववाचक संज्ञा	विशेषण	भाववाचक संज्ञा
सुन्दर	सुन्दरता	कठोर	कठोरता
कुरूप	कुरूपता	मधुर	मधुरता
गर्म	गर्मी	उष्ण	उष्णता
ठंडा	ठंडक	छोटा	छुटपन/छोटापन
सर्द	सर्दी	लम्बा	लम्बाई
चौड़ा	चौड़ाई	ऊँचा	ऊँचाई
काला	कालापन	मीठा	मिठास
लाल	लाली	चतुर	चतुराई
नीला	नीलापन	बड़ा	बड़ाई/बड़प्पन
कड़वा	कड़वाहट/कड़वापन	पवित्र	पवित्रता
मैला	मैल	शीतल	शीतलता
गंदा	गंदगी	मलिन	मलिनता
लघु	लघुता	गुरु	गुरुता
खुरदरा	खुरदरापन	लचीला	लचीलापन
धूर्त	धूर्तता	ठोस	ठोसपन
ईमानदार	ईमानदारी	दक्ष	दक्षता
कर्मठ	कर्मठता	पटु	पटुता
निपुण	निपुणता	भिन्न	भिन्नता
शिष्ट	शिष्टता	एक	एकता
वीर	वीरता	नीच	नीचता
उच्च	उच्चता	क्लिष्ट	क्लिष्टता
कायर	कायरता	सभ्य	सभ्यता
नपुंसक	नपुंसकता	शांत	शांति
उज्ज्वल	उज्ज्वलता	नम्र	नम्रता
क्षुद्र	क्षुद्रता	लोभी	लोभ
लालची	लालच	क्रोधी	क्रोध
डरावना	डर	भयावह	भय
आश्चर्य जनक	आश्चर्य	संक्षिप्त	संक्षिप्तता
दीर्घ	दीर्घता		

क्रिया से–

क्रिया	भाववाचक संज्ञा	क्रिया	भाववाचक संज्ञा
चढ़ना	चढ़ाई/चढ़ाव	विकसित होना	विकास
पढ़ना	पढ़ाई	विचारना	विचार
लड़ना	लड़ाई	निकलना	निकास
उठना	उठाव	सजाना	सजावट
बहना	बहाव	लिखना	लिखावट
खींचना	खिंचाव	दौड़ना	दौड़
लूटना	लूट	सिसकना	सिसकी
घुलना	घोल	झाड़ना	झाड़
बोलना	बोल	फूँकना	फूँक
कूदना	कूद	घबराना	घबराहट
झुकना	झुकाव	बनाना	बनावट
तनना	तनाव	मिलाना	मिलावट

लिंग (Gender)

'व्याकरण' में लिंग, पुरुष एवं स्त्री जाति के लिए प्रयुक्त चिह्न को कहा जाता है। इसे परिभाषित करते हुए कहा जा सकता है–"लिंग उसे कहते हैं जिससे संज्ञा के स्त्री या पुरुष होने का बोध हो।" दूसरे शब्दों में–"जिस चिह्न से व्यक्ति या वस्तु की स्त्री या पुरुष जाति का ज्ञान हो, उसे लिंग कहते हैं।"

लिंग-भेद

हिन्दी में लिंग के दो भेद मान्य हैं–*(i)* पुल्लिंग *(ii)* स्त्रीलिंग

(i) **पुल्लिंग (Masculine Gender) :** 'पुल्लिंग' संज्ञा के उस रूप को कहा जाता है, जिससे उसके पुरुष होने का बोध होता है। जैसे–राजेश, मुकेश, प्रमोद, सूर्य, चाँद, बैल, घोड़ा इत्यादि।

(ii) **स्त्रीलिंग (Feminine Gender) :** स्त्रीलिंग से आशय संज्ञा के उस रूप से है जिससे उसके स्त्री होने का पता चले। जैसे–राधा, शीला, घोड़ी, बकरी, तितली, मैना, कोयल, मुर्गी आदि।

लिंग-निर्णय के नियम

पुल्लिंग शब्दों के पहचान के लिए नियम :

1. हिन्दी में वे तत्सम शब्द जो अकारान्त हैं, साधारणतः पुल्लिंग होते हैं।
   जैसे–ग्रंथ, हल, फल, जल, सूर्य, अध्यक्ष आदि।
   अपवाद–पुस्तक।
2. प्राणियों में मनुष्य, बड़े पशु आदि में नर पुल्लिंग होते हैं और नारी स्त्रीलिंग होती हैं।
   जैसे–आदमी, बैल, घोड़ा, बकरा, कुत्ता, गधा, हाथी आदि। क्योंकि ये सभी नर बोधक शब्द हैं।
3. कुछ प्राणियों के लिंग-निर्णय का आधार व्यवहार है। व्यवहार के आधार पर लिंग-निर्णय विशेषतः कीड़ों, छोटे पक्षियों या जिनमें नर-मादा का अन्तर कठिन है–का होता है।
   जैसे–बन्दर, तीतर, बटेर, चीता आदि पुल्लिंग हैं जबकि मछली, मैना, गौरैया, कोयल स्त्रीलिंग हैं।

4. अप्राणिवाचक संज्ञाओं का लिंग-निर्णय रूप के आधार पर होता है। पुल्लिंग शब्दों के उदाहरण के तौर पर निम्नलिखित शब्द दिये जाते हैं-
   (क) द्रव पदार्थों (liquid) के नाम–दही, पानी, शर्बत, घी, तेल, सिरका इत्यादि।
   (ख) धातुओं के नाम–लोहा, ताम्बा, सोना, पीतल, जस्ता आदि। **अपवाद**–चाँदी।
   (ग) ग्रहों के नाम–मंगल, बुध, शुक्र, शनि, आदि। **अपवाद**–पृथ्वी।
   (घ) वनस्पतियों के नाम–सागौन, अशोक, महुवा, पीपल, आम, ताड़, बाँस आदि। **अपवाद**–नीम, जामुन, आदि।
   (ङ) अनाजों के नाम–चना, उड़द, जौ, गेहूँ, चावल, धान, मटर, आदि। **अपवाद**–अरहर, मक्का, ज्वार, मूँग, आदि।
   (च) रत्नों के नाम–हीरा, मोती, माणिक, नीलम, मूँग, जवाहर आदि। **अपवाद**–मणि
   (छ) दिनों के नाम–सोम, मंगल, रवि, गुरु आदि।
   (ज) पहाड़ों के नाम–विन्ध्याचल, हिमालय, हिन्दुकुश आदि।
   (झ) जल और स्थल भागों के नाम–नगर, द्वीप, देश, समुद्र, घर, आकाश, पाताल आदि। **अपवाद**–नदी, झील, घाटी आदि।
   (ञ) भाव वाचक संज्ञाएँ–जिनके अन्त में ना, वा, पा, आव, पन, आ होते हैं प्रायः पुल्लिंग होते हैं। जैसे :–घेरा, डेरा, बसेरा, बुढ़ापा, बड़प्पन, बहाव, चढ़ाव आदि।
   (ट) हिन्दी की वे संज्ञाएँ जिनके अन्त में आकार होता है पुल्लिंग होती हैं। परन्तु इसमें संस्कृत के तत्सम शब्द शामिल नहीं होंगे और न हिन्दी के 'इया' प्रत्यय को लगाकर बने हुए शब्द ही।
   जैसे–रुपया, छाता, आटा, पैसा, पहिया, कपड़ा, चमड़ा आदि।
   (ठ) कृदन्त संज्ञाएँ–जिनके अन्त में 'आन' होता है। जैसे–नहान, उठान, मिलान आदि।

स्त्रीलिंग शब्दों की पहचान

1. हिन्दी में जिन संज्ञाओं के अन्त में आ, इ, उ, हो, वे स्त्रीलिंग मानी जाती हैं। हिन्दी की ये संज्ञाएँ संस्कृत से हिन्दी में आयी हैं।
   उदाहरण :
   आ वन्दना, प्रार्थना, कविता, दया, क्षमा, कृपा, रेखा आदि।
   इ सिद्धि, मति, गति, रीति, नीति, विधि, निधि आदि।
   उ मृत्यु, रेणु, धेनु, आदि।
2. ऐसी भाव वाचक संज्ञाएँ जिनके अन्त में ट, वट, आई, ता हट, हो स्त्रीलिंग होती हैं।
   उदाहरण :
   ट खाट, बाट, हाट आदि।
   वट मिलावट, लिखावट, सजावट आदि।
   आई लड़ाई, मिठाई, भलाई, चढ़ाई आदि।
   ता लघुता, प्रभुता, ममता, क्षमता आदि।
   हट अकुलाहट, घबड़ाहट, आहट आदि।
3. हिन्दी की उन संज्ञाओं को स्त्रीलिंग माना जाता है जिनके अन्त में ई, इया, ऊ, ख, त, स, हो। जैसे-
   ई नदी, चिट्ठी, टोपी, धोती, रोटी, चलनी आदि।
   अपवाद–घी, दही, जी, मोती, पानी, यही।
   इया खटिया, डिबिया, मचिया, पुड़िया, बुढ़िया, आदि।
   ऊ लू, बालू, झाड़ू, गेरू, दारू आदि।
   ख राख, भूख, कोख, साख, आँख, ईख, रेख आदि।
   अपवाद–रूख।
   त बात, रात, लात, छत आदि।
   स मिठास, रास (लगाम), ओस, प्यास, साँस, आदि।
   अपवाद–निकास, निवास।
4. कृदन्त की अकारान्त संज्ञाएँ भी स्त्रीलिंग होती हैं।
   जैसे–लूट, दौड़, चमक, पुकार, छाप, मार, समझ आदि।
   अपवाद–मेल, बिगार, नाच, खेल।
5. अनुस्वारांत संज्ञाएँ भी स्त्रीलिंग होती हैं।
   जैसे–खड़ाऊँ, चूँ आदि।
6. नदियों के नाम स्त्रीलिंग होते हैं।
   जैसे–गंगा, यमुना, गोमती, कृष्णा, बेतवा आदि
   अपवाद–ब्रहमपुत्र, सोन, सिन्धु।
7. नक्षत्रों के नाम स्त्रीलिंग होते हैं।
   जैसे–अश्विनी, रोहिणी, अनुराधा, कृत्तिका आदि।
8. तिथियों के नाम स्त्रीलिंग होते हैं।
   जैसे–प्रतिपदा, दूज, तीज, चौथ, अष्टमी, नवमी आदि।
9. किराने के पदार्थों के नाम स्त्रीलिंग होते हैं।
   जैसे–इलायची, सुपारी, लौंग, दालचीनी आदि। **अपवाद**–जीरा नमक, कपूर, केसर आदि।
10. भोजनों के नाम स्त्रीलिंग होते हैं।
    जैसे–खीर, दाल, खिचड़ी, कढ़ी, पकौड़ी, पूड़ी, कचौड़ी, आदि
    अपवाद–भात, रायता, दूध, पराठा, हलुआ आदि।

वचन (Number)

वचन का शाब्दिक अर्थ है–बोली। परन्तु हिन्दी में व्याकरण की दृष्टि में वचन का अर्थ संख्या से लिया जाता है। इसलिए वचन को परिभाषित करते हुए कहा जा सकता है–संज्ञा, सर्वनाम, विशेषण और क्रिया के जिस रूप से संख्या का बोध होता है, उसे वचन कहते हैं।

वचन के भेद

हिन्दी में वचन के दो भेद माने गए हैं–(1) एकवचन (2) बहुवचन

(1) एकवचन (Singular Number) : जैसा कि नाम से स्पष्ट है एकवचन विकारी शब्द का वह रूप है जिससे एक ही व्यक्ति

या वस्तु का बोध होता है। उदाहरण—घोड़ा दौड़ता है। गाय चरती है। इन वाक्यों में 'घोड़ा' और 'गाय' से एक जानवर का बोध होता है। अतः ये एकवचन हैं।

(2) **बहुवचन (Plural Number) :** बहुवचन वह विकारी शब्द है जिससे एक से अधिक वस्तुओं, व्यक्तियों आदि का बोध होता है। जैसे—घोड़े चरते हैं। गायें दौड़ती हैं। 'घोड़े' और 'गायें' कहने से एक से अधिक जानवरों का बोध होता है। अतः ये बहुवचन हैं।

वचन के रूपान्तर : यद्यपि वचन के कारण संज्ञा, सर्वनाम, विशेषण और क्रिया के रूप में परिवर्तन होता है तथापि सर्वनाम, विशेषण और क्रिया के रूप मूलतः इनसे जुड़ी संख्या पर ही आधारित होते हैं। अतएव वचन में संज्ञा शब्दों के रूपान्तर की ही प्रमुखता है।

वचन के अधीन संज्ञा के रूप दो तरह से परिवर्तित होते हैं—

(1) विभक्ति रहित

(2) विभक्ति सहित

विभक्ति रहित संज्ञाओं के बहुवचन बनाने के नियम

विभक्ति रहित संज्ञाओं का बहुवचन साधारणतः निम्नलिखित नियमों के अन्तर्गत बनाया जाता है-

1. पुल्लिंग संज्ञा के आकारान्त को एकारान्त कर बहुवचन बनाया जाता है। यथा-

एकवचन	बहुवचन	एकवचन	बहुवचन
घोड़ा	घोड़े	गधा	गधे
लड़का	लड़के		

अपवाद—मामा, नाना, बाबा, पिता, योद्धा, आत्मा, देवता, जामाता आदि। इन शब्दों के रूप दोनों वचनों में समान होते हैं।

2. पुल्लिंग आकारान्त शब्दों के अतिरिक्त अन्य मात्राओं से अन्त होने वाले शब्दों के रूप दोनों वचनों में एक समान रहते हैं। जैसे—

एकवचन	बहुवचन	एकवचन	बहुवचन
एक बालक	चार बालक	एक डाकू	चार डाकू
एक भाई	चार भाई	एक जौ	चार जौ

3. आकारान्त स्त्रीलिंग शब्दों के अन्त में 'एँ' जोड़ने से बहुवचन बनता है। जैसे—

एकवचन	बहुवचन	एकवचन	बहुवचन
शाखा	शाखाएँ	लता	लताएँ
माता	माताएँ	महिला	महिलाएँ

4. अकारान्त स्त्रीलिंग संज्ञा के बहुवचन शब्द में आगत अंतिम अ को यें कर देने से बनता है। जैसे—

एकवचन	बहुवचन	एकवचन	बहुवचन
गाय	गायें	रात	रातें
बात	बातें	आँख	आँखें
याद	यादें		

5. दीर्घ या ह्रस्व इकारान्त संज्ञाओं को ह्रस्व इकारान्त कर उनके अन्त में याँ जोड़ देने से बहुवचन बनता है। जैसे—

एकवचन	बहुवचन	एकवचन	बहुवचन
नारी	नारियाँ	पहेली	पहेलियाँ
लड़की	लड़कियाँ	सहेली	सहेलियाँ
नीति	नीतियाँ	नदी	नदियाँ
घड़ी	घड़ियाँ	छड़ी	छड़ियाँ
धोती	धोतियाँ	साड़ी	साड़ियाँ

6. जिन स्त्रीलिंग शब्दों के अन्त में 'या' आता है, 'या' पर चन्द्रबिन्दु लगाकर बहुवचन बनाया जाता है जैसे—

एकवचन	बहुवचन	एकवचन	बहुवचन
बुढ़िया	बुढ़ियाँ	चिड़िया	चिड़ियाँ
गुड़िया	गुड़ियाँ	डिबिया	डिबियाँ
दुनिया	दुनियाँ		

7. ह्रस्व या दीर्घ ऊकारान्त स्त्रीलिंग संज्ञाओं को ह्रस्व उकारान्त बनाकर अन्त में 'एँ' लगाने से बहुवचन का निर्माण होता है। जैसे-

एकवचन	बहुवचन	एकवचन	बहुवचन
धेनु	धेनुएँ	वस्तु	वस्तुएँ
बहू	बहुएँ	ऋतु	ऋतुएँ

8. कुछ शब्द समष्टि मूलक होते हैं। जैसे—गण, कुल, वृन्द, समूह, वर्ग, लोग, जन, मण्डल, दल, ग्राम, मण्डली आदि। ये शब्द विशेषतः वहाँ जोड़े जाते हैं, जहाँ दोनों वचनों में पुल्लिंग अथवा स्त्रीलिंग में एक ही रूप होते हैं।

उदाहरण :

एकवचन	बहुवचन	एकवचन	बहुवचन
पाठक	पाठकगण	आप	आप लोग
तुम	तुम लोग	छात्र	छात्रगण
विद्यार्थी	विद्यार्थीगण		

विभक्ति सहित संज्ञाओं के बहुवचन बनाने के नियम

सविभक्ति संज्ञाओं के बहुवचन बनाने के सामान्य नियम निम्नलिखित हैं—

1. संस्कृत शब्दों को छोड़कर हिन्दी के अकारान्त, आकारान्त तथा एकारान्त संज्ञाओं के अन्तिम अ, आ, ए के बदले बहुवचन बनाने में इसे 'ओं' कर दिया जाता है। जैसे-

एकवचन	बहुवचन
नर	नरों (का)
चीता	चीतों (द्वारा)
चोर	चोरों (ने)
घोड़ा	घोड़ों (को)

विभक्ति चिह्नों के साथ प्रयोग :

(क) नरों की कहानी।

(ख) चीतों का भय।

(ग) चोरों की पकड़।

(घ) घोड़ों की हिनहिनाहट।

2. संस्कृत आकारान्त संज्ञाओं तथा हिन्दी एवं संस्कृत की सम्पूर्ण अकारान्त, उकारान्त, ऊकारान्त तथा आकारान्त संज्ञाओं को बहुवचन बनाने के लिए अन्त में 'ओं' जोड़ना पड़ता है। ऊकारान्त में 'ओं' सम्पृक्त करने के पूर्व उसे उकारान्त करना पड़ता है। जैसे–

एकवचन	बहुवचन	विभक्ति चिह्नों के साथ प्रयोग
कला	कलाओं	कलाओं का प्रदर्शन
घर	घरों	घरों में जाओ
वधू	वधुओं	वधुओं का सम्मेलन

3. समस्त इकारान्त और ईकारान्त संज्ञाओं का बहुवचन बनाने के लिए अन्त में 'यों' जोड़ना पड़ता है। ईकारान्त संज्ञाओं में 'यों' जोड़ने के पूर्व ई का इ कर दिया जाता है। जैसे–

एकवचन	बहुवचन	विभक्ति चिह्नों के साथ प्रयोग
नारी	नारियों	नारियों की स्थिति
नदी	नदियों	नदियों का प्रवाह
कवि	कवियों	कवियों की वाणी
कपि	कपियों	कपियों का समूह

कारक (Case)

संज्ञा या सर्वनाम के उस रूप को कारक कहते हैं जिससे उसका सम्बन्ध वाक्य के अन्य शब्दों विशेषतः क्रिया के साथ प्रकट होता है। वास्तव में, विभक्ति चिह्नों से युक्त संज्ञा या सर्वनाम शब्द ही वाक्य में अन्य शब्दों से सम्बन्ध प्रकट करते हैं।

ने, को, से, द्वारा–आदि विभक्ति चिह्न हैं। कारक का एक उदाहरण इस प्रकार है–'मोहन ने बाग में डण्डे से आम तोड़ा।' इस वाक्य में मोहन ने, डण्डे से, और आम संज्ञाओं के रूपान्तरण हैं। जिस तत्त्व के द्वारा इन रूपान्तरित संज्ञाओं का सम्बन्ध तोड़ा, क्रिया से स्पष्ट होता है, वही कारक है।

कारक-चिह्न

हिन्दी में कारक के आठ भेद माने जाते हैं :

	कारक	विभक्ति या कारक चिह्न
1.	कर्त्ता	ने
2.	कर्म	को
3.	करण	से, द्वारा
4.	सम्प्रदान	को, के लिए
5.	अपादान	से
6.	सम्बन्ध	का, के, की, रा, रे, री, ना, ने, नी
7.	अधिकरण	में, पर
8.	सम्बोधन	हे, हो, अरे, अजी, अहो आदि।

कारक-चिह्न/विभक्ति/परसर्ग

हिन्दी में कारक का ज्ञान कराने के लिए संज्ञा या सर्वनाम के साथ जो प्रत्यय लगाये जाते हैं, उन्हें ही व्याकरण में विभक्ति कहते हैं। हिन्दी में चूँकि विभक्ति चिह्न पद से अलग प्रयुक्त होते हैं इसलिए इन्हें 'परसर्ग' भी कहा जाता है। परसर्ग का शब्दिक अर्थ है–पीछे जुड़ना। कारक चिह्न सदैव संज्ञा या सर्वनाम के पीछे जुड़ते हैं।

(*i*) **कर्त्ता कारक :** कर्त्ता का अभिप्राय है, करने वाला। वाक्य में जो क्रिया सम्पन्न करता है, उसे कर्त्ता कहा जाता है। जैसे–राम पढ़ता है। सुरेश पत्र लिखता है। इन वाक्यों में राम और सुरेश कर्त्ता कारक हैं क्योंकि ये ही क्रिया को सम्पादित करने वाले हैं।

(*ii*) **कर्म कारक :** कर्त्ता द्वारा सम्पादित क्रिया का फल जिस प[illegible] पड़ता है, उसे 'कर्म' कहते हैं। जैसे–शीला ने राजेश को पढ़ाया इस वाक्य में कर्त्ता है–शीला, क्रिया है–पढ़ाना। पढ़ाना क्रि[illegible] का फल राजेश पर स्पष्ट पड़ रहा है। इसलिए यहाँ राजेश क[illegible] कारक की स्थिति में है।

(*iii*) **करण कारक :** वाक्य में करण कारक उस शब्द को कहते [illegible] जो क्रिया को पूर्ण करने में साधन के रूप में कर्ता का सहाय[illegible] होकर आता है। जैसे–मैं कलम से लिखता हूँ। इस वाक्य [illegible] 'कलम से' करण कारक है क्योंकि लेखन-क्रिया में कलम साध[illegible] है।

(*iv*) **सम्प्रदान कारक :** कर्त्ता क्रिया की सिद्धि जिसके लिए करता [illegible] अथवा जिसको कुछ देता है, उसे प्रकट करने वाले शब्द रू[illegible] को सम्प्रदान कारक कहते हैं। जैसे–श्याम मीरा के लिए खिलौ[illegible] लाया। राकेश शीला के लिए रोता है। इन वाक्यों में ला[illegible] और रोना क्रियाएँ क्रमशः मीरा और शीला के लिए सम्पादि[illegible] की जा रही हैं। इसलिए मीरा और शीला के लिए शब्द रू[illegible] सम्प्रदान कारक है।

(*v*) **अपादान कारक :** वाक्य में अलगाव सूचित करने वाला श[illegible] अपादान कारक कहलाता है। जैसे–शारदा नहर गंगा नदी [illegible] निकली है। पेड़ से पत्ते गिरते हैं। इन वाक्यों में निकलना औ[illegible] गिरना क्रियाओं के अलग होने का भाव क्रमशः गंगा नदी औ[illegible] पेड़ से स्पष्ट हो रहा है। अतएव इन दोनों शब्दों की स्थि[illegible] अपादान कारक में है।

(*vi*) **सम्बन्ध कारक :** संज्ञा, सर्वनाम का वह रूप जिससे वाक्य [illegible] आगत अन्य शब्द के साथ जुड़ाव या सम्बन्ध का बोध [illegible] सम्बन्ध कारक कहलाता है। सम्बन्ध कारक का सम्बन्ध क्रि[illegible] के साथ प्रत्यक्ष नहीं होता है। जैसे–शीला की पुस्तक। रमे[illegible] का घोड़ा। मेरी कलम।

इन वाक्यों में शीला की, रमेश का, मेरी–क्रमशः पुस्त[illegible] घोड़ा, कलम से लगाव स्पष्ट करते हैं। अतः ये सम्बन[illegible] कारक हैं।

(*vii*) **अधिकरण कारक :** संज्ञा या सर्वनाम के उस रूप को अधिकर[illegible] कारक कहते हैं जिससे वाक्य में क्रिया के आधार का बो[illegible]

होता है। जैसे—गाय बाग में चरती है। विद्यालय में 400 विद्यार्थी हैं। इन वाक्यों में 'बाग में' और 'विद्यालय में' अधिकरण कारक हैं। क्योंकि वे क्रमशः गाय के चरने के लिए तथा विद्यार्थियों के लिए आधार का काम करते हैं।

(viii) **सम्बोधन कारक :** वाक्य में वक्ता श्रोता का ध्यान अपनी ओर खींचने के लिए अथवा उसे सचेत करने के लिए संज्ञा के जिस रूप को प्रयुक्त करता है उसे सम्बोधन कारक कहते हैं। जैसे—अरे राकेश, तुमने यह क्या हाल कर रखा है। इस वाक्य में 'अरे राकेश' सम्बोधन कारक है, क्योंकि इस पद द्वारा ध्यानाकृष्ट किया गया है। सम्बोधन कारक का सम्बन्ध क्रिया के साथ नहीं होता है। इसका प्रयोग बिना चिह्न के भी हो सकता है। जैसे गुरुदेव, क्षमा करें। यहाँ गुरुदेव सम्बोधन कारक है।

सर्वनाम (Pronoun)

सर्वनाम दो शब्दों से मिलकर बना है—सर्व + नाम। सर्व का अर्थ है 'सब' और 'नाम' का अर्थ 'संज्ञा' है। जिन विकारी शब्दों का प्रयोग संज्ञा के बदले में होता है, उन्हें सर्वनाम कहते हैं। जैसे—तुम, मैं, आप, यह, वह, जो, सो, कोई, कुछ, कौन, क्या इत्यादि।

सर्वनाम का प्रयोग कर वाक्य को संज्ञा के पुनरुक्ति दोष से बचाया जाता है। सर्वनाम की सर्वोपरि विशेषता यह है कि उससे उसी संज्ञा का बोध होता है जिससे उसका पूर्वापर सम्बन्ध होता है। किन्तु संज्ञा से केवल उसी का बोध होता है, जिसका वह नाम है। उदाहरण के लिए 'घोड़ा' कहने से मात्र घोड़ा का ही बोध होता है, पुस्तक, गाय आदि का ज्ञान नहीं होता। लेकिन 'वह' कहने से पूर्वापर सम्बन्ध के अनुरूप ही संज्ञा का पता चलता है।

सर्वनाम के भेद

सर्वनाम के सात भेद माने गये हैं :

(1) पुरुषवाचक सर्वनाम
(2) निजवाचक सर्वनाम
(3) निश्चयवाचक सर्वनाम
(4) अनिश्चयवाचक सर्वनाम
(5) सम्बन्धवाचक सर्वनाम
(6) प्रश्नवाचक सर्वनाम
(7) साकल्पवाचक सर्वनाम

(1) **पुरुषवाचक सर्वनाम**—जो सर्वनाम—बोलने वाले, सुनने वाले और जिसके विषय में कुछ कहा जाए—का बोध कराते हैं, उन्हें पुरुषवाचक सर्वनाम कहते हैं।
जैसे—मैं, तुम, वह आदि।
पुरुषवाचक सर्वनाम तीन प्रकार के होते हैं :
(क) उत्तम पुरुष (ख) मध्यम पुरुष (ग) अन्य पुरुष

(क) उत्तम पुरुष—उत्तम पुरुष में वक्ता या लेखक आते हैं। जैसे—मैं, हम।

(ख) मध्यम पुरुष—मध्यम पुरुष में—तू, तुम, आप, आते हैं। जिससे कोई बात बोली या कही जाती है उसे मध्यम पुरुष कहते हैं।

(ग) अन्य पुरुष—जिसके विषय में कुछ कहा, लिखा या सुना जाए—वह अन्य पुरुष कहलाता है। जैसे—वह, वे।

(2) **निजवाचक सर्वनाम**—जो सर्वनाम स्वयं या निज का बोध कराने वाले हैं उन्हें निजवाचक सर्वनाम कहते हैं। जैसे—मैं आप चला जाऊँगा। तुम आप वहाँ चले जाना। मैं अपने को सुधार लूँगा। यहाँ 'आप' निजवाचक सर्वनाम है।
निजवाचक सर्वनाम 'आप' एक ही तरह दोनों वचनों में आता है और तीनों पुरुषों में इसका प्रयोग किया जा सकता है।

(क) निजवाचक सर्वनाम 'आप' का प्रयोग किसी संज्ञा, सर्वनाम के निश्चय के लिए होता है। जैसे—मैं आप आया हूँ।

(ख) निजवाचक 'आप' का प्रयोग दूसरे व्यक्ति के निराकरण के लिए होता है। जैसे—उन्होंने मुझे रहने को कहा और आप चलते बने।

(ग) सर्वसाधारण के अर्थ में भी आप का प्रयोग होता है। जैसे—आप भला तो जग भला।

(घ) निश्चय के अर्थ में कभी-कभी 'आप' के साथ 'ही' जोड़ा जाता है। जैसे—मैं आप ही चला आया था।

निजवाचक आप और पुरुषवाचक आप में अन्तर

पुरुषवाचक आप मध्यम पुरुष में आदर सूचक के रूप में प्रयुक्त होता है। इसका रूप तू के स्थान पर होता है। जैसे—आप कब आयेंगे? आप कहाँ जा रहे हैं?

निजवाचक 'आप' शब्द स्वयं या खुद के लिए होता है। जैसे—वह अपने आप आ जायेगा। मैं आप ही बुरा हूँ।

(3) **निश्चयवाचक सर्वनाम**—जिस सर्वनाम से किसी निश्चित व्यक्ति या वस्तु का बोध होता है, उसे निश्चयवाचक सर्वनाम कहते हैं। जैसे—यह, वह आदि। यह का बहुवचन 'ये' और 'वह' का बहुवचन 'वे' है।

(4) **अनिश्चयवाचक सर्वनाम**—जिस सर्वनाम से किसी निश्चित व्यक्ति, वस्तु या स्थान का बोध न हो, उसे अनिश्चयवाचक सर्वनाम कहते हैं।
जैसे—कोई, कुछ आदि।
उदाहरण : कोई आ रहा है। कुछ भी लेते आना।
साधारणतः 'कोई' अनिश्चित व्यक्ति के लिए आता है और 'कुछ' अनिश्चित वस्तु के लिए।

(5) **सम्बन्धवाचक सर्वनाम**—जिस सर्वनाम से संज्ञा या अन्य सर्वनाम के साथ सम्बन्ध जाना जाता है, उसे सम्बन्धवाचक सर्वनाम कहते हैं। जैसे—जो आयेगा सो जायेगा। जिसकी लाठी उसकी भैंस। यहाँ 'जिस' और 'उस' सम्बन्ध वाचक सर्वनाम हैं। वर्तमान हिन्दी में 'सो', 'तिस', 'तिन' शब्दों के स्थान पर 'यह' और 'उन' का प्रयोग भी शुद्ध माना जाता है।

(6) **प्रश्नवाचक सर्वनाम**–जिस सर्वनाम शब्द से प्रश्न का बोध हो, उसे प्रश्नवाचक सर्वनाम कहते हैं। जैसे–क्या, कौन आदि।

उदाहरण :

तुम्हारा नाम क्या है?
आप क्या चाहते हैं?
कौन आ रहा है?

'कौन' शब्द व्यक्ति के विषय में तथा 'क्या' शब्द वस्तु के विषय में प्रश्न के निमित्त प्रयोग में लाया जाता है।

(7) **साकल्पवाचक सर्वनाम**–इस सर्वनाम में साकल्प या समूह का बोध होता है। जैसे–सब, कुल, सकल आदि। इसे समूह बोधक भी कहते हैं।

सर्वनाम की विशेषताएँ

(1) सर्वनाम का लिंग के अनुसार रूपात्मक परिवर्तन नहीं होता है। मैं, तुम, यह, वह इत्यादि सर्वनाम पुरुष और स्त्री दोनों के लिए प्रयोग में लाये जाते हैं।

(2) सर्वनाम के कारकीय रूपों में सम्बन्ध कारक नहीं होता है।

(3) सर्वनाम के कारकीय रूपों में सम्बन्ध कारक का केवल 'का' रूप लिंग से प्रभावित होता है।

जैसे–उसकी पुत्री। उसका पुत्र।
मेरी पुत्री। मेरा पुत्र।

सर्वनाम का लिंग

लिंग की दृष्टि से सर्वनाम में किसी प्रकार का परिवर्तन उपस्थित नहीं होता। उसका रूप सदैव एक-सा विद्यमान रहता है। वाक्य में उनका प्रयोग चाहे पुल्लिंग के लिए हो या स्त्रीलिंग के लिए। मैं, तुम, हम, वह, वे आदि सर्वनामों का प्रयोग दोनों लिंगों में एक जैसा होता है।

जैसे– मैं खेलता हूँ। लड़का कहेगा।
मैं खेलती हूँ। लड़की कहेगी।

लड़का और लड़की पुल्लिग स्त्रीलिंग संज्ञाओं के स्थान पर प्रयुक्त 'मैं' सर्वनाम के रूप में किसी प्रकार का परिवर्तन नहीं हुआ।

सर्वनाम का वचन

सर्वनाम का प्रयोग दोनों वचनों में संज्ञा की तरह ही होता है। जैसे–

एकवचन	**बहुवचन**
वह	वे
यह	ये
मैं	हम

विशेषण (Adjective)

संज्ञा या सर्वनाम शब्दों की विशेषता बताने वाले शब्दों को विशेषण कहते हैं। जैसे–लाल पैण्ट, पाँच आम, मोटा लड़का, अच्छी लड़की आदि। ऊपर के उदाहरणों में लाल, पाँच, मोटा, अच्छी आदि विशेषण हैं।

विशेषण के भेद

विशेषण के निम्नलिखित भेद हैं–

(1) सार्वनामिक विशेषण
(2) संख्यावाचक विशेषण
(3) गुणवाचक विशेषण
(4) परिमाणवाचक विशेषण
(5) व्यक्तिवाचक विशेषण
(6) प्रविशेषण

(1) **सार्वनामिक विशेषण**–ऐसे सर्वनाम शब्द जो विशेषण के रूप में प्रयुक्त किये जाते हैं, वे सार्वनामिक विशेषण कहे जाते हैं। क्या, कोई, कुछ, यह, वह, कौन, जो, सो, जैसा, कैसा, इतना, उतना आदि सार्वनामिक विशेषण के उदाहरण हैं। वस्तुतः ऐसे शब्द सर्वनाम और विशेषण दोनों ही का कार्य करते हैं। जब क्रिया के पूर्व उन शब्दों का प्रयोग होता है तब वे सर्वनाम होते हैं और जब उनका प्रयोग किसी संज्ञा के साथ होता है तब उन्हें विशेषण कहा जाता है। जैसे–

सर्वनाम	**विशेषण**
वह पढ़ रहा है।	वह लड़का पढ़ रहा है।
यह देखो।	यह घोड़ा देखो।

सार्वनामिक विशेषण के दो भेद हैं–

(क) मूल सार्वनामिक विशेषण
(ख) यौगिक सार्वनामिक विशेषण

(क) **मूल सार्वनामिक विशेषण**–मूल सार्वनामिक विशेषण वे हैं जिनमें वचन एवं कारक के कारण किसी प्रकार का परिवर्तन उपस्थित नहीं होता जैसे–यह, वह, कौन, जो, सो, कोई कुछ, क्या आदि।

(ख) **यौगिक सार्वनामिक विशेषण**–ये मूल सर्वनाम में प्रत्यय लगाकर बनाये जाते हैं तथा इनका रूप कारक एवं वचन के अनुसार बदलता रहता है। जैसे–कैसा, कैसी, ऐसा, ऐसे, ऐसी, जैसा, जैसे, जैसी। इसी प्रकार वैसा, तैसा, इतना, उतना, जितना, कितना आदि।

(2) **संख्यावाचक विशेषण**–संख्यावाचक विशेषण के द्वारा संज्ञा या सर्वनाम की संख्या का ज्ञान होता है। संज्ञा-सर्वनाम की संख्यात्मक विशेषता स्पष्ट करने के कारण ही इसे संख्यावाचक विशेषण कहा जाता है। जैसे–दस घोड़े, चालीस गायें, कुछ आदमी, सब अध्यापक। यहाँ दस, चालीस, कुछ, सब–संख्यावाचक विशेषण हैं। क्योंकि इनसे संख्या की संख्यात्मक स्थिति का आभास मिलता है।

संख्यावाचक विशेषण के दो प्रकार हैं–

(क) निश्चित संख्यावाचक
(ख) अनिश्चित संख्यावाचक

(क) **निश्चित संख्यावाचक विशेषण**–निश्चित संख्या का बोध कराने वाले विशेषण को निश्चित संख्यावाचक विशेषण कहते हैं। जैसे–आठ लड़कियाँ, तीस रुपये।

(ख) **अनिश्चित संख्यावाचक विशेषण**–संज्ञा या सर्वनाम की निश्चित संख्या का बोध न कराने वाले विशेषण को अनिश्चित संख्यावाचक विशेषण कहा जाता है। जैसे–कुछ मकान, सब घोड़े।

(3) **गुणवाचक विशेषण**–जिस शब्द से संज्ञा या सर्वनाम का गुण स्पष्ट होता है, उसे गुणवाचक विशेषण कहते हैं। गुण के अन्तर्गत संज्ञा या सर्वनाम के रूप, रंग, स्थान, स्वभाव आदि स्थितियों का स्पष्टीकरण होता है। गुण से आशय अच्छे और बुरे दोनों से है। जैसे–सुन्दर पुरुष, गरीब किसान, दुष्ट आदमी, काला घोड़ा, मोटी स्त्री, सूखा खेत, शान्त अध्यापक।

(4) **परिमाणवाचक विशेषण**–जिन शब्दों के द्वारा परिमाण अर्थात् माप, तौल इत्यादि का बोध होता है, उन्हें परिमाणवाचक विशेषण कहते हैं। जैसे–बहुत पानी, थोड़ा दूध, कुछ अनाज, सब तेल। इसके दो भेद हैं–(क) निश्चित परिमाणवाचक (ख) अनिश्चित परिमाणवाचक।

(क) **निश्चित परिमाणवाचक**–जिससे परिमाण की निश्चित स्थिति का पता चलता है, उसे निश्चित परिमाणवाचक विशेषण कहते हैं। जैसे–दो किलो दूध, चार गज कपड़ा।

(ख) **अनिश्चित परिमाणवाचक**–जिससे निश्चित परिमाण का बोध नहीं होता है, उसे अनिश्चित परिमाणवाचक विशेषण कहते हैं।

जैसे–कुछ अनाज, सब तेल।

(5) **व्यक्तिवाचक विशेषण**–व्यक्तिवाचक संज्ञा से निर्मित विशेषणों को व्यक्तिवाचक विशेषण कहते हैं।

जैसे–कानपुर-कानपुरी, बनारस-बनारसी, पटना-पटनियाँ, कलकत्ता-कलकतिया आदि।

(6) **प्रविशेषण**–विशेषण की एक नयी कोटि भी बनायी गयी है। इसका नाम प्रविशेषण है। प्रविशेषण वे शब्द हैं जो विशेषण की विशेषता बताते हैं।

जैसे–शीला अति सुन्दर है।

राणा प्रताप बड़े साहसी थे।

राजेश अत्यन्त मेधावी छात्र है।

विशेषण का पद परिचय

विशेषण के पद-परिचय में लिंग, वचन, विशेषण, विशेषण का भेद, विशेष्य और कारक बताए जाते हैं।

जैसे–मानव श्रेष्ठतम कृति है।

श्रेष्ठतम–विशेषण, गुणवाचक विशेषण, पुल्लिंग, एकवचन, विशेष्यकृति, उत्तमावस्था, विशेष्य विशेषण।

क्रिया (Verb)

क्रिया–वाक्य में जिस शब्द से किसी काम का होना या करना ज्ञात होता है, उसे क्रिया कहते हैं। जैसे–लिखना, पढ़ना, खाना, खेलना, दौड़ना, रोना, आना, जाना आदि।

क्रिया विकारी शब्द है जिसके रूप, लिंग, वचन और पुरुष के अनुसार बदलते हैं।

धातु

क्रिया जिस मूल शब्द से बनती है, उसे धातु कहते हैं। क्रिया का निर्माण 'धातु' में 'ना' जोड़ने से होता है। क्रिया से 'ना' हटा देने पर जो शेष बचता है, वही धातु कहलाता है। जैसे–लिख, खा, आ, जा, पढ़ आदि धातु हैं।

धातु के भेद–धातु मुख्यतः दो प्रकार के होते हैं–

(1) मूल धातु

(2) यौगिक धातु

(1) **मूल धातु**–मूल धातु किसी पर आधारित न होकर स्वतंत्र होता है। जैसे–पढ़, लिख, खा, देख इत्यादि।

(2) **यौगिक धातु**–यौगिक धातु का निर्माण प्रत्येक के जुड़ाव से होता है। यौगिक धातु का निर्माण मुख्यतः तीन प्रकार से होता है–

(*i*) धातु में जब प्रत्यय का योग किया जाता है तब अकर्मक से सकर्मक और प्रेरणार्थक धातु की रचना होती है।

(*ii*) धातु के साथ धातु को संपृक्त करने से संयुक्त धातु की रचना होती है।

(*iii*) संज्ञा या विशेषण से नाम धातु का निर्माण होता है।

प्रेरणार्थक क्रिया–(धातु)–जिससे यह ज्ञात होता हो कि कर्त्ता स्वयं नहीं कर रहा है बल्कि कार्य करने के लिए किसी अन्य को प्रेरित कर रहा है, वह प्रेरणार्थक क्रिया कहलाती है।

जैसे–पढ़ना = पढ़ाना/पढ़वाना।

चलना = चलाना/चलवाना।

यौगिक क्रिया–(धातु)–दो या दो से अधिक धातुओं के मेल से जिस क्रिया का निर्माण होता है, उसे यौगिक क्रिया कहते हैं। जैसे–गिर पड़ना, मार देना, रख देना इत्यादि।

नाम धातु–जिस धातु की रचना संज्ञा या विशेषण से होती है, उसे नाम धातु कहते हैं। जैसे–हाथ से हथियाना, लात से लतियाना इत्यादि।

क्रिया के भेद

साधारणतः क्रिया के भेद दो आधारों पर किये जाते हैं–

(*i*) रूप के आधार पर (*ii*) अर्थ के अनुसार

रूप के अनुसार क्रिया के भेद

रूप के अनुसार क्रिया के दो भेद हैं–

(क) सकर्मक क्रिया (ख) अकर्मक क्रिया

(क) **सकर्मक क्रिया**–जिस क्रिया के साथ कर्म के प्रयोग की अपेक्षा होती है, अथवा जो क्रिया कर्म के साथ आती है, उसे सकर्मक क्रिया कहते हैं। सकर्मक क्रिया को सम्पादित करने वाला यद्यपि कर्त्ता ही होता है, किन्तु उसके कार्य का फल कर्म पर पड़ता है। जैसे–राम रोटी खाता है। इस वाक्य में प्रयुक्त क्रिया खाता है–सकर्मक है, क्योंकि उसका एक कर्म है। रोटी खाने वाला राम है लेकिन उसकी क्रिया खाना का फल रोटी पर पड़ता है। वह जाता है। यहाँ जाना क्रिया सकर्मक है। इस वाक्य में यद्यपि कर्म का प्रयोग नहीं हुआ है लेकिन कर्म के प्रयोग की आवश्यकता है। 'जाता है' के पहले घर, गाँव, स्कूल, मंदिर या किसी विशेष स्थान का बोधक शब्द रखा जा सकता है।

(ख) **अकर्मक क्रिया**–जिस क्रिया का प्रयोग बिना कर्म के होता है अर्थात् जिस क्रिया के साथ कर्म का प्रयोग न हो, वह अकर्मक क्रिया कहलाती है। अकर्मक क्रिया के कर्त्ता का फल कर्त्ता पर ही पड़ता है। जैसे–वह रोता है। यहाँ प्रयुक्त 'रोना' क्रिया अकर्मक है। क्योंकि इस वाक्य में न तो कोई कर्म है और न उसके प्रयोग की आवश्यकता ही महसूस होती है। रोना क्रिया का फल कर्त्ता 'वह' पर ही पड़ रहा है।

अर्थ के अनुसार क्रिया के भेद

(क) समापिका क्रिया
(ख) असमापिका क्रिया

(क) **समापिका क्रिया**–समापिका क्रिया वह क्रिया है जिससे पूर्णता का भाव प्रकट होता है। दूसरे शब्दों में कहा जा सकता है–"वह क्रिया जो संदेह या आकांक्षा को समाप्त कर देती है, समापिका क्रिया है।" जैसे–रमेश मैदान में खेलता है। इस वाक्य में 'खेलता है' समापिका क्रिया है क्योंकि इसके बाद रमेश क्या करता है, इस तरह का संदेह नहीं रह जाता।

(ख) **असमापिका क्रिया**–असमापिका क्रिया वह है जिससे अपूर्णता का भाव जाना जाता है। इस क्रिया से सन्देह या आकांक्षा का समापन नहीं होता और आगे जानने की जरूरत महसूस होती है। जैसे–'राम ने आते ही...।' यदि इस वाक्य को यहीं छोड़ दिया जाए तो आकांक्षा होगी कि 'क्या किया'? इस आकांक्षा की समाप्ति तभी होगी जब आगे वाक्य जोड़ दिया जाए–'बच्चों को प्यार किया।' अब पूरा वाक्य हुआ। राम ने आते ही बच्चों को प्यार किया। इस प्रकार आते ही, आते हुए, आकर इत्यादि असमापिका क्रियाएँ हैं।

काल (Tense)

काल क्रिया के उस रूपान्तरण को कहते हैं जिससे कार्य-व्यापार का समय और उसके पूर्ण अथवा अपूर्ण अवस्था का बोध हो।

जैसे– राम खाता है।
राम जायेगा।
मोहन ने खाया।

काल के भेद

क्रिया के मुख्यतः तीन काल हैं–(1) वर्तमान काल (2) भूतकाल (3) भविष्यत् काल

(1) वर्तमान काल

'वर्तमान काल' में क्रिया से कार्य होने का बोध होता है अर्थात् इसमें क्रिया के व्यापार की निरन्तरता का स्पष्टीकरण होता है। जैसे–'वह पढ़ता है।' –इस वाक्य में पढ़ने की क्रिया हो रही है।

वर्तमान काल के भेद

(क) सामान्य वर्तमान
(ख) अपूर्ण वर्तमान/तात्कालिक वर्तमान
(ग) पूर्ण वर्तमान
(घ) संभाव्य वर्तमान

(क) **सामान्य वर्तमान**–सामान्य वर्तमान उसे कहते हैं जिसमें क्रिया का वर्तमान काल में होना जाना जाता है।

जैसे– मोहन जाता है।
राम पढ़ता है।
गीता देखती है।

(ख) **अपूर्ण वर्तमान**–इसका दूसरा नाम तात्कालिक वर्तमान भी है। अपूर्ण वर्तमान में इस बात का बोध होता है कि क्रिया वर्तमान काल में जारी है। जैसे–मैं पत्र लिख रहा हूँ। सुरेश गाना गा रहा है।

(ग) **पूर्ण वर्तमान**–इस काल से यह ज्ञात होता है कि क्रिया वर्तमान काल में सम्पन्न हो चुकी है। जैसे–राम गया है। रमेश ने रोटी खायी है।

(घ) **संभाव्य वर्तमान**–इस काल में कार्य के पूर्ण होने की संभावना रहती है। जैसे–राम खाया हो। वह सोया हो।

(2) भूतकाल

भूतकाल का अर्थ है–बीता हुआ समय अर्थात् क्रिया के जिस रूपान्तरण से कार्य के समापन का बोध हो, उसे भूतकाल की क्रिया कहते हैं। जैसे–राम खा चुका था। वह सोया था। सीता ने गाया।

भूतकाल के भेद

भूतकाल के छः भेद हैं–

(क) सामान्य भूत (घ) अपूर्ण भूत
(ख) आसन्न भूत (ङ) संदिग्ध भूत
(ग) पूर्ण भूत (च) हेतु हेतु मद् भूत

(क) **सामान्य भूत**–इस काल की क्रिया से यह ज्ञात होता है कि कार्य स्वाभाविक रीति से हुआ अर्थात् क्रिया के विशेष समय का बोध नहीं होता। जैसे–राम ने पत्र लिखा। मोहन गया।

(ख) **आसन्न भूत**–इस बात के द्वारा यह ज्ञात होता है कि क्रिया की समाप्ति निकट भूत में तत्काल हुई। जैसे–राम पत्र लिख चुका है। वह अभी आया था।

(ग) **पूर्ण भूत**–पूर्ण भूत की क्रिया से यह स्पष्ट पता चलता है कि क्रिया की समाप्ति सुदूर भूत में ही हो चुकी है अर्थात् क्रिया के सम्पादित होने के समय का स्पष्ट ज्ञान होता है।
जैसे–राम ने रावण को मारा था। आशा ने गीत गाया था।

(घ) **अपूर्ण भूत**–इस काल की क्रिया से यह ज्ञात होता है कि भूतकाल में कार्य निरन्तर जारी था।
जैसे–रमेश पुस्तक पढ़ रहा था। सुरेश खाना खा रहा था।

(ङ) **संदिग्ध भूत**–संदिग्ध भूत में इस बात का सन्देह बना रहता है कि कार्य समाप्त हुआ या नहीं। जैसे–तुमने लिखा होगा। उसने चुराया होगा।

(च) **हेतु हेतु मद् भूत**–इस काल में यह पता चलता है कि यद्यपि क्रिया का समापन भूतकाल में होना था। परन्तु किसी कारणवश नहीं हो सका।
दूसरे शब्दों में हम कह सकते हैं कि इस काल में कार्य के होने की शर्त लगी रहती है अर्थात् एक क्रिया की सिद्धि में दूसरी क्रिया शर्त बनकर प्रयुक्त होती है।
जैसे– यदि तुम पढ़ते तो परीक्षा पास करते।
यदि वर्षा होती तो पैदावार अच्छी होती।

(३) **भविष्यत् काल**

वह क्रिया जो भविष्य में होनी है, उसे भविष्यत् काल की क्रिया कहा जाता है।

जैसे– वह खाएगा।
वह नौकरी करेगा।
रमेश व्यापार करेगा।

भविष्यत् काल के भेद

(क) सामान्य भविष्यत् (ख) हेतु हेतु मद् भविष्यत्
(ग) सम्भाव्य भविष्यत्

(क) **सामान्य भविष्यत्**–इस काल की क्रिया से यह पता चलता है कि कार्य स्वाभाविक रीति से भविष्य में पूरा होगा।
जैसे–मैं लिखूँगा। वह गाँव जायेगा।

(ख) **हेतु हेतु मद् भविष्यत्**–इस काल की क्रिया से यह प्रकट होता है कि भविष्य में एक क्रिया का होना दूसरी क्रिया पर निर्भर करता है।
जैसे– अध्यापक आएं तो पढ़ाएं।
विद्यार्थी पढ़े तो परीक्षा उर्त्तीण करे।

(ग) **संभाव्य भविष्यत्**–इस काल की क्रिया से भविष्यत् काल में कार्य के होने की संभावना का बोध होता है।
जैसे– सम्भव है, वह पत्र लिखे।
सम्भवतः वह कल आए।

अव्यय (Indeclinable)

'अव्यय' ऐसे शब्द या शब्दांश को कहते हैं जिसके रूप में लिंग, वचन, कारक इत्यादि के कारण कोई विचार (परिवर्तन) उत्पन्न नहीं होता। जैसे–जब, तब, यहाँ, वहाँ, कब, क्यों, वाह, आह, ठीक, अरे, और, तथा, एवं, किन्तु, परन्तु, बल्कि, इसलिए, अतः, अतएव, चूँकि, अर्थात्, इत्यादि।

अव्यय के भेद

अव्यय के चार भेद हैं–

(1) क्रिया विशेषण (Adverb)
(2) सम्बन्ध बोधक (Preposition)
(3) समुच्चय बोधक (Conjunction)
(4) विस्मयादि बोधक (Interjection)

क्रिया-विशेषण

'क्रिया-विशेषण' ऐसे अविकारी शब्दों को कहा जाता है जो क्रिया-विशेषण या दूसरे क्रिया-विशेषण की विशेषता बतलाते हैं। दूसरे शब्दों में–क्रिया के अर्थ में विशेषता उत्पन्न करने वाले शब्दों को क्रिया विशेषण कहते हैं।

जैसे– तुम तेज दौड़ते हो।
राम वहाँ जा रहा है।

उपर्युक्त वाक्यों में 'तेज' और 'वहाँ' विशेषता बताने वाले शब्द हैं। कभी-कभी क्रिया-विशेषण, विशेषण या दूसरे क्रिया-विशेषण शब्दों की विशेषता बतलाते हैं।

जैसे– वह बहुत अच्छा लड़का है।
तुम बहुत जल्दी आए।

क्रिया-विशेषण के भेद

क्रिया-विशेषण का विभाजन निम्नलिखित तीन आधारों पर होता है–

(*i*) प्रयोग के आधार पर (*ii*) रूप के आधार पर
(*iii*) अर्थ के आधार पर

(*i*) क्रिया-विशेषण के भेद (प्रयोग के आधार पर)

प्रयोग के अनुसार क्रिया-विशेषण के तीन भेद हैं :–

(क) साधारण क्रिया-विशेषण (ख) संयोजक क्रिया-विशेषण
(ग) अनुबद्ध क्रिया-विशेषण

(क) **साधारण क्रिया-विशेषण**–वाक्य में स्वतंत्र रूप से प्रयोग किये जाने वाले क्रिया-विशेषण शब्द साधारण क्रिया-विशेषण कहलाते हैं।
जैसे– रमेश, जल्दी जाओ।
अरे, ठग कहाँ गया।
हाय! अब वह क्या करेगा।

(ख) **संयोजक क्रिया-विशेषण**–जो क्रिया विशेषण दो उपवाक्यों को जोड़ने के लिए प्रयुक्त होते हैं, उन्हें संयोजक क्रिया-विशेषण कहते हैं।
जैसे– जब अध्यापक आयेंगे, तब बच्चे पढ़ेंगे।
जहाँ अभी कानपुर शहर है, वहाँ किसी समय जंगल था।

(ग) **अनुबद्ध क्रिया-विशेषण**—अनुबद्ध क्रिया विशेषण वे हैं जिनका प्रयोग वाक्य में अवधारण (निश्चय) के लिए किसी भी शब्द-भेद के साथ होता है।

जैसे—मैं उसका पता मात्र जानता हूँ।
यह तो किसी ने चालाकी की है।
शीला मुझे जानती तक नहीं।

—ही, भर, केवल, मात्र, भी आदि अवधारण के लिए आते हैं, अतः ये अनुबद्ध क्रिया-विशेषण हैं।

(*ii*) क्रिया-विशेषण के भेद (रूप के आधार पर)

रूप के अनुसार क्रिया-विशेषण को तीन भागों में वर्गीकृत किया गया है—

(क) मूल क्रिया-विशेषण
(ख) यौगिक क्रिया-विशेषण
(ग) स्थानीय क्रिया-विशेषण

(क) **मूल क्रिया-विशेषण**—मूल क्रिया-विशेषण ऐसे क्रिया-विशेषण हैं जो किसी शब्द के मेल से नहीं बनते हैं।
जैसे—नीचे, नजदीक, दूर, ऊपर, अभी, फिर, पुनः आदि।

(ख) **यौगिक क्रिया-विशेषण**—यौगिक क्रिया-विशेषण दूसरे शब्दों के मेल से बनते हैं। दूसरे शब्दों के योग से निर्मित होने के कारण इन्हें यौगिक क्रिया-विशेषण कहते हैं।
जैसे—साल भर, रात भर, प्रति वर्ष, हर दिन, हृदय से आदि।
यौगिक क्रिया-विशेषण का निर्माण संज्ञा, सर्वनाम, विशेषण, धातु और अव्यय के मेल से होता है।

यौगिक क्रिया-विशेषण का निर्माण—यौगिक क्रिया-विशेषण साधारणतः निम्नलिखित शब्दों के मेल से बनते हैं :

संज्ञा द्विरुक्ति से—साल-साल, घर-घर, वन-वन, बीच-बीच, हाथों-हाथ।
दो संज्ञाओं के मेल से—हाथ-पाँव, घर-बाहर, एड़ी-चोटी, नख-शिख, सुबह-शाम।
विशेषणों की द्विरुक्ति से—साफ-साफ, ठीक-ठीक, थोड़ा-थोड़ा।
संज्ञा और विशेषणों के मेल से—हर-घड़ी, एक-साथ, एक-बार।
क्रिया-विशेषणों की द्विरुक्ति से—धीरे-धीरे, बैठे-बैठे, पहले-पहले, कभी-कभी।
दो क्रिया-विशेषणों के मेल से—नीचे-ऊपर, दूर-पास, आजकल, आस-पास, जब-तब।
अनुकरण वाचक शब्दों की द्विरुक्ति-धड़ाधड़, फटाफट, खटाखट, टनाटन, भनाभन।
अव्ययों के मेल से—यथाशक्ति, यथाक्रम, अनुक्रम, प्रतिदिन, अजन्म, भरपेट।
पूर्वकालिक कृदन्त और विशेषण के मेल से—विशेषकर, एक-एक कर, मुख्यकर।

(ग) **स्थानीय क्रिया-विशेषण**—ऐसे दूसरे शब्द, जो बिना परिवर्तन के किसी विशेष स्थान पर क्रिया-विशेषण के स्थान पर प्रयुक्त होते हैं स्थानीय क्रिया-विशेषण कहलाते हैं।
जैसे—वह अपना सिर पढ़ेगा।

(*iii*) क्रिया-विशेषण के भेद (अर्थ के आधार पर)

अर्थ के अनुसार क्रिया-विशेषण के निम्नलिखित भेद हैं—

(क) **परिमाणवाचक क्रिया-विशेषण**—जिन शब्दों के द्वारा परिमाण का बोध होता है, उन्हें परिमाणवाचक क्रिया विशेषण कहते हैं। ये निम्नलिखित प्रकार से वर्गीकृत हो सकते हैं।
वे परिमाणवाचक क्रिया विशेषण जो कम मात्रा काबोध कराते हैं।

(*i*) अधिकता बोधक—बहुत, भारी, खूब, अत्यन्त, अतिशय, बड़ा।
(*ii*) न्यूनता बोधक —कम, अल्प, अत्यल्प, कुछ, जरा, किंचित्।
(*iii*) पर्याप्ति बोधक—केवल, बराबर, बस, काफी, यथेष्ठ।
(*iv*) तुलना-वाचक—अधिक, कम, जितना, उतना, कितना, बढ़कर।
(*v*) श्रेणी-वाचक—क्रम-क्रम से, बारी-बारी से, यथा-क्रम, थोड़ा-थोड़ा, तिल-तिल आदि।

(ख) **रीतिवाचक क्रिया-विशेषण**—इनकी संख्या बहुत अधिक है। नीचे मुख्य रीतिवाचक क्रिया-विशेषण दिये जाते हैं।

(क) प्रकार — यथा, तथा, ऐसे, कैसे, जैसे, सहज, अनायास, साक्षात्, हौले, पैदल।
(ख) निश्चय — सचमुच, सही, निस्सन्देह, अवश्य, वस्तुतः इत्यादि।
(ग) स्वीकार — हाँ, जी, ठीक, सच।
(घ) अनिश्चय — शायद, कदाचित, यथासंभव।
(ङ) कारण — किसलिए, क्यों, काहे को।
(च) निषेध — न, नहीं, मत।
(छ) अवधारण — भी, ही, मात्र, भर, तक, तो, सा।

(ग) **स्थान वाचक क्रिया-विशेषण**—इसके द्वारा स्थान का ज्ञान होता है। इसके दो भेद हैं :—

(1) स्थितिवाचक—यहाँ, वहाँ, ऊपर, नीचे, पीछे, बाहर, भीतर, पास, सर्वत्र इत्यादि।
(2) दिशावाचक—इधर, उधर, किधर, दाएँ, बाएँ, इस तरफ, उस तरफ आदि।

(घ) **कालवाचक क्रिया-विशेषण**—इसके द्वारा समय का ज्ञान होता है। इसका वर्गीकरण तीन भागों में किया गया है :—
समय वाचक—आज, कल, परसों, नरसों, तरसों, जब, तब, सबेरे, शाम, तुरन्त इत्यादि।
अवधि वाचक—आजकल, नित्य, सदा, लगातार, दिनभर, कब का।
पौनः पुन्य वाचक—प्रतिदिन, एक, दूसरे, तीसरे, बार-बार, बहुधा इत्यादि।

(ङ) **गुणवाचक क्रिया-विशेषण**—जिन शब्दों से क्रिया का गुण प्रकट होता है, उनको गुण वाचक क्रिया-विशेषण कहते हैं। जैसे—वह तेज भागता है।

सम्बन्ध-बोधक

सम्बन्ध-बोधक वे अविकारी शब्द हैं जो संज्ञा या सर्वनाम के अनन्तर प्रयुक्त होकर वाक्य में आगत अन्य शब्दों के साथ उसका सम्बन्ध प्रकट

करते हैं। जैसे–परिश्रम के बिना सफलता नहीं मिलती। उसने कक्षा पाँच तक पढ़ा। इन वाक्यों में 'बिना' और 'तक' शब्द सम्बन्ध-बोधक हैं।

सम्बन्ध-बोधक के भेद–सम्बन्ध-बोधक अव्यय का वर्गीकरण प्रयोग, अर्थ और व्युत्पत्ति के आधार पर अधोलिखित रूप में किया गया है–

प्रयोग के अनुसार भेद–प्रयोग के अनुसार सम्बन्ध-बोधक के दो भेद हैं–(*i*) सम्बद्ध, (*ii*) अनुबद्ध

(*i*) **सम्बद्ध-सम्बन्ध-बोधक**–सम्बद्ध सम्बन्ध-बोधक अव्यय का प्रयोग वाक्य में संज्ञा की विभक्तियों के बाद होता है।
जैसे–परिश्रम के बिना, पूजा से पहले, घर के बाहर, घोड़े के ऊपर।

(*ii*) **अनुबद्ध सम्बन्ध-बोधक**–अनुबद्ध सम्बन्ध-बोधक अव्यय वाक्य में संज्ञा के विकृत रूप के अनन्तर प्रयुक्त होता है।
जैसे–मित्रों सहित, कटोरे भर, पाँचवी तक, सैनिकों समेत।

अर्थ के अनुसार सम्बन्ध-बोधक के भेद

(*i*) काल-वाचक–आगे, पीछे, पूर्व, पश्चात्, लगभग, बाद, उपरान्त आदि।
(*ii*) स्थान-वाचक–आगे, पीछे, नीचे, तले, सामने, पास, निकट, भीतर, यहाँ, वहाँ, बीच, बाहर, दूर।
(*iii*) दिशा-वाचक–प्रति, ओर, तरफ, पार, आरपार, आसपास।
(*iv*) साधन-वाचक–जरिये, द्वारा, मारफत, हाथे, सहारे, बल करके।
(*v*) हेतु-वाचक–लिए, वास्ते, सीमित, खातिर, कारण, हेतु, मारे।
(*vi*) विषय-वाचक–बाबत, बनिस्बत, विषय, भरोसे इत्यादि।
(*vii*) व्यतिरेक-वाचक–सिवाय, अलावा, बिना, अतिरिक्त, रहित, बगैर।
(*viii*) विरोध-वाचक–समान, तरह, तुल्य, अनुसार, अनुरूप, भाँति, नाई, सरीखा, खिलाफ, प्रतिकूल, विपरीत, उल्टे।
(*ix*) विनिमय-वाचक–बदले, पलटे, एवज, जगह।
(*x*) सहचर-वाचक–संग, समेत, साथ, वश, स्वाधीन, सहित, अधीन।
(*xi*) संग्रह-वाचक–तक, भर, मात्र, पर्यंत।
(*xii*) तुलना-वाचक–अपेक्षा, बनिस्बत, आगे, सामने।

व्युत्पत्ति के अनुसार सम्बन्ध-बोधक के भेद

व्युत्पत्ति के अनुसार सम्बन्ध-बोधक के निम्नलिखित भेद हैं–

(*i*) मूल सम्बन्ध-बोधक
(*ii*) यौगिक सम्बन्ध-बोधक

(*i*) **मूल सम्बन्ध-बोधक**–हिन्दी में मूल सम्बन्ध-बोधक अव्यय वे हैं जो दूसरे शब्दों के योग से नहीं बनते हैं।
जैसे बिना, पर्यंत, नाईं, पूर्यक, समेत इत्यादि।

(*ii*) **यौगिक सम्बन्ध-बोधक**–यौगिक सम्बन्ध-बोधक वे हैं जो दूसरे शब्दों के योग से बनते हैं।
जैसे–उपेक्षा, मारफत, भीतर, दरम्यान।

यौगिक सम्बन्ध-बोधक का निर्माण–इसका निर्माण अधोलिखित शब्दों से होता है :–

संज्ञा से–पलटे, मारफत, लेखे, बदले, विषय, पालते, नाच आदि।
विशेषण से–समान, तुल्य, उल्टा, ऐसा, जैसा, योग्य, सरीखा आदि।
क्रिया-विशेषण से–ऊपर, भीतर, यहाँ, बाहर, पास, पीछे, इत्यादि।
क्रिया से–करके, लिए, मारे, जाने।

समुच्चय बोधक

जो अव्यय दो या दो से अधिक शब्दों, वाक्यांशों अथवा वाक्यों को जोड़ता या अलग करता है, उसे 'समुच्चय बोधक' अव्यय कहते हैं। जैसे–"राम और लक्ष्मण वन गए।" यहाँ 'और' अव्यय दो वाक्यों 'राम वन गए', 'लक्ष्मण वन गए' को जोड़ता है। इस वाक्य में और समुच्चय बोधक है।

समुच्चय बोधक अव्यय के भेद

समुच्चय बोधक अव्यय के दो प्रमुख भेद हैं–(*i*) समानाधिकरण समुच्चय बोधक, (*ii*) व्यधिकरण समुच्चय बोधक

(*i*) **समानाधिकरण समुच्चय बोधक**–समानाधिकरण समुच्चय बोधक उन अव्ययों को कहते हैं जो दो मुख्य वाक्यों या समान स्थिति वाले पदों अथवा वाक्य खण्डों को जोड़ते हैं। इनके चार उपभेद निम्नलिखित हैं–
संयोजक–और, तथा एवं, अब और व।
विभाजक–या, वा, अथवा, किंबा, कि, न कि, नहीं तो, न न, चाहे....चाहे।
विरोध दर्शन–बल्कि, मगर, परन्तु, किन्तु, लेकिन, पर, वरन्।
परिमाण दर्शक–इसलिए, अतः, अतएव, सो।

(*ii*) **व्यधिकरण समुच्चय बोधक**–व्यधिकरण समुच्चय बोधक अव्यय उसे कहते हैं जिसका प्रयोग प्रधान वाक्य या उसके समानाधिकरण वाक्य खण्डों को जोड़ने के लिए होता है। इनके भी चार भेद हैं–
कारक वाचक–क्योंकि, चूँकि, कि, कारण, इसलिए, जो कि।
उद्देश्य वाचक–कि, जो, इसलिए, ताकि।
संकेत वाचक–जो....तो, यदि....तो, चाहे, परन्तु, यद्यपि, तो... भी, अगर, कि।
स्वरूप वाचक–कि, जो, अर्थात्, याने, मानो।

विस्मयादि बोधक अव्यय

'विस्मयादि बोधक अव्यय' वे पद हैं जिनका प्रयोग वक्ता के शोक, हर्ष आदि मनोभावों की अभिव्यक्ति के लिए होता है। किन्तु उनका सम्बन्ध वाक्य या उसके किसी विशेष पद से नहीं होता है।

जैसे–हाय! अब वह नहीं रहा। इस वाक्य में हाय विस्मयादि बोधक अव्यय है। इसका सम्बन्ध न तो वाक्य से है और न किसी पद से।

विस्मयादि बोधक अव्यय के भेद

विस्मयादि बोधक अव्ययों का वर्गीकरण अधोलिखित रूप में किया गया है–

(*i*) हर्ष बोधक –आहा! वाह-वाह! धन्य-धन्य! शाबाश! जय-जय! कैसा मनोरम दृश्य!
(*ii*) शोक बोधक –आह! ऊह! हा-हा! दइया रे! राम-राम! बाप रे! आदि।
(*iii*) आश्चर्य बोधक –वाह! हैं! ऐ! ओहो! क्या! वाह वा!
(*iv*) अनुमोदन बोधक–ठीक! वाह! शाबाश! हाँ-हाँ! अच्छा!
(*v*) तिरस्कार बोधक–छिः! हट! अरे! धिक्! दुर्! चुप!
(*vi*) स्वीकार बोधक–हाँ! जी हाँ! अच्छा! जी! ठीक! बहुत अच्छा!
(*vii*) सम्बोधन बोधक–अरे! रे! लो! हे! अहो! अजी! जी! अरी!

वस्तुनिष्ठ प्रश्नोत्तर

1. कौन-से शब्द अविकारी होते हैं?
A. सर्वनाम B. देशज
C. क्रिया-विशेषण D. यौगिक

2. निम्नलिखित वाक्यों में से किस वाक्य में अकर्मक क्रिया है?
A. राम आम खाता है B. उसने कमीज पहनी
C. पुष्पा रोती है D. मैंने उसे पुस्तक दी

3. संज्ञा के स्थान पर प्रयुक्त होने वाले शब्द को क्या कहते हैं?
A. सर्वनाम B. सार्थक
C. अविकारी D. अव्यय

4. मुख्यतः काल कितने हैं?
A. पाँच B. चार
C. तीन D. दो

5. 'वह पढ़ रहा है'—यह कौन-सा काल है?
A. भूतकाल B. भविष्यत् काल
C. वर्तमान काल D. अपूर्ण काल

6. मूल क्रिया के अतिरिक्त वाक्य में जितनी भी क्रियाएँ आती हैं, उन्हें क्या कहते हैं?
A. अकर्मक क्रिया B. सहायक क्रिया
C. गौण क्रिया D. रंजक क्रिया

7. 'इधर-उधर कहीं मत जाना' में 'इधर-उधर' व्याकरण की दृष्टि से क्या है?
A. क्रिया-विशेषण B. विशेषण
C. सर्वनाम D. क्रिया

8. निम्नलिखित शब्दों में से कौन-सा शब्द अविकारी है?
A. घोड़ा B. आजकल
C. संकेत D. नदी

9. निम्नलिखित शब्दों में से कौन-सा शब्द स्त्रीलिंग है?
A. दही B. मधु
C. मोती D. धातु

10. 'कक्षा' कौन-सी संज्ञा है?
A. जातिवाचक B. भाववाचक
C. समुदायवाचक D. व्यक्तिवाचक

11. हिन्दी में कितने 'कारक' होते हैं?
A. दस B. आठ
C. पाँच D. तीन

12. विशेषण उन शब्दों को कहते हैं, जो—
A. संज्ञा के स्थान पर इस्तेमाल किए जाएं
B. संज्ञा की विशेषता प्रकट करें
C. क्रिया की विशेषता प्रकट करें
D. अपने आप में पूर्ण हों

13. नीचे कुछ शब्दों के पुल्लिंग और स्त्रीलिंग के जोड़े दिए हुए हैं। कौन-सा जोड़ा गलत है?
A. शूद्र-शूद्रा B. ग्वाला-ग्वालिन
C. कबूतर-कबूतरी D. बाल-बाली

14. सतीश ने आम खाये। इसमें 'आम' शब्द—
A. एकवचन है B. बहुवचन है
C. दोनों है D. दोनों में से कोई नहीं है

15. 'दया' भाववाचक संज्ञा है। इससे विशेषण बनेगा—
A. दयालु B. दीनता
C. दयात्व D. दयता

16. 'पढ़ना' से भाववाचक संज्ञा क्या बनेगी?
A. पाठ B. पठनीय
C. पढ़ाई D. पाठक

17. निम्नलिखित में से कौन-सा शब्द विशेषण है?
A. पशुता B. यौवन
C. चातुर्य D. दुष्ट

18. गली में 'तीसरा' मकान श्याम का है। यहाँ 'तीसरा' व्याकरण की दृष्टि से क्या है?
A. बहुवचन B. विशेषण
C. संज्ञा D. अव्यय

19. 'ने' किस कारक की विभक्ति है?
A. करण B. कर्म
C. कर्ता D. सम्प्रदान

20. 'यश' व्याकरण की दृष्टि से क्या है?
A. विशेषण B. संज्ञा
C. क्रिया D. क्रिया-विशेषण

21. 'श्रीमान' का स्त्रीलिंग है—
A. पत्नी B. श्रीमती
C. देवी D. महोदया

22. निम्न में से कौन-सा शब्द तद्भव है?
A. अग्नि B. हाथ
C. रात्रि D. कर्ण

23. निम्न वाक्यों में से किस वाक्य में क्रिया कर्मवाच्य है?
A. राम के पिता अध्यापक हैं
B. वे सब काश्मीर जायेंगे
C. उत्सव में राष्ट्रीय गीत गाया गया
D. बच्चे पार्क में खेल रहे हैं

24. 'उसे' का बहुवचन है—
A. उसको B. उससे
C. उन्हें D. उसका

25. 'हमें' का एकवचन है—
A. हम B. हमको
C. मुझे D. मुझसे

26. निम्न में से कौन-सा शब्द तत्सम नहीं है?
A. दुग्ध B. चूर्ण
C. क्षेत्र D. माता

27. निम्न में से कौन-सा शब्द अविकारी नहीं है?
A. आज B. कल
C. ऊपर D. घोड़ा

28. 'मीठा' विशेषण है। इससे भाववाचक संज्ञा बनेगी–
A. मीठात्व B. मीठापन
C. मिठास D. मिठाई

29. 'राधा तेज दौड़ती है'। इसमें तेज शब्द क्या है?
A. क्रिया B. क्रिया-विशेषण
C. विशेषण D. उपरोक्त में से कोई भी नहीं

30. जो शब्द संज्ञा के बदले प्रयुक्त होता है, उसे कहते हैं–
A. सर्वनाम B. क्रिया
C. विशेषण D. क्रिया-विशेषण

31. निम्न में से कौन-सा शब्द सर्वनाम है?
A. मेरी B. उन्होंने
C. हमारे D. उपरोक्त तीनों

32. निम्न में से भाववाचक संज्ञा है–
A. मोहन B. खिलाड़ी
C. बचपन D. मैदान

33. निम्न में से कौन-सा शब्द विशेषण है?
A. रोग B. घोड़ा
C. गाँव D. शोक

34. निम्न में से कौन-सी अकर्मक क्रिया है?
A. चुराना B. माँगना
C. लेना D. हँसना

35. निम्न में से कौन-सी सकर्मक क्रिया है?
A. सोना B. हँसना
C. रोना D. देखना

36. पंडित की भाववाचक संज्ञा है–
A. पंडित्व B. पंडिताइन
C. पंडिताऊ D. पांडित्य

37. 'विद्वान्' का स्त्रीलिंग है–
A. विद्वानी B. विद्यावती
C. विदुषी D. विदुषिनी

38. निम्नलिखित में से कौन-सा शब्द भाववाचक संज्ञा नहीं है?
A. बन्धुत्व B. प्रभुता
C. मानवता D. कुशल

39. 'दैनिक' क्या है?
A. संज्ञा B. सर्वनाम
C. क्रिया D. विशेषण

40. 'श्रद्धा' का विशेषण क्या बनता है?
A. श्रद्धास्पद B. श्रद्धेय
C. श्रद्धालु D. उपर्युक्त में से कोई भी नहीं

41. उपसर्ग का प्रयोग होता है, शब्द के–
A. मध्य में B. आदि में
C. अन्त में D. आदि और अंत दोनों में

42. सर्वनाम का प्रयोग किसके बदले किया जाता है?
A. क्रिया-विशेषण B. क्रिया
C. विशेषण D. संज्ञा

43. व्याकरण की दृष्टि से 'प्रेम' शब्द क्या है?
A. भाववाचक संज्ञा B. विशेषण
C. अव्यय D. क्रिया

44. 'मैंने' कौन-सा कारक है?
A. कर्ता B. कर्म
C. करण D. सम्प्रदान

45. 'सेवक' का स्त्रीलिंग है–
A. सेवका B. सेवकाइन
C. सेवकी D. सेविका

उत्तरमाला

1	2	3	4	5	6	7	8	9	10
C	C	A	C	C	B	A	B	D	C
11	**12**	**13**	**14**	**15**	**16**	**17**	**18**	**19**	**20**
B	B	D	B	A	C	D	B	C	B
21	**22**	**23**	**24**	**25**	**26**	**27**	**28**	**29**	**30**
B	B	C	C	C	D	D	C	B	A
31	**32**	**33**	**34**	**35**	**36**	**37**	**38**	**39**	**40**
D	C	D	D	D	D	C	D	D	C
41	**42**	**43**	**44**	**45**					
B	D	A	A	D					

★ ★ ★

6

अशुद्ध वाक्य को शुद्ध करना

	अशुद्ध वाक्य		शुद्ध वाक्य
1.	कई रेलवे कर्मचारियों की गिरफ्तारी हुई।	–	रेलवे के कई कर्मचारियों की गिरफ्तारी हुई।
2.	वह दण्ड देने योग्य है।	–	वह दण्डित होने योग्य है/वह दण्ड पाने योग्य है।
3.	सौ रुपए सधन्यवाद प्राप्त हुए।	–	सौ रुपए प्राप्त हुए। धन्यवाद!
4.	महाविद्यालय की ओर से प्रधानमंत्री को अभिनन्दन पत्र प्रदान किया गया।	–	महाविद्यालय की ओर से प्रधानमंत्री को अभिनन्दन पत्र अर्पित किया गया।
5.	कुत्ता दरवान की तरह दुम हिलाता हुआ दरवाजे पर खड़ा रहता था।	–	कुत्ता दुम हिलाता हुआ दरवान की तरह दरवाजे पर खड़ा रहता था।
6.	इन बातों के बावजूद भी वह नहीं समझ सका।	–	इन बातों के बावजूद वह नहीं समझ सका।
7.	ये बातें केवल दिखावा भर थीं।	–	ये बातें केवल दिखावा थीं/ये बातें दिखावा भर थीं।
8.	दक्षिण का अधिकांश भाग पठार है।	–	दक्षिण का अधिक भाग पठार है।
9.	मेरी निगाह मेरे मित्र की ओर थी।	–	मेरी निगाह मित्र की ओर थी।
10.	प्रधानाध्यापक लड़के चुनेंगे।	–	प्रधानाध्यापक लड़कों को चुनेंगे।
11.	मैंने लिख चुका था।	–	मैं लिख चुका था।
12.	मैंने इस गाड़ी से जाना है।	–	मुझे इस गाड़ी से जाना है।
13.	कर्ण बहुत बड़े दायक थे।	–	कर्ण बहुत बड़े दाता थे।
14.	इसका कोई अर्थ नहीं होता।	–	इसका कुछ अर्थ नहीं होता।
15.	आओ, तुम भी कोई काम कर लो।	–	आओ, तुम भी कुछ काम कर लो।
16.	श्री कृष्ण के अनेकों नाम हैं।	–	श्री कृष्ण के अनेक नाम हैं।
17.	उसकी गर्दन शर्म से नीचे थी।	–	उसकी गर्दन शर्म से नीची थी।
18.	मैं आपकी श्रद्धा करता हूँ।	–	मैं आप पर श्रद्धा रखता हूँ।
19.	सरकार शान्ति-व्यवस्था के लिए पुलिस पर निर्भर करती है।	–	सरकार शान्ति-व्यवस्था के लिए पुलिस पर निर्भर रहती है।
20.	मैं अपने गुरु के उँपर बहुत श्रद्धा रखता हूँ।	–	मैं अपने गुरु पर बहुत श्रद्धा रखता हूँ।
21.	कृष्ण और सुभद्रा भाई-बहन थीं।	–	कृष्ण और सुभद्रा भाई-बहन थे।
22.	राम और श्याम विद्यालय जा रहा है।	–	राम और श्याम विद्यालय जा रहे हैं।
23.	राम और सीता वन को जा रही थीं।	–	राम और सीता वन को जा रहे थे।
24.	शायद वे जरूर जाएँगे।	–	शायद वे जाएँगे/वे जरूर जाएँगे।
25.	मेरी स्त्री बीमार है।	–	मेरी पत्नी बीमार है।
26.	शरीफ पुरुष किसी को तंग नहीं करते।	–	शरीफ लोग किसी को तंग नहीं करते/सज्जन पुरुष किसी को तंग नहीं करते।
27.	इस समस्या का कोई उपाय नहीं है।	–	इस समस्या का कोई समाधान नहीं है।
28.	हो सकता है वह अवश्य पास हो जाए।	–	हो सकता है वह पास हो जाए।
29.	किसी और दूसरे आदमी को भेज दीजिए।	–	किसी और को भेज दीजिए/किसी दूसरे को भेज दीजिए।
30.	यह दवा बहुत तत्काल असर दिखाती है।	–	यह दवा तत्काल असर दिखाती है।
31.	यहाँ तरुण नवयुवकों की शिक्षा का प्रबन्ध है।	–	यहाँ नवयुवकों की शिक्षा का प्रबन्ध है।
32.	प्रत्येक दिन स्नान करना चाहिए।	–	प्रतिदिन स्नान करना चाहिए।

	अशुद्ध वाक्य		शुद्ध वाक्य
33.	सैनिकों ने खूँखार अस्त्र-शस्त्रों से हमला किया।	—	सैनिकों ने विनाशकारी अस्त्र-शस्त्रों से हमला किया।
34.	हैजे आदि से हजारों लोग मर गए।	—	हैजा आदि से हजारों लोग मर गए।
35.	पूज्यनीय पिताजी को प्रणाम।	—	पूज्य पिताजी/पूजनीय पिताजी को प्रणाम।
36.	उसकी सौन्दर्यता पर सब मुग्ध थे।	—	उसके सौन्दर्य पर सब मुग्ध थे। या, उसकी सुन्दरता पर सब मुग्ध थे।
37.	अत्याधिक कार्य स्वास्थ को बिगाड़ देता है।	—	अत्यधिक कार्य स्वास्थ्य को बिगाड़ देता है।
38.	भिखारी ने राजा को आशीर्वाद प्रदान किया।	—	भिखारी ने राजा को आशीर्वाद दिया।
39.	प्राणीमात्र पर दया करो।	—	प्राणिमात्र पर दया करो।
40.	झगड़े का श्री गणेश तब हुआ जब जुलूस पर किसी ने पत्थर फेंक दिया।	—	झगड़े का आरम्भ तब हुआ जब जुलूस पर किसी ने पत्थर फेंक दिया।
41.	मेरा पतलून मैला है।	—	मेरी पतलून मैली है।
42.	उसकी दादी अभी जिन्दी है।	—	उसकी दादी अभी जिन्दा है।
43.	राम ने बाजार जाना है।	—	राम को बाजार जाना है।
44.	आज की ताजी खबर पढ़िए।	—	आज की ताजा खबर पढ़िए।
45.	हमने उनकी योजनाओं को दुम दबाकर स्वीकार कर लिया।	—	हमने उनकी योजनाओं को विवश होकर स्वीकार कर लिया।
46.	वह विद्वान महिला थीं।	—	वह विदुषी थीं।
47.	इसका उत्तरदाइत्व आपके उँपर है।	—	इसका उत्तरदायित्व आप पर है।
48.	उनकी मृत्यु से नगर की अपूर्व क्षति हुई।	—	उनकी मृत्यु से अपूरणीय क्षति हुई।
49.	साहित्य और जीवन का घोर सम्बन्ध है।	—	साहित्य और जीवन का घनिष्ठ सम्बन्ध है।
50.	ईश्वर उसकी मृत आत्मा को शान्ति दें।	—	ईश्वर उसकी आत्मा को शान्ति दें।
51.	आप खाना खाने आ जाओ।	—	आप खाना खाने आ जाएँ।
52.	आप कहोगे।	—	आप कहेंगे।
53.	अगर मैं गलती करूँ तो आप मुझे दुरुस्त कर दें।	—	अगर मैं गलती करूँ तो आप मुझे सुधार दें।
54.	काँग्रेस ने भारत की अच्छाई के अनेक कार्य किए।	—	काँग्रेस ने भारत की भलाई के लिए अनेक कार्य किए।
55.	उसका पैर गरम आग पर पड़ गया।	—	उसका पैर आग पर पड़ गया।
56.	शब्द केवल संकेत मात्र होते हैं।	—	शब्द केवल संकेत होते हैं। या, शब्द संकेत मात्र होते हैं।
57.	उसकी दृष्टि चित्र में गड़ी थी।	—	उसकी दृष्टि चित्र पर गड़ी थी।
58.	वे लगन के साथ देश की सेवा कर रहे हैं।	—	वे लगनपूर्वक देश की सेवा कर रहे हैं।
59.	फिर, कुछ देर से उसने कहा।	—	फिर, कुछ देर बाद उसने कहा।
60.	केवल कहने मात्र से कुछ नहीं होता।	—	केवल कहने से कुछ नहीं होता।
61.	चाहे जैसे भी हो, तुम वहाँ जाओ।	—	चाहे जैसे हो, तुम वहाँ जाओ।
62.	सभी प्रकार की चीज मौजूद थी।	—	सभी प्रकार की चीजें मौजूद थीं।
63.	आपके एक-एक शब्द तुले हुए होते हैं।	—	आपके एक-एक शब्द नपे-तुले होते हैं।
64.	आपकी राय से यह काम जरूरी है।	—	आपकी राय में यह काम जरूरी है।
65.	आपकी पुस्तक धन्यवाद सहित लौटाता हूँ।	—	आपकी पुस्तक धन्यवादपूर्वक लौटाता हूँ।
66.	हमारे बाप-दादाओं ने कभी ऐसा नहीं किया।	—	हमारे बाप-दादा ने कभी ऐसा नहीं किया।
67.	सबों ने यही राय दी।	—	सबने यही राय दी।
68.	संज्ञा की प्रशंसा करने वाले शब्द विशेषण होते हैं।	—	संज्ञा की विशेषता बताने वाले शब्द विशेषण होते हैं।
69.	मुझे प्रायः समस्त काम अपने हाथों करना पड़ता है।	—	मुझे प्रायः सम्पूर्ण काम अपने हाथों करना पड़ता है।
70.	सूरदास के उँपर डॉ॰ हजारी प्रसाद द्विवेदी ने एक उत्तम ग्रंथ लिखा है।	—	सूरदास के सम्बन्ध में डॉ॰ हजारी प्रसाद द्विवेदी ने एक उत्तम ग्रंथ लिखा है।
71.	अधिकांश धन व्यर्थ गया।	—	धन का अधिकांश व्यर्थ गया।
72.	राम का भविष्य शंकर के उँपर निर्भर है।	—	राम का भविष्य शंकर पर निर्भर है।
73.	इन दोनों में केवल यही अन्तर है।	—	इन दोनों में यही अन्तर है।
74.	उसे एक चिट्ठी लिखना होगा।	—	उसे एक चिट्ठी लिखनी होगी।

	अशुद्ध वाक्य		शुद्ध वाक्य
75.	यह बात हृदय से सम्भव है वे न मानें।	–	सम्भव है यह बात वे हृदय से नहीं मानें।
76.	आज उपशिक्षा मंत्री जी नगर में पधार रहे हैं।	–	आज शिक्षा उपमंत्री जी नगर में पधार रहे हैं।
77.	अधिकांश उर्दू के कवि शृंगारी कविता लिखते हैं।	–	उर्दू के अधिकतर कवि शृंगारी कविता लिखते हैं।
78.	उसकी आवाज कान में सुनाई पड़ी।	–	उसकी आवाज सुनाई पड़ी/उसकी आवाज कान में पड़ी।
79.	वह कहते हैं।	–	वे कहते हैं।
80.	थोड़ी देर बाद वे वापस लौट आए।	–	थोड़ी देर बाद वे लौट आये। या, थोड़ी देर बाद वे वापस आए।
81.	उन्हें मृत्युदण्ड की सजा मिली।	–	उन्हें मृत्युदण्ड मिला।
82.	उसी आदमी को, जो आपके पास जायेगा, यह पुस्तक दे दिजिए।	–	उसी आदमी को, जो आपके पास जाएगा, यह पुस्तक दे दीजिए।
83.	मेरा विश्वास मेरी आँखों पर भी नहीं है।	–	मेरा विश्वास अपनी आँखों पर भी नहीं है।
84.	वह अनेक प्रकार के बहाने बनाने लगा।	–	वह अनेक बहाने बनाने लगा।
85.	आप अपनी ताकत के बल पर यह काम करना चाहते हैं।	–	आप अपने बल पर यह काम करना चाहते हैं। या, आप अपनी ताकत पर यह काम करना चाहते हैं।
86.	मैं आज प्रातःकाल के समय वहाँ गया था।	–	मैं आज प्रातःकाल वहाँ गया था।
87.	कृपया यह बताने का अनुग्रह करें।	–	कृपया यह बतलावें। या, यह बतलाने की कृपा करें। या, यह बतलाने का अनुग्रह करें।
88.	सारे देशभर में यह बात फैल गई।	–	सारे देश में यह बात फैल गई/या, देशभर में यह बात फैल गई।
89.	वह इस बात की व्यवस्था का कोई प्रबन्ध नहीं कर सकता।	–	वह इस बात की व्यवस्था नहीं कर सकता/या, वह इस बात का प्रबन्ध नहीं कर सकता।
90.	देश की रक्षा का भार तुम्हारे उँपर है।	–	देश की रक्षा का भार तुम पर है।
91.	दंगे में दस मनुष्य मरे और पन्द्रह आदमी घायल हुए।	–	दंगे में दस आदमी मरे और पन्द्रह घायल हुए।
92.	कुछ पशु खेती के काम में आने के सिवा वे धर्म की दृष्टि से भी पूज्य हैं।	–	कुछ पशु खेती के काम में आने के अतिरिक्त धर्म की दृष्टि से भी पूज्य हैं।
93.	वह खाने-पीने के व्यंजन बना रही थी।	–	वह व्यंजन बना रही थी।
94.	प्रायः ऐसे अवसर आते हैं जिसमें लोगों को कभी-कभी अपना मत बदलना पड़ता है।	–	प्रायः ऐसे अवसर आते हैं जिनमें लोगों को अपना मत बदलना पड़ता है।
95.	आगरा के निकट दो रेलगाड़ियाँ लड़ गईं।	–	आगरा के निकट दो रेलगाड़ियों की टक्कर हो गई।
96.	वृक्ष में फल लगे हैं।	–	वृक्ष पर फल लगे हैं।
97.	उसने उधर देखा और बोला।	–	उसने उधर देखा और कहा।
98.	वहाँ पूड़ियाँ और झरने का पानी पीकर हमलोग आगे बढ़े।	–	वहाँ पूड़ियाँ खाकर और झरने का पानी पीकर हमलोग आगे बढ़े।
99.	मैं यह काम किया चाहता हूँ।	–	मैं यह काम करना चाहता हूँ।
100.	मेरे को ऐसा मत कहो।	–	मुझको ऐसा मत कहो।
101.	वे कोई स्कूल नहीं खोले थे।	–	उन्होंने कोई स्कूल नहीं खोला था।
102.	पंजाब के मुसलमान वहाँ प्रवेश किए थे।	–	पंजाब के मुसलमानों ने वहाँ प्रवेश किया था।
103.	लड़ाई के द्वारा लोगों ने खूब धन कमाया।	–	लड़ाई के समय लोगों ने खूब धन कमाया।
104.	यह बीमारी देश में लड़ाई के द्वारा फैली थी।	–	देश में यह बीमारी लड़ाई के कारण फैली थी।
105.	उन्होंने सरलता के साथ उत्तर दिया।	–	उन्होंने सरलतापूर्वक उत्तर दिया।
106.	उनके विरुद्ध मुकदमा चलाया गया।	–	उन पर मुकदमा चलाया गया।
107.	पूर्व इसके कि कोई हँसे, हम हँस पड़े।	–	किसी के हँसने के पहले हम स्वयं हँस पड़े।
108.	परीक्षा की प्रणाली बदलना चाहिए।	–	परीक्षा की प्रणाली बदलनी चाहिए।
109.	मैं तुम्हारे साथ नहाकर चलूँगा।	–	मैं नहाकर तुम्हारे साथ चलूँगा।
110.	शुद्ध गाय का दूध सेवन करो।	–	गाय का शुद्ध दूध सेवन करो।
111.	इतने वेतन से केवल दाल-रोटी हो जाती है।	–	इतने वेतन से केवल दाल-रोटी ही मिल पाती है।

	अशुद्ध वाक्य		शुद्ध वाक्य
112.	प्रेमचन्द जी ने पर्याप्त मात्रा में कहानी और उपन्यास लिखे।	–	प्रेमचन्द जी ने पर्याप्त संख्या में कहानी और उपन्यास लिखे।
113.	अनेकों बार समझाने पर भी वह नहीं समझा।	–	अनेक बार समझाने पर भी वह नहीं समझा।
114.	वह आगामी वर्ष हरिद्वार गया था।	–	वह गत् वर्ष हरिद्वार गया था।
115.	वह धर्मशालें में गया है।	–	वह धर्मशाला में गया है।
116.	मित्रों! उसकी भाग्य फूट गई।	–	मित्रों! उसका भाग्य फूट गया।
117.	हमें अपने माता-पिता का आदर करना चाहिए।	–	हमें माता-पिता का आदर करना चाहिए।
118.	उन्हें व्यर्थ रुपए देने से कोई लाभ नहीं है।	–	उन्हें रुपए देने से कोई लाभ नहीं/ अथवा, उन्हें रुपए देना व्यर्थ है।
119.	शास्त्रीजी की मृत्यु से हमें बड़ा खेद हुआ।	–	शास्त्री जी के निधन से हमें बहुत दुःख हुआ।
120.	शोक है कि आपने मेरे पत्रों का उत्तर नहीं दिया।	–	दुःख है कि आपने मेरे पत्रों के उत्तर नहीं दिए।
121.	एक-एक करके सभी चले गए।	–	एक-एक कर सभी चले गए।
122.	यह ग्रंथ दोहा और चौपाइयों में लिखा गया है।	–	यह ग्रंथ दोहे और चौपाइयों में लिखा गया है।
123.	मैं माता का दर्शन करने गया था।	–	मैं माता के दर्शन करने गया था।
124.	यही वे कारण हैं जिनके कारण देश में अशान्ति बढ़ रही है।	–	यही वे कारण हैं जिनसे देश में अशान्ति बढ़ रही है।
125.	ऐसी एकाध बातें और देखने में आती हैं।	–	ऐसी एकाध बात और देखने में आती है।
126.	प्रत्येक छोटी-मोटी विशेषताओं को देखना चाहिए।	–	प्रत्येक छोटी-मोटी विशेषता को देखना चाहिए।
127.	उन्होंने हाथ जोड़ा।	–	उन्होंने हाथ जोड़े।
128.	हम तो शादी में अवश्य ही जाएँगे।	–	हम शादी में अवश्य जाएँगे।
129.	तुम्हारा सब काम गलत होता है।	–	तुम्हारे सब काम गलत होते हैं।
130.	वह तो केवल आप ही पर निर्भर है।	–	वह तो केवल आप पर निर्भर है।
131.	उनकी आँखों की दृष्टि शून्य आकाश की ओर थी।	–	उनकी दृष्टि शून्य आकाश की ओर थी। या, उनकी आँखें शून्य आकाश की ओर थीं।
132.	वे सब काल-चक्र के पहिए के नीचे दब गए।	–	वे सब काल-चक्र में डूब गए।
133.	लड़का मिठाई लेकर भागता घर आया।	–	लड़का मिठाई लेकर दौड़ता हुआ घर आया।
134.	उसके अंग-अंग में सौन्दर्यता भरी थी।	–	उसके अंग-अंग में सौन्दर्य था।
135.	दो दिन की बदली के पीछे आज सूर्य निकला है।	–	दो दिन की बदली के बाद आज सूर्य निकला है।
135.	कोयला जलकर राख हो गई।	–	कोयला जलकर राख हो गया।
136.	सारा राज्य उसके लिए एक थाती थी।	–	सारा राज्य उसके लिए एक थाती था।
137.	मैं अपनी बात का स्पष्टीकरण करने के लिए तैयार हूँ।	–	मैं अपनी बात के स्पष्टीकरण के लिए तैयार हूँ।
138.	यह चित्र, गाँधी जी जब यहाँ पधारे थे। उस समय लिया गया था।	–	यह चित्र उस समय लिया गया था, जब गाँधी जी यहाँ पधारे थे।
139.	शत्रु उस पर टूट गए।	–	शत्रु उस पर टूट पड़े।
140.	लोग रविवार के दिन छुट्टी मनाते हैं।	–	लोग रविवार को छुट्टी मनाते हैं।
141.	उनकी एक आँख कानी थी।	–	वे काने थे।
142.	भीष्म पितामह आजन्म ब्रह्मचारी रहे।	–	भीष्म पितामह आजीवन ब्रह्मचारी रहे।
143.	वह अपनी विद्या समाप्त करके ही कुछ काम करेगा।	–	वह अपनी शिक्षा समाप्त करके ही कुछ काम करेगा।
144.	चावल का चिन्तनीय अभाव है।	–	चावल का अभाव चिंतनीय है।
145.	वह व्यक्ति ही क्या, जो कभी दुःख नहीं उठाया।	–	वह व्यक्ति ही क्या, जिसने कभी दुःख नहीं उठाया।
146.	यहाँ सर्वोत्कृष्ट ज्वर की चिकित्सा होती है।	–	यहाँ ज्वर की सर्वोत्कृष्ट चिकित्सा होती है।
147.	घड़ा और लोटा में पानी है।	–	घड़े और लोटे में पानी है।
148.	नौकर से कहो कि मेरा सामान तैयार रखो।	–	नौकर से कहो कि मेरा सामान तैयार रखे।
149.	गाँधी का देश सदैव आभारी रहेगा।	–	देश गाँधी का सदैव आभारी रहेगा।
150.	मैंने यह बात उनके द्वारा सुनी थी।	–	मैंने यह बात उनसे सुनी थी।

वस्तुनिष्ठ प्रश्नोत्तर

निर्देश (प्रश्न संख्या 1 से 4 तक): *निम्नलिखित अशुद्ध वाक्यों के शुद्ध रूप का नीचे दिए विकल्पों में से चयन कीजिए।*

1. मैं तेरे को बता दूँगा
A. मैं बता तुझको दूँगा B. मैं तुम्हें बता दूँगा
C. मैं तुझको बता दूँगा D. सभी वाक्य सही हैं

2. पेड़ों पर कोयल बोल रही थी
A. पेड़ पर कोयलें बोल रही थीं
B. पेड़ पर कोयल बोल रही थी
C. पेड़ों पर कोयल थी
D. सभी वाक्य सही हैं

3. मुझे भारी दुःख हुआ
A. मुझे बहुत दुःख हुआ
B. मुझे दुःखी हुआ
C. मुझे ज्यादा दुःख हुआ
D. सभी वाक्य सही हैं

4. वह पूर्णतया उत्तीर्ण हो गया
A. वह एकदम उत्तीर्ण हो गया
B. वह उत्तीर्ण हो गया
C. वह एकदम पास हो गया
D. सभी वाक्य सही हैं

निर्देश (प्रश्न संख्या 5 से 31 तक): *निम्नलिखित में शुद्ध वाक्य का चयन कीजिए।*

5. A. एक गीतों की पुस्तक ला दो
B. गीतों की एक पुस्तक ला दो
C. पुस्तक एक गीतों की ला दो
D. पुस्तक गीतों की एक ला दो

6. A. बन्दर को काटकर चाकू से फल खिला दो
B. चाकू से बन्दर को काटकर फल खिला दो
C. चाकू से फल काटकर बन्दर को खिला दो
D. फल काटकर चाकू से बन्दर को खिला दो

7. A. बाघ और बकरी एक घाट पर पानी पीती हैं
B. बाघ और बकरी एक घाट पर पानी पीते हैं
C. बाघ और बकरी पानी पीते हैं एक घाट पर
D. बाघ और बकरी पीते हैं पानी एक घाट पर

8. A. मैं गाने की कसरत कर रहा हूँ
B. मैं गाने का अभ्यास कर रहा हूँ
C. मैं गाने का शौक कर रहा हूँ
D. मैं गाने का व्यायाम कर रहा हूँ

9. A. उसकी अवस्था चालीस वर्ष की है
B. उसकी आयु चालीस वर्ष की है
C. उसका बात मत करो
D. आपका पत्र सधन्यवाद मिला

10. A. मैं जाते-जाते रुक गया
B. मैं जा रहा था पर रुक गया
C. मैं जा रहा था और रुक गया
D. अचानक जाते-जाते रुक गया

11. A. उसे जाने दो, रोको मत
B. रोको मत, उसे जाने दो
C. मत रोको, उसे जाने दो
D. उसे जाने ही दो, रोको नहीं

12. A. रात दस बजे गाड़ी आएगी
B. दस बजे रात में गाड़ी आएगी
C. रात में दस बजे गाड़ी आएगी
D. गाड़ी रात में दस बजे आएगी

13. A. रामचन्द्रजी को दशरथ ने चौदह वर्ष का वनवास दिया
B. दशरथ ने राम को चौदह वर्षों के लिए वनवास दिया
C. चौदह वर्षों का वनवास दशरथ ने राम को दिया
D. दशरथ ने राम को चौदह वर्षों का वनवास दिया

14. A. सम्भवतः कल तक वर्षा हो जाएगी
B. सम्भवतः कल तक अवश्य वर्षा हो जाएगी
C. कल तक निश्चित रूप से वर्षा होने की संभावना है
D. सम्भावना है कि कल तक निश्चय ही वर्षा होगी

15. A. हिन्दी के विकास के मुख्य तीन काल हैं, केवल
B. हिन्दी के विकास के तीन ही मुख्य काल हैं
C. तीन मुख्य काल हिन्दी के विकास के हैं
D. हिन्दी के विकास के तीन काल मुख्य हैं

16. छात्र द्वारा अवकाश के प्रार्थना-पत्र के अन्त में लिखा जाना चाहिए
A. आपका शिष्य B. आपका आज्ञाकारी शिष्य
C. आपका छात्र D. आपका स्नेही

17. A. जो जैसा कभी बोता है वैसा काटता है
B. वह जैसा कभी बोएगा है वैसा काटेगा
C. जो जैसा बोएगा वैसा ही काटेगा
D. जिसने जब जैसा बोया उसने तब वैसा काटा

18. A. मेरे को घर जाना चाहिए
B. मैंने घर जाना चाहिए
C. मुझे घर जाना चाहिए
D. मुझको घर को जाना चाहिए

19. 'मुझे केवल दस रुपए मात्र मिले' वाक्य अशुद्ध है, क्योंकि
A. वाक्य में **मुझे** नहीं होना चाहिए
B. वाक्य में **मिले** अन्त में नहीं होना चाहिए
C. वाक्य में **रुपए** मात्र से पूर्व नहीं होना चाहिए
D. वाक्य में **केवल** नहीं होना चाहिए

20. A. हमारे यहाँ तरुण नवयुवकों को काम सिखाया जाता है
B. पंडित जी की मृत्यु का हमें खेद है
C. यही नहीं, बल्कि वे वहाँ से चले भी आए
D. मुझसे यह काम सम्भव नहीं हो सकता

21. A. वहाँ भारी-भरकम भीड़ जमा थी
B. जो धन का भूखा है, वह साधु नहीं है
C. मुझे इस अधिवेशन का समाचार नहीं मिला था
D. मेरी कविता मुद्रित हो रही है

22. सही वाक्य का चयन कीजिए
A. देश सदा महात्मा गांधी का ऋणी रहेगा
B. महात्मा गांधी का देश सदा ऋणी रहेगा
C. महात्मा गांधी का सदा देश ऋणी रहेगा
D. देश महात्मा गांधी का सदा ऋणी रहेगा

23. A. परिवर्तन का यह अर्थ नहीं कि कदापि अतीत की सर्वथा उपेक्षा की जाए
B. परिवर्तन का अर्थ यह कदापि नहीं कि अतीत की सर्वथा उपेक्षा की जाए
C. परिवर्तन का अर्थ यह कदापि नहीं कि अतीत की सर्वथा अपेक्षा की जाए
D. परिवर्तन का यह अर्थ कदापि नहीं कि अतीत की सर्वथा उपेक्षा की जाए

24. A. जानते हैं किसी को कि इस बात को सताया न जाए
B. जानते हैं इस बात को किसी को सताया न जाए
C. इस बात को जानते हैं किसी को कि सताया नहीं जाए
D. इस बात को जानते हैं कि किसी को सताया न जाए

25. A. सीटी की आवाज जिधर से आ रही थी मैं उधर ही दौड़ पड़ा
B. बस सीटी की आवाज जिधर से आ रही थी मैं उधर ही दौड़ पड़ा
C. सीटी की आवाज जिधर से आ रही थी बस उधर ही मैं दौड़ पड़ा
D. जिधर से सीटी की आवाज आ रही थी मैं उधर ही दौड़ पड़ा

26. A. अधिकारियों ने कागजात का निरीक्षण किया
B. अधिकारियों ने कागजात का परीक्षण किया
C. अधिकारियों ने कागजात की जाँच की
D. अधिकारियों ने कागजात का अन्वेषण किया

27. A. भारत में अनेकों जातियाँ हैं
B. भारत में अनेक जातियाँ हैं
C. भारत में अनेकों जाति हैं
D. भारत में अनेक जाति हैं

28. A. वह दण्ड देने योग्य है
B. वह दण्ड के योग्य है
C. वह दण्ड लेने योग्य है
D. वह दण्ड पाने योग्य है

29. A. फल बच्चे को काटकर खिलाओ
B. बच्चे को काटकर फल खिलाओ
C. बच्चे को फल काटकर खिलाओ
D. काटकर फल बच्चे को खिलाओ

30. A. उसे अनुत्तीर्ण होने की आशा है
B. उसे अनुत्तीर्ण होने की आशंका है
C. उसे अनुत्तीर्ण होने का शक है
D. उसे अनुत्तीर्ण होने का संशय है

31. A. कल पाठ पढ़कर आइए
B. पाठ पढ़कर कल आइए
C. पाठ पढ़कर आइए कल
D. कल पाठ पढ़कर आइए

निर्देश (प्रश्न संख्या 32 से 46 तक): *निम्नलिखित अशुद्ध वाक्य के लिए चार-चार विकल्प दिए गए हैं। सही विकल्प चुनिए।*

32. जो मिठाइयाँ पसन्द हों आप खा लो
A. जो मिठाई पसन्द हों आप खा लो
B. जो मिठाई पसन्द हो तुम खा लो
C. जो मिठाइयाँ पसन्द हों तुम खा लो
D. जो मिठाइयाँ पसन्द हों उन्हें आप खाइए

33. हम बचपन में वहाँ जाता रहा
A. हम बचपन में वहाँ जाएंगे
B. हम बचपन में वहाँ जाते रहे हैं
C. मैं बचपन में वहाँ जाता रहा
D. मैं बचपन में वहाँ जाऊँगा

34. प्रत्येक व्यक्ति कविता नहीं कर सकते
A. प्रत्येक व्यक्ति कविता कर सकते हैं
B. प्रत्येक व्यक्ति कविता नहीं कर सकते हैं
C. प्रत्येक व्यक्ति कविता नहीं कर सकता
D. हर व्यक्ति कविता कर सकते हैं

35. हेम नरेश को पुस्तक दिया
A. हेम नरेश की पुस्तक दी
B. हेम ने नरेश को पुस्तक दी
C. हेम नरेश का पुस्तक देगा
D. हेम ने नरेश का पुस्तक दिया

36. मन्त्री ड्राइवर को कार चलवाता है
A. मन्त्री ड्राइवर से कार चलवाता है
B. मन्त्री ड्राइवर की कार चलवाता है
C. मन्त्री ड्राइवर के लिए कार चलवाता है
D. मन्त्री ड्राइवर पर कार चलवाता है

37. A. जीवन और साहित्य का घोर सम्बन्ध है
B. जीवन और साहित्य का निकट सम्बन्ध है
C. जीवन और साहित्य का घनिष्ठ सम्बन्ध है
D. जीवन और साहित्य का गहरा सम्बन्ध है

38. A. सूर्य पश्चिम को अस्त होता है
B. मुझे विद्यालय जाना है
C. मैं तो आप के ऊपर निर्भर हूँ
D. लड़ाई में लोगों ने खूब कमाया

39. A. यह अध्यापक बहुत श्रेष्ठ पढ़ाता है
B. आज गोपाल उसके अपने काम से शहर गया
C. यह गाय बहुत प्यासी है
D. मानव ईश्वर की सबसे उत्कृष्टतम कृति है

40. A. रमेश के अन्दर बहुत विद्वता है
B. रमा विदुषी महिला है
C. सभी श्रेणियों के लोग वहाँ उपस्थित थे
D. धन्यवाद देता हूँ मैं उन्हें

41. A. आवश्यकता आविष्कार की जननी है
B. आविष्कार की जननी आवश्यकता है
C. आविष्कार आवश्यकता की जननी है
D. जननी है आविष्कार की आवश्यकता

42. A. मैं आपसे कुछ नहीं कह सकता हूँ
B. कुछ नहीं कह सकता हूँ मैं आपसे
C. आपसे मैं कुछ नहीं कह सकता हूँ
D. आपको मैं कुछ नहीं कह सकता हूँ

43. A. गंगा का उद्गम स्थल गंगोत्री में है
B. गंगा का उद्गम स्थल गंगोत्री पर है
C. गंगा का उद्गम स्थल गंगोत्री से है
D. गंगा का उद्गम स्थल गंगोत्री है

44. A. मुझे आज की बैठक का समाचार नहीं था
B. मैंने अभी लखनऊ जाना है
C. पाप को डरो, पानी से नहीं
D. एक कप चाय मुझे भी देना

45. A. विष्णु के अनेकों नाम हैं
B. कन्या पराया धन होती है
C. वह पढ़ता-पढ़ता सो गया
D. मैं रोज गाने की कसरत करता हूँ

46. A. आज हमारी सौभाग्यवती कन्या का विवाह है
B. उसने गीत की दो-चार लड़ियाँ ही सुनाई
C. देखो, कहीं उसकी नींद न खुल जाए
D. यह कार्य आप पर निर्भर करता है

निर्देश (प्रश्न संख्या 47 से 50 तक): *निम्नलिखित प्रश्नों के दिए गए वाक्यों के काले भाग में कुछ न कुछ त्रुटि है। उसके शुद्ध रूप को नीचे के विकल्प से ज्ञात कीजिए। यदि काले भाग में कोई गलती न हो तो अपने उत्तर के रूप में (D) अर्थात् कोई सुधार आवश्यक नहीं है, को इंगित कीजिए।*

47. समाज एवं देश के बहुमुखी विकास के लिए तन, मन, धन से प्रयत्न करना होगा **केवल मात्र कागजी योजनाओं** से कोई लाभ नहीं होगा
A. केवल सिर्फ कागजी योजनाओं
B. सिर्फ मात्र कागजी योजनाओं
C. मात्र कागजी योजनाओं
D. कोई सुधार आवश्यक नहीं है

48. बढ़ती महंगाई के कारण **देशी घी खरीदने** की सार्थकता लोगों में नहीं रह गई
A. देशी घी खरीद सकने
B. देशी घी खरीद करने
C. देशी सामान खरीद सकने
D. कोई सुधार आवश्यक नहीं है

49. बैठक कक्ष **केवल महिलाओं के उपयोग के लिए है**
A. केवल महिलाओं द्वारा इसका उपयोग होना चाहिए
B. केवल महिलाओं के उपयोग में लाना चाहिए
C. इसका उपयोग केवल महिलाओं द्वारा हो
D. कोई सुधार आवश्यक नहीं है

50. सभी घायल **भर्ती किए गए तथा ध्यान रखा गया**
A. अन्दर दाखिल हुए और ध्यान दिया गया
B. दाखिल हुए और ध्यान दिया गया
C. भर्ती किए गए और ध्यान रखा गया
D. कोई सुधार आवश्यक नहीं

उत्तरमाला

1	2	3	4	5	6	7	8	9	10
C	B	A	B	B	C	B	B	A	A
11	**12**	**13**	**14**	**15**	**16**	**17**	**18**	**19**	**20**
B	A	D	A	A	B	C	C	D	D
21	**22**	**23**	**24**	**25**	**26**	**27**	**28**	**29**	**30**
D	A	D	D	D	C	B	B	D	B
31	**32**	**33**	**34**	**35**	**36**	**37**	**38**	**39**	**40**
B	D	C	C	B	A	C	B	C	B
41	**42**	**43**	**44**	**45**	**46**	**47**	**48**	**49**	**50**
A	A	D	D	B	C	C	D	D	D

★ ★ ★

7

वाक्य रचनान्तरण (सरल/संयुक्त/मिश्र)

वाक्य

वाक्य सार्थक शब्दों का वह समूह है जिससे बोलने अथवा लिखने वाले का तात्पर्य पूरी तरह स्पष्ट हो जाता है। जैसे : वह निर्धन लेकिन परिश्रमी बालक है। रीता गीत गाती है।

उपवाक्य

जब किसी एक भाव को स्पष्ट करने के लिए किसी एक वाक्य के अंश-रूप में दो या दो से अधिक वाक्यों का उपयोग किया जाता है, तब उन अंश या खण्ड वाक्यों में प्रत्येक को उपवाक्य कहा जाता है।

जैसे– 'मैं जानता हूँ कि वे मेरे मित्र हैं।'

इस वाक्य में 'मैं जानता हूँ' तथा 'वे मेरे मित्र हैं' दोनों ही उपवाक्य या खण्डवाक्य कहलाएँगे।

उपवाक्य के भेद

उपवाक्य के दो भेद हैं :

1. प्रधान उपवाक्य, 2. आश्रित उपवाक्य

1. प्रधान उपवाक्य–जो उपवाक्य पूरे वाक्य से पृथक होकर भी अपना स्वतन्त्र एवं पूर्ण अर्थ रखता है उसे प्रधान उपवाक्य कहते हैं। जैसे–'मैं जानता हूँ कि वे मेरे मित्र हैं।' इस वाक्य में 'मैं जानता हूँ'–प्रधान उपवाक्य है।

2. आश्रित उपवाक्य–जो उपवाक्य प्रधान उपवाक्य के बिना अपना अर्थ स्पष्ट नहीं कर सकता वह 'आश्रित उपवाक्य' कहलाता है। आश्रित उपवाक्य अर्थ के लिए वस्तुतः प्रधान उपवाक्य पर आश्रित रहता है।

जैसे–'मैं जानता हूँ कि वे मेरे मित्र हैं'–में 'वे मेरे मित्र हैं' –आश्रित उपवाक्य है।

आश्रित उपवाक्य के भेद

1. संज्ञा उपवाक्य
2. विशेषण उपवाक्य
3. क्रिया उपवाक्य

1. संज्ञा उपवाक्य–जो आश्रित उपवाक्य संज्ञा का दायित्व निर्वाह करता है उसे 'संज्ञा उपवाक्य' कहते हैं।

जैसे–'मैं नहीं जानता कि वे कब लौटेंगे।'–इस वाक्य का उपवाक्य 'वे कब लौटेंगे' 'जानता' क्रिया के कर्म के रूप में कार्य कर रहा है इसलिए संज्ञा उपवाक्य है।

2. विशेषण उपवाक्य–जो आश्रित उपवाक्य विशेषण का कार्य करता है, उसे विशेषण उपवाक्य कहते हैं।

जैसे–वह लड़का **जो कल यहाँ आया था** बीमार है।

वह अपने नौकर को **जिसने चोरी की है** पीट रहा है।

वह अपने नौकर को उस छड़ी से पीट रहा है **जिसे उसने कल ही खरीदी है**। इनमें प्रत्येक रेखांकित उपवाक्य विशेषण का कार्य कर रहा है।

विशेषण उपवाक्य मुख्यतः जो, जिसको, जिससे, जिसके लिए, जिसका, जिसमें आदि से प्रारम्भ होता है।

3. क्रिया उपवाक्य–जो उपवाक्य क्रिया विशेषण का कार्य करे उसे क्रिया विशेषण उपवाक्य कहते हैं।

जैसे–**जब पानी बरसता है** तब मेढक बोलता है।

जहाँ वह मन्दिर बना हुआ है वहाँ एक दिन यज्ञ हुआ था।

इन वाक्यों में प्रत्येक रेखांकित उपवाक्य क्रिया विशेषण उपवाक्य हैं। क्यों ये उपवाक्य क्रिया विशेषण का कार्य करते हैं। क्रिया विशेषण उपवाक्य का आरम्भ विशेषतः निम्नलिखित शब्दों से होता है– जब, ज्योंही, जब-जब, जहाँ-कहाँ, जिधर, जैसे, मानो, ज्यों-ज्यों, जैसे-जैसे, जहाँ तक, चूँकि, ताकि, शायद, तथापि आदि।

वाक्य के भेद

वाक्यों के भेद सामान्यतः दो आधारों पर किए जाते हैं–

(क) रचना के आधार पर

(ख) अर्थ के आधार पर

रचना के आधार पर

रचना के आधार पर वाक्य के तीन भेद होते हैं–1. सरल वाक्य 2. मिश्र वाक्य 3. संयुक्त वाक्य

1. सरल वाक्य–जिस वाक्य में एक ही उपवाक्य होता है, उसे सरल वाक्य कहते हैं। इसमें केवल एक कर्त्ता और एक क्रिया होती है।

जैसे– राम ने रावण का वध किया।

बच्चे खेल रहे हैं।

वह मेरा मित्र है।

1. मिश्र वाक्य–जिस वाक्य में एक प्रधान उपवाक्य तथा एक या अधिक आश्रित उपवाक्य हो उसे मिश्र वाक्य कहते हैं।

जैसे–तुम वहाँ आ सकते हो जहाँ मैं रहता हूँ।
मैं उस व्यक्ति को जानता हूँ जो तुम्हारा मित्र है।
हमसे वह पुस्तक खो गई है जो तुमने हमें दी थी।

3. **संयुक्त वाक्य**–जिस वाक्य में दो या दो से अधिक प्रधान उपवाक्य हों और वे परस्पर किसी अव्यय द्वारा जुड़े हों तो वह संयुक्त वाक्य कहलाता है।
जैसे– मैं आया और वह चल दिया।
उसने परिश्रम किया किन्तु असफल रहा।
संयुक्त वाक्य में सरल तथा मिश्र दोनों प्रकार के वाक्य प्रविष्ट हो सकते हैं। प्रधान उपवाक्यों को जोड़ने वाले शब्द प्रायः निम्नलिखित होते हैं।
यथा–और, तथा, एवं, व, वा, या, अथवा, परन्तु, पर, किन्तु, बल्कि, इसलिए, सो, अतः आदि।

अर्थ के आधार पर

अर्थ के आधार पर वाक्य के मुख्यतः आठ भेद होते हैंः–

1. **विधि वाचक वाक्य**–जिस वाक्य से किसी बात के होने का बोध हो उसे विधि वाचक वाक्य कहते हैं।
जैसे–अच्छे लोग सदा मधुर भाषण करते हैं।
2. **निषेध वाचक वाक्य**–जिस वाक्य से आज्ञा, अनुरोध, आदेश आदि का भाव प्रकट हो, उसे आज्ञा वाचक वाक्य कहते हैं।
जैसे–परिश्रम कभी व्यर्थ नहीं जाता।
3. **आज्ञा वाचक वाक्य**–जिस वाक्य से आज्ञा, अनुरोध, आदेश आदि का भाव प्रकट हो, उसे आज्ञा वाचक वाक्य कहते हैं।
जैसे– कभी चोरी न करो।
यहाँ आइये।
4. **प्रश्न वाचक वाक्य**–जिस वाक्य से किसी प्रकार के प्रश्न का बोध हो उसे प्रश्न वाचक वाक्य कहते हैं।
जैसे– तुम क्या चाहते हो?
5. **विस्मयादि बोधक वाक्य**–जिस वाक्य से हर्ष, शोक, विस्मय आदि का बोध हो उसे विस्मयादि बोधक वाक्य कहते हैं।
जैसे– अहा! कितना सुन्दर फल है।
6. **इच्छा वाचक वाक्य**–जिस वाक्य से इच्छा या आशंका का बोध हो उसे इच्छा वाचक वाक्य कहते हैं।
जैसे– भगवान, आपको दीर्घायु करें।
7. **संदेह वाचक वाक्य**–जिस वाक्य से किसी प्रकार के संदेह का बोध हो उसे संदेह वाचक वाक्य कहते हैं। जैसे–वे लोग आ रहे होंगे। वह शायद बीमार है।
8. **संकेत वाचक वाक्य**–जिस वाक्य से किसी शर्त या संकेत का बोध हो उसे संकेत वाचक वाक्य कहते हैं।
जैसे–यदि वह पढ़ता तो निश्चय ही उत्तीर्ण होता।

वाक्य-विस्तार

किसी भी वाक्य के मुख्य रूप से दो अंग होते हैं–

(1) उद्देश्य
(2) विधेय।

उद्देश्य

वाक्य में जिस वस्तु या व्यक्ति के बारे में कुछ कहा जाता है उसे उद्देश्य कहते हैं। वाक्य की समाविका क्रिया का कर्त्ता ही उद्देश्य होता है।

जैसे– सीता पुस्तक पढ़ती है।
मेरी माताजी इन दिनों बीमार हैं।
मैं उन्हें जानता हूँ।

इन वाक्यों में सीता, माताजी, मैं–उद्देश्य अथवा कर्त्ता शब्द हैं। उद्देश्य का अपना विस्तार भी होता है। संज्ञा, सर्वनाम, विशेषण, क्रिया विशेषण, क्रियार्थक संज्ञा, वाक्यांश आदि सभी उद्देश्य का रूप ले सकते हैं।

जैसे–

1. संज्ञा–गाय रँभाती है।
2. सर्वनाम–वे घर जाते हैं।
3. विशेषण–मेहनती छात्र सफलता पाते हैं।
4. क्रिया–धीरे-धीरे चलो।
5. क्रियार्थक संज्ञा–टहलना स्वास्थ्यप्रद होता है।
6. वाक्यांश–दूसरे की निन्दा अच्छी नहीं होती।

उद्देश्य का विस्तार–उद्देश्य की विशेषता वाले शब्दों को उद्देश्य का विस्तार कहते हैं।

जैसे–दुष्ट जनों की संगति अच्छी नहीं होती है। विस्तार शब्दों के भिन्न-भिन्न रूप होते हैं।

जैसे–

1. विशेषण–दुष्टजन त्याज्य हैं।
2. सम्बन्ध कारक–मेरी पुस्तक खो गई है।
3. क्रिया द्योतक–सोता हुआ व्यक्ति जाग उठा।
4. प्रश्न बोधक–क्या चाहते हो?
5. वाक्यांश–निरन्तर परिश्रम करने वाला छात्र सुखी होता है।
6. संबोधनात्मक–हे भाई! तुम कौन हो?

विधेय

उद्देश्य के सम्बन्ध में जो कुछ कहा जाता है उसे विधेय कहते हैं। जैसे–राम-श्याम खेल रहे हैं। विधेय 'साधारण और जटिल' दो प्रकार के होते हैं। विधेय के साथ यदि पूरक शब्द आता है तब विधेय 'जटिल' कहलाता है। संज्ञा, विशेषण, सम्बन्ध वाचक तथा क्रिया विशेषण प्रायः पूरक शब्दों के रूप में आते हैं।

1. संज्ञा–मेरे मित्र अध्यापक हैं।
2. विशेषण–वह छात्र मेधावी है।
3. सम्बन्ध वाचक–यह पुस्तक तो आपकी है।
4. क्रिया विशेषण–तुम कहाँ खो गए थे।

विधेय का विस्तार–विधेय के सम्बन्ध में जो कुछ कहा या लिखा जाए उसे विधेय का विस्तार कहते हैं। जैसे–घोड़ा धीरे-धीरे दौड़ रहा है। वह घर लौटते ही गिर पड़ा।

विधेय का विस्तार निम्नलिखित रूपों में होता है–

कर्म	–	बच्चा सेब खाता है।
विशेषण	–	आभा विदुषी है।
क्रिया विशेषण	–	घोड़ा धीरे-धीरे दौड़ रहा है।
सम्बन्ध सूचक	–	पुत्र के साथ माँ चली गई।
क्रिया द्योतक	–	मोटर पों-पों करती चली गई।

पूर्वकालिक क्रिया – वह उठकर दौड़ पड़ा।
पद वाक्यांश – बाजार से लौटने के बाद वह सो गया।
करण कारक – उसने मुझे बेंत से मारा।
सम्प्रदान कारक – गरीबों के लिए उसने दान दिया।
अपादान कारक – वृक्ष से पत्ते गिरते हैं।
अधिकरण कारक – वह पिता पर आश्रित है।

मिश्र वाक्य से सरल वाक्य में रूपान्तरण

मिश्र वाक्य		सरल वाक्य
1. सीता ने कहा कि मैं घर जाऊंगी।	–	1. सीता ने घर जाने के लिए कहा।
2. 'संशय की एक रात' खंडकाव्य है, वैसे ही 'प्रवाद पर्व भी खंडकाव्य है।	–	2. 'संशय की एक रात' की भांति 'प्रवाद पर्व भी खंडकाव्य है।
3. जब बारिश होती है, तब फूल लिखते हैं।	–	3. बारिश होने पर फूल खिलते हैं।
4. जो लोग अध्ययन करते हैं, वे अच्छा लिख पाते हैं।	–	4. अध्ययन करने वाले लोग अच्छा लिख पाते हैं।
5. जितना सुख हमें घर में मिलता है, उतना और जगह नहीं।	–	5. घर जितना सुख हमें और जगह नहीं मिलता।

सरल वाक्य से मिश्र वाक्य में रूपान्तरण

सरल वाक्य		मिश्र वाक्य
1. परिश्रमी को सफलता मिलती है।	–	1. जो परिश्रमी होता है, उसे सफलता मिलती है।
2. गंभीर संवेदनाओं के कवि का सम्मान सभी करते हैं।	–	2. जिनके पास गंभीर संवेदनाएं होती हैं, ऐसे कवि का सम्मान सभी करते हैं।
3. हमारे परिवार ने अपने सम्मानित कवि के नाम पर पुस्तकालय बनवाया।	–	3. हमारे परिवार ने एक पुस्तकालय बनवाया, जो हमारे सम्मानित कवि के नाम पर है।

संयुक्त वाक्य से सरल वाक्य में रूपान्तरण

संयुक्त वाक्य		सरल वाक्य
1. वे अब दिखाई नहीं देते, क्योंकि बाजार जाते हैं।	–	1. वे बाजार जाने के कारण अब दिखाई नहीं देते।
2. तुम इतनी उछल-कूद मचा रहे हो, लेकिन यह व्यर्थ है।	–	2. तुम व्यर्थ ही इतनी उछल-कूद मचा रहे हो।
3. वह न केवल पढ़ता, अपितु पढ़ाता भी है।	–	3. वह पढ़ने के साथ-साथ पढ़ाता भी है।
4. वह दिनभर पढ़ता है और रात में सोता है।	–	4. वह दिनभर पढ़कर रात में सोता है।
5. बारिश हो रही थी इसलिए छुट्टी भी मिली।	–	5. बारिश होने पर ही छुट्टी मिली।
6. वह बहुत भागा, परंतु असफल रहा।	–	6. बहुत भागने पर भी वह असफल रहा।

मिश्र वाक्य से संयुक्त वाक्य में रूपान्तरण

मिश्र वाक्य		संयुक्त वाक्य
1. मैंने जो पुस्तक लिखी थी, वह छप गई।	–	1. मैंने पुस्तक लिखी थी और वह छप गई।
2. हालांकि मुझे लिखना था, फिर भी नहीं लिख पाया।	–	2. मुझे लिखना था किंतु नहीं लिख पाया।
3. जब दुर्घटना की खबर सुनी, तब मन दुखी हो गया।	–	3. दुर्घटना की खबर सुनी और मन दुखी हो गगा।
4. जब भी मैं विकास के घर गया, मेरा आदर सत्कार हुआ।	–	4. विकास के घर मेरा आदर भी हुआ और सत्कार भी।

संयुक्त वाक्य से मिश्र वाक्य में रूपान्तरण

संयुक्त वाक्य		मिश्र वाक्य
1. वे मेधावी छात्रा हैं, इसलिए उन्हें सफलता अवश्य मिलेगी।	–	1. वे मेधावी छात्रा हैं, उन्हें सफलता अवश्य मिलेगी।
2. वहाँ सब तरफ हरियाली है और वहीं वह नदी है।	–	2. जहाँ सब तरफ हरियाली है, वहीं वह नदी है।
3. विशाल ने एक मोबाइल खरीदा है और वह नया है।	–	3. विशाल ने जो मोबाइल खरीदा है, वह नया है
4. शिक्षक ने सबको गृहकार्य करने को कहा एवं स्वयं करने को कहा।	–	4. शिक्षक ने कहा कि सबको गृहकार्य स्वयं करना है।

वस्तुनिष्ठ प्रश्नोत्तर

1. आज बहुत पानी गिरा।—यह कैसा वाक्य है?
A. साधारण वाक्य B. मिश्र वाक्य
C. संयुक्त वाक्य D. उपवाक्य

2. 'उससे अब अकेले नहीं रहा जाता है'। यह कैसा वाक्य है?
A. कर्तृवाक्य B. कर्मवाच्य
C. भाववाच्य D. इनमें से कोई नहीं

3. 'वहाँ जाओ'। यह कैसा वाक्य है?
A. निषेधवाचक B. प्रश्नवाचक
C. आज्ञावाचक D. अनुरोधवाचक

4. 'उसने कहा कि मैं घर जाऊँगा'। यह कैसा वाक्य है?
A. सरल वाक्य B. संयुक्त वाक्य
C. मिश्र वाक्य D. प्रश्नवाचक वाक्य

5. 'तुम यह काम मत करो।' यह कैसा वाक्य है?
A. आज्ञावाचक B. निषेधवाचक
C. प्रश्नवाचक D. विस्मयवाचक

6. 'हो सकता है राम का काम बन जाय।' यह कैसा वाक्य है?
A. निषेधवाचक B. प्रश्नवाचक
C. संदेहवाचक D. आज्ञावाचक

7. 'अरे! उसने तो कमाल कर दिया।' यह कैसा वाक्य है?
A. प्रश्नवाचक B. निषेधवाचक
C. विस्मयवाचक D. इच्छावाचक

8. 'राम क्रिकेट खेलता है पर अच्छा नहीं।' यह कैसा वाक्य है?
A. सरल वाक्य B. संयुक्त वाक्य
C. मिश्र वाक्य D. इनमें से कोई नहीं

9. 'ज्यों ही मैंने दरवाजा खोला कि वह आ गया।' यह कैसा वाक्य है?
A. सरल वाक्य B. संयुक्त वाक्य
C. मिश्र वाक्य D. इनमें से कोई नहीं

10. 'वह आए तो काम बन सकता है।' यह कैसा वाक्य है?
A. इच्छाबोधक B. संदेहसूचक
C. संकेतार्थक D. विधानार्थक

11. तुम विद्यालय के लिए यह कर दो या रमेश को बोल दो।
A. संयुक्त वाक्य B. मिश्र वाक्य
C. सरल वाक्य D. इनमें से कोई नहीं

12. मजदूर मेहनत करता है, किंतु उसके लाभ से वंचित रहता है।
A. सरल वाक्य B. मिश्र वाक्य
C. संयुक्त वाक्य D. इनमें से कोई नहीं

13. प्रत्येक धर्म सिखाता है कि आपस में भाई-चारे से रहो।
A. मिश्र वाक्य B. संयुक्त वाक्य
C. सरल वाक्य D. इनमें से कोई नहीं

14. मुझे विश्वास है कि आप अवश्य आएँगे।
A. मिश्र वाक्य B. संयुक्त वाक्य
C. सरल वाक्य D. इनमें से कोई नहीं

15. अल्प ज्ञानी व्यक्ति बुद्धिमान की कद्र करना क्या जाने।
A. सरल वाक्य B. संयुक्त वाक्य
C. मिश्र वाक्य D. इनमें से कोई नहीं

16. नीति कहती है कि तुम गलत के साथ गलत मत करो।
A. सरल वाक्य B. संयुक्त वाक्य
C. मिश्र वाक्य D. इनमें से कोई नहीं

17. दुष्ट व्यक्ति की मित्रता स्थायी नहीं होती।
A. सरल वाक्य B. संयुक्त वाक्य
C. मिश्र वाक्य D. इनमें से कोई नहीं

18. अमर के रहते विद्यालय के किसी छात्र को सर्वश्रेष्ठ खिलाड़ी की पदवी नहीं मिल सकती।
A. मिश्र वाक्य B. संयुक्त वाक्य
C. सरल वाक्य D. इनमें से कोई नहीं

19. मैंने किरायेदार नहीं रखे, मुसीबत मोल ले ली।
A. सरल वाक्य B. मिश्र वाक्य
C. संयुक्त वाक्य D. इनमें से कोई नहीं

20. समय पर पश्चाताप करना ही बुद्धिमानी की बात है।
A. सरल वाक्य B. मिश्र वाक्य
C. संयुक्त वाक्य D. इनमें से कोई नहीं

21. रचना की दृष्टि से वाक्य के कितने भेद होते हैं?
A. तीन B. पाँच
C. छह D. आठ

22. सरल वाक्य में कितने कर्ता और कितनी क्रिया होती है?
A. एक कर्ता, एक क्रिया
B. एक कर्ता, एक क्रिया, एक सहायक क्रिया
C. दो क्रिया एक कर्ता
D. दो कर्ता दो क्रिया

23. अधोलिखित में से वाक्य के (रचना के आधार पर) भेद कौन-से हैं?
A. सरल वाक्य B. मिश्र वाक्य
C. संयुक्त वाक्य D. उपर्युक्त तीनों

24. **धूप निकली है** में कितने उद्देश्य और कितने विधेय हैं?
A. एक उद्देश्य एक विधेय B. एक उद्देश्य दो विधेय
C. उपर्युक्त दोनों D. कोई नहीं

25. सरल वाक्य में कितने उद्देश्य और कितने विधेय होते हैं?
A. एक उद्देश्य एक विधेय B. दो उद्देश्य एक विधेय
C. दो विधेय दो उद्देश्य D. उपर्युक्त में से कोई ठीक नहीं

26. मिश्र वाक्य में कितनी समापिका क्रियाएँ होती हैं?

A. दो B. एक या एक से अधिक

C. कोई D. कोई ठीक नहीं

27. वह कौन ऐसा भारतीय है जो गाँधीजी को नहीं जानता। कौन-सा वाक्य है?

A. सरल वाक्य B. मिश्र वाक्य

C. संयुक्त वाक्य D. कोई नहीं

28. मिश्र वाक्य में कितने वाक्य होते हैं?

A. एक मुख्य वाक्य एक उपवाक्य

B. दो मुख्य वाक्य

C. दो उपवाक्य

D. कोई ठीक नहीं

29. मुख्य वाक्य और उपवाक्य में किसकी संगति होती है?

A. भाव की B. ध्वनि की

C. अर्थ की D. किसी की नहीं

30. जहाँ साधारण और मिश्र वाक्यों का मेल संयोजक अव्ययों द्वारा होता है, उसे कहते हैं–

A. सरल वाक्य B. मिश्र वाक्य

C. संयुक्त वाक्य D. विधि वाक्य

31. संयुक्त वाक्य में कैसे वाक्य अव्ययों द्वारा संयुक्त किए जाते हैं?

A. सरल वाक्य B. मिश्र वाक्य

C. उपर्युक्त दोनों D. कोई ठीक नहीं

32. मैं नहा चुका तब वह साबुन लाया। कौन-सा वाक्य है?

A. विधिवाचक, सरल वाक्य

B. विधिवाचक, मिश्र वाक्य

C. विधिवाचक, संयुक्त वाक्य

D. कोई नहीं

33. तुम नहाओ और तुम्हारे बाद सभी नहायें। कौन-सा वाक्य है?

A. आज्ञावाचक सरल वाक्य

B. आज्ञावाचक मिश्र वाक्य

C. आज्ञावाचक संयुक्त वाक्य

D. कोई नहीं

34. राम घर पहुँच गया होगा। कैसा वाक्य है?

A. विधि वाक्य B. विस्मयवाचक वाक्य

C. संदेहवाचक वाक्य D. संकेतवाचक वाक्य

35. वह परीक्षा में उत्तीर्ण हो। कैसा वाक्य है?

A. विधिवाचक वाक्य B. इच्छावाचक वाक्य

C. संकेतवाचक वाक्य D. संदेहवाचक वाक्य

36. तुम न बचाते तो वह डूब जाता। कैसा वाक्य है?

A. संकेतवाचक वाक्य B. इच्छावाचक वाक्य

C. संदेहवाचक वाक्य D. विस्मयवाचक वाक्य

37. संकेतवाचक वाक्य निर्भर रहता दूसरे वाक्य की–

A. संभावना पर B. धारणा पर

C. अवधारणा पर D. इच्छा पर

38. जिस वाक्य में किसी बात के होने का बोध हो उसे कहते हैं–

A. आज्ञावाचक वाक्य B. संदेहवाचक वाक्य

C. इच्छावाचक वाक्य D. विधिवाचक वाक्य

39. जिस वाक्य में दुख एवं सुख का बोध हो उसे कहते हैं–

A. संकेतवाचक वाक्य B. संदेहवाचक वाक्य

C. विस्मयवाचक वाक्य D. विधिवाचक वाक्य

40. अहा! तुम्हारे आने से सभी प्रसन्न हैं। वाक्य में कौन-सा भाव है?

A. संदेह का B. विस्मय का

C. इच्छा का D. संकेत का

उत्तरमाला

1	2	3	4	5	6	7	8	9	10
A	C	C	C	B	C	C	B	C	C
11	**12**	**13**	**14**	**15**	**16**	**17**	**18**	**19**	**20**
A	C	A	A	A	C	A	C	C	A
21	**22**	**23**	**24**	**25**	**26**	**27**	**28**	**29**	**30**
A	A	D	A	A	B	B	A	C	C
31	**32**	**33**	**34**	**35**	**36**	**37**	**38**	**39**	**40**
C	B	C	C	B	A	A	A	C	B

★ ★ ★

8

मुहावरा

मुहावरा का शाब्दिक अर्थ 'अभ्यास' है। किन्तु उस वाक्यांश अथवा शब्द समूह को मुहावरा कहते हैं जो अपने साधारण अर्थ को त्याग कर एक विशेष अर्थ प्रकट करने लगता है। मुहावरों के प्रयोग से भाषा का सौंदर्य एवं उसकी शीलता बढ़ जाती है।

नीचे कुछ मुहावरे, उसका अर्थ तथा वाक्यों में प्रयोग दिया जा रहा है–

- **अंग-अंग ढीला होना**—*बहुत थक जाना*
  अपनी बहिन की शादी में काम करते-करते मेरा ***अंग-अंग ढीला*** हो गया।
- **अंगारे उगलना**—*क्रोध में अति कठोर शब्द कहना*
  जब औरंगजेब के दरबार में शिवाजी ने अपना अपमान होते देखा तो वे ***अंगारे उगलने*** लगे।
- **अँगूठा दिखाना**—*इनकार करना*
  स्वार्थी मित्र संकट के समय सहायता माँगे जाने पर ***अँगूठा दिखाकर*** चले जाते हैं।
- **अंधे की लकड़ी होना**—*एकमात्र सहारा*
  अब तो बेटा तुम ही हमारे लिए ***अन्धे की लकड़ी*** के समान हो।
- **अँधेरे घर का उजाला होना**—*इकलौता बेटा*
  रामू मेरे छोटे भाई की एकमात्र संतान है। वही उसके ***अँधेरे घर का उजाला*** है।
- **अक्ल के पीछे लाठी लिए फिरना**—*हमेशा उल्टा काम करना*
  हमारा एक साथी तो हर समय ***अक्ल के पीछे लाठी लिए फिरता*** है।
- **अक्ल पर पत्थर पड़ना**—*बुद्धि नष्ट हो जाना*
  तुम्हारी तो ***अक्ल पर पत्थर पड़*** गए हैं जो तुम मेरी बात समझते ही नहीं।
- **अपना उल्लू सीधा करना**—*स्वार्थ सिद्ध करना*
  वह ***अपना उल्लू सीधा करके*** चलता बना।
- **अपना-सा मुँह लेकर रह जाना**—*लज्जित होना*
  हम वहाँ बड़ी उम्मीद लेकर गए थे, किन्तु उसने ऐसी निराशापूर्ण बात कही जिससे हमें ***अपना-सा मुँह लेकर रह जाना*** पड़ा।
- **अपनी खिचड़ी आप पकाना**—*सबसे अलग रहना*
  कुछ लोग ऐसे स्वभाव के होते हैं कि वे किसी से मिलना ही नहीं चाहते; ***अपनी खिचड़ी आप ही पकाते*** हैं।
- **अपने मुँह मियाँ मिट्ठू बनना**—*अपनी प्रशंसा स्वयं करना*
  अपने मुँह मियाँ मिट्ठू बनने से क्या होता है, दूसरे लोग तुम्हारी प्रशंसा करें तब बात है।
- **अपने पैरों पर खड़े होना**—*आत्मनिर्भर होना*
  जब तक तुम इस योग्य न हो जाओ कि ***अपने पैरों पर खड़े हो*** सको तब तक तुम्हें विवाह के बारे में सोचना भी नहीं चाहिए।
- **आँख की किरकिरी होना**—*अप्रिय होना*
  राम व्यर्थ में ही मुझे अपनी ***आँख की किरकिरी*** समझता है।
- **आँख चुराना**—*सामने आने से घबराना*
  जब से उसने मेरा पेन लिया है, तब से वह ***आँखें चुराता*** फिरता है।
- **आँखें नीली-पीली करना**—*क्रोध में आना*
  मैंने ऐसा कोई गलत काम नहीं किया है; आप व्यर्थ में ***आँखें नीली-पीली न करें***।
- **आँखें फेर लेना**—*उपेक्षा करना*
  स्वार्थी मित्र संकट के समय में ***आँखें फेर लेते*** हैं।
- **आँखों का तारा होना**—*अत्यन्त प्रिय*
  कृष्ण अपने माँ-बाप की ***आँखों का तारा*** है।
- **आँखों का पानी ढल जाना**—*बेशर्म हो जाना*
  उसके माँ-बाप उसे बहुतेरा समझाते-बुझाते हैं, किन्तु उसकी ***आँखों का तो पानी ढल*** गया है। उस पर किसी बात का असर होता ही नहीं।
- **आँखों में धूल झोंकना**—*धोखा देना*
  जो लोग दूसरों की ***आँखों में धूल झोंकने*** की कोशिश करते हैं, वे वस्तुतः अपने को ही धोखा देते हैं।
- **आकाश-पाताल एक करना**—*बहुत अधिक परिश्रम करना*
  राम ने नौकरी प्राप्त करने के लिए ***आकाश-पाताल एक कर*** दिया।
- **आग पर घी डालना**—*क्रोध को बढ़ाना*
  तुम्हारा टोकना तो ***आग पर घी डालने*** जैसा था।
- **आटे-दाल का भाव मालूम होना**—*जीवन में कष्टों का अनुभव करना*
  अब तक तो तुम अकेले थे, कुछ पता ही नहीं चला; अब तुम्हें ***आटे-दाल का भाव मालूम होगा***।
- **आम के आम और गुठलियों के दाम**—*दोहरा लाभ*
  मूँगफली के व्यापार में ***आम के आम और गुठलियों के दाम*** मिलते हैं; क्योंकि उसकी गिरी से तेल निकाल कर खली बिक जाती है और मूँगफली का छिलका भी बिक जाता है।
- **आस्तीन का साँप**—*विश्वासघाती*
  उस पर कभी विश्वास मत करो, वह ***आस्तीन का साँप*** है।
- **ईंट से ईंट बजाना**—*नष्ट-भ्रष्ट कर देना*
  शिवाजी ने मुगल साम्राज्य की ***ईंट से ईंट बजा*** दी।

- **ईद का चाँद होना**—*बहुत कम दिखाई पड़ना*
  तुम तो ***ईद के चाँद हो गए*** हो; कभी इधर आते ही नहीं।
- **उड़ती चिड़िया पहचानना**—*मन की बात ताड़ लेना*
  मुझसे क्यों छिपाते हो, ***मैं उड़ती चिड़िया पहचान*** लेता हूँ।
- **उल्लू सीधा करना**—*काम निकालना*
  अधिकांश लोग ***उल्लू सीधा*** होते ही बात नहीं करते।
- **ऊँट के मुँह में जीरा**—*आवश्यकता से बहुत कम देना*
  एक रोटी से उसका क्या बनेगा, यह तो उसके लिए ***ऊँट के मुँह में जीरा*** की तरह है।
- **एक अनार सौ बीमार**—*किसी चीज की माँग आपूर्ति से अधिक होना*
  यह वस्तु मैं किस-किस को दूँ, इसके माँगने वाले इतने अधिक हैं कि यह ***एक अनार सौ बीमार*** वाली बात हो रही है।
- **एक तीर से दो शिकार करना**—*एक साथ दो मतलब पूरे करना*
  तुम्हारे ऐसा कहने से ***एक तीर से दो शिकार*** होंगे, सबके सामने उसकी पोल खुल जाएगी और तुम्हारा काम भी बन जाएगा।
- **एक थैली के चट्टे-बट्टे होना**—*एक ही स्वभाव के*
  तुम सब ***एक ही थैली के चट्टे-बट्टे हो***, कोई किसी से कम नहीं।
- **एक हाथ से ताली न बजना**—*किसी काम के लिए एक ही व्यक्ति उत्तरदायी नहीं होता*
  एक हाथ से ताली नहीं बजती, तुमने भी अवश्य कुछ-न-कुछ ऐसी बात जरूर की होगी, जिसका यह परिणाम निकला।
- **ओखली में सिर देना**—*जानते हुए किसी कष्ट में पड़ना*
  अब तो ***ओखली में सिर दे ही दिया*** है, इस काम को पूरा करना ही है।
- **कच्ची गोलियाँ खेलना**—*अनुभव की कमी होना*
  मैंने कोई ***कच्ची गोलियाँ नहीं खेली*** हैं, जो मैं तुम्हारी बातों में आ जाऊँ।
- **कटे पर नमक छिड़कना**—*दु:खी को और दु:खी करना*
  तुम यह बात कहकर ***कटे पर नमक छिड़कना*** चाहते हो।
- **कठपुतली की तरह नाचना**—*किसी के कहने के अनुसार कार्य करते रहना*
  पता नहीं उसने महेश पर कैसा जादू किया है कि वह उसके सामने ***कठपुतली की तरह नाचता*** रहता है।
- **कब्र के मुर्दे उखाड़ना**—*पुरानी बातों की याद दिलाना*
  जो बात हो गई सो हो गई; ***कब्र के मुर्दे उखाड़ने*** से क्या लाभ।
- **कलई खुलना**—*सच्ची बात प्रकट हो जाना*
  तुम कब तक अपने फेल होने की बात को छिपाओगे, एक न एक दिन तो ***कलई खुलेगी*** ही।
- **कलेजा दो टूक होना**—*बहुत दु:खी होना*
  तुमने आज जैसी बातें कही हैं, उनसे मेरा ***कलेजा दो टूक हो*** गया है।
- **कलेजे पर साँप लोटना**—*डाह से जलना*
  मेरी तरक्की देखकर उसके ***कलेजे पर साँप लोट*** गया।
- **काँटे बिछाना**—*रुकावटें पैदा करना*
  जो दूसरे के मार्ग में ***काँटे बिछाता*** है, वह स्वयं ही उसमें उलझता है।
- **काटो तो खून नहीं**—*डर से पीला पड़ जाना*
  चोरी करते पकड़े जाने पर उसकी दशा ऐसी हो गई कि ***काटो तो खून नहीं***।
- **काठ का उल्लू**—*मूर्ख*
  वह पढ़ा-लिखा तो बहुत है, किन्तु सांसारिक मामलों में ***काठ का उल्लू*** है।
- **कान का कच्चा**—*बिना जाँच किये प्रत्येक बात पर विश्वास कर लेना*
  जो व्यक्ति ***कान के कच्चे*** होते हैं वे मित्र बनाने योग्य नहीं होते।
- **कान पर जूँ न रेंगना**—*तनिक भी ध्यान न देना*
  मैंने उसे बार-बार समझाया कि पढ़ाई-लिखाई की ओर ध्यान दो, परन्तु उसके ***कान पर जूँ तक न रेंगी***।
- **कान में तेल डालना**—*किसी की बात न सुनना*
  कृष्णा के नौकरी कर लेने पर सबने उसकी टीका-टिप्पणी की, किन्तु वह ***कान में तेल डाले*** रही।
- **किताब का कीड़ा होना**—*दिन-रात पढ़ते रहना*
  रवीन्द्र किसी बात से मतलब नहीं रखता, वह तो ***किताब का कीड़ा*** है।
- **किस खेत की मूली**—*अत्यन्त तुच्छ*
  तुम हो ***किस खेत की मूली***, मैं तुम जैसों की बिल्कुल परवाह नहीं करता।
- **कोल्हू का बैल बनना**—*दिन-रात काम में लगे रहना*
  तुम तो हर समय ***कोल्हू के बैल ही बने*** रहते हो, तभी तो तुम्हारा स्वास्थ्य ठीक नहीं रहता।
- **कौड़ी-कौड़ी को मोहताज होना**—*पास में एक पैसा न होना*
  जबसे उसकी नौकरी छूटी है, तबसे वह ***कौड़ी-कौड़ी को मोहताज*** हो गया है।
- **खटाई में पड़ना**—*उलझ जाना*
  तुम्हारी तरक्की का मामला ***खटाई में पड़*** गया है।
- **खाने दौड़ना**—*झल्ला उठना*
  मैंने कुछ कहा भी है कि आप ***खाने दौड़*** रहे हैं।
- **खून-पसीना एक करना**—*अत्यधिक परिश्रम करना*
  तुम्हारे इस मामले में तो कृष्ण ने ***खून-पसीना एक कर*** दिया।
- **गंगाजली उठाना**—*हाथ में गंगाजल लेकर सौगन्ध खाना*
  मैं ***गंगाजली उठाकर*** कहता हूँ कि मैं बिल्कुल निर्दोष हूँ।
- **गज-भर की छाती होना**—*उत्साह से भर जाना*
  अपनी पुत्री के परीक्षा में प्रथम आने से उसकी ***गज-भर की छाती हो*** गई।
- **गहरा हाथ मारना**—*बहुत माल प्राप्त करना*
  जगदीश ने अपने पुत्र के विवाह में ***गहरा हाथ मारा*** है।
- **गाँठ का पूरा**—*धनी व्यक्ति*
  वह ऊपर से कैसा ही प्रतीत हो, किन्तु है ***गाँठ का पूरा***।
- **गागर में सागर भरना**—*थोड़े शब्दों में बहुत-कुछ कह देना*
  वह बहुत कम बोलता है किन्तु जब भी बोलता है तो उसकी बातों में ***गागर में सागर भरा*** होता है।
- **गाजर-मूली समझना**—*बहुत तुच्छ समझना*
  शिवाजी मुगल सैनिकों को ***गाजर-मूली की तरह समझते*** थे।
- **गाढ़े पसीने की कमाई**—*मेहनत से कमाया हुआ धन*
  यह मेरे ***गाढ़े पसीने की कमाई*** है, मैं नहीं चाहता कि इसे व्यर्थ में पानी की तरह बहाया जाए।

- **गिरगिट की तरह रंग बदलना**—*कभी कुछ कहना और कभी कुछ*
आजकल विधान सभाओं के अनेक सदस्य ***गिरगिट की तरह रंग बदलते*** दिखाई देते रहते हैं।
- **गुड़ गोबर करना**—*बना काम बिगाड़ देना*
तुमने ये शब्द कहकर सारा ***गुड़ गोबर कर*** दिया।
- **गोबर गणेश**—*मूर्ख*
तुम बिल्कुल ***गोबर गणेश*** हो, अपने हित की बात ही नहीं समझते।
- **घड़ों पानी पड़ना**—*अति लज्जित होना*
चुगली करने की बात खुल जाने पर उस पर ***घड़ों पानी पड़*** गया।
- **घर का दिया बुझ जाना**—*इकलौते पुत्र की मृत्यु होना*
दीपक उसका इकलौता पुत्र था, उसके मर जाने से उसके ***घर का दिया ही बुझ*** गया।
- **घाट-घाट का पानी पीना**—*जगह-जगह से अनुभव प्राप्त करना*
मुसीबत के दिनों में उसे ***घाट-घाट का पानी पीना*** पड़ा है।
- **घाव पर नमक छिड़कना**—*दुःखी को (कठोर शब्दों से) और दुःखी करना*
तुम्हारे ये शब्द ***घाव पर नमक छिड़कने*** का काम कर रहे हैं।
- **घास काटना**—*किसी काम को लापरवाही से करना*
घास मत काटो, जरा धीरे-धीरे अच्छी तरह पढ़ो।
- **घी के दीये जलाना**—*खूब खुशियाँ मनाना*
जिस दिन मेरे भाई की नौकरी लग जायेगी उस दिन मैं ***घी के दीये जलाऊँगा***।
- **घुटने टेक देना**—*हार मान लेना*
सैल्युकस ने चन्द्रगुप्त मौर्य के आगे ***घुटने टेक दिये***।
- **घोड़े बेचकर सोना**—*निश्चिन्त होकर सोना*
बहिन का विवाह करने के पश्चात् वह ऐसे सो गया मानो ***घोड़े बेचकर सोया*** हो।
- **चलता पुर्जा**—*चालाक व्यक्ति*
चन्द्र बड़ा ही ***चलता पुर्जा*** है, उससे बचकर रहना।
- **चाँदी का जूता मारना**—*रुपये के बल पर दबाना*
वह तो ***चाँदी का जूता मारती*** है और सबसे अपना काम करा लेती है।
- **चाँदी होना**—*अत्यधिक लाभ होना*
आजकल महँगाई के जमाने में व्यापारियों की ***चाँदी*** है।
- **चादर देखकर पाँव फैलाना**—*अपनी शक्ति के अनुसार कार्य करना*
बुद्धिमानी इसी में है कि ***चादर देखकर पाँव फैलाये*** जायें अन्यथा जीवन में बड़ी कठिनाई का सामना करना पड़ता है।
- **चार चाँद लगना**—*शोभा बढ़ना*
वह सुन्दर तो है ही, पर इस साड़ी को पहनने पर उसकी सुन्दरता में ***चार चाँद लग*** जाते हैं।
- **चार दिन की चाँदनी**—*थोड़े दिनों का सुख*
तुम इतना घमण्ड क्यों करते हो, यह सुख तो ***चार दिन की चाँदनी*** है, कभी दुःख के दिन भी आ सकते हैं।
- **चिकना घड़ा होना**—*किसी बात का असर न पड़ना*
वह तो बिल्कुल ***चिकना घड़ा हो*** गया है, उस पर कहे-सुने का असर पड़ता ही नहीं।
- **चिराग लेकर ढूँढना**—*बहुत छानबीन करना*
तुम यदि ***चिराग लेकर भी ढूँढो,*** तब भी तुम्हें ऐसा सज्जन नहीं मिलेगा।
- **चुल्लू भर पानी में डूब मरना**—*मुँह दिखाने योग्य न रहना*
तीसरी बार भी परीक्षा में फेल होने पर उसे ***चुल्लू भर पानी में डूब मरना*** चाहिए।
- **चूना लगाना**—*धोखा देना*
कितनी ही सावधानी से काम लो, किन्तु कभी-कभी दुकानदार ***चूना लगा*** ही देते हैं।
- **चोली-दामन का साथ होना**—*अटूट सम्बन्ध होना*
भारत और नेपाल का ***चोली दामन का साथ*** है।
- **छक्के छूटना**—*हिम्मत हार जाना*
भारतीयों की वीरता देखकर पाकिस्तानी सैनिकों के ***छक्के छूट*** गए।
- **छठी का दूध याद आना**—*घोर कष्ट में पड़ना*
मैं तुम्हें ऐसी मार लगाऊँगा कि ***छठी का दूध याद आ*** जायेगा।
- **छप्पर फाड़कर देना**—*बिना परिश्रम किए धन मिलना*
भगवान् जब देता है तो ***छप्पर फाड़कर देता*** है।
- **छाती पर मूँग दलना**—*हमेशा दुःख देना*
तू इस तरह ***छाती पर मूँग ही दलता*** रहेगा या कहीं जाकर कुछ काम खोजने की कोशिश भी करेगा?
- **जरा-सा मुँह निकल आना**—*दुर्बल हो जाना*
उस पर इन दिनों इतना काम पड़ा है कि उसका ***जरा-सा मुँह निकल आया*** है।
- **जली-कटी कहना**—*कठोर बातें कहना*
वह हमेशा ***जली-कटी कहता*** रहता है, पता नहीं वह क्या चाहता है।
- **जहर का घूँट पीकर रह जाना**—*अपमान को चुपचाप सहन कर लेना*
यद्यपि उसने सबके सामने मेरा अपमान किया किन्तु फिर भी मैं आपका ख्याल करके ***जहर का घूँट पीकर रह*** गया।
- **जहर की पुड़िया**—*उपद्रवी व्यक्ति*
वह सीधी नहीं है, ***जहर की पुड़िया*** है।
- **झंडा गाड़ना**—*अधिकार करना*
शिवाजी ने तोरण के किले को जीतकर उस पर अपना ***झंडा गाड़*** दिया।
- **टोपी उछालना**—*अपमानित करना*
महेश ने सबके सामने मेरी ***टोपी उछाली,*** यह उसने ठीक नहीं किया।
- **ठोकना-बजाना**—*अच्छी तरह परखना*
जिस तरह तुम हरेक वस्तु परख कर खरीदते हो उसी तरह मित्र भी ***ठोक-बजाकर*** बनाना चाहिए।
- **डंके की चोट पर**—*खुल्लमखुल्ला स्पष्ट शब्दों में कहना*
मैं ***डंके की चोट पर*** कहता हूँ कि किसी भी हालत में उसका साथ नहीं छोड़ूँगा।
- **डूबते को तिनके का सहारा**—*असहाय को थोड़ी सहायता भी काफी काम कर जाती है*
तुम्हारी थोड़ी सहायता ही ***डूबते को तिनके का सहारा*** के समान सिद्ध हुई।

- **डेढ़ चावल की खिचड़ी पकाना**—*सबसे अलग रहकर कार्य करना*
कुछ लोग ऐसे होते हैं जो ***डेढ़ चावल की खिचड़ी पकाना*** चाहते हैं, परन्तु समाज ऐसे लोगों का सम्मान नहीं करता।
- **ढेर हो जाना**—*मर जाना*
उसने डाकू पर लाठी का एक ही प्रहार किया कि वह ***ढेर हो*** गया।
- **तलवार के घाट उतारना**—*तलवार से मारना*
हल्दीघाटी के मैदान में राजपूतों ने असंख्य मुगल सैनिकों को ***तलवार के घाट उतार*** दिया।
- **तारे गिनना**—*रात-भर जागना*
मैं उसकी स्मृति में रात-भर ***तारे गिनता*** रहा, एक पल को भी नींद नहीं आई।
- **तिल का ताड़ बनाना**—*छोटी-सी बात को बहुत बढ़ाना*
बहुत लोगों को ***तिल का ताड़ बनाने*** में बड़ा आनन्द आता है।
- **तिलों में तेल न होना**—*कोई आशा न होना*
तुम किससे पार्टी (दावत) माँग रहे हो; इन ***तिलों में तेल नहीं*** है।
- **तेली का बैल होना**—*रात-दिन काम में लगा रहना*
तुम तो हमेशा ***तेली के बैल*** के समान काम में लगे रहते हो।
- **थाली का बैंगन होना**—*स्वार्थवश कभी किसी का साथ देना और कभी किसी का*
तुम तो बिल्कुल ***थाली के बैंगन हो***, तुम्हारा कोई भरोसा नहीं।
- **दाँत काटी रोटी**—*गहरी मित्रता*
जोशी और कैलाश में ***दाँत काटी रोटी*** थी किन्तु पता नहीं क्यों आजकल वे एक-दूसरे से दूर-दूर रहते हैं।
- **दाँत खट्टे करना**—*हरा देना*
शिवाजी ने औरंगजेब की सेना के ***दाँत खट्टे कर*** दिए।
- **दाल में काला होना**—*किसी बात की शंका होना*
वह बार-बार इधर आता है, अवश्य कुछ ***दाल में काला*** है।
- **दिन दूनी रात चौगुनी**—*बहुत तेज गति से*
स्वतन्त्रता मिलने के उपरान्त भारत ने ***दिन दूनी रात चौगुनी*** उन्नति की है।
- **दूध का दूध पानी का पानी**—*सच्चा न्याय*
राजा विक्रमादित्य अत्यन्त पेचीदे मामलों में भी ***दूध का दूध पानी का पानी*** कर देते थे।
- **दो नावों में पैर रखना**—*दोनों पक्षों का समर्थन करना*
जो लोग ***दो नावों पर पैर रखते*** हैं, वे किसी के भले नहीं बन पाते।
- **धूप में बाल सफेद न करना**—*बहुत अनुभवी होना*
मेरे ***बाल धूप में सफेद नहीं*** हुए हैं, मैं सबकुछ जानता हूँ।
- **नाक पर मक्खी न बैठने देना**—*किसी को कुछ कहने का अवसर न देना*
वह बहुत ही सिद्धान्तवादी है, ***नाक पर मक्खी भी नहीं बैठने*** देता।
- **पाँचों उँगलियाँ घी में होना**—*बहुत लाभ होना*
आजकल व्यापारियों की ***पाँचों उँगलियाँ घी*** में हैं।
- **पाँव उखड़ जाना**—*हारकर भागना*
राणा सांगा की विशाल सेना को देखकर बाबर की सेना के ***पाँव उखड़*** गए।
- **पापड़ बेलना**—*मुसीबत झेलना (परिश्रम करना)*
मैंने अपनी जिन्दगी में बड़े ***पापड़ बेले*** हैं, तब कहीं जाकर यह दिन देखने को मिला है।
- **पेट का हल्का होना**—*किसी बात को छिपा न सकना*
जो मनुष्य ***पेट के हल्के होते*** हैं, वे सबके बुरे बन जाते हैं।
- **पौ बारह होना**—*लाभ ही लाभ होना*
आजकल व्यापारियों की ***पौ बारह*** है।
- **बाल की खाल निकालना**—*सूक्ष्म विवेचन करना*
तर्क करने वाले प्रत्येक बात में ***बाल की खाल निकालते*** हैं।
- **बाल बाँका न होना**—*तनिक भी हानि न होना*
आग में प्रहलाद का तो ***बाल भी बाँका न हुआ*** किन्तु उसकी बुआ होलिका जलकर भस्म हो गई।
- **मुँह में पानी भर आना**—*लालच आना*
लोमड़ी ने जब अंगूर लटकते हुए देखे तो उसके ***मुँह में पानी भर आया***।
- **मुट्ठी गरम करना**—*रिश्वत देना*
तुम्हें इस काम के लिए अधिकारियों की ***मुट्ठी गरम करनी*** पड़ेगी।
- **रंग में भंग पड़ना**—*मजा किरकिरा होना*
उत्सव के समय यकायक पानी बरसने से ***रंग में भंग पड़*** गया।
- **लकीर का फकीर होना**—*पुरानी रीति पर चलना*
तुम तो बिल्कुल ***लकीर के फकीर हो,*** किसी बात को तर्क की कसौटी पर कसना ही नहीं चाहते।
- **सफेद झूठ बोलना**—*सरासर झूठ बोलना*
तुम ***सफेद झूठ बोलते*** हो; ऐसा कभी नहीं हो सकता।
- **सिर पर कफन बाँधना**—*मरने के लिए तैयार होना*
भारत को स्वतन्त्र कराने के लिए अनेक वीरों ने ***सिर पर कफन बाँध*** लिया था।
- **सिर पर भूत सवार होना**—*किसी धुन पर अड़े होना*
जब शान्ति के ***सिर पर भूत सवार होता*** है, तो फिर उसे कोई नहीं समझा सकता।
- **सूर्य को दीपक दिखाना**—*महान् व्यक्ति का परिचय देने की कोशिश करना*
स्वामी विवेकानन्द के सम्बन्ध में कुछ कहना ***सूर्य को दीपक दिखाना*** ही है।
- **हाथ धोकर पीछे पड़ना**—*बुरी तरह सताना*
वह तो ***हाथ धोकर मेरे पीछे पड़*** गया है, मैं कितना ही अच्छा काम करूँ, वह कोई-न-कोई गलती निकाल ही देता है।
- **हाथ-पाँव फूल जाना**—*बहुत घबरा जाना*
दंगाइयों के अचानक घर में घुस जाने पर मेरे ***हाथ-पाँव फूल*** गए।
- **हाथों के तोते उड़ जाना**—*सुध-बुध खोना*
दुकान खोलते ही जब सेठ जी ने देखा कि तिजोरी खुली पड़ी है, तो उनके ***हाथ के तोते उड़*** गए।

वस्तुनिष्ठ प्रश्नोत्तर

निर्देश : *नीचे प्रत्येक प्रश्न में एक मुहावरा दिया गया है और उसके नीचे A, B, C, D विकल्प के सामने उसका (मुहावरे का) अर्थ दिया गया है। चारों अर्थों में से जो अर्थ आपको सर्वाधिक उपयुक्त लगे, उस पर सही का निशान लगाइये।*

1. आँख नीली-पीली करना
A. उत्सुकता से देखना B. सावधान हो जाना
C. बहुत क्रुद्ध होना D. हैरानी प्रकट करना

2. आन की आन में
A. एकदम B. अपमान करते हुए
C. इज्जत देना D. अपने आप

3. एक की चार लगाना
A. गप्प मारना B. अपनी बात ऊपर रखना
C. अनेक बहाने बनाना D. झूठी शिकायत करना

4. कसर निकालना
A. कमी पूरी करना B. उदारता दिखाना
C. बदला लेना D. चैन से न बैठने देना

5. खटपट होना
A. झगड़ा होना B. शोर होना
C. आवाज होना D. शान्ति भंग होना

6. अन्धे की लकड़ी
A. सबसे बड़ा सहारा
B. एक मात्र आशा
C. आशा की किरण
D. असहाय व्यक्ति का एकमात्र सहारा

7. अक्ल पर पत्थर पड़ना
A. अक्ल का उपयोग न करना B. बुद्धि काम न देना
C. बुद्धि नष्ट हो जाना D. मंद बुद्धि होना

8. अपना उल्लू सीधा करना
A. अपना काम निकालना
B. अपने को विपत्ति से मुक्त करना
C. अपना काम पूरा होने पर मुँह फेर लेना
D. दूसरे को उल्लू बनाकर अपना हित साधना

9. अपना-सा मुँह लेकर रह जाना
A. पराजित होना B. लज्जित होना
C. निराश होना D. हिम्मत पस्त होना

10. अपने मुँह मियाँ मिट्ठू बनना
A. डींग मारना B. रोब जमाना
C. स्वयं अपनी प्रशंसा करना D. अपने माल की तारीफ करना

11. आँख चुराना
A. आँखें न मिलाना B. शरमाना
C. सामने न आना D. डराना

12. आँखें फेर लेना
A. बेमुरव्वत
B. शिष्टाचार न बरतना
C. मिलना-जुलना बंद कर देना
D. उपेक्षा करना

13. आँधी के आम
A. सस्ती वस्तु
B. खराब वस्तु
C. बिना परिश्रम के प्राप्त वस्तु
D. मुफ्त मिली वस्तु

14. आग उगलना
A. मारने को दौड़ना B. खरी-खोटी सुनाना
C. बहुत क्रोध दिखाना D. क्रोध से पागल होना

15. आस्तीन का साँप
A. छिपा रुस्तम B. गुदड़ी का लाल
C. समय पर साथ न देना D. विश्वासघाती

16. ईद का चाँद होना
A. बहुत कम दिखाई देना B. बहुत प्रिय होना
C. बहुत सुन्दर होना D. बहुत लाड़ला होना

17. एक थैली के चट्टे-बट्टे
A. एक ही गुट के B. एक जैसी प्रकृति के
C. एक ही जाति-धर्म के D. एक से एक बढ़ कर

18. कागजी घोड़े दौड़ाना
A. मंसूबे बाँधना B. लिखा-पढ़ी करना
C. कागज काला करना D. व्यर्थ का काम करना

19. कान का कच्चा
A. दूसरों की बात न सुनने वाला
B. एक कान से सुनना दूसरे से निकाल देना
C. बिल्कुल बर्दाश्त न करना
D. दूसरों की बातों पर सहज विश्वास करना

20. गच्चा खाना
A. धोखे में ठगा जाना B. पराजित होना
C. हार मानना D. आरोप में फँस जाना

21. कोल्हू का बैल
A. दिन-रात काम करते रहना
B. बड़ी मेहनत व ईमानदारी से काम करना
C. एक ही काम करने लायक होना
D. एक ही काम करते-करते ऊब जाना

22. खरी-खोटी सुनाना
A. गाली देना B. भला-बुरा कहना
C. खबरदार करना D. बड़े-छोटे का लिहाज न करना

23. गंगा नहाना
A. पुण्य कमाना
B. किसी बड़े काम को पूरा करके राहत महसूस करना
C. भविष्य में अच्छा काम करने का संकल्प लेना
D. स्वास्थ्य-लाभ करना

24. गाल बजाना
A. स्वाद ले-लेकर खाना B. डींग मारना
C. प्रसन्न होना D. अशिष्ट व्यवहार करना

25. घास काटना
A. छोटा-मोटा काम करना
B. व्यर्थ समय गँवाना
C. ऐसा काम करना, जिसमें परिश्रम के अनुसार लाभ न हो
D. किसी काम को बेपरवाही से करना

26. घुटने टेकना
A. प्रणाम करना B. पराजय स्वीकार करना
C. गुलामी स्वीकार करना D. हिम्मत हारना

27. चूना लगाना
A. चापलूसी करके अपना काम निकालना
B. धोखा देना
C. कठोर बात कहना
D. सफाई करना

28. जहर का घूँट पीकर रह जाना
A. पराधीन होना
B. बड़ा अपमान सहकर भी चुप रहना
C. क्रोध दबा जाना
D. स्वयं मुसीबत मोल लेना

29. गले मढ़ना
A. पीछे पड़ना B. आगा-पीछा न सोचना
C. मुसीबत मोल लेना D. जबरदस्ती दे देना

30. टोपी उछालना
A. अपमान करना B. अत्यधिक खुशी व्यक्त करना
C. अच्छी तरह परखना D. इज्जत करना

31. डंके की चोट पर कहना
A. अपमानित करना B. खुल्लमखुल्ला कहना
C. कोई लिहाज न करना D. भला-बुरा सब कह डालना

32. तारे गिनना
A. व्यर्थ का काम करना
B. असम्भव काम की कोशिश करना
C. रात-भर जागना
D. सोने की भरसक कोशिश करना

33. दाँत काटी रोटी
A. जूठा भोजन
B. गहरी दोस्ती
C. चारों तरफ से संकटों से घिरा
D. रूखा-सूखा भोजन

34. दाल में काला होना
A. मजा न आना
B. किसी बात का संदेह होना
C. किसी संकट की शुरुआत
D. संकट की घड़ी में नई मुसीबत आ जाना

35. नौ-दो ग्यारह होना
A. लेन-देन पूरा होना B. भाग जाना
C. पूरा ध्यान रखना D. सौदेबाजी करना

36. पहाड़ टूट पड़ना
A. बहुत नुकसान होना B. भारी मुसीबत आ जाना
C. असम्भव बात होना D. उथल-पुथल होना

37. पाँचों उँगलियाँ घी में होना
A. रोज बढ़िया भोजन मिलना B. गुलछर्रे उड़ाना
C. अत्यधिक लाभ होना D. चैन से दिन गुजरना

38. पेट का हल्का होना
A. अपच होना
B. क्रोधी होना
C. किसी बात को गुप्त न रख पाना
D. जल्दी ही घबरा जाना

39. पेट में दाढ़ी होना
A. बहुत लालची होना
B. धूर्त होना
C. बहुत मोटा होना
D. छोटी आयु में ही बहुत चतुर-चालाक होना

40. बट्टा लगना
A. कीमत घट जाना B. कलंक लगना
C. घाटा होना D. पोल खुल जाना

41. बहती गंगा में हाथ धोना
A. आसानी से काम पूरा कर लेना
B. दूसरों को मौके का लाभ उठाते देखकर खुद भी मौके का लाभ उठा लेना
C. सबकी हाँ में हाँ मिलाना
D. मौका हाथ से न जाने देना

42. बातों में आना
A. झूठ पर विश्वास करना
B. बात को पी जाना
C. भेद प्रकट कर देना
D. किसी की बातों पर विश्वास कर लेना

43. भंडा फूटना
A. बेइज्जती होना B. भेद खुल जाना
C. बँटवारा होना D. मन की भड़ास निकालना

44. भूत सवार होना
A. पागल होना
B. किसी के वश में होना
C. किसी बात/काम के पीछे पड़ जाना
D. जी-तोड़ मेहनत करना

45. मक्खियाँ मारना
A. गंदे काम करना
B. खाली बैठे रहना
C. समय व्यतीत करने हेतु कुछ-न-कुछ करते रहना
D. आनन्द करना

46. माथा ठनकना
A. क्रोध आना B. याद आना
C. सन्देह होना D. उपाय सूझना

47. मुँह में पानी भर आना
A. लालच आना B. खाने की इच्छा होना
C. हड़पने का उपाय सोचना D. प्रसन्न हो जाना

48. रफूचक्कर हो जाना
A. बचकर भाग जाना B. मैदान छोड़कर भाग जाना
C. छिप जाना D. सरपट भागना

49. लट्टू होना
A. लोट-पोट होना B. मुग्ध होना
C. प्रभावित होना D. आगे-पीछे चक्कर लगाना

50. शेखी बघारना
A. बड़ी-बड़ी बातें करना B. बढ़ा-चढ़ाकर आत्मप्रशंसा करना
C. घमंड करना D. कोरी बातें करना

51. सब्ज़ बाग दिखाना
A. खुश करना B. सांत्वना देना
C. झूठी आशा बँधाना D. सफेद झूठ बोलना

52. साँप का बच्चा
A. जहरीला B. दुश्मन
C. स्वभाव से दुष्ट D. तेज गति से भागने वाला

53. सितारा गर्दिश में होना
A. घाटा होना B. बुरे दिन होना
C. पराजित होना D. पतन होना

54. सिर धुनना
A. पछताना B. लज्जित होना
C. तंग करना D. शोक मनाना

55. हवा बाँधना
A. सबको दबाकर रखना B. धाक जमाना
C. खुशामद करना D. साँस रोकना

56. हाथ तंग होना
A. कंजूस होना B. किफायत करना
C. रुपये पैसे की कमी होना D. कंगाल हो जाना

57. शह देना
A. दुलराना B. डराना
C. उकसाना D. धमकाना

58. सिर खाना
A. परेशान करना B. रट लगाना
C. शोर करना D. शरारत करना

59. सीधा करना
A. पीटना B. आदत सुधारना
C. अकड़ दूर करना D. रास्ते पर लाना

60. सौ बात सुनाना
A. लम्बी बात करना B. भला-बुरा कहना
C. मीन-मेख निकालना D. जिद करना

उत्तरमाला

1	2	3	4	5	6	7	8	9	10
C	A	D	C	A	D	C	A	B	C
11	**12**	**13**	**14**	**15**	**16**	**17**	**18**	**19**	**20**
C	D	C	C	D	A	B	B	D	A
21	**22**	**23**	**24**	**25**	**26**	**27**	**28**	**29**	**30**
A	B	B	B	D	B	B	B	D	A
31	**32**	**33**	**34**	**35**	**36**	**37**	**38**	**39**	**40**
B	C	B	B	B	B	C	C	D	B
41	**42**	**43**	**44**	**45**	**46**	**47**	**48**	**49**	**50**
B	D	B	C	B	C	A	A	B	B
51	**52**	**53**	**54**	**55**	**56**	**57**	**58**	**59**	**60**
C	C	B	A	B	C	C	A	C	B

★★★

9

लोकोक्ति

लोकोक्ति पूर्ण वाक्य हुआ करती है। यह किसी घटना विशेष का निष्कर्ष होती है। यह एक ओर वास्तविकता का संकेत देती है तो दूसरी ओर तीखी आलोचना या व्यंग्य प्रस्तुत करती है। कथन को प्रभावशाली बनाने में लोकोक्तियाँ बहुत महत्व रखती हैं। नीचे कुछ वाक्य प्रयोग सहित लोकोक्तियाँ दी जा रही हैं–

- **अपनी करनी पार उतरनी**–*अपना कार्य ही फलदायक होता है।*
  जीवन में दूसरों का सहारा ढूँढने से क्या होता है, अपनी करनी पार उतरनी।
- **अंधेर नगरी चौपट राजा**–*अन्याय का बोलबाला।*
  अयोग्य अधिकारी होने पर सभी कामों में धांधली चलती है, ठीक ही कहा गया है–अंधेर नगरी चौपट राजा।
- **हाथ पतला होना**–*दयनीय दशा होना।*
  व्यापार में घाटा हो गया इसलिए आजकल उसका हाथ पतला है।
- **अपनी-अपनी ढपली, अपना-अपना राग**–*मनमानी।*
  संगठन के अभाव में लोग अपनी-अपनी ढपली, अपना-अपना राग अलापते हैं।
- **लाल गुदड़ी में नहीं छिपते**–*होनहार का व्यक्तित्व छिपा नहीं रह सकता।*
  राजीव अपने जीवन में संघर्ष कर रहा है। असाधारण प्रतिभा के बावजूद उसे मंजिल नहीं मिल रही, लेकिन उसके साथी भरोसा दिलाते हैं–लाल गुदड़ी में भी नहीं छिपते।
- **खेल खिलाड़ी का, पैसा मदारी का**–*मेहनत किसी की, लाभ दूसरे का।*
  पूँजीवादी व्यवस्था की सबसे बड़ी बुराई यही है कि खेल खिलाड़ी का, पैसा मदारी का।
- **कंगाली में आटा गीला**–*एक मुसीबत पर दूसरी मुसीबत आ पड़ना।*
  विजय की नौकरी छूट गई, ऊपर से घर में नल खराब हो गया। इस पर विजय की पत्नी कहने लगी–कंगाली में आटा गीला।
- **गोदी में बैठकर दाढ़ी नोंचे**–*भला करने वाले के साथ दुष्टता करना।*
  समय ऐसा आ गया है कि लोग गोदी में बैठकर दाढ़ी नोंचने लगते हैं।
- **चोर को कहें चोरी कर और साह से कहें जागते रहो**–*दो पक्षों को लड़ाने वाला।*
  संजीव ने पड़ोसी से कहकर रामपाल के यहाँ छापा डलवा दिया और फिर रामलाल को बता दिया कि छापा किसने डलवाया है। उसकी हरकत पर लोग कह उठे चोर को कहें चोरी कर और साह से कहें जागते रहो।
- **दादा कहने से बनिया गुड़ देता है**–*मधुर वाणी से काम बन जाता है।*
  आजकल समय ऐसा आ गया है जब दादा कहने से ही बनिया गुड़ देता है।
- **दीवार के भी कान होते हैं**–*रहस्य की बात गुपचुप करनी चाहिए।*
  अजय, विजय को विनय की चोरी की दास्तान सुनाने लगा तो विजय ने अजय से कहा–धीरे बोलो, दीवार के भी कान होते हैं।
- **न रहेगा बाँस न बजेगी बाँसुरी**–*मूल कारण को रफा-दफा करे तो झगड़ा-फसाद ही न हो।*
  अध्यापक ने विद्यार्थी से कहा, तुम आलस्य त्याग दो इससे तुम्हें सफलता एवं उत्तम स्वास्थ्य प्राप्त होगा क्योंकि न रहेगा बाँस न बजेगी बाँसुरी।
- **तबेले की बला बंदर के सिर**–*अपराध करे कोई, पकड़ा जाये कोई और।*
  पुलिस वालों की तबेले की बला बंदर के सिर रखने की आदत हो गई है।
- **रानी रूठेगी तो अपना सुहाग लेगी**–*रूठने से अपना ही नुकसान होता है।*
  पुत्र के विवाह में दामाद के न आने से दुखी शर्मा जी को कहना पड़ा, 'रानी रूठेगी तो अपना सुहाग लेगी।'
- **अपना रख पराया चख**–*अपनी नहीं दूसरों की चीज का इस्तेमाल करना।*
  संजय बहुत चालाक है, वह अपना रख पराया चख की नीति पर चलता है।
- **आए थे हरि भजन को ओटन लगे कपास**–*उच्च लक्ष्य लेकर चलना पर कोई घटिया काम करने लगना।*
  पार्टी के कार्यकर्ता जागृति अभियान पर निकले लेकिन रास्ते में शराब और जुए में मस्त हो गए तो नेताजी को कहना पड़ा–आए थे हरि भजन को ओटन लगे कपास।
- **खग जाने खग ही की भाषा**–*एक साथ काम करने वाले एक-दूसरे के भाव-इशारे समझ जाते हैं।*
  दलाल के इशारे दूसरा दलाल समझ जाता है और किसान देखता रह जाता है, सच है–खग जाने खग ही की भाषा।
- **कोयला होय न ऊजला सौ मन साबुन धोय**–*दुष्ट व्यक्ति की प्रकृति में कोई परिवर्तन नहीं होता उसे चाहे कितनी ही सीख दी जाए।*
  मास्टर जी ने गाँव के विकास को हर प्रकार से समझाया कि वह बुरी आदतें छोड़ दें लेकिन वह नहीं माना। हारकर मास्टर जी को मानना पड़ा कोयला होय न ऊजला सौ मन साबुन धोय।

- **चमड़ी जाय पर दमड़ी न जाय**–*बहुत कंजूसी।*
  सेठ लालाराम स्टेशन से पैदल घर सामान उठाकर आ गए तो बीबी बोली सेठ जी आप भी चमड़ी जाय पर दमड़ी न जाय कहावत में विश्वास रखते हैं।
- **गागर में सागर भरना**–*संक्षेप में विस्तृत बात कह देना।*
  बिहारी ने अपने दोहों में गागर में सागर भर दिया है।
- **गुड़ खाए गुलगुलों से परहेज**–*बनावटी त्याग।*
  स्वामीजी प्याज नहीं खाते, परन्तु प्याज की बनी पकौड़ियाँ खा लेते हैं, ऐसे ही लोगों के लिए कहा गया है–गुड़ खाए गुलगुलों से परहेज।
- **मार के आगे भूत भागे**–*मार से सब डरते हैं।*
  पुलिस ने उसे मारा तो उसने अपराध कबूल लिया। सच है, मार के आगे भूत भागता है।
- **होनहार बिरवान के होत चीकने पात**–*होनहार बालक के लक्षण आरम्भ से ही दिखाई देने लगते हैं।*
  विकास के कार्यकलाप देखकर सभी यही कहते हैं–होनहार बिरवान के होत चीकने पात।
- **चौबे गये छब्बे बनने दुब्बे बनकर आये**–*लाभ के बदले हानि हो जाना।*
  प्रेस में प्रश्न-पत्र छापने वाले शर्मा जी ने मॉडल पेपर निकालकर प्रकाशक बनने का प्रयास किया जिसमें घाटा हो गया और उनकी दशा पर लोग कहने लगे, चौबे गये छब्बे बनने दुब्बे बनकर आये।
- **हाथ मलना**–*कुछ प्राप्त न होना।*
  विनय को इनाम मिला और मैं हाथ मलता रह गया।
- **अब पछताए होत क्या जब चिड़ियाँ चुग गईं खेत**–*नुकसान हो जाने के बाद पछताना बेकार।*
  परीक्षा के दिनों में अरविन्द ने पढ़ाई नहीं की, फेल तो होना ही था, जब वह रोने लगा तो पिता ने कहा–अब पछताए होत क्या जब चिड़ियाँ चुग गईं खेत।
- **आम के आम गुठलियों के दाम**–*दोहरा लाभ।*
  राजेश गन्ने का रस बेचता है और छीलन गौशाला वाले खरीदकर ले जाते हैं। इस प्रकार उसके तो आम के आम गुठलियों के दाम हैं।
- **उल्टा चोर कोतवाल को डांटे**–*दोषी होने पर धौंस जमाना।*
  राजेश से कक्षा में देर से आने के लिए मॉनीटर ने कारण पूछा तो राजेश ने कहा, 'तुम्हें मतलब'? तुम क्या अध्यापक हो, जाओ अपना काम करो। उसका जवाब सुनकर एक लड़का कह उठा, उल्टा चोर कोतवाल को डाँटे।
- **अपना ही पैसा खोटा तो परखने वाले का क्या दोष**–*अपनी ही चीज खराब हो तो दूसरे को दोष देना उचित नहीं।*
  अजय ने पड़ोसी की लड़की छेड़ दी। इस पर उसकी माँ अजय के घर आकर उसे बुरा भला कहने लगी, इस पर उसके पिताजी बोले अपना ही पैसा खोटा हो तो परखने वाले का क्या दोष।
- **न अंधे को न्यौता देते न दो जने आते**–*न यह काम करते न बवाल खड़ा होता।*
  संजीव ने एक विधवा से विवाह किया, जिसके दो बच्चे थे। फिर जब अपने दो बच्चे हो गए तो गुजारा कठिन हो गया, इस पर मित्र ने समझाया न अंधे को न्यौता देते न दो जने आते।
- **चोरी का माल मोरी में**–*गलत ढंग से अर्जित धन गलत ढंग से ही खर्च होता है।*
  मनोहर ने रिश्वत लेकर खूब धन कमाया, लेकिन बच्चे की बीमारी में सब खर्च हो गया, इस प्रकार चोरी का माल मोरी में चला गया।
- **घर की मुर्गी दाल बराबर**–*घर की वस्तु का आदर नहीं होता।*
  व्यक्ति कितना ही महान् हो, घर में उसका मूल्यांकन उतना नहीं हो सकता है, क्योंकि घर की मुर्गी दाल बराबर होती है।
- **कहीं की ईंट कहीं का रोड़ा, भानुमती ने कुनबा जोड़ा**–*इधर-उधर की सामग्री एकत्र करके कोई रचना करना।*
  राजग गठबंधन की सरकार कहीं की ईंट कहीं का रोड़ा, भानुमती ने कुनबा जोड़ा वाली सरकार थी।
- **काठ की हाण्डी बार-बार नहीं चढ़ती**–*अन्याय बार-बार नहीं चलता।*
  जितेन्द्र बिना टिकट यात्रा के अपराध में पकड़ा ही गया, ठीक ही कहा गया है कि काठ की हाण्डी बार-बार नहीं चढ़ती।
- **काला अक्षर भैंस बराबर**–*निरक्षर व्यक्ति के लिए पुस्तकें व्यर्थ हैं।*
  हमें कागज क्यों दिखाते हो, हमारे लिए काला अक्षर भैंस बराबर।
- **खरबूजे को देखकर खरबूजा रंग बदलता है**–*जब कोई व्यक्ति अपने साथी के अनुसार आचरण करने लगता है तब यह कहावत कही जाती है।*
  राहुल द्रविड़ को शानदार बल्लेबाजी करते देख लक्ष्मण ने भी शानदार बल्लेबाजी करके भारत को ऑस्ट्रेलिया के विरुद्ध मैच जिता दिया, तब ऑस्ट्रेलिया के खिलाड़ियों को कहना पड़ा–खरबूजे को देखकर खरबूजा रंग बदलता है।
- **खुदा गंजे को नाखून नहीं देता**–*अयोग्य को अधिकार नहीं मिलता।*
  अकर्मण्य व्यक्ति को अधिकार नहीं मिल पाते हैं, क्योंकि खुदा गंजे को नाखून नहीं देता।
- **इस हाथ दे उस हाथ ले**–*कर्म का फल शीघ्र मिलता है।*
  दूसरों का सम्मान करने से स्वयं को सम्मान मिलता है। ठीक ही है–इस हाथ दे उस हाथ ले।
- **आधी छोड़ सारी को धावै, आधी मिलै न पूरी पावै**–*अधिक लोभ करने से हानि ही होती है।*
  भाजपा ने समयपूर्व चुनाव करा दिये कहीं हार न जाये, सच भी है आधी छोड़ सारी को धावै, आधी मिलै न पूरी पावै।
- **ईश्वर की माया, कहीं धूप कहीं छाया**–*संसार में कहीं दुख है कहीं सुख है।*
  किसी घर दूध घी की बहार है और किसी घर सूखी रोटी भी नहीं है, ठीक ही कहा गया है–ईश्वर की माया कहीं धूप कहीं छाया।
- **उल्टे बाँस बरेली को**–*विपरीत कार्य करना।*
  शीला फिरोजाबाद गयी तो चूड़ियाँ ले गई तब रीना बोली–दीदी तुमने तो उल्टे बाँस बरेली वाली कहावत चरितार्थ कर दी, फिरोजाबाद तो चूड़ियों का शहर है।
- **आज का बनिया कल का सेठ**–*काम करते रहने से आदमी बड़ा हो ही जाता है।*
  अजय ने सुनील से कहा निराश मत हो मित्र, मेहनत से कार्य करते रहो एक दिन इसी फर्म में तरक्की पा जाओगे। कहावत भी है आज का बनिया कल का सेठ।

- **एक सड़ी मछली सारे तालाब को गन्दा कर देती है**–*अच्छे समाज को एक बुरा व्यक्ति कलंकित कर देता है।*
मुहल्ले में एक धंधा करने वाली के बस जाने से पूरा मुहल्ला बदनाम हो गया। सच है एक सड़ी मछली सारे तालाब को गन्दा कर देती है।
- **एक तो करेला फिर नीम चढ़ा**–*दोहरा कटुत्व।*
सुधा एक तो पढ़ने में कमजोर है और दूसरे शिक्षकों के प्रति उसका व्यवहार ठीक नहीं है, ऐसे लोगों के लिए कहा गया है–एक तो करेला फिर नीम चढ़ा।
- **एक पंथ दो काज**–*एक उपाय से दो कार्यों का होना।*
रामू हिन्दी विषय में एम.ए. की तैयारी कर रहा था। उसने साहित्यरत्न का भी फार्म भर दिया, इस प्रकार उसकें एक पंथ दो काज हो गए।
- **ऊँची दुकान फीका पकवान**–*केवल बाहरी दिखावा।*
हमने अन्नपूर्णा होटल का नाम बहुत सुना था, लेकिन जब हमने वहाँ खाना खाया तो न अच्छा खाना था न सफाई। सोचकर रह गये ऊँची दुकान फीका पकवान।
- **आप मियाँ जी माँगते द्वार खड़े दरवेश**–*अति दरिद्र के यहाँ भिक्षा माँगने वालों का आना।*
विजय कर्ज के बोझ से दबा था, फिर भी उसकी पत्नी साधुओं को प्रतिदिन खिलाती थी। यह देखकर लेनदार ने कहा आप मियाँ जी माँगते द्वार खड़े दरवेश।
- **अपना हाथ जगन्नाथ**–*स्वयं किया हुआ कार्य फलदायी होता है।*
घर का कार्य नौकरों से कराने की अपेक्षा स्वयं करना अच्छा है। अपना हाथ जगन्नाथ।
- **घी का लड्डू टेढ़ा भला**–*काम की वस्तु कम अच्छी रहने पर भी ठीक रहती है।*
राज का व्यवहार अजीबो-गरीब है लेकिन वह बहुत योग्य है। अतः नियोक्ता उसे घी का लड्डू टेढ़ा भला अनुसार सहन करते हैं।
- **आटे के साथ घुन भी पिसता है**–*दोषी व्यक्ति का साथी निर्दोष भी मारा जाता है।*
सोनू ने चोरी नहीं की लेकिन वह मोनू का साथी तो है, अतः पुलिस उसे भी पकड़कर ले गई। इसे कहते हैं आटे के साथ घुन भी पिसता है।
- **अंधे के हाथ बटेर**–*अनायास कोई वस्तु मिल जाना।*
मंजू की शादी गुड्डू से हो गई तो दोनों को जानने वाला कह उठा अंधे के हाथ बटेर लग गई।
- **कहाँ राजा भोज कहाँ गंगू तेली**–*छोटे आदमी की बड़े आदमी से क्या तुलना।*
मदर टेरेसा की सिस्टर निर्मला से तुलना क्या चीज है? कहाँ राजा भोज कहाँ गंगू तेली।
- **खिसयानी बिल्ली खम्भा नोचे**–*शर्म के मारे क्रोध करने लगना।*
विजय चोरी करते पकड़ा गया तो माता-पिता को कोसने लगा कि मुझे अच्छी सीख क्यों नहीं दी। सही है खिसयानी बिल्ली खम्भा नोचे।
- **थोथा चना बाजे घना**–*कम ज्ञान या गुण रखने वाला बातें बढ़-चढ़कर करता है।*
जब कोई गुणहीन व्यक्ति अपनी प्रशंसा करने लगता है तब यह कहावत चरितार्थ होती है।
- **आँख के अंधे नाम नैनसुख**–*नाम बड़ा और गुण उसके विपरीत।*
माता-पिता ने बालक का नाम धनीराम रखा, लेकिन बड़ा होकर धनीराम को दो जून की रोटी जुटानी भारी पड़ रही है, अतः किसी ने सही कहा है–आँख के अंधे नाम नैन सुख।
- **धोबी का कुत्ता घर का न घाट का**–*निकम्मा व्यक्ति।*
नीरज ने नौकरी छोड़ दी और व्यापार में भी असफल रहा तो माता-पिता ने कहा–धोबी का कुत्ता घर का न घाट का।
- **दूर के ढोल सुहावने**–*दूर की वस्तु अच्छी लगना।*
सुनील को चीन का बना कपड़ा अधिक पसन्द है, जबकि भारत का बना कपड़ा काफी अच्छा होता है, ठीक ही कहा गया है–दूर के ढोल सुहावने।
- **मान न मान मैं तेरा मेहमान**–*जबरदस्ती का मेहमान।*
सुरेश ने राजेश को पार्टी में आने का न्यौता नहीं दिया लेकिन वह फिर भी आ धमका तो इस पर लोग कहने लगे मान न मान मैं तेरा मेहमान।
- **अंधे की लकड़ी**–*बेसहारे का सहारा।*
विनय अपने बूढ़े बाप का इकलौता पुत्र था, अचानक कल उसका देहान्त हो गया तो रामलाल ने कहा–अंधे की तो लकड़ी ही टूट गई।
- **भागते भूत की लँगोटी भली**–*जिस व्यक्ति से कुछ भी मिलने की आशा न हो, उससे यदि थोड़ा भी मिल जाता है, तब यह कहावत प्रयुक्त होती है।*
अजय ने विकास को 500 रुपये उधार दिए थे, बड़ी मुश्किल से 100 रुपये विकास ने वापस दिये तो अजय ने सोचा भागते भूत की लँगोटी ही भली।
- **मन चंगा तो कठौती में गंगा**–*यदि मन शुद्ध है तो तीर्थाटन की आवश्यकता नहीं है।*
मनुष्य मन से पवित्र है तो सभी तीर्थ उसके पास हैं अतः भक्त रविदास ने कहा है–मन चंगा तो कठौती में गंगा।
- **मुल्ला की दौड़ मस्जिद तक**–*सीमित क्षेत्र तक पहुँच।*
पवन अधिक-से अधिक ग्राम प्रधान के पारा जाएगा, गुल्ला की दौड़ मस्जिद तक।
- **यह मुँह और मसूर की दाल**–*जब कोई व्यक्ति अपनी योग्यता से अधिक पाने की अभिलाषा करता है तब यह कहावत चरितार्थ होती है।*
बी.ए. में तृतीय श्रेणी में पास हुआ विवेक पी.सी.एस. की बात करने लगा तो अजय ने उससे कहा–यह मुँह और मसूर की दाल।
- **क्या काबुल में गधे नहीं होते**–*अच्छे स्थान पर बुरे लोग भी होते हैं।*
दफ्तर में सचिन का मोबाइल चोरी हो गया–जब उसने कहा कि किसी बाहरी आदमी ने चोरी की है तो अजय ने कहा–क्या काबुल में गधे नहीं होते।

वस्तुनिष्ठ प्रश्नोत्तर

निर्देश (प्रश्न संख्या 1 से 10 तक): *नीचे प्रत्येक प्रश्न में एक लोकोक्ति दी गई है और उसके नीचे A, B, C, D विकल्प के सामने उसका (लोकोक्ति का) अर्थ दिया गया है। चारों अर्थों में से जो अर्थ आपको सर्वाधिक उपयुक्त लगे, उस पर सही का निशान लगाइये।*

1. काठ की हाँडी बार-बार नहीं चढ़ती
A. किसी भी व्यक्ति को बार-बार धोखा नहीं दिया जा सकता
B. धोखा देने की एक ही तरकीब बार-बार सफल नहीं होती
C. धोखा देने की सब तरकीबें हर बार सफल नहीं होतीं
D. ठगने वाला हर बार अपनी तरकीब बदलता रहता है

2. खिसियानी बिल्ली खंभा नोचे
A. निराश व्यक्ति किसी-न-किसी वस्तु का सहारा ढूँढता है
B. किसी काम में सफल न होने पर अपना क्रोध अन्य किसी पर अकारण प्रकट करना
C. असफल व्यक्ति ऊटपटाँग काम करने लगता है
D. असफलता का दोष किसी अन्य व्यक्ति के सिर मढ़ना

3. खोदा पहाड़ निकली चुहिया
A. साधारण कार्य के लिए असाधारण प्रयत्न करना
B. असाधारण प्रयत्न के बाद अति छोटी सफलता मिलना
C. ऐसा फल निकलना, जिसकी अपेक्षा न हो
D. परिणाम, प्रयत्न के बिल्कुल विपरीत हो

4. घर की मुर्गी दाल बराबर
A. घर में विद्यमान चीज खूब जमकर (इफरात) इस्तेमाल होती है
B. घर का खाना सबसे बढ़िया होता है चाहे मुर्गी हो या दाल हो
C. घर में उपलब्ध वस्तु को अधिक महत्व नहीं दिया जाता
D. घर में पली मुर्गी को दाल भी खिलाई जाती है

5. चोर की दाढ़ी में तिनका
A. चोर सदैव सशंकित रहता है
B. चोर को लगता है कि सब उसके बारे में जानते हैं
C. पापी को अपने पाप का भय बना रहता है
D. चोर चोरी करते समय अपना कुछ-न-कुछ सबूत जरूर छोड़ जाता है

6. जिसकी लाठी उसकी भैंस
A. जबरदस्त सबसे अपनी बात मनवा लेता है
B. जबरदस्त को जो वस्तु पसन्द आ जाती है, वह उसे लेकर ही दम लेता है
C. जबरदस्त किसी की परवाह नहीं करता
D. जबरदस्त की लाठी में बल होता है

7. दूध का दूध—पानी का पानी
A. निष्पक्ष न्याय
B. जैसे को तैसा
C. अन्यायी को दण्ड
D. ऐसा न्याय, जिससे दोनों पक्ष संतुष्ट हों

8. नौ नकद न तेरह उधार
A. नकद के नौ और उधार के तेरह बराबर होते हैं
B. नकद के नौ अच्छे, उधार के तेरह नहीं अच्छे
C. अधिक लाभ के लोभ में उधार देना हानिकारक होता है
D. उधार की दुकान अधिक दिन नहीं चल पाती

9. बन्दर क्या जाने अदरक का स्वाद
A. गँवार व्यक्ति को गुणों की पहचान नहीं होती
B. गँवार व्यक्ति के गुण छिपे ही रहते हैं
C. गँवार व्यक्ति गुण-दोष पहचानने की कोशिश नहीं करता
D. गँवार व्यक्ति को कोई उत्तम वस्तु मिल जाये तो भी वह उसकी कद्र नहीं करता

10. साँप मरे न लाठी टूटे
A. असम्भव कार्य
B. दोनों प्रकार के लाभ मिलना
C. काम भी हो जाये और नुकसान (हानि) भी न उठानी पड़े
D. बिना नुकसान उठाये कोई बड़ा काम नहीं होता

निर्देश (प्रश्न संख्या 11 से 15 तक): *निम्नलिखित वाक्यांशों के लिए उपयुक्त लोकोक्तियाँ बताइए।*

11. अल्प समय के लिए अधिकार हाथ में आने पर मनमानी करना
A. सौ दिन चोर का एक दिन साहूकार का
B. बंदर की आशनाई घर में आग लगाई
C. अंधे को अंधेरे में बहुत दूर की सूझी
D. एक दिन का बादशाह बनना और चमड़े का सिक्का चलाना

12. सत्ता सम्पन्न व्यक्ति मदांध हो ही जाते हैं
A. प्रभुता पाय काह मद नाहीं
B. फटे में पाँव दफ्तर में नाव
C. आँख न दीदा काढ़े कसीदा
D. ऊँट मक्का की ओर भागता है

13. हराम की कमाई व्यर्थ जाती है
A. आदमी जानै बसे, सोना जाने कसै
B. आप मियाँजी माँगते दूर खड़े दरवेश
C. चोरी का माल मोरी में
D. अन्धी पीसे कुत्ते खाएं

14. विपदा सब पर आती है
A. चाँद को भी ग्रहण लगता है
B. इब्तदाए इश्क है रोता है क्या, आगे आगे देखिए होता है क्या
C. एक तवे की रोटी, क्या छोटी क्या मोटी
D. आसमान से गिरा, खजूर में अटका

15. केवल दिखावे से नाम नहीं मिलता
A. जोग जुगत व जानी, कपड़े रंग भये बिरागी
B. खेत खाए गदहा, मारा जाए जुलहा
C. आप मरे बिना स्वर्ग नहीं मिलता
D. कहने से कुम्हार गधे पर नहीं चढ़ता

निर्देश (प्रश्न संख्या 16 से 20 तक): *प्रत्येक प्रश्न में दी गई गहरे काली छपी लोकोक्तियों के अर्थ के लिए सही विकल्प का चयन कीजिए।*

16. रीता की पड़ोसी उसे रोज **जली-भुनी** सुनाती है
A. किसी वस्तु का जलाना
B. भला-बुरा कहना
C. कड़वी बात करना
D. सब कुछ कहना

17. घर से निकलने के बाद राजेश को **आटे-दाल का भाव मालूम हो गया**
A. आटे-दाल के लिए लाइन में खड़े होना
B. आटे-दाल का भाव ज्ञात करना
C. आटा-दाल खरीदना
D. वास्तविकता का ज्ञान होना

18. नीतू के लिए **काला अक्षर भैंस बराबर** है
A. अल्प ज्ञान रखना
B. अक्षरों का काला होना
C. अक्षर व भैंस का बराबर होना
D. बिल्कुल निरक्षर होना

19. रेखा को जरा भी चिन्ता नहीं थी, क्योंकि उसका तो यह हाल है कि **सावन सूखे न भादो हरे**
A. नुकसान न होना
B. अत्यधिक लाभ प्राप्त होना
C. हमेशा एक-सी दशा में रहना
D. कपटपूर्ण व्यवहार

20. मोहन बेकार में अदालत के चक्कर लगा रहा है, जबकि उसे **लेना एक न देना दो**
A. किसी से कोई मतलब न होना
B. गुप्त बात भी छिपी नहीं रह सकती
C. सार रहित
D. एक लेकर दो देना

निर्देश (प्रश्न संख्या 21 से 30 तक): निम्नलिखित लोकोक्तियों को उचित शब्दों से पूर्ण करें।

21. होनहार .... के होत चीकने पात
A. पुरुष B. बिरवान
C. जवान D. पंडित

22. ऊँची दुकान .... पकवान
A. अच्छे B. पूरे
C. फीके D. मीठे

23. एक पन्थ दो ....
A. काम B. काज
C. पाठ D. राह

24. दिन-दूना .... चौगुना
A. माह B. रात
C. चार D. काम

25. सब .... बाईस पसेरी
A. आम B. नाम
C. पान D. धान

26. घर आया .... भी नहीं निकाला जाता
A. मेहमान B. कुत्ता
C. रिश्तेदार D. ब्राह्मण

27. धोये जो सौ बार तौ .... होये ना सेत
A. कपड़ा B. आदमी
C. काजर D. गन्दा

28. ज्यों-ज्यों भीजे .... त्यों-त्यों भारी होय
A. कामरी B. कमली
C. उधारी D. कर्जा

29. सौ सुनार की एक .... की
A. कुम्हार B. मल्लाह
C. इस्पात D. लोहार

30. करम के बलिया पकाई .... हो गया दलिया
A. भात B. रोटी
C. खीर D. मेवा

उत्तरमाला

1	2	3	4	5	6	7	8	9	10
B	B	B	C	B	A	A	C	A	C
11	**12**	**13**	**14**	**15**	**16**	**17**	**18**	**19**	**20**
D	A	C	A	A	B	D	D	C	A
21	**22**	**23**	**24**	**25**	**26**	**27**	**28**	**29**	**30**
B	C	B	B	D	B	C	A	D	C

★★★

(ख) अपठित बोधात्मक प्रश्न

अभ्यास 1

प्रेममार्गी शाखा के प्रमुख कवि मलिक मोहम्मद जायसी संसार से इतने विरक्त नहीं थे। वे लोक तथा परलोक दोनों की साधना चाहते थे। उन्होंने अपने 'पद्मावत' में मसनवी परम्परा के अनुकूल शेरशाह की वंदना की है। उन्होंने लौकिक प्रेमगाथाओं के रूपक द्वारा परमार्थिक प्रेम की साधना की है। पद्मावती की प्रेम-कथा जो पृथ्वीराज रासो में वीर रस के आश्रित गौण थी, वह जायसी की 'पद्मावत' में मुख्यता प्राप्त कर लेती है। पद्मावत में कथा भी है और रूपक के द्वारा अलौकिक तत्त्वों की व्यंजना भी है। यद्यपि जायसी मुसलमान थे तथापि वे भारतीय संस्कृति से पूर्णतया परिचित थे। थोड़े बहुत हेर-फेर के साथ उनके काव्य में भारतीय अन्तर-कथाओं और धार्मिक परम्पराओं का उल्लेख हुआ है। उसमें रासो की अपेक्षा अन्विति अधिक है और आरंभ से लेकर अन्त तक शैली और भाषा की एकरसता है। पद्मावत प्रबंधकाव्य का एक अच्छा उदाहरण कहा जा सकता है।

—काव्य के रूप, डॉ. गुलाब राय

1. मलिक मोहम्मद जायसी थे :
- A. अवधी भाषा के प्रथम कवि
- B. सूफी सन्त कवि
- C. शेरशाह सूरी के सभासद्
- D. जायस के नागरिक

2. जायसी के सर्वोत्कृष्ट ग्रंथ का नाम है :
- A. आखिरी कलाम
- B. अखरा बट
- C. पद्मावत
- D. मधुमालती

3. उक्त गद्य खण्ड का उपयुक्त शीर्षक हो सकता है :
- A. पद्मावत का कथानक
- B. पद्मावत परिचय
- C. जायसी और उनका पद्मावत
- D. कविवर जायसी

4. पद्मावत महाकाव्य की भाषा है :
- A. ब्रजभाषा
- B. भोजपुरी
- C. खड़ी बोली
- D. अवधी

5. अवधी भाषा के सर्वाधिक लोकप्रिय महाकाव्य का नाम है :
- A. रामचरितमानस
- B. पद्मावत
- C. मधुमालती
- D. मृगावती

अभ्यास 2

सामान्य दुष्टों की वन्दना में या तो भय रहता है, या व्यंग्य। परन्तु जहाँ हम हानि होने के पहले ही हानि के कारण की वन्दना करने लगते हैं, वहाँ हमारी वन्दना के मूल में भय नहीं बल्कि उसकी स्थायी दशा की आशंका है। इस वंदना में दुष्टों को थपकी देकर सुलाने की चाल है जिसमें विघ्न-बाधाओं से जान बच सके। आशंका से उत्पन्न यह नम्रता गोस्वामी जी को आश्रय से आलंबन बना देती है। जब स्फुट अंशों के संचारीभावों तथा अनुभवों को छोड़कर वंदना के पीछे निहित भावना की दृष्टि से देखते हैं तो यह आश्रय से संक्रमित आलंबन का उदाहरण बन जाता है। सन्तों, देवताओं तथा राम की वन्दना पर्याप्त नहीं इसलिए दुष्टों की भी वन्दना की जाती है। इससे दुष्टों के महत्त्व की मायिक सृष्टि होती है और वह उन्हें और भी उपहास्य बना देती है।

—हास्य के सिद्धान्त तथा मानस में हास्य
प्रो. जगदीश पाण्डेय

1. दुष्ट वन्दना के पीछे कवि का उद्देश्य है :
- A. दुष्टों को लज्जित करना
- B. दुष्टों को थपकी देकर सुलाना
- C. दुष्टों से अपना बचाव करना
- D. दुष्टों का सहयोग प्राप्त करना

2. रामचरितमानस एक भक्ति काव्य है। इसमें दुष्ट वंदना का रहस्य है :
- A. तुलसी की व्यापक दृष्टि
- B. तुलसी का सभी को राममय देखना
- C. तुलसी की उदारता
- D. तुलसी का शील-सौजन्य

3. उपरोक्त अवतरण का उपयुक्त शीर्षक हो सकता है :
- A. तुलसी की दुष्ट वंदना
- B. तुलसी की उदारता
- C. तुलसी का मानवीय दृष्टिकोण
- D. उपर्युक्त तीनों

4. देवताओं, महापुरुषों, सज्जनों के साथ दुष्टों की वंदना इसलिए सार्थक कही जाएगी कि महाकवि तुलसी :
- A. संत कवि थे
- B. उदार चेता थे
- C. हित-अनहित और अपने-पराये की भावना से ऊपर उठ चुके थे
- D. निर्वैरता चाहते थे

5. जीवन में हास्य का महत्त्व इसलिए है कि वह जीवन को :
- A. प्रेरणा देता है
- B. आनन्दित करता है
- C. आगे बढ़ाता है
- D. सरस बनाता है

अभ्यास 3

इन्द्र यह सुनकर स्वयं महर्षि दधीचि के आश्रम में गए और उन्हें मजबूरी कह सुनायी। ऋषि जग-कल्याण के लिए सहर्ष अपना शरीर त्यागने के लिए तैयार हो गए। उनकी हड्डियों से त्वष्ठा ने वज्र बनाया। इस वज्र को हाथ में लेकर इन्द्र दुगुने उत्साह से वृत्रासुर के सम्मुख गए। उनके मेघरूपी रथ के गर्जन से एक बार वृत्रासुर का कलेजा काँप गया। उनके साथ चलते हुए मरुत जोर-जोर से उनकी जयजयकार कर रहे थे। इन्द्र ने सबसे पहले अपने वज्र से वृत्रासुर की माया को काट दिया। फिर भी वह दैत्य बड़ा शक्तिशाली था। अपनी माया से विछिन्न होकर भी वह बहुत देर तक इन्द्र से जूझता रहा। लेकिन अन्त में इन्द्र ने वज्र के प्रहार से वृत्रासुर का सिर काट दिया। वृत्रासुर के मरते ही रुका हुआ जल बह निकला, नदी-नाले फिर से भर उठे और देखते-ही-देखते खेत लहलहा उठे।

1. महर्षि दधीचि एक ऐसे ऋषि थे जिन्होंने :
- A. देवताओं की रक्षा के लिए अपने शरीर का त्याग किया था
- B. योग बल से अपने शरीर को त्याग कर वृत्रासुर के वध हेतु वज्र बनाने के लिए इन्द्र को अपनी अस्थियाँ सुलभ करा दी थीं
- C. वृत्रासुर के वध में इन्द्र की सहायता की थी
- D. वृत्रासुर का वध किया था

2. हमें इस अवतरण से यह प्रेरणा मिलती है कि परोपकार के लिए आवश्यकता पड़ने पर :
- A. अपने शरीर भी दे देना चाहिए
- B. अपना सर्वस्व दे देना चाहिए
- C. अपनी अस्थियाँ दे देनी चाहिए
- D. अपनी सम्पत्ति दे देनी चाहिए

3. इस गद्यांश का उपयुक्त शीर्षक हो सकता है :
- A. दधीचि का आत्मदान
- B. दधीचि का सर्वस्व दान
- C. वृत्रासुर वध
- D. इन्द्र का कोप

4. निम्नलिखित में से सही कथन पर निशान लगाइए :
- A. वृत्रासुर इन्द्र का प्रतिद्वन्द्वी था
- B. वृत्रासुर एक आततायी राक्षस था
- C. वृत्रासुर एक महाप्रतापी राक्षस था, जिसने जलावरोध कर रखा था
- D. वृत्रासुर उपर्युक्त में से कोई नहीं था

इस उद्धरण में प्रयुक्त निम्नलिखित शब्दों के सही अर्थों पर निशान लगाइए :

5. महर्षि
- A. मुनि
- B. ऋषि जो ब्राह्मण न हो
- C. ऋषि जो ब्राह्मण हो
- D. ऋषियों का एक पद विशेष

6. जगकल्याण :
- A. संसार का हित
- B. संसार की भलाई
- C. संसार को सुख देना
- D. संसार के लिए आनन्द की व्यवस्था करना

7. वज्र :
- A. एक प्रकार का बाजा
- B. एक प्रकार का शस्त्र
- C. एक प्रकार का आघात
- D. पत्थर गिरना या बिजली गिरना

अभ्यास 4

महाकवि सूरदास का 'सूर-सागर' भागवत के आधार पर लिखा हुआ ग्रंथ है। इसीलिए महाकवि 'सूर' ने भी ब्रह्म का यही स्वरूप ग्रहण किया और भगवान श्रीकृष्ण को अपनी उपासना का केन्द्र मानकर वैष्णव सम्प्रदाय के सिद्धान्तों का ही प्रतिपादन किया है। वास्तव में वैदिक ऋचाओं में वर्णित सिद्धान्त ही वैदिक धर्म के प्रकाण्ड आचार्यों द्वारा प्रचारित हुए हैं। काल और स्थिति के अनुसार धार्मिक सिद्धान्तों में भी परिवर्तन होना आवश्यक है। सर्वप्रथम दृष्टि से भगवान कृष्ण ने इन वैदिक सिद्धान्तों में कुछ परिवर्तन कर सूरकालीन वैष्णव धर्म का शिलान्यास किया। अतः भगवान कृष्ण को ही वैष्णव धर्म का प्रथम आचार्य कहना अनुचित न होगा। धार्मिक और ऐतिहासिक अनुसंधानों के अनुसार वेदों और संहिताओं की रचना भिन्न-भिन्न काल में हुई है। उदाहरणार्थ—यजुर्वेद संहिता में केशी नामक राक्षस का कृष्ण द्वारा वध किए जाने का उल्लेख है। इससे प्रमाणित होता है कि यह संहिता कृष्ण जन्म के बाद लिखी गई है।

—सूरदर्शन, डॉ. कृष्ण लाल 'हंस'

1. उक्त गद्यांश का सारांश एक पंक्ति में इस प्रकार हो सकता है :
- A. श्रीमद्भागवत ग्रंथ सूर-सागर की रचना का आधार है
- B. श्रीमद्भागवत नहीं अपितु ब्रह्म वैवर्त्त पुराण सूर-सागर का आधार है
- C. महाभारत ग्रंथ सूर-सागर का आधार है
- D. वैदिक ऋचाएँ सूर-सागर का आधार हैं

2. हिन्दी साहित्य में भक्ति तथा रीति काल को सम्मिलित करके तीन उत्तम कवि माने गए हैं, जिनमें प्रथम स्थान :
- A. सूरदास का है
- B. तुलसीदास का है
- C. केशवदास का है
- D. देव का है

3. महाकवि सूरदास भक्तिकाल में सगुण भक्ति की :
- A. कृष्ण भक्ति शाखा के कवि थे
- B. राम कृष्ण दोनों की भक्ति शाखा के कवि थे
- C. स्मार्त्त कवि थे
- D. उपर्युक्त किसी शाखा के कवि नहीं थे

4. इस गद्यांश का उपयुक्त शीर्षक हो सकता है :
- A. सूर-सागर का प्रणयन
- B. वैष्णव धर्म के प्रथम आचार्य श्रीकृष्ण
- C. परब्रह्म श्रीकृष्ण
- D. वैष्णव धर्म का शिलान्यास

5. सूर-सागर की कथा श्रीमद्भागवत के :
- A. दशम स्कंध से ली गई है
- B. एकादश स्कंध से ली गई है
- C. नवम स्कंध से ली गई है
- D. उपर्युक्त किसी स्कंध से नहीं ली गई है

अभ्यास 5

''पर्वतीय पथ और पत्थरों की चोट से टूटे नाखून और चुटीली उँगलियों के बीच में ढाल बनी मूँज की चप्पल मानो मनुष्य को पशु बनाकर खुर न देने वाले परमात्मा का उपहास कर रही हो। पाँव से दो बालिश्त ऊँचा और ऊनी-सूती पैबन्दों से बना हुआ पाजामा मनुष्य की लज्जाशीलता की विडम्बना जैसा लगता था। किसी से कभी मिले हुए पुराने कोट में, नीचे के मटमैले स्तर की झाँकी देती हुई, ऊपरी तह तार-तार फटकर झालरदार हो उठी थी और सब अपने पहनने वाले को एक झबरे जन्तु की भूमिका में उपस्थित करती थी। अस्पष्ट रंग और अनिश्चित रूप वाली दोपलिया टोपी के छेद से रूखे बाल जहाँ-तहाँ झाँककर मैले पानी और उसके बीच-बीच में झाँकते हुए सेवार की स्मृति करा देते थे।'' **—स्मृति की रेखाएँ, महादेवी वर्मा**

1. श्रीमती महादेवी वर्मा द्वारा किया गया उक्त रेखांकन 'स्मृति की रेखाएँ' नामक पुस्तक से है। यह रेखांकन :
   A. एक निर्धन व्यक्ति का है
   B. एक पहाड़ी नागरिक का है
   C. एक पहाड़ी मजदूर का है
   D. उपरोक्त में से किसी का नहीं है
2. उपर्युक्त गद्यांश का सार्थक शीर्षक हो सकता है :
   A. एक विपन्न कुली
   B. एक पर्वतीय श्रमिक
   C. निर्धनता एक अभिशाप
   D. करुणा की मूर्ति
3. महादेवी वर्मा की शैली की समीक्षा-मात्र एक पंक्ति में कर पाना असंभव है। फिर भी, कहा जा सकता है कि उनकी काव्य-शैली की तरह उनकी गद्य शैली भी :
   A. भावना प्रधान है B. चित्रांकन प्रधान है
   C. कल्पना प्रधान है D. मनोरम है
4. महादेवी वर्मा विरचित अनेक काव्यग्रंथ, निबन्ध तथा रेखाचित्र हैं। कुछ एक के नाम हैं :
   A. दीपशिखा, यामा
   B. अतीत के चलचित्र, स्मृति की रेखाएँ
   C. नीरजा, नीहार
   D. उपरोक्त सभी
5. इस गद्य कृति के अतिरिक्त महादेवी वर्मा द्वारा रचित प्रमुखतम गद्य कृति का नाम है :
   A. अतीत के चलचित्र B. मेरा परिवार
   C. पथ के साथी D. शृंखला की कड़ियाँ

अभ्यास 6

''आरोग्य रक्षा के नियम माँ-बाप को न मालूम रहने के कारण उनके बाल-बच्चों को भोग भुगतने पड़ते हैं। उनकी जो दुर्गति होती है, उन पर जो आफतें आती हैं उनका ठौर-ठिकाना नहीं। हजारों बच्चे तो माँ-बाप की असावधानी और मूर्खता के कारण पैदा होते ही मर जाते हैं। जो बचते हैं उनमें लाखों अशक्त, निर्बल और जन्म-रोगी होते हैं और करोड़ों ऐसे नीरोग और सबल नहीं होते जैसे होने चाहिए। अब इन सबको आप जोड़ डालिए तो आपको मालूम हो जाएगा कि माँ-बाप की नादानी के कारण सन्तति को कितनी हानि उठानी पड़ती है; कितना दुःख सहना पड़ता है।''

—शिक्षा, आचार्य महावीर प्रसाद द्विवेदी

1. इस गद्य खण्ड का उपयुक्त शीर्षक हो सकता है :
   A. स्वास्थ्य रक्षा
   B. माता-पिता और उनके बच्चों का स्वास्थ्य
   C. नीरोग रहने के उपाय
   D. स्वस्थ कैसे रहें?
2. आचार्य पं. महावीर प्रसाद द्विवेदी अपने समय के :
   A. श्रेष्ठ विद्वान् थे
   B. शीर्षस्थ समालोचक थे
   C. हिन्दी भाषा के प्रबल पक्षधर और आचार्य थे
   D. श्रेष्ठ आयुर्वेदाचार्य थे
3. हिन्दी के निबन्ध साहित्य के विकास में आचार्य द्विवेदी का स्थान :
   A. शीर्षस्थ था B. समालोचक जैसा था
   C. प्रवर्तक जैसा था D. उन्नायक जैसा था
4. आचार्य पं. महावीर प्रसाद द्विवेदी निम्नलिखित में से किस/किन पत्रिका/पत्रिकाओं के सम्पादक थे?
   A. साहित्य संदेश B. सरस्वती
   C. विशाल भारत D. उपर्युक्त तीनों
5. सन्तति का अर्थ होता है :
   A. पत्नी तथा पुत्र B. आत्मीय जन
   C. सम्बन्धी लोग D. औलाद (बाल-बच्चे)

अभ्यास 7

''अन्तिम क्षण थे, सर्वदा के लिए वियोग हो रहा था। देखती आँखों शाहजहाँ का सर्वस्व लूट रहा था और वह भारत सम्राट हताश हाथ-पर-हाथ धरे बेबस बैठा था और अपनी किस्मत को रो रहा था। सिंहासनारूढ़ हुए कोई तीन वर्ष भी नहीं बीते थे कि उसकी प्रियतमा इस लोक से विदा लेने की तैयारी कर रही थी। शाहजहाँ की सभी आशाओं पर, उसकी सारी उमंगों पर पाला पड़ रहा था।...''

''हाय अन्त हो गया, सर्वस्व लुट गया! प्रेमी, जीवन-यात्रा का एकमात्र साथी सर्वदा के लिए छोड़कर चल बसा। भारत सम्राट शाहजहाँ की प्रेयसी, साम्राज्ञी मुमताज महल सदा के लिए इस लोक से विदा हो गई। शाहजहाँ भारत का सम्राट था, जहान का शाह था, किन्तु वह भी अपनी प्रेयसी को जाने से रोक न सका।'' **—ताज, महाराज कुमार रघुबीर सिंह**

1. इस गद्यांश में अभिव्यक्ति के लिए प्रयुक्त शैली को हम क्या कहेंगे?
   A. विचार प्रधान शैली B. व्यास शैली
   C. भाव प्रवण शैली D. कल्पना प्रधान शैली
2. इस गद्यांश में व्यक्त विचार यह दर्शाते हैं कि कोई व्यक्ति कितना ही साधन-सम्पन्न, सक्षम तथा सबल क्यों न हो, किन्तु वह महाबली काल के समक्ष :
   A. एक भुनगा-सा होता है

B. अति तुच्छ होता है

C. किंकर्त्तव्यविमूढ़ हो जाता है

D. चुप हो जाता है

3. उक्त गद्यांश का सर्वाधिक उपयुक्त शीर्षक हो सकता है :

A. महाबली काल   B. मुमताज की मृत्यु

C. शाहजहाँ की बेबसी   D. प्रेयसी वियोग

4. उक्त गद्यांश में लेखक को शाहजहाँ की मन:स्थिति को चित्रित करने में :

A. बहुत कम सफलता मिली है

B. अत्यधिक सफलता मिली है

C. किंचित् सफलता मिली है

D. प्रशंसनीय सफलता मिली है

5. वियोग से तात्पर्य है:

A. वैमनस्य   B. विलाप

C. मेल-मिलाप   D. बिछुड़ना

अभ्यास 8

आचार्य शुक्ल जी के गंभीर निबंध 'चिंतामणि' में संग्रहीत हैं। उनमें दो प्रकार के निबंध हैं, एक तो भावों के विश्लेषण से सम्बन्ध रखने वाले निबंध जो भाव-विषयक होते हुए भी आवश्यक नहीं हैं वरन् उच्चकोटि के विचारात्मक हैं, दूसरे साहित्यिक जिनमें कुछ सैद्धांतिक आलोचना से संबंध रखते हैं, जैसे—'साधारणीकरण और व्यक्ति वैचित्र्यवाद' और कुछ व्यावहारिक आलोचनाओं के हैं, जैसे 'भारतेन्दु हरिश्चन्द्र'। आचार्य शुक्ल जी के मनोवैज्ञानिक निबंधों की भी अन्विति उनकी आलोचनाओं से की जा सकती है, वे भारतीय रस सिद्धान्त पर अवलम्बित हैं और उनका सम्बन्ध जीवन सागर के निजी अवगाहन से है। इन निबंधों के भावों का विश्लेषण पर्याप्त मात्रा में हुआ है किन्तु जीवन से चुने हुए उपयुक्त उदाहरणों के कारण यह विश्लेषण दुरूह नहीं होने पाया है। 'लज्जा और ग्लानि' का आधार भारत की आत्मग्लानि है, 'लोभ और प्रीति' का अन्तर समझ लेने पर जायसी के 'रत्नसेन' के प्रेम की आलोचना भली प्रकार समझी जा सकती है।

—काव्य के रूप, डॉ. गुलाब राय

1. उक्त गद्यांश का सम्यक् अनुशीलन करने से पता चलता है कि लेखक ने :

A. शुक्ल जी को समझने में काफी प्रयास किया था

B. शुक्ल जी के साहित्य का सम्यक् अध्ययन किया था

C. शुक्ल जी से दिशाबोध ग्रहण किया था

D. शुक्ल जी को समीप से देखा था

2. डॉ. गुलाब राय की शैली थी :

A. कथा शैली   B. भावना प्रवण शैली

C. विवेचना प्रधान शैली   D. विश्लेषणात्मक शैली

3. डॉ. गुलाब राय ने आचार्य शुक्ल की शैलियों का जो वर्गीकरण किया है वह :

A. अत्यन्त वैज्ञानिक है   B. शोधपूर्ण है

C. सर्वांगीण है   D. यथातथ्य है

4. उक्त गद्यांश के लिए उचित शीर्षक होगा :

A. आचार्य शुक्ल की निबंध-शैली

B. शुक्ल जी की निबंध-कला

C. निबंध कला और शुक्ल जी

D. हिन्दी के श्रेष्ठ निबंधकार शुक्ल जी

5. अन्विति का अर्थ है :

A. अनुरक्ति   B. तालमेल

C. आलोचना   D. अर्चना

अभ्यास 9

चीन में न तो वर्ण व्यवस्था थी न जाति-पाँति का भेदभाव। परम्परा के अनुसार सम्मान के मुख्य पात्र क्रमश: विद्वान्, राज्य पदाधिकारी, योद्धा और अध्यापक थे। साधारण लोगों में नौ श्रेणियाँ थीं। अन्न उत्पन्न करने वाले, माली, लकड़हारे, पशु-पक्षी पालने वाले, बुनकर, नौकर-चाकर, कारीगर, व्यापारी और फुटकर काम करने वाले। कुलीनों तथा साधारण लोगों में अथवा श्रेणियों और व्यवसायों में ऊँच-नीच का भेद कायम था। पर यह विभेद नगण्य-सा था। अपनी योग्यता के अनुसार मनुष्य का स्थान घटता-बढ़ता था। लोग आपस में विवाह आदि बिना किसी बाधा के करते थे। चीनियों में विद्वान् और सेनापति विशेष आदर के पात्र समझे जाते थे। हिजड़े, भाँड, गुलाम, हरकारे, वेश्याएँ नीचे के स्तर के लोग थे। चीन में गुलामों की दशा उतनी खराब नहीं थी जितनी रोम तथा यूरोप के देशों के मध्य युग में थी। गुलामों से घरेलू काम कराये जाते थे। उनकी विशेष जाति नहीं थी। उन्हें यद्यपि खरीदा-बेचा जा सकता था तथापि उनसे न तो नीच काम कराए जाते थे और न उन्हें सताया जाता था।

—विश्व इतिहास, डॉ. रामप्रसाद त्रिपाठी

1. उक्त उद्धरण के अध्ययन से पता चलता है कि मध्यकालीन चीन में :

A. जाति प्रथा प्रचलित थी

B. सामाजिक जीवन काफी समुन्नत था

C. सामाजिक जीवन वैभवपूर्ण था

D. वर्ण-व्यवस्था से रहित था

2. उक्त उद्धरण का उपयुक्त शीर्षक हो सकता है :

A. मध्यकालीन चीन का सामाजिक जीवन

B. मध्यकालीन चीन में सामाजिक व्यवस्था

C. चीनी समाज में विविधता

D. चीनी समाज में गिरावट

3. उक्त गद्य खण्ड का सारांश एक पंक्ति में इस प्रकार व्यक्त किया जा सकता है :

A. अन्य तत्कालीन समाजों की तुलना में मध्यकाल में चीन का सामाजिक जीवन समुन्नत था

B. चीन का मध्यकालीन समाज विकास के शिखर पर था

C. चीन मध्यकालीन राज्यों में अग्रणी था

D. मध्यकालीन चीन का सामाजिक जीवन विकासोन्मुख था

4. चीन के सामाजिक इतिहास का अनुशीलन करने से पता चलता है कि चीन में :

A. सामाजिक भेदभाव अवश्य था भले ही वहाँ वर्ण-व्यवस्था नहीं थी

B. समाज के सभी सदस्य एक-सा जीवन नहीं जीते थे

C. चीनी समाज गुलामों को उत्पीड़ित करता था

D. मध्यकालीन चीन में नागरिक सुविधाओं का अभाव था

5. चीन में विशेष आदर के पात्र समझे जाते थे :

A. हिजड़े और भाँड B. विद्वान् और वेश्याएँ

C. विद्वान् और सेनापति D. कारीगर और व्यापारी

अभ्यास 10

''मनुष्य जब नई-नई सच्चाइयों को देखता है तब वह अपना नैतिक कर्त्तव्य समझता है कि उनके अनुसार व्यवहार करे परन्तु ऐसे मौकों पर धर्म उसके रास्ते में रुकावट बनकर खड़ा होता रहा है। जब गैलीलियो ने इस बात का पता लगाया कि सूर्य पृथ्वी के इर्द-गिर्द नहीं घूमता, पृथ्वी सूर्य के गिर्द घूमती है, तो उसने अपना नैतिक कर्त्तव्य समझा कि सच्चाई को जाहिर करे। उसने जब इस सत्य को प्रकट किया तो धर्म के ठेकेदारों ने उसे जेल में डाल दिया, और उसे तब छोड़ा जब उसने कह दिया कि उसका विचार गलत था। संसार का इतिहास इस बात का साक्षी था कि धर्म सत्य को दबाता रहा है। रूढ़िवाद ने बुद्धिवाद का विरोध किया। इस दृष्टि से धर्म और विज्ञान की लड़ाई एक तरह से धर्म और नीति की लड़ाई है।''

—समाजशास्त्र के मूल तत्त्व, सत्यव्रत सिद्धान्तालंकार

1. ''धर्म और विज्ञान की लड़ाई, धर्म और नीति की लड़ाई है।'' इस कथन का आशय है :

A. धर्म ने सत्य को स्वीकार नहीं किया

B. धर्म और नीति ने मिलकर सत्य को दबाया

C. धर्म और नीति ने सत्य को स्वीकार नहीं किया

D. रूढ़िवाद ने बुद्धिवाद को नकारा

2. उक्त गद्यांश का आशय है :

A. धर्म और सत्य का सनातन संघर्ष

B. ज्ञान के रास्ते में धर्म बाधक

C. धर्म और नीति द्वारा विज्ञान की अवहेलना

D. विज्ञान द्वारा धर्म और नैतिकता का पर्दाफाश

3. इस गद्यांश का उपयुक्त शीर्षक हो सकता है :

A. धर्म और विज्ञान

B. धर्म और नैतिकता पर विज्ञान का प्रभाव

C. विज्ञान की लड़ाई

D. नैतिकता

4. समाजशास्त्र का अध्ययन आवश्यक है :

A. जीवन की सफलता के लिए

B. सामाजिक पुनर्निर्माण के लिए

C. सामाजिक सुव्यवस्था के लिए

D. उपर्युक्त किसी के लिए नहीं

5. 'जाहिर' से अभिप्राय है :

A. प्रकाशित B. धूमिल

C. स्थापित D. उजागरीप्रकट

उत्तरमाला

अभ्यास-1

1	2	3	4	5
B	C	C	D	A

अभ्यास-2

1	2	3	4	5
B	B	A	B	D

अभ्यास-3

1	2	3	4	5	6	7
B	B	C	C	C	A	B

अभ्यास-4

1	2	3	4	5
A	B	A	B	A

अभ्यास-5

1	2	3	4	5
C	B	A	D	A

अभ्यास-6

1	2	3	4	5
B	C	C	B	D

अभ्यास-7

1	2	3	4	5
C	C	C	D	D

अभ्यास-8

1	2	3	4	5
B	C	D	A	B

अभ्यास-9

1	2	3	4	5
D	B	A	A	C

अभ्यास-10

1	2	3	4	5
D	B	A	B	D

★ ★ ★